Nicholas II –
of Russia after his father
Alexander III (1894–1917)

Abdicates throne
Mar. 15, 1917

Russian Revol. took place
here in March 1917 –
due to military defeat,
internal problems, unstable
international position with allies,
unstable govt, strikes, food lines,
military mutiny – in St. Petersburg

Bolsheviks seized power Nov. 7, 1917

The Young Voter's Manual

A Topical Dictionary of
American Government and Politics

The Young Voter's Manual

A Topical Dictionary of American Government and Politics

by

Leon W. Blevins

El Paso Community College

1974

Rowman and Littlefield

Totowa, New Jersey

Library of Congress Cataloging in Publication Data

Blevins, Leon W. 1937-
   The Young Voter's Manual

   (A Littlefield, Adams Quality Paperback No. 260)
   1. United States—Politics and government—Hand-
books, manuals, etc.   I. Title.
JK274.B623   320.4'73   73-10377
ISBN 0-87471-572-5

This volume is a reflection of "time stolen" from those to whom I should give instead of from whom I should take. It is natural that the work should therefore be dedicated to Shannah, Tab, Keith, and Shaleah—my co-partners in faith, scholarship, politics, and art.

Table of Contents

Preface

This manual is a product of university student demand to satisfy a need expressed in 1970 by Texas Tech University students facing the awesome yet mundane prospect of active participation in the electoral process. That prospect became a reality in 1971 with the addition of the Twenty-sixth Amendment to the United States Constitution permitting 18-year-old individuals to vote in both federal and state elections. Undergraduate students were demanding a "companion" volume which could be used with traditional textbooks which regularly touched upon various concepts without specifically identifying particular terms used. This manual has been compiled to be of assistance to such student voters. It should be useful to any person who wishes to know more about American government.

The students continually requested four things: (1) A concise, readable, and well-balanced volume containing basic facts about government, (2) A volume grouping numerous items by subject rather than through pure alphabetical listings, (3) A book grouping U.S. Supreme Court cases and U.S. federal agencies in separate chapters for easy reference, and (4) A work clearly cross-referenced for better conceptual understanding of American government.

The Young Voter's Manual should meet all four criteria. It seeks readability through precision and clarity in both word choice and sentence structure. It seeks factual substance through inclusion of items which are most frequently discussed in basic political science and American government textbooks used across the United States. It seeks structural integrity by grouping subjects together by chapter. Finally, it seeks to provide conceptual understanding through provision of cross-references based upon the use of italics, numbers, a general index, and specialized indexing of Supreme Court cases in the topical chapters. Explanations for use of the material may be found at the beginning of each chapter.

This reference manual is an attempt to help balance both facts and concepts related to American government. If that has been achieved perhaps we shall be better students and also more knowledgeable and effective voters and citizens. Few should doubt that to be an admirable goal for young and old alike.

Acknowledgments

The incentive for the preparation of this manual came from my former students in American government at Texas Tech University. Without them I would not have begun this particular project which occupied a major portion of three years of my life. An appreciation of their needs doubtlessly kept me on course toward the objective.

Credit goes to Patricia Campbell and Ann Carmichael of Texas Tech University and Eulastine Williams of West Texas State University for typing the rough drafts of this terribly technical manuscript. Thanks goes to Gloria Rosales of El Paso Community College and to Tab Blevins for assisting in putting together the index.

I am indebted to numerous library workers at Texas Tech and West Texas State and to the most consistently helpful individual in my research, Mrs. Annette Cook, documents assistant in the library of West Texas State University.

Some of my colleagues who continually gave me encouragement throughout this project are professors Melvin Straus and Edward Leonard of U.T. El Paso, Eugene Jones of Angelo State University, Lynwood Holland and Ed Fuchs of Texas Tech, Jesse Moses and Walter Shelly of West Texas State, and Gerald Money of El Paso Community College. It is impossible to name all of my colleagues and students who encouraged and helped me over the past three years.

Finally, I thank the editorial advisers of Littlefield, Adams & Company. Their many hours of toil over the pages of this volume have truly transformed an idea into a literary reality.

It is hoped that I shall share what I have gained from my former and present students, colleagues, and editorial advisers with those who use this volume.

The Young Voter's Manual

A Topical Dictionary of
American Government and Politics

Chapter 1

United States
Supreme Court Cases

Note to the reader: Cross-referenced terms are in italics. The superscript number refers to the chapter in which the entry may be found. In addition, its placement indicates the word under which the term is alphabetized. (For example, in *electoral*[4] *college*, information on the electoral college may be found in Chapter 4 under "electoral.") Because italics are used in cross-references, they are not used for terms in which they would ordinarily be used: Supreme Court cases and titles of books, journals, plays, and so forth.

Listings of Supreme Court cases relating to material in Chapters Four through Twelve are at the end of each of these chapters.

Ableman v. Booth, 21 How. 506 (1859). Held that a prisoner in *federal*[3] custody for violating the Fugitive Slave Law of 1850 could not be released by a writ of *habeas*[8] *corpus* issued by a *state*[3] court. The *Supreme*[8] *Court* held that each court system is supreme in its appropriate sphere and that federal courts cannot enter into cases of state courts unless they involve *constitutional*[3] matters. See also *Roger Brooke Taney*[8].

Abrams v. U.S., 250 U.S. 616 (1919). Upheld *federal*[3] *authority*[3] to restrict the circulation of pamphlets urging *strikes*[10] by munitions workers during time of *war*[12]. In the decision upholding the *Sedition*[9] *Act of 1918*, the *Supreme*[8] *Court* incorporated the *bad*[9] *tendency doctrine* and held that pamphlets opposing U.S. action in *World*[12] *War I* excited disaffection, *sedition*[12], riots, and *revolution*[3]. Such actions were not protected by the *First*

Amendment[9]. In his famous minority opinion dissent, Justice *Oliver Wendell Holmes, Jr.*[8] rejected the bad tendency doctrine and supported the *clear*[9] *and present danger* doctrine. He defined a "clear and present danger" as one that "imminently threatens immediate interference with the lawful and pressing purposes of the *law*"[8].

Adderly v. Florida, 385 U.S. 39 (1967). Upheld state *authority*[3] to restrict public demonstrations on public *property*[10] of a security nature. The *Supreme*[8] *Court* emphasized that the *power*[3] of the *state*[3] to regulate general trespass was validly used against student demonstrations in this instance because the students were occupying a driveway designated for jail use only.

Adkins v. Children's Hospital, 261 U.S. 525 (1923). Ruled as *unconstitutional*[3] a *District of Columbia*[4] *minimum*[10] *wage law* for women. The decision

1

was based on the right of *contract*[10] between an employer and his employees. The *Supreme*[8] *Court* held that the administrative standards regulating such wages were too vague and imprecise, especially the section dealing with the wage levels claimed necessary to maintain adequate health and moral standards for women. The Adkins decision was overruled in *West*[1] *Coast Hotel Co. v. Parrish*. See also *Oliver Wendell Holmes, Jr.*[8]

Adler v. Board of Education, 342 U.S. 485 (1952). Upheld the Feinberg Law of the state of New York, a *statute*[8] that acccepted membership of a public school teacher in a subversive *organization*[6] as prima facie evidence of support of violent overthrow of the *government*[3]. The *Supreme*[8] *Court* held that such *state*[3] *legislation*[7] did not find persons *guilty*[9] *by association,* but provided protection to the sensitive field of public education through the removal of persons belonging to subversive organizations. The Adler decision was reversed in *Keyishian*[1] *v. Board of Regents*. See also *prima*[8] *facie case.*

Afroyim v. Rusk, 387 U.S. 253 (1967). Ruled that the citizenship clause of the *Fourteenth Amendment*[4] protects every *citizen*[3], natural born or *naturalized*[3], against divestment of his right to citizenship unless it is by "voluntary renunciation." In this decision the *Supreme*[8] *Court* ruled that a person could not lose his citizenship by voting in a foreign election. The decision reversed *Perez*[1] *v. Brownell.*

Albertson v. Subversive Activities Control Board, 382 U.S. 70 (1965). Held that compulsory registration of individual members of the *Communist Party*[5] or Communist action groups was *self-incrimination*[9] and forbidden by the *Fifth Amendment*[9]. The decision invalidated the portion of the *Internal*[9] *Security (McCarran) Act of 1950* which required such reg-

istration. See also *Subversive*[2] *Activities Control Board.*

Alexander v. Holmes, 396 U.S. 802 (1969). Unanimously held in a Mississippi case that *integration*[9] of the public schools should proceed with "all deliberate speed." The decision modified the decision in *Green*[1] *v. County School Board of New Kent County, Virginia* by declaring all *freedom*[9] *of choice plans* to be unacceptable. The *Supreme*[8] *Court* declared that dual school systems must end "at once" and that unitary systems must be instituted.

American Communications Assn. v. Douds, 339 U.S. 382 (1950). Upheld the anti-Communist *loyalty*[9] *oath* of the *Labor-Management*[10] *Relations (Taft-Hartley) Act* of 1947, an oath which, if not taken by leaders of an *organization*[6], denied the organization access to the assistance of the *National*[2] *Labor Relations Board* during labor disputes. The *Supreme*[8] *Court's* decision was based on the right of the federal *government*[3] to protect *interstate commerce*[10] against politically motivated *labor*[10] *union strikes*[10]. The controversial loyalty oath of section 9(h) was eventually repealed. See also *balancing*[9] *doctrine.*

Aptheker v. Secretary of State, 378 U.S. 500 (1964). Declared the *Internal*[9] *Security (McCarran) Act of 1950* *passport*[12] restrictions on *Communist Party*[5] members *unconstitutional*[3] because such regulations might be used by the *government*[3] to restrict the travel of persons belonging to an *organization*[6] regardless of the reasons given for traveling abroad. The *Supreme*[8] *Court* invalidated the broad restrictions, on the grounds that the *Fifth Amendment*[9] *due*[4] *process clause* guarantees a person the right to travel.

Argersinger v. Hamlin (1972). Declared in a Florida case that all criminal *defendants*[8] facing even minor *misdemeanor*[8] trials involving possible short sentences in jail must be provided legal counsel regardless of ability to pay for such counsel. The decision broadened to the fullest extent the right to legal counsel begun in *Johnson*[1] v. *Zerbst* and *Gideon*[1] v. *Wainwright*. See also *Sixth Amendment*[9]; *Betts*[1] v. *Brady*; *Powell*[1] v. *Alabama*.

Ashcraft v. Tennessee, 322 U.S. 143 (1944). Held that confessions obtained through psychologically coercive methods are not admissible as evidence in a *state*[3] trial because they are in violation of the *due*[4] *process clause* of the *Fourteenth Amendment*[4]. See also *third*[9] *degree*.

Ashwander v. Tennessee Valley Authority, 297 U.S. 288 (1936). Upheld *federal government*[3] action in undertaking a valley authority development program that involved constructing hydroelectric plants in the Tennessee River basin. The *Supreme*[8] *Court* cited the federal government's powers related to *war*[12] and internal improvements to uphold the TVA and the right of the *federal government*[3] to generate and sell electrical power. The Court held that the government may dispose of federal *property*[10] and may also act during times of peace to prepare to protect national interests. In a *concurring opinion*[8] Justice Brandeis reviewed the role of the Supreme Court with regard to *judicial*[4] *review*. He stated that the Court: (1) will not decide the constitutionality of *legislation*[7] in nonadversary proceeding, (2) will not deal with or "anticipate" the constitutionality of legislation apart from the process of *litigation*[8], (3) will not formulate a rule of *constitutional law*[8] broader than is actually required by the "precise facts to which it is applied," (4) will not deal with a matter on a *constitutional*[3] ground if there is some other basis, statutory or otherwise, on

which the case may be decided, (5) will not deal with a statute unless it can be shown that the party questioning it may actually be damaged by its enforcement, (6) will not deal with the question of constitutionality of a statute on the demand of someone who has benefited from the *law*[8], (7) will seek to avoid having to deal with the constitutionality of a statute, even a questionable statute, if there is any way "fairly possible by which the question may be avoided."

Avery v. Midland County, 390 U.S. 474 (1968). Applied the *one-man*,[5] *one-vote rule* to the local level by holding that a *county*[11] legislative body must be *apportioned*[7] according to equal population *districts*[7]. See also *Baker*[1] v. *Carr* and *Reynolds*[1] v. *Sims* for the basis of the Avery decision.

Bailey v. Drexel Furniture Company, 259 U.S. 20 (1922). Declared *unconstitutional*[3] the Federal Child Labor Tax Act (1919) provisions levying a 10 percent tax on businesses knowingly using *child*[10] *labor*. The *Supreme*[8] *Court* held that the "tax" was in reality a regulatory device violating the *reserved powers*[4] of the *states*[3] as guaranteed by the *Tenth Amendment*.[4] See *Hammer*[1] v. *Dagenhart* and *U.S.*[1] v. *Darby Lumber Co.* for amplification of the child labor cases. See also *regulatory tax*.[10]

Baker v. Carr, 369 U.S. 186 (1962). Held that a complaint in Tennessee involving *state*[3] legislative malapportionment was justiciable and could be heard in *federal government*[3] courts under the *Fourteenth Amendment*[4] *equal*[4] *protection clause*. The *Supreme*[8] *Court* abandoned the *political*[4] *question* argument it had used in *Colgrove*[1] v. *Green* to avoid dealing with *apportionment*[7] cases, and laid the basis for future decisions that eventually developed the *one-man*,[5] *one-vote rule* of legislative apportionment. See also *Avery*[1] v. *Midland*

County; Gray[1] v. Sanders; justiciable[4] question; Kirkpatrick[1] v. Preisler; Reynolds[1] v. Sims; Earl Warren[8]; Wesberry[1] v. Sanders.

Bantam Books, Inc. v. Sullivan, 372 U.S. 58 (1963). Declared a Rhode Island *statute*[8] *unconstitutional*[3] because it permitted prior restraint of publications considered *obscene*.[9] The *law*[8] created a *state*[3] *commission*[6] empowered to circulate lists of objectionable books and warn distributors of prosecution if such books were distributed for sale to minors under 18 years of age. The *Supreme*[8] *Court* held that such action violated the *First Amendment*[9] as applied to the *states*[3] by the *Fourteenth Amendment*[4]. See also *prior*[9] *restraint doctrine*.

Barenblatt v. U.S., 360 U.S. 109 (1959). Declared that the *power*[3] of a congressional *investigating committee*[7] and its concern for the preservation of the *nation*[3] against subversive activity on the part of the *Communist Party*[5] overrides a witness's right to use the *Fifth Amendment*[9] to refuse to answer questions pertaining to subversive activities or to abuse *First Amendment*[9] freedoms in the college classroom in the name of *academic*[9] *freedom*. See also *balancing*[9] *doctrine*.

Barron v. Baltimore, 7 Pet. 243 (1833). Held that the *due*[4] *process clause* of the *Fifth Amendment*[9] was written to apply only to the *federal government*[3] and not to the *states*[3]. The *Supreme*[8] *Court* held that the *amendments*[3] within the *U.S. Bill*[4] *of Rights* contain no direct references to state *governments*[3]. See also *Gitlow*[1] *v. New York* for changes in the Barron ruling.

Bartkus v. Illinois, 355 U.S. 281 (1958). Held that two trials for the same offense in separate *federal*[3] and *state*[3] courts did not constitute *double*[9] *jeopardy* as prohibited by the *due*[4]

process clauses of the *Fifth Amendment*[9] and *Fourteenth Amendment*[4]. See also *shocking*[9] *to the conscience doctrine*.

Beauharnais v. Illinois, 343 U.S. 250 (1952). Established the principle that groups as well as individuals may be protected against *libel*[9]. The decision upheld an Illinois *statute*[8] making it illegal to libel "a class of *citizens*[3]", of any race, color, creed or religion."

Benton v. Maryland, 395 U.S. 784 (1969). Held that the *Fifth Amendment*[9] protection against *double*[9] *jeopardy* applies to the *states*[3] under the *due*[4] *process clause* of the *Fourteenth Amendment*[4]. The Benton decision overruled *Palko*[1] *v. Connecticut*. See also *shocking*[9] *to the conscience doctrine*.

Berger v. New York, 388 U.S. 41 (1967). Declared a New York *statute*[8] providing for court-approved *wiretapping*[9] *unconstitutional*[3] on the grounds that it violated the *Fourth Amendment*[9] *search*[9] and *seizure* provisions. The *Supreme*[8] *Court* abandoned its earlier *Olmstead*[1] rule, which had declared that words were not "things" and therefore were not protected by the Fourth Amendment.

Berman v. Parker, 348 U.S. 26 (1954). Held that under *eminent*[9] *domain* a *government*[3] may condemn *property*[10] for public use and redevelop it through the use of private *free*[10] *enterprise*. The *Supreme*[8] *Court* upheld *urban*[11] *renewal* through the Berman decision, emphasizing that the main consideration in using eminent domain is that just compensation be paid.

Betts v. Brady, 316 U.S. 455 (1942). Held that a Maryland *state*[3] court did not err in failing to appoint legal counsel in a trial involving a noncapital offense since the proceedings were conducted fairly as prescribed by state *law*[8]. In essence the *Supreme*[8]

Court said the Powell rule of 1932, requiring state-appointed counsel, dealt with specific circumstances of a particular case rather than with a general principle involving legal counsel. In 1963 *Gideon*[1] *v. Wainwright*, a Florida case, actually reversed Betts and held that the state must provide counsel for all *defendants*[8] in noncapital criminal trials. Legal counsel was established as a basic right for *misdemeanor*[8] offenses involving possible short jail sentences in *Argersinger*[1] *v. Hamlin*. See also *capital*[8] *punishment*; *criminal law*[8]; *Powell*[1] *v. Alabama*.

Board of Education v. Allen, 392 U.S. 236 (1968). Upheld a New York *statute*[8] providing for nonsectarian textbooks for religious schools on the basis that such books benefit children rather than religion. See also *child*[9] *benefit doctrine*; *Everson*[1] *v. Board of Education*.

Bolling v. Sharpe, 347 U.S. 497 (1954). Held that the use of racially *segregated*[9] public schools in the *District of Columbia*[4] was in violation of the *due*[4] *process clause* of the *Fifth Amendment*[9].

Brown v. Board of Education of Topeka, 347 U.S. 483 (1954). Overturned the *separate*[9] *but equal doctrine* of *Plessy*[1] *v. Ferguson* and declared racial *segregation*[9] within public schools in violation of the *equal*[4] *protection clause* of the *Fourteenth Amendment*[4]. The *Supreme*[8] *Court* declared segregated facilities to be "inherently unequal" and called for the elimination of the segregated system with "all deliberate speed." See also *National*[5] *Association for the Advancement of Colored People*; *Earl Warren*[8].

Brown v. Louisiana, 383 U.S. 131 (1966). Upheld the right of peaceful protest and demonstration within a public place such as a library as a guaranteed right to the freedom of expression covered by the *First Amendment*[9].

Brown v. Maryland, 12 Wheat. 419 (1827). Established the *original*[10] *package doctrine* which holds that the *federal government*[3] may regulate a foreign commodity as *interstate commerce*[10] as long as it stays within the original shipping container. The commodity may be regulated by the *state*[3] as *intrastate commerce*[10] upon opening for the purposes of sale or use within the state.

Brown v. Mississippi, 297 U.S. 278 (1936). Forbade the use of coerced (*third*[9] *degree*) confessions in *state*[3] criminal proceedings. The Brown decision brought the *Fifth Amendment*[9] protection against *self-incrimination*[9] under the protection of the *due*[4] *process clause* of the *Fourteenth Amendment*[4] as applied to the states.

Buchanan v. Warley, 245 U.S. 60 (1917). Held a Louisville, Kentucky city *ordinance*[8] requiring racial *segregation*[9] in housing *unconstitutional*[3] on the grounds that it interfered with individual rights to own and dispose of real *property*[10].

Bunting v. Oregon, 243 U.S. 426 (1917). Upheld a *state maximum*[10] *hour law* for both men and women engaged in general industrial employment. The *law*[8] permitted three hours employment past a regular 10-hour day and required overtime pay for the extra three hours. The decision of the *Supreme*[8] *Court*, although not citing the previous case, overturned the decision in *Lochner*[1] *v. New York*.

Burstyn v. Wilson, 343 U.S. 495 (1952). Overruled the rights of *state*[3] *censorship*[9] of films as established earlier in Mutual Film Corporation v. Industrial Commission of Ohio. The Burstyn case involved "The Miracle," a film deemed "sacrilegious" because of its portrayal of Roman Catholics. The *Supreme*[8] *Court* held that the

First Amendment[9] and *Fourteenth Amendment*[4] provisions protecting free expression applied to movies.

Calder v. Bull, 3 Dall. 383 (1798). Held that the *constitutional*[3] restrictions on *ex*[9] *post facto laws* apply only to *criminal laws*[8] and not to *civil law*[8] matters.

Cantwell v. Connecticut, 310 U.S. 296 (1940). Reversed a *breach*[8] *of the peace* conviction of a Jehovah's Witness adherent who had without violence played a phonograph record verbally attacking Roman Catholics. The *Supreme*[8] *Court* upheld such actions under the *First Amendment*[9] protection of speech and religion. See also *free exercise of religion*[9] *clause.*

Carrington v. Rash, 380 U.S. 89 (1965). Held *unconstitutional*[3] a Texas *statute*[8] prohibiting nonresident U.S. military personnel from voting within the *state*[3] as long as they remained in the armed services.

Carter v. Carter Coal Company, 298 U.S. 238 (1936). Declared *unconstitutional*[3] the Bituminous Coal Conservation (Guffey-Snyder) Act of 1935 because it appeared to regulate production rather than commerce. Production was viewed as local in nature and as affecting *interstate commerce*[10] only indirectly. The Carter decision was reversed after personnel changes on the *Supreme*[8] *Court* and the threat of a *court-packing*[8] plan by *President*[6] *Franklin D. Roosevelt*[6]. See also *National*[1] *Labor Relations Board v. Jones and Laughlin Corp.*; *Sunshine*[1] *Anthracite Coal Co. v. Adkins.*

Chaplinsky v. New Hampshire, 315 U.S. 568 (1942). Held that a person has no right to violate a *state*[3] *statute*[8] prohibiting the public use of abusive and profane language which could inflict injury or incite a *breach*[8] *of the peace. The Supreme*[8] *Court* held that such speech contained no "social value" worthy of *constitutional*[3] protection under the *First Amendment*[9].

Charles River Bridge v. Warren Bridge, 11 Pet. 420 (1837). Held, in a conflict between a publicly enfranchised but privately owned toll bridge and a publicly incorporated bridge destined to become a free passage, that the toll bridge was not given an exclusive *monopoly*[10] of a *state*[3]. *The Supreme*[8] *Court* held that contracts confer only the rights specifically granted. It also held that a state has the right to care for the welfare of its *citizens*[3] and that the building of the free bridge for the people of Massachusetts was not an impairment of *contract*[10]. See also *contract*[4] *clause; Roger Brooke Taney*[8].

Chisholm v. Georgia, 2 Dall. 419 (1793). Permitted *federal*[3] courts to have *jurisdiction*[8] over any case involving a suit of a private *citizen*[3] within one *state*[3] against the *government*[3] of another state. Such cases were removed from federal jurisdiction by the adoption of the *Eleventh Amendment*[4] in 1795. See *diversity*[4] *of citizenship question.*

Civil Rights Cases, 109 U.S. 3 (1883). Held congressional *legislation*[7] of 1871 and 1875 invalid in attempting to enforce the *equal*[4] *protection* and *due*[4] *process* clauses of the *Fourteenth Amendment*[4] on the actions of private individuals within a *state*[3]. The *Supreme*[8] *Court* held that the *amendment*[3] applied only to racially *discriminatory*[9] actions of states and that any *federal*[3] legislation must be designed to correct state discriminatory legislation rather than establishing a positive program of legislative protection for Negroes. See also *civil*[9] *rights; Civil*[9] *Rights Act of 1875.*

Cohens v. Virginia, 6 Wheat. 264 (1821). Held that *state*[3] court decisions involving claims of individuals against a state may be reviewed by *federal*[3] courts if the decisions involve federal *laws*[8], *treaties*[12], or the *U.S. Constitution*[4]. *The Supreme*[8] *Court* declared that such appeals based on *federal*[4] *questions* were not in violation of the *Eleventh Amendment*[4] provision prohibiting suits against states by *citizens*[3] of other states. See also *diversity*[4] *of citizenship question*; *John Marshall*[8].

Cole v. Young, 351 U.S. 536 (1956). Held that a *federal*[3] employee may not be dismissed under loyalty security measures unless the position held is clearly one affecting national security. See also *Attorney*[9] *General's list*; *loyalty*[9] *oath*.

Coleman v. Miller, 307 U.S. 433 (1939). Held that the process of amending the *U.S. Constitution*[4] is basically political in nature and not a question for judicial consideration. The *Supreme*[8] *Court* ruled that a *state*[3] may *ratify*[3] an *amendment*[3] after once rejecting it and that determination of how long a proposed amendment should be left before a state is a *political*[4] *question* best left to the *U.S. Congress*[4].

Colgrove v. Green, 328 U.S. 549 (1946). Held that the question of legislative malapportionment was not justiciable but a *political*[4] *question*. The *Supreme*[8] *Court* refused to enter a controversy involving unequal legislative *districts*[7] within the state of Illinois. The Colgrove decision was overruled in *Baker*[1] *v. Carr* when the Court took *jurisdiction*[8] over a *state*[3] *legislative apportionment*[7] controversy in the state of Tennessee. See also *Avery*[1] *v. Midland County*; *justiciable*[4] *question*; *Kirkpatrick*[1] *v. Preisler*; *Reynolds*[1] *v. Sims*; *Wesberry*[1] *v. Sanders*.

Collector v. Day, 11 Wall. 113 (1871). Declared that a *state*[3] judge in Massachusetts was exempt from paying a *federal*[3] income tax under the doctrine of *intergovernmental tax*[4] *immunity* enunciated in *McCulloch*[1] *v. Maryland*. Many subsequent decisions changed the nature of the immunity doctrine in order to allow both *federal*[3] and state *governments*[3] to tax the salaries of public employees. See also *tax*[10] *exemption*; *graduated income tax*[10].

Communist Party v. Subversive Activities Control Board, 367 U.S. 1 (1961). Upheld the registration provisions of the *Internal*[9] *Security (McCarran) Act of 1950* which required subversive action or *front organizations*[5] to register with the *Subversive*[2] *Activities Control Board*. The *Supreme*[8] *Court* stated that the sanctions available to the *government*[3] against those failing to register were only "speculative" and would have to be dealt with individually in order to determine *constitutionality*[3]. In *Aptheker*[1] *v. Secretary of State* the Court declared the *passport*[12] restrictions to be *unconstitutional*[3] sanctions.

Cooley v. Board of Port Wardens, 12 How. 299 (1851). Upheld a Pennsylvania *state*[3] pilotage fee placed on foreign ships using local port facilities within the state. The *Supreme*[8] *Court* held that matters local in nature and not yet regulated by the *U.S. Congress*[4] may receive state regulation as long as the action does not hinder foreign or *interstate commerce*[10]. The "*Cooley*[10] *doctrine*" held that as soon as Congress acted on such a matter affecting interstate commerce, state *legislation*[7] must conform with *federal*[3] *law*[8].

Cooper v. Aaron, 358 U.S. 1 (1958). Held that the *state*[3] governor and *legislature*[7] of Arkansas were required to observe the 1954 *Supreme*[8] *Court* decision in *Brown*[1] *v. Board of Education of Topeka* calling for racially integrated public schools. In the Cooper case, the Court traced the violent resistance to *integration*[9] to actions of the *governor*[6] and state legislature and defended its own Brown decision on the grounds of *judicial*[4] *review* enunciated in *Marbury*[1] *v. Madison.*

Cox v. Louisiana, 379 U.S. 559 (1965). Reversed the conviction of a *civil*[9] *rights* leader arrested for *breach*[8] *of the peace* and obstructing public passages. The *Supreme*[8] *Court* held that the arrest violated the right of free speech and assembly because the action of the civil rights group did not meet normal criteria for a breach of the peace, the *state*[3] *statute*[8] allowing arrest for breach of the peace was too broad, and the *city*[11] officials could too easily prohibit parades and demonstrations.

Cox v. New Hampshire, 312 U.S. 569 (1941). Upheld the right of a *state*[3] to require parade permits before allowing processions on a public thoroughfare. The *Supreme*[8] *Court* held that if traffic regulations are reasonable and nondiscriminatory, they are not in violation of the free expression guarantees of the *First Amendment*[9].

Coyle v. Smith, 221 U.S. 559 (1911). Held that a *state*[3] recently admitted to the *federal*[3] union cannot be bound by limitations established by the *U.S. Congress*[4] prior to admission, if such limitations may be viewed after admittance as part of the *reserved powers*[4] of the states. In the Coyle case, the *Supreme*[8] *Court* said that issue was a state *political*[4] *question* and Oklahoma could move its state capital even though Congress had specified a certain location before admittance and designated that the capital could not be moved before 1913. See also *statehood*[4] *admission; Stearns*[1] *v. Minnesota* for a case involving a prior restriction that could not be changed.

Dartmouth College v. Woodward, 4 Wheat. 518 (1819). Held that a *corporate*[10] charter, in this case an educational charter, was a *contract*[10] and could not be violated by a *state*[3] because of the obligation of *contract*[4] *clause* contained within the *U.S. constitution*[4]. The decision was later applied to charters incorporating business enterprises and became a major protection for *property*[10] rights. See also *John Marshall*[8].

Debs, In re, 158 U.S. 564 (1895). Upheld the conviction of Eugene V. Debs, a *labor*[10] *union* leader, for violating a *federal*[3] court *injunction*[8] designed to keep open the free flow of the mail. In essence, the decision upheld the right of *President*[6] Cleveland to send federal troops into Illinois against the wishes of the *state*[3] *governor*[6] in order to assure the movement of federal mail in the face of a threatened *strike*[10] against the Pullman Company.

Dennis v. U.S., 341 U.S. 494 (1951). Sustained the conviction of 11 American *Communist Party*[5] leaders who had been tried in a federal court for conspiring to teach and to advocate the forcible overthrow of the *federal government*[3]. The *Supreme*[8] *Court* upheld the *Alien*[4] *Registration (Smith) Act of 1940* and the government's right to limit the freedom of expression under the powers of government to protect itself. In the Dennis decision, the Court narrowed the *clear*[9] *and present danger doctrine* and stated that government could act in restricting expression even before a conspiracy reached the point of *revolutionary*[3] action. The decision was later modified in *Yates*[1] *v. U.S.*

Dred Scott v. Sandford, 19 How. 393 (1857). Ruled that *diversity*[4] *of citizenship*[4] cases could not apply to Negroes because they were not defined as *citizens*[2] in the *U.S. constitution*[4]. Therefore Negroes had no standing with which to sue in a *federal*[3] court of *law*[8]. Dred Scott, a Negro slave, had brought suit for his freedom against his master who had taken him into *territory*[3] designated by the *Missouri*[4] *Compromise* of 1820 as "free" territory. Dred Scott sued for his freedom after having been brought back to a slave *state*[3]. The *Supreme*[8] Court declared the Missouri Compromise *unconstitutional*[3] because it violated the *Fifth Amendment*[9] and deprived men of *property*[10] without *due*[9] *process of law*. The *Fourteenth Amendment*[4] overruled the Dred Scott decision and declared "all persons born or naturalized in the United States" to be citizens. See also *diversity*[4] *of citizenship question, Roger Brooke Taney*[8].

Duncan v. Kahanamoku, 327 U.S. 304 (1946). Held that a declaration of *martial*[8] *law*, in this instance in Hawaii under the *federal*[3] Hawaii Organic Act, which permitted the *governor*[6] of Hawaii to declare martial law, did not destroy an individual's right to a civilian trial once civilian courts had been reopened in an area previously designated as a theater of *war*[12]. See also *Milligan*[1], *Ex parte*.

Duncan v. Louisiana, 391 U.S. 145 (1968). Held that the *Sixth Amendment*[9] right to a *jury*[8] trial in criminal proceedings involving serious crimes is also guaranteed in *state*[3] trials by the *Fourteenth Amendment*[4] *due*[4] *process clause*. See also *shocking*[9] *to the conscience doctrine*.

Edwards v. California, 314 U.S. 160 (1941). Declared as an *unconstitutional*[3] restriction on *interstate commerce*[10] a California *statute*[8] making it a *misdemeanor*[8] for any person to assist an "indigent" nonresident to enter the *state*[3]. Four justices felt that such *laws*[8] also violated the *privileges*[4] *and immunities clause* of the *Fourteenth Amendment*[4].

Endo, Ex parte, 323 U.S. 283 (1944). Held that a person of Japanese ancestry whose loyalty had been fully established by the *government*[3] during a time of *war*[12] with Japan could not be denied a *writ of habeas*[8] *corpus* and held in a government relocation camp beyond a reasonable time. The case did not decide the issue of whether detention camps as such were *unconstitutional*[3]. See also *war*[12] *powers*.

Engel v. Vitale, 370 U.S. 421 (1962). Declared the official public school prayer composed by the New York State *Board of Regents*[11] to be an *unconstitutional*[3] prescription violating the *establishment of religion*[9] *clause* of the *First Amendment*[9] as applied to the *states*[3] by the *Fourteenth Amendment*[4].

Erie Railroad v. Tompkins, 304 U.S. 64 (1938). Held that there is no federal *common law*[8], but that in *federal*[3] court cases involving diversity of citizenship, matters of *litigation*[8] are to be settled on the basis of *state*[3] laws of the state in which the dispute originates. The Erie decision overruled Swift v. Tyson, which allowed for federal discretion in *diversity*[4] *of citizenship* questions and accepted the idea of a federal common law.

Escobedo v. Illinois, 378 U.S. 478 (1964). Held that a person charged with violation of a *state*[3] criminal *statute*[8] must be allowed to consult with counsel during interrogation. States denying such a right were declared to be in violation of the "assistance of counsel" provision of the *Sixth Amendment*[9] as applied to the states by the *Fourteenth Amendment*[4] *due*[4] *process clause*.

Estes v. Texas, 381 U.S. 532 (1965). Held that widespread courtroom reporting through the use of live television cameras within the courtroom was prejudicial to a fair trial and in violation of the *due*[9] *process of law* guaranteed by the *Fifth Amendment*[9] as applied to the *states*[3] by the *Fourteenth Amendment*[4]. See also Billie Sol *Estes*[10] *investigation*.

Everson v. Board of Education, 330 U.S. 1 (1947). Upheld a New Jersey *statute*[8] that made it possible for parents sending their children to religious schools by bus to be reimbursed from public funds. The *Supreme*[8] *Court* held that such action was not in violation of the *establishment of religion*[9] *clause* of the *First Amendment*[9], but was instead designed to assist children seeking to secure an accredited education. The Court used reasoning now known as the "child-centered," "pupil-centered," or "*child*[9] *benefit*" doctrine.

"Fanny Hill" Case. A Book Named "John Cleland's Memoirs of a Woman of Pleasure" v. Attorney General of Massachusetts, 383 U.S. 413 (1966). Held that before a book could be declared obscene it must meet all three criteria established by the *Supreme*[8] *Court* as determinants of *obscenity*[9]. The three criteria recognized were: the total work appeals to a *prurient*[9] *interest* in sex, it is patently offensive to contemporary *community*[3] standards, and it is utterly without redeeming social value.

Feiner v. New York, 340 U.S. 315 (1951). Held that a person has a right to speak but has no right to use speech as an instrument to *incite to riot*[8]. The *Supreme*[8] *Court* also held that local officials are generally qualified to determine whether a situation is tending toward riot and to know when to act to prevent it.

Flast v. Cohen, 392 U.S. 83 (1968). Overruled the *Frothingham*[1] *v. Mellon* decision, holding that taxpayers could challenge *federal*[3] grants to the *states*[3] on *constitutional*[3] grounds. The Frothingham case dealt with *grants-in-aid*[10] appropriated under the *general*[4] *welfare clause*, whereas the Flast ruling involved the *establishment of religion*[9] *clause* and *free exercise of religion*[9] *clause* of the *First Amendment*[9]. The federal *law*[8] in question in the Flast ruling was the *Elementary*[11] *and Secondary Education Act of 1965*, a *statute*[8] permitting

the use of federal funds for parochial schools on the basis of the *child*[9] *benefit doctrine*. See also *Everson*[1] *v. Board of Education*.

Fletcher v. Peck, 6 Cr. 87 (1810). Presented the first occasion for the U.S. *Supreme*[8] *Court* to declare a *state*[3] *law*[8] *unconstitutional*[3]. It was also the first time for the Court to interpret the *contract*[4] *clause* of the *U.S. Constitution*[4]. The Supreme Court held that a state legislative action in the form of a *contract*[10] could not be rescinded by a subsequent *session*[8] of the *legislature*[7]. The case upheld the corrupt action of the Georgia legislature in the Yazoo Land Fraud of 1795 because of the protection afforded contracts by the contract clause of the U.S. Constitution. See also *John Marshall*[8].

Fong Yue Ting v. U.S., 149 U.S. 698 (1893). Held that deportation of *aliens*[3] is an *exclusive power*[4] of the *federal government*[3] and that deported individuals are not guaranteed formal trial procedures.

Frothingham v. Mellon, 262 U.S. 447 (1923). Established the principle that an individual taxpayer cannot challenge in a *federal*[3] court the use of federal funds going to *states*[3] through conditional *grants-in-aid*[10] programs. The *legislation*[7] in question in the Frothingham case was the *Sheppard-Towner*[10] *Act of 1921*, a *statute*[8] passed under the *general*[4] *welfare clause* in order to provide maternity care programs within the states. The *Supreme*[8] *Court* held that an individual taxpayer's portion going to a challenged grant would be too small to be considered in a court of *law*[8]. The Frothingham rule was changed in *Flast*[1] *v. Cohen*. The Sheppard-Towner Act was challenged on different *constitutional*[3] grounds by a state in *Massachusetts*[1] *v. Mellon*.

Furman v. Georgia, Jackson v. Georgia, Branch v. Texas (1972). The

Supreme[8] Court decisions which declared that in most instances in which capital[8] punishment is used in the U.S., it constitutes a *cruel and unusual punishment*[9] as prohibited by the *Eighth Amendment*[9] of the *U.S. Constitution*[4]. The 5 to 4 decisions directly affected 600 prisoners and 39 state[3] capital punishment *laws*[8]. The decisions involving murder and rape elicited *majority*[8] and *minority opinions*[8] from all the members of the Court. They appeared to leave open the possibility for the use of capital punishment under fair and equitable judicial and administrative procedures related to particular *crimes*[8].

Garner v. Board of Public Works, 341 U.S. 176 (1951). Upheld the *power*[3] of a municipal *government*[3] to require public employees to take a *loyalty*[9] *oath* declaring nonmembership in the *Communist Party*[5].

Gault, In re, 387 U.S. 1 (1967). The first juvenile case decided by the *Supreme*[8] *Court* on *constitutional*[3] grounds. The Court held that *due*[9] *process of law protections* guaranteed by the *Fifth Amendment*[9] and *Fourteenth Amendment*[4] apply to state[3] legal proceedings directed against juveniles. Such rights include notification of charges, provision of legal counsel, cross-examination of witnesses, and the right to remain silent. See also *due*[4] *process clause*.

Gibbons v. Ogden, 9 Wheat. 1 (1824). Upheld the right of the *federal government*[3] to regulate commerce among the *states*[3] as an exclusive and absolute right that could not be burdened by state *legislation*[7]. The case defined commerce as "intercourse between nations, and parts of *nations*[3]" and laid the basis for the eventual distinctions between *interstate commerce*[10] and *intrastate commerce*[10]. See also *John Marshall*[8].

Gideon v. Wainwright, 372 U.S. 335 (1963). Held that legal assistance is guaranteed to *defendants*[8] in all state[3] criminal trials, even if the defendants are unable to provide their own counsel. The *Supreme*[8] *Court* overruled *Betts*[1] *v. Brady*, stating that the *Sixth Amendment*[9] provision for counsel was brought under protection from state violation by the *Fourteenth Amendment*[4]. The right to counsel had been assured in *federal*[3] criminal trials in *Johnson*[1] *v. Zerbst*. See also *criminal law*[8]; *shocking*[9] *to the conscience doctrine*; *Earl Warren*[8]; *Argersinger*[1] *v. Hamlin*.

Gillette v. U.S., 401 U.S. 437 (1971). Held that the *Selective*[2] *Service* Act does not permit individuals about to be drafted to claim *conscientious*[9] *objector* status, on the grounds that they oppose a particular *war*[12] rather than war in general. The *Supreme*[8] *Court* dealt with the argument that there may be "just" and "unjust" wars and that individuals may selectively determine which war to serve in. The Court upheld the *draft*[12] conviction of Guy P. Gillette, a self-proclaimed humanist, who declared he would participate in a war of national defense or a peacekeeping mission sponsored by the *United*[12] *Nations*, but that he would not serve in the *Vietnam*[12] *War*. The Court held that to permit selectivity in such a matter would violate congressional ability to devise a "fair" system for determining "who serves when not all serve." See also *U.S.*[1] *v. Seeger*.

Ginsberg v. New York, 390 U.S. 629 (1968). Upheld the right of a state[3] to prohibit the selling of publications to minors if the materials portray sex or nudity in an *obscene*[9] way.

Ginzburg v. U.S., 383 U.S. 463 (1966). Held that materials that are not in themselves *obscene*[9] but which are advertised in an obscene way, may forfeit the protection of the *First Amendment*[9] guarantee of free expression. The Ginzburg case upheld a *federal*[3] *obscenity*[9] *statute*[8].

Gitlow v. New York, 268 U.S. 652 (1925). Declared that freedom of speech and the press as guaranteed by the *First Amendment*[9] to the *U.S. Constitution*[4] are "fundamental personal rights" and protected by the *due*[4] *process clause* of the *Fourteenth Amendment*[4] from impairment by the *states*[3]. The *Supreme*[8] *Court* overturned a decision made in *Barron*[1] v. *Baltimore* in 1833 and began what became known as the "nationalization" of the U.S. *Bill*[4] *of Rights*. The decision, announced by Justice Sanford, also incorporated various theories of constitutional interpretation. The *bad*[9] *tendency doctrine* was used in reference to items of expression that might have a tendency to "corrupt public morals, incite to crime, or disturb the public peace." The *reasonable*[9] *man doctrine* was evident in the statement, "Every presumption is to be indulged in favor of the validity of the statute." In other words, legislation should be declared *unconstitutional*[3] only if it acts "arbitrarily or unreasonably." In the Gitlow case a New York criminal *anarchy*[3] law was upheld as *constitutional*[3] on the grounds that it was a valid abridgement of free expression. See also *Bill*[9] *of Rights nationalization*; *subsequent*[9] *punishment doctrine*.

Gomillion v. Lightfoot, 364 U.S. 339 (1960). Declared in violation of the *Fifteenth Amendment*[9] a Tuskegee, Alabama *municipal*[11] *gerrymander*[7] arrangement that effectively excluded Negroes from the electoral process.

Graves v. New York ex rel O'Keefe, 306 U.S. 466 (1939). Overruled the principle enunciated in *Collector*[1] v. *Day*, holding that employees of *federal*[3] agencies could not be exempt from a *state*[3] income tax on the basis of *intergovernmental tax*[4] immunity as established in *McCulloch*[1] v. *Maryland*. See also *Helvering*[1] v. *Gerhardt* for modifications related to state agencies; *tax*[10] *exemption*; *graduated income tax*[10].

Gray v. Sanders, 372 U.S. 368 (1963). Held the Georgia county unit system of primary elections to be *unconstitutional*[3] because of a deliberate structural design that favored *rural*[11] *minority*[9] *groups* within the *state*[3]. The case was the first to be decided on the basis of the *one-man*[5], *one-vote rule* after the *Baker*[1] v. *Carr* decision declared such issues to be justiciable. The decision in both cases was based on the *equal*[4] *protection clause* of the *Fourteenth Amendment*[4]. See also *Avery*[1] v. *Midland County*; *justiciable*[4] *question, Kirkpatrick*[1] v. *Preisler*; *political*[4] *question, primary*[5], *direct*; *Reynolds*[1] v. *Sims*; *Westberry*[1] v. *Sanders*.

Green v. County School Board of New Kent County, Virginia, 389 U.S. 1003 (1968). Held that *integration*[9] of the public schools within the *states*[3] had been given time to meet the "all deliberate speed" clause of the *Brown*[1] v. *Board of Education of Topeka* decision and that school boards must present realistic integration plans "now." In the process the *Supreme*[8] *Court* questioned *freedom*[9] *of choice plans* as they were in operation within the states. Such plans were acceptable only as long as they could help move toward *desegregation*[9]. Freedom of choice plans were eventually declared *unconstitutional*[3] and "unitary school systems" called for in *Alexander*[1] v. *Holmes*.

Griffin v. County Board of Prince Edward County, 337 U.S. 218 (1964). Held in violation of the *Fourteenth Amendment*[4] *equal*[4] *protection clause* several Virginia *statutes*[8] that made it possible for a *state*[3] to provide tax credits to parents whose children were attending nonsectarian private schools in order to avoid public school *integration*[9]. Since such *laws*[8] had been passed to allow Prince Edward County to close its public schools rather than integrate them, the *Supreme*[8] *Court* declared it *unconstitutional*[3] for one *county*[11] to close its public schools while all other counties in the state kept theirs open. See also *tax*[10] *exemption.*

Griswold v. Connecticut, 381 U.S. 479 (1965). Declared *unconstitutional*[3] a Connecticut *statute*[8] making it illegal for anyone, married or single, to use or to advise others on how to use contraceptive devices. The *Supreme*[8] *Court* declared such *legislation*[7] to be in violation of the *right of privacy*[9] as guaranteed by the *Ninth Amendment*[9].

Grossman, Ex parte, 267 U.S. 87 (1925). Upheld the right of the *U.S. President*[6] to fully *pardon*[6] a person declared in *contempt*[8] *of court* as well as persons convicted for legal offenses. However, the *Supreme*[8] *Court* held that such pardons were restricted to criminal contempt citations. See also *criminal law*[8].

Grovey v. Townsend, 295 U.S. 45 (1935). Held that a *political party*[5] could exclude persons from participation in a *direct primary*[5] on the basis of race since a political party is a private association. The *Supreme*[8] *Court* held that such action did not violate the *equal*[4] *protection clause* of the *Fourteenth Amendment*[4] since *discrimination*[9] was by a party rather than a *state*[3]. The Grovey decision abandoned the Court's move toward equality in primary elections as evidenced in *Nixon*[1] *v. Herndon* and *Nixon*[1] *v. Condon.* It was later reversed in *Smith*[1] *v. Allwright.*

Guinn v. U.S., 238 U.S. 347 (1915). Declared in violation of the *Fifteenth Amendment*[5] an Oklahoma *statute*[8] known as the *"grandfather*[5] *clause,"* a legal device used to bar Negroes from voting who could otherwise pass the requirements of the *literacy*[5] *test.* The literacy test was upheld in *Williams*[1] *v. Mississippi* as a *constitutional*[3] method of determining voter qualifications.

Hague v. C.I.O., 307 U.S. 496 (1939). Upheld the right of individuals and *organizations*[6], in this instance a *labor*[10] *union,* to hold peaceful meetings in public streets and parks or in private halls rented for the purpose of peaceful assembly. The *Supreme*[8] *Court* declared that public officials could not arbitrarily restrict such assemblage designed for discussion of public issues on the grounds that they might become disorderly.

Hammer v. Dagenhart, 247 U.S. 251 (1918). Declared the federal Child Labor Act of 1916 *unconstitutional*[3] because of its restrictions on the interstate shipment of goods produced in plants employing *child*[10] *labor.* The *Supreme*[8] *Court* held that such *federal*[3] restrictions were in effect regulating not commerce but production, a matter reserved to the *states*[3]. See also *Bailey*[1] *v. Brexel Furniture Company; Oliver Wendell Holmes*[8], *Jr.; interstate commerce*[10]; *reserved powers*[4]; *U.S.*[1] *v. Darby Lumber Co.*

Hampton & Co. v. U.S., 276 U.S. 394 (1928). Upheld the right of the U.S. *President*[6] to use a legislative *delegation of authority*[6] to adjust *tariffs*[10] on certain items. The *Supreme*[8] *Court* also held that the fact that a tax acted as a regulatory device at the same time it brought in revenue could not invalidate the *power*[3] of the *Congress*[4] to levy such a tax. See also *regulatory tax*[10].

Hannegan v. Esquire, 327 U.S. 146 (1946). Held that the U.S. postmaster general had been granted no power of *censorship*[9] with regard to second-class mailing privileges. The *Supreme*[8] *Court* declared that the postmaster general could determine only if submitted publications were of an informational or "public" character.

Harper v. Virginia State Board of Elections, 383 U.S. 663 (1966). Declared the state poll tax *law*[8] of Virginia, a *statute*[8] requiring a *poll tax*[5] for elections involving *state*[3] officials, in violation of the *equal*[4] *protection clause* of the *Fourteenth Amendment*[4]. See also *Twenty-fourth Amendment*[5].

Harris v. New York, 401 U.S. 222 (1971). Held that the protection against *self-incrimination*[9] does not include the right to commit *perjury*[9]. The *Supreme*[8] *Court* modified the *Miranda*[1] *v. Arizona* ruling, deciding that confessions illegally gained may be permitted as evidence in a criminal case if the *defendant*[8] takes the stand in his own defense. The prosecutor may introduce the illegally obtained confession in order to prove the defendant perjured himself.

Hawke v. Smith, 253 U.S. 221 (1920). Held that a *state*[3] may not submit a proposed *amendment*[3] to the *U.S. Constitution*[4] to the *citizens*[3] of a state through a popular *referendum*[3]. A state must follow the procedures outlined in Article V of the Constitution. The word *"legislatures"*[7] in the article means the general lawmaking bodies of the states.

Heart of Atlanta Motel v. U.S., 379 U.S. 41 (1964). Upheld the *constitutionality*[3] of Title II of the *Civil*[9] *Rights Act of 1964*, the section making it illegal for a business or public accommodation engaged in *interstate commerce*[10] to *discriminate*[9] against any customer because of color, race, religion, or national origin.

Helvering v. Gerhardt, 304 U.S. 405 (1938). Overruled the principle enunciated in *Collector*[1] *v. Day*, holding that employees of *state*[3] agencies could not be exempt from the *federal*[3] *graduated income tax*[10] on the basis of *intergovernmental tax*[4] *immunity* as established in *McCulloch*[1] *v. Maryland*. See also *Graves*[1] *v. New York ex rel O'Keefe* for modifications related to federal agencies; *tax*[10] *exemption*.

Hepburn v. Griswold, 8 Wall. 603 (1870). Held *unconstitutional*[3] the *Legal*[10] *Tender Act of 1862* as a denial of *due*[9] *process of law* to those creditors whose *property*[10] rights were adversely affected by *legislation*[7] creating paper currency usable to pay debts made before the passage of the *law*[8]. The *Supreme*[8] *Court* held that only gold and silver could be used to pay such debts, even if made during a time of *civil war*[12]. The Hepburn decision was overruled in the *Legal*[1] *Tender Cases* of 1871.

Home Building and Loan Assn. v. Blaisdell, 290 U.S. 398 (1934). Upheld a Minnesota *statute*[8] passed during the *Great Depression*[10] to protect debtors facing mortgage foreclosures. The *Supreme*[8] *Court* held that a *state*[3] could not impair mortgage *contracts*[10], but that it could delay their fulfillment during times of financial crisis. The Court declared that states may exercise an inordinate amount of *power*[3] to protect their *citizens*[3] during times of emergency. See also *emergency powers*[4].

Humphrey's Executor (Rathbun) v. U.S., 355 U.S. 107 (1935). Held that the *U.S. president's*[6] *power*[3] of removal does not apply to members of *independent regulatory commissions*[6] endowed with *quasi-legislative*[6] *and quasi-judicial* functions. The Humphrey case involved President *Franklin D. Roosevelt's*[6] politically motivated removal of a member of the *Federal*[2] *Trade Commission* in violation of a provision of the *Federal*[10] *Trade Commission Act of 1914*, which stated that members could be removed only for causes specified by *law*[8]. See also *removal*[6] *powers*.

Hurtado v. California, 110 U.S. 516 (1884). Held that *states*[3] are not required to use *grand jury*[8] proceedings in order to bring persons to trial as long as proper procedures are used in the filing of an *"information"*[8] against the accused. See also *shocking*[9] *to the conscience doctrine*.

Hylton v. U.S., 3 Dall. 171 (1796). Held that a tax on carriages was an *indirect tax*[10] ("excise") and thus is not subject to apportionment among the *states*[3] on the basis of population. The *Supreme*[8] Court declared two taxes, capitation and land, to be *direct taxes*[10] capable of apportionment on the basis of population. A third direct tax, income, was added in *Pollock*[1] *v. Farmers' Loan and Trust Co.*, which led to the adoption of the *Sixteenth Amendment*[9]. See also *excise tax*[10].

James v. Valtierra, 402 U.S. 137 (1971). Held that the *state*[3] of California could by constitutional *amendment*[3] permit local *communities*[3] to determine by *referendum*[3] whether to institute or reject *public*[11] *housing* authorities within their legal *jurisdictions*[8]. The *Supreme*[8] Court held that such a process was not in violation of the *Federal Housing*[11] *Act of 1937*. It also held that rejection of such programs was not in itself racially *discriminatory*[9] or a denial of "the equal protection of the laws" guaranteed by the *Fourteenth Amendment*[4]. See also *local*[11] *public authority*; *urban*[11] *renewal*.

Jencks v. U.S., 353 U.S. 657 (1957). Declared that a *defendant*[8] in a *federal*[3] court has the right to examine written statements made against him prior to his trial and introduced in the trial by the prosecution if such statements relate to the witness's testimony on the stand. The decision required the opening of *Federal*[2] *Bureau of Investigation* files to reveal the prior statements of paid informants who testified against the defendant and revealed his activities with the *Communist Party*[5]. The so-called *Jencks*[9] *Act of 1957* was passed in order to allow a trial judge to delete unrelated materials before allowing

the defendant to see the prior testimony against him.

Johnson v. Zerbst, 304 U.S. 458 (1938). Held that in *federal*[3] *criminal law*[8] cases the trial court must appoint legal counsel for all persons, even indigents, in order to meet the *Sixth Amendment*[9] criteria for "assistance of counsel." The same criterion was applied to *state*[3] criminal trials in *Gideon*[1] *v. Wainwright*.

Jones v. Alfred H. Mayer Co., 389 U.S. 968 (1968). Upheld a *federal*[3] open housing provision in the *Civil*[9] *Rights Act of 1866*, an act based on the *Thirteenth Amendment*[4]. The *Supreme*[8] Court stated that the *U.S. Congress*[4] had the authority to abolish slavery and the "badges of slavery" and that black *citizens*[3] had the same rights as whites in the buying, selling, and renting of real and personal *property*[10]. See also *open*[9] *occupancy law*.

Katz v. U.S., 389 U.S. 347 (1967). Declared that *federal*[3] officials *wiretapping*[9] a public telephone booth used by an individual for interstate gambling purposes was an *unreasonable search*[9] *and seizure* because a person has the right to the private use of public facilities without *government*[3] invasion, physical or otherwise. The *Supreme*[8] Court mentioned that *constitutionality*[3] in such situations could be met with prior judicial approval if reasonable justification for eavesdropping could be shown. The Katz decision and *Berger*[1] *v. New York* both emphasized that the *Fourth Amendment*[9] was designed to protect people, not places. They essentially reversed an earlier decision in *Olmstead*[1] *v. U.S.*

Kendall v. Stokes, 12 Pet. 524 (1838). Held that *federal*[3] officials appointed by the *U.S. president*[6] are not always under the exclusive control of presidential *power*[3], especially with regard to actions of a purely ministerial character established by the *U.S. Congress*[4].

Kent v. Dulles, 357 U.S. 116 (1958). Declared that the word "liberty" in the *Fifth Amendment*[9] protects a *citizen's*[3] right to travel abroad. The *Supreme*[8] *Court* held that the *U.S. Congress*[4] had not given the secretary of state the right to restrict *passports*[12] because of political beliefs or associations. Restrictions based on geography and foreign *policy*[6] interests were upheld in *Zemel*[1] *v. Rusk*.

Kentucky v. Dennison, 24 How. 66 (1861). Held that a *federal*[3] court possessed no *authority*[3] to issue a *writ of mandamus*[8] to compel a state *governor*[6] to *extradite*[12] a fugitive from *justice*[8] who had entered his *state*[3].

Kentucky Whip and Collar Co. v. Illinois Central Railroad Company, 299 U.S. 334 (1937). Upheld the *Ashurst-Sumners*[10] *Act of 1935*, a *federal*[3] *statute*[8] prohibiting the shipment of prison-made goods into any *state*[3] barring such goods by state *law*[8]. The *Supreme*[8] *Court* held that such *legislation*[7] was not a *delegation of authority*[6] to states but an acceptable device designed to help states use their own *police powers*[4].

Keyishian v. Board of Regents, 385 U.S. 589 (1967). Reversed an earlier decision upholding New York's Feinberg Law and finally declared the *law*[8] *unconstitutional*[3] because its *loyalty*[9] *oath* section was too vague for public employees to determine what constituted *seditious*[12] acts and utterances. The *Supreme*[8] *Court* also indicated that dismissal under the *statute*[8] gave no opportunity for a person to prove nonactive membership in an *organization*[6] listed as subversive or to reveal disagreement with illegal aims of the *Communist Party*[5]. See also *Adler*[1] *v. Board of Education*, which upheld the Feinberg Law; *board of education*[11].

Kilbourn v. Thompson, 103 U.S. 168 (1881). Declared that the *U.S. Congress*[4] did not possess general *investigative powers*[7] to examine private business affairs, that it could not jail through congressional *resolution*[7] those uncommunicative witnesses cited for *contempt*[7] of Congress unless proper judicial procedures were followed, and that legislative investigations must deal with subjects Congress is capable of legislating upon. The case dealt with a *District of Columbia*[4] real estate pool. In settling the basic conflict over the *investigative power*[7] of Congress, the *Supreme*[8] *Court* also held that members of Congress could not be sued for statements or actions taken in their official capacities as *legislators*[7].

King v. Smith, 392 U.S. 309 (1968). Declared *unconstitutional*[3] an Alabama "substitute father" regulation related to the *federal*[3] *Aid*[11] *for Dependent Children* (AFDC) program on the grounds that the rule violated the *Social*[11] *Security Act of 1935* and the *equal*[4] *protection clause* of the *Fourteenth Amendment*[4]. The *substitute*[11] *father rule* denied AFDC payments to any woman "cohabiting" with any single or married man. The *Supreme*[8] *Court* held that the *state*[3] could not regulate illicit sexual behavior or declare a person "father" when he had no legal duty to contribute to a child's support.

Kirkpatrick v. Preisler, 394 U.S. 526 (1969). Held that *congressional districts*[7] must be exactly the same size in population. The *Supreme*[8] *Court* declared a Missouri *redistricting*[7] plan varying 3.1 percent between districts *unconstitutional*[3] because the *state*[3] could not prove such variations unavoidable.

Klopfer v. North Carolina, 386 U.S. 213 (1967). Held that the speedy trial provision of the *Sixth Amendment*[9] applied to the *states*[3] through the *due*[4] *process clause* of the *Fourteenth Amendment*[4].

Korematsu v. U.S., 323 U.S. 214 (1944). Upheld the "relocation" of United States *citizens*[3] of Japanese ancestry during *World*[12] *War II.* The *Supreme*[8] *Court* upheld the action on the grounds that during a time of national military crisis the *government*[3] may take actions necessary to prevent espionage and sabotage and meet any military exigencies at hand. In essence, the Court declared that during time of national crisis the *war*[12] *powers* may supersede the *Bill*[4] *of Rights* of the *U.S. Constitution*[4].

Lamont v. Postmaster General, 381 U.S. 301 (1965). Held *unconstitutional*[3] a *federal*[3] *statute*[8] requiring postal addressees to request in writing that the Post Office Department release any of their mail classified as "*Communist*[3] political *propaganda*[5]." The *Supreme*[8] *Court* held such a *law*[8] in violation of the *First Amendment*[9] freedom of expression. See also *United*[2] *States Postal Service.*

Legal Tender Cases (Knox v. Lee and Parker v. Davis), 12 Wall. 457 (1871). Overruled the *Hepburn*[1] *v. Griswold* decision of 1870 and upheld the right of the *federal government*[3] to permit the payment of debts, public and private, by proper currency. *The Supreme*[8] *Court* upheld such *government*[3] action under the *war*[12] *powers* borrowing power, and the *power*[3] to coin money.

Leisy v. Hardin, 135 U.S. 100 (1890). Held that the *original*[10] *package doctrine* enunciated in *Brown*[1] *v. Maryland* applied to *interstate commerce*[10] as well as to foreign commerce. In the Leisy ruling the *Supreme*[8] *Court* declared that the *police powers*[4] of the *states*[3] could not be used to restrict the shipment of liquor as long as the liquor was a part of *interstate commerce*[10] and remained in the original package. See also *divestment*[10] *theory.*

Lemon v. Kurtzman, 403 U.S. 602 (1971). Declared *unconstitutional*[3] a 1968 Pennsylvania *statute*[8] which permitted *state*[3] financial reimbursement of a portion of teachers' salaries, textbooks, and other "secular" subjects provided under the *purchase*[9] *of services doctrine* operating in religious schools. The statute was viewed as a violation of the *establishment of religion*[9] *clause* of the *First Amendment*[9] because it provided direct state aid to church-related elementary and secondary schools. A companion case, also declaring a state *law*[8] unconstitutional involved a Rhode Island statute permitting state salary supplements for nonpublic elementary school teachers. The Court held that the state could not pay 15 percent of the salary of such teachers. A third decision handed down on the same day upheld the *federal*[3] Higher Education Facilities Act of 1963 which permitted federal funds to be used in constructing academic facilities on religious campuses. The Court held that such facilities could be considered "religiously neutral."

Lochner v. New York, 198 U.S. 45 (1905). Declared a New York *maximum*[10] *hour law* (10-hour day) for bakery employees an *unconstitutional*[3] invasion of individual rights to *contract*[10] for gainful employment. The *Supreme*[8] *Court* held that such *legislation*[7] was not validly under the *police powers*[4] of the *state*[3] and was not really designed to protect health but to regulate labor. Such a condition placed the *law*[8] in violation of the *due*[4] *process clause* of the *Fourteenth Amendment*[4]. Justice *Oliver Wendell Holmes,*[8] *Jr.,* in a *dissenting opinion*[8], stated: "The Fourteenth Amendment does not enact Mr. *Herbert Spencer's*[3] Social Statics." Justice Holmes' views eventually prevailed. *Federal*[3] *legislation*[7] that would have earlier been declared in violation of the police powers of the state, the *contract*[4] *clause*, and the due process clause of the Fourteenth Amendment was upheld as *constitutional*[3]. Maximum hour laws were upheld for women in *Muller*[1] *v. Oregon* in 1908 and for men receiving overtime pay in industrial jobs in *Bunting*[1] *v. Oregon* in 1917. See also *Social*[11] *Darwinism*.

Loving v. Virginia, 388 U.S. 1 (1967). Declared a Virginia *antimiscegenation*[9] *law* a violation of individual decision-making in marriage and a deprivation of liberty without *due*[9] *process of law*. See also *discrimination*[9].

Luther v. Borden, 7 How. 1 (1849). Held that the question of whether a *state*[3] possesses a republican form of *government*[3] as guaranteed by the *U.S. Constitution*[4] is a political matter to be decided by a branch of government other than the judiciary. The case involved *Dorr's*[4] *Rebellion*, an uprising challenging whether the existing government of Rhode Island was republican in nature because of its restrictive voter qualifications. *President*[6] Tyler supported the regular government and its use of *martial*[8] *law* to avoid domestic violence, thereby acknowledging the government as republican in character. See also *republic*[3]; *Roger Brooke Taney*[8].

Mallory v. U.S., 352 U.S. 449 (1957). A highly publicized *District of Columbia*[4] rape-murder case in which the *Supreme*[8] *Court* reaffirmed the *McNabb*[1] rule and held that undue delay in arraignment may void a conviction based on a confession gained before *arraignment*[8]. The Court declared that the confession should have been excluded as evidence during the trial.

Malloy v. Hogan, 378 U.S. 1 (1964). Held that the *Fifth Amendment*[9] guarantee against *self-incrimination*[9] applied to the *states*[3] through the *Fourteenth Amendment*[4] *due*[4] *process clause*. The decision overruled *Twining*[1] *v. New Jersey*. See also *shocking*[9] *to the conscience doctrine*.

Mapp v. Ohio, 367 U.S. 643 (1961). Held that the so-called *exclusionary*[9] *rule* disallowing as evidence in *federal*[3] court any evidence or materials gained through *unreasonable search*[9] *and seizure* also applied to the actions of the *states*[3]. The decision overruled *Wolf*[1] *v. Colorado*, which had avoided incorporating the exclusionary rule in the *Fourteenth Amendment*[4] *due*[4] *process clause*.

Marbury v. Madison, 1 Cr. 137 (1803). Held for the first time in American history that an *act*[8] of the U.S. *Congress*[4] was *unconstitutional*[3]. Although the *Supreme*[8] *Court* had exercised *judicial*[4] *review* in upholding a *federal*[3] *statute*[8] in 1796, the Marbury decision is frequently cited as the real turning point in the development of the *power*[3] of the Court. The Court held unconstitutional the portion of the *Judiciary*[4] *Act of 1789* which added the right of issuing *writs of mandamus*[8] to the *original jurisdiction*[8] of the Supreme Court. In the event of a conflict between the *U.S. Constitution*[4] and a federal *law*[8], the Court stated that it must accept the Constitution as the supreme law of the land. See also *John Marshall*[8]; *national*[4] *supremacy clause*; *national*[4] *supremacy doctrine*.

Marchetti v. U.S., 390 U.S. 39 (1968). Held that the *federal*[3] *law*[8] requiring a person to declare for income tax purposes all income illegally gained through gambling was an *unconstitutional*[3] violation of the *Fifth Amendment*[9] *self-incrimination*[9] clause. See also *graduated income tax*[10].

Martin v. Hunter's Lessee, 1 Wheat. 304 (1816). Held that *state*[3] court decisions involving suits between private *citizens*[3] could be reviewed by *federal*[3] courts if the decisions involved federal *laws*[8], *treaties*[12], or the

U.S. *Constitution*[4]. The *Supreme*[8] *Court* for the first time declared that it had the *power*[3] to review the actions and decisions of state judicial bodies. See also *judicial*[4] *review*.

Massachusetts v. Mellon, 262 U.S. 447 (1923). Established the principle that a *state*[3] may not challenge a *federal*[3] conditional *grants-in-aid*[10] program as a violation of the *reserved powers*[4] of the states guaranteed by the *Tenth Amendment*[4]. In the Massachusetts v. Mellon case, a companion case of *Frothingham*[1] *v. Mellon*, the *Supreme*[8] *Court* held that it did not have *jurisdiction*[8] to settle a question basically political in nature. The federal *legislation*[7] challenged by the state of Massachusetts was the *Sheppard-Towner*[10] *Act of 1921*, an *act*[8] passed under the *general*[4] *welfare clause* of the *U.S. Constitution*[4] to provide maternity care programs within the states. See also *political*[4] *question*.

McCardle, Ex parte, 7 Wall. 506 (1869). Upheld the legislative action of the *U.S. Congress*[4] which, in changing an existing *law*[8], withdrew a case under active judicial consideration from the appellate calendar of the *Supreme*[8] *Court*. The post-Civil War Congress dominated by the Radical Republicans feared that the case of a Mississippi editor seeking release from trial before a military *commission* (see *board*[6]) on a *writ of habeas*[8] *corpus* could lead to a declaration that the *Reconstruction*[4] program was *unconstitutional*[3]. Rather than face such an eventuality, the Congress changed a section of an 1867 law over the *president's*[3] *veto*[7] in order to modify the Supreme Court's *appellate jurisdiction*[8] with regard to controversies involving release of prisoners through the writ of habeas corpus. See also *Civil*[4] *War*.

McCollum v. Board of Education, 333 U.S. 203 (1948). Declared *unconstitutional*[3] a "released time" program of religious instruction operating in Champaign, Illinois on the grounds that it violated the *establishment of religion*[9] *clause* of the *First Amendment*[9] as applied to the *states*[3] by the *Fourteenth Amendment*[4]. The program in question permitted religious instruction on campus during the school day by off-campus religious personnel who were paid by separate religious institutions. The *Supreme*[8] *Court* held that such religious use of public facilities was *unconstitutional*[3]. See also *released*[9] *time doctrine*.

McCulloch v. Maryland, 4 Wheat. 316 (1819). Upheld, in the first major decision involving the *implied powers*[4] of the *federal government*[3] the right of the U.S. government to establish a bank authorized to issue bank notes that could not be taxed by *state*[3] governments. The decision of the *Supreme*[8] *Court* emphasized the nature of implied powers, upheld the national supremacy of the central government to carry out legitimate functions assigned to it by the *U.S. Constitution*[4], and laid the basis for the development of the doctrine of *intergovernmental tax*[4] *immunity*. In the decision, *Chief*[8] *Justice John Marshall*[8] declared that "The power to tax is the power to destroy." See also *national*[4] *supremacy clause*; *national*[4] *supremacy doctrine*; *Veazie*[1] *Bank v. Fenno* for modification with regard to *federal*[3] taxes on state bank notes.

McGrain v. Daugherty, 273 U.S. 135 (1927). Upheld the right of congressional *investigating committees*[7] to compel witnesses to attend hearings, to require witnesses to produce appropriate records, to inquire into matters clearly related to *legislation*[7], and to cite individuals for *contempt*[7] *of Congress*. See also *investigative*[7] *powers*.

McLaurin v. Oklahoma State Regents, 339 U.S. 637 (1950). Held that racial *segregation*[9] of public graduate schools within the *state*[3] of Oklahoma was in violation of the *equal*[4] *protection clause* of the *Fourteenth Amendment*[4]. See also *Board of Education*[11].

McNabb v. U.S., 318 U.S. 332 (1943). Held that *federal*[3] officials must take persons suspected of violating federal *laws*[8] before legal magistrates "without unnecessary delay." The *Supreme*[8] *Court* declared *unconstitutional*[3] the conviction of a man who had been detained and interrogated for two days without the opportunity for legal counsel, even though he had confessed to shooting a federal revenue officer. The Court held such action in violation of the *due*[4] *process clause* of the *Fifth Amendment*[9].

Merryman, Ex parte, 17 Fed. Cases 9487 (1861). A decision rendered by *Chief Justice Taney*[8] while sitting in the circuit court in Baltimore, Maryland, in which the Chief Justice held that the *writ of habeas*[8] *corpus* could not be suspended by the U.S. *President*[6], but that it could be suspended by the *Congress*[4].

Milligan, Ex parte, 4 Wall. 2 (1866). Held that the *President*[6] had no *authority*[3] to suspend the *writ of habeas*[8] *corpus* and order civilians to be tried by military courts in areas where the regular courts were in operation. The *Supreme*[8] *Court* said the *Congress*[4] was also forbidden the use of such military *commissions*[6] outside an actual theater of *war*[12]. See also *Duncan*[1] *v. Kahanamoku; martial*[8] *law*.

Minersville School District v. Gobitis, 310 U.S. 586 (1940). Upheld a local public school regulation requiring all pupils to salute the U.S. flag as a part of the regular school day. The *Supreme*[8] *Court* declared that the practice challenged by adherents of the Jehovah's Witnesses was not in violation of the *free exercise of religion*[9] *clause* of the *First Amendment*[9]. The Minersville decision was reversed in *West*[1] *Virginia State Board of Education v. Barnette*.

Miranda v. Arizona, 384 U.S. 436 (1966). Elaborated on principles dealt with earlier in *Escobedo*[1] *v. Illinois* and extended *Fifth Amendment*[9] protections as applicable to the *states*[3] under the *Fourteenth Amendment*[4]. The *Supreme*[8] *Court* held that a person must be advised of his right to remain silent, warned that *self-incriminating*[9] statements may be used against him, given counsel prior to questioning, questioned in counsel's presence if desired, and provided counsel if unable to afford a lawyer. See also *Harris*[1] *v. New York; Earl Warren*[8].

Mississippi v. Johnson, 4 Wall. 475 (1867). Held that the *Supreme*[8] *Court* had no *authority*[3] to enjoin the U.S. *President*[6] from enforcing the *Reconstruction*[4] *acts*[8], on the grounds that they were *unconstitutional*[3]. The Court held that the President possessed "executive discretion" in the enforcement of *federal*[3] *law*[8].

Missouri v. Holland, 252 U.S. 416 (1920). Upheld a *federal*[3] *statute*[8] enforcing protection of migratory birds within the *states*[3], on the basis that the statute was passed to fulfill the obligations of a *treaty*[12] with Great Britain on behalf of Canada. The *Supreme*[8] *Court* held that such a treaty was not in violation of the *police powers*[4] or *reserved powers*[4] of the states, but was a valid exercise of the treaty-making power related to foreign relations, a *power*[3] clearly vested in the central *government*[3]. See *Bricker*[12] *Amendment; diplomatic*[6] *powers*.

Missouri ex rel. Gaines v. Canada, 305 U.S. 337 (1938). Declared *unconstitutional*[3] a *state*[3] *law*[8] making available state tuition payments to resident Negroes who were attending *integrated*[9] colleges outside the state. The *Supreme*[8] *Court* held that such a public *policy*[6] could not meet the test of the *separate*[9] *but equal doc-*

trine and was in violation of the *Fourteenth Amendment*[4] *equal*[4] *protection clause.*

Monitor Patriot v. Roy, 401 U.S. 265 (1971). Held that a political candidate who has been *libeled*[9] may not collect damages from a publication unless the publication knowingly printed false statements of actual malice. The *Supreme*[8] *Court* held that allegations of criminal practices, regardless of how remote, may be made about political candidates unless actual malice is involved. In the Monitor case the Court upheld a particular situation involving a long-existing rule sometimes referred to as the *thick*[5] *skin doctrine*, a doctrine which holds that persons who enter public life or expose themselves to the public must possess a "thick skin" with regard to criticism. By the very fact of going into public life, such individuals make a personal choice to "live in a glass house."

Moore v. Dempsey, 261 U.S. 86 (1923). Held in violation of the right to a fair trial a conviction obtained in a *state*[3] court dominated by mob action. Such a condition violated the *due*[4] *process clause* of the *Fifth Amendment*[9] as applied to the states by the *Fourteenth Amendment*[4].

Morgan v. Virginia, 328 U.S. 373 (1946). Declared a Virginia *law*[8] requiring *segregated*[9] accommodations on all public transportation facilities within the *state*[3] an *unconstitutional*[3] burden on *interstate commerce*[10] and travel, especially as it affected interstate bus transportation.

Mulford v. Smith, 307 U.S. 38 (1939). Upheld the marketing quota provisions of the second Agricultural Adjustment Act of 1938 (see *Agricultural*[2] *Adjustment Administration*), on the grounds that they were legitimately related to regulations on *interstate commerce*[10] and *conservation*[10]. See *U.S.*[1] *v. Butler.*

Muller v. Oregon, 208 U.S. 412 (1908). Unanimously upheld a *state*[3] *maximum*[10] *hour law* for women which restricted women to a 10-hour day in industrial employment. The *law*[8] was upheld as a legitimate function of the *police powers*[4] of the state that may protect the general welfare of the *citizens*[3] of the state, especially female citizens whose physical differences require legislative protection. The decision, generously recognizing the "Brandeis brief" presented by legal counsel and later justice of the *Supreme*[8] *Court* Louis Brandeis, took "judicial cognizance" of the sociological and medical data related to the question at hand. It was the first Supreme Court decision accepting such material rather than pure "legal" arguments.

Munn v. Illinois, 94 U.S. 113 (1877). Held that an Illinois *law*[8] fixing minimum rates allowable for storage of grain within privately owned elevators open to public use was not in violation of the *due*[4] *process clause* of the *Fourteenth Amendment*[4]. The *Supreme*[8] *Court* held that such *legislation*[7] did not take private *property*[10] without due process. The Court also held that a *state*[3] may use its *police powers*[4] to regulate businesses *affected with a public*[10] *interest*. Munn v. Illinois, one of the major cases resulting from the so-called *Granger*[10] *Movement*, was significantly weakened in Wabash, St. Louis and Pacific Railroad Company v. Illinois in 1886. The Court declared certain *state*[3] regulatory devices invalid on the grounds that they interfered with *federal*[3] control over *interstate commerce*[10]. Other cases in Minnesota, Texas, and other states weakened *rate-making*[10] activities of states on the grounds that such activities deprived individuals of property without *due*[9] *process of law.*

Myers v. U.S., 272 U.S. 52 (1926). Held *unconstitutional*[3] an 1876 *federal*[3] *law*[8] requiring U.S. *Senate*[7] "advice and consent" before the *U.S. President*[6] could remove appointed postmasters who were serving four-year terms of office as set by law. The *Supreme*[8] *Court* upheld the action of President *Woodrow Wilson*[6] who removed Myers, the first-class postmaster of Portland, Oregon, without Senate action and before Myers' term of office had expired. See also *advice*[7] *and consent powers*; *appointment*[6] *powers*; *removal*[6] *powers*.

Nardone v. U.S., 308 U.S. 338 (1939). Held that Section 605 of the *Federal*[9] *Communications Act of 1934*, a section stating: "No person not being authorized by the sender shall intercept any communication and divulge or publish the evidence, contents, substance, purport, effect or meaning of such intercepted communication to any person," made wiretapping a *federal*[3] offense and barred *wiretap*[9] evidence from use in a federal court of *law*[8]. See also *Olmstead*[1] *v. U.S.*

National Association for the Advancement of Colored People (NAACP) v. Alabama, 357 U.S. 449 (1958). Upheld the right of the NAACP as a New York based *corporation*[10] operating in the *state*[3] of Alabama to maintain a secret list of its members even though an Alabama *law*[8] required public disclosure of membership lists of out-of-state corporations. The basis of the decision was the right of association of a group generally recognized as legally acceptable.

National Labor Relations Board v. Jones and Laughlin Corp., 301 U.S. 1 (1937). Upheld the *constitutionality*[3] of the *National*[10] *Labor Relations (Wagner) Act of 1935*, which guaranteed labor the right to organize and bargain collectively and which created the *National*[2] *Labor Relations Board (NLRB)* to handle labor-management disputes. Although the case did not directly overrule earlier decisions declaring manufacturing and production to be local in nature, it

did broaden the *Federal*[3] *power*[3] over production by holding that the NLRB could handle labor disputes of companies whose business production and labor problems affected the movement of goods in *interstate commerce*[10]. See also *Carter*[1] *v. Carter Coal Co.*; *collective*[10] *bargaining*; *Charles Evans Hughes*[8]; *Schechter*[1] *Poultry Corp. v. U.S.*; *Sunshine*[1] *Anthracite Coal Co. v. Adkins*; *U.S.*[1] *v. E. C. Knight Co.*

Neagle, In re, 135 U.S. 1 (1890). Upheld the right of a federal *executive*[6] official under presidential *authority*[3] to take action in the absence of specific federal *legislation*[7] which may be necessary to maintain order and protect *federal*[3] officials and *property*[10]. Neagle, a *United*[8] *States marshal*, had been assigned by the *Attorney*[8] *General* to protect Justice Field of the *Supreme*[8] *Court*. Neagle was arrested by a California official when he carried out his duty to the fullest and killed a man named Terry who attacked Justice Field. The Court upheld the *prerogative*[6] *theory* which holds that the executive may act on his own in some instances without specific legislation because of his oath to "preserve, protect, and defend the *Constitution*[4] of the United States."

Near v. Minnesota, 283 U.S. 697 (1931). Declared *unconstitutional*[3] a Minnsota "*gag*[9] *law*" designed to suppress printed criticism of public officials. The *Supreme*[8] *Court* held that *government*[3] could not place a "prior restraint" on general public expression although abuses of such expression could be dealt with after the fact. Prior restraint was viewed as a violation of the *First Amendment*[9] freedom of the press as applied to the *states*[3] by the *Fourteenth Amendment*[4]. See also *prior*[9] *restraint doctrine*; *subsequent*[9] *punishment doctrine*.

Nebbia v. New York, 291 U.S. 502 (1934). Upheld a New York state *law*[8] regulating milk prices as a valid exercise of *power*[3] by a *state*[3] to regulate businesses *"affected with a public*[10] *interest"*, thereby broadening the idea of "public interest" beyond the areas generally classified as *public*[10] *utilities*. The Nebbia case also marked the turning point of the *Supreme*[8] *Court's* rejection of *substantive due*[9] *process* as the basic guideline for interpreting *Fifth Amendment*[9] and *Fourteenth Amendment*[4] guarantees.

Newberry v. U.S., 256 U.S. 232 (1921). Held that primary elections were not elections in the pure sense of the word, but instead were *political party*[5] functions designed simply for the nomination of party candidates. The *Supreme*[8] *Court* thereby invalidated a portion of the Corrupt Practices Act of 1910 which set limitations on expenditures of *federal*[3] candidates in primary elections. It also laid the framework for *state*[3] *legislation*[7], creating what came to be known as the *white primary*[5]. The Newberry decision was reversed in *U.S.*[1] *v. Classic*. See also *direct primary*[5].

New York Times Co. v. Sullivan, 376 U.S. 254 (1964). Held in a case involving a factually inaccurate paid advertisement in the New York Times that a newspaper cannot be sued for *libel*[9] if there is no evidence of malice and if the erroneous statements were "honestly made." The inaccurate advertisement in question was directed against the racial attitudes and practices of *city*[11] officials of Montgomery, Alabama and led to libel awards in *state*[3] courts ranging up to $500,000 each. The *Supreme*[8] *Court* declared such action in violation of freedom of speech and press.

New York Times Co. v. U.S., 403 U.S. 713 (1971). Held that the United States *government*[3] could not continue to restrain the New York Times or the Washington Post from publishing material from a top secret classi-

fied government study entitled "History of U.S. Decision-Making Process on Vietnam Policy." The *Supreme*[8] *Court* held that the prior restraint placed upon the publications by temporary *federal*[3] court *injunctions*[8], the first such restraint in U.S. history, violated the freedom of the press as guaranteed by the *First Amendment*[9]. Mr. Justice Black wrote of the First Amendment in a *concurring opinion*[8]: "The press was protected so that it could bare the secrets of government and inform the people. Only a free and unrestrained press can effectively expose deception in government." Only *Chief*[8] *Justice* Burger and Justices Blackmun and Harlan dissented. Chief Justice Burger stated the government's position by holding that the Court acted with too little knowledge, too much haste, and on a matter involving "complex modern government, and specifically the effective exercise of certain constitutional powers of the Executive." See also *prior*[9] *restraint doctrine*; *subsequent*[9] *punishment doctrine*; *Pentagon*[12] *Papers*; *Vietnam*[12] *War*.

Nixon v. Condon, 286 U.S. 73 (1932). Held *unconstitutional*[3] a Texas *statute*[8] permitting an executive *committee*[7] of a *political party*[5] to establish the criteria for party membership and participation in party primaries. The *Supreme*[8] *Court* voided the statute on the grounds that it was designed to bar Negroes from voting and to circumvent the previous decision of *Nixon*[1] *v. Herndon*. Such *discrimination*[9] was declared in violation of the *Fourteenth Amendment*[4] *equal*[4] *protection clause* because the party *executive*[6] committee serves as an agent of the *state*[3] in election matters. See *direct primary*[5]; *Grovey*[1] *v. Townsend*; *Smith*[1] *v. Allwright*.

Nixon v. Herndon, 273 U.S. 536 (1927). Held that a Texas *statute*[8] prohibiting Negroes from voting in *Democratic Party*[5] primary elections was a denial of the equal protection of the laws as guaranteed by the *Fourteenth Amendment*[4]. See also *direct primary*[5]; *equal*[4] *protection clause*; *Grovey*[1] *v. Townsend*; *Nixon*[1] *v. Condon*; *Smith*[1] *v. Allwright*.

Olmstead v. U.S., 277 U.S. 438 (1928). Held that the use of *wiretapping*[9] of telephone lines by *federal*[3] agents to enforce federal *law*[8] (prohibition) was not a violation of the *Fourth Amendment*[9] *unreasonable search*[9] *and seizure* provision because there was no physical invasion of the *property*[10] of the *defendants*[8] in question. The *Supreme*[8] *Court* declared that conversation was not protected since it did not have the character of objects. The *Federal Communications*[9] *Act of 1934* made the use of evidence gained through such methods inadmissible in a federal court of law. The *legislation*[7] was upheld in *Nardone*[1] *v. U.S.* The Olmstead rule was essentially reversed by *Berger*[1] *v. New York* and *Katz*[1] *v. U.S.*

Opp Cotton Mills v. Administrator of Wage and Hour Division, 312 U.S. 126 (1941). Upheld the congressional *delegation of authority*[6] to administrative agencies to establish minimum wages in particular industries. The case, one of many dealing with administrative rule-making, upheld the *Fair*[10] *Labor Standards Act of 1938* and the right of the *U.S. Congress*[4] to establish guidelines of *authority*[3] which may be filled in by administrative detail. See also *minimum*[10] *wage law*; *administrative*[6] *order*.

Oregon v. Mitchell, 400 U.S. 112 (1970). Upheld the provision within the *Voting*[5] *Rights Act of 1970* which permits persons 18 years old or older to vote in elections involving *federal*[3] officials. The *Supreme*[8] *Court* held that the *U.S. Congress*[4] could not establish age qualifications for *state*[3] elections. The decision stimulated the rapid addition of the *Twenty-sixth Amendment*[5] (1971) to the *U.S. Constitution*[4]. The amendment established the *18-year-old*[5] *vote* as the standard voting age classification throughout the United States for both federal and state elections.

Pacific States Telephone and Telegraph Co. v. Oregon, 223 U.S. 118 (1912). Refused to decide whether the *initiative*[3] and *referendum*[3] provisions within the Oregon *state*[3] *constitution*[3] violated the *federal*[3] provision guaranteeing to each state a republican form of *government*[3]. The *Supreme*[8] *Court* held that such a question was not answerable within a federal court of *law*[8] but could best be answered by the *U.S. Congress*[4] in acceptance or rejection of a state's congressional *delegation*[5]. See also *legislative*[7] *delegation*; *political*[4] *question*; *republic*[3].

Palko v. Connecticut, 302 U.S. 319 (1937). Held that the *Fifth Amendment*[9] provision against *double*[9] *jeopardy* was not protected against encroachment by *states*[3] under the *Fourteenth Amendment*[4] *due*[4] *process clause*. The *Supreme*[8] *Court* held that not all of the *U.S. Bill*[4] *of Rights* had been "nationalized" by the Fourteenth Amendment. Speech, press, religion, and assembly, the basic rights essential to the "concept of ordered liberty," were listed as the basic rights protected from impairment by either *federal*[3] or state *governments*[3]. The Palko case established what came to be known as the *selective*[9] *incorporation doctrine*. It was also a leading case involving what came to be known as the *shocking*[9] *to the conscience doctrine*, a judicially enunciated theory of human rights. The Palko decision was reversed in *Benton*[1] *v. Maryland* and double jeopardy was nationalized under the Fourteenth Amendment. See also *Bill*[9] *of Rights nationalization*.

Panama Refining Co. v. Ryan, 293 U.S. 388 (1935). Declared *unconstitutional*[3] the provisions of the *National*[10] *Industrial Recovery Act of*

1933, which gave the *U.S. President*[6] the *power*[3] to regulate petroleum ("hot oil") shipments in *interstate commerce*[10] if such shipments exceeded quotas set by *state*[3] *legislation*[7]. The *Supreme*[8] *Court* held that the *U.S. Congress*[4] had delegated legislative *authority*[3] without establishing adequate guidelines for its use. See also *delegation of authority*[6]; *New*[6] *Deal*.

Passenger Cases, 7 How. 283 (1849). Declared *unconstitutional*[3] *state*[3] *legislation*[7] within Massachusetts and New York which required taxes on shipmasters for immigrants brought into port. The stated purpose of the taxes was to pay for medical examinations and services provided immigrants. The decisions emphasized that the *federal government*[3] has *exclusive jurisdiction*[8] over *immigration*[3].

Pennsylvania v. Nelson, 350 U.S. 497 (1956). Held that the *federal government*[3], acting in permissible areas of *legislation*[7] also occupied by *state*[3] legislation, may present a condition whereby federal legislation becomes so pervasive as to leave no room for further state action. The *Supreme*[8] *Court* declared that a Pennsylvania antisedition *act*[8] had been superseded by a federal *law*[8], the *Alien*[4] *Registration (Smith) Act of 1940*. The Court also declared that control of *seditious*[12] practices had become basically national in scope and that state legislation might conflict with federal programs designed to control seditious activities. See also *preemption*[4] *doctrine*.

Perez v. Brownell, 356 U.S. 44 (1958). Upheld *federal*[3] legislation which deprived native-born *citizens*[3] of their citizenship for voting in foreign elections. The *Supreme*[8] *Court* upheld the *legislation*[7] on the grounds that the *U.S. Congress*[4] had acted under its *implied powers*[4] related to foreign affairs. The decision was reversed in *Afroyim*[1] *v. Rusk*.

Pierce v. Society of Sisters, 268 U.S. 510 (1925). Held *unconstitutional*[3] an Oregon *statute*[8] requiring all children between the ages of eight and sixteen to attend public rather than private or religious schools. The *Supreme*[8] *Court* said such action by the *state*[3] was an unconstitutional invasion of the parents' right to guide the education of their children, a right guaranteed by the *Fourteenth Amendment*[4] *due*[4] *process clause*.

Pierce v. U.S., 252 U.S. 239 (1920). The *Supreme*[8] *Court* case which introduced the use of the *bad*[9] *tendency doctrine* in determining the extent of restriction on free expression. The case involved the *Espionage*[9] *Act of 1917* and pamphlets attacking *World*[12] *War I* and the *draft*[12]. The Court held in the *majority opinion*[8] that such pamphlets might "have a tendency to cause insubordination, disloyalty, and refusal of duty in the military and naval forces of the United States." Justices Louis Brandeis and *Oliver Wendell Holmes*[8], *Jr.* dissented, preferring to use the *clear*[9] *and present danger doctrine* as the basis for any limitations on free expression.

Plessy v. Ferguson, 163 U.S. 537 (1896). Held that a Louisiana *statute*[8] requiring racially *segregated*[9] public transportation facilities did not violate the *Fourteenth Amendment*[4] *equal*[4] *protection clause* as long as facilities were "separate but equal." The *"separate*[9] *but equal" doctrine* was abandoned in *Brown*[1] *v. Board of Education of Topeka* in 1954.

Pointer v. Texas, 380 U.S. 400 (1965). Held that the *Sixth Amendment*[9] right of confrontation of witnesses is protected from impairment by the *state*[3] through the *due*[4] *process clause* of the *Fourteenth Amendment*[4].

Pollock v. Farmers' Loan and Trust Co., 157 U.S. 429, 158 U.S. 601 (1895). Declared the *federal*[3] income tax *law*[8] of 1894 an *unconstitutional*[3] levy of a *direct tax*[10] because it was not, as specified by Article I, Section 9 of the *U.S. Constitution*[4], apportioned among the various *states*[3] on the basis of population. The *Sixteenth Amendment*[10] was added to the Constitution in 1913 in order to remove the need for apportionment of a *graduated income tax*[10] on the basis of population.

Pollock v. Williams, 322 U.S. 4 (1944). Held that a *state*[3] cannot use the threat of imprisonment to force a person to work in order to repay a debt. Such a state action violates the *Thirteenth Amendment*[9] provision against *peonage*[9].

Powell v. Alabama, 287 U.S. 45 (1932). Upheld the right to legal counsel during a *state*[3] trial as protected by the *due*[4] *process clause* of the *Fourteenth Amendment*[4]. The Powell case was one of the "Scottsboro cases" involving nine Negro boys accused of raping two white girls on a train near Scottsboro, Alabama. The *Supreme*[8] *Court* held that if the *defendants*[8] were unable to secure legal assistance, the trial court should "assign counsel." The decision did not establish a general rule related to counsel but instead dealt with the particular circumstances of the illiterate Negro youths charged by the Alabama legal authorities. See also *Betts*[1] *v. Brady*; *Gideon*[1] *v. Wainwright*.

Powell v. McCormack, 266 F. Supp. 354 (1967). Held that the *United States House*[7] *of Representatives* may not deny a seat to a duly elected member who meets the three qualifications of age, citizenship, and residency as prescribed in the *Constitution*[4]. See also *exclusion*[7]; *Adam Clayton Powell*[7] *investigation*.

Prize Cases, 2 Black 635 (1863). Upheld *President*[6] *Abraham Lincoln's*[6] blockade of southern ports and the seizure of foreign vessels running the *blockade*[12] during the *U.S. Civil*[4] *War*.

The *Supreme*[8] *Court* held that such action was valid even without an official *declaration of war*[12] because of the realities of the crisis. See also *war*[12] *powers*.

Red Lion Broadcasting Co. v. Federal Communications Commission, 395 U.S. 367 (1969). Held that the "*fairness*[5] *doctrine*" of the *Federal*[2] *Communications Commission*, a doctrine requiring that both sides of public issues be fairly presented by broadcasters, was not in violation of the free expression clause of the *First Amendment*[9].

Reid v. Covert, 354 U.S. 1 (1957). Held that *military*[8] *law* does not generally apply to military dependents who are abroad with the armed services. The *Supreme*[8] *Court* emphasized in the decision that the *constitutional*[3] provisions related to *civil*[9] *rights* are not changed by *treaties*[12] or *laws*[8] related to treaties.

Reitman v. Mulkey, 387 U.S. 369 (1967). Declared an *amendment*[3] to the California state *constitution*[3] which guaranteed a homeowner the right to *discriminate*[9] in the rental and selling of his real *property*[10] an *unconstitutional*[3] *state*[3] violation of the *equal*[4] *protection clause* of the *Fourteenth Amendment*[4].

Reynolds v. Sims, 377 U.S. 533 (1964). Held that both houses of the Alabama *legislature*[7], and by implication all other *bicameral*[7] state legislative bodies must be *apportioned*[7] on the basis of population under the "*one-man*[5], *one-vote*" *rule* in order to provide the voters of the *state*[3] the equal protection of the *laws*[3] guaranteed to them by the *Fourteenth Amendment*[4]. Upon his retirement from the U.S. *Supreme*[8] *Court*, *Chief*[8] *Justice Earl Warren*[8] indicated that Reynolds v. Sims was perhaps the most significant decision he was associated with because it was basic to the operation of a *democratic*[3] system of *government*[3]. See also *equal*[4] *protection clause.*

Reynolds v. U.S., 98 U.S. 145 (1879). Held that the *free exercise of religion*[9] *clause* of the *First Amendment*[9] does not extend to actions that are clearly unacceptable to *society*[3] at large and which may be validly regulated to maintain public order. The *Supreme*[8] *Court* thereby upheld the *federal*[3] *statute*[8] making the practice of polygamy illegal in federal *territories*[3], a practice officially recognized by the Mormons until 1890.

Robinson v. California, 370 U.S. 660 (1962). Held that a California *law*[8] making it a *crime*[8] to be a drug addict was a *cruel and unusual punishment*[9] prohibited by the *Eighth Amendment*[9] and *Fourteenth Amendment*[4].

Rochin v. California, 342 U.S. 165 (1952). Declared in violation of *due*[9] *process of law* the conviction of a man who was found guilty of narcotics violations, on the basis of evidence obtained when his stomach was pumped under orders of *state*[3] officials. The action was declared an *unreasonable search*[9] *and seizure* and in violation of the *Eighth Amendment*[9] and *Fourteenth Amendment*[4]. See also *due*[4] *process clause.*

Roth v. U.S., 354 U.S. 476 (1957). Held that *obscenity*[9] could not warrant *constitutional*[3] protection since it could not be claimed that obscenity has "redeeming social importance." The case overruled the use of the *Hicklin*[9] *test*, an English concept which held that anything tending to corrupt immature minds could be *censored*[9], and established what has come to be known as the *Roth*[9] *test*. The Roth test determines obscenity on the grounds of "whether to the average person, applying contemporary *community*[3] standards, the dominant theme of the material taken as a whole appeals to *prurient*[9] *interest*".

Rowan v. United States Post Office Department, 397 U.S. 728 (1969). Upheld a *federal*[3] *statute*[8] permitting individuals to ask the U.S. Postmaster General to cease delivering offensive and "sexually provocative" materials to the homes of those not wanting such materials. See also *obscenity*[9]; *pornography*[9].

Scales v. U.S., 367 U.S. 203 (1961). Upheld the membership clause of the *Alien*[4] *Registration (Smith) Act of 1940* which makes it a *crime*[8] to knowingly belong to an *organization*[6] advocating violent overthrow of the *government*[3]. The *Supreme*[8] *Court* held that such active membership is not *constitutionally*[3] protected by the *First Amendment*[9] rights of free expression and association or by the *Fifth Amendment*[9] rights protected under *due*[9] *process of law.*

Schechter Poultry Corp. v. U.S., 295 U.S. 495 (1935). Invalidated the *National*[2] *Recovery Administration (NRA)*, which was designed to create codes of fair practices in business competition. The *Supreme*[8] *Court* held that the *National*[10] *Industrial Recovery Act of 1933* which created the NRA, was regulating in the name of *interstate commerce*[10] an area basically local in nature. Also, the *legislation*[7], a basic portion of President *Franklin D. Roosevelt's*[6] *New*[6] *Deal*, was declared in violation of the *constitutional*[3] *separation*[3] *of powers* because it delegated unwarranted *legislative powers*[6] to the *U.S. President*[6]. The major shift in the idea that production could be regulated by the *federal government*[3] came in the case of *National*[1] *Labor Relations Board v. Jones and Laughlin Corp.* See also *delegation of authority*[6]; *Charles Evans Hughes*[8].

Schenck v. U.S., 249 U.S. 47 (1919). Upheld the *Espionage*[9] *Act of 1917* and the conviction of a man arrested under the Act for circulating pamphlets critical of U.S. involvement in

World[12] *War I* and for seeking to persuade men to resist the military *draft*[12]. Justice *Oliver Wendell Holmes*[8], *Jr.*, speaking for the *majority*[3] of the *Supreme*[8] *Court*, distinguished between restrictions on free expression during peacetime and during wartime and enunciated the famous *"clear*[9] *and present danger" doctrine* which states that materials and actions must be examined as to "whether the words used are used in such circumstances and are of such a nature as to create a clear and present danger that they will bring about the substantive evils that *Congress*[4] has a right to prevent."

School District of Abington Township v. Schempp, 374 U.S. 203 (1963). Forbade *state*[3] prescribed recitation of the Lord's Prayer or reading of portions of the Bible as part of the regular school day. The *Supreme*[8] *Court* held that such exercises violated the *establishment of religion*[9] *clause* of the *First Amendment*[9] as applied to the states by the *Fourteenth Amendment*[4].

Selective Draft Law Cases, 245 U.S. 366 (1918). Upheld the *Selective*[2] *Service* Act of 1917 and the right of the *federal government*[3] to use a compulsory military *draft*[12] to raise an army. The *Supreme*[8] *Court* held that such action was not "involuntary servitude" prohibited by the *Thirteenth Amendment*[4].

Shapiro v. Thompson, 394 U.S. 618 (1969). Held that *states*[3] could not require a residency period of one year before granting welfare benefits to residents within their *boundaries*[12]. The *Supreme*[8] *Court* held such a requirement to be in violation of the *Fourteenth Amendment*[4] *equal*[4] *protection clause*. See also *welfare*[11] *migration*.

Shelley v. Kraemer, 334 U.S. 1 (1948). Held that racially *discriminatory*[9] *restrictive*[9] *covenants* in housing cannot be enforced in a *state*[3] court because state action in such matters would be in violation of the *Fourteenth Amendment*[4] *equal*[4] *protection clause*. See also *covenant*[3].

Sheppard v. Maxwell, 384 U.S. 383 (1966). Held in the highly publicized case of Dr. Sam Sheppard of Cleveland, Ohio that the carnival atmosphere surrounding his trial for the murder of his wife which was generated by the press and accepted by the trial judge was in violation of the *constitutional*[3] guarantee to a fair trial.

Sherbert v. Verner, 374 U.S. 398 (1963). Declared *unconstitutional*[3] *state*[3] *laws*[8] denying unemployment benefits to religious adherents who refused to work on Saturday because of religious beliefs. See also *unemployment*[11] *insurance*.

Slaughterhouse Cases, 16 Wall. 36 (1873). A series of cases involving a *state*[3] sanctioned slaughterhouse *monopoly*[10] operating in New Orleans, Louisiana. The cases presented for the first time the argument that the *Fourteenth Amendment*[4] protects general *property*[10] rights of all *citizens*[3] as well as the citizenship rights of Negroes. Those challenging the monopoly argued that they were denied their "privileges and immunities," denied the "equal protection of the laws," and deprived of liberty (property) without *"due*[9] *process of law"*. The *Supreme*[8] *Court* held that the rights contained within the *Fourteenth Amendment*[4] were applicable to the *federal government*[3] only. The decision upheld the concept of *dual citizenship*[3] and left the states free to regulate local matters related to the privileges and immunities, equal protection, and liberty of their own citizens. See also *due*[4] *process clause*; *equal*[4] *protection clause*; *privileges*[4] *and immunities clause*.

Slochower v. Board of Education, 350 U.S. 551 (1956). Held that a person may not be fired by a *state*[3] agency simply for invoking the *Fifth Amendment*[9] guarantee against *self-incrimination*[9] before a congressional *investigating committee*[7]. Such dismissal violates the *due*[4] *process clause* of the *Fifth Amendment*[9] and *Fourteenth Amendment*[4].

Smith v. Allwright, 321 U.S. 649 (1944). Held that the exclusion of Negroes from Texas primary elections was in violation of the *Fifteenth Amendment*[5] because a *political party*[5] functions not as a private association in such a process but as an agent of the *state*[3]. *Discrimination*[9] by the party, therefore, is tantamount to discrimination by the state. The *Supreme*[8] *Court* reversed the *Grovey*[1] *v. Townsend* decision through such reasoning and moved back toward decisions made earlier in *Nixon*[1] *v. Herndon* and *Nixon*[1] *v. Condon*. The Smith decision was possible largely because of the nonwhite primary case of *U.S.*[1] *v. Classic*, a decision which held that primary elections are an integral part of the election process and may be regulated as such. See also *direct primary*[5]; *white primary*[5].

Smyth v. Ames, 169 U.S. 466 (1898). Held in a Nebraska railroad *ratemaking*[10] case that several criteria must be considered in determining the nature of a fair return on private investments of *public*[10] *utility* companies. Some of the criteria mentioned by the *Supreme*[8] *Court* were original cost, reproduction cost, improvements, operating expenses, market value of securities, and earning capacity.

South Carolina v. Katzenbach, 383 U.S. 301 (1966). Upheld the provisions of the *Voting*[5] *Rights Act of 1965* and the *power*[3] of the *federal government*[3] to regulate voting requirements within the *states*[3] if such requirements are clearly designed to fulfill guarantees made by the *Fifteenth Amendment*[5].

South Carolina v. U.S., 199 U.S. 437 (1905). Held that *state*[3] operated enterprises viewed as regular business operations being conducted under *proprietary powers*[4] may not be exempt from *federal*[3] taxation. See also *tax*[10] *exemption*.

Stanley v. Georgia, 394 U.S. 557 (1969). Held *unconstitutional*[3] a *state*[3] *law*[8] making it a *crime*[8] to possess *obscene*[9] materials, even within the privacy of one's home. The *Supreme*[8] *Court* held such a law in violation of the freedom of expression clause of the *First Amendment*[9] as applied to the states by the *Fourteenth Amendment*[4].

Stearns v. Minnesota, 179 U.S. 223 (1900). Upheld *federal*[3] preadmission requirements placed on the state of Minnesota once the *state*[3] attempted to tax land previously belonging to the *federal government*[3], land specifically declared exempt as part of the requirements for admission into the Union. The *Supreme*[8] *Court* held that such an agreement involved contractual relationships related to *property*[10] rather than to the nature of political *power*[3]. See also *contract*[10]; *Coyle*[1] *v. Smith*; *statehood*[4] *admission*; *tax*[10] *exemption*.

Steward Machine Co. v. Davis, 301 U.S. 548 (1937). Upheld the unemployment compensation provisions of the *Social*[11] *Security Act of 1935* provisions establishing a *tax*[10] *offset* arrangement whereby the *federal government*[3] agreed not to apply *withholding tax*[10] programs within *states*[3] providing their own unemployment compensation tax programs. See also *unemployment*[11] *insurance*.

Sunday Closing Cases, 366 U.S. 420 (1961). Held that state *statutes*[8] requiring Sunday closing of businesses were not in violation of the *free exercise of religion*[9] *clause* of the *First Amendment*[9] because Sunday closing *laws*[8] had shifted from a religious to a secular emphasis and were valid exercises of the *police powers*[4] of the *state*[3], to protect the welfare of the *citizens*[3] of the states. See also *blue*[9] *law*; *general*[4] *welfare clause*.

Sunshine Anthracite Coal Co. v. Adkins, 310 U.S. 381 (1940). Sustained portions of the Guffey-Vinson Act (1937) regulating prices and marketing practices of bituminous coal. The decision came after changes in *Supreme*[8] *Court* personnel and threats of a *court-packing*[8] *plan* by *President*[6] *Franklin D. Roosevelt*[6]. It essentially reversed an earlier decision in *Carter*[1] *v. Carter Coal Co.*, a decision supporting the idea that manufacturing is local in nature and cannot be regulated as affecting *interstate commerce*[10]. See also *National*[1] *Labor Relations Board v. Jones and Laughlin Corp.*

Swann v. Charlotte-Mecklenburg Board of Education, 402 U.S. 1 (1971). Unanimously declared *unconstitutional*[3] a North Carolina *statute*[8] prohibiting the use of "busing" to achieve compulsory racial *integration*[9]. The decision, frequently cited as the most significant *desegregation*[9] decision since *Brown*[1] *v. Board of Education of Topeka*, held that *federal*[3] courts possessed "broad" *powers*[3] to assure that racial integration of the public schools eventually be achieved. The *Supreme*[8] *Court* held that under the *equal*[4] *protection clause* of the *Fourteenth Amendment*[4] that court orders could require reasonable "busing," altered school *boundaries*[12] and "pairing" of school zones without common boundaries. It also held the *community*[3] racial ratios could be used as a starting point for integration of public schools, that one-race schools could be questioned as to the validity of their existence, and that school construction could not

be used to continue segregated school systems.

Sweatt v. Painter, 339 U.S. 629 (1950). Held that the creation of a separate law school for Negroes in the state of Texas was in violation of the *equal*[4] *protection clause* of the *Fourteenth Amendment*[4] because the facilities and faculty of the Negro school were not equal to those provided the white persons within the *state*[3]. The Court held that no *segregated*[9] law school could meet the *separate*[9] *but equal doctrine*.

Terminiello v. Chicago, 337 U.S. 1 (1949). Held that a local *ordinance*[8] classifying controversial speeches and actions creating conditions of unrest as subject to restrictions under *breach*[8] *of the peace* was an *unconstitutional*[3] restriction on free expression as guaranteed by the *First Amendment*[9].

Texas v. White, 7 Wall. 700 (1869). Held that the *federal*[3] Union created by the *U.S. Constitution*[4] of 1787 was an "indissoluble" arrangement and that the *states*[3] in *rebellion*[3] during the *Civil*[4] *War* were never really out of the Union.

Thornhill v. Alabama, 310 U.S. 88 (1940). Invalidated an Alabama *law*[8] prohibiting peaceful *picketing*[10] as an *unconstitutional*[3] restraint on the freedom of expression protected by the *First Amendment*[9] and *Fourteenth Amendment*[4].

Times Film Corp. v. Chicago, 365 U.S. 43 (1961). Upheld a local *ordinance*[8] requiring prior approval of all films before permits for public exhibition could be granted. In this instance the *Supreme*[8] *Court* proved unwilling to place films under a rule prohibiting prior restraint of free expression. See also *prior*[9] *restraint doctrine*.

Tinker v. Des Moines School District, 393 U.S. 503 (1969). Upheld the right of public school students to wear black armbands as symbolic protest to U.S. involvement in the *Vietnam*[12] *War*. The *Supreme*[8] *Court* held that such symbolic expressions were *constitutionally*[3] protected under the free speech guarantees of the *First Amendment*[9] and *Fourteenth Amendment*[4].

Torcaso v. Watkins, 367 U.S. 488 (1961). Declared *unconstitutional*[3] a Maryland state *constitutional*[3] provision requiring a declaration of belief in the existence of God as a prerequisite for holding a *state*[3] office. The *Supreme*[8] *Court* held such a requirement an unconstitutional restriction on the *free exercise of religion*[9] as protected by the *First Amendment*[9] and *Fourteenth Amendment*[4].

Toth v. Quarles, 350 U.S. 11 (1955). Held that *military*[8] *law* does not apply to former servicemen charged with offenses committed while in the armed forces.

Trop v. Dulles, 356 U.S. 86 (1958). Held *unconstitutional*[3] various *federal*[3] *statutory*[8] provisions depriving a person of *citizenship*[3] if he was convicted of wartime desertion by a *court-martial*[8] proceeding. The *Supreme*[8] *Court* held that the deprivation of citizenship under such conditions constituted a *cruel and unusual punishment*[9] prohibited by the *Eighth Amendment*[9].

Twining v. New Jersey, 211 U.S. 78 (1908). Held that exemption from *self-incrimination*[9] was not a guaranteed right at the *state*[3] level and was not incorporated in the *due*[4] *process clause* of the *Fourteenth Amendment*[4]. The Twining decision was overruled in *Malloy*[1] *v. Hogan*, and the self-incrimination provision was applied to the *states*[3]. See also *shocking*[9] *to the conscience doctrine*.

Ullmann v. U.S., 350 U.S. 422 (1956). Upheld the *Federal*[3] Immunity Act of 1954, which may compel testimony from witnesses being questioned by appropriate legal bodies investigating security matters. When witnesses are compelled to testify, they may be granted immunity through an *immunity*[9] *bath* and escape future criminal prosecution by federal or *state*[3] *governments*[3] on the basis of testimony given. The *Supreme*[8] *Court* held that immunity and forced testimony may be gained by court order and that witnesses who continue to remain silent may be jailed for *contempt*[8] *of court*. See also *investigative*[7] *powers*.

U.S. v. Belmont, 301 U.S. 324 (1937). Upheld the right of the *U.S. President*[6] to make *executive*[12] *agreements* with foreign *nations*[3], agreements having essentially the same force as international *treaties*[12]. The *Supreme*[8] *Court* specifically upheld President *Franklin D. Roosevelt's*[6] recognition of the Soviet Union in 1933 by executive agreement. See also *diplomatic*[12] *recognition*.

U.S. v. Brown, 381 U.S. 437 (1965). Voided a 1959 *Federal*[3] *statute*[8] which made it illegal for a member of the *Communist Party*[5] to be an officer or employee of a *labor*[10] *union*. The *Supreme*[8] *Court* held that such a restriction was *unconstitutional*[3] because it was in the form of a *bill of attainder*[9].

U.S. v. Butler, 297 U.S. 1 (1936). Declared the first *Agricultural*[10] *Adjustment Act of 1933 unconstitutional*[3] on the grounds that the regulation of farm prices through the use of processing taxes collected on crops covered by the program was an invasion of the *reserved powers*[4] of the *state*[3] and that such taxes were not true taxes but *regulatory taxes*[10] which could not be justified under the *general*[4] *welfare clause* of the *U.S. Constitution*[4]. The second AAA of 1938 was upheld in *Mulford*[1] *v. Smith* under the *commerce*[4] *clause* of the *Constitution*[4].

U.S. v. Carolene Products Co., 304 U.S. 144 (1938). Held that judicial action was available to individuals or groups who could not find legal protection for their rights through the legislative process. Justice Harlan F. Stone argued on the basis of what has come to be known as the *preferred*[9] *freedom*, or "absolute freedom" doctrine that the *First Amendment*[9] freedoms have a special place within the system of *constitutional*[3] values.

U.S. v. Classic, 313 U.S. 299 (1941). Upheld the *power*[3] of the *U.S. Congress*[4] to regulate primary elections within the *states*[3]. The *Supreme*[8] *Court* declared that elections involving congressional candidates may be regulated under Article I, Section 4, a section securing to Congress the right to assure that proper procedures are used in the selection of members. The Court overruled the *Newberry*[1] *v. U.S.* decision and held that state primaries could be regulated by the *federal government*[3] because of their integral relationship to the election process. See also *direct primary*[5].

U.S. v. Curtiss-Wright Export Corp., 299 U.S. 304 (1936). Upheld congressional action permitting the *U.S. President*[6] to exercise broad powers restricting the shipment of arms to foreign *belligerents*[12]. The issue before the *Supreme*[8] *Court* involved President *Franklin D. Roosevelt's*[6] *embargo*[12] on weapons destined for a conflict between Paraguay and Bolivia. In interpreting the president's action, the Court recognized that the *U.S. Congress*[4] could delegate to the president broader powers in foreign affairs than it could in domestic affairs. The Court also admitted, for the first time in U.S. history, that the president possessed an *inherent power*[4] with regard to foreign affairs. See also *delegation of authority*[6].

U.S. v. Darby Lumber Co., 312 U.S. 100 (1941). Upheld the *Fair*[10] *Labor Standards Act of 1938* and its regulations of conditions, wages, and hours of employees engaged in manufacture

destined for *interstate commerce*[10]. The decision also overruled *Hammer*[1] *v. Dagenhart* and upheld *federal*[3] restrictions on the interstate shipment of goods produced by *child*[10] *labor*.

U.S. v. E.C. Knight Co., 156 U.S. 1 (1895). Held that provisions of the *Sherman*[10] *Antitrust Act of 1890* could not be applied to the *merger*[10] of five Pennsylvania sugar refineries controlled by a nationwide sugar *monopoly*[10] because such an action only indirectly affected *interstate commerce*[10]. The *Supreme*[8] *Court* declared that such activities were primarily controlled by *state*[3] *statutes*[8] regulating manufacturing, an activity considered local in nature. The major shift from the E. C. Knight decision came in *National*[1] *Labor Relations Board v. Jones and Laughlin Corp.*, when the Court held that the *federal government*[3] could handle labor disputes of local companies whose business production and labor problems affected the movement of goods in interstate commerce.

U.S. v. E.I. Du Pont deNemours & Co., 366 U.S. 316 (1961). Held that Du Pont had to divest itself of a large block of General Motors stock because control of such stock gave the chemical company an unfair advantage and had a considerable economic effect on the supplying of automobile paints and fabrics. See also *monopoly*[10].

U.S. v. Harriss, 347 U.S. 612 (1954). Upheld the *Federal*[5] *Regulation of Lobbying Act of 1946* and the *power*[3] of the *U.S. Congress*[4] to regulate those directly seeking to influence *legislation*[7]. The decision denied Congress the right to regulate those seeking to indirectly influence its activities through the swaying of *public opinion*[5].

U.S. v. Robel, 389 U.S. 258 (1967). Held that a person's *First Amendment*[9] right of association meant that he could not be barred from working in a defense facility just because he belonged to the *Communist Party*[5].

U.S. v. Seeger, 380 U.S. 163 (1965). Held that a person could qualify as a *conscientious*[9] *objector* even if he did not hold an orthodox belief in God. The *Supreme*[8] *Court* stated that the main criterion must be a consistent ethical belief rejecting *war*[12]. See also *Gillette*[1] *v. U.S.*

U.S. v. U.S. District Court of the Eastern District of Michigan (1972). The *U.S. Supreme*[8] *Court* decision which held in a case involving the *Omnibus*[8] *Crime Control and Safe Streets Act of* 1968 that the *U.S. President*[6] or agents under his authority may not authorize or use *wiretaps*[9] against so-called "domestic subversives" without federal judicial authorization. The 8–0 decision involved the issue of *unreasonable search*[9] *and seizure* as prohibited by the *Fourth Amendment.*[9] See *Berger*[1] *v. N.Y.* and *Katz*[1] *v. U.S.*

U.S. v. Wong Kim Ark, 169 U.S. 649 (1898). Held that the *Fourteenth Amendment*[4] guarantees the right of *citizenship*[3] to all children who are natural born within the U.S. even if their parents are *aliens*[3] who are ineligible for U.S. citizenship through the process of *naturalization*[3]. See also *natural-born citizen*[3].

Veazie Bank v. Fenno, 8 Wall. 533 (1869). Upheld a 10 percent *federal*[3] tax on *state*[3] bank notes as an acceptable regulatory and nonrevenue measure designed to provide a uniform currency throughout the U.S. See also *McCulloch*[1] *v. Maryland* for modifications with regard to state taxes on federal bank notes; *regulatory tax*[10].

Walz v. Tax Commission of the City of New York, May 4, 1970. Held that tax exempt status for religious *property*[10] used primarily for religious purposes was not in violation of the *establishment of religion*[9] or *free exercise of religion*[9] clauses of the *First Amendment*[9]. The *Supreme*[8] *Court* held that *tax*[10] *exemption* is not a form of *government*[3] aid, but primarily a freedom from government interference. The Court did not hold that such exemption had to be granted but that it could be granted by a state.

Watkins v. U.S., 354 U.S. 178 (1957). Reversed a legislative contempt citation which penalized a witness for refusing to answer questions related to acquaintances' past *Communist Party*[5] affiliations. The *Supreme*[8] *Court* held that legislative *committees*[7] must operate within reasonably defined areas of legislative competence and may not conduct investigations purely for the sake of exposure. The Court also said that Watkins had been denied *due*[9] *process of law* as guaranteed by the *Fifth Amendment*[9] *due*[4] *process clause* and that witnesses have the right to refuse to answer questions that are not relevant to the investigation. See also *investigating committee*[7]; *contempt*[7] *of Congress*; *guilt*[9] *by association*; *investigative*[7] *powers*.

Weeks v. U.S., 232 U.S. 383 (1914). Held inadmissible in *federal*[3] court any evidence gained through illegal or *unreasonable search*[9] *and seizure*. The Weeks decision established what is known as the *exclusionary*[9] *doctrine*. See also *Wolf*[1] *v. Colorado* and *Mapp*[1] *v. Ohio* for application to the *states*[3].

Wesberry v. Sanders, 376 U.S. 1 (1964). Held in a Georgia case that United States *congressional districts*[7] must be *apportioned*[9] on the basis of approximately equal population figures. The *Supreme*[8] *Court* thereby applied the *one-man*[5], *one-vote rule* to the *House*[7] *of Representatives*. The basis of the decision was Article I, Section 2 of the *Constitution*[4], which declares that *congressmen*[7] shall be elected "by the people of the several States." See also *Avery*[1] *v. Midland*

County; *Baker*[1] *v. Carr*; *Gray*[1] *v. Sanders*; *Kirkpatrick*[1] *v. Preisler*; *Reynolds*[1] *v. Sims*; *Earl Warren*[8].

West Coast Hotel Co. v. Parrish, 300 U.S. 379 (1937). Upheld a Washington state *minimum*[10] *wage law* for women and thereby overruled the *Adkins*[1] *v. Children's Hospital* decision, which had said that *state*[3] minimum wages violated the right of *contract*[10] as protected by the *Fourteenth Amendment*[4] *due*[4] *process clause*. The West Coast Hotel decision followed personnel changes in the *Supreme*[8] *Court* and the *court-packing*[8] *plan* of *President*[6] *Franklin D. Roosevelt*[6].

West Virginia State Board of Education v. Barnette, 319 U.S. 624 (1943). Reversed the *Minersville*[1] *School District v. Gobitis* decision of 1940 and held that the public school requirement of compulsory flag salute to the U.S. flag was in violation of the *First Amendment*[9] clause guaranteeing the *free exercise of religion*[9].

Wickard v. Filburn, 317 U.S. 111 (1942). Upheld the right of the *U.S. Congress*[4] to regulate local agricultural production under the *Agricultural*[10] *Adjustment Act of 1938* on the grounds that local production above established quotas, even if used for local consumption, exerts a major influence on *interstate commerce*[10] and may be regulated as such.

Williams v. Mississippi, 170 U.S. 213 (1898). Upheld the use of *literacy*[5] *tests* to establish voter qualifications within the *states*[3].

Williams v. North Carolina, 325 U.S. 226 (1945). Declared that a *state*[3] does not have to legally recognize an out-of-state divorce decree granted to one of its residents if the decree was gained through nominal residence in the state granting the divorce. See also *comity*[3]; *full*[4] *faith and credit clause*.

Witherspoon v. Illinois, 389 U.S. 1035 (1968). Held that persons conscientiously opposed to *capital*[8] *punishment* may not be automatically excluded from *juries*[8] hearing capital cases.

Wolf v. Colorado, 338 U.S. 25 (1949). In a case involving an abortionist who had been convicted in a *state*[3] court on evidence illegally obtained from his office, the *Supreme*[8] *Court* held for the first time that the *Fourth Amendment*[9] search and seizure provision protects a person from state encroachment as well as from *federal*[3] violation. The Court decided, however, that evidence gained through an illegal or *unreasonable search*[9] *and seizure* could still be admitted as evidence in a state court although it would not be admissible in a federal court, a principle established earlier in *Weeks*[1] *v. U.S.* The *"exclusionary*[9] *doctrine"* was eventually "nationalized" and the Wolf decision was modified in *Mapp*[1] *v. Ohio*. See also *Bill*[9] *of Rights nationalization*.

Yates v. U.S., 354 U.S. 298 (1957). Held that an abstract or philosophical belief in the doctrine of the *revolutionary*[3] overthrow of an existing *government*[3] differs from actual advocacy of and preparation for such an eventuality. The *Supreme*[8] *Court* overturned the convictions of several members of the *Communist Party*[5] who had been convicted of violating provisions of the *Alien*[4] *Registration (Smith) Act of 1940*. The Court reversed the convictions on the grounds that abstract beliefs are protected by the *First Amendment*[9] freedom of expression. The Yates decision was a modification of the *clear*[9] *and present danger doctrine* as interpreted in *Dennis*[1] *v. U.S.*

Youngstown Sheet & Tube Co. v. Sawyer, 343 U.S. 579 (1952). Held *unconstitutional*[3] *President*[6] *Harry S Truman's*[6] *executive*[6] *order* directing his Secretary of Commerce to seize privately owned steel mills in an effort to avert a threatened nationwide *strike*[10]. President Truman's claim that he validly used his *inherent power*[4] and *Commander-in-chief powers*[6] in order to protect the *nation's*[3] security during the *Korean*[12] *War* was rejected by the *Supreme*[8] *Court* on the grounds that the *U.S. Congress*[4] had not included in the *Labor-Management*[10] *(Taft-Hartley) Act of 1947* or any other *legislation*[7] any provisions for the *U.S. President*[6] to seize private *property*[10] under such conditions.

Zemel v. Rusk, 381 U.S. L (1965). Upheld the power of the *Department of State*[2] to place restrictions on travel to *Communist*[3] *nations*[3]. The *Supreme*[8] *Court* held that such restrictions are designed to protect U.S. foreign *policy*[6] interests and are geographical in nature rather than based on membership in a subversive *organization*[6]. Restrictions based on political beliefs or associations were not upheld in *Kent*[1] *v. Dulles*.

Zorach v. Clauson, 343 U.S. 306 (1952). Upheld a *released*[9] *time* program of religious education in the public school system of New York City. The *Supreme*[8] *Court* held that such an arrangement differed from the released time program declared *unconstitutional*[3] in *McCollum*[1] *v. Board of Education*, in that the New York arrangement released students from classes during the school day in order to permit religious exercises and classes off campus. The program, based on written permission of parents and on off-campus participation, was viewed as acceptable because public funds and buildings were not used for religious purposes. Such action was not in violation of the *establishment of religion*[9] *clause* of the *First Amendment*[9].

Chapter 2

United States Government Agencies

Note to the reader: Cross-referenced terms are in italics. The superscript number refers to the chapter in which the entry may be found. In addition, its placement indicates the word under which the term is alphabetized. (For example, in *electoral*[4] *college*, information on the electoral college may be found in Chapter 4 under "electoral.") Because italics are used in cross-references, they are not used for terms in which they would ordinarily be used: Supreme Court cases and titles of books, journals, plays, and so forth.

ACTION, 1971– . An *independent agency*[6] within the *federal government*[3] created in 1971 to consolidate various federal volunteer service agencies operating throughout the U.S. and other *nations*[3]. The agency, headed by a director, is headquartered in *Washington*[4], *D.C.* and maintains regional offices throughout the *country*[3]. The agency contains *Volunteers*[11] *In Service To America* (VISTA), the *Peace*[2] *Corps*, Foster Grandparents Program, Retired Senior Volunteer Program (RSVP), and the Office of Voluntary Action. A number of these programs and agencies were moved from other *government*[3] agencies in 1971. ACTION also operates in a liaison capacity with the *Small*[2] *Business Administration (SBA)* in providing volunteer services through the Service Corps of Retired Executives (SCORE) and the Active Corps of Executives.

Administrative Conference of the United States, 1964– . An *independent agency*[6] established to improve legal procedures within the various *federal*[3] agencies and to protect the rights of federal employees. The Administrative Conference is headed by a *chairman*[7] appointed by the *U.S. President*[6] and *confirmed*[6] by the *U.S. Senate*[7] for a five-year term of office.

Administrative Office of the United States Courts, 1939– . An agency operating under the *Judicial*[8] *Conference of the United States* which is responsible for supervising administrative matters related to *federal*[3] court personnel, supplies, docket schedules, records, compensation, retirement programs, general business, and other items essential for efficient judicial procedures. The agency handles administrative matters for all federal courts except the *Supreme*[8] *Court*.

Agency for International Development (AID), 1961– . A *Department of State*[2] agency established to carry out U.S. overseas programs of economic and technical assistance to less developed *countries*[3]. The agency handles loans and grants, administers food distribution programs, assists foreign health programs, and encourages private capital investments abroad. See also *Food*[10] *for Peace Program; foreign*[12] *aid.*

Agricultural Adjustment Administration (AAA), 1933 and 1938. A *New*[6] *Deal* agency established in 1933 to help raise and regulate farm prices by reducing production and balancing the domestic market. The first AAA was declared *unconstitutional*[3] by the *Supreme*[8] *Court* in *U.S.*[1] *v. Butler*, on the grounds that the processing taxes being used were not true taxes and that the crop control measures invaded the *reserved powers*[4] of the *states*[3]. The second AAA, in 1938, was upheld in *Mulford*[1] *v. Smith* as a device used for soil *conservation*[10] purposes and storage programs. The programs operated under the AAA brought about much emotional upheaval due to the destruction of crops in the midst of the *Great Depression*[10]. See also *price*[10] *support program; soil*[10] *bank.*

Agriculture, Department of, 1862– . The *executive*[6] department of the *federal government*[3] charged with assisting the national economy through comprehensive agricultural programs in the areas of research, education, *conservation*[10], marketing, inspection, agricultural adjustment, surplus disposal, *rural*[11] development, and general regulatory work. The Department of Agriculture was the first "*clientele*[6] centered" *cabinet*[6] addition, a *department*[6] created to serve and regulate a specific portion of *society*[3] and the economy. The agency is headed by a cabinet-level Secretary of Agriculture. See also *Commodity*[2] *Credit Corporation; Forest*[2] *Service; price*[10] *support program; Rural*[2] *Electrification Administration.*

Atomic Energy Commission (AEC), 1946– . An *independent regulatory commission*[6] created to assist national *policy*[6] through the development, use, and control of atomic energy. The AEC is composed of five civilian members *appointed*[6] by the *President*[6]

and *confirmed*[6] by the *Senate*[7]. See also *Atomic*[12] *Energy (McMahon) Act of 1946; atomic*[12] *war; National*[2] *Aeronautics and Space Council.*

Census, Bureau of the, 1902– . An agency within the *Department of Commerce*[2] established for the purpose of determining population figures to be used in *apportioning*[7] membership within the *House*[7] *of Representatives*. The Bureau is one of the major statistical agencies within the *federal government*[3].

Central Intelligence Agency (CIA), 1947– . An agency under the *National*[2] *Security Council* responsible for coordinating *intelligence*[12] operations of the various *federal*[3] agencies charged with guarding national security. See also *Bay*[12] *of Pigs crisis of 1961; Watergate*[5].

Civil Aeronautics Board (CAB), 1938– . An *independent regulatory commission*[6] responsible for regulating private airline operations within the U.S. and abroad. The CAB is responsible for the encouragement of civil aviation, the designation of air traffic routes, and the regulation of rates and other economic and business aspects of the airline industry.

Civilian Conservation Corps (CCC), 1933. The temporary *New*[6] *Deal* agency designed to provide public employment for young people during the *Great Depression*[10]. The CCC emphasized road building, flood control, *conservation*[10], fire prevention, construction of dams, and similar projects.

Civil Rights, Commission on, 1957– . The *federal*[3] agency responsible for investigating and reporting violations of federal *civil*[9] *rights statutes*[8] and civil liberties in matters of voting rights, legal rights, education, housing, and other related areas. See also *Civil*[9] *Rights Acts of 1957, 1960, 1964, and 1968.*

Commerce, Department of, 1913– .
The *executive*[6] *department*[6] of the
federal government[3] created to promote the full development of the economic resources of the United States.
The Department of Commerce,
headed by the *cabinet*[6] level Secretary of Commerce, sponsors programs
of data collection, research, promotion, and technical assistance. It also
operates a *patent*[10] service, controls
export operations, establishes standards, carries out materials priorities
and industrial mobilization programs,
and generally oversees activities related to *interstate* and *intrastate commerce*[10]. See also *Bureau of the Census*[2]; *Civil*[9] *Rights Act of 1964;
Maritime*[2] *Administration*.

**Commodity Credit Corporation
(CCC), 1933– .** An agency, created
as part of *President*[6] *Franklin D.
Roosevelt's*[6] *New*[6] *Deal*, which is
within the *Department of Agriculture*[2]
and charged with responsibility for
agricultural price support and stabilization programs. A major portion of
the CCC program is the acquisition
of surplus commodities on the domestic market and the disposal of them
through *foreign*[12] *aid* and exchange
programs. See also *Food*[10] *for Peace
Program; parity*[10]; *price*[10] *support
program; soil*[10] *bank.*

**Comptroller of the Currency, Office
of, 1863– .** An agency within the
Department of the Treasury[2] responsible for regulating national banks.

Consumer Affairs, Office of, 1971– .
An *Executive*[2] *Office* agency which
advises the *President*[6] on matters of
consumer protection and coordinates
various *federal*[3] programs related to
consumer interests. The agency handles general consumer complaints and
publishes information of interest to
consumers.

Cost of Living Council, 1971– . A
cabinet[6] level agency established in
August 1971 for administering *President*[6] Richard M. Nixon's *wage-
price*[10] *freeze* instituted by *executive*[6]
order under authorization of the Economic Stabilization Act of 1970. The
agency was created as an emergency
structure with Secretary of the Treasury John Connally as its director. Four
other leading economic and administrative specialists within the Nixon
administration[6] were assigned to the
council to help direct the "temporary"
wage-price freeze. The council was
given *authority*[3] to make decisions involving economic arrangements and
practices in both the public and private sectors. Its original mandate was
to use the 90-day freeze to begin long-
range planning in economic affairs.

**Council of Economic Advisers
(CEA), 1946– .** An *Executive*[2] *Office*
agency established by the *Employment*[10] *Act of 1946* as a three-member
council to analyze the national economy, advise the *President*[6] on economic developments, appraise the
economic programs and *policies*[6] of
the *federal government*[3], recommend
policies for national economic growth
and stability, and assist the President
in preparing economic reports to be
presented to the *Congress*[4]. See also
fiscal policy[10]; *monetary policy*[10].

Customs, Bureau of, 1927– . A *decentralized organization*[5] within the
Department of the Treasury[2] responsible for developing and administering programs related to *customs*[10]
duties. See also *Customs Court*[8] *(U.S.).*

**Defense, Department of (DOD),
1949– .** The *executive*[6] *department*[6]
of the *federal government*[3] specifically charged with designing and
leading a comprehensive military program to protect national security. The
major emphasis of the department is
on providing and training manpower
for the armed forces of the United
States. Within the Department of De-

fense, headed by a *cabinet*[6] level Secretary of Defense, are the Departments of the Army, Navy, Air Force, as well as other agencies created to protect national security. See *Joint*[2] *Chiefs of Staff; Pentagon*[12]; *Pentagon*[12] *Papers.*

Domestic Council, 1970– . A *cabinet*[6] level council within the *federal government*[3] which is composed of the *President*[6], *Vice-President*[6], the director of the *Office of Economic*[2] *Opportunity*, and all cabinet-level officials except the Secretary of State, the Secretary of Defense, and the director of the *Office of Management*[2] *and Budget.* The Domestic Council acts as a *staff organization*[6] to coordinate and direct domestic programs throughout the U.S. It conducts research programs, directs resource allocation, reviews programs in effect, and carries out other tasks common to federal domestic programs. See also *Advisory*[6] *Council on Executive Reorganization.*

Economic Opportunity, Office of (OEO), 1964– . An *Executive*[2] *Office* agency created as part of the *Great*[6] *Society* of *President*[6] Lyndon B. *Johnson*[6] in order to coordinate *federal*[3] efforts to eliminate the causes and conditions of poverty within the U.S. The OEO, created partially through stimulation by a book entitled The Other America by *Michael Harrington*[11], contains numerous programs operated under the *Community*[11] *Action Agencies.* Some of the programs originally created as part of the OEO were the *Job*[11] *Corps, Neighborhood*[11] *Youth Corps, Legal*[11] *Services Program, Project Headstart*[11] and *Upward*[11] *Bound. Volunteers*[11] *in Service to America* was part of OEO, but was transferred to a new agency called ACTION[2] in 1971. President Richard M. Nixon began dismantling OEO in 1973 although various programs were continued under other agencies. See also *War*[11] *on Poverty.*

Emergency Preparedness, Office of (OEP), 1968– . An *Executive*[2] *Office* agency charged with advising the *President*[6] on the determination and coordination of *policy*[6] for all emergency preparedness activities. The agency is concerned with emergency conditions related to manpower, resources, industry, transportation, communications, *civil*[12] *defense*, and other vital areas important to *government*[3] operations during times of crisis. See also *mobilization*[12]; *National*[2] *Security Council.*

Engineers, Corps of, 1802– . An agency within the U.S. Army responsible for planning and construction of various *public*[10] *works* on navigable rivers and streams throughout the United States. The Corps of Engineers is one of the major agencies involved in the development of flood control projects and the construction of hydroelectric plants.

Environmental Protection Agency (EPA), 1970– . A *federal*[3] agency established in order to consolidate and coordinate various anti-pollution and environmental programs already in existence. The *organization*[6] is directed by an administrator appointed by the *President*[6] and *confirmed*[6] by the *Senate*[7]. It regulates such areas as air pollution, water pollution, and pesticide usage. The EPA was created with the monumental task of coordinating scientific, medical, industrial, economic, social, and political factors surrounding pollution. See also *Advisory*[6] *Council on Executive Reorganization; urban ecology*[11].

Equal Employment Opportunity Commission (EEOC), 1965– . The only agency within the *federal government*[3] vested with *statutory*[8] *authority*[3] to deal with discriminatory employment practices outside the federal government. The agency was created to end *discrimination*[9] in private employment practices and to provide new job opportunities for *minority*[9] groups. See also *Civil*[9] *Rights Act of 1964.*

Executive Office of the President, 1939– . The office containing the major *staff organizations*[6] of the *President*[6]. The agencies composing the Executive Office in late 1972 were the *White*[2] *House Office,* the *Office of Management*[2] *and Budget, Council*[2] *of Economic Advisers, National*[2] *Security Council, Domestic*[2] *Council, National*[2] *Aeronautics and Space Council, Office of Economic*[2] *Opportunity, Office of Emergency*[2] *Preparedness, Office of Science*[2] *and Technology, Office of the Special*[2] *Representative for Trade Negotiations, Office of Intergovernmental*[2] *Relations, Office of Consumer*[2] *Affairs,* Council on Environmental Quality, Office of Telecommunications Policy, Council on International Economic Policy, Special Action Office for Drug Abuse Prevention, and the *Cost*[2] *of Living Council.* See also *Brownlow Commission*[6]; *Watergate*[5].

Export-Import Bank of the United States, 1934– . A bank operating under *federal*[3] charter as a *government corporation*[6]. It makes direct loans to domestic and foreign businesses in order to facilitate foreign trade. See also *balance*[10] *of payments.*

Farm Credit Administration (FCA), 1916– . An *independent agency*[5] created to regulate and coordinate farm credit programs for farmers and farmer *organizations*[6]. See also *price*[10] *support program.*

Federal Aviation Administration (FAA), 1967– . A formerly *independent agency*[5] which became part of the *Department of Transportation*[2] in 1967. The FAA is responsible for regulating air commerce development and formulating air safety standards. It also maintains a system of air traffic control, establishes aircraft production and maintenance standards, certifies pilots, and investigates air traffic mishaps.

Federal Bureau of Investigation (FBI), 1908– . An agency within the *Department of Justice*[2] charged with investigating all violations of *federal*[3] *laws*[8] except those specifically assigned to particular federal agencies. The FBI, for many years led by J. Edgar Hoover, is responsible for investigating offenses such as subversion, *sedition*[12], sabotage, kidnaping, extortion, bank robbery, interstate transportation of stolen vehicles, and numerous other federal offenses. See also *Jencks*[9] *Act of 1957; Jencks*[1] *v. U.S.; Watergate*[5].

Federal Communications Commission (FCC), 1934– . An *independent regulatory commission*[6] created to regulate foreign and *interstate commerce*[10] in communications by wire and radio and to provide a comprehensive and inexpensive system of communications for the U.S. See also *Federal*[9] *Communications Act of 1934.*

Federal Deposit Insurance Corporation (FDIC), 1933– . A *government corporation*[6] created during the *Great Depression*[10] as part of the *New*[6] *Deal* in order to insure bank deposits of all banks entitled to the benefits of insurance under the law. The agency is responsible for regulating and correcting unsound banking practices, handling bank affairs during time of economic disaster, regulating *merger*[10] arrangements, and insuring accounts up to a specified limit.

Federal Housing Administration (FHA), 1934– . An agency within the *Department of Housing*[2] *and Urban Development* responsible for loan and mortgage insurance programs. The FHA was created as part of *President*[6] *Franklin D. Roosevelt's*[6] *New*[6] *Deal.* See also *Housing*[11] *and Urban Development Act of 1965;*

Housing[11] *and Urban Development Act of 1968; Housing*[11] *Act of 1937.*

Federal Maritime Commission (FMC), 1961– . An *independent regulatory commission*[6] charged with protecting the interests of the American public by regulating domestic and foreign related waterborne shipping. The agency regulates shipping agreements, rates, practices, licenses, safety, and other matters related to water carriers. See also *interstate commerce*[10]; *admiralty law*[8]; *Maritime*[2] *Administration.*

Federal Mediation and Conciliation Service (FMCS), 1947– . An *independent regulatory commission*[6] charged with assisting labor and management in peacefully settling disputes that could hinder the free flow of *interstate commerce*[10]. See also *labor arbitration*[10]; *National*[2] *Mediation Board.*

Federal Power Commission (FPC), 1920– . An *independent regulatory commission*[6] created to regulate the interstate aspects of the electric power and natural gas industries. The agency regulates construction, operation, and rates of interstate facilities within the U.S. See also *interstate commerce*[10]; *public*[10] *power; Public*[10] *Utility Holding Co. Act of 1935.*

Federal Reserve System, Board of Governors (FRS), 1913– . An *independent regulatory commission*[6] created to provide a system of Federal Reserve banks, to furnish an elastic currency, afford means of rediscounting commercial paper, and establish a more effective means of supervising banking in the U.S. The Board of Governors determines general *monetary policy*[10] and regulates interest rates within the U.S. The Federal Reserve System is composed of 12 regional banks coordinating and regulating the activities of member banks within each district. See also *Federal*[10] *Reserve note; rediscount*[10] *rate; reserve*[10] *ratio.*

Federal Trade Commission (FTC), 1915– . An *independent regulatory commission*[6] organized to maintain an economic system based upon *free*[10] *enterprise* and economic competition. The agency is charged with investigating and reporting on deceptive trade practices and *monopolistic*[10] arrangements within the U.S. See also *Federal*[10] *Trade Commission Act of 1914; restraint of trade*[10].

Food and Drug Administration (FDA), 1931– . An agency within the *Department of Health*[2], *Education, and Welfare* created to protect the health of the people of the U.S., especially as it is affected by foods, drugs, cosmetics, and other household substances sold as consumer products. Among the basic tasks of the FDA are research and inspection. See also *Pure*[11] *Food and Drug Act of 1906.*

Foreign Service, 1924– . An agency within the *Department of State*[2] responsible for providing the basic staff of the *department's*[6] operations, a staff directly involved in implementing U.S. foreign *policy*[6] in the various *countries*[3] around the world. See also *Rogers*[12] *Act of 1924; country*[12] *mission, diplomacy*[12], *closed*[6] *career system.*

Forest Service, 1905– . An agency within the *Department of Agriculture*[2] responsible for promoting the *conservation*[10] and best use of the U.S. forest lands. The Forest Service conducts research, regulates the commercial use of *federal*[3] timber reserves, develops recreation programs, conducts fire safety programs, and undertakes other programs related to forest preservation.

General Accounting Office (GAO), 1921– . An *independent agency*[6] within the legislative branch of the *federal government*[3] which was created to assist the *Congress*[4] in providing legislative control over the receipt, disbursement, and application of public funds. The agency's primary functions are in the fields of *auditing*[10] accounting, legal decisions, special assistance to the Congress, records management and services, and settlement of claims against the U.S. government.

General Services Administration (GSA), 1949– . An *independent agency*[6] created to manage *federal*[3] property and records. The GSA supervises construction and operation of buildings, procurement and distribution of supplies, disposal of surplus *property*[10], traffic and communications facilities, stockpiling of strategic and critical materials, and the preservation and disposal of records.

Health, Education, and Welfare, Department of (HEW), 1953– . The *executive*[6] *department*[6] of the *federal government*[3] established for the purpose of improving the *administration*[6] of those agencies responsible for promoting the general welfare in the fields of health, education, and *Social*[11] *Security*. HEW is headed by a *cabinet*[6] level Secretary, and contains agencies concerned with retirement programs, family assistance, public health, food and drug quality, *vocational*[11] *rehabilitation*, and other related interests. See also *Central*[11] *Cities Project*; *Food*[2] *and Drug Administration*; *general*[4] *welfare clause*; *Social*[2] *Security Administration*; *Work*[11] *Experience Program*; *Work*[11] *Study Program*.

Housing and Urban Development, Department of (HUD), 1965– . The *executive*[6] *department*[6] of the *federal government*[3] created to help coordinate the various federal programs related to housing and *urban*[11] problems. HUD is headed by a *cabinet*[6] level Secretary, and contains agencies concerned with mortgage credit, *urban*[11] *renewal, public housing*[11], and

related areas. It was created as part of *President*[6] *Lyndon B. Johnson's*[6] *Great*[6] *Society* in order to deal with social and urban problems. See also *Federal*[2] *Housing Administration*.

Immigration and Naturalization Service, 1891– . The agency within the *Department of Justice*[2] responsible for administering the *laws*[8] related to *immigration*[3], *naturalization*[3], exclusion, and deportation of *aliens*[3]. See also *Immigration*[4] *and Naturalization (McCarran-Walter) Act of 1952; Immigration*[4] *Act of 1965.*

Intergovernmental Relations, Office of, 1969– . An *Executive*[2] *Office* agency serving as a clearinghouse for the rapid handling and solution of problems common to *federal*[3], *state*[3], and *municipal* [see *city*[11]] governments. Such problems are brought to the attention of the *President*[6] or *Vice-President*[6] by *executive*[6] and legislative officers of state and local *governments*[3]. The agency coordinates various federal assistance programs designed to assist state and local agencies. See also *grants-in-aid*[10]; *intergovernmental*[11] *agreement; interstate*[11] *compact; interstate*[11] *relations.*

Interior, Department of the, 1849– . The *executive*[6] *department*[6] of the *federal government*[3] serving as the custodian of the natural resources of the U.S. and its dependencies. The Department is headed by a Secretary of the Interior, and contains agencies concerned with Indian affairs, mining, fish and wildlife, geologic research, land management, national parks and monuments, *territories*[3], flood control, *conservation*[10], *public*[10] *works*, and related areas.

Internal Revenue Service (IRS), 1862– . An agency within the *Department of the Treasury*[2] responsible for the determination, assessment, and collection of all internal revenue and taxes levied within the U.S. The agency also supervises the enforcement of *statutes*[8] related to the legal alcohol industry and the use of firearms. See also *Tax Court*[8] (U.S.); *graduated income tax*[10].

Interstate Commerce Commission (ICC), 1887– . The first *independent regulatory commission*[6] organized by the *federal government*[3], an agency created to regulate *common*[10] carriers engaged in foreign and *interstate commerce*[10] affecting the U.S. The ICC regulates rates, services, and other operations of air, rail, water, trucking, and pipeline facilities handling either goods or persons. See also *National*[5] *Grange*.

Joint Chiefs of Staff (JCS), 1949– . An agency within the *Department of Defense*[2] which serves as the immediate military staff of the Secretary of Defense and acts as chief military counsel for the *President*[6]. The *staff organization*[6] provides strategic military plans, makes recommendations for military reorganization, reviews military operations, and makes recommendations with regard to long-range manpower, research, and budgetary needs. The JCS consists of the chairman of the Joint Chiefs of Staff and the chief of staff of each branch of the U.S. armed forces.

Justice, Department of, 1870– . The *executive*[6] *department*[6] of the *federal government*[3] created to provide means for the enforcement of federal *laws*[8], to furnish legal counsel in federal cases, and to construe the laws under which other departments act. The department is headed by the *Attorney*[8] *General*. Various duties of the department are to supervise *pardons*[6] and *paroles*[8], supervise federal penal institutions, supervise *United*[8] *States attorneys* and *United*[8] *States marshals*, investigate and detect violations of federal laws, and conduct suits in the *Supreme*[8] *Court* on behalf of the federal government. The department is the principal agency charged with enforcing laws related to subversive ac-

tivities and *civil*[9] *rights*. One of the most famous agencies within the department is the *Federal*[2] *Bureau of Investigation*. See also *Civil*[9] *Rights Acts of 1957, 1960, 1964,* and *1968*; *Immigration*[2] *and Naturalization Service*.

Labor, Department of, 1913– . The *executive*[6] *department*[6] of the *federal government*[3] charged with administering and enforcing *statutes*[8] designed to advance the public interest by promoting the welfare of the wage earners of the U.S. The Department is headed by a Secretary of Labor, and contains divisions concerned with manpower needs, retraining, labor-management relations, international trade, working conditions, safety, and other related subjects. See also *job*[11] *training program*.

Law Enforcement Assistance Administration (LEAA), 1968– . An agency within the *Department of Justice*[2] which is headed by an administrator appointed by the *President*[6] and *confirmed*[6] by the *Senate*[7]. LEAA is charged with assisting *state*[3] and local *law*[8] enforcement agencies in *crime*[8] prevention and detection. The agency works through *grants-in-aid*[10], comprehensive planning, academic assistance, research, and statistical services. See also *Omnibus*[8] *Crime Control and Safe Streets Act of 1968*.

Management and Budget, Office of, 1970– . A *federal*[3] agency within the *Executive*[2] *Office* that replaced the Bureau of the Budget, which was created in 1921 to handle the preparation of the annual *budget*[10]. The agency, the largest within the Executive Office, is chaired by a director selected by the *President*[6], who is directly responsible to the President in assisting in the preparation of the budget. The office deals with continuing fiscal analysis, program evaluation, interagency cooperation, and intergovernmental programs. It advises on management systems, reviews organizational structures, and makes recommendations for *administrative reorganization*[6]. The Office of Management and Budget also handles data systems, career *executive*[6] programs, statistical services, and legislative reference functions. It also evaluates and coordinates all federal programs handled by the various *cabinet*[6] level *departments*[6]. See also *Budget*[10] *and Accounting Act of 1921*; *Advisory*[6] *Council on Executive Reorganization*; *grants-in-aid*[10]; *intergovernmental*[11] *agreement*; *interstate*[11] *relations*.

Maritime   Administration   (MA), 1950– . An agency within the *Department of Commerce*[2] which promotes and regulates the activities of the U.S. merchant marine. The Maritime Administration directs emergency operations related to merchant marine activities, establishes specifications for shipbuilding and design, determines routes, and manages other areas of merchant operations. See also *Federal*[2] *Maritime Commission*; *admiralty law*[8].

National Aeronautics and Space Administration (NASA), 1958– . An *independent regulatory commission*[6] designed to develop and coordinate programs for the peaceful exploration of outer space through research, development, and operational systems. The agency was successful in actually placing American research teams on the moon. See also *National*[2] *Aeronautics and Space Council*.

National   Aeronautics   and   Space Council (NASC), 1958– . An *Executive*[2] *Office* agency created to advise and assist the *President*[6] regarding a comprehensive space program. The Space Council consists of the *Vice-President*[6], the Secretary of State, the Secretary of Defense, the administrator of the *National*[2] *Aeronautics and Space Administration*, and the *chairman*[7] of the *Atomic*[2] *Energy Commission*.

National Foundation on the Arts and the Humanities, 1965– . A *federal*[3] *independent agency*[6] created in the Arts and Humanities Act of 1965 to encourage the development of artistic achievement in the U.S.

National   Labor   Relations   Board (NLRB), 1935– . An *independent regulatory commission*[6] created during the *Great Depression*[10] as part of the *New*[6] *Deal*. The agency was created to carry out the provisions of the *National*[10] *Labor Relations (Wagner) Act of 1935* and other *federal*[3] *legislation*[7] passed to permit laborers to organize and carry out *collective*[10] *bargaining*. The NLRB regulates unfair labor practices and supervises *labor*[10] *union* elections. See also *National*[1] *Labor Relations Board v. Jones and Laughlin Corp.*

National Mediation Board (NMB), 1934– . An *independent agency*[6] established during the *New*[6] *Deal* to mediate labor-management problems in the fields of railway and airline transportation. The NMB assists in problems of *collective*[10] *bargaining* and seeks to protect the national economy and national security by keeping rail and air traffic operating. See also *Railway*[10] *Labor Act of 1926*; *labor arbitration*[10]; *Federal*[2] *Mediation and Conciliation Service*.

National   Recovery   Administration (NRA), 1933. The former *New*[6] *Deal* agency created by the *National*[10] *Industrial Recovery Act of 1933* to enforce "codes of fair competition" in labor-management relations and business competition. The NRA, a major agency designed to help overcome the problems of the *Great Depression*[10], was   declared   *unconstitutional*[3]   in *Schechter*[1] *Poultry Corp. v. U.S.* and *Panama*[1] *Refining Co. v. Ryan* as an unwarranted *delegation of authority*[6] to the *President*[6] and an invasion of the *reserved powers*[4] of the *states*[3].

National Science Foundation (NSF), 1950– . An *independent agency*[6] created to encourage and expand scientific endeavors in research, education, and development.

National Security Council (NSC), 1947– . An *Executive*[2] *Office* agency charged with advising the *President*[6] on matters related to national security. The NSC is composed of the President, the *Vice-President*[6], the Secretary of State, the Secretary of Defense, and the Director of the *Office of Emergency*[2] *Preparedness*. See also *Central*[2] *Intelligence Agency*.

Occupational Safety and Health Review Commission, 1970– . A three-member independent *executive*[6] agency created by the *Occupational*[11] *Health and Safety Act of 1970* in order to insure fair and equitable enforcement of *federal*[3] health and safety standards. Members are appointed by the *President*[6] and *confirmed*[6] by the *Senate*[7] for six-year terms of office. See also *independent agency*[6].

Peace Corps, 1961– . An *executive*[6] agency operating under the *federal*[3] consolidated volunteer agency known as ACTION[2]. The Peace Corps, originally promoted and created during the *administration*[6] of *President*[6] John F. Kennedy, is designed to promote international friendship through the placement abroad of American *citizens*[3] qualified in various job specialties. Placement of volunteers is in developing *nations*[3] seeking skilled manpower. The agency was created as part of the *New*[6] *Frontier* in order to help overcome the foreign problem known as *Ugly*[12] *Americanism*. It operated within the *Department of State*[2] until 1971.

Public Health Service (PHS), 1944– . A *federal*[3] agency created in 1798, named the Public Health Service in 1912, and enlarged and re-

organized in 1944. The PHS is involved in numerous programs related to hospital construction, medical research, medical surveys, federal medical and research grants to *states*[3], alcoholic and narcotic rehabilitation, and other specialized programs related to the health needs and problems of the people of the U.S. See also *closed*[6] *career system*.

Rural Electrification Administration (REA), 1935– . An agency created in the midst of the *Great Depression*[10] in order to provide loan programs for *rural*[10] *electrification* and telephone service. The agency is located within the *Department of Agriculture*[2] and operates primarily through *cooperatives*[10] and *public service commissions*[10].

Science and Technology, Office of (OST), 1962– . An *Executive*[2] *Office* agency created to advise and give assistance to the *President*[6] in the areas of science and technology in the interests of national security and general welfare.

Secret Service, United States: see *United*[2] *States Secret Service*.

Securities and Exchange Commission (SEC), 1934– . An *independent regulatory commission*[6] charged with protecting the interests of the public and investors against malpractices in the securities and financial markets of the U.S. The agency regulates stock exchange transactions, *holding*[10] *company* arrangements, *monopolies*[10], *trusts*[10], investment companies, and *bankruptcy*[10] reorganization proceedings. The SEC was one of the major agencies created during the *Great Depression*[10] as part of *President*[6] *Franklin D. Roosevelt's*[6] *New*[6] *Deal*. See also *Public*[10] *Utility Holding Company Act of 1935*.

Selective Service System (SSS), 1947– . A *federal*[3] agency within the

Executive[2] *Office* responsible for the registration and *drafting*[12] into military service all male *citizens*[3] meeting specifications set by *law*[8]. In *World*[12] *War* I the Selective Service Act of 1917, the second compulsory draft *legislation*[7] in U.S. history, authorized the *President*[6] to require the registration of all males between the ages of 21 and 30, males who were considered available for military service. The law expired at the end of World War I. Selective Service was revived in the Selective Service Act of 1940. Through that law and subsequent legislation, a Selective Service System headed by the Director of Selective Service was created. It operated through local selective service draft *boards*[6] who examined and classified potential draftees. The registration liability varies from time to time. However, it begins primarily at the age of 19 and ends at the age of 35. A major revision in the Selective Service System was instituted in 1969 when a draft lottery was created. Young men reaching their nineteenth birthday received a number drawn by lottery. That number was used to determine draft eligibility. Various exemptions and deferments were allowed for such things as medical deficiencies, family hardship, and mental disorders. In 1973 the draft ended and legislation became effective which instituted an all-volunteer army, a system still requiring registration with the Selective Service. See also *Gillette*[1] *v. U.S.*; *U.S.*[1] *v. Seeger.*

Small Business Administration (SBA), 1953– . An *independent regulatory commission*[6] created to aid, counsel, assist, and protect the interests of small business concerns within the U.S. The agency helps small businesses acquire *government*[3] *contracts*[10], makes loans during times of disaster, helps improve the management skills of owners of small businesses, makes loans to *state*[3] and local development companies, and funds

analysis and research projects designed to assist small businesses. See also *ACTION*[2]; *free*[10] *enterprise.*

Social Security Administration (SSA), 1946– . The *federal*[3] agency established to combine the various programs covered by the *Social*[11] *Security Act of 1935* and subsequent *legislation*[7] passed to help provide for the general welfare. The agency administers federal retirement, survivors, disability, and health insurance programs. It presently operates within the *Department of Health*[2], *Education, and Welfare.*

Special Representative for Trade Negotiations, Office of the, 1963– . An *Executive*[2] *Office* agency headed by an official with *ambassador*[12] rank. The agency is concerned with international trade *policies*[6] and directs U.S. participation in trade agreement negotiations with other *countries*[3]. See also *tariff*[10]; *United*[2] *States Tariff Commission.*

State, Department of, 1789– . The oldest *executive*[6] *department*[6] of the *federal government*[3], a department responsible for formulating and executing U.S. foreign *policy*[6]. The Department is led by the Secretary of State, and contains agencies responsible for such functions as *Foreign*[2] *Service* staff, handling *passports*[12] and *visas*[3], enforcing *immigration*[3] and *naturalization*[3] *laws*[8], operating *foreign*[12] *aid* programs, providing *intelligence*[12] services, and guiding international organization. See also *Agency*[2] *for International Development*; *United*[2] *States Information Agency.*

Subversive Activities Control Board (SACB), 1950– . An independent *executive*[6] agency established to register and investigate "Communist-action" and "Communist-front" organizations within the U.S. A basic assignment of the SACB is to prevent the "worldwide *Communist*[3] conspiracy" from "accomplishing its purpose in the United States." The *organization*[6] has been weakened to almost a useless position because of various *Supreme*[8] *Court* decisions involving *constitutionally*[3] guaranteed *civil*[9] *rights* related to free expression and association. See also *Albertson*[1] *v. SACB*; *Communist*[1] *Party v. SACB*; *Internal*[9] *Security (McCarran) Act of 1950*; *front organization.*[5]

Tax Court of the United States: see *Tax Court*[8] (U.S.).

Tennessee Valley Authority (TVA), 1933– . A *government corporation*[6] created to provide for the development of the Tennessee River and its tributaries in the interest of navigation, the control of floods, and the generation and disposition of hydroelectric power. The TVA generates electric power which is distributed to the public through private companies, *cooperatives*[10], and local *governments*[3]. It also manufactures and sells fertilizers, produces nitrates destined for defense usage, and conducts forest preservation and *conservation*[10] projects. The TVA was created as a major *New*[6] *Deal public*[10] *works* project designed to employ persons during the *Great Depression*[10]. See also *Ashwander*[1] *v. TVA*; *public*[10] *power*; *war*[12] *powers*.

Transportation, Department of (DOT), 1966– . The *executive*[6] *department*[6] of the *federal government*[3] created for the express purpose of developing national transportation *policies*[6] and programs related to the transportation needs of the U.S. The Department combined the administrative machinery of numerous agencies formerly devising and regulating Federal transportation policies. DOT is led by the Secretary of Transportation, and was created as part of *President*[6] *Lyndon B. Johnson's*[6] *Great*[6] *Society* in order to deal with major social and *urban*[11] problems. See also *Federal*[2] *Aviation Administration.*

Treasury, Department of the, 1789– . The *executive*[6] *department*[6] of the *federal government*[3] responsible for formulating domestic and international financial *policy*[6], devising general tax policy, guiding general economic policies, and managing the public debt. The Department is led by the Secretary of the Treasury, and handles matters of accounting, processing of government checks, collecting tax revenues and *customs*[10] *duties*, regulating banks, producing money, regulating forgery and counterfeiting, and providing protection for the *President*[6] and the *Vice-President*[6] and their families. See also *Bureau of Customs*[2]; *Alexander Hamilton*[4]; *Office of Comptroller*[2] *of the Currency*; *United*[2] *States Secret Service.*

United States Arms Control and Disarmament Agency (USACDA), 1961– . An *independent agency*[6] responsible for *policy-formulation*[7] and international negotiations in the area of arms control and disarmament. See also *atomic*[12] *war*; *arms*[12] *race.*

United States Civil Service Commission, 1883– . An *independent regulatory commission*[6] created to administer the *federal*[3] merit system, an arrangement established to fill public offices without political considerations. See also *civil*[6] *service*; *Civil*[6] *Service (Pendleton) Act of 1883*; *merit*[6] *system.*

United States Information Agency (USIA), 1953– . An *independent agency*[6] designed to help achieve foreign *policy*[6] objectives through the use of communications media such as broadcasting, books, movies, cultural exchanges, library facilities, and exhibits. The USIA works closely with the *Department of State*[2]. See also *mass*[5] *media*; *propaganda.*[5]

United States Postal Service, 1970– . A *government corporation*[6] created to supersede the Post Office Department, which had been in existence since

1872. The United States Postal Service is charged with providing efficient nationwide postal service capable of promoting the general welfare and advancing the national economy. The agency may set rates, raise money through the issuance of *bonds*[10], and handle employee bargaining and personnel practices. The *organization*[6] was created in an effort to improve postal service, remove the postal operations from political pressures, and eliminate previous abuses involving *patronage*[6]. The government corporation is directed by a Postmaster General, a Deputy Director, and a nine-man *board*[6] appointed by the *President*[6] and *confirmed*[6] by the *Senate*[7]. Members of the board serve staggered terms of office.

United States Secret Service, 1860– . An agency within the *Department of the Treasury*[2] charged with protecting the *President*[6] and the *Vice President*[6] and their immediate families. Since 1968 the presidential and vice-presidential candidates of the major *political parties*[5] have been assured protection during presidential elections. The Secret Service also enforces *laws*[8] related to coins, obligations, and securities of the U.S. and foreign *governments*[3].

United States Tariff Commission, 1916– . An independent advisory staff agency serving the *President*[6] and the *Congress*[4] in *tariff*[10] matters. The Tariff Commission is responsible for conducting research, *hearings*[6], and investigations. Upon the basis of its findings the agency makes recommendations with regard to international trade. See also *Customs Court*[8]; *Court*[8] *of Customs and Patent Ap-*

peals; Office of the Special[2] *Representative for Trade Negotiations.*

Urban Mass Transportation Administration, 1968– . A *federal*[3] agency within the *Department of Transportation*[2] created to assist in the planning and development of mass transportation systems throughout the U.S. The agency works primarily through *grants-in-aid*[10] designed to assist research, planning, design, and personnel training.

Veterans Administration (VA), 1930– . An *independent agency*[6] created to administer *laws*[8] authorizing benefits for former members of the armed forces and their dependents. The VA administers hospitals, retirement benefits, rehabilitation programs, and other related matters. See also *G.I.*[12] *Bill of Rights.*

White House Office. A basic *staff organization*[6] within the *Executive*[2] *Office of the President*, which contains the personal staff of the *President*[6]. The staff includes administrative assistants, secretaries, physicians, military aides, and other related personnel. See also *Watergate*[5].

Works Progress Administration (WPA), 1935. The temporary *New*[6] *Deal* agency which provided general public employment during the *Great Depression*[10]. The WPA combined the efforts of other temporary agencies and provided employment on projects such as hospitals, schools, bridges, and slum clearance. The WPA also assisted the fine arts, music, and other economically depressed portions of *society*[3].

Chapter 3

Statehood and Constitutionalism

Note to the reader: Cross-referenced terms are in italics. The superscript number refers to the chapter in which the entry may be found. In addition, its placement indicates the word under which the term is alphabetized. (For example, in *electoral[4] college*, information on the electoral college may be found in Chapter 4 under "electoral.") Because italics are used in cross-references, they are not used for terms in which they would ordinarily be used: Supreme Court cases and titles of books, journals, plays, and so forth.

alien. A person within a *state[3]* who is a *citizen[3]* of a foreign *country[3]* or who has not become a *naturalized[3]* citizen of the state in which he resides. See also *enemy alien[12]*; *Immigration[2] and Naturalization Service*; *Fong[1] Yue Ting v. U.S.*; *U.S.[1] v. Wong Kim Ark*.

alienation. The feeling of an individual or a portion of *society[3]* that there is estrangement between the self, individual or social, and those who possess *power[3]*.

amendment. A change made in a *constitution[3]*, proposed *bill[7]*, *act[8]*, *resolution[7]*, *administrative[6] order*, or other written document. The process of proposing amendments to the *U.S. Constitution[4]* requires acceptance by a two-thirds vote of both houses of the *Congress[4]* or by a *convention[3]* requested by two-thirds of the state *legislatures[7]*. The process of *ratifying[3]* amendments to the Constitution requires acceptance by three-fourths of the *state[3]* legislatures or by conventions in three-fourths of the states.

Some factors concerning the amending process of the Constitution are: a state legislature may reject an amendment and later accept it; a state legislature may not reject an amendment it has once accepted; an amendment may not be submitted to the voters of a state on a popular *referendum[3]*; Congress may set a limit on the time an amendment may circulate among the states for consideration; and the *President[6]* may not *veto[7]* an amendment. See also *flexible constitution[3]*; *Coleman[1] v. Miller*; *Hawke[1] v. Smith*.

anarchism. The *theory[3]* that *government[3]* is unnecessary for a meaningful arrangement and operation of *society[3]*, especially since coercive elements within government are restrictive of individual liberty and expression. See also *Michael Bakaunin[3]*; *Pierre Proudhon[3]*.

anarchy. A social system devoid of *government[3]* and characterized by political disorder. In a *society[3]* characterized by a condition of anarchy, there is often chaos, mob rule, and general uncertainty about political and social rules.

annexation: see Chap. 11.

Aquinas, St. Thomas, 1225–74. The major writer of medieval European scholasticism and author of Summa Theologica (1265–74). His work shifted church doctrine and commitments from mystical *Platonic*[3] thought as interpreted by *St. Augustine*[3] to legalistic *Aristotelian*[3] logic. Aquinas taught that *government*[3] originated before the battle of good and evil, that it is directed toward the otherworldly life with God, that secular government should be subservient to spiritual values as taught by the church, that the best ruler is a *monarch*[3] accountable to God and removable through official public action, and that the church and *state*[3] have different functions but are both designed to work toward the salvation of lost souls. See also *Mosaic Code*[8].

aristocracy. Political control by those viewed as the upper or superior strata of *society*[3], regardless of the social criteria used to designate "upper" (wealth, art, education, etc.). See also *elitism*[3]; *plutocracy*[3].

Aristotle, 384–322 B.C. The author of Politics, one of the earliest known systematic analyses of the *state*[3]. Aristotle viewed man as a "political animal" and the state as the highest social *community*[3], a living organism with a life separate from the individuals composing it. He believed the state was created for the greatest good of man and that the best state would incorporate *aristocratic*[3] virtues. He felt that the state could operate effectively under one man or several, but that the most stable *government*[3] would be based on a *mixed constitution*[3] balancing wealth and population through the existence of a middle class. He felt the worst possible government would be *tyranny*[3].

Aristotle laid the framework for the study of *politics*[3] as a science by analyzing the state, *revolution*[3], *property*[10], slavery, *law*[8], comparative government, and other basic elements of social and political *organization*[6]. See also *St. Thomas Aquinas*[3]; *organic state*[3].

Augustine, St. Aurelius, 354–430 A.D. The most influential writer of early Christianity and the author of The City of God (413–427 A.D.). St. Augustine contrasted the heavenly city (city of God) and the earthly city (city of man) and discussed the nature of divided loyalties between church and *state*[3]. He incorporated *Platonic*[3] dualism in his arguments and developed the idea that history is a struggle between good and evil, body and spirit, *justice*[8] and injustice. He taught that the state should have a spiritual base and should serve God and man. He especially stressed the need for social order, peace, and the good life. Because of his views on the orderly universe he declared that there is a difference between "just" and "unjust" wars. He laid the base for the belief that Christians should obey *tyrants*[3] rather than rebel against them. He also taught that the church acts as God's representative in earthly affairs. See also *Mosaic Code*[8]; *Gillette*[1] *v. U.S.*

autarchy (autarky). A condition of national self-sufficiency, usually attained through *state*[3] policies carefully regulating imports and exports in order to avoid dependency on strategic goods available only from foreign nations. A *nation*[3] seeking autarchy is also careful to avoid becoming dependent upon *foreign*[12] *aid*.

authoritarianism. A social arrangement wherein political control is based on the *theory*[3] that political subjects owe absolute obedience to those possessing political *power*[3]. Usually such a system is more concerned with controlling the political views and activities of its subjects than in regulating all areas of social and economic life that do not threaten the political power of the dominant group. See also *Communism*[3]; *fascism*[3]; *Nazism*[3].

authority. The *constitutionally*[3] or legally acknowledged right to formulate rules and enforce obedience to them.

autocracy. Unlimited *government*[3] vested in one person.

autonomy. The quality of possessing self-*government*[3].

Bakaunin, Michael, 1814–76. The Russian *anarchist*[3] who was the leading exponent of philosophical *nihilism*[3]. In his book, God and the State (1882), Bakaunin supported the total destruction of the *state*[3], absolute *individualism*[3], atheism, *radicalism*[3], insurrection, a total rejection of political action, and a *society*[3] based on a loose federation of cooperative associations.

Bentham, Jeremy, 1748–1832. The Englishman sometimes referred to as the "Father of *utilitarianism*"[3]. The basic premise of Bentham's works such as An Introduction to the Principles of Morals and Legislation (1789) and A Catechism of Parliamentary Reform (1809) was that *government*[3] and social actions are structured by man's desire for happiness, not by some organic or divine purpose. Bentham's ideas led him directly into battles for *constitutional*[3], legislative, and social reform and he is generally recognized as the major English social reformer of the nineteenth century. See also *organic state*[3]; *divine right theory*[3].

Bill of Rights (England, 1689). An English *statute*[8] officially known as "An Act declaring the Rights and Liberties of the Subjects, and settling the Succession of the Crown." The Bill of Rights settled the succession

of William and Mary after the *Glorious Revolution*[3] and became a cornerstone for the unwritten English *constitution*[3]. It held that *laws*[8] could not be suspended or taxes levied without Parliamentary approval. On the positive side, it granted frequent Parliaments, free elections, freedom of speech within Parliament, the right of petition, the right to bear arms, and the right to trial for *treason*[3]. On the negative side, it abolished excessive *bails*[8] and fines, *cruel and unusual punishment*[9], and peacetime armies unless approved by Parliament. See also *unwritten constitution*[3]; *parliamentary government*[3]; *Magna*[3] *Carta*.

Bill of Rights (United States): see Chap. 4.

Blackstone, William, 1723–80. The author of the most famous and most readable systematization of English *common law*[8] ever compiled by a single individual. The work, entitled Commentaries on the Laws of England (1765–69), is a recording of legal history as well as a practical analysis of the nature of *law*[8] and *government*[3]. Blackstone's analysis of law, *natural rights*[3], personal liberties, and *property*[10] ownership greatly influenced the writing of the American *Declaration*[4] *of Independence* and the *U.S. Constitution*[4].

Bodin, Jean, 1530–96. The French political and economic philosopher whose book, The Six Books on the State (1576), is frequently acclaimed as the first modern volume on the science of *politics*[3] and political economy. Bodin believed that sovereign *power*[3] originated from human needs rather than from a positive act of God. He supported *environmental determinism*[3], a *theory*[3] of *natural law*[8], a theory of *force*[3] for the operation of *society*[3], a society based on practical *legislation*[7], religious toleration, human rights, a *mixed constitution*[3], a benevolent *monarchy*[3], industrial development, and passive *civil*[9] *disobedience*.

Bolshevik. A Russian designation of the accepted *state*[3] *party*[5] of the Soviet Union. The word literally means *majority*[3]. The *Marxist*[3] oriented party operating under such a designation supported social change through violent *revolution*[3] and was led to political victory under *Lenin*[3] in 1917. See also *Menshevik*[3].

Bonapartism. An interpretation of *popular sovereignty*[3], which contends that a personal *dictatorship*[3] may be conferred on a person by the people according to *constitutional*[3] rules. In essence, popular sovereignty may suppress itself. Such an idea came from Napoleon's desire, even while acting as a dictator, to demonstrate that his *power*[3] came from the people.

bourgeoisie. The social class owning the means of production. A member of the middle class who is concerned with *capitalistic*[3] interests. See also *proletariat*[3].

Burke, Edmund, 1729–97. The Englishman sometimes referred to as "The Father of Modern Conservatism." Burke's writings, such as Reflections on the Revolution in France (1790), indicted *wars*[12], *tyranny*[3], corruption, and *radical*[3] social change. His Reflections, an indictment of the excesses and *anarchic*[3] conditions of the French Revolution of 1789, is still recognized as the outstanding English work of political *conservatism*[3]. Burke believed in an organic theory of the *state*[3], *government*[3] by a wealthy *aristocracy*[3], the sanctity of private *property*[10], and a *society*[3] based on traditions. He rejected ideas of equality, *proportional representation*[5], and *popular sovereignty*[3]. See also *organic state*[3].

Calvin, John, 1509–64. The creator of the religious, philosophical, and political movement known as Calvinism.

John Calvin compiled the Institutes of the Christian Religion (1536), the most systematic theological work of the Protestant Reformation. He stressed the *authority*[3] of the Bible, the sovereignty of God, the depravity of man, and the salvation of the elect. In *politics*[3] he stressed natural order, *natural rights*[3], the institution of church and *state*[3] to glorify God, the use of *tyrants*[3] to punish wicked men and *societies*[3], limited resistance to tyrants, and *government*[3] through *covenants*[3]. Calvin's ideas laid the framework for Puritanism, a rigid political-religious movement whose adherents helped settle New England. See also *Mosaic Code*[8]; *Protestant*[4] *Ethic*.

capitalism. An economic system based on privately owned methods of production designed for profit making through economic competition. See also *free*[10] *enterprise*.

centralization. The concentration of political *power*[3] within one central *government*[3]. See also *unitary government*[3].

checks and balances. An arrangement of governmental *power*[3] in such a way as to permit various branches and *departments*[6] of *government*[3] to participate in the affairs of other departments in an effort to balance political power. Examples of checks and balances within the United States *constitutional*[3] system are the presidential *veto*[7], the *veto*[7] *override* possessed by the *Congress*[4], *Senate*[7] *confirmation*[6] of *treaties*[12] and executive *appointments*[6], and *judicial*[4] *review* of legislative and *executive*[6] actions.

citizen. A person who is recognized as a member of a *state*[3]. Such a person is entitled to the general rights guaranteed by the state (voting, economic rights, etc.) and is required to fulfill certain obligations as a member of the state (military service, obedience to the *laws*[8], etc.). Citizenship may be gained either through birth or *naturalization*[3]. Citizenship determined by the parent's citizenship is known as *jus*[3] *sanguinis* and that determined by place of birth is known as *jus*[3] *soli*. The basic determinant of U.S. citizenship is jus soli and is defined in the *Fourteenth Amendment*[4] of the U.S. *Constitution*[4]. The most common method of loss of citizenship is by voluntary renunciation, a process known as *expatriation*[3]. See also *Afroyim*[1] *v. Rusk*; *Dred*[1] *Scott v. Sandford*; *Immigration*[4] *Act of 1965*; *Immigration*[4] *and Nationality Act of 1952*; *Perez*[1] *v. Brownell*; *Trop*[1] *v. Dulles*.

citizen, natural-born. A *citizen*[3] born within the legal *jurisdiction*[8] of a *state*[3].

citizenship: see *citizen*[3].

citizenship, dual. The condition of being accepted as a *citizen*[3] of two legal *jurisdictions*[8]. Such a condition is possible when a person is born while his parents are abroad. He may be accepted as a citizen in the *state*[3] where he is born, while also being accepted as a citizen of the state where his parents reside. In the United States *constitutional*[3] *system* a person may be considered a citizen of the U.S. and a citizen of a separate state within the Union at the same time. See also *privileges*[4] *and immunities clause*.

city-state. An *urban*[11] or metropolitan center possessing the characteristics of a *state*[3]. Athens and Sparta were known as Greek city-states.

civil disobedience: see Chap. 9.

coexistence. The political reality of two or more *nations*[3] of extreme political, economic, and *ideological*[3] differences existing in an international social order by seeking to avoid competition that could be detrimental to all parties concerned. See also *peaceful coexistence*[12]; *ideological warfare*[12].

collectivism. The social arrangement based on collective or group ownership of *property*[10] and the means of production. See also *Brook*[4] *Farm*; *communism*[3]; *Charles Fourier*[3]; *Robert Owen*[3]; *Claude Saint-Simon*[3]; *New*[4] *Harmony*; *socialism*[3].

colonialism. The practice of one political *state*[3] maintaining political control over foreign *countries*[3] in order to exploit natural resources and open foreign markets. See also *Daniel Leonard*[4]; *Monroe*[12] *Doctrine*; *mercantilism*[3].

comity. The cooperative practice between *states*[3] or *nations*[3] designed to allow reciprocal action concerning various *executive*[6], legislative, and judicial matters such as *extradition*[12] of fugitives, *diplomatic*[12] *immunity*, and recognition of legal documents and judicial decisions. See also *full*[4] *faith and credit clause*; *privileges*[4] *and immunities*; *Williams*[1] *v. N.C.*

commonwealth. A *society*[3] organized around political institutions, agencies, and practices. The term is most frequently used to designate a body politic governed by the people through elected *representatives*[7]. See also *dominion*[3]; *representative government*[3].

communism. A term designating a social arrangement in which *society*[3] shares *property*[10], land, and political *power*[3] for the benefit of all the members of the *community*[3]. See also *collectivism*[3].

Communism. A general *theory*[3] of social and political *organization*[6] based on Marxian *socialism*[3] as developed by *Lenin*[3] through *revolutionary*[3] means. The doctrine developed by *Karl Marx*[3] and Lenin interprets history as class warfare which will eventually end in the victory of the working class and the creation of the *dic-*

tatorship[3] *of the proletariat.* It stresses total social control through a single *authoritarian*[3] party and absolute opposition to *capitalistic*[3] systems. It also emphasizes the ultimate development of a classless society based on a socialistic economic structure. See also *bourgeoisie*[3]; *collectivism*[3]; *economic determinism*[3]; *labor*[10] *theory of value*; *proletariat*[3]; *Joseph Stalin*[3].

community. A social group residing in a particular area under some form of acknowledged social or political structure and sharing a common cultural environment. See also *society*[3].

compact: see *covenant*[3].

condominium. A shared sovereignty held by two or more *states*[3] over a dependent or subject *territory*[3]. See *state (constitutional) sovereignty*[3].

consensus. General agreement by members of a social and political system on the fundamentals of *government*[3] or social values, structures, and actions.

conservatism. General opposition to change in institutions or practices within a *society*[3]. The leading exponent of philosophical conservatism was the English political theorist, *Edmund Burke*[3]. Burke argued for social and political change in graduated steps, based on carefully tested practices and institutions. The U.S. brand of conservatism usually emphasizes the *status*[3] quo in race relations, opposition to governmental interference in economic affairs, *states'*[4] *rights*, lower taxes, and fewer social programs financed by *government*[3]. See also *reactionary*[3]; *right*[3].

constitution. The fundamental *law*[8] of a *state*[3], written or unwritten, which organizes *government*[3], assigns and limits political *power*[3], and clarifies the relationship between the people and their political leaders. The *U.S.*

Constitution[4] became effective on March 4, 1789. It contains seven articles, has been *amended*[3] 26 times, and has been modified considerably through *custom*[3], usage, and judicial interpretation. See also *constitutional*[3]; *constitutional*[3] *system*; *polity*[3]; *preamble*[3]; *unconstitutional*[3].

constitutional. A part of or in agreement with a *constitution*[3]. See also *constitutionalism*[3]; *unconstitutional*[3]; *Ashwander*[1] *v. TVA*.

constitutionalism. The principle of *government*[3] which holds that political *power*[3] should be defined and limited by fundamental rules, either written or unwritten. See also *constitutional*[3]; *limited government*[3]; *constitutional law*[8]; *unconstitutional*[3].

constitutional system. A basic set of rules by which a population conducts its own affairs within its own *boundaries*[12]. A *constitution*[3], written or unwritten, is usually the basis for a larger constitutional system modified through *custom*[3], usage, *legislative*[4] *elaboration*, *executive*[6] action, judicial interpretation, and popular ideas and actions. See also *unwritten constitution*[3]; *state (constitutional) sovereignty*[3].

constitution, flexible. A *constitution*[3] that is easily *amended*[3]. See also *rigid constitution*[3].

constitution, mixed (balanced). A *theory*[3] of *government*[3] that holds that the best method of assuring that government will be responsible to the people and serve their needs is to mix or balance *powers*[3] between functional agencies of government. Present theories of mixed constitutions contain various elements of *separation*[3] *of powers* and *checks*[3] *and balances*.

constitution, rigid. A *constitution*[3] that makes no allowance for *amendments*[3] or that requires a procedure so difficult that it is almost impossible to add amendments. See also *flexible constitution*[3].

constitution, unwritten. A *constitution*[3] that consists primarily of *custom*[3], convention, or *common law*[8] that has not been written down in one comprehensive document of *government*[3]. In most political systems a written constitution composed of one document or several is usually supplemented by unwritten *constitutional*[3] elements. The *U.S. Constitution*[4] has added *political parties*[5], the presidential *cabinet*[6], *senatorial*[6] courtesy, the legislative *committee*[7] system, *judicial*[4] *review*, and other unwritten elements to the *constitutional*[3] system.

constitution, written. The fundamental *law*[8] of a *state*[3], which is contained in one or more written documents. See also *U.S. Constitution*[4].

continental shelf. The submerged shelf of land which slopes from the exposed edge of a continent to the place where the steep descent to the bottom of the ocean begins. The continental shelf is frequently disputed *territory*[3] between national *states*[3]. Within the U.S. there have been controversies over whether the *federal government*[3] or the various state governments control the continental shelf. See also *Tidelands*[4] *Oil controversy*.

convention. An assembly of persons meeting for a specific purpose. A convention is generally composed of certified *delegates*[5] empowered to discuss or act upon certain matters of interest to those who selected the delegates. The word "convention" is also commonly used to mean *custom*[3] or accepted usage. See also *Annapolis*[4] *Convention*; *Constitutional Convention*[4] *of 1787*; *Hartford*[4] *Convention*; *Mount*[4] *Vernon Convention*; *party convention*[5]; *preprimary convention*[5]; *rump convention*[5].

country. An area of land or the definable *territory*[3] of a *state*[3] or *nation*[3].

county: see Chap. 11.

coup d'état. A sudden political move, frequently by persons possessing some *authority*[3], to overthrow an existing *government*[3] by *force*[3]. See also *rebellion*[3]; *revolution*[3]; *war*[12].

covenant (contract, compact). A binding agreement between two or more persons, groups, *organizations*[6], or other collective bodies to do or refrain from doing a particular thing. See also *contract*[10]; *contract theory*[3].

custom. A conventional or accepted practice which may be recognized as part of a *constitutional*[3] system and which may be partially circumscribed and reinforced through legal actions of the *state*[3]. See also *convention*[3].

czarism. Absolutist or *tyrannical*[3] rule under one political figure, a rule resembling that of the Russian czars prior to the Russian *revolution*[3] of October 1917.

decentralization. The dispersion of *power*[3] over a broad area. See also *decentralized organization*[5].

Defense of Liberty Against Tyrants, A (1579). An anonymous French Huguenot tract published under the pseudonym of Stephen Junius Brutus. The tract analyzed government by *contract*[10], *popular sovereignty*[3], *property*[10] rights, trusteeship government, and *revolution*[3]. The author contended that God *covenants*[3] with the ruler and the people collectively in order to form *government*[3]. The *monarch*[3] then covenants with the people, and the people agree to obey faithfully only as long as the king rules justly and does not become a *tyrant*[3] or violate the *laws*[8] of God. If a ruler is a tyrant and violates the trust the people have given him, then they may revolt. The

Defense was in direct opposition to sixteenth-century arguments that revolution was in violation of the will of God. See also *limited government*[3]; *representative government*[3]; *contract theory*[3]; *higher law theory*[3].

democracy. A system of *government*[3] in which political *authority*[3] rests with the people. Direct democracy is evidenced when all persons within the political system participate in the formulation of rules for society. Indirect is the most widely used type of democracy and is based on the principle of *representation*[7]. Some of the basic characteristics of democratic political systems are: (1) a belief in the dignity and worth of the individual, (2) *constitutional*[3] government, (3) the freedom of expression, (4) the acknowledgment of equal rights for all persons, (5) political and social control by *majority*[3] *rule* and (6) political liberty and choice. A government using indirect democracy sometimes refers to itself as a *representative government*[3] or a *republic*[3]. Concepts of democracy are generally traced to the small Greek *city-states*[3] of ancient times. Basic to democratic philosophy was the idea of *citizen*[3] participation. The Greek word "demos" literally meant "people." *Aristotle*[3] and *Plato*[3] did not particularly care for democracy because of their fear of mob rule and political emotionalism. Modern concepts of democracy find their roots in the seventeenth and eighteenth centuries, particularly during the *Enlightenment*[3]. Leading exponents of various modifications of democratic *theory*[3] were *Jean Jacques Rousseau*[3], *John Locke*[3], and *Thomas Jefferson*[6]. They based their theories on *empiricism*[3], an optimistic view of man, an educated citizenry, popular elections, and the assumption that common goals and the "common good" could be achieved within the political system. See also *constitutionalism*[3]; *Jacksonian democracy*[4]; *Jeffersonian democracy*[4]; *general*[3] *will*; *Friederich Hayek*[10]; *majoritarianism*[3]; *majority*[3];

John Stuart Mill[3]; *Revolution*[5] *of 1800*, *Alexis de Tocqueville*[4]; *Frederick Jackson Turner*[4]; *tyranny*[3] *of the majority*.

deportation. Legal expulsion of an *alien*[3] from the *state*[3] in which he is residing to the *country*[3] or state of origin. See also *Fong*[1] *Yue Ting v. U.S.*

despotism. A *government*[3] dominated by a person or group possessing absolute political *power*[3]. See also *dictatorship*[3]; *tyranny*[3].

determinism, economic. The concept that the economic *laws*[8] and structures within a population determine the political and social structures within the *state*[3]. *Karl Marx*[3] and Friedrich Engels put forth the most famous *theory*[3] of economic determinism in The Communist Manifesto (1848). See also *Communism*[3]; *dialectical*[3] *materialism*.

determinism, environmental. The concept that overall environmental factors such as ethnic characteristics, weather, cultural practices, geography, and other interrelated variables largely determine the political structures of the *state*[3]. *Charles Montesquieu*[3], *Robert Owen*[3], and a number of other political philosophers held such a *theory*[3]. See also *Arthur Bentley*[5]; *Jean Bodin*[3].

determinism, geographical. The concept that the geographic location in which a population finds itself determines the political and social structures within the *state*[3]. See also *geopolitics*[3].

devolution. The delegation of *authority*[3] by a central *government*[3] or official to subordinate officials, agencies, or geographical *jurisdictions*[8].

dialectical materialism. The Marxist concept of the dynamics of man's interaction with *society*[3], especially productive society. *Karl Marx*[3] believed that the relationships of production affect *politics*[3], education, religion, and other social institutions. People act the way they do because of their economic arrangements. Existing economic arrangements create continual tension between owners and workers and such tension brings about change and progress. Marx held that each class, owners and workers, seeks to gain the economic advantage. Materialism moves forward from the dialectical process within history. The dialectical process is essentially a process of continual interaction between thesis (idea), antithesis (opposing idea), and synthesis (a new idea composed of the original thesis and antithesis). See also *bourgeoisie*[3]; *economic determinism*[3]; *dictatorship*[3] *of the proletariat*; *Hegel*[3]; *labor*[10] *theory of value*; *proletariat*[3].

dictatorship. A governmental system dominated by an individual or a small group wielding absolute political *power*[3]. See also *despotism*[3]; *tyranny*[3].

dictatorship of the proletariat. The Marxist-Leninist concept of a classless *society*[3] governed by the *proletariat*[3] (workers). *Lenin*[3] visualized a ruling class consisting of *urban*[11] and industrial workers, a class which would eventually destroy the *power*[3] of *capitalism*[3]. He believed such a rule would come into being only through *force*[3] because the *bourgeoisie*[3] (owners of the means of production) controlled the *state*[3]. See also *dialectical*[3] *materialism*; *labor*[10] *theory of value*; *Karl Marx*[3]; *Joseph Stalin*[3].

dominion. Political control over the inhabitants of a particular *territory*[3]. The term is frequently used to describe a member of the British *Commonwealth*[3].

egalitarianism (equalitarianism). The belief that all persons should possess equal social, political, economic, and legal rights. See also *liberalism*[3].

elitism. The concept that the major economic, social, and political decisions should be made by a group considered superior to the masses, regardless of the criteria used to determine superiority (wealth, education, physical ability, etc.). See also *aristocracy*[3].

empiricism. The belief that knowledge is derived from experience and observation. See also *behavioral political*[3] *science*; *systems theory*[3].

Enlightenment, the. The eighteenth century European philosophical movement dominated by a rational search for knowledge, skeptical acceptance of positive *authority*[3], and an *empirical*[3] methodology in almost every area of life. The Age of Enlightenment, a period extending from approximately 1680 through 1800, was dominated by political and philosophical greats such as Voltaire, *Locke*[3], *Montesquieu*[3], and *Rousseau*[3]. See also *liberalism*[3]; *state*[3] *of nature*; *contract theory*[3].

equalitarianism: see *egalitarianism*[3].

Establishment, the. The group of individuals within a social or political system who clearly possesses the major portion of *power*[3] and are the most influential in directing public *policy*[6]. See also *radicalism*[3].

ethnic. A cohesive social group characterized by common features of race, religion, language, cultural heritage, or other recognizable traits.

ethnocentrism. The belief that one's own race or *nation*[3] is superior to all others. See also *chauvinism*[12]; *arrogance*[12] *of power doctrine*; *nationalism*[3]; *Pax*[12] *Americana*; *xenophobia*[3].

expatriation. The act of being banished from one's own *country*[3] or the voluntary renunciation of *citizenship*[3].

faction. A small, relatively homogeneous group of individuals within a larger *organization*[6] which holds opinions different from the larger group or seeks to control *power*[3] presently lodged elsewhere in the total organization. A faction seeks to gain power through internal dissension or by influencing the organization through opportunistic political maneuvers. See also *The Federalist*[5] *No. 10*; *fifth*[12] *column*; *Washington's*[12] *Farewell Address*.

fascism. A particular form of *totalitarianism*[3] which arose in Italy around 1922 under the leadership of Benito Mussolini. Fascism as a political philosophy advocates a one-party *dictatorship*[3] under a glorified leader, violent suppression of political opposition, extreme *nationalism*[3], racism, and private ownership of production under *centralized*[3] governmental control. The term "fascism" is most often applied to so-called *right-wing*[3] totalitarian movements. See also *Nazism*[3].

federal: see *federal government*[3].

feudalism. The social, political, and economic system that dominated the major European *nations*[3] between the ninth and fifteenth centuries. The system was based upon a servile relationship between a "vassal" and a "lord." The vassal paid homage and service to the lord and the lord provided land and protection to the vassal.

force. *Power*[3] or strength, physical or otherwise, to motivate or restrain individuals, *organizations*[6], or objects. See also *coup*[3] *d'état*; *rebellion*[3]; *revolution*[3]; *war*[12].

Fourier, Charles, 1772–1837. The French social philosopher whose idealistic writings such as Domestic and Agricultural Association (1822) influenced the founding of various social experiments within the U.S. during the 1840's. *Brook*[4] *Farm*, Massachusetts (1840) was the most famous

of these "Associations." Each Association formed as a "phylanx," or a balanced *community*[3] of 1,600 people, was based on Fourier's premise that basic *laws*[8] of human nature are conducive to harmony. The laws of human nature may be discovered and arranged for the benefit of all. Fourier's most famous American followers were Horace Greeley, Ralph Waldo Emerson, *Henry David Thoreau*[4], and Nathaniel Hawthorne. See also *collectivism*[3]; *socialism*[3]; *utopia*[1].

general will. The expression most often associated with the name of *Jean Jacques Rousseau*[3] because of his use of it to describe the collective political will of the people. See also *democracy*[3]; *majoritarianism*[3]; *majority*[3] *rule*.

geopolitics. The study of the effect of geography on *politics*[3]. See also *geographical determinism*[3].

gerontocracy. A *government*[3] basically controlled by the oldest men within the social and political system.

government. The *organization*[6] of processes and institutions within a *state*[3] for the political and administrative control of the people.

government, confederate. A *league*[3] of sovereign *states*[3] grouped together around a central *government*[3] for the *administration*[6] of common matters. The central government may use only the *powers*[3] delegated to it by the member states and may not act directly on member states without their consent. See also *Articles*[4] *of Confederation*; *Confederate*[4] *States of America*.

government, de facto. A *government*[3] recognized as actually controlling the affairs of a *state*[3] even though it has not been granted legal *authority*[3] to do so nor recognized by foreign states. A government possessing complete legal recognition is referred to as *de*[8] *jure* government. See also *de*[8] *facto*; *diplomatic*[12] *recognition*.

government, federal. A system of *government*[3] in which there is a geographical division of political *power*[3] based on one central government supreme in its appropriate sphere of operations and other regional governments acting in their respective spheres as designated through *constitutional*[3] processes. Both parts of the system act directly on the same individuals rather than on geographical districts or other structural arrangements. The central government of the United States, which is located in *Washington*[4], *D.C.*, is frequently referred to as the "federal government," the "central government," or the "national government." The regional governments in the U.S. are often called the "*state*[3] governments." See *national*[4] *supremacy clause*; *metropolitan*[11] *federation*.

government, limited. The political concept that there are certain areas in the people's lives that are beyond the *power*[3] of *government*[3]. Limited government is usually sought through the use of *written constitutions*[3] outlining what government may and may not do. See also *constitutionalism*[3]; *representative government*[3]; *republic*[3]; *consent theory*[3].

government, parliamentary. A system of *government*[3] in which there is a combination of legislative and *executive*[6] functions within a formal *power*[3] structure. In a parliamentary system the executive's power is contingent upon the fact that he and his *cabinet*[6] must command the support of a *majority*[3] of the members of Parliament or else face the electorate or restructure the executive branch. See also *responsible party government*[5]; *prime*[3] *minister*.

government, presidential. A system of *government*[3] in which the *executive*[6] and legislative functions are separated and the executive serves a fixed term of office and is generally selected on a basis different from legislative members. See also *president*[3]; *U.S. President*[6].

government, representative. A system of *government*[3] which places the basic legislative *power*[3] within a *legislature*[7] whose members are elected by the people of the body politic. Representative government is sometimes referred to as indirect *democracy*[3], and a *state*[3] using such government sometimes refers to itself as a *republic*[3] or a *commonwealth*[3]. See also *constitutionalism*[3]; *limited government*[3].

government, republican: see *republic*[3].

government, unitary. A governmental structure in which all political *power*[3] belongs to a central *government*[3] and in which any geographical subdivisions may use only the powers assigned to them or permitted them by the central government. See also *centralization*[3]; *centralized organization*[5].

government, world. The *theory*[3] that the nature of world problems has created the need for one central political unit capable of insuring peace and preserving the health and safety of the entire population of the world. Some see either a *totalitarian*[3] or a *federal*[3] system guiding world affairs.

Harrington, James, 1611–77. The author of The Commonwealth of Oceana (1656), an English *utopia*[3] which carefully analyzed the relationships between economic *power*[3], political power, and *revolution*[3]. Harrington argued for a stable *government*[3] based on a *written constitution*[3], *limited government*[3], widespread *property*[10] distribution, a *separation*[3] *of powers*, a secret ballot, frequent rotation in public office, and a carefully regulated military force. He was widely read by the American *colonists*[4] and many of his ideas were incorporated into the U.S. *Constitution*[4].

Hegel, Georg Wilhelm Friedrich, 1770–1831. The metaphysical German philosopher who is best remembered for his ideas on dialectical knowledge, ideas on which *Karl Marx*[3] built a system of *dialectical*[3] *materialism*. In The Philosophy of Law (1821), Hegel's most systematic work, the individual was viewed as important only as he was related to the *state*[3]. The state's primary duty is self-preservation and the leader's first duty is to preserve the *power*[3] of the state. Hegel interpreted the movement of history through dialectical knowledge. A thesis (concept) attracts an antithesis (opposing concept) and a synthesis (conceptual interaction) becomes a new thesis. Such interaction, according to Hegel, moves history in a progressively upward spiral toward perfect freedom of the spirit. Hegel and his followers visualized the German *nation*[3] as the personification of the "World Spirit." *Adolf Hitler*[3] distorted Hegel's ideas in an effort to develop the German nation through *fascist*[3] *totalitarianism*[3]. See *Nazism*[3].

Hitler, Adolf, 1889–1945. The German *fascist*[3] *dictator*[3] and author of Mein Kampf (1925–27). Mein Kampf, Hitler's autobiography, laid the plans for world conquest on the framework of *propaganda*[5], *diplomatic*[12] deception, and military might. Hitler, the "Father of *Nazism*[3]," emphasized the racial superiority of the Aryan people, outlined the nature of the *totalitarian*[3] state, laid plans for total governmental control of education, advocated the use of the "big lie" in leading the ignorant masses, visualized *state*[3] family planning, sought to solidify national support by indicting external enemies, and laid the psychological base for blaming Jews for all social ills.

Hobbes, Thomas, 1588–1679. The English political philosopher generally credited with writing the first general *theory*[3] of *politics*[3] written in the English language. Hobbes' Leviathan, or the Matter, Form and Power of a Commonwealth Ecclesiastical and Civil (1651), published soon after the execution of King Charles I (1649), emphasized strong *government*[3] providing social order, an organic and mechanistic *state*[3], self-preservation as the first law of human existence, a "brutish" *state*[3] *of nature* existing before government, and a *monarchy*[3] resting on powers given to a ruler by the people purely for the preservation of order and the protection of life and *property*[10]. He did not believe in the right of *revolution*[3], the *separation*[3] of *powers*, or a state religion. See also *mechanistic state*[3]; *organic state*[3]; *contract theory*[3].

ideology. The theoretical and conceptual arrangement of the body of ideas of a group of people, an arrangement which generally determines the social, economic, and political structures and actions of a *society*[3]. See also *ideological warfare*[12].

immigration. The act or process of a person or a group of persons moving into and establishing residence in a *country*[3] or *territory*[3] which is considered foreign. In the United States the regulation of immigration is exclusively a *power*[3] of the central *government*[3]. Immigration and *naturalization*[3] are regulated by the *Department of State*[2] and the *Department of Justice*[2]. The *federal government*[3] began to restrict the immigration of *aliens*[3] into the U.S. in 1882. Persons with criminal records, the insane, and various other undesirable categories were excluded from entering the country at that time. The *quota*[3] system, based on national origins, was created by *law*[8] in 1924. The system was abolished in the *Immigration*[4] Act of 1965. The *Immigration*[4] and Naturalization (McCarran-Walter) Act of 1952 restricted the immigration of persons adhering to *Communist*[3] or *totalitarian*[3] beliefs and made provision for divesting naturalized persons of their *citizenship*[3] if they joined such *organizations*[6]. With regard to restrictions on immigration, the number of persons admitted from the Eastern Hemisphere was limited in 1921. Oriental immigrants were largely prohibited in 1924 and immigrants from the Western Hemisphere were limited for the first time in 1965. See also *Immigration*[2] *and Naturalization Service*; *exclusive powers*[4]; *U.S.*[1] *v. Wong Kim Ark*.

imperialism. The *policy*[6] of a *state*[3] designed to extend the sovereign *authority*[3] of the state over persons and *territory*[3] in foreign areas in an effort to extend economic markets and exploit natural resources. See also *state (constitutional) sovereignty*[3].

individualism. The doctrine or practice which emphasizes that individual interests and needs are more important than the collective interests or needs of the social or political *community*[3]. The doctrine also holds that the foundation of *society*[3] and the *state*[3] is the individual rather than a philosophical or religious abstraction.

initiative. An electoral process whereby designated percentages of the electorate may initiate legislative or *constitutional*[3] changes through the filing of formal petitions to be acted on by the *legislature*[7] or the total electorate. Various methods are used to permit the electorate to initiate legislative proposals. A "direct" initiative is acted on by the people during the next general election. An "indirect" initiative requires legislative approval before presentation to the total electorate. See also *Pacific*[1] *States Telephone and Telegraph Co. v. Oregon*; *referendum.*[3]

iron law of oligarchy. The social and political concept that one dominant class inevitably succeeds another and that small-group domination of social

and political units is a natural fact of life. The *theory*[3] is generally attributed to various European philosophers such as Robert Michels and Vilfredo Pareto. See also *interest*[5] *group*; *oligarchy*[3]; *pressure*[5] *group.*

irredentism. The *policy*[6] or desire to recover *territory*[3] occupied by persons of similar *ethnic*[3] characteristics or that was previously part of the *state*[3] and which is presently controlled by a foreign *government*[3].

jus sanguinis. The principle that a person's *citizenship*[3] is determined by the citizenship of the parents.

jus soli. The principle that a person's *citizenship*[3] is determined by place of birth rather than by the citizenship of one's parents.

laissez faire. The theory that *government*[3] should not interfere in private economic affairs unless it is to provide protection or necessary governmental services. The *theory*[3] enunciated by the French physiocrats and elaborated on by *Adam Smith*[3] in The Wealth of Nations (1776) stressed a free market economy and the creation of wealth through production and consumption. See also *capitalism*[3]; *free*[3] *enterprise*; *Herbert Spencer*[3].

law, constitutional (fundamental, organic): see Chap. 8.

law, customary: see Chap. 8.

law, natural: see Chap. 8.

law, positive: see Chap. 8.

league. An agreement between two or more *states*[3] to unite in a limited fashion in order to achieve common goals. See also *Articles*[4] *of Confederation*; *Confederate*[4] *States of America*; *confederate government*[3].

left (leftist, left-wing). The political designation of persons or groups supporting extremely *liberal*[3] or *radical*[3] economic and political programs within a social system. See also *Black*[5] *Panthers*; *Communist Party*[5] *of the U.S.*; *Progressive Party*[5] *of 1948*; *Socialist Party*[5]; *Socialist Labor Party*[5]; *Socialist Worker's Party*[5]; *Youth International Party*[5]; *Students*[5] *for a Democratic Society*; *right*[3].

legitimacy. A condition accepted by the general populace as lawful or in accord with accepted or customary practices. Legitimacy within any given social or political system is largely determined by existing cultural and political patterns. Legitimacy may be determined by *custom*[3], popular consent, periodic elections, positive *authority*[3], or other accepted methods determined by the cultural context or political setting. See also *constitutionalism*[3]; *positive law*[8]; *popular sovereignty*[3]; *consent theory*[3].

Lenin, Vladimir Ilyich Ulyanov, 1870–1924. The professional *revolutionary*[3] largely responsible for thrusting *Marxist*[3] *dialectical*[3] *materialism* and *Communist*[3] *ideology*[3] on Soviet Russia. Lenin emphasized the revolutionary victory of the *proletariat*[3] over the *bourgeoisie*[3] in his early political work, What Is to Be Done? (1902). In his major political treatise, State and Revolution (1918), Lenin detailed the origin, structure, and *powers*[3] of the *state*[3]. He pointed to the state's demise, predicted a violent death for *capitalism*[3], prophesied the development of the *dictatorship*[3] *of the proletariat*, and stressed the need for the transitional existence of the state before the proletariat could fully possess power and the state could wither away. Leninism is the popular designation of the philosophical, *ideological*[3], and political programs advocated by Lenin.

liberalism. A political and social philosophy that stresses the rational nature of man and the freest expression of individual development. Liberal-

ism also emphasizes progress, change, the basic goodness of man, and the ability of man to give capable direction to his own affairs through *constitutional*[3] political action. Leading European liberals such as *Locke*[3], *Rousseau*[3], and Voltaire dominated the eighteenth century intellectual environment. The U.S. brand of liberalism usually emphasizes *civil*[9] *rights* protection for minorities, *centralization*[3] of governmental *authority*[3] in the *federal government*[3], governmental control of economic affairs, and broader social programs financed by *government*[3]. See also *egalitarianism*[3]; *the Enlightenment*[3]; *left*[3]; *radicalism*[3].

Locke, John, 1632–1704. The leading English philosophical *liberal*[3] of the seventeenth century, and author of the Second Treatise on Government (1690), a major general *theory*[3] of *government*[3]. The First Treatise on Government (1690) was a justification of the *Glorious Revolution*[3] of 1688. The Second Treatise analyzed the *state*[3] *of nature* and man's move into civil *society*[3] through a social contract. Locke believed that the state of nature was basically good, that man moved into civil society in order to attain predictability through *law*[8], that government should be by consent of the people, that *power*[3] should be vested in a *legislature*[7] possessing no positive rights of its own, and that the people possess the right of *revolution*[3] against oppressive governments. Locke's ideas on *inalienable rights*[3], *natural law*[8], and *due*[9] *process of law* were adopted as the major justification for both the *American Revolution*[4] (1776) and the French Revolution (1789). His language was incorporated directly into the American *Declaration*[4] *of Independence* (1776). Before the revolutionary period, Locke received some recognition for helping Lord Ashley, a founder of Carolina colony, compose the *Fundamental*[4] *Constitutions of Carolina* (1669). See also the *the Enlighten-*

ment[3]; *representative government*[3]; *positive law*[8]; *instrumental state*[3]; *consent theory*[3]; *contract theory*[3].

Luther, Martin, 1483–1546. The leading European theological figure of the period known as the Protestant Reformation (1517–1648). In An Address to the Christian Nobility of the German Nation (1520), Luther indicted the Roman Catholic Church and its leadership and called on the German Emperor, Charles V, to lead in the social reform of Germany. In Secular Authority: To What Extent It Should Be Obeyed he analyzed *government*[3] and Christian responsibility. He held that government is ordained by God and that men must obey secular *authority*[3], even if leaders are *tyrants*[3]. He taught that tyrants may be used to punish wicked men and preserve social order. Luther also taught that Christians as a *minority*[3], are ruled by faith, while the masses are ruled largely by external *force*[3]. His ideas on *politics*[3] and religion greatly affected the early American *colonists*[4] and every succeeding generation of Americans. See also *Mosaic Code*[8]; *Protestant*[4] *Ethic*; *minority*[9] *group*.

Machiavelli, Niccolo, 1469–1527. The outstanding advocate of the political *theory*[3], "might makes right," and author of The Prince (1532), a volume sometimes cited as the first systematic work of *political*[3] *science* to point out precisely how political *power*[3] may be acquired and retained. Machiavelli is sometimes referred to as "the father of modern political science." He stressed *empirical*[3] analysis, political absolutism, practical political action, the corruption and selfishness of man, the nature of power, and the role of the political leader. "Machiavellianism" is the popular designation of programs of political deception and opportunism similar to those advocated by Machiavelli.

Magna Carta (England, 1215). The "Great Charter" signed by King John of England. The document granted to English barons the basic political and *civil*[9] *rights* that eventually became a part of the *constitutional*[3] *system* protecting the liberties of all English *citizens*[3]. See also *Bill*[3] *of Rights* (England).

majoritarianism. The belief and practice of vesting the conduct of *government*[3] in the *majority*[3] of the people and the acceptance of every man as equal and capable of directing the process of government. See also *democracy*[3]; *general*[3] *will*; *majority*[3] *rule*; *Rousseau*[3].

majority, absolute (simple). A number that is one more than half the number of votes cast on a given question or nomination. See also *minority*[3], *plurality*[3].

majority, extraordinary. A number that is listed *constitutionally*[3] as politically effective for electoral or legislative purposes, but which may be used for change only if the margin between an *absolute majority*[3] (50% + 1 person) and the specified figure is reached (50% + 25% for a ¾ majority, 50% + 17% for a ⅔ majority, etc.).

majority rule. A political principle which holds that the political decisions of the larger portion of a *society*[3] should prevail in electing officials and formulating *policies*[6]. See also *democracy*[3]; *general*[3] *will*; *majoritarianism*[3]; *policy*[7] *formulation*; *Rousseau*[3].

Mao Tse-tung, 1883– . Chinese revolutionary *Marxist*[3], *guerrilla war*[12] tactician, a founder of the Chinese Communist Party (1921), and Chairman of the People's Republic of China (1949–). Mao gained his leadership position upon the strength of the Chinese peasant revolt against Chiang Kai-shek. Mao led China in a cultural *revolution*[3] that transformed

China from a peasant *society*[3] into a *collectivist*[3] worker's *state*[3]. He was the source of what has come to be known as the "little red book," a volume entitled Quotations from Chairman Mao Tse-tung (1964). The book is a basic work of revolutionary *Communist*[3] *ideology*[3]. What has come to be known as "Maoism" is the Marxist-Leninist philosophy as interpreted by Chairman Mao. He emphasized the peasant revolutionary uprising, the combination of peasants with small businessmen and intellectuals in a new revolutionary *party*[5], and guerrilla warfare against the *bourgeoisie*[3]. See also *Bamboo*[12] *Curtain*.

Marx, Karl, 1818–83. The German economic philosopher whose works entitled The Communist Manifesto (1848) and Das Kapital (1867) laid the philosophical framework for modern *totalitarian*[3] *Communism*[3]. The Communist Manifesto by Karl Marx and Friedrich Engels argued that the history of man is the history of class struggle. The *proletariat*[3] (oppressed workers) will climax history by defeating the *bourgeoisie*[3] (wealthy oppressors). Marx traced the struggle on the basis of the Hegelian dialectic, a process of class struggle between economic opposites. He visualized the destruction of *capitalism*[3], the institution of the *dictatorship*[3] *of the proletariat*, the abolition of private *property*[10], the *nationalization*[10] of major economic and industrial institutions, and the spread of education and other social benefits. "Marxism" is the popular term used to indicate the philosophical ideas and political programs advocated by Marx. Karl Marx's basic *theories*[3] were placed in a *revolutionary*[3] setting by *Lenin*[3] in the Russian *Revolution*[3] of 1917. See also *dialectical*[3] *materialism*; *Hegel*[3]; *labor*[10] *theory of value*.

matriarchy. A form of *government*[3] in which women possess the political *power*[3].

Menshevik. The Russian *party*[5] split opposed to the *Bolsheviks*[3] during the struggle for *power*[3] which led to *Lenin's*[3] victory in October 1917. The word literally means *"minority"*[3]. The *Marxist*[3]-oriented party supported *revolution*[3] through *democratic*[3] processes.

mercantilism. An arrangement of economic activity designed to benefit the *state*[3] rather than individuals within the state, especially by encouraging exports over imports in order to build up wealth in the form of precious metals and gems. Mercantilism dominated the economic lives of the larger European states between the fifteenth and nineteenth centuries. It was characterized by the development of large merchant fleets, military adventures, exploration, and *colonization*[4].

Mill, John Stuart, 1806–73. One of the major English proponents of the political and social philosophy known as *utilitarianism*[3]. One of Mill's major works was entitled Utilitarianism (1836); in it he emphasized that "the greatest happiness for the greatest number" comes primarily when man is least hampered by arbitrary social rules. He believed that the *state*[3] with the greatest liberty is the state with the most liberated individuals. In his work On Liberty (1859), he expressed fear of group action capable of forcing nonconformists to accept the social *tyranny*[3] of the masses, action frequently referred to as the *"tyranny*[3] *of the majority."* See also *majoritarianism*[3].

minority. Any number which is less than one-half of a total figure. See also *absolute majority*[3]; *plurality*[3].

monarchy. A form of *government*[3] in which political *power*[3] is vested, practically or ostensibly, in a king or other royal personality. An absolute monarch possesses full political power, whereas a *constitutional*[3] monarch serves as a figurehead or shares powers with elected officials.

Montesquieu, Charles, 1689–1755. The French political theorist best remembered in the U.S. for his theories of the *separation*[3] *of powers* and *checks*[3] *and balances* as outlined in The Spirit of the Laws (1748). Montesquieu's general *theory*[3] of *government*[3] analyzed political institutions, religion, *custom*[3], geography, economics, *war*[12], and almost every other area affecting *politics*[3]. He accepted the idea of a *state*[3] *of nature* governed by *natural laws*[8], a civil *society*[3] based on legal relationships, an enlightened *monarchy*[3], *civil*[9] *rights*, and a system of checks and balances based on legislative, *executive*[6], and judicial functions. Many of Montesquieu's ideas were adopted as a formal part of the United States *constitutional*[3] *system*. See also *environmental determinism*[3]; *the Enlightenment*[3].

More, Sir Thomas, 1478–1535. The imaginative English writer who indicted the political actions and social *customs*[3] of sixteenth century England in his work, Utopia (1516). More's *utopia*[3] was the first work of political and social idealism of its kind in modern western civilization; it is an analysis of what life might be like in an ideal *state*[3]. More visualized simple *government*[3], *community*[3] ownership of *property*[10], simple culture, enjoyable labor, a perfect social order, *socialized medicine*[11], state-regulated family life, tolerant religion, a world of peace, and a *society*[3] without need for money. His writings stimulated numerous European and American volumes of political idealism and various community social experiments.

nation. A group of people united, usually within the framework of a *state*[3], through a common culture and sense of social consciousness. The national bond is generally held together through ties of race, religion, language, culture, and traditions.

nationalism. A feeling of extreme devotion to the political, social, economic, and cultural characteristics of a particular social group, a feeling which generally unites a people against outside *forces*[3] or *powers*[3], either real or imagined. See also *chauvinism*[12]; *fascism*[3]; *nation*[3]; *Nazism*[3]; *statism*[3].

nativism. The practice of using the *power*[3] and *authority*[3] of the *state*[3] to favor native-born individuals over *immigrants*[3].

naturalization. The legal process used by a *state*[3] to grant full citizenship to *aliens*[3], either individually or collectively. An individual may become a U.S. *citizen*[3] by meeting various qualifications and the background investigation conducted by the *Immigration*[2] *and Naturalization Service* of the *Department of Justice*[2]. To become a U.S. citizen through naturalization, a person must be 18 years old, file a formal petition for naturalization, be able to read, speak, and write English, possess a fundamental understanding of U.S. *government*[3], provide proof of acceptable moral character, possess no memberships in or reveal support of subversive *organizations*[6], and take an oath renouncing citizenship in his former homeland and acknowledging allegiance to the government of the United States. The oath of citizenship may be administered by a *federal*[3] court or a state *court*[8] *of record*. See also *Afroyim*[1] *v. Rusk*; *Immigration*[4] *and Naturalization Act of 1952*; *Immigration*[4] *Act of 1965*; *Perez*[1] *v. Brownell*; *quota*[3] *system*; *Department of State*[2]; *U.S.*[1] *v. Wong Kim Ark*.

Nazism. A particular form of *totalitarian*[3] fascism founded in Germany in 1933 under the leadership of *Adolf Hitler*[3]. Nazism, or National Socialism, stressed the general elements of *fascism*[3], but added race as a major *ideological*[3] base, especially glorification of Aryans and rejection of Jews. See also *discrimination*[9].

Nietzsche, Friedrich Wilhelm, 1844–1900. The German philosopher who is remembered as the "Father of the Superman." In Thus Spake Zarathustra (1883–84) and Beyond Good and Evil (1886), Nietzsche expressed a *nihilistic*[3] view because he believed traditional human values and institutions kept man in bondage. He spoke against *nationalism*[3], *democracy*[3], equality, social welfare, and Christianity ("God is dead"). Nietzsche's major thesis was that the creative man can be a noble spirit and create his own values. The creation of noble values can lead to an *aristocracy*[3] of supermen. Kaiser Wilhelm and *Adolf Hitler*[3] both falsely interpreted Nietzsche for nationalistic and *totalitarian*[3] purposes by claiming that the Nordic, or "Aryan," race was the master race of supermen who were destined to dominate history through their "will to *power*[3]."

nihilism. The doctrine that all existing political and social institutions must be destroyed by whatever means possible in order to create improved conditions for individual men and future social relationships. See also *Bakunin*[3]; *Nietzsche*[3].

oligarchy. A form of *government*[3] in which political control is exercised by a few persons. See also *iron*[3] *law of oligarchy.*

Owen, Robert, 1771–1858. The English social reformer and *utilitarian*[3] who founded New[4] Harmony, Indiana (1825), an unsuccessful social enterprise based on the example of his progressive, successful, and "ideal" industrial *community*[3] known as New Lanark, Scotland. In A New View of Society, or, Essays on the Formation of the Human Character (1813–16)

Owen expressed a belief in *environmental determinism*[3] and the perfectibility of the human spirit through education and proper social planning. See also *collectivism*[3]; *socialism*[3].

passport: see Chap. 12.

paternalism. A system of *government*[3] in which the ruler acts toward the people as a father would toward his children. Paternalism may be characterized by expressions of fatherly affection toward the citizenry, *tribalism*[3] directed by some form of "father figure," evidence of a *welfare*[11] state, or other similar political variables.

Petition of Right (England, 1628). A Parliamentary document signed by Charles I which declared that taxes would be levied only with the consent of Parliament, there would be no imprisonment without cause, there would be no public quartering of soldiers with private *citizens*[3], and there would be no *martial*[8] *law* during times of peace. See *Quartering*[4] *Act of 1766, parliamentary government*[3]; *consent theory*[3].

philosopher king. The leadership designation used by *Plato*[3] in The Republic to describe the ideal leader, a benevolent personage possessed of true and complete wisdom and knowledge.

Plato, 427–347 B.C. The Greek political philosopher best remembered as the author of The Republic, the earliest known systematic analysis of political and social ideas and the earliest conceptualization of the ideal *state*[3]. Plato's political idealism was based on concepts of *justice*[8] and a good life. He believed that "just" men and "just" *societies*[3] should be whole and balanced systems. Justice, with each person being in the proper relationship to the state and other individuals within the state, could best be achieved through the leadership of a *philosopher*[3] *king*. The state should have rulers, warriors, and producers. The purpose of the state should be to achieve a good life for all men. Plato's ideal state was based on the philosophical ideas of forms, especially the concept of the duality of the universe (good and evil, justice and injustice, etc.). Plato's philosophical and political ideas influenced the modern world, primarily through theologians such as *Augustine*[3], *Calvin*[3] and *Luther*[3].

plebiscite. A direct *popular vote*[5] of the people on any given subject placed before them by the appropriate *authorities*[3]. Plebiscites are most often concerned with the choice of a ruler, *annexation*[11] to a foreign *power*[3], acceptance or rejection of a parliamentary program, or other related issues. See also *parliamentary government*[3].

pluralism. The condition of *society*[3] in which there are heterogeneous social and political groups possessing distinct economic, *ethnic*[3], religious, and cultural differences. A pluralistic system is generally dynamic and possesses interests within the *state*[3] which may be utilized for balancing political *power*[3].

plurality. The largest number of votes cast for any one candidate in an election, a number sometimes indicated as acceptable for electoral victory. See *absolute majority*[3]; *minority*[3].

plutocracy. A form of *government*[3] in which political *power*[3] is exercised by persons of wealth. See also *aristocracy*[3]; *elitism*[3].

polarization. The process in which differing viewpoints, attitudes, or political positions move to opposite extremes of one another. See also *bipolarity*[12]

political science. The study of the *state*[3] and its institutions. The discipline of political science includes such specialized areas as *political*[3] *theory*, *constitutional law*[8], public *administration*[6], *political parties*[5], international relations, and comparative *government*[3]. See also *American*[5] *Political Science Association, Arthur Bentley*[5]; *Robert A. Dahl*[11]; *V. O. Key*[5]; *Harold D. Lasswell*[5]; *Seymour Lipset*[5]; *E. E. Schattschneider*[5]; *Woodrow Wilson*[6].

political science, behavioral. The approach to the study of the *state*[3] and its institutions, which is characterized by the use of methods of *empirical*[3] science. The approach is general, analytic, and explanatory and avails itself of modern techniques of problem solving, quantification, and systematization. It is also interdisciplinary in recognizing that *political*[3] *science* is closely related to and affected by other areas of knowledge and human behavior. See also *V. O. Key*[5]; *Harold Lasswell*[5]; *The People's*[5] *Choice*; *Survey*[5] *Research Center*; *systems theory*[3].

political science, traditional. The approach to the study of the *state*[3] and its institutions, which is characterized by normative value assumptions and historical and particular descriptions of political institutions, processes, and ideas.

political socializaton. The process wherein an individual becomes aware of and active in the political life of his *society*[3]. See also *Americanization*[4]; *benevolent*[12] *assimilation*; *Seymour Lipset*[5]; *The People's*[5] *Choice*; *Survey*[5] *Research Center*.

political theory. A specialized area of *political*[3] *science* concerned with ideas about the origin, nature, and operation of the *state*[3]. Political *theory*[3] of the past was generally normative and speculative, while modern political theory is frequently *empirical*[3] in nature.

politics. The science and art of manipulating or managing affairs of *government*[3]. See also *theory*[3].

polity. The governmental structure of any social *organization*[6]. See also *constitution*[3]; *constitutional*[3] *system*; *society*[3].

power. The ability to manipulate ideas, persons, *organizations*[6], or circumstances to one's own advantage. The word "power" is sometimes used to indicate a particular national or political entity exercising influence in world affairs.

pragmatism. The philosophical and political concept that ideas and actions are to be judged by their practical results. Pragmatism, a philosophy popularized by *William James*[4], generally holds that that which works in a particular circumstance is useful and that which does not work is of no benefit. See also *political*[5] *pragmatism*.

preamble. An introductory statement attached to a *constitution*[3] or other formal document explaining the reason for the writing of the document.

prerogative. An exclusive right inherent within a position or office. See *inherent powers*[4]; *prerogative*[6] *theory*.

president. The chief *executive*[6] officer of a *state*[3] or *organization*[6] designating its basic form of *government*[3] as a presidential system. The *power*[3] possessed by the president of any system is largely determined by *constitutional*[3] structures. Written documents, *custom*[3], and political actions usually qualify such things as selection, length of term in office, succession, relationships to other branches of government, *appointive*[6] *powers*, *removal*[6] *powers*, *war*[12] *powers*, *diplomatic*[6] *powers* and other variables of office. See also *presidential government*[3]; *U.S. President*[6]; *presidential*[6] *disability*; *presidential*[6] *succession*.

prime minister. The chief *executive*[6] officer of a *state*[3] or *organization*[6] listing its basic form of *government*[3] as

parliamentary. See also *parliamentary government*[3].

proletariat. The poorest class of people within a *society*[3], a group dependent on individual labor for an existence. See also *bourgeoisie*[3]; *dictatorship*[3] *of the proletariat*; *labor*[10] *theory of value*.

protectorate. A governmental arrangement in which a strong *state*[3] maintains partial control over a smaller *power*[3], especially the smaller power's foreign affairs.

Proudhon, Pierre Joseph, 1809–65. The French *socialist*[3] who is often referred to as the "father of *anarchism*[3]." In What is Property? or an Inquiry into the Principle of Right and of Government (1840), Proudhon stated that "*property*[10] is theft." He supported *radicalism*[3] and denounced *capitalism*[3] and the *centralization*[3] of governmental *power*[3]. He advocated what he called "mutualism," a *federal*[3] system wherein each industry would be operated by a voluntary association of producers who would benefit from their own efforts.

quota system. The process of acting on the basis of numerical figures specified as maximum or minimum allowables. Some *nations*[3] base their *immigration*[3] *laws*[8] on a quota system limiting the number of immigrants allowable to geographic and time factors. See also *naturalization*[3].

radicalism. The philosophical or practical belief in extreme change. A radical is a person who opposes, in the extreme, the *status*[3] *quo* or existing institutions. A radical is in direct, and sometimes violent, opposition to what is known as *the Establishment*[3]. See also *Michael Bakaunin*[3]; *left*[3]; *nihilism*[3]; *reactionary*[3]; *revolution*[3].

ratification. Validation, acceptance, or approval of an action of an official or agency of *government*[3]. Ratification is generally the final process in officially accepting a *treaty*[12], *amending*[3] a *constitution*[3], or formalizing other actions of government. See also *Coleman*[1] *v. Miller*; *Hawke*[1] *v. Smith*.

reactionary. A person who opposes in the extreme any progressive social or political change. See also *radicalism*[3]; *status*[3] *quo*.

rebellion. Organized, open, and violent opposition to existing *authority*[3] or *government*[3]. See also *Bacon's*[4] *Rebellion*; *coup*[3] *d'etat*; *Dorr's*[4] *Rebellion*; *revolution*[3]; *war*[12]; *Shays'*[4] *Rebellion*; *Whiskey*[4] *Rebellion*.

referendum. An electoral process in which legislative or *constitutional*[3] questions are referred to the total electorate for its acceptance or rejection. A referendum may have the *force*[3] of *law*[8] or it may be used in an advisory capacity to inform *government*[3] officials of public feelings on particular subjects. In many areas of concern, the referendum is optional. In other areas such as *amending*[3] the *constitution*[3] of a *state*[3], the referendum may be mandatory. See also *Hawke*[1] *v. Smith*; *initiative*[3]; *James*[1] *v. Valtierra*.

regionalism. The *theory*[3] that separate political units located in close proximity to one another can work together in solving common problems and reaching common goals.

representation: see Chap. 7.

republic. A *state*[3] or *nation*[3] in which supreme *power*[3] resides in the people and is exercised by *representatives*[7] directly responsible to the general electorate. See also *democracy*[3]; *limited government*[3]; *representative government*[3].

revolution. The action of one portion of a population which radically changes the social or political struc-

ture through *force*[3], *authoritarian*[3] tactics, or other obvious methods. A revolution is more than simply a change in the form of *government*[3] or of governmental leadership; it is a *radical*[3] change in the total system. See also *coup*[3] *d'etat*; *rebellion*[3]; *American Revolution*[4]; *Glorious Revolution*[3]; *war*[12].

Revolution, Glorious (England, 1688–89). The "Bloodless Revolution" which deposed James II and brought William and Mary to the English throne. The major points of significance of the *revolution*[3] were the rejection of the *theory*[3] of the divine right of kings, the acceptance of parliamentary supremacy, and the acceptance of the English *Bill*[3] *of Rights*. *John Locke*[3] was the major theorist who developed arguments justifying the Glorious Revolution. See also *parliamentary government*[3]; *divine right theory*[3].

right (rightist, right-wing). The political term used to indicate persons or groups supporting extremely *conservative*[3] or *reactionary*[3] economic and political programs within a political or social system. See also *left*[3].

rights, inalienable. Rights which are by nature nontransferrable to another person. See also *Mosaic Code*[8]; *Declaration*[3] *of Independence*; *natural rights*[3].

rights, natural. Rights that are viewed as inherent and inalienable because of the nature of man and the universe. See also *Mosaic Code*[8]; *Declaration*[3] *of Independence*; *inalienable rights*[3].

Rousseau, Jean Jacques, 1712–78. One of the major French political theorists of the eighteenth century and author of The Social Contract (1762). Rousseau is remembered as the major *majoritarian*[3] theorist and the father of the modern concepts of natural man. He argued in some of his writings that natural man is purer and more human than civilized man. In The Social Contract, a major general *theory*[3] of *politics*[3], Rousseau argued for the existence of a simple *state*[3] *of nature*, a social contract designed to provide civil liberty and social order, *popular sovereignty*[3] to allow the people to exercise *power*[3] through *majority*[3] *rule*, an *organic state*[3] functioning through knowledge of the *"general*[3] *will"*; *government*[3] arranged to provide man with a good life, *civil*[9] *rights* for all, protection for *property*[10] rights, and the right of *revolution*[3] against despotic government. Rousseau became one of the most famous writers of the period known as *the Enlightenment*[3]. His influence on political, philosophical, and educational *liberalism*[3] is incalculable. Rousseau's ideas were used to justify the *American Revolution*[4] (1776) and the French Revolution (1789). *Thomas Jefferson*[6] admitted that Rousseau's ideas were incorporated in the *Declaration*[4] of *Independence* (1776). See also *democracy*[3]; *natural law*[8]; *contract theory*[3].

Saint-Simon, Claude Henri, 1760–1825. The French social and political philosopher who was the leading French advocate of *Christian socialism*[3]. He was also the father of a "positive organicist" *theory*[3] of *society*[3], a theory of social order based on conscience or mutual benefit. In The New Christianity, Saint-Simon advocated the use of social science to restructure society, the abolition of class structures, a planned industrial *state*[3], scientifically managed welfare programs, and the use of religious motivation to achieve a true brotherhood of man. See also *socialism*[3].

sedition: see Chap. 12.

separation of powers. The placement of *power*[3] in separate institutions charged with particular political responsibilities. The most common separation of powers is between legislative, *executive*[6], and judicial functions. In such a separation no branch is entirely independent of or supreme over the other branches. The separation of powers allows for a system of *checks*[3] *and balances* to avoid the concentration of political power within one branch of *government*[3]. See also *centralization*[3]; *Michael Harrington*[11]; *John Locke*[3]; *Charles Montesquieu*[3].

Smith, Adam, 1723–90. The "father of laissez faire economics" and author of An Inquiry into the Nature and Causes of the Wealth of Nations (1776). The Wealth of Nations, the outstanding volume of *laissez*[3] *faire* economic philosophy, set forth the idea that a nation's wealth is determined by production, consumption, worker skills, and product distribution within a free market setting. Smith believed that beneath the economic system lay human self-interest and the desire for wealth. He analyzed the division of labor, economic exchange, the *labor*[10] *theory of value*, *government*[3] responsibilities toward *citizens*[3], and citizen responsibilities toward government. He concluded that the *nation*[3] prospers as individual men prosper through economic competition and *free*[10] *enterprise*. Smith also argued that the wealthiest nation is the most efficient one. Because of this he rejected restrictive *colonial*[3] *policies*[6], *mercantilism*[3], and the concentration of wealth within the ruling classes.

socialism. An economic and social *theory*[3] which holds that the economic system and all means of production and distribution of goods should be owned and controlled by the *state*[3] for the collective good of *society*[3]. See also *Brook*[4] *Farm*; *collectivism*[3]; *Communism*[3]; *Charles Fourier*[3]; *Lenin*[3]; *Karl Marx*[3]; *Robert Owen*[3]; *Claude Saint-Simon*[3].

socialism, Christian. A nineteenth century European reform movement which favored trade unions, cooperatives, and welfare, education, and voting reforms. A basic premise of the movement was that *socialism*[3] had its beginning in Judeo-Christian tradition. *Saint-Simon*[3] is generally referred to as the "father of Christian socialism."

socialism, creeping. A term used to indicate legislative measures and economic realities which gradually move unannounced into a *socialistic*[3] economic structure.

socialism, democratic. The *theory*[3] that the production and distribution of goods should be owned and controlled by the *state*[3] within a governmental system based on *democratic*[3] principles.

socialism, guild. A *theory*[3] of *socialism*[3] advocating that the production and distribution of goods should be publicly owned but should be regulated through guilds or unions within each industry.

society. An organized *community*[3] of individuals acting on the basis of shared interests. See also *contract theory*[3].

society, closed. A *society*[3] which conducts itself on the basis of a narrow range of information available from limited sources, usually from *authoritarian*[3] or *totalitarian*[3] individuals or agencies controlling communications and educational facilities. See also *Bamboo*[12] *Curtain*; *Iron*[12] *Curtain*; *propaganda*[5].

society, open. A *society*[3] which conducts itself on the basis of a wide range of information available from numerous sources both inside and outside formal *government*[3] *organizations*[6]. See also *Madison*[5] *Avenue*; *mass*[5] *media*; *N.Y.*[1] *Times Co. v. U.S.*; *public opinion*[5]; *propaganda*[5]; *United*[2] *States Information Agency*.

sovereignty, divided (dual). The *theory*[3] that within a *federal*[3] system the central *government*[3] and the *state*[3] governments each possess sovereign *power*[3] within their respective spheres. See also *national sovereignty*[4]; *state (southern interpretation) sovereignty*[4].

sovereignty, popular. A doctrine popularized by the *natural rights*[3] and contract *theorists*[3] that all *power*[3] issues from the people and may be exercised and altered by them at will. See also *Bonapartism*[3]; *constitutionalism*[3]; *Declaration*[4] *of Independence*; *democracy*[3]; *legitimacy*[3]; *squatter sovereignty*[4]; *contract theory*[3].

sovereignty, state (constitutional). The concept that a geographical, social, or political subdivision is free to organize its basic institutions and conduct its own affairs without external control. Sovereignty is sometimes referred to as *constitutional*[3] independence. A population may be considered constitutionally independent if the ultimate *power*[3] to govern is vested somewhere within its own people and within its own *territory*[3]. See also *constitutional*[3] *system*.

soviet. A Russian term meaning "council." The basic governmental unit in the *Communist*[3] *government*[3] of the Soviet Union is the soviet (council). Soviets were arranged primarily along industrial lines at the lowest level of worker classification within industrial complexes. Theoretically, the arrangement of *power*[3] flows from the single soviets up through the *hierarchy*[6] to the Supreme Soviet at the top. In reality, the power flows from the top to the bottom.

Spencer, Herbert, 1820–1903. The leading modern advocate of *theories*[3] of *laissez*[3] *faire* economics, politics, and social interaction. Spencer, an English social and economic theorist, is remembered as "the father of *Social*[11] *Darwinism*" because of the theories he advocated in Social Statics (1851) and The Man Versus the State (1884). He believed in natural social and economic *laws*[8], rugged *individualism*[3], social evolution, and the primacy of *property*[10]. He opposed powerful *legislatures*[7], state welfare programs, the *bureaucracy*[6], and extreme taxation. See also *natural law*[8]; *welfare*[11] *state, Lochner*[1] *v. N.Y.*

Stalin, Joseph, 1879–1953. The Russian *Communist*[3] revolutionary leader who succeeded *Lenin*[3] in the position of top leadership of the Soviet Union. Stalin is best remembered for his oppressive and *totalitarian*[3] solidification of political *power*[3]. His writings, such as Foundations of Leninism (1924) and Problems of Leninism (1926), stressed the need for *centralized*[3] world *Communist*[3] control, the nature of Communist-*capitalistic*[3] conflict, exported Communist *revolution*[3], and the *"encirclement theory"*[3], which became useful for continuing a Communist *dictatorship*[3] and deferring political leadership for the *proletariat*[3]. See also *dictatorship*[3] *of the proletariat; Iron*[12] *Curtain.*

state. A *community*[3] of individuals politically organized upon a definite *territory*[3], possessing organized *government*[3], possessing *constitutional*[3] independence (sovereignty) reasonably free from external control, and exercising general *authority*[3] on the inhabitants within the political system. The United States of America came into existence as a state upon *ratification*[3] of the *Constitution*[4] of the United States of America. The "states" within the *federal*[3] Union meet all of the qualifications of statehood except constitutional independence. See also *state (constitutional) sovereignty*[3].

state, corporative. The arrangement of the *state*[3] in which the division of *power*[3] is vested in functional *corporations*[10] or businesses exercising power upon individuals within their respective *jurisdictions*[8]. The concept of the corporative state accepts the idea that the total system receives

basic direction through acknowledged agencies of *government*[3].

state, instrumental. The *theory*[3] of the *state*[3] that holds that the state is a creation of man and is designed for his service. The state is viewed as an instrument of man rather than as a being with a separate life of its own. See also *John Locke*[3]; *organic state*[3].

state, mechanistic. A *theory*[3] of the *state*[3] which holds that the state is a machine designed for higher purposes beyond itself. *Thomas Hobbes'*[3] general political *theory*[3] entitled Leviathan presents a mechanistic view of the state, an artificial man operating according to mechanical principles. The theory is frequently viewed as simply a modification of the theory of the *organic state*[3].

state of nature. The concept that man existed at some time in the past without formal social and political *organization*[6]. The *theory*[3] was popularized during the eighteenth century by European writers such as *Rousseau*[3], *Locke*[3], and *Hobbes*[3]. See also *the Enlightenment*[3]; *contract theory*[3].

state, organic. A *theory*[3] of the *state*[3] which holds that the state is a natural living organism with a life separate from the persons who compose it. Writers such as *Aristotle*[3], *Hobbes*[3], *Rousseau*[3], *Marx*[3], *Lenin*[3], and *Stalin*[3] presented various views of the organic state. See also *mechanistic state*[3]; *statism*[3].

state, satellite. A *state*[3] generally possessing the normal characteristics of statehood but which has to adjust its own foreign and domestic *policies*[6] to suit a more powerful state threatening intervention.

statism. An organic *theory*[3] of the *state*[3] which holds that the national state deserves and demands supreme allegiance and that social and political objectives are best achieved through *centralized*[3] *authority*[3] rather than through individual action. See also *chauvinism*[12]; *nationalism*[3]; *organic state*[3].

status quo. The existing state of affairs. A term used to describe the *conservative*[3] attitude that things are best left as they are. See also *reactionary*[3].

syndicalism. The *theory*[3] of political and economic action that advocates bringing economic production and distribution of goods under the control of *federations*[3] of *labor*[10] *unions* through direct action. The *radical*[3] political philosophy, which was most influential during nineteenth century European labor movements, stressed the use of the general *strike*[10] and sabotage to shift political *power*[3] from the *state*[3] to the trade unions (syndicates).

technocracy. A form of *government*[3] in which political *power*[3] is no longer fully controlled by persons but instead is dominated largely by the machines built by the people. Persons supporting technocracy generally amplify the role of scientists, engineers, and technicians in economic and social management.

territory. An area of land or water designated as under the *jurisdiction*[8] of an individual sovereign *state*[3] or *nation*[3]. The term is also used to refer to a portion of land belonging to a governmental jurisdiction and which is being settled in preparation for inclusion within a larger *constitutional*[3] *system* such as the United States of America. See also *boundary*[12]; *territorial court*[8]; *state (constitutional) sovereignty*[3].

theocracy. A system of *government*[3] based on the rule of a divine personality who transmits his will through human agents who are usually clerical or religious leaders. Ancient Israel operated under such a system of government before the anointing of Saul as the first king of Israel and the acceptance of *monarchy*[3].

theory. A systematic and speculative explanation of reality or some other set of principles or phenomena. A theory is an abstract model or frame of reference for understanding particular situations or objects. A theory of *politics*[3] is an abstract model that seeks to explain political reality. See also *political*[3] *theory*.

theory, consent. The political *theory*[3] which holds that *government*[3] possesses no *powers*[3] beyond those given to it through the consent of the governed. See also *Stamp Act Congress*[4]; *Declaration*[4] *of Independence*; *John Dickinson*[4]; *limited government*[3]; *legitimacy*[3]; *John Locke*[3]; *Mayflower*[4] *Compact*.

theory, contract. The concept that fundamental governmental *organization*[6] and operations are based on contractual obligations between those possessing political *power*[3] and those feeling the weight of political *authority*[3]. Contract theorists such as *Rousseau*[3], *Locke*[3], and *Hobbes*[3] generally stressed life in the *state*[3] *of nature*, the move from the state of nature into civil *society*[3], and the nature of contractual obligations within civil society. See also *constitutionalism*[3]; *contract*[10]; *covenant*[3]; *A Defense*[3] *of Liberty Against Tyrants*; *the Enlightenment*[3]; *John Wise*[4].

theory, divine right. The *theory*[3] that political *authority*[3] resides in a *monarch*[3] who gained *power*[3] through divine appointment or through inheritance from family members who themselves had been divinely appointed. The theory was especially popular throughout Europe between the twelfth and seventeenth centuries.

Leading English exponents of the theory were James I, Charles I, and Charles II.

theory, encirclement. The Communist *theory*[3] of *Lenin*[3] and *Stalin*[3], which holds that the Soviet *dictatorship*[3] controlling the *proletariat*[3], rather than being controlled by the proletariat, must continue as long as the *Communist*[3] states are "encircled" by *capitalistic*[3] states. Such a belief means that the withering away of the *state*[3] and full political control by the proletariat must wait until total Communist control of the world is a reality. The doctrine is basically a theoretical camouflage for a *totalitarian*[3] dictatorship. See also *dictatorship*[3] *of the proletariat*; *world government*[3].

theory, higher law. A *theory*[3] which holds that there exists within the universe certain principles of *justice*[8] which are superior to man-made *positive laws*[8]. Such laws are viewed as superior because they rest upon nature, reason, or God rather than imperfect formulations of men. See also *Book*[4] *of the General Lawes*; *Mosaic Code*[8]; *natural law*[8].

theory, rule of law. The *theory*[3] that stresses the predictable operation of social and political rules which are designed to limit the *power*[3] of public officers.

theory, systems. The approach to the study of *political*[3] *science* which analyzes variables and interrelationships within a total political system. Systems theory frequently seeks to analyze or explain cause-effect relationships. See also *empiricism*[3]; *behavioral political*[3] *science*.

totalitarianism. A political and social characteristic of a *state*[3] exercising *centralized*[3], total control over the life of persons and *organizations*[6] within it. A totalitarian system is usually characterized by the *dictatorship*[3] principle, one-*party*[5] dominance, and the use of physical *force*[3]. See also *despotism*[3]; *fascism*[3]; *Nazism*[3]; *police*[9] *state*; *tyranny*[3].

treason. Violation of allegiance to one's own *state*[3]. Treason against the U.S. is defined in Article III, Section 3 of the *U.S. Constitution*[4] and is a *concurrent power*[4] between *federal*[3] and *state*[3] *governments*[3], since individual states may punish for treason against their own *constitutions*[3] and *laws*[8]. See also *crime*[8].

tribalism. The *organization*[6] and practices of a tribe of people basing their social organization upon common ancestry, culture, language, or other notable features within the tribe. See also *paternalism*[3].

tyranny. A governmental system dominated by an absolute ruler who arbitrarily exercises political *power*[3]. See also *authoritarianism*[3]; *czarism*[3]; *despotism*[3]; *dictatorship*[3]; *fascism*[3]; *Nazism*[3]; *totalitarianism*[3].

tyranny of the majority. Absolute and arbitrary political and social control through the use of *majority*[3] action, action used to *force*[3] *minority*[3] elements and interests to conform to majority desires. See also *John Stuart Mill*[3].

unconstitutional. Not in accord with accepted principles or practices established by the *constitution*[3] of a *state*[3]. See also *constitutional*[3]; *constitutionalism*[3].

utilitarianism. The doctrine that stresses that value is determined by the usefulness of objects, actions, or ideas, especially if reality is dominated by the "greatest good for the greatest number." *Jeremy Bentham*[3], "the father of utilitarianism," and *John Stuart Mill*[3] popularized the concept through widespread circulation of *Cesare Beccaria's*[8] expression, "the greatest good for the greater number."

utopia. A social and political order characterized by perfection. The concept of a utopian *society*[3] was popularized in classical Greece in *Plato's*[3] Republic and was introduced into modern thinking by Sir *Thomas More's*[3] volume entitled Utopia (1516). The word "utopia" is a Greek word literally meaning "no place." See also *Edward Bellamy*[4]; *Brook*[4] *Farm*; *New*[4] *Harmony*; *Robert Owen*[3].

visa. An official stamp or signature on a *passport*[12] which authorizes a person to enter a *country*[3] or national *state*.[3]

xenophobia. A fear or hatred of foreigners. See also *chauvinism*[12]; *ethnocentrism*[3]; *nationalism*[3].

Chapter 4

United States Constitutional History and Development

Note to the reader: Cross-referenced terms are in italics. The superscript number refers to the chapter in which the entry may be found. In addition, its placement indicates the word under which the term is alphabetized. (For example, in *electoral*[4] *college,* information on the electoral college may be found in Chapter 4 under "electoral.") Because italics are used in cross-references, they are not used for terms in which they would ordinarily be used: Supreme Court cases and titles of books, journals, plays, and so forth.

Supreme Court cases relating to material in this chapter are listed at the end of the chapter (see page 103).

Adams, John: see Chap. 6.

Albany Plan of Union (1754). *Benjamin Franklin's*[4] proposal at the *Albany Congress*[4] *of 1754.* Franklin sought to establish a confederation with *power*[3] to regulate Indian affairs, western lands, and taxation designed to support a common military establishment. He asked for colonial *representation*[7] in the system on the basis of population and wealth. The council would be presided over by a president-general appointed by the King of England. Franklin's plan got a cool reception from the *colonies*[4] and from Great Britain. See also *confederate government*[3].

Alien and Sedition Acts of 1798. A series of short-lived *federal*[3] *laws*[8] passed by the *Federalists*[4] and directed against *Democratic-Republican Party*[5] supporters and pamphleteers. The *legislation*[7] stiffened residency requirements for *citizenship*[3], allowed presidential deportation of any *alien*[3] during peacetime, permitted the presidential jailing of *enemy aliens*[12] during wartime, and provided severe penalties for *seditious*[12] writings or speeches critical of the *government*[3].

Alien Registration (Smith) Act of 1940. An *act*[8] requiring the annual registration of *aliens*[3] over the age of 14 and making it unlawful to teach or advocate the forceable overthrow of *government*[3] or to organize or knowingly join *organizations*[6] advocating such action. See also *Dennis*[1] *v. U.S.; Penn*[1] *v. Nelson; Yates*[1] *v. U.S.*

Amendment, Eighteenth (1919). The *amendment*[3] to the U.S. *Constitution*[4] which prohibited the manufacture or sale of "intoxicating liquors." The amendment was repealed by the *Twenty-first Amendment*[4] in 1933. It is the only amendment that has been added to the Constitution and then repealed. See also *Anti-Saloon*[5] *League of America*; *Prohibition Party*[5]; *Women's*[5] *Christian Temperance Union.*

Amendment, Eleventh (1798). The *amendment*[3] to the U.S. *Constitution*[4] that removed from the *jurisdiction*[8] of the U.S. *Supreme*[8] *Court* any private lawsuits directed against *states*[3] by *citizens*[3] of other states. The amendment was added to avoid private suits such as the one which arose in the Supreme Court case of *Chisholm*[1] *v. Georgia.* See also *diversity*[4] *of citizenship question*; *Cohens*[1] *v. Virginia.*

Amendment, Fourteenth (1868). The *amendment*[3] to the U.S. *Constitution*[4] which was intended to override the decision in the Dred Scott (see *Dred*[1] *Scott v. Sandford*) case of 1857, a *Supreme*[8] *Court* decision which held that Negroes possessed no rights of *citizenship*[3]. The Fourteenth Amendment allowed for reduction in congressional *representation*[7] for *states*[3] denying adult males the right to vote, disqualified former officials "in *rebellion*"[3] from holding *federal*[3] offices until qualified by congressional action, validated Union *war*[12] debts and voided Confederate ones, denied claims for losses incurred from the emancipation of slaves, and granted citizenship to all persons "born or naturalized in the United States." The amendment's most famous phrases are "privileges and immunities," "*due*[9] *process of law,*" and "equal protection of the laws." They have been used in federal judicial interpretation for broadening civil liberties protections for *citizens*[3] within the states. Since the Supreme Court decision of *Gitlow*[1] *v. New York*, numerous rights have been "nationalized." They are not only guaranteed protection against federal encroachment by the U.S. *Bill*[4] *of Rights*, but are now protected against state impairment by the separate states under Fourteenth Amendment provi-

sions. The amendment has been modified primarily through the *due*[4] *process clause* of the *Fifth Amendment*[9]. See also *First Amendment*[9]; *Fourth Amendment*[9]; *Bill*[9] *of Rights nationalization*; *civil*[9] *rights*; *Civil*[4] *War*; *Confederate*[4] *States of America*; *equal*[4] *protection clause*; *nationalized rights*[9]; *naturalization*[3]; *privileges*[4] *and immunities clause*; *separate*[9] *but equal doctrine.*

Amendment, Tenth (1791). The *amendment*[3] to the U.S. *Constitution*[4] which declares that the *"reserved" powers*[4] belong to the *states*[3].

Amendment, Thirteenth (1865). The *amendment*[3] to the U.S. *Constitution*[4] which prohibits slavery. See also *peonage*[9]; *Pollock*[1] *v. U.S.*

Amendment, Twenty-first (1933). The only *amendment*[3] to the U.S. *Constitution*[4] which was *ratified*[3] by *conventions*[3] within the *states*[3] rather than by state *legislatures*[7], an addition which repealed the *Eighteenth Amendment*[4] prohibiting the manufacture and sale of "intoxicating liquors." See also *Anti-Saloon*[5] *League of America*; *Prohibition Party*[5]; *Women's*[5] *Christian Temperance Union.*

Americanization. The assimilation of *alien*[3] elements into the already existing sociopolitical structure of the United States, especially through the process of academic and civic education. See also *political*[3] *socialization.*

Annapolis Convention (1786). A meeting of 12 *delegates*[5] from five states united under the *Articles*[4] *of Confederation*, which was called in an effort to overcome commercial problems existing between the various states of the *"league*[3] of friendship." The primary result of the meeting was a call for a formal *convention*[3] at Philadelphia in 1787, a meeting which eventually drafted the U.S. *Constitution*[4]. See also *Constitutional Convention*[4] *of 1787*; *Mount*[4] *Vernon Convention.*

Antifederalists. The name used to indicate persons opposing the newly drafted *Constitution*[4] of the United States during the period between 1787 and 1789.

Articles of Confederation (1781–89). The instrument of *government*[3] that served as the basic document of government for the American *states*[3] that had broken away from Great Britain between 1775 and 1781. The Articles served as a *"league*[3] of friendship" from 1781 until 1789, when the *U.S. Constitution*[4] was officially *ratified*[3]. The Articles were characterized by the fact that they had weak taxation *powers*[3] (essentially an authorization to requisition), weak commerce powers (no central regulation of *interstate commerce*[10]), and a rigid *amending*[3] process (unanimous consent). See also the *Critical*[4] *Period*; *confederate government*[3].

Association, The (1774). The agreement of the *delegates*[5] to the *First Continental Congress*[4] to boycott British goods in an effort to get the British Parliament to revise the *Intolerable*[4] *Acts of 1774*, which burdened the American *colonies*[4].

Bacon's Rebellion (1676). An unsuccessful *rebellion*[3] led by Nathaniel Bacon against the sometimes questionable and insensitive *administration*[6] of Virginia by Sir William Berkeley. *Governor*[6] Berkeley continually raised taxes and ignored *citizens'*[3] pleas for help against Indians on the frontier. Although Bacon's movement eventually failed, the Virginia House of Burgesses passed what became known as "Bacon's Laws," *legislation*[7] extending the *suffrage*[5], *liberalizing*[3] officeholding requirements, and revising taxation procedures.

Beard, Charles A, 1874–1948. The American political historian who wrote An Economic Interpretation of the Constitution (1913), a classic and controversial analysis of the *Constitutional Convention*[4] *of 1787* and the *U.S. Constitution*[4]. Beard's thesis was that the Constitution was molded primarily by the economic self-interests of the *delegates*[5] to the *convention*[3] rather than by the political philosophies of the day. He contended that the authors of the document sought a strong central *government*[3] to protect their own interests and to provide *law*[8] and order. See also *centralization*[3].

Bellamy, Edward, 1850–98. The author of the leading *utopia*[3] written in nineteenth century America. Bellamy's utopia, Looking Backward, 2000–1887, published in 1888, was a social commentary visualizing a United States of total social cooperation. He believed there would be a system of total *state*[3] control with the political *power*[3] residing in the people and the economic power being managed by an industrial army. Bellamy analyzed economic structures, political power, natural resource usage, family relationships, and nearly every other area of *society*[3]. Bellamy's utopia had no money, no competition, and almost no *politics*[3]. The society was a peaceful, classless, and secure system based on scientific and social cooperation. The end result of such a planned state was progress and equality.

Bill of Rights, United States (1791). The first ten *amendments*[3] to the *U.S. Constitution*[4]. The Bill of Rights was introduced in the First *U.S. Congress*[4] in 1789 as a concession to those who had objected to the proposed *constitution*[3] on the grounds that it did not provide enough civil liberty protections. The Bill of Rights assures such things as trial by *jury*[8], the *writ of habeas*[8] *corpus*, freedom of expression, freedom of religion, freedom of assembly, and numerous other guarantees related to *property*[10] and human rights. The Bill of Rights applies primarily to the *federal government*[3].

However, since the *Supreme*[8] *Court* case of *Gitlow*[1] *v. New York,* numerous rights have been "nationalized" under the *Fourteenth Amendment*[4] and now apply to the *states*[3]. See also *Bill*[9] *of Rights nationalization, civil*[9] *rights; nationalized rights*[9].

Bill of Rights, Virginia (1776). The legal guarantees provided the *citizens*[3] of Virginia as part of their *state*[3] *constitution*[3]. The rights of trial by *jury*[8], *writ of habeas*[8] *corpus,* etc. were drawn from English *common law*[8] and were used along with rights contained in other state constitutions as examples in drafting the *U.S. Bill*[4] *of Rights.*

Book of the General Lawes and Libertyes concerning the Inhabitants of the Massachusets (1648). A work by some of the inhabitants of the Massachusetts Bay Colony which called for *Governor*[6] Winthrop and the religious leadership of the *colony*[4] to acknowledge that public acts made by self-governing freemen should take precedence over the *laws*[8] of God. See also *higher law theory*[3].

Book of the States: See Chap. 11.

Brook Farm (1840–47). A communal social experiment established in Massachusetts in 1840 along the lines advocated by the French social philosopher *Charles Fourier*[3]. The members of Brook Farm followed Fourier's ideas in establishing an "association," or balanced *community*[3], known as a "phalanx." Brook Farm and similar experiments were more romantic than successful. All failed primarily because of prevailing ideas of *individualism*[3]. See also *collectivism*[3]; *socialism*[3].

Calhoun, John C., 1782–1851. The most outstanding, systematic southern defender of the social institution of slavery and the leading defender of *states'*[4] *rights* and the doctrines of *nullification*[4] and *secession*[4]. Calhoun, a U.S. *Senator*[7] from South Carolina,

a *vice-president*[6] of the United States, and the "father of the *concurrent majority*"[4], attacked the *natural rights*[3] philosophy in A Disquisition on Government (1850). He argued strongly for a *government*[3] based on order, refused to believe in a *state*[3] *of nature* without formal government, accepted social and political inequality as a natural fact of life, and viewed slavery as the basis for civilization and progress. See also *state (southern interpretation) sovereignty*[4]; *Civil*[4] *War.*

Charter of Privileges (1701). A *liberalization*[3] *of government*[3] in the *colonial*[4] *territory*[3] of William Penn. The assembly became the real body of government *power*[3], subject primarily to the *veto*[7] power of the *governor*[6]. Penn had already established a *bicameral*[7] *legislature*[7] elected by freemen. He had also given nearly all freemen the right to vote.

Civil War, U.S. (1861–65). The internal conflict within the U.S. which pitted 11 southern *states*[3] against the remaining states located north of what was known as the *Mason-Dixon*[4] *Line.* The rebelling states called themselves the *Confederate*[4] *States of America.* The primary causes of the *war*[12] were slavery, *tariff*[10] regulations, social differences, and political differences over the nature of the *federal*[3] Union. The war began with a southern attack on Fort Sumter, South Carolina on April 12, 1861, and ended with the surrender of General Robert E. Lee's army at Appomattox, Virginia in April 1865. The war was immediately followed by what came to be known as the *Reconstruction*[4]. During Reconstruction, the *U.S. Supreme*[8] *Court* held in *Texas*[1] *v. White* that the states in *rebellion*[3] were never legally out of the Union. See also *Kansas-Nebraska*[4] *Act of 1854; Missouri*[4] *Compromise; states'*[4] *rights.*

colony, charter. A *colony*[4] created through royal charter and granted general control over its own affairs, subject primarily to provisions stated within the charter. Connecticut, Rhode Island, and Massachusetts were charter colonies.

colony, proprietary. A *colony*[4] created through a grant of *power*[3] to one or more individuals or *organizations*[6] and which possessed full rights of governmental organization and control over its own affairs. Pennsylvania and Carolina were proprietary colonies. See also *Fundamental*[4] *Constitutions of Carolina.*

colony, royal. A *colony*[4] created through the action of a *monarch*[3] appointing a *governor*[6] directly responsible to royal *authority*[3]. Royal colonies generally possessed appointed councils and popularly elected assemblies. Virginia (1624), Georgia (1752), and South Carolina (1721) became royal colonies after unsuccessful ventures under proprietors. See also *proprietary colony*[4].

Columbia, District of. The capital of the United States of America. The *city*[11] designed by a French engineer named Pierre Charles L'Enfant, operates as a *municipal corporation*[11] under *federal*[3] control. It has a *mayor*[11] and *city*[11] *council* appointed by the *President*[6]. Its financial affairs are controlled primarily by the *Congress*[4]. The District of Columbia, frequently referred to as Washington, D.C., was granted the right to participate in presidential elections by the addition of the *Twenty-third Amendment*[5] to the *Constitution*[4] (1961). The city has a nonvoting *representative*[7] seated in the *House*[7] of Representatives. See also *Compromise*[4] of 1850.

commerce clause (Art. I, Sec. 8, Cl. 3). The provision within the *U.S. Constitution*[4] that permits the *U.S. Congress*[4] to regulate commerce with foreign *nations*[3] and among the several *states*[3]. The commerce clause has been broadly interpreted by the *U.S. Su-*

preme[8] *Court* in permitting the *federal government*[3] to regulate the movement of goods across state lines, manufacturing, *child*[10] *labor, civil*[9] *rights,* and other areas considered national in scope. See also *Brown*[1] *v. Maryland; interstate commerce*[10]; *intrastate commerce*[10]; *liberal construction*[4]; *Cooley*[1] *v. Board of Port Wardens; Gibbons*[1] *v. Ogden; NLRB*[1] *v. Jones and Laughlin Corp.; U.S.*[1] *v. E. C. Knight Co.*

Commerce Compromise (1787). The compromise agreed upon at the *Constitutional Convention*[4] *of 1787,* which involved the issues of domestic and foreign commerce and the slave trade. It was agreed that the national *government*[3] could regulate commerce with foreign *nations*[3], among the several states[3], and with Indian tribes. The *U.S. Congress*[4] could not tax exports and it could not regulate the slave trade before 1808, except to place a $10 tax on each imported slave. See also *interstate commerce*[10]; *federal government*[3]; *import tax*[10].

committees of correspondence. A group of *committees*[7] led by Samuel Adams of Massachusetts, which acted as the primary system of intercolonial communications just prior to the *American Revolution*[4]. The system laid the framework for an *intelligence*[12] gathering operation active during the American Revolution.

Compromise of 1850. A congressional compromise proposed by *Senator*[7] Henry Clay, the "Great Compromiser." The Compromise of 1850 was designed to alleviate the problems developing between northern and southern *states*[3] and which eventually led to the *Civil*[4] *War.* The compromise admitted California as a free state, established New Mexico and Utah as separate *territories*[3] with the slavery question within them to be decided through *"popular sovereignty"*[3], assumed the debts of the former *republic*[3] of Texas and paid $10 million for land ceded to New Mexico, prohibited the slave trade within the *District of Columbia*[4], and passed a fugitive slave *law*[8] to help southerners recover runaway slaves. See also, *Mexican*[12] *War*.

Confederate States of America (1861–65). The *league*[3] of southern *states*[3] which *seceded*[4] from the United States of America and organized as a separate governmental system with its capital at Montgomery, Alabama. *President*[6] Jefferson Davis and *Vice-President*[6] Alexander H. Stephens led the Confederate states in a *civil war*[12] against United States control. The *constitution*[3] of the Confederate States of America provided for a nonrenewable presidential term of six years' duration, an *item veto*[7], *cabinet*[6] member expression before the Confederate congress, and a mandatory *constitutional*[3] *convention*[3] session on the call of any three member states. See also *Civil*[4] *War*; *confederate government*[3]; *Reconstruction*[4].

Congress, Albany (1754). An intercolonial meeting of *delegates*[5] from New Hampshire, Massachusetts, Connecticut, Rhode Island, Pennsylvania, and Maryland who met with the *lieutenant*[6] *governor* of New York, members of the lieutenant governor's council, and several Iroquois chiefs. The Congress was called by the English Privy Council in an effort to restore Iroquois confidence in British activities and to gain their support against the French. The Congress adopted a plan which was eventually rejected by the English *government*[3] and the *colonies*[4] themselves. See also *Albany*[4] *Plan of Union*; *Benjamin Franklin*[4].

Congress, First Continental (1774). The unofficial meeting of *colonial*[4] leaders in Philadelphia, Pennsylvania. The Congress met in direct reaction to the *Intolerable*[4] *Acts of 1774*. The Congress, composed of *delegates*[5] from all the colonies except Georgia, voted to support *"The Association"*[4]

which was formed to *boycott*[10] British goods. The First Continental Congress and its unsuccessful boycott proved to be the last peaceful attempt at reconciling differences between the colonies and Great Britain.

Congress, Second Continental (1775–81). The unofficial and *revolutionary*[3] meeting of colonial leaders at Philadelphia, Pennsylvania under the leadership of John Hancock. The Congress united all 13 British *colonies*[4] in their break with Great Britain through the *American Revolution*[4] (1775–81). Although the Continental Congress was not a recognized *government*[3], it asserted itself and declared independence from Great Britain, raised an army, borrowed money from foreign sources in order to conduct a *war*[12], developed a national currency, and regulated domestic affairs during the time of crisis. See also *Declaration*[4] *of Independence*; *de facto government*[3].

Congress, Stamp Act (1765). A meeting of *delegates*[5] from nine *colonies*[4] called to discuss the problems created by the passage of the *Stamp*[4] *Act of 1765*. The New York meeting issued a "Declaration of Rights and Grievances" which stated that internal taxation should be levied only with the consent of the people or their *representatives*[7]. See also *Sons*[4] *of Liberty*; *consent theory*[3].

Congress, U.S. (1789–). The official legislative body of the *government*[3] of the United States of America. Congress is composed of a *Senate*[7], known as the *upper chamber*[7], and a *House*[7] *of Representatives*, known as the *lower chamber*[7]. The Senate is presided over by its president, the *Vice-President*[6] of the United States. The presiding officer of the House is selected from the House and is known as the *Speaker*[7] *of the House*. The houses are both part of the regular lawmaking process. However, revenue measures are restricted to introduction in the House of Representatives. The

Senate is vested with specialized *power*[3] to give "advice and consent" to the *U.S. President*[6] on international *treaties*[12] and *executive*[6] *appointments*[6]. During an *impeachment*[7] proceeding against the President, the House is responsible for bringing charges, and the Senate tries the case. In choosing a President when there is no clear *majority*[3] vote in the *electoral*[4] *college*, the House votes by states and chooses the President from among the top three candidates. The Senate votes by members and chooses the Vice-President from among the top two candidates. Beyond these specialized functions both houses have general legislative powers outlined in the *U.S. Constitution*[4] or in their respective rules of *parliamentary*[7] *procedure*. See also *Connecticut*[4] *Compromise*; *advice*[7] *and consent powers*; *delegated powers*[4]; *implied powers*[4].

Connecticut Compromise (1787). The major ("Great") compromise of the *Constitutional Convention*[4] *of 1787*, a compromise arranged by the *delegates*[5] from Connecticut. The compromise involved the issue of *representation*[7]. It was decided that the national *congress*[4] would consist of two houses, one based on geographical units and the other based on population figures. The *U.S. Senate*[7] would contain two members from each *state*[3] and would represent states. The *U.S. House*[7] *of Representatives* would be based on population and would represent people. The compromise was necessary in order to balance the interests of the small states and large states competing for *power*[3].

Constitution, United States (1789). The fundamental *law*[8] of the national *state*[3] officially known as the United States of America. The Constitution of the United States became effective on March 4, 1789. It is one written document containing seven basic articles and 26 *amendments*[3]. The document distributes *power*[3] within a *federal*[3] system of *government*[3] consisting of one national government and 50 state governments. It contains *delegated powers*[4] granted to the central government and *reserved powers*[4] granted to the states. It contains *implied powers*[4] derived from those delegated to the central government and *concurrent powers*[4] belonging to both governments. It also has some powers belonging exclusively to one government and some powers denied to one or both parts of the federal structure. Since the *Supreme*[8] *Court* case of *United*[1] *States v. Curtiss-Wright Export Corporation*, it has been recognized that the Constitution contains an *"inherent" power*[4] related to foreign affairs. The *written constitution*[3] has been greatly modified through formal amendments, *custom*[3] and usage, judicial interpretation, *legislative*[4] *elaboration*, and *executive*[6] action. See also *federal government*[3]; *constitutional law*[8]; *denied powers*[4]; *exclusive powers*[4].

construction, liberal (loose). The interpretation of a *constitution*[3] which holds that the usage of *power*[3] lies not just in powers expressly stated within a written document, but within broad and reasonably acceptable *implied powers*[4]. During early U.S. history the *Federalist Party*[5], under the leadership of *Alexander Hamilton*[4], *John Adams*[6], and *George Washington*[6] adopted a *liberal*[3] construction of the *U.S. Constitution*[4]. The *Federalists*[4] championed the use of implied powers as derived from the *necessary*[4] *and proper clause* (Art. I, Sec. 8, Cl. 18) of the Constitution. They used these powers to strengthen the central government and shift power away from the states. See also *written constitution*[3]; *federal government*[3]; *delegated powers*[4]; *McCulloch*[1] *v. Maryland*.

construction, strict (rigid). The interpretation of a *constitution*[3] which holds that the usage of *power*[3] lies primarily in powers expressly delegated to the *government*[3], generally through a written document. During early U.S. history the *Democratic-Republican Party*[5] led by *Thomas Jefferson*[6], supported a strict construction of the *U.S. Constitution*[4]. A person who defends such a viewpoint is usually considered a *conservative*[3] and a defender of *states'*[4] rights. See also *written constitution*[3]; *delegated powers*[4]; *McCulloch*[1] *v. Maryland*.

contract clause (Art. I, Sec. 10, Cl. 1). The provision within the *U.S. Constitution*[4] which prohibits the *U.S. Congress*[4] from impairing the obligation of *contracts*[10]. The contract clause applies to the *federal government*[3], *state*[3] governments, and individuals. Various *Supreme*[8] *Court* cases have established that state *legislatures*[7] may not change *corporate*[10] charters because they are in the nature of contracts, a state legislature may not revoke land grants with subsequent *legislation*[7] because such grants are in the nature of contracts, and contracts must be strictly construed. See also *Charles*[1] *River Bridge v. Warren Bridge*; *Dartmouth*[1] *College v. Woodward*; *Fletcher*[1] *v. Peck*.

Convention of 1787, Constitutional. An unofficial *convention*[3] of *delegates*[5] from all the member states except Rhode Island, which were united under the *Articles*[4] *of Confederation*. The secret meeting was held in Philadelphia, Pennsylvania from May 25 to September 17, 1787. It was called to revise the Articles of Confederation. Instead, the 55 delegates, led by *George Washington*[6], drafted the *U.S. Constitution*[4] and submitted it to the *states*[3] for *ratification*[3]. The primary business of the convention revolved around the issues of *representation*[7], *executive*[6] *power*[3], commerce, and slavery. The major divisions evident at the meeting were large states versus small states, southern states versus northern states, slave states versus free states, agricultural states versus manufacturing states, and *aristocratic*[3] ideas versus *democratic*[3] ideas. The primary plans presented at the convention were the *Virginia*[4] *Plan* (large states) and the *New*[4] *Jersey Plan* (small states). The major conflicts were settled through compromises: *Connecticut*[4] ("*Great*") *Compromise* on representation, *Three-fifths*[4] *Compromise* on slavery, and the *Commerce*[4] *Compromise*. The best record of the struggles of the Constitutional Convention is *Madison's*[4] *Journal of the Federal Convention*.

Council of Revision (New York). A governmental body with *authority*[3] to *veto*[7] *acts*[8] passed by the *legislature*[7] of the *state*[3] of New York. The Council of Revision was composed of the *governor*[6], the chancellor, and the judges of the state supreme court. It was in existence from 1777 until 1821 and served as a model for the Council of Revision proposed in the *Virginia*[4] *Plan* for inclusion within the *U.S. Constitution*[4]. See also *Council*[4] *of Revision (Virginia Plan)*.

Council of Revision (Virginia Plan). A national governmental body proposed as part of the *Virginia*[4] *Plan*, which was presented to the *Constitutional Convention*[4] of 1787. The Council, rejected as part of the *U.S. Constitution*[4], would have been composed of members from the *executive*[6] and judicial branches and would have possessed a *veto*[7] over regular *legislation*[7]. A vetoed national legislative *act*[8] could be overridden by a simple *majority*[3] vote of both houses. A national legislative veto of a *state*[3] *law*[8], a *power*[3] proposed in the Virginia Plan, could also be vetoed by the Council of Revision. The Council of Revision proposal was patterned after the Council of Revision operating in the state of New York. It was proposed as a "*fourth*[4] *branch of government*" designed to *force*[3] officials to give more careful consideration to the lawmaking process. See also *Council*[4] *of Revision (New York)*; *veto*[7] *override*.

Council of State Governments: see Chap. 11.

Critical Period, the (1781–89). The popular designation of the period during which the 13 separate North American *states*[3] operated under the *Articles*[4] *of Confederation*. There was a weak central *government*[3], with almost no *taxing power*[4] and no control over the extreme commercial rivalry between the states. There were numerous disputes over western land claims, continual economic problems at home, and military threats from abroad. See also *confederate government*[3].

Declaration of Independence (1776). A document issued by the *Second Continental Congress*[4], which was the result of a *resolution*[7] introduced on June 7, 1776 by *Richard Henry Lee*[4]. Lee's resolution stated that "the United Colonies are and of right ought to be free and Independent *states*[3]." The Declaration of Independence, written primarily by *Thomas Jefferson*[6], was officially drafted by a *committee*[7] composed of Jefferson, *Benjamin Franklin*[4], *John Adams*[6], Robert Livingston, and Roger Sherman. The document was adopted by the Congress on July 4, 1776. The Declaration of Independence was directed against the *tyrannical*[3] acts of King George III and the British Parliament. It is considered a classic statement of *popular sovereignty*[4], *natural law*[8], *inalienable rights*[3], and *revolution*[3]. Thomas Jefferson admitted that the English political philosopher *John Locke*[3] had greatly influenced the ideas and language contained within the famous document. See also *colonialism*[4]; *natural rights*[3].

democracy, Jacksonian. The term used to describe the period of U.S. history between approximately 1820 and 1860, when there was a decline in *aristocratic*[3] elements and a movement toward *democratization*[3] of political, social, and economic institutions. Some of the major characteristics of the period in which the people elected the popular hero *Andrew Jackson*[6] as *U.S. President*[6] were *suffrage*[5] extension, removal of various restrictive *state*[3] *constitutional*[3] barriers, acceptance of a longer ballot, rotation in office, development of the national nominating *convention*[3], destruction of *King Caucus*[5], extension of the *spoils*[6] *system*, extensive use of the *executive*[6] *veto*[7], executive battles with a *federal*[3] judiciary dominated by *property*[10] interests, and large-scale movement into western lands. See also *long ballot*[5]; *party convention*[5].

democracy, Jeffersonian. The term used to describe the period of U.S. history between approximately 1800 and 1820 when *democratic*[3] political philosophy was dominated by the ideas of *Thomas Jefferson*[6]. Jeffersonian democracy was characterized by unequivocal support of human rights, support of the elective principles resting in the hands of a popular electorate, rejection of strong *centralized*[3] government and support of *states'*[4] *rights* as part of the division of *power*[3], balanced *budgets*[10] under simple *government*[3], and simple military and foreign *policies*[6]. Jeffersonians warned against large-scale *urbanization*[11] and industrialization and emphasized that the best *society*[3] is one composed of an educated population engaged in agricultural activities.

Dickinson, John, 1732–1808. A leading *colonial*[4] pamphleteer and the author of Letters from a Farmer in Pennsylvania to the Inhabitants of the British Colonies (1767), the major indictment of the British *Townshend*[4] *Acts of 1767*. Dickinson's work was a treatise defining parliamentary *authority*[3] and an analysis of the *un-*

constitutionality[3] of the British suspension of the legislative functions of the New York *legislature*[7] and the levying of taxes on the colonies without their permission. See also *parliamentary government*[3]; *consent theory*[3].

diversity of citizenship question. A question or conflict between *citizens*[3] of different *states*[3] which may be subject to judicial action. The *U.S. Constitution*[4] (Art. III, Sec. 2, Cl. 1) permits *federal*[3] courts to hear such cases. However, *Supreme*[8] *Court* decisions and federal *legislation*[7] have given state courts widespread *authority*[3] to hear diversity of citizenship cases. See also *Eleventh Amendment*[4]; *Chisholm*[1] *v. Georgia*; *Cohens*[1] *v. Virginia*; *Dred*[1] *Scott v. Sandford*; *Erie*[1] *Railroad v. Tompkins*.

divestment: see *divestment*[10] *theory*.

Dorr's Rebellion (1841–42). A popular *rebellion*[3] led by Thomas W. Dorr against a largely unrepresentative Rhode Island *government*[3] operating under the *colonial*[4] charter of 1663. Dorr's followers drafted a "People's Constitution" which was unofficially *ratified*[3] by a large number of *citizens*[3] of the *state*[3]. They immediately elected Dorr *governor*[6]. The official governor declared *martial*[8] *law*, *President*[6] Tyler supported the official government, and Dorr was tried and sentenced to life imprisonment. In 1843 Rhode Island *liberalized*[3] the state *constitution*[3] and in 1845 Dorr's sentence was withdrawn. In 1849, in the case of *Luther*[1] *v. Borden*, the *U.S. Supreme*[8] *Court* refused to determine whether Rhode Island had a *republican government*[3]. See also representative *government*[3].

due process clauses (Amendment 5 and Amendment 14, Section 1). The separate but related provisions within the *U.S. Constitution*[4] which guarantee the basic *common law*[8] protections related to life, liberty, and *prop-*

erty[10]. The *Fifth Amendment*[9] due process clause restricts the *federal government*[3] from using arbitrary methods of *government*[3] against the people. The *Fourteenth Amendment*[4] due process clause was originally interpreted as applying only to the *states*[3]. However, since 1925 numerous rights contained within the U.S. *Bill*[4] *of Rights* have been "nationalized." It is now held that the Fourteenth Amendment due process clause protects individuals within the states in the same way the Fifth Amendment due process clause protects individuals against federal encroachment. See also *Bill*[9] *of Rights nationalization*; *procedural due*[9] *process*; *substantive due*[9] *process*; *nationalized rights*[9]; *Barron*[1] *v. Baltimore*; *Gault*[1], *In re*; *Gitlow*[1] *v. N.Y.*; *Palko*[1] *v. Conn.*

electoral college. The group of individuals chosen every four years by the popular electorate within the separate *states*[3] and the *District of Columbia*[4] who vote on the *President*[6] and *Vice-President*[6]. The electors of the electoral college meet within their separate *jurisdictions*[8] in December after the November *general election*[5]. Their ballots are opened and certified before a *joint session*[7] of *Congress*[4] when it convenes in January. Each state *delegation*[5] has the same number of members that the state has in its national congressional delegation (Senate and House). The *Twenty-third Amendment*[5] permits the District of Columbia to have electors on the same basis as a state. The electoral delegation within each state is determined by a *plurality*[3] of the *popular vote*[5]. Electors pledge to vote for the candidates heading the *political party*[5] ticket, but they cannot be held to that pledge. Originally the presidential candidate receiving the highest number of *electoral votes*[5] became President and the one receiving the second highest number became Vice-President. The *Twelfth Amendment*[5] (1804) changed the electoral college and placed the presidential and vice-presidential candidates on "distinct" and separate ballots as teams. In the event there is no clear *majority*[3] for a team, the *House*[7] *of Representatives* votes by state and chooses the President from among the top three candidates. The *Senate*[7] votes by member and chooses the Vice-President from among the top two candidates. See also *Lodge-Gossett Amendment*[5]; *legislative delegation*[7]; *electoral power*[7]; *minority president*[5]; *Revolution*[5] *of 1800*.

enabling act. A *federal*[3] *law*[8] permitting the residents of a federal *territory*[3] to hold a *constitutional*[3] *convention*[3] and to take all steps necessary in preparing for statehood. See also *federal government*[3]; *state*[3]; *statehood*[4] *admission*.

equal protection clause (Amendment 14, section 1). The provision within the U.S. *Constitution*[4] which declares that the separate *states*[3] must provide *citizens*[3] the equal protection of the *laws*[8]. The clause has made its presence known largely through judicial interpretation. The U.S. *Supreme*[8] *Court* held in the *Civil*[1] *Rights Cases* (1883) that the provisions of the *Fourteenth Amendment*[4] did not allow for a positive program of federal *legislation*[7] affecting private actions abridging personal liberties. The Court said the *amendment*[3] restricted only *discriminatory*[9] state actions. In the *Slaughterhouse*[1] *Cases* (1873) the Court held that the Fourteenth Amendment provision applied to the *federal government*[3] only. However, numerous recent cases have been decided in the areas of civil liberties, voting rights, legal rights, and legislative *apportionment*[7] on the grounds that the Fourteenth Amendment equal protection clause protects citizens within the states in the same way liberties within the U.S. *Bill*[4] *of Rights* protect citizens against federal encroachment. See also *Baker*[1] *v. Carr*; *Bill*[9] *of Rights nationalization*; *Brown*[1] *v. Board of Education of Topeka*; *civil*[9] *rights*; *nationalized rights*[9].

federalism, cooperative (creative). The view of federalism that stresses the interrelationships of the *federal*[3] system and the mutual cooperation between the central *government*[3] and the *states*[3]. Emphasis is placed on cooperation in areas of *law*[8] enforcement, judicial practices, election practices, public health, *urban*[11] problems, and other common interests. See also *intergovernmental*[11] *agreement*; *interstate*[11] *compact*; *interstate*[11] *relations*; *interstate*[11] *trade barrier*.

federalism, dual. The view of federalism which maintains that the *Constitution*[4] created a *federal*[3] system with national and *state*[3] governments of equal sovereignty possessing separate and distinct *powers*[3]. The *theory*[3], adopted and enforced by the *Supreme*[8] *Court* between the late 1800's and 1937, holds that the *reserved powers*[4] of the states limit the *delegated powers*[4] of the national *government*[3]. See also *state (constitutional) sovereignty*[3].

Federalist: A Collection of Essays Written in Favor of the New Constitution, The (1788). A series of essays written by *James Madison*[6], *Alexander Hamilton*[4], and John Jay and first published in New York newspapers in an attempt to win support for the *U.S. Constitution*[4]. The Federalist was the outstanding pro-*Federalist*[4] point-by-point analysis of how the proposed *constitution*[3] would operate in providing an orderly and effective *government*[3]. The 85 essays were published anonymously under the pseudonym "Publius"; they are still the best analysis of the *federal*[3] system of government ever written. They called for a strong central government, a division of *power*[3] between the central government and the *states*[3], *limited government*[3] based on a well-balanced system of *checks*[3] *and balances*, and control of various *factions*[3] within a *pluralistic*[3] *society*[3]. See also *centralization*[3]; *Federalist Party*[5].

✓ **Federalists.** The name used to indicate persons supporting *ratification*[3] of the newly drafted *U.S. Constitution*[4] during the period between 1787 and 1789. The name was later used as a *party*[5] label to identify persons supporting a strong central *government*[3]. See also *centralization*[3]; *The Federalist*[4]; *federal government*[3]; *Federalist Party*[5].

federal question. A question or conflict in *law*[8] or *equity*[8], which may be subject to judicial action because it involves the *U.S. Constitution*[4], Federal *legislation*[7], or an international *treaty*[12] *ratified*[3] by the United States. Such cases are subject to *federal*[3] judicial action in accordance with Article III, Section 2, Clause 1 of the Constitution. See also *Cohens*[1] *v. Virginia*.

Federal-State Joint Action Committee: see Chap. 11.

fourth branch of government. The popular designation of public *administration*[6] or "the *Bureaucracy*"[6]. Numerous political observers contend that the Bureaucracy, especially the bloc of *independent regulatory commissions*[6], has gained *power*[3] as influential on occasion as the three formal branches of *government*[3]. Some writers occasionally refer to the congressional *committee*[7] *system* or some other power center as the fourth branch of government. However, the most frequently cited power center is public administration. See also *Council*[4] *of Revision (Virginia Plan)*.

Franklin, Benjamin, 1706–90. The American *statesman*[5], philosopher, scientist, and writer who published the Pennsylvania Gazette and Poor Richard's Almanack (1732–57). The

Pennsylvania resident was a *delegate*[5] to the *Albany Congress*[4] (1754), where he introduced the *Albany*[4] *Plan of Union*. He was a minister to England in 1757, a member of the committee appointed to draft the *Declaration*[4] *of Independence* in 1776, a minister to France (1776–85), a commissioner during the negotiations on the *Treaty*[12] of Paris, which officially ended the *American Revolution*[4] in 1783, and the oldest delegate to the *Constitutional Convention*[4] of 1787. His life is chronicled in his Autobiography (1771–90).

Freeport Doctrine (1858). The doctrine enunciated by *Senator*[7] Stephen A. Douglas during his senatorial campaign debates with *Abraham Lincoln*[6] at Freeport, Illinois. Abraham Lincoln gained fame from the encounter and Douglas lost southern support for the presidency due to his statement that the Dred Scott decision (1857) made slavery legally acceptable in *federal*[3] territories but that, in practice, the people of the *territories*[3] could keep slavery out through local *squatter sovereignty*[4] regulations unfavorable to the institution.

full faith and credit clause (Art. IV, Sec. 1). The clause within the *U.S. Constitution*[4] which holds that the various *states*[3] must recognize legislative *acts*[8], public records, and judicial decisions of the other states within the United States. The principal exception to date, as decided by the *U.S. Supreme*[8] *Court* in *Williams*[1] *v. North Carolina*, is that divorce decrees do not have to be recognized elsewhere unless one of the parties to a divorce was a legal resident of the state granting the divorce. See also *comity*[3].

Fundamental Constitutions of Carolina (1669). A *constitutional*[3] *system* designed with the help of *John Locke*[3] for Lord Ashley, one of 8 proprietors of the Carolina Colony. The system provided for a *governor*[6] appointed by the proprietors, a *unicameral*[7] *legislature*[7] composed of major landholders, a system of political rights based on heredity and wealth, and an established Church of England. The *feudalistic*[3] system eventually developed a *bicameral*[7] legislature with an *upper chamber*[7] for nobles and a *lower chamber*[7] for commoners. The system was never fully developed, and in 1721 the area became a *royal colony*[4] under the name South Carolina.

Fundamental Orders of Connecticut (1639). A document claimed by some as the first *written constitution*[3] of civil *government*[3] drafted in America. The constitution between the *towns*[11] of Windsor, Wethersfield, and Hartford contained 11 articles providing for election of a *governor*[6] by *majority*[3] vote of freemen, for the selection of magistrates to care for the "public good," for the removal of religious qualifications for *citizenship*[3], and for a *bicameral*[7] legislative body. After 1645 the *upper chamber*[7] was allowed to *veto*[7] actions of the *lower chamber*[7].

general welfare clause (Art. I, Sec. 8, Cl. 1). The provision within the *U.S. Constitution*[4] which declares that the *U.S. Congress*[4] may tax and pay debts in order to provide for the "general welfare of the United States." The clause has been broadly interpreted by the *Supreme*[8] *Court* in permitting the Congress to regulate various activities within the *states*[3]. In providing for the general welfare, the *federal government*[3] frequently uses conditional *grants-in-aid*[10] and other taxation and spending programs that may be regulatory as well as revenue-producing in scope. See also *liberal construction*[4]; *regulatory tax*[10]; *Frothingham*[1] *v. Mellon*; *Massachusetts*[1] *v. Mellon*; *U.S.*[1] *v. Butler*.

Grants-in-aid: see Chap. 10.

Great Fundamentals (1636). The first basic system of *laws*[8] actually formulated in the American *colonies*[4]. The laws were designed to provide a system of *representation*[7] for Plymouth colony. The *suffrage*[5] was extended and a *unicameral*[7] *legislature*[7] was provided to work with the *governor*[6]. See also *Mayflower*[4] *Compact*.

Hamilton, Alexander, 1757–1804. American *statesman*[5], resident of New York, one of the authors of *The Federalist*[4] (1788), a major leader of the *Federalist Party*[5], and the first Secretary of the Treasury. Hamilton established the economic pattern for the U.S. through his support of the *assumption of state*[10] *debts* incurred during the *American Revolution*[4], through the establishment of the *Bank*[10] *of the United States*, through his *Report*[10] *on the Subject of Manufacturers* (1791) calling for *government*[3] planning and protective *tariffs*[10] to encourage manufacturing, and through his leadership in crushing the *Whiskey*[4] *Rebellion* (1794). See also *Department of the Treasury*[2].

Hartford Convention (1814–15). A secret meeting of *representatives*[7] from five New England *states*[3] which was called to protest U.S. involvement in the *War*[12] *of 1812*, a *war*[12] especially disruptive of New England trade. The *delegates*[5], largely *Federalists*[4], protested the ready acceptance of foreign *immigrants*[3], the easy admission of new states into the Union, *centralized*[3] military forces, the *Three-fifths*[4] *clause* of the *U.S. Constitution*[4], and the unlimited number of presidential terms of office. The delegates advocated *interposition*[4], the passing of state laws protecting state *citizens*[3] against *unconstitutional*[3] national action. The War of 1812 ended before the *resolutions*[7] were delivered. The *Federalist Party*[5], however, was characterized as *treasonous*[3] because of its part in the meeting. See also *convention*[3]; *statehood*[4] *admission*; *states'*[4] *rights*.

Holmes, Oliver Wendell, Jr.: see Chap. 8.

Hughes, Charles Evans: see Chap. 8.

Immigration Act of 1965. An *act*[8] undertaking major revisions of U.S. immigration *policies*[6]. It eliminated the use of a *quota*[3] *system* based on national origin, stressed the admittance of persons on the basis of skills and the need to reunite families, and established limits on the number of immigrants to be admitted annually. The act was the first *law*[8] to place a ceiling on *immigration*[3] from the Western Hemisphere. See also *Immigration*[4] *and Nationality Act of 1952*; *Immigration*[2] *and Naturalization Service*.

Immigration and Nationality (McCarran-Walter) Act of 1952. An *act*[8] which maintained an *immigration*[3] *quota*[3] *system* based on national origin and which placed restrictions on immigrants adhering to *Communist*[3] or *totalitarian*[3] beliefs. The *law*[8] stated that Communists could be denied *naturalization*[3] and that naturalized *citizens*[3] could lose their citizenship by joining subversive *organizations*[6] or refusing to testify before congressional committees investigating such activities. The quota system was eventually abolished by the *Immigration*[4] *Act of 1965*. See also *investigating committee*[7]; *Immigration*[2] *and Naturalization Service*; *Communist Party*[5].

ingress and egress. The process of going into and out of a *state*[3]. The right of ingress and egress across state lines is protected by the *privileges*[4] *and immunities clauses* of the U.S. Constitution[4] (Article 4, Sec. 2, Cl. 1, and Amendment 14, Sec. 1). See also *comity*[3].

interposition. The doctrine that a *state*[3] within the *federal*[3] Union may "interpose" its *authority*[3] between its *citizens*[3] and the national *government*[3] in order to protect its citizens from unwarranted or allegedly "*unconstitutional*"[3] actions. The doctrine originated with the *Kentucky*[4] *and Virginia Resolutions* (1798–99) by *Thomas Jefferson*[6] and *James Madison*[6] when they argued that the states did not have to obey the federal *Alien*[4] *and Sedition Acts of 1798*. It was advocated by the *Federalists*[4] at the *Hartford*[4] *Convention* of 1814–15 as a means of protesting the *War*[12] *of 1812*. The doctrine was renewed by southerners prior to the *Civil*[4] *War* and after the school *desegregation*[9] decision of *Brown*[1] *v. Board of Education of Topeka* in 1954. In *Cooper*[1] *v. Aaron* the *Supreme*[8] *Court* rejected any further claim to interposition within the federal Union. See also *nullification*[4].

interstate compact: see Chap. 11.

interstate relations: see Chap. 11.

interstate rendition: see Chap. 11.

interstate trade barrier: see Chap. 11.

Intolerable Acts of 1774. A series of English *statutes*[8] popularly referred to by the American *colonists*[4] as "intolerable" because of their subject matter. They were designed to close the port of Boston until the colonists paid the East India Company for losses incurred during the Boston Tea Party (1773), provide for trials in England for officers indicted in Massachusetts for capital offenses committed while enforcing British *laws*[8], halt *town*[11] meetings, allow the king or *governor*[6] to fill offices previously elective, and allow for further quartering of soldiers. See also *Quartering*[4] *Act*; *The Association*[4]; *First Continental Congress*[4].

Jackson, Andrew: see Chap. 6.

James, William, 1842–1910. The American philosopher remembered as the individual most responsible for popularizing the approach to life known as *"pragmatism"*[3]. In his famous volumes entitled Pragmatism: A New Name for Some Old Ways of Thinking (1907) and The Meaning of Truth (1909), James emphasized the practical consequences of specific actions. His views on pragmatism and truth, that which can be verified or that which is workable, were easily adapted to the political realm, especially by persons commonly known as "practical politicians." See also *political*[5] *pragmatism*.

Jefferson, Thomas: see Chap. 6.

judicial review. The *power*[3] of a court, in the course of *litigation*[8], to declare the actions of other branches of *government*[3] *unconstitutional*[3]. The power was not cited in the *Constitution*[4], but has been an accepted part of the United States *constitutional*[3] *system* since the *Supreme*[8] *Court* case of *Marbury*[1] *v. Madison.* See also *Ashwander*[1] *v. TVA; Martin*[1] *v. Hunter's Lessee.*

Judiciary Act of 1789. The *federal*[3] *legislation*[7] that created the federal court system below the *U.S. Supreme*[8] *Court.* The *act*[8] specified the number of justices to sit on the Supreme Court, created a system of appellate courts, spelled out areas of *jurisdiction*[8], and filled in other details necessary for the *administration*[6] of *justice*[8]. In the Supreme Court case of *Marbury*[1] *v. Madison,* the first major case involving *judicial*[4] *review* of federal *legislation*[7], a portion of the Judiciary Act of 1789 was declared *unconstitutional*[3] because it added to the *original jurisdiction*[8] of the Supreme Court. See also *U.S. Court*[8] *of Appeals; appellate jurisdiction*[8].

justiciable question. A question or conflict which may be subject to judicial action. A justiciable question may be one involving individuals, groups, or a *state*[3]. It may be validly dealt with by a court of *law*[8] in accordance with *constitutional*[3] or *statutory*[8] provisions. See also *Baker*[1] *v. Carr; Colgrove*[1] *v. Green; Gray*[1] *v. Sanders.*

Kansas-Nebraska Act of 1854. The controversial *federal*[3] *legislation*[7] introduced by *Senator*[7] Stephen A. Douglas, which created the territories of Kansas and Nebraska with an understanding that the slavery question would be determined by *popular sovereignty*[3] within each *territory*[3]. The action thus repealed the portion of the *Missouri*[4] *Compromise* (1820) prohibiting slavery in such territory. Attempts by both "free" and "slave" proponents to settle the area led to open warfare and laid the stage for the *Civil*[4] *War.* Three years after the Kansas-Nebraska Act, the *Dred*[1] *Scott v. Sandford* decision declared the Missouri Compromise *unconstitutional*[3].

Kentucky and Virginia Resolutions (1798–99). A series of *resolutions*[7] written by *Thomas Jefferson*[6] and *James Madison*[6] and adopted by the *state*[3] *legislatures*[7] in Kentucky and Virginia. The resolutions (Jefferson's in Kentucky and Madison's in Virginia) declared that the federal *Alien*[4] *and Sedition Acts of 1798* were void since they violated the *U.S. Constitution*[4]. The resolutions supported the idea of *interposition*[4], a doctrine which held that *federal*[3] *power*[3] consisted of a *delegation of authority*[6] from the states and that *unconstitutional*[3] use of such *authority*[3] justified states "interposing" their authority between their *citizens*[3] and the national *government*[3]. See also *state (southern interpretation) sovereignty*[4]; *states'*[4] *rights.*

Lee, Richard Henry, 1732–94. The author of Letters from a Federal Farmer (1787), the best known *Antifederalist*[4] criticism of the proposed *U.S. Constitution*[4]. Lee rejected the Constitution and sought reform of the *Articles*[4] *of Confederation*, primarily because he feared the loss of *state* sovereignty[3] and the consolidation of power[3] in a central government[3]. He criticized the Constitution because he felt it was drawn up by men who did not fully understand the sentiments of the "men of middling property[10]", because of its "national[4] supremacy clause", and because it lacked a bill[4] of rights. See also centralization[3]; federal government[3]; state (southern interpretation) sovereignty[4].

legislative (congressional) elaboration. The developmental process of a constitutional[3] system which takes place through direct legislative action. Legislative elaboration is part of the "informal" amending process. Examples of legislative action affecting constitutional[3] growth and development within the U.S. are the creation of a federal[3] court system, a national banking system, and a system of independent regulatory commissions[6].

Leonard, Daniel, 1740–1829. One of the leading and most systematic Tory[4] writers prior to the American Revolution[4]. Leonard's Massachusettensis, Letters Addressed to the Inhabitants of the Province of Massachusetts Bay (1775) expressed the belief that government[3] originated to establish social order. His series of Letters defended the English mixed constitution[3] as the "most perfect system that the wisdom of ages has produced." In them he held: that nations[3] have the right to colonize[4] other lands and regulate their affairs as part of that right, that powers[3] of regulation lie within the parliament of the parent state[3], that colonial charter grants establish the principle that legislation[7] must be obeyed, and that if men rebel and throw off legitimate rule, they will revert to a harsh state[3] of nature and find themselves under a local tyranny[3]. See also John Adams[4]; parliamentary government[3].

Lincoln, Abraham: see Chap. 6.

Madison, James: see Chap. 6.

Madison's Journal of the Federal Convention (1840). The most accurate account of the Constitutional Convention[4] of 1787, a volume best known as Madison's Journal. The informal and extensive notes by James Madison[6] were kept secret and published four years after the death of the former President[6] and statesman[5].

majority, concurrent. The theory[3] of power[3] distribution set forth by John C. Calhoun[4] in his A Disquisition on Government (1850). Calhoun's theory of the concurrent majority was an argument for a power distribution designed to avoid centralized[3] and absolute majority[3] rule. To keep power in check, each portion of society[3] affected by government[3] should register its desires; then the various interests should concur in accepting or rejecting centralized proposals. Major interests should therefore be able to negate major proposals affecting them. Calhoun's immediate concern was in defending states'[4] rights against centralized control affecting the slavery issue and other southern interests. See also state (southern interpretation) sovereignty[4].

Manifest Destiny. The term used by expansionists[12] to signify that the western expansion of the U.S. across the North American continent was part of providential design. The height of feelings about Manifest Destiny came between 1845 and 1860. It was a major cause of the Mexican[12] War. It also led to increased social and political conflicts over the extension of slavery.

Marshall, John: see Chap. 8.

Mason-Dixon Line (1763–67). The popular designation of the dividing line between slave and free states[3] or territories[3]. Charles Mason and Jeremiah Dixon, two Englishmen, surveyed the line in 1763–67. The line became a popular symbol of the political and social divisions between

North and South during the *Civil*[4] *War*.

Mayflower Compact (1620). A written document of *government*[3] based on the *consent theory*[3] of government. The Compact, promulgated at Plymouth, Massachusetts, in 1620, is generally recognized as the earliest written document of government in the American *colonies*[4]. The document was written for the "general good of the Colony" and was the first American attempt at self-government. Earlier colonial governmental structures had been established and empowered by outside *authority*[3]. See also *Great*[4] *Fundamentals*.

Mayhew, Jonathan, 1720–66. The earliest American writer to develop a rational justification for *revolution*[3] against *governments*[3] that neglect the good of the people or that fail to recognize that legitimate *power*[3] rests on the consent of the governed. Mayhew's writings, especially Unlimited Submission and Non-Resistence to the Higher Powers (1750), placed *natural law*[8] over divine law and stressed that man possesses certain *inalienable rights*[3] which emanate from natural law. He admitted that good rulers should be obeyed, but felt that *tyrannical*[3] ones should be resisted. See also *consent theory*[3]; *divine right theory*[3].

Mecklenberg Declaration (1775). A declaration of independence of questionable authenticity, based on a series of *resolutions*[7] adopted in Mecklenberg County, North Carolina. The resolutions declared certain commissions of the British *government*[3] null and void. The work is frequently compared to the American *Declaration*[4] *of Independence*.

Missouri Compromise (1820). A series of measures passed by the *U.S. Congress*[4] in order to balance northern and southern interests threatening warfare over the institution of slavery. The Compromise brought Maine into the Union as a free *state*[3]; Missouri became a slave state; and the extension of slavery was prohibited north of the geographic line of 36° 30'. The restriction on the spread of slavery into *federal*[3] *territory*[3] was declared *unconstitutional*[3] in *Dred*[1] *Scott v. Sandford*, and the *Civil*[4] *War* was soon forthcoming.

Model State Constitution. A *state*[3] constitutional plan proposed by the *National*[11] *Municipal League* and regularly revised to meet the changing needs of the states. The *constitution*[3] is composed of basic *constitutional*[3] elements, and it suggests the use of a *unicameral*[7] *legislature*[7], a strong *executive*[6], a unified judiciary, the use of the *initiative*[3] and *referendum*[3], a flexible *amending*[3] process, *home*[11] *rule* for local *governments*[3], and the use of modern administrative techniques. See also *flexible constitution*[3].

Mount Vernon Convention (1785). A conference composed of commissioners from Virginia and Maryland which was called for discussions concerning navigation problems on the Potomac River. The meeting led to the *Annapolis*[4] *Convention of 1786*. See also *convention*[3].

national supremacy clause (Art. VI, Cl. 2). The provision within the *U.S. Constitution*[4] which declares that the Constitution, *laws*[8], and *treaties*[12] of the U.S. are the "supreme law of the land." The clause has been interpreted to mean that national laws passed within their appropriate sphere may override *state*[3] laws in conflict with national action. The clause does not specify who decides when there is a conflict over supremacy. The *U.S. Supreme*[8] *Court* early assumed such a role in the settlement of conflicts between national and state *power*[3]. See also *Cooper*[1] *v. Aaron*; *federal govern-*

ment[3]; *McCulloch[1] v. Maryland*; *Marbury[1] v. Maryland*; national[4] supremacy doctrine.

national supremacy doctrine. The doctrine developed through judicial interpretation and *civil war[12]*, which holds that the United States *government[3]* is itself a sovereign *power[3]* within its appropriate sphere of activities. The national government is not dependent upon a *delegation of authority[6]* from separate sovereign *states[3]*. The doctrine was in opposition to *theories[3]* of *states'[4]* rights. See also *Civil[12] War*; *federal government[3]*; *McCulloch[1] v. Maryland*; *state (constitutional) sovereignty[3]*; *Texas[1] v. White*.

Navigation Acts of 1651–1750. A series of economic regulations related to the American *colonies[4]*. The enforcement of the *acts[8]* after 1660 led to colonial dissatisfaction, which in turn led eventually to the *American Revolution[4]*. Nearly all of the measures were designed for the economic advantage of Britain or British merchants.

necessary and proper clause (Art. I, Sec. 8, Cl. 18). The provision within the *U.S. Constitution[4]* frequently referred to as the "elastic" or *implied powers[4]* clause. The clause permits the *U.S. Congress[4]* to "make all *laws[8]* which shall be necessary and proper for carrying into execution" the powers listed in clauses 1 through 17 of Article I, Section 8 of the Constitution. The clause has been broadly interpreted in developing the *powers[3]* of the *federal government[3]*. See also *liberal construction[4]*; *McCulloch[1] v. Maryland*.

New England Confederation (1643–84). The earliest colonial attempt to combine into some form of a governmental union. The New England Confederation was created for the purpose of defense against the Indians,

the French, and the Dutch. It was composed of Massachusetts Bay, Plymouth, Connecticut, and New Haven. Each *colony[4]* had two *representatives[7]* within the *organization[6]*. See also *confederate government[3]*.

New Harmony (1825–28). An unsuccessful *utopian[3]* communal experiment in Indiana based on the ideas of the British social reformer *Robert Owen[3]*. See also *collectivism[3]*; *socialism[3]*.

New Jersey Plan (1787). The small-*state[3]* plan presented at the *Constitutional Convention[4]* of 1787 by William Paterson of New Jersey. The plan was presented in opposition to the *Virginia[4] Plan*; it advocated a revision of the *Articles[4] of Confederation*, a *unicameral[7]* legislative body, a plural *executive[6]* elected by *Congress[4]* and without *veto[7]* power, and a national judiciary.

Northwest Ordinances (1784–87). Three measures passed by the American *Congress[4]* operating under the *Articles[4] of Confederation*. They granted certain rights and privileges to settlers in the Northwest Territory and established a method whereby new *states[3]* could enter the *confederate government[3]*. New states were to be admitted to the Union on an equal footing with the original 13 states, slavery was prohibited in the *territories[3]*, and designated public lands were set aside for educational purposes. The basic provisions were carried over into the *government[3]* of the United States of America under the *U.S. Constitution[4]*.

nullification. The doctrine that a *state[3]* within the *federal[3]* Union may declare a federal *law[8]* null and void and of no effect on the *citizens[3]* of a state making such a declaration. The doctrine, as formulated by *John C. Calhoun[4]*, resembled the earlier *theory[3]* of *interposition[4]*, in that it held that the national *government*[3] possessed only those *powers*[3] delegated to it by separate sovereign states. Federal laws interpreted as in violation of such a *delegation of authority*[6] need not be obeyed. South Carolina took such a stance with regard to the Tariff Acts of 1828 ("Tariff of Abominations") and 1832. See also *delegated powers*[4]; *state (southern interpretation) sovereignty*[4]; *Civil*[4] *War*.

Otis, James, 1725–83. One of the American *colonial*[4] writers challenging the British restrictive colonial *legislation*[7] of the 1760's and the author of The Rights of the British Colonies Asserted and Proved (1764). Otis argued that *government*[3] was based on *natural laws*[8], formalized through *compact*[3], clarified through *laws*[8] by men, and occasionally swept by *revolution*[3]. He believed that government was a trust designed to give man a good life. He also argued for colonial *representation*[7] in the British Parliament and for local taxes to be levied by local *legislators*[7]. See also *limited government*[3]; *parliamentary government*[3]; *representative government*[3]; *contract theory*[3].

Paine, Thomas, 1737–1809. The *colonial*[4] *revolutionary*[3] pamphleteer who wrote Common Sense (1776), which has been recognized as the publication most responsible for convincing the American colonists to revolt against English rule. Paine discussed the origin and nature of *government*[3], delineated between *society*[3] and government, and discussed *natural law*[8], *representation*[7], and human rights. He believed government arose because of man's wickedness and that *monarchy*[3] was an unnatural structure. After stressing colonial needs, he maintained that the colonists were both willing and able to wage a successful *war*[12] against Great Britain. After the *American Revolution*[4] Paine was rejected for the *radical*[3] view-

points he expressed in The Age of Reason (1792) and other works.

Paterson Plan (1787): see *New*[4] *Jersey Plan*.

Pinckney Plan (1787). A proposal presented at the *Constitutional Convention*[4] of 1787 which called for a *bicameral*[7] *legislature*[7] composed of one house selected by the people and a second house selected by members of the first, a *president*[3] elected by the legislature for a seven-year term of office, a national court of appeals, and a national legislative *power*[3] to approve or reject *acts*[8] of *state*[3] legislatures. See also *Courts*[8] *of Appeals* (U.S.).

political question. A judicially pronounced doctrine which holds that questions of a political nature are not "justiciable" within *federal*[3] courts, but are best left to other branches of *government*[3] for decision. The *Supreme*[8] *Court* has employed the doctrine when cases involved political controversy or presented problems of enforcement. Some of the more famous cases in which the doctrine has been used have involved the issues of *republican government*[3] within *states*[3], the *amending*[3] process, and state legislative *apportionment*[7]. See also *Coleman*[1] *v. Miller*; *Colgrove*[1] *v. Green*; *Luther*[1] *v. Borden*; *Pacific*[1] *States Telephone and Telegraph Co. v. Oregon*.

powers, concurrent. *Power*[3] or *authority*[3] which may be validly exercised over a particular subject area by more than one *government*[3] at a time. Within the United States *federal*[3] system, such things as taxation, *bankruptcy*[10], banking, and judicial action are concurrent powers.

powers, delegated (expressed, enumerated). *Power*[3] or *authority*[3] that is specifically given by *constitutional*[3] or legal action to a recognized *government*[3]. Within the United States *constitutional*[3] *system* the delegated powers are cited in the first three articles of the *U.S. Constitution*[4], especially in Article I, Section 8, Clauses 1 through 17. The delegated powers are clearly designed to limit government. Examples of such powers given to the *federal government*[3] are the power to tax, regulate commerce, establish post offices, declare *war*[12], and govern *territories*[3]. See also *commerce*[4] *clause*; *limited government*[3]; *taxing powers*[4]; *war* [12] *powers*.

powers, denied. *Power*[3] or *authority*[3] that may not be exercised by a specified *government*[3]. In the United States *constitutional*[3] *system* neither the central nor the *state*[3] governments may tax exports, grant titles of nobility, pass *ex*[9] *post facto laws*, or enact *bills of attainder*[9]. In other instances the states are denied power in areas specifically delegated to the national government, and the *federal government*[3] may not invade powers reserved to the states. See also *reserved powers*[4]; *export tax*[10].

powers, emergency. *Power*[3] or *authority*[3] that is not ordinarily exercised except during times of crisis. Emergency power is most frequently used during times of *war*[12], economic upheaval, and natural disaster. It may be used by the *President*[6] directly or conferred on him by the *Congress*[4], in some cases conferred retroactively. The *Supreme*[8] *Court* has declared that an emergency does not create power but that it may call forth the need for extraordinary use of power already in existence. Presidents *Lincoln*[6], *Wilson*[6], *Franklin Roosevelt*[6], and *Truman*[6] used extraordinary emergency powers during times of war. On some occasions the use of such powers was contested in the Supreme Court; presidential action was upheld in some cases and declared *unconstitutional*[3] in others. In cases where the power

was held unconstitutional, the decision was frequently made after the emergency was past. See also *Home*[1] *Building and Loan Assn. v. Blaisdell*; *retroactive legislation*[7]; *war*[12] *powers*; *Prize*[1] *Cases*; *Youngstown*[1] *Sheet and Tube Co. v. Sawyer*.

powers, exclusive. *Power*[3] or *authority*[3] that is specifically delegated to a *government*[3] which may not be exercised by any other governmental unit. In the United States *constitutional*[3] *system*, the central government has the exclusive power to print money, declare *war*[12], and conduct foreign relations. See also *federal government*[3]; *delegated powers*[4]; *war*[12] *powers*.

powers, implied. *Power*[3] or *authority*[3] that is not specifically expressed as belonging to a particular *government*[3], but which may be assumed to exist because of its close relationship to specifically *delegated powers*[4]. Since the United States *constitutional*[3] *system* gives the delegated powers to the central government in the *necessary*[4] *and proper clause* (Art. I, Sec. 8, Cl. 18), it indirectly gives the central government the implied powers. The principle of implied powers was officially accepted by the *Supreme*[8] *Court* in *McCulloch*[1] *v. Maryland*. Examples of implied powers are the chartering of a national bank, *drafting*[12] military personnel, and spending money on internal improvements. See also *Bank*[10] *of the United States*; *federal government*[3].

powers, inherent. *Power*[3] or *authority*[3] that is not specifically enumerated or derived through implication from *delegated powers*[4], but which exists as part of the nature of sovereignty. The *Supreme*[8] *Court* has recognized that the *federal government*[3] has the power to conduct foreign relations without a specific delegation of power. See also *diplomatic*[6] *powers*; *prerogative*[3]; *state (constitutional) sovereignty*[3]; *U.S.*[1] *v. Curtiss-Wright Ex-*

port Corp.; *Youngstown*[1] *Sheet and Tube Co. v. Sawyer.*

powers, police. *Power*[3] or *authority*[3] which may be used by a *government*[3] to regulate the personal activities of its *citizens*[3] for the public good. Within the United States *constitutional*[3] *system* the police powers belong to the *states*[3] as part of their *reserved powers*[4]. Under the police powers, each state has the power to promote the public health, safety, welfare, morals, and conveniences of its own citizens. Police powers must conform to both *federal*[3] and state *constitutional*[3] provisions, especially the requirements of *due*[9] *process of law* as outlined in the *U.S. Constitution*[4] (Amendment 5 and Amendment 14, Section 1). See also *resulting powers*[4]; *Lochner*[1] *v. N.Y.*; *Missouri*[1] *v. Holland*; *Muller*[1] *v. Oregon.*

powers, proprietary. The *power*[3] of a *government*[3] to engage in what is generally considered a business activity. Proprietary powers are most often used by local governments. It is frequently difficult to distinguish between purely governmental and proprietary activities. Items generally recognized as proprietary in nature are the operation of recreational facilities, utility services, and liquor outlets. See also *public*[10] *utility*; *South*[1] *Carolina v. United States.*

powers, reserved (residual). *Power*[3] or *authority*[3] that is not specifically enumerated within a written document of *government*[3], delegated to a specific government, or reasonably implied from powers which are delegated to a recognized government. Within the United States *constitutional*[3] *system* the reserved powers are granted to the *states*[3] by the *Tenth Amendment*[4] of the *Constitution*[4]. *Police powers*[4] are generally recognized as reserved powers belonging to the states. See also *delegated powers*[4]; *implied powers*[4]; *Massachusetts*[1] *v. Mellon*; *Missouri*[1] *v. Holland.*

powers, resulting. *Power*[3] or *authority*[3] evidenced from a combination of powers either enumerated or implied or developed from a combination of powers reserved to a *state*[3]. On the national level, the *war*[12] *power* is a combination of specifically *delegated powers*[4] given to both the legislative and *executive*[6] branches of *government*[3]. During times of crisis numerous powers "result" from the combination of powers in action. On the state level numerous *police powers*[4] may combine to operate in a specific area of concern and "result" in a concentration of power. See also *implied powers*[4].

powers, taxing. The *power*[3] which may be *constitutionally*[3] granted to *government*[3] to levy and collect taxes from the general population. The taxing power is normally based on the need to raise revenue for the general operation of government. However, taxes are frequently used as regulatory devices. The principal kinds of taxes permitted to the *federal government*[3] of the United States are *direct taxes*[10] and *indirect taxes*[10]. The first specifically *delegated power*[4] cited in Article I, Section 8, Clause 1 of the *U.S. Constitution*[4] is: "The Congress shall have the power to lay and collect taxes, duties, imposts, and excises, to pay the debts and provide for the common defense and general welfare of the United States; but all duties, imposts, and excises shall be uniform throughout the United States." See also *Sixteenth Amendment*[10]; *regulatory tax*[10].

preemption doctrine. The doctrine developed through judicial interpretation, which holds that the *federal government*[3], acting in permissible areas of *legislation*[7] also occupied by *state*[3] legislation, may present a condition whereby federal legislation becomes so pervasive as to leave no room for further state action. See also *interstate commerce*[10]; *intrastate commerce*[10]; *Pennsylvania*[1] *v. Nelson.*

privileges and immunities clauses
(Art. IV, Sec. 2, Cl. 1, and Amendment 14, Sec. 1). Two separate but related provisions within the *U.S. Constitution*[4]. The Article IV provision generally applies to an individual's relationship to the *federal*[3] Union. A *citizen*[3] of one *state*[3] visiting in another state is guaranteed the general rights afforded to the citizens of the host state. This means the right to cross state lines, to own *property*[10], to have access to courts, and to have legal protection. The *Fourteenth Amendment*[4] provision generally applies to the same kinds of things the *Fourth Amendment*[9] covers. It restricts arbitrary methods the state might use against U.S. citizens. However, the *Supreme*[8] *Court* has recognized a *dual citizenship*[3] and has narrowly interpreted both privileges and immunities clauses. The Court has never fully elaborated on either of the two clauses. For this reason they are sometimes referred to as "the forgotten clauses." See also *comity*[3]; *ingress*[4] and *egress*; *Slaughterhouse*[1] *Cases*.

Protestant Ethic. The religious, social, and *ideological*[3] pattern which dominates the life of the American people. Although the pattern is not based upon "pure" religious orthodoxy or active religious participation in Protestant Christianity, the pattern is dominated by an acceptance of God, a belief in the importance of church attendance, and acceptance of the Bible as a meaningful and inspired work of religion. The Protestant Ethic has greatly influenced American ideas of *natural law*[8], *democracy*[3], *Manifest*[4] *Destiny*, the dignity of the individual, the dignity of work, and the importance of social order. See also *John Calvin*[3]; *Martin Luther*[3]; *Max Weber*[6]; *Roger Williams*[4].

public domain. That which is available to general public use, such as *property*[10] belonging to the *community*[3] at large or material not protected by *patent*[10] or *copyright*[10]. Public

lands under the ownership of the U.S. government are part of the public domain. The land is composed of national parks, national forests, grazing land, Indian reservations, and *government*[3] installations of various types. Public lands are generally regulated by the *Department of the Interior*[2] and the *Department of Agriculture*[2].

Quartering Act of 1766. The English *act*[8] providing that British troops could be garrisoned in public inns and private homes at the American *colonists'*[4] expense if regular barracks were insufficient. See also *Intolerable*[4] *Acts of 1774*; *Townshend*[4] *Acts*.

Quebec Act of 1774. An English *statute*[8] which organized and enlarged the *territory*[3] of Quebec and recognized certain portions of French *law*[8] operating in the area. Such action recognized trials without *juries*[8] and political equality for Catholics. The *act*[8] also extended the newly organized territory over disputed territory claimed by Massachusetts, Connecticut, and Virginia. The American *colonists*[4] saw the act as a threat to their rights and liberties.

Randolph Plan (1787): see *Virginia*[4] *Plan*.

Reconstruction (1865–77). The period of U.S. history when the *federal government*[3] undertook to rebuild the Union, which had been torn by the *Civil*[4] *War*. Some of the major problems of Reconstruction were the transition from military to civil rule, the assimilation of former Negro slaves into a totally "free" society, and the rebuilding of a stable economic system. The period was dominated by conflict between the *Congress*[4] and the *President*[6] as to which branch of the federal government should lead in rebuilding the *nation*[3]. Major social problems were created by harsh "Radical Reconstruction" measures directed against former Confederate *states*[3] and officials, by the movement of northern "*carpetbaggers*"[5] into the South, and by southern attempts to evade full acceptance of the emancipation of the slaves. See also *black*[9] *code*; *Civil*[9] *Rights Act of 1866*; *Civil*[9] *Rights Act of 1875*; *Confederate*[4] *States of America*; *Emancipation*[9] *Proclamation*; *Scalawag*[5]; *Jim*[9] *Crow law*; *McCardle*[1], *Ex parte*; *Mississippi*[1] *v. Johnson*; *Texas*[1] *v. White*.

Revolution, American (1775–81). The *war*[12] *of rebellion*[3] between Great Britain and her 13 *colonies*[4] located on the North American continent. The war began at Lexington, Massachusetts on April 19, 1775, and the last major battle was fought at Yorktown, Virginia, on October 19, 1781. Basic causes of the conflict were political, economic, and *nationalistic*[3] as England allowed the colonies little self-*government*[3], as she unwisely taxed the colonists, and as the colonists began to think of themselves as a separate *nation*[3]. The war was officially ended with the *Treaty*[12] of Paris in 1783. See also *Navigation*[4] *Acts of 1651–1750*; *Tory*[4]; *Whig*[4].

Revolutionary Conservatives. A term used to describe the *majority*[3] of *delegates*[5] in attendance at the *Constitutional Convention*[4] *of 1787*, a group seeking revision of the political system without a social and economic *revolution*.[3] The group was led by *George Washington*[6], *John Adams*[6], *Benjamin Franklin*[4], *James Madison*[6], and *Alexander Hamilton*[4].

Revolutionary Radicals. A term used to describe those individuals who either *boycotted*[10] the *Constitutional Convention*[4] *of 1787* or who were unable to attend and who supported a total social and economic *revolution*[3]. *Thomas Paine*[4], Patrick Henry, and *Richard Henry Lee*[4] were usually classified as Revolutionary Radicals.

Revolution, Glorious: see *Glorious*[3] *Revolution*.

Roosevelt, Franklin D.: see Chap. 6.

Roosevelt, Theodore: see Chap. 6.

secession. The doctrine expressed by southern political leaders, especially *John C. Calhoun*[4], that *states*[3] within the *federal*[3] Union possessed the same sovereign *power*[3] to withdraw from the United States that they had in *ratifying*[3] the *U.S. Constitution*[4] and joining the Union. Southern states dissatisfied with federal action related to slavery, *tariffs*[10], and political *representation*[7] declared themselves to be seceded from the United States. Their action precipitated the *Civil*[4] *War*. After the *war*[12] the *U.S. Supreme*[8] *Court* declared secession an *unconstitutional*[3] and meaningless action. It did so in *Texas*[1] *v. White* in 1869, on the grounds that the Union is an "indissoluble" union composed of "indestructible" states.

Shays' Rebellion (1786–87). A violent debtor's uprising in western Massachusetts led by Daniel Shays and other veterans of the *American Revolution*[4] who had lost faith in a state *government*[3] dominated by *property*[10] and commercial interests. The rebellious debtors first expressed their grievances through *county*[11] *conventions*[3] and then turned to mob action against the civil courts trying debtor cases and criminal courts holding debtors for criminal actions. The *rebellion*[3] emphasized to *conservatives*[3] the need for a stronger central government to protect property interests. The rebellion convinced some that they should support the *constitutional*[3] changes advocated at the *Constitutional Convention*[4] *of 1787*.

Sons of Liberty (1765–66). An inter*colonial*[4] *organization*[6] of persons actively and violently engaged in opposition to the *Stamp*[4] *Act of 1765*. Numerous members of the secret and subversive Sons of Liberty destroyed the *property*[10] of tax collectors and eventually attended the *Stamp Act Congress*[4] (1765) to protest British taxation measures. Samuel Adams was one of the principal leaders of the Sons of Liberty.

sovereignty, national. The doctrine supported by *Daniel Webster*[4], *Abraham Lincoln*[6], and other northern *statesmen*[5] and writers prior to the *Civil*[4] *War*. The doctrine held that the United States possessed a life of its own before it divided into separate *states*[3] within the *federal*[3] Union. Therefore the Union was considered sovereign over the states because of its position relative to their creation. See also *state (constitutional) sovereignty*[3], *state (southern interpretation) sovereignty*[4]; *states'*[4] *rights*.

sovereignty, squatter (1854–61). The doctrine championed by *U.S. Senator*[7] Stephen A. Douglas, which held that the inhabitants of a *federal*[3] *territory*[3] could decide the slavery question for themselves. See also *Freeport*[4] *Doctrine*.

sovereignty, state (southern interpretation). The doctrine held by numerous southern *statesmen*[5] and writers prior to the *Civil*[4] *War*, which argued that the separate *states*[3] within the United States were sovereign before they joined the Union. Those states used that sovereignty to create a national *government*[3] of *delegated powers*[4]. If the central government violated its *authority*[3], then the separate states could nullify *federal*[3] *legislation*[7] affecting them or even *secede*[4] from the Union. See also *nullification*[4]; *national sovereignty*[4]; *state (constitutional) sovereignty*[3]; *states'*[4] *rights*.

Stamp Act of 1765. The English *act*[8] which levied the first *direct tax*[10] on the American *colonists*[4]. Taxes were imposed on newspapers, legal documents, pamphlets, playing cards, and other similar items sold in the *colonies*[4]. The act implied the creation of

ecclesiastical courts for the colonies, allowed for violators to be tried in *admiralty courts*[8], and levied heavy fines on violators. See also *Stamp Act Congress*[4]; *Sons*[4] *of Liberty*.

statehood admission. The *constitutional*[3] process of accepting new *states*[3] into the *federal*[3] Union known as the United States of America. The *U.S. Constitution*[4] makes provision (Art. IV, Sec. 3) for new states to enter the Union on an equal basis with previous states. General entrance procedures are for a *territory*[3] to petition the *Congress*[4] for admission, for Congress to pass an *enabling*[4] *act* permitting the territory to draft a *constitution*[3], for Congress to pass an *act*[8] of admission, and for the *President*[6] to proclaim that a new state has entered the Union. The Constitution declares that new states may not be "formed or erected within the *jurisdiction*[8] of any other State, nor any State be formed by the junction of two or more States or parts of States" without approval of the States involved. Vermont, Kentucky, Tennessee, Maine, and West Virginia were formed by separating from other states. Texas entered the Union through a *joint resolution*[7] of Congress and moved from the status of a *republic*[3] to that of a state. California entered the Union as a part of the Mexican Cession (1848) and the *Compromise*[4] *of 1850*. Congress has occasionally set prior conditions on statehood admission, but it has not been able to enforce all of them after states have entered the Union. See also *Coyle*[1] *v. Smith*; *Northwest*[4] *Ordinances*; *Stearns*[1] *v. Minnesota*.

states' rights. A *theory*[3] holding that *centralization*[3] of *power*[3] within the national *government*[3] of the United States violates sovereign power belonging to the separate *states*[3]. Advocates of states' rights have supported programs ranging from mere protest of centralization to outright *secession*[4]. Supporters of states' rights have emphasized such things as individual *property*[10] ownership, local control over public education, and rejection of conditional *grants-in-aid*[10]. See also *Hartford*[4] *Convention; federal government*[3]; *interposition*[4]; *Kentucky*[4] *and Virginia Resolutions; concurrent majority*[4]; *nullification*[4]; *state (southern interpretation) sovereignty*[4].

Taney, Roger Brooke: see Chap. 8.

tax immunity, intergovernmental. The doctrine that one governmental *jurisdiction*[8] within the U.S. cannot tax purely governmental agencies or properties of another governmental jurisdiction. The doctrine has been developed and modified primarily through judicial action. See also *Collector*[1] *v. Day; Graves*[1] *v. New York Ex Rel O'Keefe; Helvering*[1] *v. Gerhardt; McCulloch*[1] *v. Maryland; South*[1] *Carolina v. U.S.; Veazie*[1] *Bank v. Fenno.*

territory, incorporated. A United States *territory*[3] designated by the *Congress*[4] as capable of claiming only procedural and substantive *constitutional*[3] rights appertaining to regular *states*[3] within the Union. See also *procedural due*[9] *process; substantive due*[9] *process.*

territory, unincorporated. A United States *territory*[3] designated by the *Congress*[4] as capable of claiming only the substantive rights guaranteed by the *Constitution*[4]. Procedural rights such as trial by *jury*[8] may be delayed until statehood is granted or the area is listed as an *incorporated territory*[4]. See also *procedural due*[9] *process; substantive due*[9] *process.*

Thoreau, Henry David, 1817–62. The New England philosopher and author of the famous and influential volume entitled Civil Disobedience (1849). Thoreau's work was a polemic against the *federal government's*[3] support of the institution of slavery and its involvement in the *Mexican*[12] *War.* He viewed *government*[3] as a necessary evil created for the benefit of individuals. He believed that if government passed unjust *laws*[8] or acted in an evil way, then individuals had a moral duty to disobey the *state*[3]. His direct *civil*[9] *disobedience* took the form of nonpayment of taxes which Thoreau claimed were being used to support evil activities of the state. Civil Disobedience became the philosophical framework for Gandhi's "Satyagraha" in India's struggle for independence from Great Britain and for *Martin Luther King*[9] *Jr.'s* black *civil*[9] *rights revolution*[3] in the United States. Thoreau's influence has also been felt through his volume entitled Walden (1854), a philosophical treatise on rugged *individualism*[3].

three-fifths clause: see *Three-fifths*[4] *Compromise.*

Three-fifths Compromise (1787). The compromise agreed upon at the *Constitutional Convention*[4] *of 1787* which involved slavery, taxation, and *representation*[7]. It was decided that three-fifths of the slaves in each state would be counted in determining the *apportionment*[7] figures for each state's representation in the *U.S. House*[7] *of Representatives.* The same basis and the same figure would be used in levying *direct taxes*[10] within the separate states.

Tidelands Oil controversy. A complex dispute between the United States *government*[3] and the *states*[3] of California, Louisiana, Florida, and Texas over offshore oil reserves. In 1947 and 1950 the *Supreme*[8] *Court* ruled that the oil rights belonged to the *federal government*[3], even though the states were developing them. *President*[6] *Harry Truman*[6] *vetoed*[7] a *bill*[7] that would return the lands to the states. President Eisenhower campaigned partly on the tidelands issue, and signed the Submerged Lands (Tidelands Oil) Act in 1953, which returned to the states the mineral reserves under their historic *bounda-*

ries[12]. The *act*[8] recognized U.S. control over the outer fringes of the *continental*[3] shelf.

Tocqueville, Alexis de, 1805–59. The French historian who wrote Democracy in America (1835–40), one of the most perceptive analyses of American political and social institutions ever made by a foreigner. De Tocqueville traveled within the U.S. and analyzed *public opinion*[5], individual rights, religion, *law*[8], the press, industry, education, governmental structures— nearly every segment of American life. He believed the success of *democracy*[3] lay in the balance between *centralized*[3] and *decentralized*[3] government as established in the American *constitutional*[3] system. He visualized the U.S. as a world leader and industrial *power*[3]. He warned of democracy's excesses, internal threats to liberty through *majority*[3] *rule* conformity, and democratic inconsistencies. De Tocqueville believed that one of the greatest threats to American democracy lay in the institution of slavery within a system based on democratic principles. See also *Frederick Jackson Turner*[4]; *tyranny*[3] *of the majority*.

Tory (Loyalist). An English *political party*[5] name which was used to indicate American *colonial*[4] supporters of British *policies*[6]. Tories generally opposed the so-called *Whigs*[4], who supported the break from Great Britain during the *American Revolution*[4]. See also *Daniel Leonard*[4].

Townshend Acts of 1767. A series of English *acts*[8] which placed taxes on colonial imports such as lead, glass, paper, paint, and tea. A board of customs commissioners was created to enforce the acts. *Writs*[9] *of assistance* could be used, violators could be tried in *admiralty courts*[8] and tax collectors salaries were to be paid from fines collected from the colonists. The New York Assembly was to remain suspended under the *legislation*[7] until it agreed to comply with the *Quartering*[4] *Act of 1766*. See also *John Dickinson*[4]; *import tax*[10].

Truman, Harry S: see Chap. 6.

Turner, Frederick Jackson, 1861–1932. The American historian who popularized the "frontier theory of American life." Turner's article, entitled "The Significance of the Frontier in American History" (1893), was enlarged in a book entitled The Frontier in American History (1920). The major thesis of both works was that the existence of a frontier vitally affected the American character based on a *democratic*[3] philosophy. Turner held that the wilderness changed the European personality into an American personality, with its own democratic life style. He saw the frontier as a safety valve against social and political *tyranny*[3] and a stimulant for creative energy and inventiveness. See also *Homestead*[10] *Act of 1862*; *Alexis de Tocqueville*[4].

Virginia Plan (1787). The large-*state*[3] plan presented at the *Constitutional Convention*[4] *of 1787* by Edmund Randolph of Virginia. The plan, drafted primarily by *James Madison*[6], called for rejection of the *Articles*[4] *of Confederation* and the creation of a new national *government*[3], a *bicameral*[7] legislature with one house popularly elected and a second house chosen by the first, an *executive*[6] chosen by the *legislature*[7], a national judiciary, a national *veto*[7] on *state*[3] *legislation*[7], and a national *Council*[4] *of Revision* with *powers*[3] somewhat akin to *judicial*[4] *review*. See also *federal government*[3].

Warren, Earl: see Chap. 8.

Washington, D.C.: see District of Columbia[4].

Washington, George: see Chap. 6.

Webster, Daniel, 1782–1852. American *statesman*[5], renowned orator, U.S.

Senator[7] from Massachusetts, and U.S. Secretary of State. Webster is remembered for his legal defense of commercial and national interests in the *Supreme*[8] *Court* cases of *Dartmouth*[1] *College v. Woodward* and *McCulloch*[1] *v. Maryland,* his eloquent defense of the *federal*[3] Union in the *Webster-Hayne*[4] *Debates* (1830), his negotiations on the Webster-Ashburton *Treaty*[12] with Great Britain (1841), and his defense of the *Compromise*[4] *of 1850.* See also *national sovereignty*[4].

Webster-Hayne Debates (December 1829–January 1830). A series of debates in the *U.S. Senate*[7] between *Senator*[7] *Daniel Webster*[4] and Senator Robert Y. Hayne. Hayne defended *states'*[4] *rights* in general and the doctrine of *nullification*[4] in particular in his remarks on public lands and protective *tariffs*[10]. Senator Webster replied, eloquently defending the Union as a "creature of the people" rather than a *compact*[3] among sovereign *states*[3]. He closed his plea with the famous phrase: "Liberty and Union, now and forever, one and inseparable." See also *national sovereignty*[4]; *state (constitutional) sovereignty*[3]; *state (southern interpretation) sovereignty*[4].

Whig. An English *political party*[5] name which was used to indicate American *colonists*[4] who supported the *American Revolution*[4] against Great Britain. See also *Tory*[4].

Whiskey Rebellion (1794). A taxpayers' revolt in western Pennsylvania, which was viewed by national leadership as an attack on the *government*[3] of the United States in its attempts to collect an *excise tax*[10] on whiskey. Over 13,000 *federal*[3] militiamen were led by *Alexander Hamilton*[4] and visited in the field by *President*[6] *George Washington*[6]. Approximately

100 rebels were captured and two were sentenced to death. Washington eventually *pardoned*[6] those given the death sentence. Swift federal action during the *rebellion*[3] emphasized the determination of the new central government to enforce its *laws*[8].

Williams, Roger, 1604–83. A major *colonial*[4] religious leader and the founder of Rhode Island. Roger Williams is remembered as a leading religious *liberal*[3], partly because of his The Bloudy Tenent of Persecution, for Cause of Conscience (1644), which laid the framework for the idea of the separation of church and state. Williams opposed *theocratic*[3] *authoritarianism*[3], religious orthodoxy, colonial grants depriving Indians of land, religious qualifications for voting, and persecution for conscience's sake. In founding Rhode Island, Roger Williams put the *consent theory*[3] of *government*[3] into practice through the use of broad *suffrage*[5], frequent elections, a *unicameral*[7] *legislature*[7], the *initiative*[3], the *referendum*[3], the recall, the abolition of debtors' prison, the abolition of an established church, and widespread toleration in all areas of life. See also *wall*[9] *of separation doctrine; recall election*[5].

Wilson, Woodrow: see Chap. 6.

Wise, John, 1652–1729. The first American writer of *political*[3] *theory* to fully analyze the *contract theory*[3]. In A Vindication of the Government of New England Churches (1717), Wise spoke against increasingly *centralized*[3] control by the *theocratic*[3] government of the Presbyterians, led by Cotton and Increase Mather. The Presbyterians were seeking to overwhelm the Congregational churches of Massachusetts. Wise based his *theory*[3] of *government*[3] by *contract*[10] on *natural rights*[3] and *popular sovereignty*[3].

Supreme Court cases related to material in this chapter are arranged below by subject. Summaries of the cases are in Chapter One arranged alphabetically by the name of the first party in each case.

AMENDING PROCESS—
Coleman v. Miller (1939)
Hawke v. Smith (1920)

CITIZENSHIP—
Afroyim v. Rusk (1967)
Dred Scott v. Sandford (1857)
Fong Yue Ting v. U.S. (1893)
Passenger Cases (1849)
Perez v. Brownell (1958)
Trop v. Dulles (1958)
U.S. v. Wong Kim Ark (1898)

CONSTITUTIONAL RIGHTS—
Brown v. Board of Education of Topeka (1954)
Dred Scott v. Sandford (1857)

ECONOMY—(Contracts)
Charles River Bridge v. Warren Bridge (1837)
Dartmouth College v. Woodward (1819)
Fletcher v. Peck (1810)

ECONOMY—(Intergovernmental Tax Immunity)
McCulloch v. Md. (1819)

EXECUTIVE—
U.S. v. Curtiss-Wright Export Corp. (1936)
Youngstown Sheet & Tube v. Sawyer (1952)

FEDERALISM—(General)
Texas v. White (1869)

FEDERALISM—(Diversity of Citizenship)
Chisholm v. Ga. (1793)
Cohens v. Va. (1821)
Dred Scott v. Sandford (1857)
Erie Railroad v. Tompkins (1938)

FEDERALISM—(Full Faith and Credit)
Williams v. N.C. (1945)

FEDERALISM—(Implied Powers)
McCulloch v. Md. (1819)

FEDERALISM—(Inherent Powers)
U.S. v. Curtiss-Wright Export Corp. (1936)
Youngstown Sheet & Tube v. Sawyer (1952)

FEDERALISM—(Interstate Rendition)
Ky. v. Dennison (1861)

FEDERALISM—(National Supremacy)
McCulloch v. Md. (1819)

FEDERALISM—(Republican Government)
Luther v. Borden (1849)
Pacific States Telephone and Telegraph Co. v. Oregon (1912)

FEDERALISM—(Reserved Powers)
Ky. Whip and Collar Co. v. Ill. Central Railroad Co. (1937)
Missouri v. Holland (1920)
Pennsylvania v. Nelson (1956)

FEDERALISM—(Statehood Admission)
Coyle v. Smith (1911)
Stearns v. Minn. (1900)

FOREIGN POLICY AND DEFENSE—
Missouri v. Holland (1920)

Pennsylvania v. Nelson (1956)
U.S. v. Curtiss-Wright Export Corp. (1936)
Youngstown Sheet & Tube v. Sawyer (1952)

JUDICIAL REVIEW—(General)
Ableman v. Booth (1859)
Ashwander v. TVA (1936)
McCardle, Ex parte (1869)
Marbury v. Madison (1803)
Martin v. Hunter's Lessee (1816)

JUDICIAL REVIEW—(Diversity of Citizenship)
Chisholm v. Ga. (1793)
Cohens v. Va. (1821)
Dred Scott v. Sandford (1857)
Erie Railroad v. Tompkins (1938)

JUDICIAL REVIEW—(Political Question)
Baker v. Carr (1962)
Coleman v. Miller (1939)
Colgrove v. Green (1946)
Luther v. Borden (1849)
Pacific States Telephone & Telegraph Co. v. Ore. (1912)

LEGISLATIVE APPORTIONMENT—
Avery v. Midland Co. (1968)
Baker v. Carr (1962)
Colgrove v. Green (1946)
Reynolds v. Sims (1964)
Wesberry v. Sanders (1964)

Chapter 5

Political Dynamics

Note to the reader: Cross-referenced terms are in italics. The superscript number refers to the chapter in which the entry may be found. In addition, its placement indicates the word under which the term is alphabetized. (For example, in *electoral*[4] *college*, information on the electoral college may be found in Chapter 4 under "electoral.") Because italics are used in cross-references, they are not used for terms in which they would ordinarily be used: Supreme Court cases and titles of books, journals, plays, and so forth.

> *Supreme Court cases relating to material in this chapter are listed at the end of the chapter (see page 146).*

Amendment, Fifteenth (1870). The *amendment*[3] to the *U.S. Constitution*[4] which prohibits a *state*[3] from denying the right to vote to any person on the basis of race, color, or previous condition of servitude. See also *Gomillion*[1] *v. Lightfoot*; *grandfather*[5] *clause*; *Guinn*[1] *v. U.S.*; *Smith*[1] *v. Allwright*; *South*[1] *Carolina v. Katzenbach*.

Amendment, Lodge-Gossett (1948). A proposed *amendment*[3] to the *U.S. Constitution*[4] which would have reformed the method of electing the *U.S. President*[6]. Electors would be eliminated, *electoral votes*[5] would be assigned to candidates in relation to *popular votes*[5] received within the separate *states*[3], and a *plurality*[3] of at least 40 percent of the vote would be sufficient for victory. See also *electoral*[4] *college*.

Amendment, Nineteenth (1920). The *amendment*[3] to the *U.S. Constitution*[4] which gave women the right to vote. See also *suffragette*[5].

Amendment, Twelfth (1804). The *amendment*[3] to the *U.S. Constitution*[4] which changed the *electoral*[4] *college* system and placed the presidential and vice-presidential candidates on the same ballot as a team. Article 2, Section 3 of the Constitution originally allowed for the candidate with the highest number of *electoral votes*[5] to be *President*[6] and the candidate with the second highest number of votes to be the *Vice-President*[6]. The Twelfth Amendment was added to the Constitution to avoid the kind of deadlock that developed in 1800 when *Thomas Jefferson*[6] and Aaron Burr received the same number of votes. See also *electoral*[4] *college*; *Revolution*[5] *of 1800*.

Amendment, Twenty-fourth (1964). The *amendment*[3] to the *U.S. Constitution*[4] which prohibits the use of a *poll tax*[5] in elections involving *federal*[3] officials. In essence, the amendment applied only to the *states*[3] of Alabama, Arkansas, Mississippi, Texas, and Virginia. The attempt to use poll taxes in elections involving only state officials was declared *un-constitutional*[3] in 1966 in the *Supreme*[8] *Court* case of *Harper*[1] *v. Virginia State Board of Elections.*

Amendment, Twenty-sixth (1971). The *amendment*[3] to the *U.S. Constitution*[4] which established 18 as the standard voting-age qualification throughout the U.S. for both *federal*[3] and *state*[3] elections. See also *18-year-old*[5] *vote; Oregon*[1] *v. Mitchell.*

Amendment, Twenty-third (1961). The *amendment*[3] to the *U.S. Constitution*[4] which gave *citizens*[3] within the *District of Columbia*[4] the right to vote in presidential elections.

American Association of University Professors (AAUP), 1915– . An *organization*[6] designed to advance the interests of the academic profession. The AAUP has engaged at all levels in influencing public *policy*[6] related to professional standards, ethics, *academic*[9] *freedom*, faculty compensation, and *government*[3] support of higher education.

American Bar Association (ABA), 1878– . A national *organization*[6] composed of members of the legal profession. The ABA is separate from *state*[3] and local bar associations and actively seeks *legislation*[7] favorable to the legal profession. It generally supports *conservative*[3] social and economic *policies*[6] and works closely with the U.S. *Department of Justice*[2] and the *Senate*[7] *Committee*[8] *on the Judiciary* in screening prospective *federal*[3] judges. See also *Conference*[11] *of Commissioners on Uniform State Laws.*

American Civil Liberties Union (ACLU), 1920– . An *organization*[6] dedicated to the proposition that the U.S. *Bill*[4] *of Rights* applies to all *citizens*[3] in the U.S. regardless of race, religion, *politics*[3], or economic circumstances. The ACLU is a *liberal*[3], per-manent, national, and *nonpartisan*[5] legal advisory agency and has been highly visible to the public because of its defense of various persons, groups, and causes considered unpopular or subversive of *majority*[3] beliefs and practices. Among such issues have been *civil*[9] *rights* related to labor, race, religion, education, *immigration*[3], voting, and *due*[9] *process of law.*

American Farm Bureau Federation (AFBF), 1919– . The largest and most *conservative*[3] farm *organization*[6] in the U.S. The AFBF grew out of separate *county*[3] bureaus which arose between 1912 and 1914 to provide a local base for *cooperative*[10] agricultural extension programs provided under the Smith-Lever Act of 1914. The AFBF still works closely with the U.S. Agricultural Extension Service. It supports trade and marketing programs favorable to agriculture, agricultural research programs, and agricultural education programs. In recent years the organization has placed major emphasis on efficient farm management, which has frequently favored *corporate*[10] farms over family-type farms. It has also opposed mandatory production controls. See also *price*[10] *support program.*

American Federation of Labor and Congress of Industrial Organizations (AFL-CIO), 1955– . The largest labor *organization*[6] in the U.S. The labor federation was formed through the *merger*[10] of the AFL and CIO in 1955. The AFL was founded in 1886 on the basis of crafts, and the CIO was founded in 1935 by AFL affiliates seeking to unionize mass-production industries. The AFL dissidents were expelled in 1937, but the two separate groups reunited in 1955. The *constituent*[5] *labor*[10] *unions* of the federation actively *lobby*[5] at all levels in an effort to gain publicity and promote the cause of labor. The AFL and the CIO supported *New*[6] *Deal legislation*[7], have consistently supported liberal[3] Democratic Party[5] candidates and policies[6], and have recently evidenced support of civil[9] rights legislation. The political arm of the AFL-CIO, which is used to financially assist candidates friendly to labor, is the Committee[5] on Political Education (COPE).

American Federation of Teachers (AFT), 1916– . An educational labor[10] union affiliate of the AFL-CIO. The organization[6], which became most vocal in the 1960's, is generally viewed as the most radical[3] teacher organization because of its use of the strike[10] to achieve its objectives related to professional participation in policy[7] formulation, salary, and working conditions. The AFT is located primarily in the major urban[11] centers on the East and West coasts.

American Institute of Public Opinion (AIPO), 1935– : see Gallup poll[5].

American Jewish Committee, 1916– . A community[3] relations organization[6] founded in the U.S. for the specific purpose of defending religious, political, and civil[9] rights of all people in the United States. It emphasizes the religious and cultural heritage of Judaism in the U.S. and seeks support for the nation[3] of Israel.

American Legion, 1919– . The largest U.S. serviceman's organization[6], the Legion is a conservative[3] voluntary association composed of honorably discharged servicemen. It has been a primary supporter of strong national defense measures, veterans rehabilitation, the draft[12], Veterans[2] Administration, G.I.[12] Bill of Rights, benefits for veteran's children, and youth and Americanism programs. The Legion has been a major supporter of servicemen serving during the Korean[12] War and Vietnam[12] War.

American Medical Association (AMA), 1847– . The major organi-

zation[6] promoting the medical profession in the U.S. The AMA is a federation[3] of state[3] organizations and is active in research, publication, data collection, legal assistance, and other related activities. It works for political benefits through the American[5] Medical Political Action Committee (AMPAC). The AMA supports uniform state laws[8] regulating medical licenses and practices, pure food and drug laws, and laws regarding the activities of paramedical practitioners and medical quacks. The conservative[3] organization was fairly progressive until 1920; since then it has opposed federal[3] infant, maternal, and veterans care. It has also opposed federal subsidies[10] to hospitals, private group hospitalization plans, Medicare[11], Medicaid[11], socialized medicine[11], and other social insurance[11] programs. It has been an extremely conservative organization but, at the same time, it has been one of the major contributors to scientific advances in medical science. See also Pure[11] Food and Drug Act of 1906.

American Medical Political Action Committee (AMPAC). The political arm of the powerful American[5] Medical Association. The organization[6] is one of the wealthiest political action groups in the U.S. It is also one of the most conservative[3]. It has opposed various federal[3] health care programs, private group hospitalization plans, and other "inroads into socialized medicine"[11]. AMPAC generally supports Republican Party[5] candidates, although it gives political campaign contributions to any candidate supporting its objectives. In the congressional elections of 1970 the organization distributed almost $700,000 to separate state[3] AMPAC affiliates, to be spent on support for selected candidates.

American Political Science Association (APSA), 1903– . The largest professional organization[6] of political scientists in the U.S. The association is composed of university faculty members, public officials, *government*[3] researchers, and others interested in the discipline of *political*[3] *science*. It seeks to stimulate the impartial research of political science through the regular publication of the American Political Science Review. The APSA prepares reports for the *Congress*[4] and other groups, conducts a Congressional Fellowship Program, and publishes special volumes such as *Toward*[5] *A More Responsible Two-Party System* (1950), Nation-Building (1963), and Political Theory and Social Change (1967). The APSA seeks to remain an impartial, *nonpartisan*[5] observer of the governmental process, but on various occasions has recommended structural changes and reforms in governmental institutions and practices. See also *Robert Dahl*[11]; *V. O. Key*[5]; *E. Schattschneider*[5].

Americans for Democratic Action (ADA), 1947– . A *nonpartisan*[5] organization which is generally dominated by *liberal*[3] political leaders, university professors, and *labor*[10] *union* officials. The *organization*[6] contributes to the campaigns of liberal candidates and seeks to influence *legislation*[7] through educational efforts, legislative testimony, and organized *lobbying*[5].

American Society for the Prevention of Cruelty to Animals (ASPCA), 1866– . The first humane society established in the U.S., an *organization*[6] dedicated to the legal and humane protection of animals. The ASPCA *lobbies*[5] for regulations related to animal research, slaughtering practices, animal theft, and other similar areas.

The American Voter: see *Survey*[5] *Research Center*.

Anti-Saloon League of America, 1895– . A U.S. temperance *organization*[6] presently known as the National Temperance League. The *league*[3] was formed to combat the manufacture and consumption of alcoholic beverages. Its basic program rests on education, *legislation*[7], and *law*[8] enforcement. It was the major organization responsible for the passage of the so-called Prohibition Amendment, the *Eighteenth Amendment*[4] to the *U.S. Constitution*[4]. See also *Prohibition Party*[5].

availability. The status of being suitable or acceptable for office, a condition generally based on criteria separate from proper legal and *constitutional*[3] qualifications. Availability normally includes personal life, geography, religious affiliation, party acceptability, and any other informal qualifications considered by a given electorate at a given time.

backlash. A word coined during the presidential election of 1964 by Eliot Janeway, an economic writer in New York City, to describe the condition which might arise if white blue-collar workers were forced to compete with black blue-collar workers for jobs during an economic *recession*[10]. The term used by Janeway was that the white workers might "lash back" at Negroes who were in competition with them. The term was also used to point out possible political reactions to such competition. See also *American Independent Party*[5].

ballot, Australian. A ballot form introduced in the U.S. in 1888, which is presently used throughout the *country*[3] in one form or another. The major characteristics of the ballot are that it: is printed at *government*[3] expense, lists all candidates, is cast secretly, is available only at the voting booth, and usually allows for write-in candidates. The major forms of the Australian ballot used in the U.S. are the *party-column (Indiana) ballot*[5] and the *office-block (Massachusetts) ballot*[5]. See also *write-in vote*[5].

ballot, long. An electoral form or ballot which lists many positions to be filled or issues to be decided. See also *short ballot*[5].

ballot, office-block (Massachusetts). A ballot form on which the names of all candidates for a particular office are listed under the office title. Listings are made under various titles regardless of the various party affiliations of the candidates. The office-block ballot tends to encourage *split ticket*[5] voting because voters cannot vote for a single slate of political officials by *political party*[5] label by simply marking one spot on the ballot. See also *Australian ballot*[5]; *party-column ballot*[5].

ballot, party-column (Indiana). A ballot form on which the names of all candidates of each *political party*[5] are placed in separate columns under party names and symbols, regardless of the offices sought by the candidates. The party-column ballot encourages *straight ticket*[5] voting because *states*[3] using such a ballot permit voters to select all the candidates of one party by marking in a single place on the ballot. See also *Australian ballot*[5]; *office-block ballot*[5].

ballot, short. An electoral form or ballot containing relatively few offices to be filled or issues to be decided. High officials chosen through a short ballot are generally empowered to fill numerous offices through the *appointment*[6] process. See also *long ballot*[5].

Barnburners, 1843–48. A *radical*[3] element of the *Democratic Party*[5] in New York which opposed the *Hunkers*[5], a *conservative*[3] group of New York Democrats who gave the Barnburners their name. The Barnburners were named after the legendary Dutch farmer who burned his barn to get rid of the rats. The political implication of the name was that such persons would destroy *corporations*[10] and *public*[10] *works* in order to clean up the corruption within them.

Bentley, Arthur, 1870–1957. Sociologist, political scientist, editorial writer, businessman, author, and political activist who authored one of the first American political studies based on behavioral research methods. Bentley's volume, The Process of Government (1908), analyzed basic human interests, complex human patterns, and environmental determinants of human behavior. Bentley was especially fascinated in his theoretical work with social action, group pressures, and complex variables involving *legislation*[7], *lobbying*[5], *executive*[6] action, and judicial interpretations. He emphasized the *organization*[6] of *minority*[3] power and special interests in the *democratic*[3] process, as well as how such pressures tend to defeat general welfare and social needs. He *theorized*[3] that legislation issues more from specific conflicts between competing interests than from *ideological*[3] or conceptual commitments. He stressed that a major protection for the democratic process is the fact that many interests compete for *power*[3] and no one interest can permanently control *government*[3]. See also *environmental determinism*[3]; *pressure*[5] *group*; *behavioral political*[3] *science*.

bipartisan (bipartisanship). National, international, or other policy-making processes which involve two parties working together. Bipartisanship ordinarily involves suspension of criticism of one another, mutual understanding of a desired objective of benefit to both *parties*[5] or the *nation*[3], and a unified front which is presented to the general public or foreign nations.

Black Muslims (Nation of Islam in North America), 1930– . An independent American black *nationalist*[3] *organization*[6] structured along the lines of the traditional Eastern Islamic religion. The group stresses black superiority, racial pride, racial *segregation*[9], and black independence in a separate *nation*[3] within the *bounda-ries*[12] of the present United States. The Chicago-based Black Muslims have been dominated by Elijah Poole who is better known as Elijah Muhammed.

Black Panthers, 1966– . A militant, *nihilistic*[3] black *organization*[6] started in Oakland, California. The group's early philosophical leaders were Stokely Carmichael and H. Rap Brown of the *Student*[5] *Non-Violent Coordinating Committee.* Among the early organizers of the group were Huey Newton and Bobby Seale. By 1970 Carmichael and Brown had fled the U.S. because of their violent activities directed against the white *community*[3]. Seale and other leaders were in prison on various charges, some of them involving the murder of other black militant leaders vying for *power*[3]. The Black Panthers were active during several race riots of 1967, gained some attention as a *radical*[3] *minor party*[5] in some *states*[3] during the presidential election of 1968, and became less radical between 1970 and 1973. See also *black*[9] *power.*

boss. A person who heads a political *machine*[5] and who manipulates political *power*[3] in a particular area (*state*[3], *county*[11], *city*[11], etc.), especially through the use and control of *patronage*[6], influence over administrative agencies, electoral manipulation, exploitation of public funds, domination of legislative leadership, and other questionable political tactics.

cabal. A private association or *party*[5] engaged in secret political intrigues.

campaign. A series of political maneuvers on the part of a *political party*[5] or a candidate seeking to capture political offices through the winning of support of those capable of bestowing political *power*[3]. Campaign styles and tactics vary considerably according to numerous variables such as candidate personality, economic re-

sources, time, region, and party strength.

carpetbagger. An opportunistic *politician*[5] who moves from one area to another in order to gain political *power*[3] or financial advantage. The term was coined to describe northern, *radical*[3] politicians who moved to the South during the chaotic conditions of *Reconstruction*[4]. See also *scalawag*[5].

caucus. A confidential and closed meeting of *political party*[5] leaders who decide questions of *policy*[6], leadership, choice of candidate, and other party business. The caucus may be used by party members either inside or outside a legislative body. See also *caucus*[7] *(conference)*; *congressional caucus*[5]; *King Caucus*[5]; *mixed (mongrel) caucus*[5].

caucus, congressional. The term used to describe the form of *caucus*[5] used to nominate presidential candidates before the fall of what was known as *King Caucus*[5] around 1824 and before the introduction of the national nominating *party convention*[5] by the *Anti-Masonic Party*[5] in 1831. The congressional caucus of each *party*[5] was a closed meeting of party members who were members of the *legislature*[7] and who took it upon themselves to nominate candidates for public office. See also *mixed caucus*[5].

Caucus, King. The term used to describe the significant position of the *caucus*[5] during early U.S. history. Nomination by *party*[5] caucus dominated the political scene until the period between 1824 and 1828, when *Andrew Jackson*[6] attacked it as an undemocratic device. Jackson had been denied nomination for the presidential office by the congressional *Democratic Party*[5] caucus of 1824. In 1831 the *Anti-Masonic Party*[5] introduced the *party convention*[5] for making nominations. It soon replaced the caucus as a means of nominating candidates for public office. See also *congressional caucus*[5]; *mixed caucus*[5].

caucus, mixed (mongrel). A private meeting of *political party*[5] members selected from both a legislative body and *party conventions*[5]. Such a *caucus*[5], formerly used in some *states*[3], was designed to nominate candidates for public office. The mixed caucus came into being in order to assure that faithful party members would be nominated and, at the same time, overcome public criticism of nominations made strictly by party leaders within a *congressional caucus*[5] operating inside a *legislature*[7]. See also *King Caucus*[5].

chairman, party. The presiding officer and primary party figure of a particular level of *political party*[5] machinery. Since the U.S. party system is *decentralized*[3] the *chairman*[7] of each level is chosen in a manner prescribed by the party structure at his level and is empowered with duties of a particular nature. Party chairmen range from *bosses*[5] of political *machines*[5] to figureheads and political window-dressing. The principal job of a chairman at any level is the management of an election in such a way as to enhance the *power*[3] of the party and thus capture public offices. The national chairman is ostensibly chosen by the national *party convention*[5]. In reality, he is chosen by the party's presidential candidate. If the party candidate becomes *U.S. President*[6], the chairman serves at the new party leader's pleasure. If the party candidate is defeated the chairman may find his actions controlled primarily by the national *party committee*[5]. The chairman is charged with raising campaign funds, building the party image, and spearheading the election drive.

challenge. A charge by a poll watcher that a person casting his vote in a *primary*[5] or *general election*[5] is doing so in violation of *political party*[5] regulations, state *statutes*[8], or *federal*[3] con-

stitutional[3] or statutory provisions. A *bipartisan*[5] group of election officials is usually provided in states permitting challenges. The *Civil*[9] *Rights Act of 1964* and the *Voting*[5] *Rights Act of 1965* permit federal officials of the *Department of Justice*[2] to assist voters kept from participating in an election through the use of *unconstitutional*[3] challenges on the part of *state*[3] and local officials. A challenge may also be used to question the fairness of selection of convention *delegations*[5]. Challenges are generally dealt with by the credentials committee of a *party convention*[5]. See also *Mississippi Freedom Democratic Party*[5]; *South*[1] *Carolina v. Katzenbach*.

Chamber of Commerce of the United States, 1912– . A *federation*[3] of business *organizations*[6] within the U.S. The Chamber of Commerce contains *state*[3] and local organizations, trade associations, and other business groups. It is the major business organization actively seeking to influence *government*[3] with regard to broad national *policy*[6] related to business. The Chamber of Commerce generally supports free competitive enterprise, opposes *union*[10] *shop* arrangements, supports state regulation of business and industrial activities, and supports tax reductions. In the past, the *conservative*[3] organization has opposed various social and labor reforms such as compulsory medical insurance programs. See also *free*[10] *enterprise*; *Medicare*[11]; *socialized medicine*[11].

charisma. An uncommon and highly individualistic quality of personality which captures the popular imagination and inspires devotion and unswerving obedience among a large number of people.

Civil Rights Act of 1964: see Chap. 9.

coalition. A combination or temporary *alliance*[12] of *political parties*[5] or *factions*[3] united for some specific purpose. In *multi-party*[5] *systems* it is nearly always necessary to form a *coalition government*[5] composed of members of various parties in order to institute a program of *government*[3].

committee, congressional campaign. A *party committee*[5] within the *Congress*[4] designed to raise funds and lend support to the reelection of congressional candidates. Congressional campaign committees are located in both houses of the national Congress. The *Republican Party*[5] began to use such a committee in 1866 and the *Democratic Party*[5] in 1882. Congressional campaign committees are especially active in *off-year elections*[5]; they generally concentrate their efforts in areas where they have the best chance of winning seats for their *political party*[5].

Committee on Political Education (COPE), 1947– . The political action committee of the *AFL-CIO*[5]. The *organization*[6] exhibits a continuing interest in public *policies*[6] and, among all the "independent" political action organizations, is the most effectively organized occupational group working toward political ends. The union agency is most powerful in assisting the campaigns of candidates sympathetic to labor. Although COPE supports candidates of either *political party*[5], in modern times it has most frequently supported *liberal*[3] members of the *Democratic Party*[5]. COPE began in 1947 as Labor's Educational and Political League and was renamed and reorganized after the *merger*[10] of the AFL-CIO in 1955.

committee, party. A group of individuals within a *political party*[5] charged with providing leadership for party activities. Committee structure and responsibility varies greatly according to party design, location, and countless other factors. Some committees are functional, well financed, and powerful. Other committees are mere figureheads, poorly financed, and powerless. The national committee of each of the two major parties is composed of one man and one woman from each *state*[3], the Virgin Islands, and Puerto Rico. The *Republican Party*[5] adds members to its national committee on the basis of several factors indicating Republican strength within particular states. The primary job of a national committee in either party is the selection of a site for the next national *party convention*[5]. State committees resemble national committees, but rarely possess any real *power*[3]. They are dominated by key party figures within the states. *County*[11] and *precinct*[5] committees seldom function except during the few weeks prior to an election. They are also dominated by a few individuals. See also *iron*[3] *law of oligarchy*.

Common Cause, 1970– . A "citizen's lobby" founded and led by former Secretary of the *Department of Health*[2], *Education and Welfare* John Gardner. The *liberal*[3] and allegedly *nonpartisan*[5] *organization*[6] supports reforms in congressional structures and procedures, military spending, the urban society, and other areas.

Congress of Racial Equality (CORE), 1942– . A national interracial federation of *organizations*[6] dedicated to securing *civil*[9] *rights* for Negroes through direct nonviolent action. The organization, founded by James Farmer of the Fellowship of Reconciliation, began as a northern *urban*[11] movement to aid Negroes. It uses public relations campaigns, *lobbying*[5], petitions, *public opinion polls*[5], and direct action. It helped develop the *sit-in*[9], stand-in, *freedom*[9] *ride*, racial *boycott*[10], and the racial *picket*[10]. CORE has sought to change attitudes and *laws*[8] which *discriminate*[9] against black people in the U.S.

constituency. A *legislative district*[7] from which an individual or group of individuals is chosen with the charge to act in a public fashion on behalf of the persons residing within the district. The persons within the district, or the district itself, may be considered the constituency of a *legislator*[7]. See also *constituent*[5]; *constituent power*[7]; *representative*[7].

constituent. A person represented in an assembly by an elected official serving a *legislative district*[7]. See also *constituency*[5]; *legislator*[7]; *constituent power*[7]; *representative*[7].

convention: see Chap 3.

convention, party. An assembly of official *delegates*[5] representing a *political party*[5] in the discharge of some official duty such as the choice of party candidates, the adoption of *platform*[5] statements, or the selection of delegates to represent the party at a higher-level meeting. The basic convention closest to the general party supporter and voter is the precinct convention. A precinct convention is usually quite small, is dominated by the *chairman*[7] (captain), and is used to choose delegates to a higher-level party convention. County or *congressional district*[7] conventions are composed of delegates selected at a lower level who choose delegates and adopt platform statements destined for the state *convention*[3]. State conventions determine state party rules, adopt platform statements, and choose delegates to the national convention. In some cases state conventions may pledge their delegates to a *favorite*[5] *son* (in 1972 the *Democratic Party*[5] outlawed this) or to an acknowledged candidate for *U.S. President*[6]. The national convention is the highest party organ and is responsible for choosing presidential and vice-presidential candidates and adopting a national party platform. The *Anti-Masonic Party*[5] used the first national nominating convention to nominate a candidate for President in 1832 (the meeting was conducted at Baltimore, Maryland, on September 26, 1831). Delegates and alternates to modern conventions are chosen by party primaries or party conventions within the separate states and under existing state *laws*[8]. The parties within the states are permitted to choose their slates of delegates generally on the basis of *electoral*[4] *college* or congressional *delegation*[5] strength, plus bonus votes for states supporting the separate parties' candidates in the last presidential election. Candidates in both major party conventions are nominated by an *absolute majority*[3] vote of officially seated delegates. See also *legislative*[7] *delegation*; *direct primary*[5]; *Walker*[8] *Report*.

convention, preprimary. A *party convention*[5] within a *state*[3] which is conducted prior to a *primary*[5] election. Such a convention may choose party candidates and adopt *platform*[5] statements. However, in some cases, a major nominee may choose to wait for primary election results to determine whether to accept a preprimary convention nomination. In this fashion he may have a view of both *political party*[5] and general electoral support before actively campaigning against the candidates of other parties.

convention, rump. A splinter or protest group which conducts its own unofficial *convention*[3] and selects *delegates*[5] to a higher *party convention*[5] in hopes that its actions will later be accepted by an authoritative *party*[5] meeting or party officials.

county-unit system. A system of weighted voting used in the *Democratic Party*[5] *primary*[5] elections of Georgia before 1963. The system allotted a set number of electoral units to each *county*[11] (2, 4, or 6) and during a statewide election gave all units to the candidate gaining a *plurality*[3] within the county. The system gave the statewide nomination to the candidate winning the largest number of units from all counties. The county-unit system actually violated the idea of *proportional representation*[5] based on population and was held to be in violation of the *one-man*[5], *one-vote* rule in the *Supreme*[8] *Court* case of *Gray*[1] *v. Sanders*, the first decision to declare an *act*[8] of *state*[3] legislative *apportionment*[7] *unconstitutional*[3] after the Court had held such issues to be *justiciable*[4]. See also *Baker*[1] *v. Carr*; *unit*[5] *rule*.

cross-filing. An election *filing*[5] process which permits a candidate to enter more than one *primary*[5] election at the same time. Generally, such a process requires that the candidate must win the nomination of his own *political party*[5] before he can accept the nomination of another party. If the candidate is successful in winning joint nominations through such a procedure, he will have no opposition in the *general election*[5]. The state of California used the most famous system of cross-filing between 1914 and 1959.

crossover voting: see *raiding*[5].

cross pressures. Psychological or emotional factors within a voter which create contrasting feelings about electoral participation. The voter may strongly like certain characteristics of a candidate or a *political party*[5] *platform*[5] but at the same time be violently opposed to other characteristics. See also *The People's*[5] *Choice*; *political*[5] *ambivalence*.

dark horse. An unexpected compromise candidate who is nominated for office by a *political party*[5] after a series of deadlocks over more conspicuous contenders. At the presidential level, some dark horses have been James K. Polk (1840), Franklin Pierce (1852), James Garfield (1880), and Warren Harding (1920).

delegate. A person authorized or sent to act for others within a *constituent*[5] assembly or political *convention*[3]. See also *constituency*[5]; *delegation*[5]; *instructed delegate*[5]; *delegate legislator*[7].

delegate, instructed. A *convention*[3] member directed by his *constituents*[5] to vote for particular candidates or measures. See also *constituency*[5]; *delegate*[5]; *delegation*[5].

delegation. A group of individuals representing an *organization*[6] or association and acting on behalf of the larger body in making decisions and seeking to fulfill objectives sought by the organization. *Political parties*[5] select *delegates*[5] at various levels to represent the party at higher-level meetings which culminate in the national nominating *party convention*[5]. Another obvious use of delegations is found when the *U.S. House*[7] *of Representatives* is required to select a *President*[6] from the top three contenders for the office. When there is no clear *majority*[3] vote for a candidate's name before the *electoral*[4] *college*, the *representatives*[7] from the various *states*[3] vote as separate state delegations and each state casts one vote for its choice for President. See also *constituency*[5]; *constituent*[5]; *instructed delegate*[5]; *legislative*[7] *delegation*.

demagogue. A person who takes political advantage of social and political unrest through the use of highly emotional and prejudiced appeals to the general population or a particular segment of the general population. A demagogue is usually characterized by such things as scapegoating, *utopian*[3] idealism, evasiveness, egocentrism, *propaganda*[5] development, untruthfulness (with lying and half-truths), *prejudice*[9], corruption, emotional rhetoric, persecution complexes, Messianic complexes, dogmatism, and *aggression*[12]. See also *last-minute*[5] *lie*.

Dixiecrats: see *States' Rights Democratic (Dixiecrat) Party*[5].

18-year-old vote. A popular expression used to describe the fact that 18-year-old individuals may vote in state or national elections. Before 1970 both Georgia and Kentucky permitted 18-

year-olds to vote. Alaska permitted 19-year-olds to vote and Hawaii permitted 20-year-olds to exercise the *franchise*[5], although the general voting age across the *nation*[3] was 21. The 18-year-old vote was sought primarily under the slogan "old enough to fight—old enough to vote." In the *Voting*[5] *Rights Act of 1970* the *Congress*[4] stated that 18-year-olds could vote in all states. On December 21, 1970 the *Supreme*[8] *Court* upheld the 18-year-old vote for *federal*[3] elections. However, the Court held that the Congress could not set the age qualification for state elections. The *Twenty-sixth Amendment*[5] was added to the *Constitution*[4] in 1971 in order to permit 18-year-olds to vote in both federal and state elections. See also *Oregon*[1] *v. Mitchell.*

election, at-large. An election in which a public official is selected from a major election *district*[7] rather than a minor subdivision within the larger unit. A *congressman*[7] *at large* is a *legislator*[7] elected by the entire *state*[7] rather than by the voters of a particular *legislative district*[7]. The need for such an election usually arises because of the failure of a state to *redistrict*[7] once it has been granted an additional seat in the *House*[7] *of Representatives*. *U.S. Senators*[7], presidential electors, numerous city councilmen, and other public officials across the U.S. are elected at large. In contrast to election at large is election by *district*[7] or *ward*[5]. On June 7, 1971, in the *U.S. Supreme*[8] *Court* decision of Whitcomb v. Chavis, the use of at-large elections for choosing state legislators from *multi-member districts*[7] was upheld as *constitutional*[3]. The Court held in this Indiana case that states are not required to provide legislative district arrangements which guarantee that racial minorities or other distinct groups must have obvious representation or control particular districts. See also *city*[11] *council.*

election, deviating. An election in which established *political party*[5]

loyalties and structures remain intact but in which the *minority party*[5] captures *power*[3] from the *majority party*[5].

election, general. A regularly conducted election within a designated electoral *jurisdiction*[8]. General elections within the U.S. are usually conducted on a statewide basis to elect *state*[3] and national officials. The *President*[6] is elected at four-year intervals. Congressional elections for all the members of the *House*[7] *of Representatives* and one-third of the *Senate*[7] are held at two-year intervals. Some states elect their state officials at the same time *federal*[3] officials from their state are chosen. Other states choose their state and local officials in what are known as *off-year elections*[5]. See also *primary election*[5]; *special election*[5].

election, maintaining. An election in which established *political party*[5] loyalties and structures remain intact and in which relative positions of *majority*[3] and *minority parties*[5] are unchanged.

election, nonpartisan. An election in which candidates are not recognized on the ballot by *political party*[5] label. *Nonpartisan*[5] elections are most frequently used in choosing *state*[3] judges, state educational officials, and various officials of *municipal*[11] *government*[3].

election, off-year. An election conducted at a time other than the presidential election. The most obvious off-year elections are those *federal*[3] elections regularly held midway between two presidential elections. All members of the *House*[7] *of Representatives* and one-third of the *Senate*[7] are up for reelection at that time. One outstanding fact about such off-year elections is that the *political party*[5] not controlling the presidency tends to gain strength during such elections. Some *states*[3] purposely schedule their selection of officials at off-year intervals in order to emphasize their own elections and not have the public attention drawn away by national issues and personalities. See also *general election*[5].

election, primary: see *direct primary*[5].

election, realigning. An election in which established *political party*[5] loyalties and structures are fundamentally changed and *majority party*[5] and *minority party*[5] positions are reversed.

election, recall. An election which permits voters to remove a public official from office before his term has been completed. Generally, an elected official may be permitted to serve a certain length of time before a recall election may be held. After that period ends, the qualified voters may petition for a recall election. After a required percentage of voters have signed the petition, an election may be conducted. If an official is recalled, then a successor may be selected on the same ballot or in another election. The recall election is not used by the *federal government*[3], but is used in some *states*[3] and *municipalities*[11] to remove state *executive*[6] officials, *legislators*[7], judges, and municipal officers.

election, reinstating. An election in which established *political party*[5] loyalties and structures remain intact and in which the party out of *power*[3] regains the *majority*[3] position after having been replaced temporarily by the *minority party*[5] through a *deviating election*[5]. See also *maintaining election*[5]; *realigning election*[5]; *majority party*[5].

election, special (by–   ). An election held to choose a person to fill an unexpired term of office under the retirement, removal, or death of a particular official.

electoral college: see Chap. 4.

Electoral Count Act of 1887. The *federal*[3] *legislation*[7] that provides for the settlement of disputes over *electoral votes*[5] within the *electoral*[4] college. In

states[3] where two sets of electors are claiming to be the "official" slate for a *political party*[5], the *act*[8] permits the U.S. *Congress*[4] to vote as separate houses and decide which electors to certify. If the two houses cannot agree, the electors certified by the state *governor*[6] are to be accepted. The act was a result of the disputed election of 1876, the election in which an electoral commission was used and in which Rutherford B. Hayes was elected by one electoral vote.

equal time (fairness) doctrine. See *fairness*[5] *doctrine*.

Era of Good Feelings, 1817–25. A short-lived period in U.S. history referred to by the Boston Columbian Centinel (July 12, 1817) as an "era of good feelings" because of the lack of extreme *partisan*[5] conflict. The term gained popular acceptance and was used to describe the *administration*[6] of *President*[6] Monroe. Although the *Federalist Party*[5] had died around 1816 and the *Democratic-Republican Party*[5] reigned supreme, there were some basic *political party*[5] realignments taking place during the Era of Good Feelings. There were intraparty struggles within President Monroe's administration. The era ended with one of the most unpleasant elections in U.S. history, the battle between John Quincy Adams and *Andrew Jackson*[6]. The election deadlocked and John Quincy Adams was elected by a highly partisan *House*[7] of *Representatives*.

Erie County Study: see *The People's*[5] *Choice*.

faction: see Chap. 3.

fairness (equal time) doctrine. The concept within Section 315 of the *Federal*[9] *Communications Act of 1934*, which holds that major advocates of both sides of political and public issues should be given fair opportunity to broadcast their viewpoints, especially if attacked by political opposition through public airwaves. The doctrine, sometimes referred to as the "equal time" doctrine, was upheld as *constitutional*[3] in 1969 in *Red*[1] *Lion Broadcasting Company v. Federal Communications Commission.*

favorite son. A candidate favored by the political leaders from his own *state*[3] or area. See also convention[5], party.

Federal Election Campaign Act of 1972. *Federal*[3] *legislation*[7] which replaced the Corrupt Practices Act of 1925. The *act*[8], incorporating the first campaign-spending ceiling in U.S. history, was designed ostensibly to help reduce campaign expenses and make it easier to reveal campaign contributors. The *law*[8] restricts candidates from contributing over $50,000 to their own campaigns, places a 10 cents per potential voter limitation on *mass*[5] *media* expenditures, with 6 cents of that limitation covering television and radio ($8.4 million for TV and radio in 1972). Media businesses may charge political candidates no more than the lowest charges made to other advertisers for comparable services, and all personal contributions over $100 per year and *party committee*[5] collections over $1,000 per year must be reported. The *Comptroller*[10] *General* and the clerks of the *U.S. Congress*[4] file the reports.

Federalist No. 10, The. The essay in which *James Madison*[6] expressed concern over the development of political *factions*[3] within the framework of popular *government*[3]. In the essay, one of the most famous in the collection entitled *The Federalist*[4], Madison revealed his fear of the particular interests of *political parties*[5] and *pressure*[5] *groups*. He expressed the feeling that factions could be effectively controlled through *representative government*[3] incorporating a system of *separation*[3] *of powers* and *checks*[3] *and balances*. See also *limited government*[3].

Federal Regulation of Lobbying Act of 1946. Title III of the *Legislative*[7] *Reorganization Act of 1946*, a title requiring registration of persons and *organizations*[6] seeking to influence the course of *federal*[3] *legislation*[7], the filing of financial statements by *pressure*[5] *groups* and the filing of quarterly reports describing activities undertaken by registered *lobbyists*[5]. See also *U.S.*[1] *v. Harriss.*

filing. The official act of announcing, generally through the payment of a fee to a legal *authority*[3], that one intends to actively seek a particular elective office. See also *cross-filing*[5].

floater. A person who sells his vote or goes from place to place during an election and casts ballots illegally, generally through the use of previously established, falsified *registration*[5] records. See also *Tasmanian*[5] *Dodge.*

foreign agent. A person, generally an American *citizen*[3], who registers with the *federal government*[3] as a *lobbyist*[5] representing the general interests of a foreign *nation*[3] or *corporation*[10]. Foreign agents most often push trade benefits, sympathy and active support of the foreign *power*[3], and tourism.

franchise. In the area of political dynamics this means the right to vote.

Gold Democrats: see *National Democratic Party*[5].

government, coalition. A temporary *alliance*[12] or combination of political *factions*[3] designed to achieve some specific objective such as electoral victory. In a *multi-party*[5] *system* it is frequently necessary for *political parties*[5] of similar interests to form a *coalition*[5] in order to control the political system and legislative process.

government, responsible party. A governmental system operated under the concept that a *political party*[5] which holds *power*[3] should be held publicly responsible for its actions while in office. The system has to be arranged whereby the electorate knows that parties truly act as parties and that a particular party clearly holds power at any given time. England operates under responsible party government through the use of *parliamentary government*[3]. The U.S. system of *federalism*[3] does not use responsible party government because of the extreme use of *separation*[3] *of powers* and *checks*[3] *and balances*. See also *E. E. Schattschneider*[5]; *Toward*[5] *a More Responsible Two-Party System*; *Woodrow Wilson*[6].

grandfather clause. A voting rights provision contained in some southern *state*[3] *constitutions*[3] after the *Civil*[4] *War*. The provision permitted persons to vote if their ancestors had voted before a specified date. In 1896 the state of Louisiana adopted such a device to protect nonproperty-owning and illiterate whites who were barred from voting along with Negroes who owned no *property*[10] and who could not pass a *literacy*[5] *test*. Louisiana permitted a person's name to be placed on a permanent voter registration list if his father or grandfather had voted before January 1, 1867. Negroes could not meet such a requirement because their ancestors could not vote until after the *ratification*[3] of the *Fifteenth Amendment*[5] in 1870. Grandfather clauses were declared *unconstitutional*[3] and in violation of the Fifteenth Amendment by the *Supreme*[8] *Court* in *Guinn*[1] *v. U.S.* See also *permanent registration*[5].

Grand Old Party (GOP). A popular term which arose around 1880 to characterize the *Republican Party*[5].

hack. An abbreviated term for "hackney horse," hack means a petty follower or henchman. A party hack is a person who carries out the basic wishes of *political party*[5] leaders.

Hare system. A systematic electoral arrangement of *Proportional Representation*[5] based on the popular preferential strength of individual candidates running for office. The system, devised in 1857 by an Englishman named Thomas Hare, uses a single preferential and transferable vote which may be cast by a qualified voter. The voter marks preference numbers beside the names of candidates (1, 2, 3, 4, etc.) running for a particular office. A quota of voter strength generally establishes which candidates will win on the basis of the preference number totals. Candidates receiving high totals or totals above the quota are elected and those receiving low totals are eliminated. Since several elective positions are available the marginal candidates are given additional or surplus votes on the basis of preferences listed on the ballots. Through this process an entire slate of elected officials may be chosen. The system affords *minority parties*[5] or groups the opportunity for *representation*[7] within a *legislature*[7]. The Hare system was popular in the U.S. between 1900 and 1950 but fell into disuse because of its complicated operation. See also *list*[5] *system*.

Hearst, William Randolph, 1863–1951). An influential newspaper publisher best remembered for popularizing what came to be known as "yellow journalism," a type of reporting which plays upon the emotional and sensational in life. Hearst greatly influenced American *public opinion*[5] through his consolidation of numerous small newspapers across the U.S. into one syndicate. His public expressions and reporting tactics were instrumental in getting the American people to support U.S. involvement in the *Spanish-American*[12] *War*. See also *mass*[5] *media*.

Hoovercrat. A southern member of the *Democratic Party*[5] who supported the *Republican Party*[5] candidate, Herbert Hoover, in the presidential election of 1928. Many Hoovercrats were actually acting in a negative way against the Democratic nominee, Alfred E. Smith, because he was a Roman Catholic and supported the repeal of prohibition. See also *Twenty-first Amendment*[4].

Hunkers, 1845–52. A *conservative*[3] element of the *Democratic Party*[5] in New York which opposed the *Barnburners*[5], a *radical*[3] group of New York Democrats who gave the Hunkers their name. The Hunkers were referred to in such a derisive way because they sought the entire "hunk" of *government*[3] *patronage*[6] and because they excessively "hunkered" for office. The Hunkers supported slavery, internal improvements, and the *spoils*[6] *system*.

incumbent. A person who presently holds an office.

independent. A person who is not connected with any *political party*[5] or *organization*[6], or a person who votes according to personal desires rather than party affiliation. See also *mugwump*[5].

initiative: see Chap. 3.

interest group. A group of individuals, either amorphous or formally organized, which reveals some agreement on a particular subject or issue. The term is sometimes used as a synonym for "*pressure*[5] group." See also *public opinion*[5].

International Brotherhood of Teamsters, 1903– . The largest independent American *labor*[10] union and the largest free union in the world. The union was expelled from the AFL CIO in 1957 after a period of sensational exposures involving corrupt leadership. Two successive *presidents*[3] of the union, David Beck and James Hoffa, were eventually sentenced to *federal*[3] penitentiaries. The union represents transportation workers, clerks, and numerous other occupations. It gained its real strength during the 1930's when truckers and warehousemen combined in their bargaining efforts against companies handling basic commercial products.

John Birch Society, 1958– . The largest "*right-wing*"[3] organization in the U.S. The *organization*[6], founded and led by Robert Welch, is headquartered in Belmont, Massachusetts. The society is named after a fundamental Baptist missionary to China, stresses opposition to a "worldwide *Communist*[3] conspiracy," supports "basic" American values and traditions, rejects social and economic reforms (*Social*[11] *Security, graduated income tax*[10], etc.) and international organizations such as the *United*[12] *Nations*. The Society advocates direct, *centralized*[3], and controversial methods to combat Communism and the loss of traditional values. One of the organization's earliest objectives was to persuade the *U.S. Congress*[4] to *impeach*[7] *Chief*[8] *Justice Earl Warren*[8] of the *U.S. Supreme*[8] *Court*. The society publishes a magazine entitled American Opinion, has an official manual known as The Blue Book (1959), and distributes great quantities of free and low-priced literature.

Key, V. O., 1908–63. Professor of *political*[3] *science*, former *president*[3] of the *American*[5] *Political Science Association*, innovator in the field of political behavior, and one of the pioneers in the development of behavioralism in political science. Key's classic text, Politics, Parties, and Pressure Groups (1942), was a major contribution to political analysis and is frequently cited as the major analysis of American *political parties*[5]. Another significant volume, Southern Politics in State and Nation (1949), won acclaim for its incisive treatment of southern political variables. In 1961, Key published Public Opinion and American Democracy, his last major contribution to the academic understanding of the structures and operation of the American political system. See also *behavioral political*[3] *science*.

Know-Nothing Party: see *American Party*[5].

Ku Klux Klan (KKK), 1866– . An *organization*[6] founded at Pulaski, Tennessee in 1866 in opposition to the *radical*[3] *policies*[6] of the *Republican Party*[5] program of *Reconstruction*[4]. The group was dedicated to maintaining "white supremacy" through support of southern white traditions and through intimidation of Negroes who tried to vote or move into "white society." The KKK was weakened during the 1870's by *federal*[3] *legislation*[7], but was reorganized in 1915, with its emphasis now anti-Negro, anti-Catholic, *anti-Semitic*[9], and anti-foreigner. Its dramatic robes and burning crosses became worldwide symbols of racial hatred and bigotry. The Klan was especially active during the 1920's, but its extreme tactics caused it to lose public favor and once again face legislative restrictions. It became public and active once again after the 1954 *Supreme*[8] *Court desegregation*[9] decision of *Brown*[1] *v. Board of Education of Topeka* and after the *civil*[9] *rights* movements of the 1960's. Between 1963 and 1966 the KKK emphasized its national scope and its middle-class composition and sought to change its basic public image. See also *lynch*[9] *law*; *vigilante*[9].

Lasswell, Harold D., 1902– . Professor of *law*[8] and *political*[3] *science* at Yale University, *government*[3] adviser, and social researcher. Lasswell was one of the earliest major exponents of the behavioral school of political science. His major emphasis has been on behavior, *decision*[8]-making processes, and psychological factors of candidates and the electorate. He has authored Psychopathology and Politics (1930), World Politics and Personal Insecurity (1935), Politics: Who Gets What, When, How? (1958),

and numerous other works on political-psychological variables. See also *behavioral political*[3] *science*.

last-minute lie. An untruth deliberately spread just before an election by persons seeking to discredit a person running for public office. A last-minute lie is difficult to deal with because of the time element involved. See also *demagogue*[5]; *propaganda*[5].

Lazarsfeld, Paul F.: see *The People's*[5] *Choice*.

League of Women Voters, 1920– . A *nonpartisan*[5] civic *organization*[6] founded to help the newly enfranchised women voters to make intelligent political decisions. The organization is designed to stimulate political interest and participation among the general populace through educational and research campaigns. It operates at all levels of *government*[3] and has supported such things as permanent voter *registration*[5], extension of *civil*[6] *service*, *unicameral*[7] *legislatures*[7] within the *states*[3], *child*[10] *labor legislation*[7], and ballot reforms. See also *franchise*[5].

Liberty Lobby, 1960– . A patriotic, *conservative*[3] "citizen's lobby." The allegedly *nonpartisan*[5] *organization*[6] supports tax reform, *individualism*[3], and *isolationism*[12]. It opposes *Communism*[3], *socialism*[3], the *United*[12] *Nations*, the "no-win" *Vietnam*[12] *War*, public school sex education courses, racial *integration*[9], and powerful *labor*[10] *unions* and banks.

Lipset, Seymour Martin, 1922– . Professor of sociology at Harvard University, political sociologist, and author of such books as Agrarian Socialism (1950), Political Man: The Social Bases of Politics (1960), and The First New Nation (1963). Lipset's Political Man is recognized as one of the major contributions to the study of *politics*[3] from a sociological perspective. It examines *democracy*[3] as a characteristic of social systems and of *nation*[3]-states. It analyzes political participation, voter behavior, values, political structures, and various social and economic structures affecting the democratic system. A major thesis of the work is that the nature of a social system determines whether democracy is a viable form of *government*[3] for a particular system and how stable it will be if introduced into the system. See also *political*[3] *socialization*; *state*[3].

list system. A systematic electoral arrangement of *Proportional Representation*[5] based on separate lists of candidates seeking political offices under *political party*[5] labels. When the election is over each party is assigned legislative seats according to electoral strength. Seats are assigned to the members of each party on the basis of the order in which the names appeared on the list. See also *Hare*[5] *system*; *minority party*[5]; *list system voting*[5].

literacy test. A voting qualification device wherein a prospective voter must read and interpret a portion of the *U.S. Constitution*[4] or a portion of the *state*[3] constitution of the state in which the prospective voter resides. Voting registrars and election judges in states using such a device frequently used arbitrary and *discriminatory*[9] judgment in determining whether a person passed the test. The literacy test was first used to keep new *immigrants*[3] from voting and was later broadened to exclude Negroes from the *franchise*[5]. The use of literacy tests was upheld by the *Supreme*[8] *Court* in 1898 in *Williams*[1] v. *Mississippi*. However, its use was suspended for five years in several southern states in the *Voting*[5] *Rights Act of 1965* on the basis that it could not be used in areas where less than 50 percent of eligible voters were registered or voting. The suspension was extended until 1975 and applied nationwide in the *Voting*[5] *Rights Act of*

1970. See also *South*[1] *Carolina v. Katzenbach*.

Literary Digest. A publication that gained nationwide political attention in 1916 when it began to publish periodical *straw polls*[5] on political issues and candidates. Between 1916 and 1936 it surveyed such things as *presidential preference primaries*[5], prohibition, *New*[6] *Deal legislation*[7], general *elections*[5], and various other issues. The Digest picked the winner in every presidential election from 1916 until 1936, but collapsed financially soon after it was publicly embarrassed by predicting a landslide victory by Alfred Landon over *Franklin D. Roosevelt*[6]. It predicted 32 states for Landon who ended up winning only 2—Maine and Vermont. The Digest used mass mail and telephone *random*[5] *samples* of an unscientific nature. Its success between 1916 and 1936 was primarily based on the fact that its mass surveys were conducted on a relatively stable and homogeneous segment of the national population, a factor which changed considerably after the *Great Depression*[10] of the 1930's. It missed the 1936 election because it mailed questionnaires to persons listed in telephone books and on automobile registration lists, forgetting that during the Depression millions of people had no telephones or automobiles. The ones who were not questioned were those who gave Roosevelt his overwhelming victory.

lobby (lobbying, lobbyist). The collective designation of persons who seek to influence *government*[3] officials (sometimes in the lobby or cloakroom outside a legislative chamber) to support particular projects or interests, either for themselves or special groups they represent. A lobby pressures all branches of government at all levels. Lobbyists testify before legislative *committees*[7] on behalf of themselves or their clients, assist *legislators*[7] in drafting *legislation*[7] in their area of specialization, and carry out a general program designed to gain favor with legislators, administrators, judicial figures, and others who affect their interests. See also *Federal*[5] *Regulation of Lobbying Act of 1946*; *foreign*[5] *agent*; *interest*[5] *group*; *pressure*[5] *group*; *U.S.*[1] *v. Harriss*.

machine. A highly organized *hierarchical*[6] or semi-hierarchical group of politically active individuals who combine in an effort to exploit the resources and *power*[3] of a *political party*[5]. The machine, led by a skillful *boss*[5] may dominate the regular party *organization*[6] within an area by capturing *party conventions*[5] and *primaries*[5], intimidating potential challengers to its power, or controlling *patronage*[6].

Madison Avenue. A major street and its adjacent commercial district (approximately 24 square blocks) in New York City that is recognized as the commercial center of the advertising, publishing, and public communications systems in the U.S. The term "Madison Avenue" is almost synonymous with *public opinion*[5], social taste, and public awareness because of its influence on *society*[3] through the use of the *mass*[5] *media*. In recent years Madison Avenue has become highly visible in political campaigns as image makers for political candidates. It was especially active in rebuilding the image of Richard Nixon during the presidential election of 1968 and in developing images for candidates of both major *political parties*[5] during the congressional elections of 1970. See also *propaganda*[5].

majority rule: see *absolute majority*[3]; *majority*[3] *rule*.

mass media. The collective grouping of all widespread public communications systems. Generally included as part of the mass media are news-papers, television, movies, magazines, and other printed, electronic, and cinematic communications systems. See also *William Randolph Hearst*[5]; *Madison*[5] *Avenue*; *propaganda*[5]; *United*[2] *States Information Agency*.

McGovern Commission. A reform *commission*[6] of the *Democratic Party*[5] created after the chaotic Democratic Party Convention of 1968. The body was originally chaired by *Senator*[7] George McGovern and named the Commission on Party Structure and Delegate Selection. *Representative*[7] Donald Fraser took over as *chairman*[7] once Senator McGovern became an active presidential candidate seeking office in the 1972 election. Representatives Fraser and James G. O'Hara, chairman of the Commission on Rules, led in modern reform of Democratic Party presidential candidate selection procedures. The basic reforms (McGovern Rules) were directed toward making the *party convention*[5] more representative, open, deliberative, and fair. The reforms involved the creation of regional platform hearings, revisions in convention practices, the adoption of party rules within the various *states*[3], the reduction of financial burdens for participants, the restriction of selection of convention delegates to the calendar year of the election, and adequate public notification of party meetings and elections. The most controversial reform incorporated a *quota*[3] *system* of proportional *representation*[7] designed to balance age, sexual, racial, and presidential preference categories present in the total population. The *revolutionary*[3] reforms led to the exclusion of numerous long-time party workers, brought to the forefront the *New*[5] *Politics*, stimulated bitter *delegation*[5] *challenges*[5] across the U.S., and helped Senator McGovern gain the Democratic Party nomination for *President*[6].

Morris Plan (1787). An electoral proposal presented during the debates of the *Constitutional Convention*[4] *of 1787* to elect presidential electors by popular ballot through an *electoral*[4] *college* vote within each *state*[3] rather than by the *U.S. Congress*[4]. The plan, advocated by Gouverneur Morris of Pennsylvania, was adopted by the Convention and became Article II, Section 1, Clauses 2, 3, and 4. Numerous *convention*[3] *delegates*[5] expected that after the election of *George Washington*[6] by unanimous action, the *House*[7] *of Representatives* would nearly always be called on to select the *President*[6].

mugwump. A derisive nickname given to *independent*[5] Republicans who withdrew their support from *Republican Party*[5] candidate James G. Blaine in 1884. "Mugwump," an Algonquin Indian word, meant a superior man. It was used to ridicule the "morally superior" position of the independents. The word eventually came to mean any person who does not strictly adhere to a *political party*[5] program, a person who is an independent voter.

multi-party system. A political system wherein a variety of *major parties*[5] and *minor parties*[5] are present on the political scene and vie for political *power*[3] and *government*[3] offices. A multi-party system is characterized chiefly by a *legislature*[7] composed of a wide variety of interests. It is generally necessary for a *coalition*[5] of interests to work together in order to carry out a program of government. See also *coalition government*[5].

National Association for the Advancement of Colored People (NAACP), 1910– . An interracial *organization*[6] composed largely of members of the black middle class who organized originally to combat lynching and voting *discrimination*[9] in the U.S. The group is generally recognized as a moderate, black *civil*[9] *rights* organization and as the one organization most successful in winning civil rights battles through *U.S. Supreme*[8] *Court*

decisions, one of the most famous being the *Brown*[1] *v. Board of Education of Topeka* decision of 1954, a decision which declared *unconstitutional*[3] the "*separate*[9] *but equal*" doctrine. See also *lynch*[9] *law*.

National Association of Manufacturers (NAM), 1895– . One of the major industrial *organizations*[6] in the U.S. The NAM was created in order to promote industrial and business interests and to assure that industry's influence was felt in *government*.[3] The *conservative*[3] organization has opposed unionization, tax increases, massive *federal*[3] spending, and governmental ownership of industries. It has supported a balanced *budget*[10], *tariff*[10] protections, and *free*[10] *enterprise*. The NAM carries on a comprehensive public relations and educational campaign and exerts great influence on government through legislative testimony and organized *lobbying*[5]. See also *nationalized property*[10].

National Catholic Welfare Conference, 1919– . An active Roman Catholic *organization*[6] designed to provide Catholic priests with an organizational framework for influencing public questions related to political, social, and economic issues of interest to Catholics.

National Council of Churches of Christ (NCC), 1950– . The largest religious *pressure*[5] *group* within the U.S. The NCC, a combination of the Federal Council of Churches (1908) and other religious bodies, has been a leading advocate of social reform. It has supported *maximum*[10] *hour laws*, *minimum*[10] *wage laws*, *collective*[10] *bargaining*, and *civil*[9] *rights legislation*[7]. The NCC has generally opposed *federal*[3] aid to private and parochial schools.

National Council of Farmer Cooperatives (NCFC), 1929– . A major farm *organization*[6] designed to act as a clearinghouse of information for member *cooperatives*[10]. The *federated*[3] organization defends the interests of cooperatives in areas of marketing, foreign trade, research, transportation, and other similar interests.

National Education Association (NEA), 1857– . A major professional association in the field of public elementary and secondary education. The *organization*[6] contains both administrators and teachers and seeks improved salaries, facilities, and working conditions for educational personnel. The NEA has been recognized as a moderate educational organization which relies primarily on public relations programs and "sanctions" (warnings of specific educational shortcomings in specific situations) to achieve its objectives.

National Farmer's Organization (NFO), 1955– . One of the most recent and militant major agricultural *pressure*[5] *groups*. The NFO has been highly visible to the public because of its "withholding actions" of crops in order to raise the price of specific farm products.

National Farmers Union (NFU), 1902– . A major farm *organization*[6] composed of farmers dedicated to continuation of the existence of individual family farms. The NFU supports farm *cooperatives*[10], *rural*[10] *electrification*, agricultural education and research programs, high levels of *parity*[10], flexible price supports, and other *government*[3] programs designed to provide farmers with a system of production management and price protection. Outside of agriculture the NFU has supported the *War*[11] *on Poverty*, *Social*[11] *Security*, comprehensive health care, antitrust *legislation*[7], and *federal*[3] aid to education. See also *price*[10] *support program*.

National Grange, 1867– . An *organization*[6] originally created in 1867 as a secret society designed to promote agricultural interests. The National Grange, originally known as the Patrons of Husbandry, developed into a major agricultural *pressure*[5] *group* which opposed *monopolies*[10], sought rate regulations for railroads, establishment of agricultural and mechanical colleges, and related items. It supported many of the programs of the *Populist Party*[5] and was influential in the passage of what came to be known as the *Granger*[10] *Laws*, *state*[3] *legislation*[7] establishing railroad and warehouse *commissions*[6]. By 1887 the *federal government*[3] had followed suit and created the *Interstate*[2] *Commerce Commission* (ICC) to regulate interstate transportation of goods and people. The National Grange is presently one of the more *conservative*[3] farm groups, although it occasionally supports certain *price*[10] *support programs*. See also *Greenback (Independent) Party*[5]; *Munn*[1] *v. Illinois*.

National Rifle Association of America (NRA) 1871– . A powerful *lobby*[5] *organization*[6] which is composed of *state*[3] and local groups containing sportsmen and gun fanciers of all types. The NRA, headquartered in *Washington*[4], *D.C.*, has been instrumental in regularly defeating strong national gun control *legislation*[7], primarily on the grounds that the *Second Amendment*[9] provision related to the right "to keep and bear arms" prohibits such restrictions. The American Rifleman is the NRA monthly publication.

National Urban League, 1911– . An interracial *organization*[6] designed to advance the social, economic, and political status of Negroes. The *league*[3] is a moderate, *federated*[3] organization which works especially hard on behalf of blacks' economic position. It draws its major membership from the black middle class.

New Left. A *radical*[3] *ideologically*[3] oriented movement which arose in the U.S. during the 1960's. The New Left is highly fragmented (*Marxists*[3], *Mao-*

ists[3], Weathermen, etc.), but in general is Marxist in outlook, violent in temperament, and *nihilistic*[3] in objective. The New Left, acting partially underground, sees present social and governmental *organizations*[6] in the U.S. as corrupt, dominated by selfish and irresponsible economic interests, unwise in international military posture, and insensitive to domestic *civil*[9] *rights* protections and welfare needs of *minority*[9] *groups*. See also *left*[3]; *Students*[5] *for a Democratic Society*; *Youth International Party*[5].

New Politics. A label attached to a group of dissident liberals, basically *liberal*[3] Democrats, in the presidential election of 1968. The group's adherents pledged support to *Senator*[7] Eugene McCarthy and Senator George McGovern once Senator Robert Kennedy was assassinated. The movement of college amateurs was characterized by participation and *individuality*[3]. It originally rejected rigid and traditional *political party*[5] *organization*[6] and operations but eventually moved into the 1972 unsuccessful campaign of Senator McGovern.

nomination by petition. The process whereby a person not officially nominated for public office by a major *political party*[5] may be nominated by mass public action through collection of a specified number of signatures of qualified voters.

nonpartisan. Not recognized as being a member or supporter of a particular *political party*[5]. See also *nonpartisan election*[5].

one-man, one-vote rule. The concept that the elective positions in a representative assembly must be based on *proportional representation*[5], an arrangement whereby each *legislator*[7] represents approximately the same number of people as every other legislator within the assembly. The one-man, one-vote rule was not legally

enforcable in the state *legislatures*[7] of the separate *states*[3] of the U.S. until after the *Supreme*[8] *Court* decisions of *Baker*[1] *v. Carr* in 1962 and *Reynolds*[1] *v. Sims* in 1964. As enunciated by the Court, the one-man, one-vote concept means that each voter's ballot must be essentially equal to every other voter's ballot or else be found in violation of the *Fourteenth Amendment*[4] *equal*[4] *protection clause*. See also *apportionment*[7]; *Avery*[1] *v. Midland County*; *Colgrove*[1] *v. Green*; *county-unit*[5] *system*; *Gomillion*[1] *v. Lightfoot*; *Gray*[1] *v. Sanders*; *Kirkpatrick*[1] *v. Preisler*; *reapportionment*[7]; *redistricting*[7]; *Wesberry*[1] *v. Sanders*.

one-party system. A political system wherein one dominant *political party*[5] clearly manipulates political activity and controls the agencies of *government*[3]. See also *Solid*[5] *South*.

opinion, public. The collective opinion of a social *community*[3] on a particular issue or any combination of issues which interest the people in general. Nearly every public is fragmented into smaller social groups holding varying shades of opinions on any given issue. In that sense, public opinion becomes the basic idea held by a selected portion of the population. Politicians, advertising agents, market researchers, religious leaders, and other active participants in political, economic, and social affairs aim their appeals for action or support at different levels of opinion according to the responses desired at a particular time. See also *interest*[5] *group*; *pressure*[5] *group*; *Madison*[5] *Avenue*; *mass*[5] *media*; *public opinion poll*[5]; *propaganda*[5]; *outside strategy*[5]; *U.S.*[1] *v. Harriss*.

organization, ad hoc. An *organization*[6] created for a specific purpose. Numerous political organizations are created on occasion to deal with a specific issue or support a particular candidate. Once the issue is settled or the election is past, the organization disbands.

organization, centralized. Any *hierarchy*[6] or organizational structure that places *power*[3] within a small group of individuals or organizational body. See also *centralization*[3]; *organization*[6].

organization, decentralized. Any *hierarchy*[6] or organizational structure that disperses *power*[3] among several scattered groups of individuals or organizational bodies. See also *decentralization*[3]; *organization*[6].

organization, front. An *organization*[6] specifically created to act as a cover for some more active or powerful organization, either legal or illegal. See also *Communist*[1] *Party v. SACB; Internal*[9] *Security Act of 1950.*

partisan. A person or *organization*[6] that acts with strong feelings about or on behalf of a *political party*[5] or *faction*[3]. See also *nonpartisan*[5].

party: see *political party*[5].

Party, American (Know-Nothing), 1840's–1860. The U.S. *political party*[5] best known as the Know-Nothing Party. The New York party referred to as the American Republican Party arose in 1843 in order to elect only native Americans to public offices. It and other similar, and secret, associations developed into the American Party. It gained a number of followers in *urban*[11] areas on the East Coast and in various *rural*[11] areas of the South. Lower-echelon party members pledged to vote for party figures helped give the party its nickname by regularly replying "I don't know" or "I know nothing" to any inquiries about party *policy*[6]. Millard Fillmore, former *U.S. President*[6], was the party's presidential candidate in 1856. The *conservative*[3] party supported the extension of slavery, electoral positions for native Americans only, and severe restrictions on *immigration*[3] and Roman Catholic *power*[3]. See also *Americanization*[4]; *right*[3].

Party, American Independent, 1968– . A *conservative*[3] *minor party*[5] led by *Governor*[6] George Wallace during the presidential election of 1968. The *political party*[5] emphasized individual choice in the use of *property*[10], local control of public schools, *law*[8] and order, *labor*[10] union changes, and a military victory in the *Vietnam*[12] *War*. It opposed racial *integration*[9] of public schools, *open*[9] *occupancy laws, centralization*[3] of *power*[3] in the *federal government*[3], and numerous *civil*[9] *rights* acts and *Supreme*[8] *Court* decisions. George Wallace drew his support largely from white blue-collar workers and ultraconservative *Republican Party*[5] members who supported Barry Goldwater for *President*[6] in 1964. He chose retired Air Force general Curtis LeMay for his vice-presidential running mate in 1968. Although there was some fear that the election would be thrown into the *House*[7] *of Representatives* because of the structure of the *electoral*[4] *college*, the situation was avoided when Wallace received only 13.5 percent of the total *popular vote*[5] and only 46 *electoral votes*[5]. See also *backlash*[5]; *right*[3].

Party, Antifederalist, 1787–89. A loosely organized group of individuals who opposed the proposed *U.S. Constitution*[4] when it was submitted to the *states*[3] for *ratification*[3]. The *Antifederalists*[4] were led by Patrick Henry, *Richard Henry Lee*[4], and other early supporters of the *American Revolution*[4]. They opposed the Constitution because of its creation of a strong central *government*[3] and its lack of a specific *U.S. Bill*[4] *of Rights*. The leading Antifederalist pamphlet was Letters from a Federal Farmer (1787) by Richard Henry Lee. The Antifederalists were not generally viewed as a formal *political party*[5]. However, numerous Antifederalists entered the

Democratic-Republican Party[5] of *Thomas Jefferson*[6] upon its creation in 1800. See also *Federalist Party*[5].

Party, Anti-Masonic, 1826–36. A short-lived United States *minor party*[5] which took as its banner a righteous crusade against the secret *organization*[6] of Freemasons after the disappearance of William Morgan of New York in 1826; Morgan had disclosed some of the secret practices of the Masons. The *political party's*[5] real opposition was directed at the rise of *Jacksonian democracy*[4] (*Andrew Jackson*[6] was also a Mason). The Anti-Masonic Party is generally recognized as the first serious *third party*[5] effort in American *politics*[3], as the first party to write a party *platform*[5], and as the first party to use a national nominating *party convention*[5], a meeting held at Baltimore, Maryland on September 26, 1831 in preparation for the election of 1832. The party nominated William Wirt, a Freemason, for *President*[6] in 1832. He won the seven *electoral votes*[5] of Vermont and recorded a *popular vote*[5] of 101,051.

Party, Bull Moose: see *Progressive Party*[5] *of 1912 (Bull Moose)*.

Party of the U.S., Communist, 1919– . A U.S. *minor party*[5] and political extension of the worldwide movement known as *Communism*[3]. The *political party*[5], a combination of the Communist and Communist Labor parties, has held varying political viewpoints such as the overthrow of *capitalism*[3], support of various social issues within the U.S., and support of Soviet *policies*[6] related to Communist *ideology*[3]. The *radical*[3] *Marxist*[3]-oriented party first ran a candidate for *U.S. President*[6] in 1924. After the passage of the *Alien*[4] *Registration (Smith) Act of 1940*, however, the *organization*[6] was not treated as a regular party by the United States *government*[3]. In 1954 the *Communist*[9] *Control Act* declared the party to be part of an illegal conspiracy and agent of a hostile foreign

government. The *left-wing*[3] party was required to register with the *federal government*[3] under the *Internal*[9] *security (McCarran) Act of 1950*. After a series of *U.S. Supreme*[8] *Court* decisions during the 1960's, which protect the right of expression and political participation, the party once again entered a candidate in a presidential election in 1968, the first they had entered since 1940. Mrs. Charlene Mitchell, a 38-year-old Negro, advocated a Communist government for the U.S., an end to the *Vietnam*[12] *War*, abolition of the *draft*[12], abolition of *corporate*[10] *monopolies*[10], an end to *discrimination*[9] against Negroes, and an end to the *Cold*[12] *War* with the Soviet Union. Gus Hall, long-time Communist leader was the presidential candidate in 1972. See also *Adler*[1] *v. Board of Education; Albertson*[1] *v. SACB; American*[1] *Communications Association v. Douds; Aptheker*[1] *v. Secretary of State; Barenblatt*[1] *v. U.S.; Communist*[1] *Party v. SACB; Dennis*[1] *v. U.S.; Garner*[1] *v. Board of Public Works; Jencks*[9] *Act of 1957; Jencks*[1] *v. U.S.; Keyishian*[1] *v. Board of Regents; Lamont*[1] *v. Postmaster General; Lenin*[3]; *Scales*[1] *v. U.S.; U.S.*[1] *v. Brown; U.S.*[1] *v. Robel; Watkins*[1] *v. U.S.; Yates*[1] *v. U.S.; Zemel*[1] *v. Rusk*.

Party, Democratic, 1800– . One of the major American parties, a *political party*[5] claiming *Thomas Jefferson*[6] and *Andrew Jackson*[6] as its early philosophical founders. The party was originally known as the Democratic-Republican Party. It early emphasized *egalitarian*[3] principles, a *strict construction*[4] of the *U.S. Constitution*[4], a liberal *immigration*[3] *policy*[6], and low *tariffs*[10]. The party supported the *spoils*[6] *system*, slavery, and various devices that placed *power*[3] in the hands of big-*city*[11] *machines*[5]. The modern Democratic Party dates from the period of *Woodrow Wilson*[6] (1912) and was especially influential in designing modern economic and social structures because of its control of power during the *Great Depres-*

sion[10] under *Franklin D. Roosevelt's*[6] *New*[6] *Deal*. In modern times the Democratic Party has supported *civil*[9] *rights, centralized*[3] control of economic and social matters, *foreign*[12] *aid, collective*[12] *security* arrangements, and *liberal*[3] economic and social policies. Its major supporters in recent years have been organized *labor*[10] *unions*, low-income groups, *minority*[9] *groups, urban*[11] dwellers, and intellectuals. See also *Revolution*[5] *of 1800; Solid*[5] *South; Watergate*[5].

Party, Democratic-Republican: see *Democratic Party*[5].

Party, Dixiecratic: see *States' Rights Democratic Party*[5].

Party, Farmer-Labor, 1920. A *political party*[5] whose influence has primarily been felt in various *states*[3] of the Midwest. It drew into its fold progressive reformists seeking *government*[3] *nationalization*[10] of *public*[10] *utilities*, banks, and other economic interests. It also supported labor and farm measures which were later adopted during the *New*[6] *Deal administration*[6] of *President*[6] *Franklin D. Roosevelt*[6]. The party eventually became *radically*[3] *socialistic*[3] and became a minor *force*[3] in American *politics*[3]. See also *nationalized property*[10].

Party, Federalist, 1788–1816. The first official *political party*[5] established in the U.S. *Alexander Hamilton*[4] was the philosophical founder of the party during the *administration*[6] of *President*[6] *George Washington*[6]. The Federalist Party supported a strong *federal*[3] Union, industrial growth, *elitist*[3] leadership, business interests, and a *liberal construction*[4] of the *U.S. Constitution*[4]. The party became highly controversial after passage of the *Alien*[4] *and Sedition Acts of 1798* and after the "midnight" *appointments*[6] of retiring Federalist President *John Adams*[6]. The *liberal*[3] party fell from public favor and disappeared from the public scene soon after the *War*[12] *of*

1812, a *war*[12] the party publicly disapproved of and secretly discussed at the *Hartford*[4] *Convention* of 1814–15. After the party's fall in 1816 its *power*[3] continued to be felt through the judicial interpretations of *Chief*[8] *Justice John Marshall*[8] of the *Supreme*[8] *Court*, a John Adams appointee who served on the Court until 1835. See also *Revolution*[5] *of 1800*.

Party, Free-Soil, 1847–54. A split from the *Democratic Party*[5] which combined with the remains of the *Liberty Party*[5] (1840–48) to oppose the extension of slavery into *territories*[3] newly acquired from Mexico. The Free-Soil's weakening of the Democratic Party made it possible for the *Whig Party*[5] to put Zachary Taylor into the presidency in 1849. After the *Compromise*[4] *of 1850*, part of the Free-Soil Party returned to the Democratic Party. However, the more vocal antislavery people were absorbed into the *Republican Party*[5] in 1854.

Party, Greenback (Independent), **1874–78.** A *minor party*[5] composed of midwestern and southern debtor farmers hurt by the *Panic*[10] of 1873. The party's primary concern was credit and currency. It sought cheap and easily available paper money, redemption of *greenbacks*[10] in gold, *government*[3] regulation of commercial and economic activities, and other economic objectives. The Greenback Party was one of the earliest political expressions of agrarian unrest in the U.S. The *party*[5] supported Peter Cooper of New York for *President*[6] in 1876, but Cooper won no *electoral votes*[5]. Soon after the election the party combined with other agrarian and labor groups and formed the *Greenback Labor (National) Party*[5]. See also *National*[5] *Grange*.

Party, Greenback Labor (National), **1878–84.** One of the first efforts to politically unite agricultural and labor interests in the U.S. within one *political party*[5]. The party supported the free coinage of silver on a *parity*[10] with gold, *immigration*[3] restrictions, *maximum*[10] *hour laws*, woman *suffrage*[5], a *graduated income tax*[10], and *federal*[3] regulation of *interstate commerce*[10]. The party nominated James B. Weaver of Iowa for *President*[6] in 1880 and General Benjamin F. Butler of Massachusetts in 1884; neither candidate won any *electoral votes*[5]. The party died out after 1884 and many of its members moved into the People's Party of the United States of America, a movement better known as the *Populist Party*[5]. See also *free*[10] *silver*; *greenback*[10]; *Greenback Party*[5].

Party, Independent: see *Greenback (Independent) Party*[5].

Party, Know-Nothing: see *American Party*[5].

Party, Liberty, 1840–48. An antislavery *political party*[5] led by James G. Birney, a *radical*[3] *abolitionist*[9] from New York. The support Birney received in 1844 helped split the *Whig Party*[5] and elect *Democratic Party*[5] candidate James K. Polk. In 1848 the party united with antislavery Democrats and Whigs and formed the *Free-Soil Party*[5]. Although the slavery issue was foremost on the Liberty Party *platform*[5], the party stressed a wide range of *democratic*[3] principles and equal rights.

party, majority. The *political party*[5] which controls a numerical and working *majority*[3] of *legislators*[7] within a *legislature*[7]. Within a *parliamentary government*[3] the *prime*[3] *minister* leads the majority party inside the parliament. Within the U.S. *constitutional*[3] *system* the majority party may differ from one house of the *Congress*[4] to the other. The majority party in either house is the party with the largest number of members registered under the same party label. The *Speaker*[7] *of the House* is the leader of the majority party in the *House*[7] of Repre-

sentatives. The *majority floor*[7] *leader* is the leader of the majority party in the *Senate*[7]. The majority party stands in contrast to the *minority party*[5] inside the legislature. See also *deviating election*[5]; *maintaining election*[5]; *realigning election*[5]; *reinstating election*[5].

party, minor. A *political party*[5] which has limited popular and financial support and which is incapable of seriously challenging elective positions. Minor parties stimulate major parties to consider political issues; they sometimes act as political innovators; and they offer distinct possibilities for future replacements for existing major parties. See also *Anti-Masonic Party*[5].

party, minority. The *political party*[5] which controls less than a numerical *majority*[3] of the members of a *legislature*[7]. It is in opposition to the *majority party*[5]. Within the U.S. *constitutional*[3] *system* the minority party is led by a *minority floor*[7] *leader* in each house of the *Congress*[4]. See also *Proportional Representation*[5]; *Hare*[5] *system*; *list*[5] *system*; *deviating election*[5]; *maintaining election*[5]; *realigning election*[5]; *reinstating election*[5].

Party, Mississippi Freedom Democratic, 1964–68. A challenge *delegation*[5] to the Democratic Convention at Atlantic City, New Jersey in 1964 and to the Democratic Convention at Chicago, Illinois in 1968. In 1964 the challenge delegation from the *state*[3] of Mississippi was led by Robert Moses. It presented 68 *delegates*[5] and alternates (all black except for four white Mississippi *civil*[9] rights workers) and sought to be seated as the official Mississippi delegation in place of the delegation composed exclusively of whites. The *party convention*[5] accepted a compromise, declaring that no Mississippi regular delegate could be seated unless he pledged to support the 1964 *Democratic Party*[5] ticket, that the challenge delegation could seat two delegates at large with voting privileges, and that at future Democratic Party conventions the state delegations could not be seated if they represented state *party*[5] machinery that was used to deprive individuals of the right to vote on the basis of race. During the 1968 convention in Chicago the Credentials Committee examined the racial composition of various state delegations and required fairness in selection.

Party, National Democratic (Gold Democrats), 1896–1900. The *political party*[5] popularly known as the Gold Democrats. It was composed of a dissident group of *Democratic Party*[5] members who opposed William Jennings Bryan's *free*[10] *silver* stand. The party's presidential nominee was *Senator*[7] J. M. Palmer of Illinois. Senator Palmer polled slightly over 130,000 votes in the election. The party dissipated before 1900.

Party, Peace and Freedom, 1968. A *radical*[3] minor party which placed candidates on some *state*[3] ballots (California, Michigan, New Jersey, Pennsylvania, etc.) in the presidential election of 1968. The *minor party*[5] was composed of a loose-knit group of *New*[5] *Left* radicals, black militants, dissident *liberal*[3] Republicans and Democrats, and anti-George Wallace adherents. Eldridge Cleaver, the Minister of Information for the *Black*[5] *Panthers*, was put forth as the Peace and Freedom presidential nominee in most states where the *political party*[5] was on the ballot. The *left-wing*[3] party advocated killing policemen ("pigs" in Black Panther terminology), acceptance of *socialism*[3], and social *justice*[8] for blacks and underprivileged whites. It opposed the *Vietnam*[12] *War*, the *military-industrial*[12] *complex*, the conventional *two-party*[5] *system*, anti-labor *legislation*[7], and "liberal materialism." It also supported a three-dollar-per-hour *minimum*[10] *wage law*, and called for an end to the use of troops during *urban*[11] rioting. See also

American Independent Party[5]; *black*[9] *power*.

Party, People's: see *Populist Party*[5].

party, political. A group of individuals acting collectively within some *organizational*[6] framework for the purpose of winning political offices with a view toward changing public *policy*[6].

Party, Populist, 1892–1900. A *political party*[5] officially named the People's Party of the United States of America. The party drew largely from southern and western agricultural and laboring interests which were previously associated with the *Greenback Party*[5] and *Greenback Labor Party*[5]. It supported public ownership and regulation of railroads and communications lines, a *graduated income tax*[10], the free and unlimited coinage of silver, widespread circulation of *greenbacks*[10], clean *government*[3], an eight-hour work day, popular election of *U.S. Senators*[7], a postal savings system, the secret ballot, the use of *initiative*[3] and *referendum*[3], and other *liberal*[3] measures. James B. Weaver, previous nominee of the Greenback Labor Party, was the party's presidential candidate in 1892. The party's most famous candidate was William Jennings Bryan, a man who accepted both the *Democratic Party*[5] and Populist Party nominations in 1896. Weaver received 22 *electoral votes*[5] in 1892 and Bryan received 176 in 1896, mostly on the basis of his Democratic Party label. Both men were hurt most by the *free*[10] *silver* issue. Although the party died out around 1900, numerous portions of its party *platform*[5] were adopted by the Democratic Party and later adopted as *constitutional*[3] *amendments*[9] or *federal*[3] *statutory*[8] provisions. See also *National*[5] *Grange*.

Party of 1912, Progressive (Bull Moose), 1912–16. A *minor party*[5] led by former *President*[6] *Theodore Roosevelt*[6] and a group of dissident Republicans opposing the *conservatism*[3] of President Taft and supporting the ideas of "New Nationalism." The Bull Moose Party, officially named the National Progressive Republican League, supported *liberal*[3] reforms such as woman *suffrage*[5], *primary*[5] elections, the use of *initiative*[3] and *referendum*[3], the use of the *recall*[5], direct election of *U.S. Senators*[7], *conservation*[10] of natural resources, creation of a national program of *social insurance*[11], the abolition of *child*[10] *labor*, and acceptance of *maximum*[10] *hour laws* and *minimum*[10] *wage laws*. The Bull Moose Party reunited with the regular *Republican Party*[5] in 1916. However, its presence on the political scene split the Republican Party in 1912 and helped elect *Democratic Party*[5] candidate *Woodrow Wilson*[6]. Many of its proposals were added to the *U.S. Constitution*[4] by formal *amendment*[3] or were enacted into *law*[8] under Democratic *administrations*[6].

Party of 1924, Progressive, 1924–28. A *minor party*[5] led by *Senator*[7] Robert LaFollette of Wisconsin and composed of dissident agricultural and labor elements from both the *Democratic Party*[5] and the *Republican Party*[5]. The reform-minded *political party*[5] supported governmental control of railroads and *public*[10] *utilities*, popular election of the U.S. *President*[6], protection for labor, and other *liberal*[3] measures. LaFollette won the 13 *electoral votes*[5] of Wisconsin in the election of 1924.

Party of 1948, Progressive. A *minor party*[5] led by former *Vice-President*[6] Henry A. Wallace and composed of *liberal*[3] and *left-wing*[3] dissidents within the *Democratic Party*[5]. The *political party*[5], greatly influenced by *Communist*[3] *front organizations*[5], opposed the foreign *policy*[6] of the *administration*[6] of *President*[6] *Harry Truman*[6]. It also advocated *civil*[9] *rights* for Negroes, called for the *nationalization*[10] of basic industries within the U.S., and urged that eco-

nomic relations with the Soviet Union be expanded. Wallace was unable to win any *electoral votes*[5] in the election of 1948. See also *nationalized property*[10].

Party, Prohibition, 1869– . The oldest existing *minor party*[5] in the U.S., a *political party*[5] which has consistently made the liquor issue the primary plank in its overall *platform*[5]. The party seeks total prohibition of the manufacture and selling of alcoholic beverages. It has supported such things as woman *suffrage*[5], abolition of *child*[10] *labor*, a *graduated income tax*[10], direct election of *U.S. Senators*[7], and other reforms that were eventually adopted within the U.S. *constitutional*[3] *system*. The party first ran a candidate for *President*[6] in the election of 1884. It consistently supported presidential candidates between 1884 and 1916. It has never had a candidate who won any *electoral votes*[5]. The party was influential in getting the *Eighteenth Amendment*[4] added to the U.S. *Constitution*[4] in 1919, an act which made it illegal to manufacture or sell "intoxicating liquors" in the U.S. The party fought a losing battle in 1933, and alcoholic beverages were legalized once again by the addition of the *Twenty-first Amendment*[4]. Since 1916 the Prohibition Party has had some presidential candidates on the ballots of various *states*[3] and has carried out an educational program related to liquor abuses, but it has had little influence as a *force*[3]. See also *Anti-Saloon*[5] *League; Women's*[5] *Christian Temperance Union.*

Party, Republican, 1854– . One of the major American parties, a *political party*[5] founded in opposition to the extension of slavery into *federal*[3] *territories*[3]. The party was originally a combination of Whigs, Free-Soilers, and northern Democrats that opposed the extension of slavery and the Fugitive Slave Law of 1850. The party supported a protective *tariff*[10], a homestead *law*[8], and a cross-continent railroad. It first won the presidency in 1860 with *Abraham Lincoln*[6] as its leader. After the *Civil*[4] *War* the party was dominated by a group of *congressmen*[7] known as "Radical Republicans." The party led in a harsh program of *Reconstruction*[4] of the South and supported high protective tariffs, programs designed to protect the dollar, and economic benefits for business and industrial interests. The Republican Party controlled federal *power*[3] between 1860 and 1932, with the exception of the *administration*[6] of *Woodrow Wilson*[6] (1912–20). In modern times the Republican Party has been the more *conservative*[3] of the two major parties. It generally supports *decentralized*[3] control of economic and social matters, economy in *government*[3], *free*[10] *enterprise*, high tariffs, and other policies which benefit business. Its major supporters have been business, management, high-income groups, *WASP'S*[5], midwestern and northern farm groups, and anti-intellectuals. See also *Homestead*[11] *Act of 1862*; *Grand*[5] *Old Party*; *Democratic Party*[5]; *Free-Soil Party*[5]; *Whig Party*[5]; *Watergate*[5].

Party, Socialist, 1901– . A U.S. *political party*[5] which began as the Social Democratic Party in 1898 and was reorganized in 1901 as the Socialist Party. It has been composed mostly of moderate *Marxists*[3]. The *socialistic*[3] and *left-wing*[3] party has regularly attacked *capitalism*[3]; supported public ownership of major businesses and public welfare programs; and sought a social order based on *law*[8] rather than *revolution*.[3] Eugene V. Debs was the party candidate for the presidency between 1900 and 1920. Norman Thomas became the party leader after 1928 and until his death in 1968. See also *Debs*[1], *In re*.

Party, Socialist Labor, 1876– . A U.S. *political party*[5] composed of individuals supporting radical *Marxist*[3]

ideas. The *left-wing*[3] party, composed mostly of Germans early in its history, appeals primarily to laboring groups. Daniel DeLeon was consistently the leader of the *radical*[3] wing of the party during its early period of development. The party advocates *socialism*[3], racial equality, and an end to *discrimination*[9] in housing, *labor*[10] *unions*, and employment. Its uncompromising conflicts with the *capitalistic*[3] system and its radical views of the *state*[3] have kept it from gaining the sympathy of the general population. The party consistently runs a candidate for *President*[6] on the ballots of a few major states, but it has never won any *electoral votes*[5] in a presidential election.

Party, Socialist Worker's, 1938– . A *radical*[3] *political party*[5] composed of followers of Russian revolutionary, Leon Trotsky. The *revolutionary*[3] American party has few active followers in the U.S. although it regularly puts up candidates in some areas of labor and social unrest. In the election of 1960 the Socialist Worker's candidate, Farrell Dobbs, polled 39,692 *popular votes*[5].

Party, States' Rights Democratic (Dixiecrat), 1948. A *right-wing*[3] splinter group of southern Democrats which broke from the *Democratic Party*[5] under the leadership of *Senator*[7] Strom Thurmond. The Dixiecrats walked out of the 1948 Democratic *Convention*[5] in protest against a strong *civil*[9] *rights* plank in the Democratic *platform*[5]. The *political party*[5] was based on white supremacy and *states'*[4] *rights*. Thurmond won 39 *electoral votes*[5] from 4 southern *states*[3] (Alabama, Louisiana, Mississippi, and South Carolina) and 1,169,-000 *popular votes*[5]. He eventually joined the *Republican Party*[5]. The Dixiecratic Party has not had a serious presidential candidate since 1948. However, a number of "white supremacy" leaders have run under the states' rights banner in recent years, but have referred to the party as the National States' Rights Party.

party, third. Any *political party*[5] which captures public attention during a campaign as a potential threat to the *power*[3] of either of the two major political parties in a *two-party*[5] *system*. Third parties tend to arise whenever both major parties are neglecting to deal realistically with particular problems in the *society*[3]. A third party is generally transitory since the issues it raises are usually preempted by the major parties. For this reason, a third party nearly always remains a *minor party*[5]. See also *Anti-Masonic Party*[5].

Party, Whig, 1834–54. A major U.S. *political party*[5] which represented general *conservative*[3] viewpoints between the period of *Andrew Jackson*[6] and *Abraham Lincoln*[6]. Whig supporters agreed primarily only on opposition to Andrew Jackson and his *policies*[6]. The party was composed of northern industrial and financial interests and southern slaveholding *aristocrats*[3]. Whigs tenuously agreed upon protective *tariffs*[10], internal improvements, and support of the *Bank*[10] *of the United States*. However, the party split apart over the slavery issue with the "Northern (Conscience)" Whigs going into the *Republican Party*[5] and the "Southern (Cotton)" Whigs going into the *Democratic Party*[5]. The Whig Party's first presidential victor, William Henry Harrison, died after only one month in office in 1840. His successor, John Tyler, was denied renomination by his own party tn 1844. The party won its second and last victory with General Zachary Taylor running as a *Mexican*[12] *War* hero in 1848.

Party, Youth International (Yippies), 1968– . An interracial, *leftist*[3], *radical*[3], anti-*Establishment*[3], and revolutionary movement founded by Abbott (Abbie) Hoffman and Jerry Rubin. The *New*[5] *Left* group emphasizes satire, sexual freedom, and ecstatic experiences through the use of psychedelic drugs. It often publicly challenges the investigations conducted by the *House*[7] *of Representatives Committee*[7] *on Internal Security* (formerly the House Committee on Un-American Activities), supports foreign *revolutionary*[3] movements, and was instrumental in provoking the riots in Chicago during the Chicago Democratic National *Convention*[5] in 1968. Both Hoffman and Rubin were tried in *federal*[3] court in Chicago with the "Chicago Seven" and were found guilty of *inciting to riot*[8]. One of the Yippies' major tactics has been outlandish social and political action designed to gain public attention through the *mass*[5] *media*. See also, *Walker*[8] *Report*.

The People's Choice: How the Voter Makes Up His Mind in a Presidential Campaign (1944). The first major behavioral study of a U.S. presidential election,, a work authored by Paul F. Lazarsfeld, Bernard B. Berelson, and Hazel Gaudet. The sophisticated survey study of the election of 1940 examined in detail the voting behavior of the electorate in Erie County, Ohio. It emphasized the effects of campaigning, the impact of mass communications, the nature of sociological variables (group identity, economic status, religion, geography, *cross*[5] *pressures*, apathy, etc.), and the nature of decision-making in voting. In their 1948 study of Elmira, New York, Lazarsfeld and his associates placed more emphasis on the nature of the *community*[3] and its institutions than they did in the Erie County study. See also *mass*[5] *media*; *behavioral political*[3] *science*; *political*[3] *socialization*.

platform. A publicly announced program of action or statement of principles adopted by a *political party*[5] or a political candidate. Platforms are generally adopted at *party conventions*[5] but are rarely binding on a strong political leader who is really responsible for determining directions and seeking to get party adherents to follow.

Political Activities (Hatch) Acts of 1939 and 1940. Two pieces of federal *legislation*[7] which placed limitations on campaign expenditures and campaign practices. A national *party committee*[5] may spend no more than $3 million per year, and individual contributions may not exceed $5,000 for any one political *committee*[7]. *Civil*[6] *Service* personnel may not actively participate in political campaigns and may not be forced to make campaign contributions. Direct contributions by *labor*[10] *unions* and *corporations*[10] are also forbidden. The 1939 *act*[8] was directed at *federal*[3] personnel, while the 1940 act applied to *state*[3] and local workers employed on federally funded projects. The Hatch Acts have been ineffective in actually regulating campaign finances because of indirect and *decentralized*[3] support for particular *political parties*[5] and candidates.

political ambivalence. Politically oriented but contradictory ideas or conduct on the part of political leaders, *organizations*[6], or voters. The ambivalent political leader holds contradictory positions at the same time and leaves his followers uncertain about the direction to move. For example, he may simultaneously seek the black northern vote and the white southern vote without clarifying how their past differences can be reconciled. The ambivalent voter may have social, geographic, and economic differences which create inner conflict with his present voting behavior and his *political party*[5] identification. Regardless of how he votes, he will go against a basic belief, economic interest, family background, or other

variable. See also *cross*[5] *pressures*; *The People's*[5] *Choice*.

political folklore. The system of political beliefs that exist within any given political and social system, regardless of their authentication as being factual or true. In the U.S. some of the more obvious items of political folklore, which differ in intensity from place to place and time to time, are: "All *politicians*[5] are crooks"; "You can't fight city hall"; "Democrats always start *wars*[12]"; and "Republicans always start *depressions*[10]." See also *Democratic Party*[5]; *Republican Party*[5].

political pragmatism. The approach to *political parties*[5] that tests ideas and actions by their practical results. The political pragmatist develops and uses political *power*[3] on the basis of political arrangements and devices which obviously work to his own advantage. The pragmatic approach to *politics*[3] may involve a process of trial and error in given situations or the adoption of previously tested political practices and arrangements. See also *William James*[4]; *pragmatism*[3].

political socialization: see Chap. 3.

politician. A person who actively engages in political affairs and public *policy*[6], generally for personal and *partisan*[5] advantage. See also *statesman*[5].

poll, Gallup. One of the oldest and most successful American *public opinion polls*[5], a poll begun during the 1920's by Dr. George Gallup. In 1933 Gallup began reporting different subjects each week, sometimes as many as four reports per week. He founded the American Institute of Public Opinion in 1935 and began to publish regular poll results on presidential elections. He was a professor of advertising at Columbia University and an advertising research consultant before creating his institute. Gallup popularized and refined statistical analysis and representative samples based on numerous variables such as age, sex, race, geographical region, and income. The AIPO not only releases poll results on all types of subjects, but the Princeton, New Jersey-based institute publishes Public Opinion Quarterly, the official journal of the *public opinion*[5]-related *organizations*[6] throughout the U.S. Gallup poll results have been phenomenally accurate, with the exception of 1948, when AIPO and the other major polling agencies predicted a Thomas Dewey victory over *Harry Truman*[6]. See also *probability*[5] *sample*; *quota*[5] *sample*; *random*[5] *sample*.

poll, Harris. One of the leading "new polls" designed to provide private customer service to businesses, political candidates, and private individuals. The polling services of Louis Harris and Associates, Inc., begun in 1956, may be hired by a political candidate in order to help him assess *public opinion*[5] on particular issues and to help him map strategy for taking political advantage of the acquired information. Louis Harris, *president*[3] of the *organization*[6], personally served as a campaign strategist for *Senator*[7] John F. Kennedy in the presidential election of 1960. Mr. Harris is a former colleague of Elmo Roper (see *Roper poll*[5]), a specialist in research analysis and marketing, and the author of Is There a Republican Majority (1954). He began publishing a regular *public opinion poll*[5] in 1963 and has done some polling through the media of television.

poll, public opinion. A systematic analysis of selected groups and individuals arranged so as to determine the nature of *public opinion*[5] on a given question at a particular time. See also *Gallup poll*[5]; *Harris poll*[5]; *Roper poll*[5].

poll, Roper. One of the oldest and most successful American *public opin-*

ion polls[5], a poll begun during the 1920's by Elmo Roper and reorganized as the Roper Public Opinion Research Center at Williams College in Massachusetts in 1957. The center's data is available to educators, *government*[3] agencies, and other nonprofit research institutes. Roper began the Fortune Survey for Fortune magazine in 1935 by predicting a *Franklin D. Roosevelt*[6] victory in the presidential election of 1936. The Roper poll surveys all areas of *society*[3], social concern, and *public opinion*[5], and regularly publishes the results.

poll, straw: see *straw vote*[5].

precinct. The primary political subdivision in the U.S., a subdivision used for basic party *organization*[6] and electoral practices. Precincts act as voting areas within each *county*[11] or major *municipality*[11] in the U.S. *Party convention*[5] activities start at this level and move upward to the county, *state*[3], and national conventions. Each *political party*[5] at the precinct level may choose precinct captains to lead party activities. State and county officials use the precinct as the basic unit for operating the electoral machinery within the state.

president, minority. A *President*[6] who is elected to the highest elective office in the U.S. on the basis of a *majority*[3] vote of the *electoral*[4] *college* even though he receives less than an *absolute majority*[3] of all the *popular votes*[5] cast in the election. Such a possibility arises because of the operation of the electoral college, which gives all the popular votes cast in a *state*[3] to the presidential candidate receiving a *plurality*[3] of that state's votes. For example, in 1968 Richard Nixon's 31,770,237 votes were less than the 41,176,674 cast for candidates Hubert Humphrey (31,270,533) and George Wallace (9,906,141) combined. However, Nixon's *electoral vote*[5] of 301 was an absolute majority when compared to the combination of Humphrey's 191 and Wallace's 46 electoral votes (total of 237).

President's Club. A *Democratic Party*[5] fund-raising *organization*[6] created in 1962 to assist *President*[6] *Lyndon Johnson*[6] and other Democratic officials in their bids for reelection in 1964. The loosely organized club operated at the *state*[3] level without *federal*[3] regulation. It was composed of over 2,500 individuals who contributed $1,000 or more to the Democratic National Committee or its affiliates. Members were given special recognition through invitations to the White House and the presentation of presidential souvenirs. The organization disbanded when President Johnson retired from office in 1968. See also *party committee*[5].

pressure group. A group of individuals, generally exhibiting some formal *organization*[6] which actively seeks to influence the process of *government*[3] to its own advantage. Pressure groups act on government in general, are most frequently concerned with economic or social issues, can rarely be held responsible for *legislation*[7] or administrative decisions, and are led by a few politically active personalities. See also *interest*[5] *group*; *iron*[3] *law of oligarchy*; *public opinion*[5]; *lobby*[5].

primary: see *direct primary*[5].

primary, blanket (wide-open). A nominating election arranged to choose *political party*[5] candidates to run for office in the *general election*[5] and in which all registered voters may participate regardless of party affiliation. Participants may vote for candidates for all available offices regardless of the candidates' party affiliations. The *state*[3] of Washington is the only state in the Union presently using such a primary. See also *direct primary*[5]; *open primary*[5]; *raiding*[5].

primary, challenge. A nomination by *party convention*[5] which may be final but which leaves open the possibility that any losing candidate with a sizable percentage of the convention vote may demand a *direct primary*[5] election.

primary, closed. A nominating election arranged to choose *political party*[5] candidates to run for office in the *general election*[5] and in which only registered party members may participate. The closed primary excludes *independent*[5] voters from the nomination process in *states*[3] using such an arrangement. However, for parties using such a device, it keeps members of an opposition party from participating in the nomination of their party candidates and avoids the possibility of the opposition nominating weak candidates which the opposition could later defeat, an action known as *raiding*[5]. See also *direct primary*[5]; *open primary*[5].

primary, direct. An election arranged to permit qualified voters to participate directly in the nomination process by voting for candidates who wish to run for public office in a *general election*[5]. The direct primary operates in different ways in different *states*[3] and in some cases is used not only to nominate candidates for office but to choose *political party*[5] officials or *delegates*[5] to *party conventions*[5]. See also *blanket primary*[5]; *challenge primary*[5]; *closed primary*[5]; *Newberry*[1] *v. U.S.*; *nonpartisan primary*[5]; *open primary*[5]; *presidential preference primary*[5]; *raiding*[5]; *running off primary*[5]; *U.S.*[1] *v. Classic*; *white primary*[5].

primary nonpartisan. A *primary*[5] election arranged to nominate candidates without regard to *political party*[5] affiliation or identification. The use of the *nonpartisan*[5] primary differs from place to place. In most instances, any nominated candidate who receives an *absolute majority*[3] vote in the primary automatically becomes the winner in the *general election*[5]. If no nominee has an absolute majority vote, the two highest nominees face one another in the general election.

primary, open. A nominating election arranged to choose *political party*[5] candidates to run for office in the *general election*[5]; it is an election in which any registered voter may participate. A qualified voter has to meet no political party qualification before casting his ballot and he may participate in the *primary*[5] of any party putting forth possible nominees. In some open primaries the voter is given the ballots of all participating parties and in the voting booth may choose one of the party's ballots and nominate candidates for the general election from that ballot. The unused ballot is returned to the election officials. The open primary permits *independent*[5] voters to participate in the nomination process, but it also permits what is known as *raiding*[5], a process in which a person may nominate weak candidates which he hopes will be defeated in the general election.

primary, presidential preference. An election used to select an individual as the *political party*[5] preference for *U.S. President*[6]. In a few *states*[3] both parties make their preferences on the same day, with a view toward influencing the choices which will be made at the national *party conventions*[5]. The primary may also be used to choose *delegates*[5] to the party's national convention. In some states such a *primary*[5] pledges the delegates to vote for a particular person at the convention. In other states the delegates are free to vote for their own choices once they meet in convention. Presidential preference primaries are physically demanding, expensive to conduct, have no binding effect, and sometimes unnecessarily bind a convention *delegation*[5] from a particular state. They sometimes, however, prove to be a testing ground for the various presidential contenders within a given party. During a

presidential campaign year the *state*[3] of New Hampshire holds the first presidential preference primary in the early spring and California and New York hold the last major ones during the summer.

primary, runoff. A *primary*[5] election necessitated because no *political party*[5] candidate for a particular office received an *absolute majority*[3] of the votes cast. A few *states*[3], noticeably in the South, use runoff primaries to make the final choice between the two party candidates receiving the greatest support in the election.

primary, white. A *primary*[5] election in which black persons are barred from participating in selection of *political party*[5] nominees to run for office in the *general election*[5]. The use of such a device effectively kept Negroes in most southern *states*[3] from having a voice in electing public officials until it was declared *unconstitutional*[3] by the *U.S. Supreme*[8] *Court* in 1944. This was true because the southern states solidly supported the *Democratic Party*[5] and were known as one-party states. State officials were generally determined in the primary elections. Supreme Court interpretations generally influenced the nature of the white primary. In 1927 the Court said that outright prohibition of Negroes from the Democratic primary in the state of Texas was in violation of the *Fourteenth Amendment*[4] *equal*[4] protection clause. In 1932 the Court declared that a Texas *statute*[8] permitting an executive *party committee*[5] of the Democratic Party to establish the criteria for party membership and participation was unconstitutional because it was designed to bar Negroes from voting and was in violation of the equal protection clause of the Fourteenth Amendment. In 1935 the Court reversed itself and held that a political party could exclude persons from participation in a primary on the basis of race since a political party is a private association. The Court held that *discrimination*[9] in such an event was not by the state but by a private party and therefore was not in violation of the equal protection clause. The Court reversed its 1935 reversal in 1944 in the Texas decision of *Smith*[1] *v. Allwright*, once again holding the white primary to be unconstitutional. In the 1944 decision, the present guideline for the white primary, the Court shifted from reference to the Fourteenth Amendment and held that the exclusion of Negroes from state primary elections was in violation of the *Fifteenth Amendment*[5], an *amendment*[3] giving the Negroes the right to vote. The Court held that the political party functions not as a private association in such a process but as an agent of the state. Discrimination by the party, in essence, becomes discrimination by the state. Before 1944 the Court had some difficulty in pointing out that the *federal government*[3] could regulate primary elections, since primaries came under state control. However, after the Court upheld the *power*[3] of the *Congress*[4] to regulate primary elections within the states in *United*[1] *States v. Classic* in 1941, it became easier to outlaw the white primary altogether in 1944. See also *civil*[9] *rights; general election*[5]; *Grovey*[1] *v. Townsend; Nixon*[1] *v. Condon; Nixon*[1] *v. Herndon.*

probability sample. A compiled gauge of *public opinion*[5] collected on the basis of statistical analysis and questioning patterns involving representative categories (age, income, sex, geographical region, race, etc.) and designed so that every person in the total population ("universe" or "sample") under consideration faces the possibility (probability) of being questioned. Once the separate variables operating within the "universe" to be sampled are determined, those taking the poll may question a limited number of individuals possessing the same social characteristics. They must follow the rigidly predetermined and

scientific criteria in order to consider the sample valid. Probability sampling has been the most successful and popular kind of public opinion survey method used since 1948. See also *public opinion poll*[5].

propaganda. Systematic representation of a particular point of view through indoctrination or mass efforts designed to elicit support. Propaganda, either true or false, may be used to elicit support for or against specific ideas, persons, programs, or *nations*[3]. It is a basic device of political persuasion in almost every form of political system, from the extremely *democratic*[3] to the extremely *totalitarian*[3]. See also *demagogue*[5]; *last-minute*[5] *lie; Madison*[5] *Avenue; public opinion*[5]; *United*[2] *States Information Agency.*

quota sample. A compiled gauge of *public opinion*[5] collected on the basis of quotas from categories preselected for analysis by anyone sampling public opnion and in which those taking the poll interview at random within the separate categories (age, income, sex, *political party*[5], etc.). The results of the sample may or may not be reliable ,depending on such factors as the bias of the interviewers in their selection of persons to interview, location of questioning, and other independent variables. The quota sample was the most popular form of *public opinion poll*[5] used in the U.S. between 1936 and 1948.

raiding (crossover voting). The process in which a group of *political party*[5] adherents switch their votes in an *open primary*[5] to candidates of the opposition party in hopes of nominating weak candidates who will later face their own party's stronger candidates in the *general election*[5]. See also *closed primary*[5].

random sample. A compiled gauge of *public opinion*[5] collected on the basis of a nonsystematic and nonscientific questioning of various individuals stopped at random and questioned about their attitudes on one or several public issues. The random sample was popularized in the area of *politics*[3] in the U.S. by the *Literary*[5] *Digest* beginning in 1916. The random sample was the most widely used sampling technique in the U.S. between 1916 and 1936. See also *public opinion poll*[5]; *straw vote*[5].

recall: see *recall election*[5].

referendum: see Chap. 3.

registration: see *periodic registration*[5]; *permanent registration*[5].

registration, periodic. A process of voter registration requiring re-registration of voters prior to each election or after a stated lapse of time (one to ten years, etc.), regardless of prior participation in elections of the same order or in the same polling place. Texas was the last *state*[3] to use the periodic registration system, a system it abandoned in 1971. See also *permanent registration*[5].

registration, permanent. A process of voter registration which requires an initial act of registration without repeated re-registration for participation in elections of the same order or in the same polling place. Texas was the last *state*[3] to adopt some form of permanent voter registration, an action taken in 1971. See also *periodic registration*[5].

representation, proportional. *Representation*[7] within a legislative body which is clearly based on the fact that each *legislator*[7] is representing approximately the same number of people as every other legislator. The concept of proportional representation has been buttressed in the U.S. through development of the *one-man*[5], *one-vote rule* and judicial decisions based on the *Fourteenth Amendment*[4] *equal*[4] *protection clause*. See also *apportionment*[7]; *reapportionment*[7]; *redistricting*[7]; *Proportional Representation*[5]; *virtual representation*[7].

Representation, Proportional (P.R.). A formal system of *minority*[3] *representation*[7] within a *legislature*[7]. The system *apportions*[7] legislative seats on the basis of the electoral strength of the various *political parties*[5] within the political system. See also *Hare*[5] *system*; *list*[5] *system*; *minority*[9] *group*; *proportional representation*[5].

Revolution of 1800. A popular term indicating the activity in 1800 which led to the adoption of a *two-party*[5] *system* in the U.S. It was the year in which *Thomas Jefferson*[6] was elected *President*[6] as the leader of the *Democratic-Republican Party*[5]. *James Madison*[6], one of the authors of *The Federalist*[4] and an early opponent of partisan *factions*[3] (*Federalist*[5] No. 10), became President Jefferson's highly *partisan*[5] Secretary of State. Madison was elected President in 1808 as the leader of the new *political party*[5]. The second part of the Revolution of 1800 involved a major change in the structure and operation of the *electoral*[4] *college* because of the electoral college tie between Thomas Jefferson and Aaron Burr. It was the first time the *House*[7] *of Representatives* had to choose the President. By 1803 the *Twelfth Amendment*[5] had been added to permit the presidential and vice-presidential candidates to run as a team and to be voted on through the use of separate ballots. The third part of the *revolution*[3] concerned the U.S. *Supreme*[8] *Court*. *John Adams*[6], the *Federalist Party*[5] leader defeated by Jefferson in 1800, appointed his partisan Secretary of State, *John Marshall*[8], as *Chief*[8] *Justice* of the Supreme Court just before the Democratic-Republicans took office in 1801. In his lengthy tenure on the Court (1801–35), Marshall influenced numerous cases in a highly partisan fashion and stamped *Federalist*[4] policies[6] on the U.S. even though his party had died out by 1816. A fourth part of the revolution involved the acceptance of *Jeffersonian democracy*[4] and general support of the common man in contrast to a favored *aristocracy*[3].

scalawag. A word used to describe a white person living in the South after the *Civil*[4] *War* who assisted northern *radicals*[3] (*carpetbaggers*[5]) who moved into the South to take advantage of the social, political, and economic dislocation during *Reconstruction*[4].

Schattschneider, E. E., 1892– . Columbia University professor of *political*[3] *science*, former *president*[6] of the *American*[5] *Political Science Association*, and author of Party Government (1942), one of the most systematic modern defenses of the party system of *government*[3]. Professor Schattschneider revived interest in the various concepts of *responsible party government*[5] and modernized the study of such governments. His careful analysis of the *two-party*[5] *system* of government led him to conclude that *political parties*[5] are the base of *democracy*[3] and that democracy continues only as long as parties effectively operate. He examined the nature of political parties, the competitive struggle between parties, party systems, internal party structures, the political struggles between the different branches of government, party leaders, and *pressure*[5] *groups*. Schattschneider has also written Politics, Pressures, and the Tariff (1935), The Semisovereign People: A Realist's View of Democracy in America (1960), numerous journal articles, and other volumes on political dynamics.

Solid South. An expression used to indicate the overwhelming support the southern *states*[3] gave to the *Democratic Party*[5] after *Reconstruction*[4] (1865–77), a period extending roughly

between 1877 and 1948. See also *one-party*[5] *system*.

Southern Christian Leadership Conference (SCLC), 1957– . The *liberal*[3] civil rights *organization*[6] brought to prominence under the leadership of Reverend *Martin Luther King*[9], *Jr*. The organization was officially formed in 1957 by King and others who had helped him fight one of the first modern nonviolent *civil*[9] *disobedience* battles in the U.S., the 1955 Montgomery, Alabama *boycott*[10] of racially *segregated*[9] *city*[11] buses. The SCLC popularized *sit-ins*[9], *freedom*[9] *rides*, *civil*[9] *rights* marches, mass civil rights demonstrations, and civil disobedience. Its major efforts came in 1963 with a civil rights march on Selma, Alabama and a mass gathering in *Washington*[4], *D.C*. In 1966 it moved into the North in an effort to *integrate*[9] Chicago *suburbs*[11]. About the same time, the leadership of the organization began to speak out against the *Vietnam*[12] *War* because of the disproportionate number of black young men who were dying there and because some of those young men could not be buried in segregated public cemeteries once they were returned from Vietnam. In 1968 King was assassinated in Memphis, Tennessee while participating in a garbage worker's *strike*[10]. Reverend Ralph David Abernathy, one of the founders of the SCLC, succeeded the fallen leader and led a previously planned poor people's march on Washington, D.C. The SCLC constructed a shanty town on the mall near the Washington Monument and called the area Resurrection City. The 1968 march was far less successful than the 1963 rally, and it raised public questions over the direction the organization would take without the *charismatic*[5] leadership of King.

stalking horse. A political candidate who campaigns ostensibly for his own interest but who in reality seeks to divide the opposition or conceal the identity of a person who will come forward at a later time as the official contender for office.

statesman. An individual who is consistently and publicly recognized as a wise and successful leader of the people. See also *politician*[5]; *statesmanship*[5].

strategy, inside. Political campaign strategy predicated on the belief that a *political party*[5] nomination may be secured through control of party machinery and *party convention*[5] delegates chosen through regular party machinery. Inside strategy such as that used by Republican Barry Goldwater in the presidential election of 1964 and by Democrat Hubert H. Humphrey in the presidential election of 1968 seeks to enlist convention *delegate*[5] support in a highly subtle fashion well in advance of the national nominating convention. See also *outside strategy*[5].

strategy, outside. Political campaign strategy predicated on the belief that a *political party*[5] nomination may be secured through an appeal to political party members and the general electorate who can *force*[3] a *party convention*[5] nomination on the basis of popular expressions of support. Outside strategy employs mass demonstrations, letter-writing campaigns, *presidential preference primaries*[5], *public opinion polls*[5], and other highly visible campaign methods. In the presidential election of 1968 *Senator*[7] Eugene McCarthy sought to gain the nomination of the *Democratic Party*[5] through the use of standard outside strategy procedures based on the active support of university students. See also *New*[5] *Politics*; *inside strategy*[5].

Student Non-Violent Coordinating Committee (SNCC), 1960– . An activist Negro *civil*[9] rights organiza-tion[6] that helped organize and coordinate the civil rights *sit-ins*[9] and Negro voter *registration*[5] drives of the 1960's. The committee was created in 1960 with Marion Barry as president. Money was raised to coordinate civil rights activities throughout the South, and *delegates*[5] were chosen from 16 *states*[3] and the *District of Columbia*[4]. In 1966 Stokley Carmichael was chosen president and began to popularize the term *black*[9] power. He was followed by an equally *radical*[3] leader named Rap Brown. The radical organization is unusual in that it considers its entire membership as a coordinating *committee*[7].

Students for a Democratic Society (SDS), 1962– . A *radical*[3], *leftist*[3], idealistic, *nihilistic*[3], and *Marxist*[3]-oriented, loose-knit *organization*[6] of university students. The SDS, composed primarily of middle-class whites, arose as part of the "free speech" and *New*[5] *Left* movements of the 1960's. The national organization was founded by Carl Oglesby, Tom Hayden, Rennard (Rennie) Davis, and other student radicals. The group, originally a fragmented collection of local student organizations seeking general social reform, became the leading radical movement of the New Left. About the time the U.S. began to bomb North Vietnam in 1965, the SDS radicalized and moved outside established avenues of political change. It began to call for violent attacks on American *society*[3] and its governmental institutions. SDS leaders were at the forefront of campus unrest during the 1960's and helped organize the violent demonstration which erupted in Chicago during the Democratic Convention of 1968. Around 1968 the SDS developed an internal *power*[3] struggle between theoreticians and activists. It also lost numerous students through university graduation, through rejection by moderate students, and through withdrawal by militant groups such as the Weathermen. The radical elements of SDS moved "underground" between 1968 and 1970 and were blamed for various destructive attacks on *government*[3] *property*[10]. The SDS actively opposed the *Vietnam*[12] *War*, general U.S. foreign and military *policy*[6], the *draft*[12], university defense research, *corporate*[5] *monopolies*[10], white racism, and other similar items. It stressed "participatory *democracy*[3]" whereby each individual helps determine his own fate. It also called for total destruction of the present American social and political system, but it rarely discussed the nature of its replacement. See also *Walker*[8] *Report*.

suffrage. The right to participate in the electoral processes of a social and political system through the use of the vote.

suffragette. A female advocate of voting rights for women. See also *suffrage*[5].

Survey Research Center (SRC), University of Michigan, 1948– . An academic research center which has distinguished itself though in-depth studies of U.S. presidential elections, especially those since 1948. The SRC is basically sociopsychological in its approach to the study of voting behavior. It relies heavily on survey field research, questionnaires, and computer analysis. The first major study by the SRC was in 1948. The first major publication of the center was The Voter Decides (1954), by Angus Campbell, Philip E. Converse, Warren E. Miller, and Donald E. Stokes. The Voter Decides, a *probability sample*[5] study of the 1952 presidential election, analyzed voter participation, *political party*[5] and socioeconomic identification, issue perception, and voter attitudes. In 1960 the SRC published The American Voter, a highly ambitious and detailed behavioral analysis of voting behavior and a work frequently

cited as the major voting study to date. The interview study, drawing largely from data collected in 1952 and 1956, emphasized voter apathy, party identification, *ideology*[3], *political*[3] *socialization*, and group interests of political participants. See also *behavioral political*[3] *science*.

Tammany Hall. The oldest political *machine*[5] in the U.S. The machine is the dominant portion of the *Democratic Party*[5] organization of New York County and was originally based on a fraternal group which met regularly in the hall of the Society of St. Tammany, an *organization*[6] founded May 12, 1789 and named after a legendary chief of the Delaware Indians. See also *Tweed*[5] *Ring*.

Tasmanian Dodge. A chain voting maneuver wherein a person steals an official ballot, marks it, and hands it to a *floater*[5] to use in voting in a regular nonmachine voting booth. The marked ballot is then exchanged for the unmarked one received at the polling place. The stolen ballot is returned to election officials while the new ballot goes to a *political party*[5] *organization*[6] man who then marks it for the next floater.

tax, poll. A *direct tax*[10] levied on individuals. In the area of elections the poll tax was at one time used in the U.S. as a prerequisite for voting. Poll taxes were used in some *federal*[3] elections in several *states*[3] until adoption of the *Twenty-fourth Amendment*[5] to the *U.S. Constitution*[4] prohibited them in 1965. Their use in state elections was declared *unconstitutional*[3] in the U.S. *Supreme*[8] *Court* case of *Harper*[1] *v. Virginia State Board of Elections* on the grounds that they violated the *equal*[4] *protection clause* of the *Fourteenth Amendment*[4].

thick skin (glass house) doctrine. The doctrine which emphasizes that persons who enter active and open political combat should develop a "thick skin" in order to survive. The doctrine is sometimes referred to as the "glass house" doctrine because *politicians*[5] live in "glass" houses, that is, most of their personal and political life is open to public scrutiny. See also *Monitor*[1] *Patriot v. Roy.*

ticket, split. A ballot on which a person votes for candidates of more than one *political party*[5]. See also *straight ticket*[5].

ticket, straight. A ballot on which a person votes for all the candidates nominated by one *political party*[5]. See also *split ticket*[5].

Tory: see Chap. 4.

Toward a More Responsible Two-Party System (1950). A significant and controversial analysis of the American *two-party*[5] *system* which was published by the *American*[5] *Political Science Association* as a supplement to the American Political Science Review of September 1950. In the report a *committee*[7] of the APSA criticized the lack of *political party*[5] discipline, the problem of party leadership, *organization*[6] weaknesses, and vague party *platforms*[5]. The committee recommended revisions in the various problem areas in order to bring about *responsible party government*[5], both inside and outside the U.S. *Congress*[4]. The report of the group was praised for its candor, but criticized by those who feared that strict and responsible party procedures would tend to *polarize*[3] the political system within the U.S.

Tweed Ring. A corrupt political *organization*[6] which operated in New York City under the leadership of William Marcy Tweed from 1868 to 1871. Boss Tweed dominated *Tammany*[5] *Hall* and was responsible for misappropriation of millions of dollars of *government*[3] funds. He died in 1876 while serving a jail term in New York City.

two-party system. A political system wherein political *power*[3] and governmental offices tend to fluctuate between two *political parties*[5] recognized as clearly offering the electorate acceptable alternatives in *government*[3]. See also *majority party*[5]; *minority party*[5]; *Revolution*[5] *of 1800.*

two-thirds rule. Any rule of any *organization*[6] which requires that two-thirds of a whole number must give assent to an action or decision before the results will be accepted by the group. One of the most famous two-thirds rules in U.S. political history was the two-thirds rule adopted by the Democratic Convention in 1832, the first *Democratic Party*[5] national nominating *party convention*[5], and abandoned in 1936. The rule required that two-thirds of the total number of votes in the convention would be "necessary to constitute a choice" for presidential and vice-presidential candidates of the party. The rule was dropped in 1936 in favor of a rule permitting choices to be made by an *absolute majority*[3] vote of the *delegates*[5].

United Farm Workers Union (UFW), 1962– . The first successful large-scale farm workers *labor*[10] *union,* begun by Caesar Chavez when he organized the transient grape pickers of California. The *organization*[6] began on the basis of "La Causa" as expressed by Mexican-American *minority*[3] workers. The union's first major strike known as "La Huelga" and the organization's efforts toward continued existence were actively supported by U.S. *Senator*[7] Robert Kennedy of New York. The union has used nation-wide *boycotts*[10] against table grapes and lettuce harvested by non-union labor. It also supports cultural unity and pride among the *minority* group referred to as Chicano.

United Mine Workers of America (UMW), 1890– . An industrial union of coal miners and related workers in the U.S. and Canada. The UMW is an independent *labor*[10] *union* which was at one time an affiliate of the AFL-CIO. It gained its major *power*[3] during the *New*[6] *Deal* under the leadership of John L. Lewis and became known as one of the most *radical*[3] unions in the U.S. between 1933 and 1950. The union seeks higher wages, better working conditions, health services for injured workers, and other things thought necessary to assist those working in one of the most dangerous industries in the U.S.

unit rule. A rule of any *organization*[6] which requires that any person or any issue receiving a *plurality*[3] of votes cast will be given all of the votes cast for all candidates or all issues in the election. It is a winner-take-all system. The unit rule operates in the separate *electoral*[4] *college* votes in the various *states*[3] and gives all of the *electoral votes*[5] in the state to the presidential and vice-presidential candidates receiving the largest number of votes, regardless of the number of *popular votes*[5] the losers received in the election. The *Democratic Party*[5] used the unit vote in Democratic national *party conventions*[5] through the Democratic Convention of 1968, at which time it was dropped for future elections. Separate state *delegations*[5] could be bound in state conventions to use the unit rule at the national convention. All of the state's *political party*[5] *delegate*[5] votes would go for one presidential aspirant regardless of individual expressions or desires within the *delegation*[5]. The unit rule is used in another context in the legislative process. The *conference committee*[7] of the *Congress*[4] uses a *unit vote*[7] in working out details of *legislation*[7] before submitting the legislation for *executive*[6] approval. See also *county-unit*[5] *system*.

Veterans of Foreign Wars (VFW), 1899– . One of the major veteran's groups, an *organization*[6] which restricts its membership to servicemen who have served overseas. The VFW was organized in Columbus, Ohio by veterans who had served overseas during the *Spanish-American*[12] *War*. Its stated objectives support a strong military establishment, the rehabilitation of disabled veterans, assistance for military dependents, and the promotion of Americanism. Recent measures the VFW has supported are: the *Vietnam*[12] *War*, *veterans'*[6] *preference* in *civil*[6] *service*, improvements in the *Veterans*[2] *Administration*, the *Cold*[12] *War G.I.*[12] *Bill of Rights*, exclusion of Red China from the *United*[12] *Nations*, strict enforcement of the *Monroe*[12] *Doctrine*, development of the *anti-ballistic*[12] *missile* (ABM), university *Reserve*[12] *Officers Training Corps* (ROTC) and military research programs, and housing and jobs for veterans returning from the *war*[12] in Vietnam. See also *two-China*[12] *theory*.

vote, electoral. A term used to describe the voting percentages of the electors of the *electoral*[4] *college* when the college votes for *President*[6]. The term also applies to any similar body used in any other election. In the presidential election, any group of electors within a *state*[3] is certified as the official slate if it receives a *plurality*[3] of *popular votes*[5] cast within the state. The presidential candidate who receives a *majority*[3]—270—of the electoral votes from all electors in all states is declared President of the United States. See also *popular vote*[5].

vote, majority: see *majority*[3].

vote, popular. A term used to describe the voting percentages of a total number of qualified voters within a given population. Electoral victory based on a popular vote generally requires an *absolute majority*[3] of qualified voters or a *plurality*[3] of votes cast in the election. See also *plebiscite*[3]; *electoral vote*[5].

vote, protest. A vote cast by a qualified voter in opposition to his general interests, desires, or *political party*[5] affiliation in order to emphasize his dissatisfaction with party policies or candidates.

Voter Decides, The. see *Survey*[5] *Research Center.*

vote, straw. A general canvass of *public opinion*[5] in certain sections of an electorate prior to an election in order to elicit their views concerning candidates and public issues. Straw votes are generally taken on the basis of *random samples*[5] through the distribution of ballots at selected locations. Straw votes, or polls, may be scientifically structured in order to obtain a reasonably accurate view of public sentiment. However, most straw votes are unsystematic and unscientific. See also *public opinion poll*[5].

vote, write-in. A vote cast by a qualified voter for a person whose name was not printed on the official ballot. Many *states*[3] and *municipalities*[11] permit voters to write in names of persons generally qualified for office but whose names do not appear on the ballot.

voting, absentee. Electoral participation by qualified voters who are permitted to mail in ballots or vote before the regular election since they will not be present in their electoral *district*[7] on election day.

voting, compulsory. Electoral participation which is required by *law*[8]. No *state*[3] in the U.S. uses such a system of voting. However, compulsory voting which transforms the vote from a right or a privilege into a legal duty is used in Australia, Belgium, the Netherlands, Austria, Brazil, Italy, and other *nations*[3] of the world.

voting, cumulative. A system of voting wherein once a quota for electoral victory is reached by a candidate, the remaining votes cast for him are transferred to another candidate. One form of cumulative voting used in *multi-member districts*[7] permits voters to cast three votes as they wish. A voter may cast all of his votes for one candidate, divide them equally among all candidates, or cast one vote for each candidate. Cumulative votes are used to designate victors. Such a system ordinarily allows *minority*[3] *representation*[7] within a *legislature*[7]. See also *Hare*[5] *system*; *list*[5] *system*; *minority*[9] *group*; *minority party*[5]; *preferential voting*[5]; *Proportional Representation*[5].

voting, list system. A form of *Proportional Representation*[5] widely used in Europe. The system permits a voter to vote for a list of candidates without indicating any order of preference. Any positions the *political party*[5] list wins are assigned to persons in the order in which their names are listed on the ballot. See also *Hare*[5] *system*; *list*[5] *system.*

voting, plural. A system of voting wherein qualified voters are assigned voting strength according to criteria selected by the voting officials. Criteria most often used in systems using plural voting are *property*[10] ownership, education, occupation, and family relationship. For example, in electoral strength or *policy-making*[7] *power*[3], a person with a higher education or greater property value may be given twice as much voting strength as a person with a low education and no property.

voting, preferential. A system of voting in which a qualified voter indicates his order of preference among several candidates listed for separate offices. Preferential voting is most useful at the local level and usually incorporates the idea of *cumulative voting*[5] to determine which candidates have won a clear *majority*[3] of all votes and preferences cast. See also *Hare*[5] *system*; *list*[5] *system.*

Voting Rights Act of 1965. The major federal *civil*[9] *rights* legislation designed specifically to remove electoral barriers and discriminatory practices keeping Negroes from participating in the electoral process. The *legislation*[7] suspended *literacy*[5] *tests* in areas where less than 50 percent of eligible voters were registered or voting. It also empowered *federal*[3] registrars to assist in voter *registration*[5] in areas of widespread *discrimination*[9]. The *act*[8] further provided for testing the *constitutionality*[3] of the use of *poll taxes*[5] in the election of *state*[3] officials. See also *Harper*[1] *v. Virginia State Board of Elections*; *South*[1] *Carolina v. Katzenbach*; *Voting*[5] *Rights Act of 1970*.

Voting Rights Act of 1970. A controversial *federal*[3] *act*[8] which extended the *Voting*[5] *Rights Act of 1965* until 1975, reduced the voting age in federal elections to 18 years, established a uniform residency requirement for federal elections, established the right to vote by absentee ballot in all federal elections, and banned the use of *literacy*[5] *tests* across the *nation*[3] rather than in selected *states*[3]. The *legislation*[7] contained a clause permitting the *Supreme*[8] *Court* to quickly decide whether the *18-year-old*[5] *vote* provision was *constitutional*[3]. On December 21, 1970 the Court held that the provision was contitutional and that the *federal government*[3] could establish age qualifications for elections of federal officials but not for state officials. See also *Oregon*[1] *v. Mitchell*.

ward. A *territorial*[3] division of municipal *government*[3] which is generally used as a voting subdivision, a representative district, or a *district*[7] designed to effectively provide *municipal*[11] services.

WASP. Stands for White Anglo-Saxon Protestant. The popular designation of a person whose political interests and activities tend to reflect the *Protestant*[4] *Ethic*. See also *the Establishment*[3].

Watergate controversy, 1972– . An election scandal frequently cited as the worst scandal in American political history. The scandal began with the arrest of seven burglars in the *Washington*[4], *D.C.* Watergate Hotel headquarters of the *Democratic Party*[5]. Among the men arrested were former *Central*[2] *Intelligence Agency* members, former *Federal*[2] *Bureau of Investigation* agents, and former participants in the *Bay*[12] *of Pigs controversy*. After all wcrc found guilty in *Federal*[3] court there were various revelations of *wiretaps*[9] of the Watergate which were paid for from *Republican Party*[5] secret campaign contributions. The burglars were also connected with the *Pentagon*[12] *Papers* trial of Daniel Ellsberg and undue *government*[3] influence led to the dismissal of charges. *President*[6] Nixon eventually revealed the existence of a secret *White*[2] *House intelligence*[12] unit designed to protect "national security." The scandal led to numerous resignations and dismissals of high-level *Executive*[2] *Office* advisers to the president, the indictment of two former Nixon *cabinet*[6] officials, a full scale *Senate*[7] investigation, and a weakening of presidential initiative. In mid-1973 some individuals were openly discussing the possible *impeachment*[7] of President Nixon because of the Watergate crisis.

Weathermen: see *Students*[5] *for a Democratic Society*.

Whig: see Chap. 4.

white citizens' councils, 1954– . A loosely organized group of "white supremacy" *organizations*[6] which arose in the South after the 1954 *U.S. Supreme*[8] *Court* decision of *Brown*[1] *v. Board of Education of Topeka*, a decision which declared *segregated*[9] public schools to be *unconstitutional*[3]. The white citizens' councils originated in Sunflower County, Mississippi in July 1954. They were copied under various names all across the South. State chapters such as the Mississippi Association of Councils help direct the work of local groups. The councils are generally composed of upper middle-class or middle-class whites opposed to *integration*[9] in any form. They oppose school integration, *socialism*[3], and racial intermarriage. *State*[3] and local chapters supply public speakers and provide a public information service. It is supposedly left up to individual members to decide what economic or social action they wish to take against those seeking to integrate the races. See also *antimiscegenation*[9] *law*.

Women's Christian Temperance Union (WCTU), 1874– . A woman's *organization*[6] dedicated to the abolition of traffic in liquor products. The WCTU has been a highly influential civic and philanthropic group and was partially responsible for the passage of the *Eighteenth Amendment*[4] to the *Constitution*[4], an *amendment*[3] which prohibited the manufacture and sale of alcoholic beverages. See also *Twenty-first Amendment*[4]; *Anti-Saloon*[5] *League*; *Prohibition Party*[5].

Yippies: see *Youth International Party*[5].

Supreme Court cases related to material in this chapter are arranged below by subject. Summaries of the cases are in Chapter One arranged alphabetically by the name of the first party in each case.

LEGISLATIVE APPOR-
TIONMENT—
Avery v. *Midland Co.*
(1968)
Baker v. *Carr* (1962)
Colgrove v. *Green* (1946)
Gomillion v. *Lightfoot*
(1960)
Gray v. *Sanders* (1963)
Kirkpatrick v. *Preisler*
(1969)
Reynolds v. *Sims* (1964)
Wesberry v. *Sanders*
(1964)

POLITICAL CAMPAIGN-
ING—(Libel)
Monitor Patriot v. *Roy*
(1971)

POLITICAL INFLUENCE
—(Fairness Doctrine)
Red Lion Broadcasting Co.
v. *FCC* (1969)

POLITICAL INFLUENCE
—(Lobbying)
U.S. v. *Harriss* (1954)

VOTING—(General)
Carrington v. *Rash* (1965)
S.C. v. *Katzenbach*
(1966)

VOTING—(Eighteen-year-
old Vote)
Oregon v. *Mitchell* (1970)

VOTING—(Gerrymander)
Gomillion v. *Lightfoot*
(1960)

VOTING—(Grandfather
Clause)
Guinn v. *U.S.* (1915)

VOTING—(Literacy Test)
Williams v. *Miss.* (1898)

VOTING—(Poll Tax)
Harper v. *Va. State Board
of Elections* (1966)

VOTING—(Primary,
General)
Newberry v. *U.S.* (1921)
U.S. v. *Classic* (1941)

VOTING—(Primary,
White)
Grovey v. *Townsend*
(1935)
Nixon v. *Condon* (1932)
Nixon v. *Herndon* (1927)
Smith v. *Allwright* (1944)

Chapter 6

The Executive Branch and Public Administration

Note to the reader: Cross-referenced terms are in italics. The superscript number refers to the chapter in which the entry may be found. In addition, its placement indicates the word under which the term is alphabetized. (For example, in *electoral*[4] *college*, information on the electoral college may be found in Chapter 4 under "electoral.") Because italics are used in cross-references, they are not used for terms in which they would ordinarily be used: Supreme Court cases and titles of books, journals, plays, and so forth.

> *Supreme Court cases relating to material in this chapter are listed at the end of the chapter (see page 170).*

Adams, John, 1735–1826. American *colonial*[4] political philosopher, Massachusetts *legislator*[7], *revolutionary*[3] leader in opposition to the *Stamp*[4] *Act of 1765*, member of the *First* and *Second Continental Congresses*[4], first U.S. *Vice-President*[6], and the second U.S. *President*[6] (1797–1801). Adams wrote Novanglus, Letters Addressed to the Inhabitants of the Colony of Massachusetts Bay (1775) in answer to the *Tory*[4] letters of *Daniel Leonard*[4]. He also wrote Thoughts on Government (1776), helped draft the *Declaration*[4] *of Independence* (1776), helped draft the *constitution*[3] of Massachusetts (1780), and wrote A Defence of the Constitutions of Government of the United States of America (1787–88). The Defence greatly influenced the members of the *Constitutional Convention*[4] *of 1787*. Adams defended *state*[3] constitutional systems, a *mixed constitution*[3], *bicameralism*[7]

based on an *aristocratic*[3] *senate*[7] and a *lower chamber*[7] composed of common men, a *popular vote*[5] for a strong chief *executive*[6], a system of *checks*[3] *and balances* containing an executive *veto*[7], a legislative *veto*[7] *override*, and a separate judiciary. John Adams served as *minister*[12] to France, the Netherlands, and Great Britain. He helped negotiate the *Treaty*[12] of Paris which ended the *American Revolution*[4]. He served as Vice-President during the *administration*[6] of *George Washington*[6], was an active leader of the *Federalist Party*[5], a major advocate of the *Alien*[4] *and Sedition Acts of 1798*, and an opponent of military conflict with France. He was defeated for reelection by *Thomas Jefferson*[6] in the so-called *Revolution*[5] *of 1800*. One of Adams' last major acts as President was his appointment of *John Marshall*[8] as *Chief*[8] *Justice* of the *U.S. Supreme*[8] *Court*, an act that had considerable influence on the development of the *federal government*[3] and the U.S. *constitutional*[3] system.

adjudication, administrative. The process whereby an administrative agency holds a *hearing*[6] and determines the dispensation of a case involving a conflict over one of its own *administrative*[6] *orders*, or a set of rules regulating a particular subject. On the *federal*[3] level, the settlement of a conflict over the violation of an administrative rule requires that the official prosecuting a case and the official judging the case be two separate persons. See also *adjudication*[8]; *Administrative*[6] *Procedures Act of 1946*; *quasi-judicial*[8].

administration. The process wherein particular agencies enforce or fulfill public *policies*[6]. Public administration is concerned with management techniques, personnel problems, financial transactions, and other areas closely related to the general management of public affairs. The period during which a chief *executive*[6] serves is frequently referred to as an "administration." See also *bureaucracy*[6]; *fourth*[4] *branch of government*; *administrative law*[8]; *Max Weber*[6].

administrative order (rule). An administrative *act*[8] having the *force*[3] of *law*[8]. Such an order is designed to clarify a law or a specific agency *policy*[6] or to apply an existing rule to a specific situation. See also *Administrative*[6] *Procedures Act of 1946*; *Federal*[6] *Register*; *administrative law*[8]; *Opp*[1] *Cotton Mills v. Administrator of Wage and Hour Division*; *quasi-legislative*[6] *and quasi-judicial*.

Administrative Procedures Act of 1946. A comprehensive federal *law*[8] designed to standardize procedures of operation for *federal*[3] agencies and provide a method of *judicial*[4] *review* for administrative decisions. The *act*[8] specifies areas of administrative *au-*

thority[3] (discretionary, administrative, and *adjudicatory*[8]) and requires: notification of meetings, publication of proposed changes in *administrative*[6] *orders*, the separation of the prosecuting and judging functions within an agency, and that administrative agencies give interested parties opportunity to attend administrative *hearings*[6] and speak on proposed changes. *Due*[9] *process of law* is to guide the basic operation of hearings and administratve appeals. Also, adverse rulings on the part of an agency may be appealed to the regular courts once regular administrative channels have been exhausted.

Advisory Council on Executive Reorganization. A six-member advisory council appointed by *President*[6] Nixon at the beginning of his *administration*[6]. The council was chaired by Roy L. Ash, President of Litton Industries. The other five members were George P. Baker, John B. Connally, Frederick R. Kappell, Richard M. Paget, and Walter N. Thayer. The "Ash Council" was served by approximately 48 staff members. The body turned in its final report in November 1970. Upon the council's recommendations, President Nixon created by *executive*[6] *order* the *Office of Management*[2] *and Budget*, the *Domestic*[2] *Council*, and the *Environmental*[2] *Protection Agency*. The council also recommended that the President undertake sweeping revisions in the structure of *independent regulatory commissions*[6], in the *cabinet*[6], in the area of international trade programs, and with regard to *grants-in-aid*[10] programs involving *state*[3] and local *governments*[3]. It was recommended that the various regulatory agencies be headed by powerful administrators rather than by independent *boards*[6]. It was further recommended that the Cabinet be reduced to eight *departments*[6]. Four departments—State, Justice, Defense, and Treasury—would deal with traditional governmental services. However, four new departments would cover community development, economic affairs, human resources, and natural resources. The basic objectives of such major *administrative reorganization*[6] proposals were to deal with major problems by purpose rather than by *constituency*[5] and to eliminate overlapping *jurisdictions*[8] and duplicated services. Major reorganization involving the Cabinet would require legislative action by the *Congress*[4].

advisoryism, creeping. The process of using numerous *citizen*[3] advisory *committees*[7] or *commissions*[6] to investigate various subject areas related to governmental and social problems. Creeping advisoryism is characterized by a proliferation of committees appointed by *executives*[6], legislative bodies, judicial bodies, and administrative agencies concerned with various subjects ranging from medicine to campus riots and *pornography*[9]. On occasion, a committee's recommendations become a part of judicial, legislative, or *administrative reorganization*[6]. However, on other occasions the lack of action on committee recommendations leads to public suspicion that problems are being hidden under constant and endless committee investigations. See also *Hoover Commission*[6]; *Campus*[11] *Unrest Report*; *Kerner*[8] *Commission Report*; *Pornography*[9] *Report*; *Walker*[8] *Report*; *Warren Commission*[6].

agency, auxiliary (service). An agency of *government*[3] charged with servicing other primary agencies of government. Servicing agencies usually specialize in accounting, personnel, purchasing or transportation.

agency, independent. A *government*[3] agency set apart from regular *cabinet*[6] level or *executive*[6] *department*[6] level agencies. An independent agency is generally listed as either an *auxiliary agency*[6] or an *independent regulatory*

commission[6]. Such agencies are usually created to remove certain matters from *partisan*[5] *politics*[3] or to provide specialized services.

Amendment, Twentieth (1933): see Chap. 7.

Amendment, Twenty-fifth (1967). The *amendment*[3] to the *U.S. Constitution*[4] which provides for the filling of a vice-presidential vacancy once the *Vice-President*[6] succeeds to the presidency, for an *"acting president"*[6] if the *President*[6] is disabled, and for the settlement of disputes which might arise if a Vice-President attempts to take *power*[3] on the grounds that the President is disabled. See also *presidential*[6] *disability*.

Amendment, Twenty-second (1951). The *amendment*[3] to the *U.S. Constitution*[4] which limits a *President*[6] to two of his own elected terms in office or a total of 10 years in office if he succeeded to the office from the vice-presidency. The Twenty-second Amendment was a reaction to strong *executive*[6] leadership under *Franklin D. Roosevelt*[6] and his winning of third and fourth terms in office. It made official a tradition begun by *George Washington*[6] in rejecting a third term as President, a *custom*[3] which had become a part of the *"unwritten constitution*[3]*."*

amnesty. A general group *pardon*[6] of offenders convicted of violating national *legislation*[7]. Amnesty usually involves political offenses and is usually granted by chief *executive*[6] officers. In some *constitutional*[3] *systems* such as the U.S., the legislative branch may also grant amnesty.

appointive powers. The *power*[3] granted to an *executive*[6] to select persons to fill other governmental positions. The *U.S. President*[6] is empowered to fill certain positions with *confirmation*[6] by an *absolute majority*[3] vote of the *Senate*[7]. The President may appoint White House aides, *federal*[3] judges, *diplomatic*[12] officials, military officers, officers holding positions on *independent regulatory commissions*[6], commissioners investigating special subjects (campus riots, *pornography*[9], etc.), and other *government*[3] officials. Some White House and minor positions may be filled without Senate approval. Some members of courts, independent regulatory agencies, *government corporations*[6], and other agencies may fill certain positions without higher approval. Numerous government positions are filled through *merit*[6] *system* testing rather than through *appointment*[6]. See also *civil*[6] *service*; *patronage*[6]; *removal*[6] *powers*; *Schedule*[6] *C*; *senatorial*[6] *courtesy*; *spoils*[6] *system*.

appointment. The process or act wherein one *government*[3] official uses *authority*[3] vested in his office to select persons to fill other government positions. See also *appointive*[6] *power*; *patronage*[6].

appointment, recess (temporary). An *appointment*[6] made by an *executive*[6] official during a *recess*[7] of the *legislature*[7] with the understanding that the appointment will expire at a specified time, usually the end of the next legislative *session*[7], unless approved by the legislature. In the *federal government*[3] such recess appointments must be approved by the *Senate*[7]. See also *appointive*[6] *power*.

authority (power), delegation of. The process or condition of one branch of *government*[3] granting certain *powers*[3] to another branch of government or governmental agency. On various occasions the *Congress*[4] has delegated *authority*[3] to the *President*[6] or *executive*[6] agencies. The *Supreme*[8] *Court* has held that Congress may not delegate any of its *policy*[7] *formulation* power to the President, but that it may grant him the power to formulate rules essential for carrying out legislatively determined *policies*[6] and standards. Delegations of authority must be exercised within clearly specified guidelines. Congress may not delegate authority to *states*[3], and delegations of authority may be broader in foreign affairs than in domestic matters. See also *Hampton*[1] *& Co. v. U.S.*; *National*[10] *Industrial Recovery Act of 1933*; *National*[2] *Recovery Administration*; *Opp*[1] *Cotton Mills v. Administrator of Wage and Hour Division*; *Panama*[1] *Refining Co. v. Ryan*; *Schechter*[1] *Poultry Corp. v. U.S.*; *U.S.*[1] *v. Curtiss-Wright Export Corp.*

board (commission). A group of individuals, generally three or more, charged by legal *authority*[3] with investigating a particular matter, carrying out *executive*[6] *policy*[6], or administering a particular governmental agency.

board of review. A *board*[6] empowered to review administrative decisions and act in an appeals capacity to correct claimed injustices or inequities. A common type of board of review examines complaints concerning *property tax*[10] assessments. See also *assessed*[10] *valuation*; *competitive*[10] *underassessment*; *appellate jurisdiction*.[8]

brain trust. A group of individuals with specialized qualifications or knowledge who are called on by political figures for advice. The term gained popularity during the *administration*[6] of *President*[6] Franklin D. *Roosevelt*[6].

Bryce, James, 1838–1922. British Lord, English historian, and British *ambassador*[12] to the U.S., 1907–13. In 1888 Lord Bryce published a scholarly volume entitled The American Commonwealth, which contained a controversial chapter entitled "Why Great Men Are Not Chosen President." Bryce suggested the debatable proposition that it is harder to draw first-rate personalities into *politics*[3] than into business, that the U.S. *political party*[5] and congressional structures allow for little personal distinction, that mediocre men are more likely to win political offices than outstanding or controversial men because mediocre men make few enemies, and that national *prejudices*[9] exclude some good candidates from becoming *President*[6].

budget (economic) message. An *executive*[6] address delivered to a legislative body at regular intervals in order to inform the *legislature*[7] of *budgetary*[10] needs and objectives. The U.S. *President*[6] is required to deliver a budgetary message in January of each legislative *session*[7]. He uses it to indicate the direction he wishes the economy to move, to arouse public support for his economic *policies*[6], and to move the legislature to enact *legislation*[7] designed to fulfill his economic policies. *State*[3] *governors*[6] use budgetary messages in a similar fashion. See also *Budget*[10] *and Accounting Act of 1921*; *Employment*[10] *Act of 1946*.

bureau. A basic operational unit of administrative *organization*[6] within a governmental structure. A bureau is usually a major subdivision of a *department*[6] or agency of *government*[3].

bureaucracy. An administrative structure based on governmental agencies charged with the conduct of routine matters. The term "bureaucracy" is frequently used to designate the concentration of *power*[3] in administrators of governmental agencies and the unresponsiveness to the public will on the part of such career officials. See also *administration*[6]; *fourth*[4] *branch of government*; *Parkinson's Law*[6]; *Pentagon*[12]; *Peter*[6] *Principle*; *administrative state*[6]; *Max Weber*[6].

cabinet. A group of *executive*[6] advisers who generally head various executive *departments*[6] within a *government*[3]. The Cabinet of the *U.S. President*[6] has become an accepted

but informal part of the *constitutional*[3] *system* of the U.S. It began with the *appointment*[6] of various presidential advisers by President *George Washington*[6]. See also *Advisory*[6] *Council on Executive Reorganization*.

cabinet, kitchen. An informal body of advisers which a chief *executive*[6] turns to on occasion rather than consulting with his regular *cabinet*[6]. *President*[6] *Andrew Jackson*[6] had a highly visible group of advisers known as the kitchen cabinet. Other Presidents who were noted for using informal advisers were *Woodrow Wilson*[6], John F. Kennedy, and *Lyndon B. Johnson*[6]. President Nixon often calls upon Henry Kissinger, a non-cabinet member.

cease and desist order. A commonly used form of *administrative*[6] *order* designed to stop an individual or group (*labor*[10] *union, corporation*[10], etc.) from further violation of a *law*[8] or administrative rule. Failure to heed a cease and desist order may lead to imposition of a fine, revocation of a license to do business, or other appropriate penalty.

certification of eligibles. An official listing by an appropriate *government*[3] agency that certain applicants for jobs are qualified for *appointment*[6]. Some form of *civil*[6] service commission generally compiles such a list through *merit*[6] *system* testing. The *commission*[6] may list several qualified candidates, generally the top three qualifiers; then the hiring officer chooses from among the candidates.

chain of command. A system of *organization*[6] involving the movement of orders and responsibility from one level of *power*[3] to another. Generally the chain of command in a *hierarchy*[6] operates from top to bottom. See also *span*[6] *of control*.

civil service. The administrative grouping of all persons employed by government[3] in a civil capacity, especially those who were originally employed by government through *merit[6] system* testing. Civil service contrasts with military employment or placement in civil employment through the use of the *spoils[6] system*. High-level *executive[6]* officials and judges appointed by the *President[6]* and *confirmed[6]* by the *Senate[7]* are not considered a part of the civil service. See also *Civil[6] Service (Pendleton) Act of 1883; Civil[6] Service (Ramspeck) Act of 1940; Classification[6] Act of 1949; certification[6] of eligibles; Federal[6] Service Entrance Examination; Parkinson's[6] Law; Peter[6] Principle; General Schedule[6]; United[2] States Civil Service Commission*.

Civil Service (Pendleton) Act of 1883. The *federal[3] legislation[7]* that created a federal *merit[6] system* for choosing specified categories of *government[3]* personnel in the U.S. The *law[8]* established the *United[2] States Civil Service Commission* and rejected the rampant use of *patronage[6]* under the *spoils[6] system*.

Civil Service (Ramspeck) Act of 1940. A piece of *federal[3] legislation[7]* which led to *civil[6] service* coverage of most federal job classifications. The *act[8]* specifically allows for the extension of civil service coverage by *executive[6] order*.

Classification Act of 1949. The *federal[3] legislation[7]* which established basic *civil[6] service* grades and salaries. The legislation's major provisions categorized jobs within the *General Schedule[6]* (GS) of civil service. The *law[8]* has been modified as salary variables have changed since 1949.

clientele. The collective grouping of all persons normally regulated or served by an administrative or *governmental[3]* agency. The clientele generally forms a *community[3]* interest seeking specialized assistance from government. The *federal[3] Cabinet[6]-*

level *departments[6]* concerned with agriculture, labor, and commerce regulate and serve particular commercial and economic interests.

closed career system. A government *organization[6]* which provides a *tenured[6]* career in *government[3]* service through *merit[6] system* testing but which generally restricts an employee to vertical rather than horizontal movement in government service. A person may move up through the *hierarchy[6]* of an organization (*Foreign[2] Service, Public[2] Health Service*, Coast Guard, etc.) more easily than he can move from one government organization to another. See also *open[6] career system*.

commission: see *board[6]*.

Commission, Ash: see *Advisory[5] Council on Executive Reorganization*.

Commission, Brownlow. A comprehensive investigation during 1937 of *federal[3]* administrative structures and processes. The *commission[6]*, which released a work entitled Report of the President's Committee on Administrative Management, was headed by Louis Brownlow and contained Charles E. Merriam, Luther Gulick, and other administrative specialists closely associated with the Public Administration Clearing House on the University of Chicago campus. The report of the group analyzed departmental arrangements, the management process, personnel practices, *budgeting[10]*, and other related areas. It called for strong *executive[6]* leadership in fiscal and administrative processes. Partially on the recommendation of the Brownlow Commission, the *Congress[4]* passed the Reorganization Act of 1939, a *bill[7]* which received major *amendments[3]* in the *Reorganization[6] Act of 1949*, in order to permit the *President[6]* to institute limited administrative changes on his own initiative. The *Executive[2] Office of the President* was created in order to assist the President in carrying out his duties.

Commission, Hoover. A *federal*[3] investigative panel which carefully examined federal administrative practices between 1947 and 1949. The *commission*[6] released a report entitled Organization of the Executive Branch of the Government, analyzing over 2,000 federal agencies over a two-year period, and uncovered much duplication of effort, waste, and in- effective management. As a result of the commission's investigation and recommendations the *Reorganization*[6] *Act of 1949* was passed to give the *President*[6] the initiative for regular administrative review and *administrative reorganization*[6]. The report called for strong presidential control of the administrative machinery, especially in the areas of *budgeting*[10] and personnel. Well over a *majority*[3] of the commission's recommendations were eventually adopted. In 1953 a second Hoover Commission investigated regulatory agencies such as *independent regulatory commissions*[6], but was less successful in getting approval of recommendations made concerning divestment of certain *powers*[3] over private businesses.

commission, independent regulatory. A governmental body possessing *quasi-legislative*[6] *and quasi-judicial powers*[3] designed to permit the agency to regulate particular matters of *government*[3] without outside legislative or *executive*[6] control. Officials serving on independent regulatory commissions receive their positions through executive *appointment*[6] and *Senate*[7] *confirmation*[6]. However, because of the commissioners' lengthy and overlapping terms of office it is extremely difficult for one *President*[6] or one *political party*[5] to gain control of the *policy*[7] *formulation* machinery of such a *commission*[6]. The *Interstate*[2] *Commerce Commission* (1887) was the first such agency created by the *federal government*[3]. See also *Advisory*[6]

Council on Executive Reorganization; *Hoover Commission*[6].

Commission, Warren. A *federal*[3] investigating *commission*[6] chaired by *Chief*[8] *Justice Earl Warren*[8], a commission which released a controversial 1964 report entitled Report of the President's Commission on the Assassination of President John F. Kennedy. The Warren Commission was appointed by President *Lyndon B. Johnson*[6] and consisted of the Chief Justice, members of the *Senate*[7], members of the *House*[7] *of Representatives*, and private *citizens*[3] retired from previous *government*[3] service. The commission conducted a comprehensive investigation, held extensive *hearings*[6] and issued a voluminous report concerning the events surrounding the assassination of President Kennedy in Dallas, Texas on November 22, 1963. The commission concluded that Lee Harvey Oswald, the alleged assassin who was himself murdered on national television by Jack Ruby, acted alone in assassinating the *President*[6]. The commission said there was no evidence of a conspiracy or of foreign involvement. The group recommended extensive review and reorganization of the *United States Secret*[2] *Service*, better coordination of federal and *state*[3] agencies in providing protection for the President, *legislation*[7] to make the assassination of a President a federal criminal offense, and the strengthening of judicial ethics with regard to news stories which might jeopardize an individual's right to a fair trial.

confirmation. The act of a *legislature*[7] in validating or approving the action of an *executive*[6]. Confirmation may involve *appointments*[6] of executive or judicial officers, *treaty*[12] *ratification*[3], or other *constitutionally*[3] designated subjects. Appointments of the *President*[6] require a simple *majority*[3] vote of the *Senate*[7]. Acceptance of a treaty requires a two-thirds vote of the Senate. See also *appointive*[6] *power*; *senatorial*[6] *courtesy*.

constitutional (Whig, caretaker) theory. A *theory*[3] of presidential leadership which holds that the *U.S. President*[6] derives his *power*[3] from *legislation*[7] and serves as a servant of the *U.S. Congress*[4] in faithfully executing the *laws*[8]. The presidential role is primarily one of *administration*[6] and management. The President may exercise only such powers as may be traced to expressed or reasonably implied grants of power. Presidents Buchanan, Taft, Coolidge, and Hoover generally followed such a theory. See also *implied powers*[4]; *delegated powers*[4]; *prerogative*[6] *theory*; *stewardship*[6] *theory*; *Whig*[4].

corporation, government. A *government*[3] agency created to carry out certain functions in a relatively business-like, *nonpartisan*[5], and semi-autonomous fashion. The stock of such a *corporation*[10] is owned by the government, but the *board*[6] of directors is allowed considerable leeway in conducting the business of the corporation. Government corporations are subject to regular *auditing*[10] practices and *civil*[6] *service* regulations. The major government corporations are the *Tennessee*[2] *Valley Authority*, the *Federal*[2] *Deposit Insurance Corporation*, and the *United*[2] *States Postal Service*.

credibility gap. A term popularized during the 1960's to describe the condition existing when the public refuses to accept at face value what the *government*[3] says. The existence of a credibility gap appears to arise most often when the government leaves room for doubt in its official pronouncements. The term was applied particularly to the *administration*[6] of *U.S. President*[6] *Lyndon B. Johnson*[6] and his conduct of the *Vietnam*[12] *War*.

department. A major governmental unit designed for the *administration*[6] of a particular area of concern. In the U.S. *government*[3] the major departments are headed by officers within

the presidential *cabinet*[6]. A department is usually divided into separate branches, known as *bureaus*[6], divisions, or similar titles.

diplomatic (foreign policy) powers. The *executive*[6] *power*[3] to direct foreign *policy*[6] and diplomatic affairs. The *U.S. President*[6] has more power in this regard than in domestic affairs. He may negotiate *treaties*[12], sign *executive*[12] *agreements*, take action to recognize a foreign *government*[3], send and receive *diplomatic*[12] officials, and take actions which could lead to or influence the conduct of a *war*[12]. The Secretary of State is officially the President's chief foreign policy adviser. The President shares the treaty-making power and the power to appoint major diplomatic officials with the *Senate*[7]. Treaties must be approved by a two-thirds vote, and an *appointment*[6] must be approved by an *absolute majority*[3] vote of the Senate. Presidential power in foreign affairs is also greatly influenced by the existence of Senate and *House*[7] *of Representatives* committees on foreign affairs. See also *advice*[7] *and consent powers*; *Committee*[12] *on Foreign Relations (U.S. Senate)*; *diplomatic*[12] *recognition*; *inherent powers*[4]; *senatorial*[6] *courtesy*; *Department of State*[2]; *U.S.*[1] *v. Belmont*; *U.S.*[1] *v. Curtiss-Wright Export Corp.*; *Youngstown*[1] *Sheet and Tube Co. v. Sawyer*.

Employment Act of 1946: see Chap. 10.

esprit de corps. A spirit of common concern and enthusiasm on the part of the members of an *organization*[6].

Establishment, the: see Chap. 3.

executive. A person or group of persons holding the chief managerial and enforcement *powers*[3] of a political or administrative subdivision. The major executive categories within the U.S. are *President*[6], *governor*[6], *mayor*[11], *cabinet*[6] officer, administrator, and *commission*[6] *chairman*[7]. Powers and duties of the various executive categories are determined and limited largely by *constitutional*[3] provisions, *statutory*[8] provisions, political interaction with other branches of *government*[3], relations with other *nations*[3], *public opinion*[5], and numerous other variables. See also *lieutenant*[6] *governor*; *executive powers*[7]; *United States President*[6]; *United States Vice-President*.[6]

executive agent. A representative of a chief *executive*[6] who is charged with carrying out a special task of *government*[3]. Generally the term applies to a person carrying out a special mission to a foreign government or another chief of *state*[3].

executive agreement: see Chap. 12.

executive order. An order of the U.S. *President*[6] or other appropriate *executive*[6] or administrative official designed to implement general *constitutional*[3] or *statutory*[8] provisions. An executive order is recognized as having the *force*[3] of *law*[8] once it has been published in the *Federal*[6] *Register*. Executive orders are frequently used to expedite *administrative reorganization*[6], to deal rapidly with highly complex governmental problems, and to implement the use of *delegations of authority*[6] granted to the President by the *Congress*[4]. See also *war*[12] *powers*.

ex officio. A term meaning "by virtue of office." *Executive*[6], legislative, and judicial officials are sometimes constitutionally categorized as belonging to a certain *organization*[6] or agency by virtue of the fact that they hold certain offices. For example, a *governor*[6] may be "ex officio" a member of a *board of education*[11] of a *state*[3] university system. *Constitutional*[3] provisions or precedent generally determine whether the governor will be an active or inactive member in the affairs of the board of regents.

expertise. Expert or technical advice used by *executive*[6] and administrative officials to help them determine what *policies*[6] to recommend and how to administer policies already formulated. See also *policy*[7] *formulation*.

Fair Deal. The legislative and *executive*[6] program of *President*[6] *Harry S Truman*[6]. The Fair Deal aimed at labor reform, agricultural reform, *urban*[11] development, improvements in race relations, and various other major problems.

***Federalist* Numbers 70 through 73, The.** Essays, generally attributed to *Alexander Hamilton*[4], which viewed the U.S. *President*[6] as a center of vigorous *power*[3]. The essays, included in *The Federalist*[4], defended a four-year term of office with an option for reelection. Hamilton argued that the *nation*[3] needed stable and continuous *government*[3] based on *executive*[6] experience. Before the adoption of the U.S. *Constitution*[4] Hamilton had argued on numerous occasions for a strong *centralized*[3] government led by a President elected for life and possessing a *veto*[7] power over congressional *legislation*[7].

Federal Register. A daily *federal*[3] publication which contains all presidential proclamation, *executive*[6] *orders*, and *administrative*[6] *orders* as they are issued. The Register also contains notices of *executive*[6] and administrative *hearings*[6]. The publication, written in highly technical language, began during the *administration*[6] of *President*[6] Franklin D. *Roosevelt*[6] whenever expanding *bureaucratic*[6] machinery necessitated some formal means of notifying businesses of proposed or new regulations.

Federal Service Entrance Examination (FSEE). A comprehensive *federal*[3] examination designed to test college students interested in *government*[3] employment. Begun in 1955, the FSEE has been used effectively to recruit college graduates into government service and to staff junior-level *civil*[6] *service* positions.

field service. Local or branch offices of an administrative agency, offices which generally function through the use of field representatives who work among the *clientele*[6].

fourth branch of government: see Chap. 4.

gobbledygook. Administrative and political jargon that is imprecise, wordy technical, and confusing. The term was reputedly coined by *U.S. Congressman*[7] Maury Maverick of Texas.

government-by-contract. An administrative arrangement wherein a *government*[3] *organization*[6] *contracts*[10] with another agency or *free*[10] *enterprise* in order to develop a particular program, produce a particular product, or achieve an objective.

governor. The chief *executive*[6] officer within a *state*[3]. The governors within states of the U.S. are popularly elected within their states, serve terms ranging from two to four years, are ordinarily limited to two terms in office (but may not succeed himself in some states), possess an *item veto*[7] (no veto *power*[3] at all in North Carolina and no item veto in several of the states), may appoint specified officials (limited in some states by the election of numerous officials), possess the power to call *special sessions*[7], may grant *pardons*[6] and *reprieves*[6], may command state military forces during emergencies, and possess wide-ranging administrative and financial powers. See also *long ballot*[5]; *national*[12] *guard*.

Governors' Conference. An annual meeting of the *governors*[6] of the various *states*[3] within the U.S.. The conference is intended to deal with problems affecting all of the states.

Great Society. The legislative and *executive*[6] program of *President*[6] *Lyndon B. Johnson*[6]. The Great Society stressed *minority*[9] *group* rights, educational advancement, housing and *urban*[11] programs, medical care, *conservation*[10] of natural resources, and programs designed to eliminate poverty in the U.S. See also *civil*[9] *rights*; *Civil*[9] *Rights Act of 1964*; *Office of Economic*[2] *Opportunity*; *Elementary*[11] *and Secondary Education Act of 1965*; *Housing*[11] *and Urban Development Act of 1965*; *Department of Housing*[2] *and Urban Development*; *Medicaid*[11]; *Medicare*[11]; *Model*[11] *Cities Project*; *Department of Transportation*[2]; *Voting*[5] *Rights Act of 1965*; *War*[11] *on Poverty*.

hearing, administrative. A meeting of an administrative agency in order to permit interested parties to advance arguments before the adoption, change, or enforcement of an *administrative*[6] *order*. Hearings may also be conducted under *quasi-judicial*[8] *powers*[3] of an agency in order to examine whether agency rules have been violated. See also *judicial hearing*[8]; *quasi-legislative*[6] *and quasi-judicial*[8].

hierarchy. A group of individuals arranged in some rank order based on specified classifications (grade, task, skill). See also *chain*[6] *of command*; *closed*[6] *career system*; *General Schedule*[6]; *Parkinson's Law*[6]; *organization*[6]; *Peter*[6] *Principle*.

impeachment: see Chap. 7.

incrementalism. The *theory*[3] of administrative decision-making which focuses on *policy*[6] choices that differ incrementally from existing policies. The process is one of continuing evaluation of each step of *administration*[6]. See also *policy*[7] *formulation*.

inferior officer. Any *government*[3] official whose office is created by *statute*[8] and classified as "inferior" to other positions.

institutionalization. The process of becoming part of an established institutional framework or pattern of operation.

interservice competition (rivalry). Competition between or among two or more branches of military service or other organizational bodies.

Jackson, Andrew, 1767–1845. Frontiersman, Indian fighter, Tennessee jurist, member of both the *House*[7] *of Representatives* and the *Senate*[7], general, and seventh U.S. *President*[6] (1829–37). Andrew Jackson, hero of the Battle of New Orleans during the *War*[12] *of 1812*, lost the presidential election of 1824 in a closely and bitterly fought battle with John Quincy Adams. Adams was selected by the House of Representatives over Jackson even though Jackson had won more *electoral votes*[5] than any other candiate. Jackson, the *Democratic Party*[5] candidate, clearly defeated Adams in the election of 1828. Jackson's *administration*[6] is remembered for such things as his support of the *spoils*[6] *system*, the use of a *kitchen cabinet*[6], rejection of the *Bank*[10] *of the United States*, rejection of *King Caucus*[5], rejection of the doctrines of *nullification*[4] and *secession*[4], and rejection of selected *U.S. Supreme*[8] *Court* decisions needing strong *executive*[6] enforcement. See also *Jacksonian democracy*[4].

Jefferson, Thomas, 1743–1826. American *colonial*[4] political philosopher, member of the Virginia House of Burgesses, *governor*[6] of Virginia, member of the *First Continental Congress*[4], *Minister*[12] to France, Secretary of State under *President*[6] *George Washington*[6], *Vice-President*[6] during the *administration*[6] of *John Adams*[6], and third *U.S. President*[6] (1801–1809). Jefferson wrote A Summary View of the Rights of British America (1774) and Notes on Virginia (1784). He was the principal draftsman of the *Declaration*[4] *of Independence* (1776).

He also wrote *Jefferson's*[7] *Manual*, a *Senate*[7] guide to *parliamentary*[7] *procedure*. In the Declaration of Independence he supported the *consent theory*[3] *of government*[3], *natural rights*[3], various democratic principles such as *due*[9] *process of law*, and *revolution*[3] against arbitrary political rule. Throughout his life he placed great emphasis on education as the basis for a workable *democracy*[3]. Jefferson opposed the *Alien*[4] *and Sedition Acts of 1798, federal*[3] support of manufacturing, the importation of slaves, and the *Bank*[10] *of the United States*. He drafted the *Kentucky*[4] *Resolutions* of 1798 and supported a *strict construction*[4] of the *U.S. Constitution*[4], *states'*[4] *rights*, and frugal government. He was one of the founders of the *Democratic-Republican Party*[5], responsible for the Louisiana Purchase of 1803, sent naval forces to fight the Barbary pirates (1801–1805), and supported the unpopular Embargo Act of 1807. See also *Jeffersonian democracy*[4].

Johnson, Lyndon Baines, 1908–1973. Member of the *House*[7] *of Representatives* (1937–48) and the *Senate*[7] (1948–69), *Vice-President*[6] under John F. Kennedy, and 36th *U.S. President*[6] (1963–68). Johnson served as the *majority floor*[7] *leader* of the Senate from 1953 to 1960. After his *Democratic Party*[5] victory of 1964 he became a leader in *legislation*[7] on domestic affairs. His *Great*[6] *Society* emphasized *civil*[9] *rights*, education, housing, *conservation*[10], medical advancements, and a *War*[11] *on Poverty*. On the international scene he acted to put down a possible *Communist*[3] takeover in the *Dominican*[12] *crisis* of 1965; used restraint in the *Pueblo*[12] *crisis* of 1968, and escalated the *Vietnam*[12] *War* after *Congress*[4] passed the *Tonkin*[12] *Gulf Resolution* in 1964. The war caused him to decide not to run for reelection in 1968. See also *Warren Commission*[6]; *Billie Sol Estes*[10] *investigation*; *Bobby Baker*[7] *investigation*.

law, administrative: see Chap. 8.

lieutenant governor. The *executive*[6] official who serves as the second in command and in the *line of succession*[6] to most *state*[3] *governors*[6] (some states do not have a lieutenant governor's position) and succeeds him upon his death, resignation, or removal from office before the expiration of his term of office. Most lieutenant governors serve as presiding officer of the *upper chamber*[7] of the state *legislature*[7]. Some states assign their lieutenant governors to *ex*[6] *officio* positions on *legislative*[7] councils and various state *boards*[6].

Lincoln, Abraham, 1809–65. Illinois lawyer and *legislator*[7], *Whig Party*[5] member of the U.S. *House*[7] of *Representatives* (1847–49), and 16th U.S. *President*[6] (1860–65). Lincoln became the first *Republican Party*[5] President, served with almost absolute *power*[3] during the *Civil*[4] *War*, and was assassinated while in office. He ranks among those who did the most to expand the *war*[12] *powers* of the President. He used military forces without a formal *declaration of war*[12], blockaded southern ports, suspended the *writ of habeas*[8] *corpus*, issued the *Emancipation*[9] *Proclamation* which declared slaves not in *territory*[3] under *federal*[3] control to be free, and made plans for a reasonable *Reconstruction*[4] of the *states*[3] in *rebellion*[3] during the Civil War. Before Lincoln could achieve his objectives of reconstruction he was assassinated by John Wilkes Booth on the evening of April 14, 1865. Lincoln is remembered not only as a great President but as a great orator. In the Gettysburg Address (1863) he gave the classic definition of *democracy*[3] as "government of the people, by the people, for the people." His Second Inaugural (1865) was a frank statement of reconciliation which contained the phrase, "with malice toward none; with charity for all." See also *Merryman*[1], *Ex parte*; *Milligan*[1], *Ex parte*; *national sovereignty*[4]; *Prize*[1] *Cases*.

loyalty order. An *executive*[6] or *administrative*[6] *order* aimed at protecting national security from subversive threats, *sedition*[12], and sabotage. Presidential orders authorized under congressional *statute*[8] have been used to remove persons from "sensitive" *government*[3] positions. Loyalty orders were used most frequently between 1947 and 1957. See also *Cole*[1] *v. Young*; *executive*[6] *order*.

Madison, James, 1751–1836. Virginia *legislator*[7] and *statesman*[5], member of the *First* and *Second Continental Congresses*[4], principal author of the *Virginia*[4] *Plan* at the *Constitutional Convention*[4] of 1787, one of the authors of *The Federalist*[4] (1788), member of the *House*[7] of *Representatives*, principal advocate of the *U.S. Bill*[4] of *Rights* (1791), author of the Virginia Resolutions (1798), U.S. Secretary of State during the *administration*[6] of *Thomas Jefferson*[6], and fourth *U.S. President*[6] (1809–17). Madison is known as "the Father of the Constitution" and is remembered as the major chronicler of the Constitutional Convention through what was posthumously published as *Madison's*[4] *Journal of the Federal Convention*. He was one of the founders of the *Democratic-Republican Party*[5] even though he had decried political *factions*[3] in *The Federalist*[5] *No. 10*. During his administration the *War*[12] *of 1812*, "Mr. Madison's War," was conducted against England. President Madison supported such things as protective *tariffs*[10] and the *Bank*[10] *of the United States*. See also *Kentucky*[4] *and Virginia Resolutions*.

merit system. A *government*[3] *organization*[6] and classification system based on competitive examinations and demonstrated qualifications. The merit system contrasts with the *spoils*[6] *system* and is designed to provide a reasonable *nonpartisan*[5] and stable administrative structure. The *federal*[3] merit system is administered by the

United[2] States Civil Service Commission. See also *certification[6] of eligibles; civil[6] service; closed[6] career system; open[6] career system; veterans'[6] preference.*

national guard, nationalization of the. The process wherein a *state[3]* militia, generally under *executive[6]* control of a *governor[6]*, is activated for national services by the *President[6]* as Commander-in-Chief of the armed forces. *Congress[4]* may legislate on the training and funding of the *national[12] guard* and on its use while under *federal[3]* control. The national guard may be nationalized during wartime (*World[12] War II,*) national emergencies (*Cuban[12] Missile crisis of 1962*), and during domestic unrest (Little Rock, Arkansas in 1957 and Oxford, Mississippi in 1962). See also *Commander-in-Chief powers[6]*.

nepotism. The granting of political favors or offices to relatives. See also *patronage[6]; Adam Clayton Powell[7] investigation; sinecure[6]*.

Neustadt, Richard E., 1919– . Former Columbia University professor, current professor of *political[3] science* at Harvard University, and presidential adviser to Presidents Truman, Kennedy, and Johnson. Neustadt is remembered for his 1960 book, Presidential Power: The Politics of Leadership, a major analysis of the structure and operation of presidential *power[3]*. Neustadt views the power of the U.S. *President[6]* as grounded in persuasion. The President exercises power through the use of his strategic position in *government[3]*, his relation to the rest of *society[3]*, and his access to the *mass[5] media*.

New Deal. The legislative and *executive[6]* program of *President[6] Franklin D. Roosevelt[6]*. The phrase "New Deal" was used by Roosevelt to characterize his programs of social and economic reform. He first used the phrase in accepting the *Democratic Party[5]* nomination for President in 1932. Roosevelt's New Deal included labor reform, development of comprehensive welfare programs, *unemployment[11] insurance*, agricultural reform, *conservation[10]* programs, and governmental regulation of major economic institutions. See also *Agricultural[10] Adjustment Act of 1933; Agricultural[10] Adjustment Act of 1938; Agricultural[2] Adjustment Administration; Ashwander[1] v. TVA; Carter[1] v. Carter Coal Co.; Civilian[2] Conservation Corps; Committee[7] on Internal Security; Commodity[2] Credit Corporation; court-packing[8] plan; Fair[10] Labor Standards Act of 1938; Federal[2] Deposit Insurance Corporation; Federal[2] Housing Administration; Food[11] Stamp Plan; Home[1] Building and Loan v. Blaisdell; Mulford[1] v. Smith; National[10] Industrial Recovery Act of 1933; National[10] Labor Relations (Wagner) Act of 1935; National[2] Labor Relations Board; National[1] Labor Relations Board v. Jones and Laughlin Corp.; National[2] Mediation Board; National[2] Recovery Administration; Norris-La Guardia[10] (Anti-Injunction) Act of 1932; Panama[1] Refining Co. v. Ryan; Public[10] Utility Holding Co. Act of 1935; Schechter[1] Poultry Corp. v. U.S.; Securities[2] and Exchange Commission; Social[11] Security Act of 1935; Steward[1] Machine Co. v. Davis; Sunshine[1] Anthracite Coal Co. v. Adkins; Tennessee[2] Valley Authority; U.S.[1] v. Butler; U.S.[1] v. Darby Lumber Co.; West[1] Coast Hotel Co. v. Parrish; Wickard[1] v. Filburn; Works[2] Progress Administration*.

New Freedom. The *executive[6]* and legislative program enunciated by *Woodrow Wilson[6]* in the presidential campaign of 1912 and published in 1913 under the title of "The New Freedom." Items of Wilson's program were: regulation of economic *trusts[10]*, reduction of *government[3]* control by special interests, *decentralization[3]* of business and industry, lowered *tariffs*[10], correction of banking and currency abuses, rugged *individualism*[3], and governmentally protected *free*[10] enterprise. See also *Seventeenth Amendment*[7]; *Sixteenth Amendment*[10]; *Clayton*[10] *Antitrust Act of 1914*; *Farm*[2] *Credit Administration*; *Federal*[2] *Reserve System Board of Governors*; *Federal*[2] *Trade Commission*; *Federal*[10] *Trade Commission Act of 1914*; *United*[2] *States Tariff Commission*.

New Frontier. The legislative and *executive*[6] program of *President*[6] John F. Kennedy. Kennedy first used the phrase "New Frontier" in accepting the *Democratic Party*[5] nomination for President in 1960. His program emphasized *civil*[9] *rights* protections for *minority*[9] *groups*, educational advancement for all persons, revitalization of America *cities*[11], economic assistance for friendly foreign *nations*[3], and communications and trade with foreign adversaries. The program was cut short by his assassination on November 22, 1963. However, parts of his program were carried out through President *Lyndon B. Johnson's*[6] *Great*[6] *Society*. See also *Area*[11] *Redevelopment Act of 1961*; *Peace*[2] *Corps*; *War*[11] *on Poverty*.

ombudsman. An official given legal *authority*[3] to investigate complaints made by private *citizens*[3] against the *government*[3] and empowered to seek a remedy for the damaged party if a remedy is allowed. Sweden established the first known ombudsman in 1819. Hawaii created the first ombudsman position in an American *state*[3] in 1969.

open career system. A government *organization*[6] which provides a *tenured*[6] career in *government*[3] service through *merit*[6] *system* testing and which permits an employee to move to other governmenal agencies with relative ease. See also *closed*[6] *career system*.

organization. An arrangement of individuals and established structures created for the purpose of carrying out some task or achieving specific objectives. Basic organizational purpose, design, continuity, membership, etc. varies greatly from organization to organization and from time to time within a single organization. Every branch and agency of *government*[3], however, strives toward effective organizational arrangement in order to achieve desired goals. The word "organization" is also used to indicate the active arrangement of particular structures of government. See also *esprit*[6] *de corps*; *hierarchy*[6]; *line organization*[6]; *Reorganization*[6] *Act of 1949*; *staff organization*[6].

organization, line. The portion of any *hierarchy*[6] of public *administration*[6] specifically charged with formulating *policy*[6] and achieving the basic objectives of the particular *organization*[6] as outlined by appropriate authorities (*U.S. President*[6], *U.S. Congress*[4], administrative agency, etc.). See also *staff organization*[6]; *policy*[7] *formulation*.

organization, staff. The portion of any *hierarchy*[6] of public *administration*[6] which serves the *policy*[7] *formulating* section of the *organization*[6] in an advisory, planning, or other peripheral capacity. See also *line organization*[6].

pardon. The act of an *executive*[6] official in granting release from further punishment for a person convicted of a legal violation. A "conditional" pardon requires the fulfillment of certain conditions, whereas an "absolute" pardon places a person in the legal position existing before conviction. The *President*[6] may pardon any person convicted of a *federal*[3] offense except someone removed from federal office through *impeachment*[7] proceedings. *State*[3] *governors*[3] possess pardoning powers of varying degree. Some governors share their *power*[3] with pardoning *boards*[6] or other specified agency of *government*[3]. See also *amnesty*[6]; *Grossman*[1], *Ex parte*; *reprieve*[6].

Parkinson's Law. The principle of expanding *bureaucracy*[6], which holds that "work expands to fill the time available." In his 1957 book entitled Parkinson's Law, C. Northcote Parkinson set forth the *theory*[3] that civil servants multiply as their duties decrease. Parkinson postulated that bureaucracy could stifle individuality and completely dominate governmental processes and institutions. See also *administrative state*[6]; *civil*[6] *service*; *Peter*[6] *Principle*.

patronage. The *power*[3] of a *government*[3] official to *appoint*[6] a person to a position not covered by *merit*[6] *system* testing. Patronage may also be used in the granting of government *contracts*[10] or other special benefits. It is most frequently used to achieve *political party*[5] support and loyalty. See also *Civil*[6] *Service (Pendleton) Act of 1883*; *nepotism*[6]; *senatorial*[6] *courtesy*; *sinecure*[6]; *spoils*[6] *system*.

Peter Principle. An administrative concept enunciated by Laurence F. Peter and Raymond Hull in a volume published in 1969 under the title, The Peter Principle. The principle holds that in any *hierarchical*[6] organizational structure every employee or staff member tends to be promoted to his level of incompetency and then to stay there. The functioning of the *organization*[6] actually goes on because a sufficient number of employees have yet to reach their levels of incompetence. Persons and organizations who have reached their maturity in incompetency continue to function but are incapable of performing truly useful tasks or accomplishing meaningful objectives. See also *civil*[6] *service*; *Parkinson's*[6] *Law*.

planning - programming - budgeting (PPB) system. A system of administrative operation which seeks to carefully define goals, establish priorities, analyze alternatives, and attain maximum results at the least cost. PPB system planning, sometimes referred to as PPBS, was first used in the *federal government*[3] under the direction of Secretary of Defense Robert McNamara in 1965 in order to achieve specific objectives systematically. See also *Department of Defense*[2]; *F-111*[12] *(TFX) controversy*.

policy. Any *organizational*[6] plan of action or rule which is designed to achieve a specific objective. An administrative policy is an agency statement, basically legislative in character, which regulates private rights or interests. See also *administrative*[6] *order*.

powers, Commander-in-Chief. The executive *power*[3] to direct the military forces of a *nation*[3]. The U.S. *President*[6] is granted power to act as the Commander-in-Chief of the U.S. armed forces. He may employ the use of military *force*[3] without an official *declaration of war*[12] from the U.S. *Congress*[4]. His power is extremely broad because of his singular position as chief *executive*[6] and because of his *authority*[3] to direct regular forces, *reserve*[12] forces, and the *national*[12] guard. The President's chief advisers in military matters are the Secretary of Defense and the members of the *Joint*[2] *Chiefs of Staff*. See also *Department of Defense*[2]; *war*[12] *powers*; *Youngstown*[1] *Sheet and Tube Co. v. Sawyer*.

powers, emergency: see Chap. 4.

powers, inherent: see Chap. 4.

powers, judicial. *Power*[3] related to the judicial process, which is possessed by a chief *executive*[6]. The U.S. *President*[6] may appoint *federal*[3] judicial officials subject to U.S. *Senate*[7] *confirmation*[6]. He may enforce U.S. *Supreme*[8] *Court* decisions, *pardon*[6] offenders of federal *statutes*[8], grant *reprieves*[6], and suggest reorganization of federal judicial structures. See also *amnesty*[6]; *court-packing*[8] *plan*; *Grossman*[1], *Ex parte*.

powers, legislative. The *power*[3] of a chief *executive*[6] to act as a part of the legislative process. The U.S. *President*[6] may recommend *legislation*[7], *veto*[7] legislation, and call *special*[7] *sessions* of the *Congress*[4]. He may use informal powers involving *public opinion*[5], *patronage*[6], *political party*[5] support, and other more subtle devices to influence legislation. See also *State*[6] *of the Union Message*; *pocket veto*[7].

powers, party leadership. The *power*[3] inherent within an *executive*[6] position because of the executive's relationship to his *political party*[5]. The U.S. *President*[6] is not only a *government*[3] official, he is the recognized leader of his political party. He guides the development of the party *platform*[5], attempts to implement party programs through the passage of *legislation*[7], seeks to unify the *decentralized*[3] party structure throughout the country, helps raise party campaign funds, appoints party adherents to available political positions, and uses his strategic position of power to generally enhance the party image and advance its causes. See also *appointive*[6] *power*; *decentralized organization*[5]; *patronage*[6]; *legislative powers*[6].

prerogative theory. A *theory*[3] of presidential leadership which holds that during times of national emergency the U.S. *President*[6] may act in direct violation of *law*[8] in order to provide for the public good. Presidents *Lincoln*[6], *Wilson*[6], *Franklin D. Roosevelt*[6], and *Truman*[6] are frequently cited as following such a theory. See also *constitutional*[6] *theory*; *Merryman*[1], *Ex parte*; *prerogative*[3]; *stewardship*[6] *theory*; *Youngstown*[1] *Sheet and Tube Co. v. Sawyer*.

president, acting. Any *government*[3] official *constitutionally*[3] empowered to act in place of the *President*[6] and to carry out his official duties. In the U.S. the *Twenty-fifth Amendment*[6] to the *Constitution*[4] empowers the *Vice-President*[6] to become acting president in the event of *presidential*[6] *disability*. The *amendment*[3] provides for the settlement of conflicts over the return of *power*[3] *to the President*[6] once the disability no longer exists. See also *Twenty-second Amendment*[6].

presidential disability. A condition wherein the U.S. *President*[6] is no longer capable of carrying out his tasks due to physical or mental impairment. No formal provision for handling such a situation existed until the addition of the *Twenty-fifth Amendment*[6] to the U.S. *Constitution*[4] in 1967. The *amendment*[3] permits the U.S. *Vice-President*[6] to become *acting president*[6] and provides for settling any possible conflict between the President and Vice-President once the President is no longer disabled. See also *presidential*[6] *succession*.

presidential succession. The arrangement whereby the U.S. *Vice-President*[6] or other designated official succeeds to the office of U.S. *President*[6] in the event that the office becomes vacant or is occupied by a "disabled" President. The present line of succession is set by the *Presidential*[6] *Succession Act of 1947* and includes the Vice-President, *Speaker*[7] *of the House* of the *House*[7] *of Representatives*, *President*[7] *pro tempore* of the *Senate*[7], and the members of the President's *Cabinet*[6]. See also, *Twentieth Amendment*[7]; *Twenty-fifth Amendment*[6]; *presidential*[6] *disability*.

Presidential Succession Act of 1947. The *federal*[3] *legislation*[7] which established the present order of *presidential*[6] *succession*. After the *Vice-President*[6], the *law*[8] provides that the order of succession will be the *Speaker*[7] of *the House* of the *House*[7] *of Represent-atives, President*[7] *pro tempore* of the *Senate*[7], and presidential *Cabinet*[6] members in a designated order. The *Twentieth Amendment*[7] and the *Twenty-fifth Amendment*[6] provide for presidential succession under special circumstances involving *presidential*[6] *disability.* The Twenty-fifth Amendment provides for an *acting president*[6] and for a method of filling a Vice-Presidential vacancy.

President, U.S. The major *constitutional*[3] officer and the chief *executive*[6] of the *government*[3] of the United States of America. Article II of the U.S. *Constitution*[4] is devoted to outlining the *powers*[3] and duties of the President. According to that article and other related provisions within the Constitution, the President: 1. is vested with the "executive power" of the *nation*[3]; 2. serves a four-year term of office; 3. has a *Vice-President*[6] who may succeed him in office; 4. is elected by a process involving an *electoral*[4] *college*; 5. must be a *natural-born citizen*[3]; 6. must be at least 35 years old; 7. must have been a resident of the U.S. for at least 14 years prior to election; 8. receives compensation which may not be changed during his term in office; 9. may not hold any other *federal*[3] position at the same time he serves as President; 10. serves as Commander-in-Chief of the armed forces; 11. may grant *reprieves*[6] and *pardons*[6] for federal offenses (except in cases of *impeachment*[7]); 12. may make *treaties*[12] with foreign nations on the condition that the *U.S. Senate*[7] approves them; 13. may appoint selected government officials with approval of the Senate (*senatorial*[6] *courtesy*); 14. must regularly inform the *Congress*[4] about the state of the Union and may recommend *legislation*[7] within his report; 15. may call special legislative *sessions*[7]; 16. may grant commissions to officers of the U.S.; 17. may be removed from office by impeachment; 18. may *veto*[7] legisla-

tion absolutely or through the use of a *pocket veto*[7]. The President is assisted by a *Cabinet*[6] in exercising his broad powers of public office. He is the leader of foreign *policy*[6] through his *inherent power*[4] as chief of *state*[3], leader of defense policy through his power as Commander-in-Chief, leader of *administration*[6] through his *appointive*[6] *powers* and *removal*[6] *powers*, and leader of his *political party*[5] through his position as the party's highest elected official. The President also possesses strong legislative and *judicial powers*[6] because of constitutional provisions related to structural and procedural items of *checks*[3] *and balances* involving the other two branches of government. The office of President has changed over time and through the exercise of power by particular individuals holding the office. For example, the *Twenty-second Amendment*[6] formalized the earlier informal concept that a President should serve no more than two full terms in office, the *Twelfth Amendment*[5] changed the method by which Presidents and Vice-Presidents are selected, the *Twenty-fifth Amendment*[6] provided for *presidential*[6] *disability* and for the position of *acting president*[6], and informal developments gave the President the Cabinet, a position of leadership in party affairs, and senatorial courtesy in the appointment process. See Chapters 1, 2, and selected entries for further amplification on the U.S. President.

quasi-legislative and quasi-judicial. Possessing both *policy*[7] *formulating* and *adjudicative*[8] powers at the same time. Some *government*[3] agencies such as *independent regulatory commissions*[6] are empowered to formulate rules having the *force*[3] of *law*[8] and to settle conflicts over their own rules in a fashion resembling the judicial process. Agencies possessing *quasi-legislative*[7] and *quasi-judicial*[8] powers may formulate rules only within the broad framework or charter of *power*[3] granted to them by *statute*[8]. Their adjudicative decisions may be appealed to regular courts. See also *Administrative*[6] *Procedures Act of 1946*; *administrative adjudication*[6]; *independent agency*[5].

red tape. A term used to indicate rigid adherence to official forms and procedures, a condition that tends to obstruct or delay action. The term originally referred to the tape used to bind official British documents. See also *bureaucracy*[6].

removal powers. The *power*[3] of an *executive*[6] to remove another person from office. The *U.S. Constitution*[4] makes no mention of a specific removal power apart from the *impeachment*[7] process. It is generally recognized, however, that the *U.S. President*[6] may remove officials under his immediate direction and control. Judges, members of *independent regulatory commissions*[6], and *civil*[6] service employees may not be summarily removed by the President. They may be removed only for cause and through regular, specified legal channels. See also *appointive*[6] *power*; *appointment*[6]; *Humphrey's*[1] *Executor (Rathbun), v. U.S.*; *Myers*[1] *v. U.S.*; *Tenure*[6] *of Office Act of 1867*.

Reorganization Act of 1949. A *federal*[3] *law*[8] that grew out of the recommendations of the first *Hoover Commission*[6] and that shifted the initiative for reorganization of the *executive*[6] branch of the *government*[3] from the *Congress*[4] to the *President*[6]. The President may propose *administrative reorganization*[6] plans which automatically become effective within 60 days unless *vetoed*[7] by an *absolute majority*[3] vote in one house of Congress. Few presidential reorganization plans have actually been vetoed by the national *legislature*[7].

reorganization, administrative. The continuous process of rearranging administrative machinery and personnel in order to improve efficiency or reduce the cost of *administration*[6]. Administrative reorganization generally stresses consolidation of administrative functions, improved supervision of personnel and finances, and the placement of *power*[3] in the hands of officials who may be held accountable for the use of power. See also *Advisory*[6] *Council on Executive Reorganization*; *Brownlow Commission*[6]; *creeping advisoryism*[6]; *Hoover Commission*[6]; *Office of Management*[2] *and Budget*; *Reorganization*[6] *Act of 1949*.

reprieve. A delay or postponement in the execution of a sentence determined by an appropriate body such as a court of *law*[8]. Reprieves of various lengths may be granted by the U.S. *President*[6] and by *state*[3] *governors*[6]. A reprieve is generally granted to allow time for the collection of new evidence.

Roosevelt, Franklin D., 1882–1945. New York *state*[3] *Senator*[7], Assistant Secretary of the Navy, *governor*[6] of New York, and 32nd U.S. *President*[6] (1932–45). Roosevelt, *liberal*[3] leader of the *Democratic Party*[5], was elected in 1932 in the midst of the *Great Depression*[10]. His *administration*[6] was characterized by the *New*[6] *Deal*, an *executive*[6] and legislative program featuring *unemployment*[11] *insurance*, *social insurance*[11], *conservation*[10], *public*[10] *works*, agricultural *price*[10] *support programs*, bank reform, and business regulation. Roosevelt, a popular and strong chief executive, suggested a "*court-packing*[8] *plan*" which eventually forced an extremely *conservative*[3] United States *Supreme*[8] *Court* to liberalize its position and accept New Deal *legislation*[7] previously declared *unconstitutional*[3]. Roosevelt instituted the *Good*[12] *Neighbor Policy* in Latin America, was President when the Supreme Court declared in *U.S.*[1] *v. Curtiss-Wright Export Corp.* that the President posesses an *inherent power*[4] in foreign affairs, and was serving at the time *World*[12] *War II* began. He promoted *Lend-Lease*[12], announced the *Atlantic*[12] *Charter*, called for a *declaration of war*[12] on Japan after the attack on U.S. military forces at Pearl Harbor, led U.S. military *policy*[6], conducted *diplomatic*[12] relations during a time of international strife, and ordered the development of the atomic bomb. He died on April 12, 1945, just before the end of World War II.

Roosevelt, Theodore, 1858–1919. New York *state*[3] assemblyman, frontiersman, member of the *United*[2] *States Civil Service Commission*, New York City police commissioner, Assistant Secretary of the Navy, founder of the *Spanish-American*[12] *War* "Rough Riders," U.S. *Vice-President*[6], and 26th *U.S. President*[6] (1901–09). Roosevelt succeeded to the presidency on the assassination of President William McKinley. His *Square*[6] *Deal administration*[6] is remembered for *federal*[3] regulation of business *monopolies*[10] and *trusts*[10], *labor*[10] *union* development, *rate-making*[10] legislation for *public*[10] *utilities*, and consumer protection *legislation*[7] such as pure food and drug laws and meat inspection *laws*[8]. In foreign affairs he is remembered for *dollar diplomacy*[12], the *Big*[12] *Stick Policy* the *Roosevelt*[12] *Corollary* of the *Monroe*[12] *Doctrine*, development of the Panama Canal, and his *mediation*[10] in helping to end the Russo-Japanese War, an act which won him the Nobel Peace Prize in 1905. Roosevelt, quick to appeal to *public opinion*[5], created the *Bull Moose Party*[5] in 1912 and ran for the presidency against his former friend and extremely *conservative*[3] Vice-President, William Howard Taft. The split in the *Republican Party*[5] helped *Woodrow Wilson*[6] win the presidency under the label of the *Democratic Party*[5]. See also *Pure*[11] *Food and Drug Act of 1906*.

Rossiter, Clinton, 1917–1970. Cornell University professor of history, expert on American *constitutional*[3] history, and author of Conservatism in America (1955), The American Presidency (1956), and Parties and Politics in America (1960). In The American Presidency, a work which has been revised regularly since its publication, Rossiter analyzed the growth of presidential *power*[3], the movement of power, limitations on power, and the role of the presidency in a modern and complex world.

Schedule A. A schedule or list of *federal government*[3] jobs not covered by *merit*[6] *system* testing but which are available as *tenured*[6] positions. Schedule A traditionally has contained attorneys and specialized personnel in various *government*[3] agencies such as the *Internal*[2] *Revenue Service* and the *Bureau of Customs*[2]. The type of personnel listed on Schedule A is generally determined by the *United*[2] *States Civil Service Commission* and has varied from time to time depending on *executive*[6] action. See also *patronage*[6]; *Schedule*[6] *B*; *Schedule*[6] *C*; *spoils*[6] *system*.

Schedule B. A schedule or list of *federal government*[3] jobs filled by noncompetitive examinations designed to assign personnel on the basis of qualifications and previous experience. Schedule B ordinarily contains listings involving technical personnel. See also *United*[2] *States Civil Service Commission*; *patronage*[6]; *Schedule*[6] *A*; *Schedule*[6] *C*; *merit*[6] *system*; *spoils*[6] *system*.

Schedule C. A controversial schedule or list of *federal government*[3] jobs filled through *patronage*[6]. The schedule contains high-level *policy*[7] *formulating* and confidential positions and was created by *executive*[6] *order* in 1953 by *President*[6] Dwight D. Eisenhower. The creation of Schedule C was in direct opposition to the philosophy of *merit*[6] *system* testing. However, the return of a *Republican Party*[5] *administration*[6] after a lengthy period of *Democratic Party*[5] control created the need to provide positions for loyal political supporters. The *United* [2] *States Civil Service Commission* largely determines what positions may be listed on Schedule C. The schedule generally contains *bureau* [6] chiefs, information officers, legal counsels, planning directors, and other policy-making positions. See also *Schedule* [6] *A*; *Schedule* [6] *B*; *spoils* [6] *system*.

Schedule, General. The *United* [2] *States Civil Service Commission* job classification list which categorizes federal employment. Jobs are assigned to various classes on the basis of job difficulty and responsibility. Classes are divided into 18 separate grades on the basis of actual duties to be performed. Maximum and minimum salaries are based on job grades and range from GS (General Schedule)-1 to GS–18. Salary levels are changed as the economy changes. In 1968 and 1969 the *President* [6] was authorized to increase federal salaries without congressional approval in order that the *federal government* [3] could compete with private business. Various federal *departments* [6] and agencies have their own job classification categories and salary schedules.

senatorial courtesy. The informal but rigid *custom* [3] whereby an *executive* [6] appointment before the *U.S. Senate* [7] for *confirmation* [6] must be cleared by the appropriate *Senator* [7] or Senators from the same *state* [3] from which the *appointment* [6] has been made. Since major presidential appointments must be approved by the Senate, the senior Senator from the state in question is consulted by the *President* [6] before the appointment is made, especially if the Senator is a member of the same *political party* [5] as the President. If the senior Senator is of the opposition party and the junior Senator belongs to the President's party, then the President usually consults the junior Senator. If the state has no Senators who are members of the President's party, the President may

even consult party leaders within the state. If such procedures are not followed, the Senator or Senators from the state may indicate that the President's nominee is unacceptable. Senators from other states normally abide by such a decision and reject the appointment. See also *advice* [7] *and consent powers*; *appointive* [6] *powers*.

sinecure. An office or assignment that requires little or no work but which provides some form of compensation. See also *Thomas Dodd* [7] *investigation*; *nepotism* [6]; *patronage* [6]; *Adam Clayton Powell* [7] *investigation*.

span of control. The administrative principal that the number of subordinates to be directed by any one person should be limited to the range of human control. Effective operation and control in any organizational *hierarchy* [6] is largely dependent on circumstances related to physical, emotional, and other related variables operating within an *organization* [6]. See also *chain* [6] *of command*.

spoils system. The administrative process which permits *government* [3] leaders to award public jobs and public *contracts* [10] to political supporters. The term "spoils system" originated with *Senator* [7] William T. Marcy of New York in 1832. He said, "To the victors belong the spoils of the enemy." The spoils system contrasts with the *merit* [6] *system* and *civil* [6] *service*. See also *patronage* [6].

Square Deal. The term used to indicate the *executive* [6], legislative, and administrative *policies* [6] of *President* [6] *Theodore Roosevelt* [6]. Roosevelt sought to regulate industry, big business, transportation, and labor for the benefit of all of *society* [3]. The term "Square Deal" was used in reference to the settlement of a coal *strike* [10], a settlement which attempted to act fairly toward both sides of the controversy. In 1903 Roosevelt was able to create a Department of Commerce and Labor designed to guide economic affairs and achieve social *justice*[8]. He led in *conservation*[10] policies, *rate-making*[10] *legislation*[7], the breaking up of *monopolies*[10] and *trusts*[10], and consumer protection. In foreign affairs he stressed the *Big*[12] *Stick Policy*, the *Roosevelt*[12] *Corollary* of the *Monroe*[12] *Doctrine*, and *dollar diplomacy*[12].

state, administrative. A *state*[3] characterized by large-scale administrative machinery staffed by a large number of bureaucrats. An administrative state is generally characterized by impersonality, *red*[6] *tape*, regimentation, and extreme public control of individual affairs. In a complex, *urbanized*[11], and industrialized *society*[3] the administrative state is often looked to as the primary tool for rational economic and social development. It is feared by some because of its control over the individual decision-making process. See also *administration*[6]; *bureaucracy*[6]; *Parkinson's*[6] *Law*; *Max Weber*[6].

State of the Union message. A *constitutionally*[3] required presidential address, usually delivered near the opening of a *session*[7] of the *Congress*[4], in which the *President*[6] informs Congress of the state of the Union. The President uses the message, delivered in a *joint session*[7] of Congress, to inform the Congress and the public of the problems facing the *nation*[3] and to outline his legislative program for meeting national problems and needs.

statesmanship. A condition of leadership wherein an official consistently reveals skill and wisdom in the management of public business. See also *politician*[5].

stewardship theory. A *theory*[3] of presidential leadership which holds that the *U.S. President*[6] is a "steward" of the people and may use *power*[3] for the good of the people as long as it does not violate the *U.S. Constitution*[4] or specific *federal*[3] *statutory*[8] provisions. The theory is usually at-

tributed to *Constitutional Convention*[4] *delegate*[5] James Wilson in 1787. It was used especially during the *administration*[6] of President *Theodore Roosevelt*[6]. See also *constitutional*[6] *theory*; *prerogative*[6] *theory*.

subgovernments. The interrelated and interdependent *organizations*[6], both public and private, that influence public *policy*[6] in a given area. Subgovernments cross *political party*[5] lines, geographical and functional divisions of *government*[3], and private economic interests. A major subgovernment is the *military-industrial*[12] *complex*.

succession, line of. The designated *constitutional*[3] or legal order of officials who may move into vacated positions of *government*[3]. See also *lieutenant*[6] *governor*; *presidential*[6] *disability*; *presidential*[6] *succession*; *Presidential*[6] *Succession Act of 1947*; *Vice-President*[6].

Taylor, Frederick Winslow, 1856–1915. An American engineer, lecturer, and author of The Principles of Scientific Management (1911). Around 1912 Taylor led a movement which came to be known as scientific management, a movement which greatly affected the operation of *bureaucratic*[6] machinery at all levels of business and *government*[3]. He stressed planning and the measurement of quantifiable units of operation and management. He was interested in how long it took to perform particular tasks. He stressed the separate roles of planning and operation. His method was criticized mostly because of its lack of emphasis on human variables and needs. See also *administrative state*[6].

tenure. The right to hold an office as long as desired without the possibility of arbitrary dismissal. Tenure is a protective device for selected *civil*[6] *service* employees and other public officials. Such officials are usually given job protection after fulfilling a probationary period or employment. The job may be guaranteed only on good behavior or on the condition that professional competence will continue at a stated level.

Tenure of Office Act of 1867. A *federal*[3] *law*[8] passed over the *veto*[7] of *President*[6] Andrew Johnson and directed at weakening his *power*[3] to remove appointed *executive*[6] officers. The law provided that *department*[6] heads should serve during the entire term of the President who appointed them, plus one month, and they could not be removed without *Senate*[7] consent. President Johnson's supposed violation of the law in his removal of Secretary of War Stanton (a *Lincoln*[6] appointee) was used in the bill of *impeachment*[7] against the President. The impeachment proceedings were unsuccessful and the law was repealed in 1887. In 1926 the *U.S. Supreme*[8] *Court* said the act had been *unconstituional*[3]. See also *advice*[7] *and consent powers*; *appointive*[6] *powers*; *removal*[6] *powers*.

Truman, Harry S 1884–1973. *U.S. Senator*[7] from Missouri, *U.S. Vice-President*[6] during the *administration*[6] of President *Franklin D. Roosevelt*[6], and 33rd *U.S. President*[6] (1945–52). Truman succeeded to the office upon the sudden death of Roosevelt in 1945. He made the decision to end *World*[12] *War II* through the introduction of *atomic*[12] *war*, negotiated an end to the *war*[12], and helped found the *United*[12] *Nations*. Operating under the banner of the *Fair*[6] *Deal* he advocated *Social*[11] *Security* extension and protections for *minority*[9] *group* rights. He *vetoed*[7] the *Labor-Management*[10] *Relations* (*Taft-Hartley*) *Act of 1947*, which was overridden by the *Congress*[4]. He advocated the *Truman*[12] *doctrine*, instituted the *Point*[12] *Four Program*, began the *Marshall*[12] *Plan*, advocated the doctrine of *containment*[12] to fight *Communism*[3], created

the *Berlin*[12] *Airlift*, helped organize the *North*[12] *Atlantic Treaty Organization*, and led in conducting the *Korean*[12] *War*. One of President Truman's most flamboyant situations involved the *Democratic Party*[5] victory over Thomas Dewey in 1948 in spite of the split in the party by the *faction*[3] that called itself the *Dixiecratic Party*[5]. Another colorful episode involved the *MacArthur*[12] *controversy* in which Truman removed his military commander in the midst of the Korean War.

United States Government Organization Manual. An annual publication of the *federal government*[3] which lists current government agencies and outlines agency structures, objectives, and functions.

veterans' preference. A *federal*[3] *civil*[6] *service* preference category based on the fact that certain applicants or their relatives have served in the U.S. military forces. Veterans have received federal civil service preference since 1919. Disability, loss of a husband in military service, and other conditions may allow veterans' preference. Age, educational, and physical requirements may be waived in hiring a veteran. Also, competitive advantages in original employment, *merit*[6] *system* testing, and special privileges related to dismissal may be a part of the preference. Certain job categories are reserved for veterans.

veto, absolute: see Chap. 7.

veto, item: see Chap. 7.

veto, pocket: see Chap. 7.

Vice-President, U.S. The public official who directly succeeds to the office of the *U.S. President*[6] when a vacancy occurs, who may become *acting president*[6] in the event of *presidential*[6] *disability*, and who serves as the presiding officer of the *U.S.*

Senate[7]. Since the addition of the *Twelfth Amendment*[5] to the *U.S. Constitution*[4] the Vice-President has campaigned along with the President as a member of a *political party*[5] team and has been chosen by *electoral*[4] *college* vote on a ballot separate from the President. The Vice-President may vote in the Senate only in the event that he is needed to break a tie vote of regular members. The *Twenty-fifth Amendment*[6] provides that the Vice-President may become acting president under certain conditions, and when the vice presidential position is vacated, the President may nominate a new Vice-President who must be *confirmed*[6] by both houses of the *Congress*[4]. The Vice-President generally acts for the President as a goodwill *ambassador*[12] to foreign *nations*[3], as a liaison figure in the Congress, and as a party speechmaker seeking to strengthen party *power*[3] across the nation. See also *Twentieth Amendment*[7]; *presidential*[6] *succession*.

Washington, George, 1732–99. Virginia *legislator*[7] and *statesman*[5], member of the *First* and *Second Continental Congresses*[4], Commander-in-Chief of the Continental Army during the *American Revolution*[4], presiding officer at the *Constitutional Convention*[4] *of 1787*, and the first *U.S. President*[6] (1789–97). During Washington's *administration*[6] the presidential *Cabinet*[6] was created, the *assumption of state*[10] *debts* was undertaken, a national currency system was instituted, a *Bank*[10] *of the United States* was chartered, a postal system was begun, manufacturing was encouraged, tax collections were enforced in such actions as the *Whiskey*[4] *Rebellion*, a *federal*[3] judicial system was created through passage of the *Judiciary*[4] *Act of 1789*, and the *Treaty*[12] of Paris (Jay Treaty) in 1793 was negotiated in order to officially end the American Revolution. Washington announced *isolationism*[12] as the official foreign *policy*[6] of the United States *government*[3];

Washington's[12] *Farewell Address*, September 17, 1796, called for the U.S. to avoid "entangling alliances" with foreign *nations*.[3]

Weber, Max, 1864–1920. German sociologist, author of The Protestant Ethic and the Spirit of Capitalism (1920) and the person generally credited with popularizing the study of administrative and bureaucratic arrangements and processes. Weber saw *bureaucracy*[6] as the social system of modern *society*[3] and man as relatively insignificant in relation to the achievements of a planned, efficient, and specialized *administrative state*[6]. See also *administration*[6]; *capitalism*[3]; *fourth*[4] *branch of government*; *Protestant*[4] *Ethic*.

Wilson, Woodrow, 1856–1924. Professor of *political*[3] *science*, president of Princeton University, *governor*[6] of New Jersey (1911–13), and 28th U.S. *President*[6] (1913–21). Wilson set forth his political philosophy in three major volumes entitled Congressional Government (1885), Constitutional Government: A Study in American Politics in the United States (1908), and The New Freedom (1913). He reversed his philosophy of the presidential role between his first two works. In Congressional Government he viewed the *U.S. Congress*[4], and especially the *standing committees*[7] of Congress, as the dominant force in the American *federal*[3] system. He proposed that the U.S. adopt a system of *responsible party government*[5] similar to British *parliamentary government*[3]. In his last two works he saw the President as the dominant force because of his unique position as the leader of the *nation*[3], a nation which had suddenly been thrust into a position of international leadership. Wilson's presidential program, the *New*[6] *Freedom*, involved lowered *tariffs*[10], passage of the *Clayton*[10] *Antitrust Act of 1914*, creation of the *Federal*[2] *Reserve System* (1913), creation of the *Federal[2] Trade Commission* (1914), and *legislation[7]* protecting labor. While Wilson was President the *U.S. Constitution[4]* was amended to permit the use of a federal *graduated income tax[10]* (*Sixteenth Amendment[10]*), to permit the direct election of U.S. *Senators[7]* (*Seventeenth Amendment[7]*), and to prohibit the sale and usage of "intoxicating liquors" (*Eighteenth Amendment[4]*).

Wilson served as President during *World[12] War I*, enunciated the *Fourteen[12] Points* as foreign *policy[6]* ideals to be achieved, and led in negotiating the *Treaty of Versailles[12]*. He was most disappointed with rejection of the *treaty[12]* by the *U.S. Senate[7]* and refusal of the U.S. to join the *League[12] of Nations*. However, in 1919 he was awarded the Nobel Peace Prize for his efforts to create a world of peace.

Supreme Court cases related to material in this chapter are arranged below by subject. Summaries of the cases are in Chapter One arranged alphabetically by the name of the first party in each case.

GENERAL—
  Debs, In re (1895)
  Kendall v. Stokes (1838)
  Miss. v. Johnson (1867)
  Neagle, In re (1890)
  N.Y. Times Co. v. U.S. (1971)
  Prize Cases (1863)
  U.S. v. District Court for the Eastern District of Michigan (1972)

HABEAS CORPUS—
  Korematsu v. U.S. (1944)
  Merryman, Ex parte (1861)
  Milligan, Ex parte (1866)

LEGISLATIVE DELEGATION OF AUTHORITY—
  Hampton & Co. v. U.S. (1928)
  Opp Cotton Mills v. Administrator of Wage & Hour Division (1941)

  Panama Refining Co. v. U.S. (1935)
  Schechter Poultry Corp. v. U.S. (1935)
  U.S. v. Curtiss-Wright Export Corp. (1936)

PRESIDENTIAL POWERS —(Appointment & Removal)
  Cole v. Young (1956)
  Humphrey's Executor (Rathbun) v. U.S. (1935)
  Myers v. U.S. (1926)

PRESIDENTIAL POWERS —(Foreign Policy)
  Missouri v. Holland (1920)
  N.Y. Times Co. v. U.S. (1971)
  U.S. v. Belmont (1936)
  U.S. v. Curtiss-Wright Export Corp. (1936)

  Youngstown Sheet & Tube v. Sawyer (1952)

PRESIDENTIAL POWERS —(Inherent)
  U.S. v. Curtiss-Wright Export Corp. (1936)
  Youngstown Sheet & Tube v. Sawyer (1952)

PRESIDENTIAL POWERS —(Pardoning)
  Grossman, Ex parte (1925)

PRESIDENTIAL POWERS —(War)
  Korematsu v. U.S. (1944)
  Merryman, Ex parte (1861)
  Milligan, Ex parte (1866)
  N.Y. Times Co. v. U.S. (1971)
  Prize Cases (1863)
  Youngstown Sheet & Tube v. Sawyer (1952)

Chapter 7

The Legislative Branch

Note to the reader: Cross-referenced terms are in italics. The superscript number refers to the chapter in which the entry may be found. In addition, its placement indicates the word under which the term is alphabetized. (For example, in *electoral*⁴ *college*, information on the electoral college may be found in Chapter 4 under "electoral.") Because italics are used in cross-references, they are not used for terms in which they would ordinarily be used: Supreme Court cases and titles of books, journals, plays, and so forth.

> *Supreme Court cases relating to material in this chapter are listed at the end of the chapter (see page 199).*

---

act (statute): see law[8].

adjournment. The ending of a legislative *session*[7]. A legislative session may adjourn at the end of a day, for several days (no more than three days in the *U.S. Congress*[4] without permission from the other house), or for a longer period. To adjourn *sine*[7] *die* means to adjourn without setting a date for reconvening the *legislature*[7]. Although the Congress has for many years been legally required to adjourn by July 31, it has rarely done so in recent times. If the two houses cannot agree on a date for adjournment, the *President*[6] is *constitutionally*[3] empowered to set a date (a situation never experienced). Since adjournment of the Congress in recent times has run almost up to the date for reconvening the legislature, the *Legislative*[7] *Reorganization Act of 1970* stipulated that the Congress may take a summer *recess*[7] during the month of August.

advice and consent powers. The power *constitutionally*[3] granted to a *legislature*[7] to act in an *executive*[6] capacity with regard to such things as *appointments*[6] and *treaties*[12]. The *U.S. Senate*[7] is given such a *power*[3] since it must *confirm*[6] presidential appointments and give "advice and consent" on treaties. It takes a simple *majority*[3] vote of *senators*[7] present and voting to confirm presidential appointments and a two-thirds vote of senators present and voting to accept a treaty. See also *Myers*[1] *v. U.S.; senatorial*[6] *courtesy.*

alderman: see Chap. 11.

Amendment, Dirksen. An unsuccessful proposed *amendment*[3] to the *U.S. Constitution*[4] which would have permitted a *state*[3], on the basis of a popular *referendum*[3], to apportion one house of its *legislature*[7] on a basis other than population. The proposal by *Senator*[7] Everett Dirksen was directed at reversing the *Supreme*[8] *Court* decision in *Reynolds*[1] *v. Sims*, a decision which held that both houses of a state legislature must be based on population. The decision was based on the *one-*

man[5], one-vote rule of legislative apportionment[7]. During 1969 as many as 33 states passed resolutions[7] calling for a constitutional[3] convention[3] to act on the Dirksen Amendment, only one state short of the number required to call such a meeting. The conservative[3] push for such a convention began to wane during 1970 as various state resolutions demanding a convention were permitted to expire or were rescinded. There was some fear that the first constitutional convention in 182 years might go far beyond simple revision of the one-man, one-vote rule.

amendment, pro forma. A legislative device whereby a legislative member may find time to debate a point even though debate should have officially ended. The member may offer an amendment[3] supposedly designed to "strike out the last word" of a section being considered. He then earns the right to speak for five minutes and the amendment offered is never actually voted on.

Amendment, Seventeenth (1913). The amendment[3] to the U.S. Constitution[4] which instituted the direct election of U.S. Senators[7] by the qualified voters within the separate states. The Constitution had originally stated that senators were to be elected by the state legislatures[7] (Art. I, Sec. 3, Cl. 1). The Seventeenth Amendment also permits state governors[6] to fill temporary Senate[7] vacancies by recess appointment[6] until the position is filled by election procedures established by the state legislatures.

Amendment, Twentieth (1933). The amendment[3] to the U.S. Constitution[4] which moved the opening of the U.S. Congress[4] from March 4 to January 3 and the inauguration of the U.S. President[6] and the Vice-President[6] from March 4 to January 20. The "lame duck amendment" eliminated the short legislative session known as the lame duck session[7], a meeting period which

regularly occurred between December and January of even-numbered years. During a lame duck session some congressmen[7] were seated who had not been reelected to office for the upcoming, normal session of the Congress. The Twentieth Amendment also clarifies certain points related to presidential[6] succession before inauguration of a newly elected President.

apportionment, legislative. The legal act wherein the number of seats within a legislature[7] are assigned on the basis of established criteria. The criteria of population within each state[3] is used in determining the number of representatives each state may send to the U.S. House[7] of Representatives. A federal[3] decennial census is used in establishing each state's representation[7] on a regular basis. Each state is guaranteed at least one representative[7]. The Reapportionment Act of 1929 legally set a permanent number of 435 members for the House of Representatives. On the basis of the 1970 census and after reapportionment[7] in 1971, each representative was representing approximately 467,000 people. See also Avery[1] v. Midland County; Baker[1] v. Carr; Colgrove[1] v. Green; Three-fifths[4] Compromise; Gomillion[1] v. Lightfoot; Gray[1] v. Sanders; Kirkpatrick[1] v. Preisler; one-man[5], one-vote rule; proportional representation[5]; Reynolds[1] v. Sims; Wesberry[1] v. Sanders.

assemblyman. A member of a legislative body. The term is most frequently used to indicate a member of the lower chamber[7] of a state[3] legislature[7].

authority (power), delegation of: see Chap. 6.

Baker investigation, Bobby (1963–65). A U.S. Senate[7] and federal[3] grand jury[8] investigation of Robert G. Baker, majority[3] secretary to Senate majority floor[7] leader Lyndon B.

Johnson[6]. Baker was charged with conflict of interest and with using his position for personal financial gain. The investigation was provoked by *Senator*[7] John J. Williams of Delaware and led by the Committee on Rules and Administration under the *chairmanship*[7] of Senator B. Everett Jordan of North Carolina. The investigation uncovered *contract*[10] manipulations involving companies doing business with the *federal government*[3] and in which Baker had a financial interest, questionable townhouse parties involving *lobbyists*[5] and government officials, vast financial deals involving stocks and land, questionable gifts to government officials, and other controversial matters. The Senate report held that Baker had embarrassed the U.S. Senate but that the Rules Committee could not deal with the matter of federal violations. The *committee*[7] turned its files over to the *Department of Justice*[2] and the *Internal*[2] *Revenue Service*. Baker was convicted in a Federal court in 1967 of income tax evasion, theft, and conspiracy to defraud the government. After a series of appeals he was eventually confined in a federal prison. He was paroled from prison on June 1, 1972.

bicameralism. A legislative arrangement which incorporates two houses or chambers. The *U.S. Congress*[4] and all *state*[3] *legislatures*[7] except Nebraska's are bicameral in structure. See also *chamber*[7], *lower*; *chamber*[7], *upper*; *unicameralism*[7].

bill. A draft of a proposed *law*[8]. Bills in the *U.S. Congress*[4] may be introduced by any member. However, a *majority*[3] of all bills are actually suggested by *executive*[6] agencies. A major *constitutional*[3] restriction on the introduction of bills is that revenue bills (and *appropriations bills*[7] by *custom*[3]) must originate in the *House*[7] of Representatives. *Public bills*[7] deal with public matters, and *private bills*[7] deal with particular individuals. Bills are designated by initials and numbers according to the house and order of origin. The first bill in a new Congress (90th, 91st, etc.) originating in the *U.S. Senate*[7] would be numbered S. 1. The first bill in the House of Representatives would be H.R. 1. The numbering of bills in consecutive order extends across both *sessions*[7] of a Congress. A bill which fails to become law dies at the end of the Congress. It may be reintroduced at a later Congress under a new number. Once a bill passes one house it is an *engrossed bill*[7], and when it passes both houses and is signed by the presiding officers it becomes an *enrolled bill*[7] and is sent to the *President*[6] for his acceptance (by signing) or *veto*[7].

bill, appropriations. A *bill*[7] related to the expenditure of *government*[3] funds. In both houses of the *U.S. Congress*[4] there are *committees*[7] specifically designed to handle appropriations measures. *Custom*[3] holds that all appropriations bills will originate in the *House*[7] of Representatives. See also *authorization bill*[7]; *Committee*[7] *on Appropriations* (*U.S. House*); *pork*[7] *barrel*.

bill, authorization. A *bill*[7] which authorizes the expenditure of public funds. A *legislature*[7] may authorize money for a program even though the program may never be funded from the public treasury. Actual funding comes through passage of an *appropriations bill*[7]. See also *Committee*[7] *on Appropriations* (*U.S. House*); *pork*[7] *barrel*.

bill, clean (committee). A *bill*[7] passed from a legislative *committee*[7] in an amended form or in a form that makes the bill essentially a new measure. A clean bill will carry a new number when it goes to the legislative chamber for consideration.

bill, engrossed. A *bill*[7] printed in final form, including *amendments*[3], for final vote of the members of one house of a legislative body. See also *enrolled bill*[7].

bill, enrolled. A *bill*[7] passed by both houses of a legislative body, printed in final form on parchment paper, and forwarded to the *executive*[6] for his signature or *veto*[7]. See also *engrossed bill*[7].

bill, omnibus. A proposed *statute*[8] which incorporates legislative proposals from various *bills*[7] involving the same subject. For example, compromise bills such as the *Compromise*[4] *of 1850*, *legislative reorganization*[7] bills such as the *Legislative*[7] *Reorganization Act of 1946*, and *crime*[8] control bills such as the *Omnibus*[8] *Crime Control and Safe Streets Act of 1968* may be classified as omnibus bills.

bill, private. A legislative proposal dealing with private individuals and matters. The introduction of private *bills*[7] was severely restricted by the *Legislative*[7] *Reorganization Act of 1946*. Private bills generally deal with such things as *property*[10] claims against the *government*[3], appeals for special treatment in *immigration*[3] and *naturalization*[3] matters, disputed land titles, and similar categories. See also *Private Calendar*[7]; *special legislation*[7].

bill, privileged. A *bill*[7] which may avoid any procedural hurdles beyond *standing committee*[7] clearance or which may interrupt the regular order of legislative business for immediate consideration. Privileged bills may take the form of revenue or *appropriations bills*[7], *conference committee*[7] reports, *special orders*[7] from the *Committee*[7] *on Rules*, and various other specified privileged items. The *U.S. House*[7] *of Representatives Committee*[7] *on Ways and Means* and the *Committee*[7] *on Appropriations* are sometimes referred to as *privileged question committees*[7] because their bills ordinarily take precedence over other *legislation*[7].

bill, public. A legislative proposal dealing with general public business, economic or otherwise. See also *House Calendar*[7]; *Union Calendar*[7].

bloc. A group of *legislators*[7] supporting or opposing particular legislative matters, regardless of *political party*[5] affiliation of the members grouped together. Examples of blocs are legislators favorable to or in sympathy with farmers, veterans, southerners, *civil*[9] *rights* advocates, and religious leaders. See also *Conservative*[7] *Coalition*.

borough. A self-governing, incorporated *municipal*[11] area. New York City calls its five major subdivisions boroughs, while Alaska calls its geographical areas similar to *counties*[11] by the same name. In England the term "borough" means a *town*[11] or geographical area which sends *representatives*[7] to Parliament. See also *municipal corporation*[11]; *parliamentary government*[3].

borough, pocket. A geographical area whose *representation*[7] in a *legislature*[7] is controlled by one person or family. Legally acknowledged pocket boroughs were abandoned in England during the parliamentary reform of 1832. See also *rotten borough*[7].

borough, rotten. A geographical area which receives *representation*[7] in a *legislature*[7] even though the area contains few people. Legally acknowledged rotten boroughs were abandoned in England during the parliamentary reform of 1832. See also *pocket borough*[7].

burgess. A term meaning, at various times, a parliamentary *representative*[7] of an English *borough*[7], a representative of a *town*[11] or some political subdivision of a town, or a member of the *lower chamber*[7] of the *legislature*[7] in either Virginia or Maryland.

calendar. A schedule of *bills*[7] awaiting formal legislative consideration.

Calendar, Consent. The *U.S. House*[7] *of Representatives calendar*[7] which schedules debate for noncontroversial *bills*[7] that are removed from the *House* or *Union Calendars*[7] upon formal written request. A bill must have been on the Consent Calendar for three *legislative*[7] *days* prior to the Monday on which it is called. The *calendar*[7] is usually called on the first and third Mondays of each month. When a bill is first called, one *objector*[7] may delay the bill for two weeks. On the second call, if three members object, then the bill is removed from the calendar. If less than three object to the bill, it is considered immediately. Any bill involving over one million dollars is automatically objected to. If there is no formal objection when a bill is called on the Consent Calendar, it is passed by *unanimous*[7] consent without debate.

Calendar, Discharge. The *U.S. House*[7] *of Representatives calendar*[7] which schedules debate for *bills*[7] that have not been approved by *standing committees*[7] but that have been removed from *committees*[7] by discharge petitions containing at least 218 signatures. The Discharge Calendar is called for on the second and fourth Mondays of each month. A seven-day waiting period is required before floor action may be taken on a discharge Monday. See also *discharge*[7] *rule.*

Calendar, Executive. The *U.S. Senate*[7] *calendar*[7] which lists presidential nominations for *appointments*[6], *treaties*[12], and other *executive*[6] matters requiring Senate action.

Calendar, House. The *U.S. House*[7] *of Representatives calendar*[7] which schedules debate for public nonrevenue measures. See also *public bill*[7].

Calendar of Bills and Resolutions. The *U.S. Senate*[7] *calendar*[7] which contains legislative items that may be considered one by one under the *five-minute*[7] *rule.* Motions by *unanimous*[7] *consent* may bring items to the floor for unlimited debate.

Calendar, Private (Calendar of the Committee of the Whole House). The *U.S. House*[7] *of Representatives calendar*[7] which schedules debate for *bills*[7] of a private nature. The calendar is called on the first and third Tuesdays of each month. Bills are called in numerical order, and each will receive immediate consideration under the *five-minute*[7] *rule* unless there are two *objectors*[7] to the measure. See also *private bill*[7].

Calendar, Union (Calendar of the Whole House on the State of the Union). The *U.S. House*[7] *of Representatives calendar*[7] which schedules debate for public taxation and *appropriations bills*[7]. See also *public bill*[7].

Calendar Wednesday. A rarely used procedure in the *U.S. House*[7] *of Representatives* designed to allow a *standing committee*[7] that has approved a *bill*[7] to get it before the entire House by circumventing the *Committee*[7] *on Rules* or *majority*[3] leadership trying to block action. On each Wednesday the *Speaker*[7] *of the House* calls the *committees*[7] in alphabetical order. A committee *chairman*[7] may call up any bill on the *House* or *Union Calendar*[7] that his committee has previously reported but which has yet to be acted on. Calendar Wednesday may be dispensed with, as it usually is, by a two-thirds vote of the House. See also *majority floor*[7] *leader.*

caucus (conference). A closed meeting of all *political party*[5] members of one house of a legislative body. The term is frequently used to describe any informal meeting of a number of *legislators*[7] of the same party. In the *U.S. Congress*[4] the Republicans call their meeting the Republican Conference. The Democrats call their meeting the Democratic Caucus. Party caucuses are used to choose party leaders, approve *standing committee*[7] assignments, and outline legislative programs. See also *steering committee*[7]; *majority floor*[7] *leader*; *minority floor*[7] *leader*; *Democratic Party*[5]; *Republican Party*[5]; *whip*[7].

censure. The act of a *legislature*[7] or other *organization*[6] formally expressing disapproval or dissatisfaction with one of its own members. Two of the most famous acts of censure were the *Senate*[7] censures of Senator Joseph McCarthy in 1954 and Senator Thomas Dodd in 1967. See also *Thomas Dodd*[7] *investigation*; *McCarthyism*[9].

chairman. The presiding officer of any meeting, *committee*[7], *convention*[3], administrative *organization*[6], or other group which refers to its leader as "chairman." A chairman's principal duties are to preside, maintain order, and generally guide the deliberations of the organization.

chamber (house), lower (second). Generally the larger of the two houses of a *bicameral*[7] *legislature*[7], a house whose membership is ordinarily chosen on the basis of population and whose members are chosen through *popular vote*[5]. The lower chamber in the United States, the *House*[7] *of Representatives*, contains members chosen to represent population within the separate *states*[3]. See also *upper chamber*[7]; *multi-member district*[7]; *representative*[7].

chamber (house), upper. Generally the smaller of the two houses of a *bicameral*[7] *legislature*[7], a house whose membership is normally recognized as possessing more influence than the *lower chamber*[7]. The upper chamber in the United States, the *Senate*[7], contains members chosen to represent geographical units (*states*[3]) whereas the lower chamber, the *House*[7] of *Representatives*, represents population. See also *lieutenant*[6] *governor*.

closed (gag) rule. A legislative rule or *special order*[7] issued by the *Committee*[7] on *Rules* of the *U.S. House*[7] *of Representatives* which prohibits the offering of *amendments*[3] to a *bill*[7] which has been reported out of *committee*[7] and placed before the entire house.

closure (cloture) rule. The process used in the *U.S. Senate*[7] whereby unlimited debate (*filibuster*[7]) may be ended. Closure requires a preliminary petition signed by 16 *senators*[7], a two-day wait for final vote, and a two-thirds *extraordinary majority*[3] vote of senators present and voting. Once closure is accepted each senator is given one hour for debate. Closure was successfully invoked only seven times between 1917 and 1965.

committee. A group of individuals chosen from a larger *organization*[6] to consider and act on specialized matters designated by the organization. Committees within the U.S. *Congress*[4] are referred to as *standing committees*[7] if they deal regularly with the same subject matter. See also *committee*[7] *system*.

committee, conference. A temporary *joint committee*[7] composed of an equal number of members from both houses of a *bicameral*[7] *legislature*[7] in order to work out differences on *legislation*[7] considered in both houses. Such committees are necessary because both houses must agree on a *bill*[7] in exactly the same form before it can be sent to the *executive*[6] for consideration. Conferees vote under a unit rule, which holds that members (managers) from each house must vote separately in order to agree on *amendments*[3] or other changes. Conference committee compromises are returned to the respective houses for vote on the bill without the possibility of amending it. If the bill is rejected it may be allowed to die or it may be returned to conference committee under a new set of managers from each house. See also *unit vote*[7].

committee, exclusive. Any major *standing committee*[7] of the U.S. *House*[7] *of Representatives* which is considered so significant and time-consuming that *committee*[7] members assigned to such a committee may not serve on any other major (exclusive) committee. Committee members may be assigned to less significant committees. The House committees considered "exclusive" are *Rules*[7], *Appropriations*[7], and *Ways*[7] *and Means*.

committee, investigating. Any legislative *committee*[7], standing or otherwise, which undertakes an investigation in order to fulfill the legislative role of *policy*[7] *formulation*. A legislative committee may compel the attendance of witnesses, require the submission of items of evidence, and punish for *perjury*[9] and *contempt*[7] *of Congress*. An investigating committee's major restriction is that its activities and questions of witnesses must clearly relate to the legislative *powers*[3] of the U.S. *Congress*[4]. A witness may not be required to answer questions irrelevant to the investigation. The U.S. *House*[7] *of Representatives Committee*[7] *on Internal Security* has been one of the most controversial investigating bodies because of its investigations involving subversive activities. *Senator*[7] Joseph McCarthy was one of the most controversial legislative investigators when, as *chairman*[7] of the U.S. *Senate*[7] Committee on Government Operations, he investigated subversive activities in the *Department of State*[2]. McCarthy engaged in extensive usage of innuendo and *guilt*[9] *by association*, activities which led to his ultimate *censure*[7] by the Senate. See also *Barenblatt*[1] *v. U.S.*; *standing committee*[7]; *investigative*[7] *powers*; *Kilbourn*[1] *v. Thompson*; *McCarthyism*[9]; *McGrain*[1] *v. Daugherty*; *Slochower*[1] *v. Board of Education*; *Watkins*[1] *v. U.S.*

committee, joint. A *committee*[7] composed of members from two legislative chambers. There are various kinds of joint committees such as *standing committees*[7], *conference committees*[7], and *special (select) committees*[7]. Joint committees are formed in order to comprehensively handle business common to both houses.

Committee of the Whole. The occasion when a legislative body sits as one large *committee*[7]. The *House*[7] *of Representatives* frequently sits as a Committee of the Whole House on the State of the Union. A person different from the *Speaker*[7] *of the House* may preside, debate may be properly divided, *amendments*[3] may be quickly handled under the *five-minute*[7] *rule*, 100 members constitute a *quorum*[7], and numerous votes are taken without recorded roll calls. All revenue and *appropriation bills*[7] must be considered in such a committee in the House of Representatives. However, the formal House must approve Committee of the Whole action. See also *roll call vote*[7].

Committee on Appropriations (U.S. House). The largest *standing committee*[7] in the U.S. *House*[7] *of Representatives* and one of the most powerful committees in the entire U.S. *Congress*[4]. The *committee*[7] gains a large portion of its *power*[3] and autonomy from the fact that revenue measures must *constitutionally*[3] originate in the House (Art. I, Sec. 7, Cl. 1), and spending or *appropriations bills*[7] originate there by *custom*[3]. All *legislation*[7] involving *appropriations*[10] must be channeled through the Committee on Appropriations. The committee is often called on to compromise *political party*[5], regional, and other differences through the funding of various *federal*[3] programs.

committee on committees. A *partisan*[5] legislative *committee*[7] responsible for the placement of *political party*[5] members on *standing committees*[7] within a *legislature*[7]. The separate committees on committees may make committee assignments to the various standing committees in their houses in the same ratio their parties hold in each house. In the *U.S. House*[7] *of Representatives* the *Republican Party*[5] has a committee on committees composed of one *representative*[7] from each *state*[3] having Republican members in the House. The members from each state are chosen by their members in the House. The members from each state are chosen by their state *delegation*[5] and they cast votes equal to their strength in the House. The *Democratic Party*[5] members of the House use the Democratic members of the House *Committee*[7] *on Ways and Means* to determine standing committee assignments. In the *Senate*[7] the Republicans use a separate committee on committees, while the Democrats use the *steering committee*[7] of their party *caucus*[5]. Because of the *seniority*[7] *rule* the primary task of a committee on committes in the *U.S. Congress*[4] is to fill vacancies with freshman members or approve committee changes for senior members when senior positions are available.

Committee on Internal Security (U.S. House). A controversial *U.S. House*[7] *of Representatives standing committee*[7] whose major task is investigative in nature because of its responsibility to investigate subversive activities within the U.S. The Internal Security Committee, an *investigating committee*[7] formerly known as the House Committee on Un-American Activities was a *conservative*[3] "thorn in the flesh" of *Franklin Roosevelt's*[6] *New*[6] *Deal*, received recognition during the late 1940's for its exposure of Alger Hiss and his subversive activities within the *Department of State*[2], and fell into some disrepute in recent years for its lack of reference to legislative matters. The *committee*[7] has been criticized for its investigations into matters of a purely private char-

acter and its use of questions irrelevant to its investigative task. See also *Barenblatt*[1] *v. U.S.*; *Watkins*[1] *v. U.S.*

Committee on Rules (U.S. House). A *standing committee*[7] of the *U.S. U.S. House*[7] *of Representatives* that recommends which of the *public bills*[7] reported by other *committees*[7] should be considered by the entire House. The Committee on Rules coordinates the movement of *legislation*[7] in the House, determines the limitations on debate and legislative *amendments*[3] made from the floor, recommends changes in the general rules of the House, and otherwise guides the activity of the entire House. The Rules Committee's *bipartisan*[5] membership was set at 15 *representatives*[7] in 1961. See also *Calendar*[7] *Wednesday*; *special order*[7]; *closed*[7] *(gag) rule*; *open*[7] *rule*; *seven-day*[7] *rule*; *twentyone*[7] *day rule*.

Committee on Ways and Means (U.S. House). A *standing committee*[7] of the *U.S. House*[7] *of Representatives* which controls the introduction of revenue bills. The Committee on Ways and Means is significant because of the *constitutional*[3] provision (Art. I, Sec. 7, Cl. 1) requiring àll revenue measures to originate in the House of Representatives, because the *majority*[3] *of bills*[7] passed by the *U.S. Congress*[4] involve monetary considerations and because the Democratic members of the *committee*[7] serve as the *committee*[7] *on committees* for the *Democratic Party*[5] members in the House.

committee, privileged question. A *committee*[7] which may interrupt the scheduled order of legislative business in a chamber in order to get immediate consideration for a committee report or other item. Within the *U.S. Congress*[4] *the U.S. House*[7] *of Representatives Committee*[7] *on Rules* may interrupt business in order to report a *bill*[7], the House *Committee*[7] *on*

Appropriations and the *Committee*[7] *on Ways and Means* may interrupt business to introduce monetary measures, *conference committees*[7] may report on their conference activities, and other committees may also be recognized in order to introduce *privileged questions*[7] or motions.

committee, special (select). A temporary legislative *committee*[7] created for a specific purpose. Special committees or *subcommittees*[7] are ordinarily assigned to investigate certain matters, coordinate or supervise legislative tasks, or to fulfill some other legislative obligation. Members of special committees are generally appointed by the presiding officers of legislative chambers. Members of special subcommittees are generally appointed by the *chairmen*[7] of *standing committees*[7]. See also *investigating committee*[7].

committee, standing. A permanent or regular *committee*[7] created by a legislative body to consider particular subjects on which the *legislature*[7] may act. During the 91st *Congress*[4] there were 16 standing committees in the *Senate*[7] and 20 in the *House*[7] of Representatives. The membership of each standing committee is based on the same *political party*[5] ratio evident in the house that created the committee. The committee *chairman*[7] is chosen under the *seniority*[7] *rule* and is a member of the *majority party*[5] controlling the chamber. The major standing committees in the House of Representatives are *Rules*[7], *Appropriations*[7], and *Ways and Means*[7]. The major committees in the *Senate*[7] are *Foreign*[12] *Relations*, *Judiciary*[8], Armed Services, and the committees controlling monetary matters. In the operation of each standing committee some of the major factors are: individual members' votes in committee may be recorded, committees have permission to sit while the House of Representatives is in *session*[7], committee meetings and *hearings*[6] are generally to

be open, regular advance notice must be given of upcoming committee meetings, there may be no *proxy voting*[7] in most cases, and a *majority*[3] of the standing committee may report a *pigeonholed*[7] *bill*[7] against the wishes of the chairman after a seven-day delay after requesting a report with the committee clerk. See also *Legislative*[7] *Reorganization Act of 1970*; *seniority*[7] *rule*; *seven-day*[7] *rule*.

committee, steering (policy). A small group of *political party*[5] leaders within the party *caucus*[7] (*conference*) of a legislative chamber. The steering committee is generally led by the *floor*[7] *leader*. It guides the assignment of party members to *standing committees*[7], directs legislative research, and advises on the development of the party's legislative program. The *Democratic Party*[5] refers to its *committee*[7] as a steering committee, and the *Republican Party*[7] refers to its committee in the *Congress*[4] as a policy committee.

committee system. The complex and formal arrangement whereby a legislative body investigates matters deemed worthy of possible legislative action through the use of *committees*[7] and *subcommittees*[7] composed of *legislators*[7]. The U.S. *Congress*[4] uses a system of *standing committees*[7] based on specialized subjects in order to investigate and move regular legislative detail through the *legislature*[7]. Various other committees are used in order to carry out specialized tasks such as working out legislative differences between two houses, investigating special matters, expediting legislative business during general debate, and choosing *political party*[5] leadership and making standing committee assignments. The committee system has always been influential in the workings of the Congress. However, the basic structures and operations of the present committee system in the Congress came into existence through the *Revolution*[7] of

1910–11 and the passage of the *Legislative*[7] *Reorganization Act of 1946* and the *Legislative*[7] *Reorganization Act of 1970*. The committee system in both houses of the Congress leaves the primary control of *power*[3] in the hands of the *majority party*[5] in the respective houses. The *seniority*[7] *rule* is a basic element in the power structure. Some of the major standing committees in the *House*[7] *of Representatives* are the *Committee*[7] *on Appropriations, Committee*[7] *on Rules,* and the *Committee*[7] *on Ways and Means.* Two of the major standing committees in the *Senate*[7] are the *Committee*[8] *on the Judiciary* and the *Committee*[12] *on Foreign Relations.* See also *conference committee*[7]; *Committee*[7] *of the Whole; committee*[7] *on committees; investigating committee*[7]; *joint committee*[7]; *special (select) committee*[7].

Congress, United States: see Chap. 4.

Congressional Directory. A regular publication of the *U.S. Congress*[4] which contains biographical and statistical data concerning the Congress and its members. The volume generally contains additional information concerning the other branches of the *federal government*[3].

Congressional Government (1885): see *Woodrow Wilson*[6].

Congressional Record. The daily unofficial record of the proceedings of both houses of the *U.S. Congress*[4]. The material contains floor debates, statements concerning rules and *resolutions*[7], speeches of *legislators*[7] (frequently edited before going to press), extraneous remarks submitted for publication although not actually delivered in Congress, and other material of interest to observers of Congress. The official record of the proceedings in each chamber of the U.S. Congress is the *Journal*[7].

congressman. A member of either house of the *U.S. Congress*[4]. The term is used most frequently to refer to a member of the U.S. *House*[7] *of Representatives.* A congressman is chosen to represent the people who reside in his *district*[7]. He is sometimes referred to as a *representative*[7] or *a legislator*[7]. In 1971 there were 100 congressmen referred to as *senators*[7] serving in the U.S. *Senate*[7] and 435 congressmen referred to as representatives serving in the U.S. House of Representatives. See also *delegate legislator*[7]; *politico legislator*[7]; *representative (trustee-legislator*[7].

congressman at large. A member of the *U.S. House*[7] *of Representatives* who is chosen by the voters of an entire *state*[3] rather than by the voters of a particular *congressional district*[7]. A congressman at large may be chosen in situations where a state has only one *representative*[7] or in a situation where a state fails to *redistrict*[7] after a decennial census and is due one additional representative. In a situation where a state loses a seat and fails to redistrict, all members may be forced by court order to run at large. See also *at-large election*[5].

Conservative Coalition. The *bloc*[7] of southern *conservative*[3] Democrats and northern conservative Republicans in either house of the *U.S. Congress*[4] who group together in support of or opposition to particular issues. For many years the Conservative Coalition dominated the House *Committee*[7] *on Rules* and killed numerous pieces of *liberal*[3] *legislation*[7] concerning social and economic issues. See also *Democratic*[7] *Study Group.*

contempt of Congress. Deliberate interference with the *powers*[3] and duties of the *U.S. Congress*[4]. Either house of Congress has the power to cite individuals for contempt when they refuse to testify before a legislative *committee*[7], obstruct or disturb legislative proceedings, or undertake other actions interfering with the *policy*[7] *formulating* powers or other legislative powers of Congress. Persons cited for contempt are dealt with in regular *federal*[3] courts. See also *contempt*[8] *of court*; *investigating committee*[7]; *judicial powers*[7]; *Kilbourn*[1] *v. Thompson*; *McGrain*[1] *v. Daugherty*; *Watkins*[1] *v. U.S.*

Democratic Study Group (DSG), 1959– . A group of *liberal*[3] Democrats in the *U.S. House*[7] *of Representatives* which arose in 1959 to challenge the *Conservative*[7] *Coalition* of southern Democrats and *conservative*[3] Republicans. The Democratic Study Group led in winning legislative victories during the 1960's related to *civil*[9] *rights*, education, social welfare, and related areas. The group was also a major advocate of legislative reform which gained momentum near the end of the 1960's.

dilatory motion. A motion from a legislative member during consideration of a *bill*[7] in order to slow down or prevent action on the bill. Dilatory motions concerning irrelevant and minor technical points are forbidden by both houses of the *U.S. Congress*[4]. However, much discretion in the matter is left to presiding officers.

discharge petition: see *discharge*[7] *rule*.

discharge rule. A legislative rule which holds that a legislative *committee*[7] may be discharged from further consideration of a *bill*[7] before it. The device, rarely used in *legislatures*[7], brings the bill in question to the floor for full consideration. In the U.S. *House*[7] *of Representatives*, if a committee does not report a bill within 30 days after receiving it, any member of the House may file a discharge petition. In order to discharge the committee from further responsibility, 218 signatures (an *absolute majority*[3] of the House) are required. Bills may

be discharged from the *Committee*[7] *on Rules* after only seven *legislative*[7] *days*. See also *seven-day*[7] *rule, twenty-one*[7] *day rule*.

district: see *legislative district*[7].

district, congressional. A geographical *district*[7] within a *state*[3] which may legally send a *representative*[7] to the *U.S. House*[7] *of Representatives*. A *congressman*[7] is not *constitutionally*[3] required to be from the district which he serves. However, in 1842 the Congress made residency within the district a legal requirement for election.

district, flotorial. A type of *legislative district*[7] found in some *states*[3] in which one district with a surplus of population for *representation*[7] purposes may combine the surplus with a sparsely populated contiguous area in order to justify an additional state *representative*[7]. It has been judicially held in some states that such districts violate the *one-man*[5], *one-vote rule*.

district, ideally equal. A *legislative district*[7] which is approximately equal in population to other districts within the *state*[3]. In 1969 the *U.S. Supreme*[8] *Court* held that United States *congressional districts*[7] must be exactly the same unless variations are absolutely unavoidable. In 1973 in a Virginia state *reapportionment*[7] case the Court upheld a 16.4 percent variation in order to give some consideration to local subdivisions such as *cities*[11] and *counties*[11]. See also *Kirkpatrick*[1] *v. Preisler*; *proportional representation*[5].

district, legislative. A geographical district in which the qualified electorate may select a *representative*[7] to serve in a *legislature*[7]. See also *congressional district*[7]; *flotorial district*[7]; *ideally equal district*[7]; *multi-member district*[7]; *safe district*[7]; *single-member district*[7].

District Mondays. The *U.S. House*[7] *of Representatives discharge calendar*[7] days of the second and fourth Mondays of each month, which allow for the *District of Columbia*[4] *committee*[7] of the U.S. House of Representatives to present District matters to the House. *Special orders*[7] from the *Committee*[7] *on Rules* are not required for such *legislation*[7].

district, multi-member. A *legislative district*[7] represented by several *legislators*[7] at the same time. Some *state*[3] *legislatures*[7] have at least one chamber, generally the *lower chamber*[7] with a multi-member arrangement. For example, a populous *county*[11] receiving several *representative*[7] seats may elect members at large rather than trying to divide the county into several *single-member districts*[7] or *wards*[5]. The *U.S. Supreme*[8] *Court* held on June 7, 1971, in Whitcomb v. Chavis, an Indiana case involving *representation*[7] in state legislatures, that states are not required to provide legislative district arrangements which guarantee that racial *minorities*[3] and other distinct *minority*[9] groups must have obvious representation or control particular districts. The Court declared, "Multi-member districts are not per se unconstitutional." See also *at-large election*[5]; *cumulative voting*[5].

district, safe. A *legislative district*[7] which has a record of reelecting the same *legislator*[7] to his position over a long period of time. A safe district is generally one in which one *political party*[5] or political *machine*[5] clearly controls *power*[3]. The use of the *seniority*[7] *rule* in choosing *standing committee*[7] *chairmen*[7] in the U.S. *Congress*[4] makes the safe district an important variable in the total power structure of the Congress. For example, in the 2nd *session*[7] of the 91st Congress (1970) *conservative*[3] southern *Democratic Party*[5] members from safe districts dominated the *committee*[7] chairmanships in both houses of Congress. See *committee*[7] *system*; *Conservative*[7] *Coalition*.

district, single-member. A *legislative district*[7] represented by one *legislator*[7]. In the U.S. *Congress*[4] the electorate of a single-member district chooses a *representative*[7] through a *plurality*[3] vote. The structure contrasts with a *multi-member district*[7] and is generally credited with continuance of a *two-party*[5] *system* because the winner of the largest block of votes wins the election. Such a condition leaves *minor parties*[5] with little chance of gaining *power*[3].

Dodd investigation, Thomas (1964–67). A U.S. *Senate*[7] investigation prompted when a legislative assistant in the office of *Senator*[7] Thomas Dodd of Connecticut turned over controversial papers from Senator Dodd's files to columnist Drew Pearson. Pearson accused the senator of influence peddling for private businesses, acceptance of gifts, the use of *federal*[3] funds for private trips, the widespread use of *sinecures*[6] for friends, and the use of campaign money for personal purposes. The Senate Ethics Committee investigated the charges, *public opinion*[5] was aroused about the conduct of the U.S. *Congress*[4], and the Senate eventually *censured*[7] Senator Dodd in 1967 by a vote of 94 to 5. Dodd was censured for the personal use of money raised in campaign testimonial dinners. He lost favor with his fellow senators, became ineffectual in *Democratic Party*[5] affairs, was defeated for reelection as an *independent*[5] in 1970, and died a broken man in 1971.

engrossment: see *engrossed bill*[7].

enrollment: see *enrolled bill*[7].

exclusion. The act of a legislative body rejecting a person who has been elected to serve as a member of the *legislature*[7]. In the U.S. *Congress*[4] a person may be excluded from membership through a simple *majority*[3] of members present and voting. Both the

Senate[7] and *House*[7] *of Representatives* have excluded persons from membership on the grounds of polygamy, bribery, *socialism*[3], and racism. However, in 1967 the *Supreme*[8] *Court* held that exclusion should rest primarily on *constitutional*[3] grounds concerning formal qualifications (age, *citizenship*[3], and residency). See also *Powell*[1] *v. McCormack.*

expulsion. The act of a *legislature*[7] expelling one of its own members for cause. Expulsion is generally recognized as the most extreme disciplinary action a legislative body may take against a member. In the *U.S. Congress*[4] either house may expel members upon a two-thirds vote of the members present and voting.

Father of the House. The person who has served in the *U.S. House*[7] *of Representatives* longer than any other current member.

filibuster rule. A time-consuming legislative device incorporating unlimited debate, *dilatory*[7] *motions*, *quorum*[7] calls, and other tactics in order to prevent a vote on a proposed *bill*[7] or *amendment*[3]. The filibuster is most noted for its past use in the *U.S. Senate*[7], especially in defeating *civil*[9] *rights legislation*[7]. It is more readily used in the Senate than in the *House*[7] *of Representatives* because of the Senate's rules permitting unlimited debate. See also *closure*[7] *rule.*

five-minute rule. A rule or *special order*[7] used to expedite debate when the *Committee*[7] *of the Whole* meets in the *U.S. House*[7] *of Representatives*. If an *open*[7] *rule* has been issued by the *Committee*[7] *on Rules*, then a *bill*[7] may be amended through allocation of debate time to members of the House. Any member may take five minutes to speak on the bill or to propose an *amendment*[3]. Any *committee*[7] member who has had a proposed

amendment printed in the *Congressional*[7] *Record* after the reporting of the bill and at least one day before floor consideration has five minutes to explain the amendment. The first person to obtain the floor has five minutes to speak in opposition to the amendment.

floor leader, majority. A *political party*[5] leader chosen in the majority party *caucus*[7] (*conference*) of his respective house and charged with guiding the party's program through the legislative process. In the *U.S. House*[7] *of Representatives* the *Speaker*[7] *of the House* overshadows the *majority floor*[7] *leader*. In the *U.S. Senate*[7] the majority floor leader is the obvious spokesman for the *majority party*[5]. See also *Bobby Baker*[7] *investigation.*

floor leader, minority. A *political party*[5] leader chosen in the minority party *caucus*[7] (*conference*) of his respective house and charged with guiding the *minority party's*[5] program through the legislative process.

franking privilege. The privilege granted to a member of the *U.S. Congress*[4] to send out a certain amount of mail under his signature and without charge. The "frank" provides an inexpensive means whereby the *legislator*[7] may maintain contact with his *constituents*[5].

gerrymander. A process wherein *boundary*[12] lines of *legislative districts*[7] are arranged in such a way as to create an inequality of political *power*[3] and give the advantage to the *political party*[5] drawing the district lines. The gerrymander, named after *Governor*[6] Elbridge Gerry of Massachusetts around 1812, is used to give the party in power control over as many districts as possible and to isolate the *minority party*[5] within a few districts. See also *silent gerrymander*[7]; *Gomillion*[1] *v. Lightfoot.*

gerrymander, silent. An informal process wherein population shifts take place within a *state*[3] and legislative *boundaries*[12] are left intact rather than rearranged to represent the new population structure. Silent gerrymandering has been used to leave political *power*[3] and *partisan*[5] advantages undisturbed over long periods of time. Beginning in 1962, the *U.S. Supreme*[8] *Court* declared that the inequitable arrangement of *legislative districts*[7] is *unconstitutional*[3] if it tends to violate the *equal*[4] *protection clause* of the *Fourteenth Amendment*[4]. The Court held that boundary lines must be redrawn as population moves in order to meet the *one-man*[5], *one-vote rule* whereby each man's vote is equal to every other man's vote. See also *Baker*[1] *v. Carr*; *gerrymander*[7]; *proportional representation*[5]; *redistricting*[7].

Hinds' Precedents. A compilation of *U.S. House*[7] *of Representatives* precedents which was arranged and published by Asher Hinds in 1907. The last major revision of the House precedents was published by Clarence Cannon in 1935. Beween 1935 and 1970 over 60,000 additional precedents and decisions were announced by various *Speakers*[7] *of the House* of the House of Representatives. See also *parliamentary*[7] *procedure*.

House of Representatives, U.S. The *lower chamber*[7] of the *U.S. Congress*[4], a chamber selected on the basis of population within the various *states*[3]. The *U.S. Constitution*[4] provides that each state shall have at least one *representative*[7] regardless of population, that a decennial census shall determine the number of representatives to be chosen from each state, that representatives shall serve two-year terms of office, that the House shall choose the *U.S. President*[6] when the *electoral*[4] *college* cannot do so with a clear *majority*[3] vote, that all revenue bills shall originate in the House, and that the House may bring

charges of *impeachment*[7] against *federal*[3] officials. The presiding officer of the House is the *Speaker*[7] *of the House*. Members of the House are ordinarily referred to as *congressmen*[7] or representatives. Members are elected from *single-member districts*[7]. The *U.S. Supreme*[8] *Court* held in 1964 that the districts are supposed to contain approximately the same number of people. See also *Wesberry*[1] *v. Sanders*.

impeachment. A formal charge of legal violation brought by the *lower chamber*[7] of a *legislature*[7] against a civil officer outside its own body. In the *U.S. government*[3] the *House*[7] *of Representatives* is the body responsible for bringing charges of impeachment against national officials. A House *committee*[7] presents evidence and acts as prosecutor. The *Senate*[7] hears the case and acts as *jury*[8]. In a trial of the *President*[6], the *Chief*[8] *Justice* of the *Supreme*[8] *Court* presides over the Senate. Conviction in any impeachment proceedings requires a two-thirds vote of the *senators*[7] and may not be *pardoned*[6] by the President. A convicted person may be removed from office and barred from future civil offices within the *federal government*[3]. He may also be liable to trial and punishment in a regular court of *law*[8]. President Andrew Johnson was charged with violating the *Tenure*[6] *of Office Act of 1867*, was impeached by the House of Representatives, but failed of conviction in the Senate by one vote. See also *Watergate*[5].

investigative powers. The *power*[3] of a *legislature*[7] to investigate matters appropriate to the legislative task. See also *Barenblatt*[1] *v. U.S.*; *investigating committee*[7]; *Kilbourn*[1] *v. Thompson*; *McGrain*[1] *v. Daugherty*; *Slochower*[1] *v. Board of Education*; *Ullmann*[1] *v. U.S.*; *Watkins*[1] *v. U.S.*

Jefferson's Manual. A volume prepared by *Thomas Jefferson*[6] during his term of service as *U.S. Vice-Presi-*

dent[6] and as presiding officer of the *U.S. Senate*[7] (1797–1801). The work is a handbook of *parliamentary*[7] *procedure* which was adopted by the *Congress*[4] for covering certain areas of parliamentary activity. Numerous *state*[3] *legislatures*[7] also use Jefferson's Manual.

journal. A regular printed account which is the official record of proceedings within a legislative chamber. The journal is kept by the clerk and generally contains *executive*[6] messages, action taken on *bills*[7] and *resolutions*[7], proposed *amendments*[3], *committee*[7] reports, petitions, and other legislative records. In the *U.S. Congress*[4] the Journal ordinarily does not contain verbatim debates or clarifications of certain things which took place within Congress since such material is contained in the *Congressional*[7] *Record*.

junket. A trip, generally extensive and taken at public expense, which is undertaken ostensibly to investigate public business.

lame duck. A *legislator*[7] who continues to serve near the end of a legislative *session*[7] even though he was defeated in a recent election and will not be reinstated once the *legislature*[7] reorganizes with the newly elected membership. See also *Twentieth Amendment*[7]; *lame duck session*[7].

law, (act, statute): see Chap. 8.

law, statutory: see Chap. 8.

legislation. The process wherein a legally authorized body makes *law*[8] and formulates *policy*[6] of a public nature. The term "legislation" may also be used to specify laws actually passed by a *legislature*[7]. See also *bill*[7]; *policy*[7] *formulation*.

legislation, direct. Action on the part of the general electorate which may

be legally recognized as part of the legislative process. Some *states*[3] within the U.S. refer selected *legislation*[7] to the electorate or permit the electorate to initiate legislative matter. The results of such action are considered legally binding once they meet the *constitutional*[3] requirements concerning their usage. See also *initiative*[3]; *referendum*[3].

legislation, retroactive. *Legislation*[7] which applies to actions or conditions existing prior to the enactment of the *law*[8]. *Civil laws*[8] may be applied retroactively. The *U.S. Constitution*[4] prohibits retroactive application of *criminal laws*[8] which work to the detriment of persons accused of violating the law. See also *ex*[9] *post facto law*; *emergency powers*[4].

legislation, special. A *law*[8] passed especially to deal with private individuals or matters or to deal with a particular area such as a local *community*[3]. See also *private bill*[7]; *Private Calendar*[7].

legislative council. A legislative agency used in some *states*[3] which is composed of *legislators*[7] and other selected officials who study legislative problems and plan legislative strategy between regular legislative *sessions*[7]. The *majority*[3] of legislative councils are composed of a select group of legislators from both houses. They carry out a regular program of research, study proposals for legislative reform, prepare legislative programs, and in general maintain the operation of the legislative machinery while the *legislature*[7] is not in session.

legislative counsel. A person or agency specifically charged with assisting *legislators*[7] in fulfilling their legislative tasks. Legislative counsel handles problems of research, drafting *bills*[7], legislative *hearings*[6], and other technical legislative detail. The *U.S. federal government*[3] created an Office of Legislative Council in 1918 in order to assist United States *congressmen*[7].

legislative day. A day on which a particular legislative chamber holds any formal *session*[7]. The *U.S. House*[7] *of Representatives* legislative day usually corresponds in length to a calendar day. The *U.S. Senate*[7] frequently avoids routine matters by calling a *recess*[7] rather than adjourning for the day; such an approach means that the legislative day may be spread across several calender days.

legislative delegation. The members of a legislative body who all come from the same *district*[7] or *state*[3]. A state legislative *delegation*[5] in the *U.S. Congress*[4] is composed of all the *senators*[7] and *representatives*[7] representing the state in Congress. In a state *legislature*[7] a group of *legislators*[7] from a particular area, *county*[11], or district might try to influence *legislation*[7] as a delegation.

legislative drafting bureau. A legislative agency created for the specific purpose of assisting *legislators*[7] in the technical aspect of drafting *bills*[7]. Such an agency is concerned with form, rules, and even with ready-made drafts of bills in particular areas of legislative interest.

legislative (congressional) elaboration: see Chap. 4.

legislative immunity. A privilege granted to *legislators*[7] which protects them from arrest for ordinary offenses while traveling to or from or serving in the *legislature*[7]. Members of the *U.S. Congress*[4] are also granted the absolute right of expression on the floor of Congress without fear of legal action being taken against them. Legislative immunity applies primarily to civil suits, although a few criminal matters may be included. See also *Kilbourn*[1] *v. Thompson*; *civil law*[8]; *criminal law*[8]; *question*[7] *of privilege*.

legislative oversight: see *oversight powers*[7].

Legislative Reference Service. An agency within the Library of Congress which was established to assist the *U.S. Congress*[4] in fulfilling its legislative task. The Legislative Reference Service's present role and scope was established in the *Legislative*[7] *Reorganization Act of 1946*. The agency coordinates research efforts for *congressmen*[7] and provides books and other materials on request, as well as printed reports on almost every subject related to the legislative process.

Legislative Reorganization Act of 1946. A major federal *statute*[8] of *legislative reorganization*[7] which reduced the number of congressional *standing committees*[7] in the *U.S. Congress*[4], limited the number of committees on which any one *congressman*[7] may serve, increased committee staffing, established a comprehensive retirement and fringe benefit program, strengthened the regulation of *lobbying*[5], increased the size and *powers*[3] of the Office of Legislative Counsel and the *Legislative*[7] *Reference Service*, provided for a legislative *budget*[10] system, restricted legislative handling of claims against the *federal government*[3], and broadened federal powers over the construction and maintenance of bridges over navigable waters of the U.S. Title III of the Legislative Reorganization Act of 1946 is referred to as the Regulation of Lobbying Act, Title IV is the Federal Tort Claims Act, and Title V is the General Bridge Act. See also *committee*[7] *system*; *Legislative*[7] *Reorganization Act of 1970*.

Legislative Reorganization Act of 1970. The first comprehensive *legislative reorganization*[7] act since 1946, a *federal*[3] *statute*[8] designed more as a "housekeeping" bill than as an act to substantively change the *organization*[6] or *power*[3] structure of the *U.S. Congress*[4]. Several controversial items were obviously avoided in the act: major changes in *committee*[7] *jurisdictions*[8], modification of the *seniority*[7] *rule*, and abuses of *lobbying*[5]. The *legislation*[7] provided for the use of electronic computer and data processing equipment in Congress, permitted recorded *teller votes*[7], permitted televised hearings in both houses of Congress, provided free tours of the Capitol building, required pages to be high school graduates, required disclosure of individual votes in committee, permitted committees to sit while the *House*[7] *of Representatives* is in *session*[7], opened committee meetings and *hearings*[6] to the public, restricted the use of *proxy votes*[7] in committee, provided for regular advance notice of committee meetings, provided enlarged *minority party*[5] committee staffing, provided for a summer *recess*[7] for Congress, and required the reporting of a *bill*[7] within seven days after called for by *majority*[3] vote of a committee. The bill included numerous "escape clauses" which permit closed and nontelevised meetings, proxy voting, and other practices supposedly prohibited by the act. A great deal of the implementation of the *act*[8] was left with the committee *chairman*[7] or a majority of the total committee in specific instances of legislative action. The act followed various outcries of *public opinion*[5] over a *conservative*[3] Congress involved with *investigations*[7] concerning *Bobby Baker*[7], *Adam Clayton Powell*[7], and *Thomas Dodd*[7]. See also *Legislative*[7] *Reorganization Act of 1946*; *seven-day*[7] *rule*; *supportive powers*[7]; *executive session*[7].

legislative supremacy. The concept that the legislative branch generally controls the political *power*[3] in a *constitutional*[3] *state*[3], or that it is at least superior to other branches of *government*[3] in a state where power is divided among separate branches. See also *state* (*constitutional*) *sovereignty*[3].

legislator: see *representative*[7].

legislator, delegate. A *legislator*[7] who views his role and exercises his *power*[3] as a *delegate*[5] of his *constituents*[5] who placed him in office. Such a *congressman*[7] acts primarily on the instructions and wishes of his constituents. See also *pork*[7] *barrel*.

legislator, politico (eclectic). A *legislator*[7] who views his role and exercises his *power*[3] in different ways at different times and on different issues. On some occasions he acts in a provincial manner for his own *constituents*[5] (playing a *delegate*[5] role) and on other occasions he acts on behalf of a larger interest (playing a *representative legislator*[7] role).

legislator, representative (trustee). A *legislator*[7] who views his role and exercises his *power*[3] primarily on the basis of interests larger than the provincial interests of his own *constituents*[5]. A trustee acts on such intangible things as "national interest," "the people," and "*justice*[8]." See also *representation*[7].

legislature. A formal governmental body *constitutionally*[3] or legally charged with formulating *policy*[6] for individuals and institutions within the legal frame of reference of the *organization*[6]. Legislatures are generally empowered to make *laws*[8] enforceable against individuals within geographical *boundaries*[12]. All of the legislatures within the U.S. federal system, with the exception of Nebraska, are *bicameral*[7] in structure. The legislature of the *federal government*[3] is called the *U.S. Congress*[4] and is composed of the *Senate*[7] and the *House*[7] *of Representatives*. See also *policy*[7] *formulation*; *representative*[7].

logrolling. Political cooperation between members of a legislative body in the passing of legislative measures, especially those of local interest and which call for the *appropriation*[10] of funds within the members' *districts*[7]. See also *pork*[7] *barrel*.

mace. A staff which serves as the symbol of *authority*[3] of a legislative leader. A mace is used in the *U.S. House*[7] *of Representatives* while the *Speaker*[7] *of the House* presides over the *lower chamber*[7]. It is a 46-inch ebony and silver staff with a silver eagle and globe apex and a white marble base.

marking up. The detailed process wherein a legislative *committee*[7] goes through a *bill*[7] section by section, revising its language and *amending*[3] the bill as desired. Extensive revision may lead to the introduction of a *clean bill*[7] under a new number. See also *executive session*[7].

objector. A legislative member assigned by his *political party*[5] to be alert to "unfavorable" *legislation*[7] on *Consent Calendar*[7] or *Private Calendar*[7] days. In the *U.S. House*[7] *of Representatives* three or four objectors from each party serve as teams to screen legislation on those days, in order to prevent them from being passed by *unanimous*[7] consent. They may object to routine passage of particular *bills*[7] and *force*[3] them to be placed back on the *House Calendar*[7] or *Union Calendar*[7].

one-man, one-vote rule: see Chap. 5.

open rule. A *special order*[7] issued by the *Committee*[7] *on Rules* of the *U.S. House*[7] *of Representatives*, which permits germane *amendments*[3] to be adopted by *majority*[3] vote of the entire House when the chamber is operating under the *five-minute*[7] *rule*.

order, special (rule). A legislative device or "rule" issued by an appropriate official or agency in order to regulate the consideration of a particular matter. Since the 1880's the *U.S. House*[7] *of Representatives Committee*[7] *on Rules* has had the *power*[3] of issuing special orders which determine what *bills*[7] will be considered, the order in which they may be introduced, whether they may be *amended*[3] during general debate, and other important matters related to the movement of *legislation*[7]. See also *closed*[7] *rule*; *open*[7] *rule*.

order, standing. A legislative "rule" that becomes a regular part of the organizational or operational machinery of the legislative process and remains in effect until rescinded by the legislative body using it.

pair. An informal arrangement between two legislative members whereby they instruct the clerk of their legislative chamber to record them as voting opposite one another on a particular *roll call vote*[7] even though they are both absent and unable to cast their votes in person. The members may agree between themselves to be absent from the chamber at the same time or to refrain from voting if the opposite member of the pair is absent. If both members are absent and announce their opposing positions ahead of time on a particular matter, the procedure is referred to as a "specific" pair. If they instruct the clerk to list them as opposing one another on all issues over the period of their absence, it is known as a "general" pair. When an issue demands a two-thirds vote, a pair may be used by matching two members for a measure against one opposing it.

parliamentarian. A person skilled in the use of *parliamentary*[7] *procedure* and who serves as a major adviser to the presiding officer of a deliberative assembly.

parliamentary procedure. The process of using established and customary rules to guide the movement of business in a deliberative assembly. Parliamentary procedure originated in the English Parliament and grew in scope as decisions and precedents became acceptable practice. Parliamentary procedure is modified by various deliberative bodies as they discover what rules best fit their own needs. See also *parliamentary government*[3]; *Hinds'*[7] *Precedents*; *Jefferson's*[7] *Manual*.

pigeonhole. The act of a legislative *committee*[7] in systematically and intentionally delaying release of a *bill*[7] to an entire legislative chamber for consideration. A pigeonhole is extremely effective in killing bills, because *legislators*[7] outside a *standing committee*[7] exercising a pigeonhole generally recognize the committee's *power*[3] over *legislation*[7] before it. Under extraordinary circumstances a pigeonhole may be broken with a *discharge*[7] rule.

point of order. A charge by a member of a deliberative assembly that the rules of the *organization*[6] are being violated. The presiding officer must deal with the charge immediately and clarify the point in question. If the presiding officer is in doubt he may refer the point of order to the total assembly.

policy formulation (policy-making). The process of examining alternatives of action within a legislative setting and then making decisions in the form of *laws*[8] which are applied to public and private matters. See also *incrementalism*[6]; *statutory law*[8]; *legislation*[7]; *policy*[6].

pork barrel. The public treasury which is frequently drawn on by public officials legislating out of special interest for their own *constituents*[5] or for their own political image. The drain on the pork barrel is most odious when funds are wastefully allocated or expended for personal *partisan*[5] gain. See also *delegate legislator*[7]; *logrolling*[7].

Powell investigation, Adam Clayton (1967). A *U.S. House*[7] of Represent-*atives* investigation of *Congressman*[7] Adam Clayton Powell of New York. The investigation revealed that Powell's wife was on the payroll in his office but did not reside in *Washington*[4], *D.C.* or collect her own checks since her husband cashed them, that damages levied against the congressman in a New York City *libel*[9] suit had never been paid, and that Congressman Powell had misapplied approximately $40,000 of *government*[3] funds. On March 1, 1967 Powell was *excluded*[7] from the *Congress*[4] on the issue of misapplication of *federal*[3] funds. He was subsequently twice reelected by his *constituents*[5] in Harlem. He satisfied the civil damages against him in New York City and eventually sued in *federal*[3] court for his seat in Congress. The *Supreme*[8] *Court* held that Powell could not be denied a seat in Congress if he met the *constitutionally*[3] prescribed qualifications of age, *citizenship*[3], and residency. Congressman Powell was readmitted to Congress in January 1969. He was fined $25,000 and was not returned to the *chairmanship*[7] of the House Education and Labor Committee. In the congressional elections of 1970 Powell lost his reelection bid in his own *legislative district*[7]. He died on April 4, 1972. See also *nepotism*[6]; *Powell*[1] *v. McCormack*; *sinecure*[6].

powers, constituent. The *power*[3] of a legislative body to be a part of writing or amending a *constitution*[3]. The U.S. Congress[4] is given *constitutional*[3] permission to introduce *amendments*[3] by a two-thirds vote of both houses, may set limitations on the number of years a proposed amendment may circulate among the *states*[3], may determine whether final acceptance of a proposed amendment should be *ratified*[3] by *legislatures*[7] or *conventions*[3] within the states, and may call a national convention for amendment purposes when requested by two-thirds of the states. State *legislatures*[7] are involved in the amendment process as it relates to their own *consti-tutional*[3] *systems*.

powers, electoral. The *power*[3] of a legislative body to be a part of the electoral process involving an *execu-tive*[6] official. The *U.S. Congress*[4] may act in an electoral capacity in the event that the *electoral*[4] *college* can-not choose a *President*[6] or *Vice-Presi-dent*[6]. The *House*[7] *of Representatives* may choose a President when there is no clear *majority*[3] in the electoral college and the *Senate*[7] may choose a Vice-President under the same con-ditions.

powers, executive: see *advice*[7] *and consent powers*.

powers, investigative: see *investigat-ing*[7] *powers*.

powers, judicial. The *power*[3] of a legislative body to act in a judicial manner. A legislative chamber ordi-narily may settle conflicts between its own members or over its own rules. On the basis of various *constitutional*[3] and legal criteria it may *expel*[7] mem-bers, *exclude*[7] newly elected members, *censure*[7] members, and cite individ-uals for *contempt*[7] of Congress. The *Congress*[4] may remove certain *fed-eral*[3] officials through the judicial process known as *impeachment*[7]. The House brings charges and the *Senate*[7] tries a case when impeachment is used.

powers, oversight. The *power*[3] of a *legislature*[7] to maintain close surveil-lance over activities taking place within administrative agencies under *executive*[6] control.

powers, supportive (housekeeping). The *power*[3] of a legislative body to determine its rules of procedure, re-organize itself, provide for clerical and technical assistance, keep records, and generally care for its internal needs. See also *Legislative*[7] *Reorgani-zation Act of 1970*.

President pro tempore. The official, ordinarily the senior member of the *majority party*[5], who is chosen by the *U.S. Senate*[7] to preside over the Sen-ate during the absence of the *Vice-President*[6]. The President pro tempore is in the line of *presidential*[6] succes-sion. A President pro tempore is gen-erally provided for in the *upper chambers*[7] of *state*[3] *legislatures*[7].

quasi-legislative. Possessing some of the characteristics of a legislative body. Public administrative agencies possess such a characteristic when-ever they formulate administrative *policies*[6] (passenger service rates, util-ity rates, *rediscount*[10] *rates*, etc.) having the *force*[3] of *law*[8]. Agencies possessing quasi-legislative powers must exercise them within the guide-lines set by the regular legislative body. See also *policy*[7] *formulation*; *quasi-judicial*[8]; *quasi-legislative*[6] *and quasi-judicial*.

question of privilege. A matter in-volving a legislative body or one of its members. Questions of privilege generally involve members' rights and procedures such as the right to speak on the floor without fear of arrest for *libel*[9]. See also *legislative*[7] *immunity*; *seven-day*[7] *rule*.

question, previous. A parliamentary motion designed to cut off all debate and bring an issue to a vote. A call for the previous question forces a vote on the subject originally under consideration and excludes further *amendments*[3]. If a motion for the previous question passes before there has been any debate, 40 minutes of debate is permitted before the vote is taken. The rules concerning un-limited debate in the *U.S. Senate*[7] ex-clude the use of previous question motions in that house. See also *par-liamentary*[7] *procedure*; *suspension*[7] *of the rules*.

question, privileged. A motion of any kind which has priority over other motions before a *legislature*[7]. For example, a motion to *table*[7] a *bill*[7] has greater priority than one to recommit the bill to *committee*[7], and a motion to *adjourn*[7] ranks higher than motions to table or recommit. Some legislative committees such as the *Committee*[7] on *Appropriations* of the U.S. *House*[7] of *Representatives* may introduce reports from committee at any time as privileged questions and may interrupt any business in progress. See also *privileged question committee*[7].

quorum. The number of members required in attendance in a *legislature*[7] before business may be conducted. The normal figure for a quorum is a simple *majority*[3] of the membership of the body. A quorum is 218 in the U.S. *House*[7] of *Representatives* and 51 in the U.S. *Senate*[7] if there are no vacancies in either house. When the House of Representatives meets as a *Committee*[7] *of the Whole*, only 100 members constitute a quorum.

ranking member. The person serving on a legislative *committee*[7] who is a member of the *majority party*[5] and who ranks just below the committee *chairman*[7] in years of uninterrupted service on the committee. See also *committee*[7] *system*; *ranking*[7] *minority member*; *seniority*[7] *rule*.

ranking minority member. The person serving on a legislative *committee*[7] who is a member of the *minority party*[5] and who has served a longer period of uninterrupted service on the committee than any of the other *minority*[3] members. Under the *seniority*[7] *rule* the ranking minority member becomes the committee *chairman*[7] once his *political party*[5] gains a *majority*[3] of the seats in the total legislative chamber. See also *committee*[7] *system*; *ranking*[7] *member*.

readings. The parliamentary requirement that each *bill*[7] must be read three times before becoming *law*[8]. In the U.S. *Congress*[4] the first reading

takes place in either house when the bill is cited simply by title and number in the *Congressional*[7] *Record*. The second reading takes place when the bill is debated on the floor after *committee*[7] consideration. The third reading, generally by title only, comes when the bill is voted on in final form. See also *parliamentary*[7] *procedure*.

reapportionment. To redistribute legislative seats assigned to various population groups or geographic areas being represented within a legislative body. The U.S. *Senate*[7] does not have to regularly reapportion because it simply adds two new *senators*[7] to its body when a new *state*[3] enters the Union. However, the U.S. *House*[7] of *Representatives* and all state *legislatures*[7] must regularly reapportion as population shifts take place. A *federal*[3] census is required every ten years in order to reapportion House of Representatives seats. See also *apportionment*[7]; *Avery*[1] *v. Midland County*; *Baker*[1] *v. Carr*; *gerrymander*[7]; *silent gerrymander*[7]; *Kirkpatrick*[1] *v. Preisler*; *one-man*[5], *one-vote rule*; *redistricting*[7]; *Reynolds*[1] *v. Sims*; *Wesberry*[1] *v. Sanders*.

recess. A pause or break during a legislative *session*[7]. Legislative bodies frequently take recesses in order to break the routine of business without officially *adjourning*[7] or ending a *legislative*[7] *day* and all business under consideration. A legislative body may recess during a session in order to campaign for reelection or handle other business and then return to complete the session. The *Legislative*[7] *Reorganization Act of 1970* provides for a summer recess for the U.S. *Congress*[4]. See also *recess appointment*[6].

redistricting. The act of drawing new *boundary*[12] lines for electoral, judicial, *representative*[7], or other purposes. See also *apportionment*[7]; *Avery*[1] *v. Midland County*; *Baker*[1] *v. Carr*; *Colgrove*[1] *v. Green*; *Gomillion*[1] *v. Light-*

foot; *silent gerrymander*[7]; *Gray*[1] *v. Sanders*; *Kirkpatrick*[1] *v. Preisler*; *one-man*[5], *one-vote rule*; *reapportionment*[7]; *Reynolds*[1] *v. Sims*; *Wesberry*[1] *v. Sanders*.

reorganization, legislative. The complex process of restructuring legislative machinery in order to achieve more efficient or economical operation. Legislative reorganization generally must go through the regular process of *legislation*[7]. Major reorganization of the *U.S. Congress*[4] in this century has taken place in what are remembered as the *Revolution*[7] of *1910–11*, the *Legislative*[7] *Reorganization Act of 1946*, and the *Legislative*[7] *Reorganization Act of 1970*.

report, majority. A document issued by a legislative *committee*[7], in the name of the majority, in order to cite the findings or conclusions of the entire committee. The report is issued on the basis of a *majority*[3] vote within the membership of the committee. See also *majority party*[5].

report, minority. A document issued by a group of members of a legislative *committee*[7] who disagree with a report issued through *majority*[3] vote of the total membership of the committee. The report may be issued by a few or all of the members who voted in the *minority*[3] and disagreed with the majority vote. See also *minority party*[5].

representation. The process, action, or condition of having someone act in a *policy*[7] *formulating* assembly on behalf of those of the political *community*[3] at large. Two major views of representation have dominated political thought related to legislative bodies. One view is that a *representative*[7] is a *delegate*[5] authorized to act only as instructed by the political *constituency*[5] electing him. The other view is that a representative is a steward or trustee chosen to serve the best interests of the total political

community. See also *Connecticut*[5] *Compromise*; *delegate legislator*[7]; *politico legislator*[7]; *representative legislator*[7]; *collective representation*[7]; *functional representation*[7]; *minority representation*[7]; *proportional representation*[7]; *virtual representation*[7].

representation, collective. The concept that a *legislator*[7] represents the interests of a political or *territorial*[3] structure (*nation*[3], *state*[3], etc.) larger than the *constituency*[5] which elected him. See also *representative legislator*[7]; *virtual representation*[7].

representation, functional. The concept that *legislators*[7] should serve social, economic, or political entities rather than geographical districts or general units of population within geographical *districts*[7].

representation, minority. The concept that *minority*[9] *groups* should be represented within the *legislature*[7] or on *committee*[7] structures within a legislature in order to protect the interest of groups incapable of gaining political *power*[3] by capturing *majority*[3] strength or influence. The *Legislative*[7] *Reorganization Act of 1970* increased the *representation*[7] of *minority*[3] staff on *standing committees*[7] of the *U.S. Congress*[4]. See also *concurrent majority*[4].

representation, proportional: see Chap. 5.

Representation, Proportional: see Chap. 5.

representation, virtual. The concept that effective and legitimate political *representation*[7] does not need to be based on proportional districts based on population figures. Virtual representation is based on the idea that an elected official serves the entire political *state*[3] or members of the state residing abroad and that every member of the state is "virtually" represented regardless of discrepancies in population between *legislative districts*[7]. See also *representative legislator*[7]; *collective representation*[7]; *proportional representation*[7].

representative. A person selected by a popular *constituency*[5] and empowered to act on behalf of that constituency in formulating *policy*[6]. Persons referred to as representatives generally serve in what are known as *lower chambers*[7] of *legislatures*[7]. Members of the *U.S. House*[7] of *Representatives* are best known as representatives or *congressmen*[7]. A representative in the House of Representatives must be at least 25 years old, a *citizen*[3] for at least seven years, and a resident of the *state*[3] in which he is elected. A U.S. representative serves a *single-member district*[7] and is elected for a two-year term of office. See also *policy*[7] *formulation.*

resident commissioner. An elected official who represents a *territory*[3] of the U.S. in the *U.S. Congress*[4]. Only one territory, Puerto Rico, presently has a resident commissioner serving in Congress. He may serve and speak in *committees*[7] and on the floor of the *U.S. House*[7] of *Representatives*, but he may not vote in either place.

resolution. A formal statement by any *convention*[3], *legislature*[7], or other body which declares or decides a certain thing. See also *Kentucky*[4] *and Virginia Resolutions*; *concurrent resolution*[7]; *joint resolution*[7]; *simple resolution*[7]; *Tonkin*[12] *Gulf resolution.*

resolution, concurrent. A *resolution*[7] which is approved by both houses of a *legislature*[7] without the need for *executive*[6] approval. The *U.S. Congress*[4] uses such a device, which has no *force*[3] of *law*[8] in order to *amend*[3] rules concerning both houses, to express the sentiment of Congress, to fix the date for *adjournment*[7], and to *veto*[7] presidential action concerning some *delegation of authority*[6] previ-

ously granted to the *U.S. President*[6]. Concurrent resolutions are ordinarily listed as H. Con. Res. or S. Con. Res., depending on which house of Congress they originate in.

resolution, joint. A *resolution*[7] of a public nature which is approved by a simple *majority*[3] vote of both houses of a *legislature*[7] and which generally requires *executive*[6] approval before becoming official. The *U.S. Congress*[4] uses joint resolutions to propose *amendments*[3] to the *U.S. Constitution*[4] (such action does not require presidential approval but does require approval by three-fourths of the *states*[3]), to avoid the two-thirds vote required on a *treaty*[12] (Texas and Hawaii entered the Union through such a process), to handle a specific *appropriations bill*[7], or to deal with other public matters. Joint resolutions are generally designated H. J. Res. or S. J. Res., depending on the house of origin.

resolution, simple. A resolution which is approved by one house of a *legislature*[7] in order to deal with internal matters or to express the sentiment of that particular house. Simple resolutions do not have the *force*[3] of *law*[8]. They are used most often to *amend*[3] rules, advise the *U.S. President*[6] on foreign *policy*[6] or other *executive*[6] matters, and to express the feelings of the house concerning its own members or employees. Simple resolutions are generally listed as H. Res. or S. Res., depending on the house of origin.

Revolution of 1910–11. An internal *power*[3] struggle within the *U.S. House*[7] of *Representatives* in which the *Speaker*[7] of the House was stripped of much of his power. The move was directed against the *autocratic*[3] leadership of Speaker Joseph G. Cannon. The Speaker lost his position as *chairman*[7] of the *Committee*[7] on Rules, his power to appoint *committee*[7] chairmen and all members of *stand-*

ing committees[7], and various other powers related to the conduct of proceedings on the floor of the House (recognition of members, etc.). See also *legislative reorganization*[7].

rider. A legislative proposal, practically assured of defeat if left to stand on its own merits, which is added to a *bill*[7] likely to become *law*[8]. Although both houses of the *U.S. Congress*[4] ban the use of riders, they are still attached to safe *legislation*[7], especially *appropriations bills*[7] assured of passage. Some *state*[3] *governors*[6] possess the *item veto*[7] in order to weed out undesirable riders. See also *Cooper-Church*[12] *Amendment*; *Platt*[12] *Amendment*.

rule (special order): see *special order*[7].

Senate, United States. The *upper chamber*[7] of the U.S. *Congress*[4], a chamber whose membership is selected on the basis of geographical units known as *states*[3]. *The U.S. Constitution*[4] provides that each state shall have two *senators*[7] regardless of population. Senators serve six-year terms and are selected on a rotating basis with one-third of them running for office every two years. The *U.S. Vice-President*[6] is the presiding officer of the Senate. The *President*[7] *pro tempore*, a member of the *majority party*[5] controlling the Senate, is chosen by the membership to preside whenever the Vice-President is absent. The Senate may choose the Vice-President when the *electoral*[4] *college* cannot do so with a clear *majority*[3], it must *confirm*[6] presidential *appointments*[6], it gives advice and consent on *treaties*[12] negotiated by the *President*[6], and it may act as a *jury*[8] in *impeachment*[7] proceedings. State senates must represent population rather than geographical units, they are usually presided over by *lieutenant*[6] *governors*, they confirm *executive*[6] appointments, try impeachment cases, and

fulfill the normal tasks of *legislation*[7]. See also *advice*[7] *and consent powers*.

senator. A person who serves as a *legislator*[7] in an upper legislative chamber referred to as a senate. A senator in the *U.S. Senate*[7] is selected by *popular vote*[5] within a *state*[3] and is empowered to act on behalf of that *constituency*[5] in formulating *policy*[6]. A senator must be at least 30 years old, a *citizen*[3] for at least nine years, and a resident of the state in which he is elected. A senator serves a six-year term of office. Before the adoption of the *Seventeenth Amendment*[7] in 1913, all U.S. senators were elected by their respective state *legislatures*[7]. Senators in state legislatures are popularly elected, represent population rather than geographical units, and in most states serve four-year terms in office. See also *upper chamber*[7]; *one-man*[5], *one-vote rule*; *policy*[7] *formulation*; *Reynolds*[1] *v. Sims*.

senatorial courtesy: see Chap. 6.

seniority rule. The customary practice used in both houses of the *U.S. Congress*[4] to assign *committee*[7] chairmanships to the members of the *majority party*[5] who served on committees for the longest period of uninterrupted service. Seniority as a principle has always been important to the U.S. Congress. However, the use of seniority to choose committee *chairmen*[7] came into prominence during the *Revolution*[7] *of 1910–11* when the *power*[3] to appoint committee chairmen was taken away from the *Speaker*[7] *of the House*. On rare occasions, seniority may be denied by the party *caucus*[7] (*conference*) for such purposes as supporting the presidential candidate of another *political party*[5]. In 1971 in the 92nd Congress the *U.S. House*[7] *of Representatives* decided that seniority did not have to be the only consideration in selecting either the chairman or the *ranking*[7] *minority member* of a committee. The *Democratic Party*[5] caucus may vote down any chairman if such a vote is demanded by 11 members of the full house. The *Republican Party*[5] caucus automatically *ratifies*[3] the top committee assignments by secret ballot. See also *ranking*[7] *member*.

sergeant at arms. An employee of a legislative chamber who, under direction from the presiding officer, polices the activities of the deliberative assembly. He may compel attendance of members, maintain order on the floor and in the galleries, arrest and confine persons guilty of disturbing action, and generally protect the decorum of the chamber.

session. The period of time in which a *legislature*[7] meets to conduct public business. The *U.S. Congress*[4] has a term of two years and the term is divided into two regular sessions. A regular session begins in January of odd-numbered years and is numbered from the First Congress, which met in 1789. The 92nd Congress met in 1971–72. The Congress may determine its own time of *adjournment*[7] and the *President*[6] may set the date to end a session if the two chambers cannot agree on a date. The President may also call either house of Congress into *special session*[7]. The President has called the *Senate*[7] into special session, but he has never called the *House*[7] *of Representatives* by itself nor set a date for Congress to adjourn. State legislatures generally have *biennial sessions*[7] and are restricted to conducting business within a specified time limit.

session, biennial. A legislative *session*[7] which is convened every two years. The *majority*[3] of *state*[3] *legislatures*[7] meet every other year and hold *special sessions*[7] as they are needed.

session, executive (secret). A legislative meeting which excludes the public. Executive sessions may be used under prescribed conditions by an entire legislative chamber or by its *committees*[7] and *subcommittees*[7]. Executive sessions are most often permitted in legislative investigations involving national security, during *marking*[7] *up* of *bills*[7] in committee, and during other times of sensitive legislative business. See also *Legislative*[7] *Reorganization Act of 1970.*

session, joint. A legislative meeting composed of both houses of a *bicameral*[7] *legislature*[7]. The *U.S. Congress*[4] generally meets in joint *session*[7] to hear the *President's*[6] *State*[6] *of the Union message* and to hear special addresses by important persons from the U.S. and abroad. It also meets in joint session to count *electoral votes*[5] and certify the election results in the presidential election. See also *electoral*[4] *college.*

session, lame duck. A short legislative *session*[7] which convenes immediately after an election and which contains members who continue to serve even though they were just defeated and will not be reinstated once the *legislature*[7] meets in a regular long session. See also *Twentieth Amendment*[7].

session, special. A legislative *session*[7] convened under the *authority*[3] of the chief *executive*[6] in order to conduct business during the interval between regular legislative sessions. The *U.S. President*[6] may call one or both chambers of the *Congress*[4] into special session, and the members may carry out any general tasks of *legislation*[7] or handle executive matters such as *treaty*[12] approval or *confirmation*[6] of *appointments*[6]. Some *states*[3] require that their chief executives call both houses at the same time and that the *legislature*[7] deal only with matters submitted to them by the *governor*[6].

session, split. A legislative *session*[7] used in some *states*[3] in an attempt to balance the introduction and consideration of legislative matter. *Legislators*[7] spend a restricted portion of the session in *organization*[6] of the chamber and in introducing *bills*[7]. They spend a second portion of the session in *committee*[7] *hearings*[6] and investigations. A third part of the session is spent in general debate and in voting on *legislation*[7]. Split sessions have not been particularly successful because some legislative bodies are permitted to waive the use of the device by an *extraordinary majority*[3] vote at the opening of the *legislature*[7], or they may permit new legislation to be introduced near the end of a session by the same vote. See also *investigating committee*[7].

seven-day rule. A *U.S. House*[7] *of Representatives special order*[7] which holds that any member of the *Committee*[7] *on Rules* may report a *bill*[7] if the *chairman*[7] fails to act within seven days after receiving the measure from another *standing committee*[7]. The individual member may report the bill as a *question*[7] *of privilege.* The *Legislative*[7] *Reorganization Act of 1970* provided that a *majority*[3] of any standing committee in either house could file a request for report with the *committee*[7] clerk, and after seven days the bill could be considered by the entire legislative chamber.

sine die. To *adjourn*[7] a legislative body without setting a date for the chamber to reassemble.

Speaker of the House. The presiding officer of the *lower chamber*[7] of a legislative assembly. The Speaker of the House of the *U.S. House*[7] *of Representatives* presides over the business of the deliberative body. He guides the program of the *majority party*[5] in the House, recognizes members desiring to speak, regulates debate, rules on *points*[7] *of order*, appoints members of *special* and *conference committees*[7], signs *bills*[7] and *resolutions*[7], refers bills to *committees*[7], and votes

when there is a tie. The Speaker of the House is chosen in the *political party*[5] *caucus*[7] (*conference*) of the majority party and is formally recognized by the entire House. The Speaker had almost *autocratic*[3] *powers*[3] until the *Congress*[4] weakened him considerably in what came to be known as the *Revolution*[7] *of 1910–11*.

special order (**rule**): see *special order*[7].

statute: see *law*[8].

Statutes at Large of the United States. An annual publication of all the *laws*[8] and *resolutions*[7] passed by the most recent *session*[7] of the *U.S. Congress*[4]. The volume contains public and private acts, *concurrent and joint resolutions*[7], presidential proclamations, and *treaties*[12]. See also *private bill*[7]; *public bill*[7].

subcommittee. A group of individuals appointed by the *chairman*[7] of a legislative *committee*[7] to investigate legislative matters and report to the larger committee. See also *investigating committee*[7].

suspension of the rules. A legislative procedure which permits a specified number, usually a two-thirds *extraordinary majority*[3], to suspend the rules and pass a *bill*[7] that has already received *standing committee*[7] approval. Once a motion to suspend the rules has passed, 40 minutes of debate is granted before a vote is taken. Each side is generally given 20 minutes each. Once the motion to suspend the rules passes, no *amendments*[3] may be offered from the floor.

table (**lay on the table**). The act, upon the motion of a member of a deliberative assembly, of postponing consideration of a legislative matter. A *majority*[3] vote of the assembly may suspend action. The legislative body may resume consideration of the matter at a later time.

tellers. Legislative members, usually one from each side of a legislative issue, who are appointed by the presiding officer of a legislative chamber to count proponents and opponents as they walk down an aisle in expression of their voting positions. Usually those in favor of the measure walk the aisle first and those opposing follow. A *teller vote*[7] was an unrecorded vote until passage of the *Legislative*[7] *Reorganization Act of 1970.* Such a vote may be called for by one-fifth of a *quorum*[7].

twenty-one day rule. A *special order*[7] used during the 81st *Congress*[4] (1949–50) and the 89th Congress (1965–66) to move a *bill*[7] to the floor of the *House*[7] *of Representatives* without approval from the *Committee*[7] *on Rules.* The rule, used only 16 times, states that a *resolution*[7] providing for the immediate consideration of a *public bill*[7] already reported and which has been before the Rules Committee 21 days without clearance, can be called up on *Discharge Calendar*[7] days by the *committee*[7] *chairman*[7] who has reported the bill. The *Speaker*[7] can then recognize the member seeking recognition for that purpose. The 81st Congress required the Speaker to act, at his discretion. In the 81st Congress a total of seven of the eight bills brought out actually became *law*[8].

unanimous consent (without objection). A legislative device used to accept noncontroversial motions, *amendments*[3], and *bills*[7] without a vote. Such a device may be used if there is no *legislator*[7] who objects to the issue at hand. Groups of noncontroversial bills are handled on specified days by placing them on the *Consent Calendar*[7]. See also *objector*[7].

unicameralism. A legislative structural arrangement whereby all *legislators*[7] are seated in one chamber. Nebraska is the only *state*[3] *legislature*[7] in the U.S. that is unicameral. Local legis-

lative bodies such as *city*[11] councils are nearly always unicameral. The *U.S. Congress*[4] is based on *bicameralism*[7].

United States Code. A regularly revised and published consolidation and codification of all the general and permanent *laws*[8] of the U.S. The United States Code, officially entitled The Code of the Laws of the United States of a General and Permanent Character, is revised every six years and is arranged by subject matter under 50 titles.

veto, absolute. The *constitutional*[3] right of a legal *authority*[3] to reject *bills*[7] passed by another branch of *government*[3]. The *U.S. President*[6] may veto any bill or *joint resolution*[7] passed by the *U.S. Congress*[4], with the exception of proposed *amendments*[3] to the *U.S. Constitution*[4].

veto, item. A veto which permits a chief *executive*[6] to remove particular items from an *act*[8] passed by a *legislature*[7] without invalidating the entire measure. Various *states*[3] within the U.S. permit their *governors*[6] to exercise the item veto, generally only on itemized *appropriations*[10] measures. The *president*[3] of the *Confederate*[4] *States of America* was given an item veto by constitutional provision.

veto override. *Constitutionally*[3] permissible action wherein the *legislature*[7] may reject an *executive*[6] veto of a legislative enactment. The *U.S. Congress*[4] may override a presidential veto by a two-thirds *roll call vote*[7] in each house.

veto, pocket. *Executive*[6] invalidation of a legislative measure through the *constitutionally*[3] permissible right of inaction on a *bill*[7] which has been passed by a legislative body within a specified number of days before *adjournment*[7]. The *U.S. President*[6] may use such a veto by failing to sign a bill passed by the *Congress*[4] within a ten-day period before adjournment.

vote, proxy. Any authorized vote cast by one person on behalf of another person. Proxy voting is restricted in many instances in the *committee*[7] system of the U.S. *Congress*[4]. See also *Legislative*[7] *Reorganization Act of 1970; standing committee*[7].

vote, roll call. A recorded vote in a legislative chamber, which requires that members respond to a proposal by stating "yea," "nay," or "present." Record votes are required in overriding a U.S. *President's*[6] *absolute veto*[7]. A record vote may be required on any measure when one-fifth of the members present desire it. Record votes may not be demanded whenever the chamber meets as a *Committee*[7] *of the Whole* unless the vote is taken through a *teller vote*[7] which is tabulated.

vote, standing. A vote of legislative members in a chamber who stand as groups divided for or against a legislative proposal. The presiding officer counts those for or against the measure and then announces the results. How individual members vote is not recorded as a *roll call vote*[7].

vote, teller. A vote of *legislators*[7] in a chamber who walk past *tellers*[7] (one from each *political party*[5]) appointed to count members for and against a particular legislative proposal. In the U.S. *Congress*[4] the teller vote is used only in the *House*[7] *of Representatives*. Since passage of the *Legislative*[7] *Reorganization Act of 1970* it has been a *roll call vote*[7]. It may be used when demanded by one-fifth of a *quorum*[7] (44 in the total House and 20 in the *Committee*[7] *of the Whole*).

vote, unit. The system of voting used in *conference committees*[7] whereby the conferees (managers) from each legislative chamber vote among themselves to determine whether they wish to agree with conferees from the other chamber. See also *unit*[5] *rule*.

vote, voice (viva voca). A vote of legislative members in a chamber who respond in unison with "yea" or "nay" whenever issued separate calls by the presiding officer. The presiding officer determines which vocal group has the greatest volume of response and makes his decision on that basis. Voice votes are frequently challenged because the *chairman*[7] is not always fair in announcing the result and because the voting method does not involve a *roll call vote*[7].

whip. A *political party*[5] leader chosen in party *caucus*[7] (*conference*) as a chief assistant to the party floor leader. A whip (majority or minority) seeks to assure that party members are present for important votes, to make the party program as palatable for as many party members as possible, and to substitute for the floor leader in his absence. See also *majority floor*[7] *leader; minority floor*[7] *leader*.

Supreme Court cases related to material in this chapter are arranged below by subject. Summaries of the cases are in Chapter One arranged alphabetically by the name of the first party in each case.

LEGISLATIVE ACTION—
Powell v. McCormack
(1967)

LEGISLATIVE APPOR-
TIONMENT—
Avery v. Midland Co.
(1968)
Baker v. Carr (1962)
Colgrove v. Green (1946)
Gomillion v. Lightfoot
(1960)
Gray v. Sanders (1963)
Kirkpatrick v. Preisler
(1969)

Reynolds v. Sims (1964)
Wesberry v. Sanders
(1964)

LEGISLATIVE DELEGA-
TION OF AUTHOR-
ITY—
Hampton & Co. v. U.S.
(1928)
Opp Cotton Mills v.
Administrator of Wage
& Hour Division
(1941)
Panama Refining Co. v.
Ryan (1935)

Schechter Poultry Corp.
v. U.S. (1935)
U.S. v. Curtiss-Wright
Export Corp. (1936)

LEGISLATIVE INVESTI-
GATION—
Barenblatt v. U.S. (1959)
Kilbourn v. Thompson
(1881)
McGrain v. Daugherty
(1927)
Slochower v. Board of
Education (1956)
Watkins v. U.S. (1957)

Chapter 8

The Judicial Branch
and the Legal Process

Note to the reader: Cross-referenced terms are in italics. The superscript number refers to the chapter in which the entry may be found. In addition, its placement indicates the word under which the term is alphabetized. (For example, in *electoral*[4] *college*, information on the electoral college may be found in Chapter 4 under "electoral.") Because italics are used in cross-references, they are not used for terms in which they would ordinarily be used: Supreme Court cases and titles of books, journals, plays, and so forth.

> *Supreme Court cases relating to material in this chapter are listed at the end of the chapter (see page 218).*

accusatorial (adversary) proceeding. A formal legal proceeding wherein charges of wrongdoing are made by one party against another. The person or *organization*[6] charged is then given the opportunity to defend himself against the charges. The judicial machinery in such a process is usually structured so as to try to determine "fault." See also *adjudication*[8]; *defendant*[8]; *ex*[8] *parte*; *plaintiff*[8].

acquittal. Declaration by accepted *authority*[3], such as that given to a formal *jury*[8], that a party is not guilty as charged in a court of *law*[8].

adjudication. The judicial process wherein a body empowered with legal *authority*[3] hears a legal controversy and renders judgment. See also *accusatorial*[8] *proceeding*.

Amendment, Eleventh: see Chap. 4.

amnesty: see Chap. 6.

appeal, writ of. A written judicial order issued by a higher court recognizing the right of a party losing a case in a lower court to move his case to the higher court through appeal. Higher courts use various types of *writs*[8] to move cases on appeal. See also *appellate jurisdiction*[8]; *Court*[8] *of Appeals*; *writ*[8] *of certiorari*; *writ of error*[8].

arraignment. The process wherein a party is accused of a legal violation and formally charged (*indicted*[8]) before a court of *law*[8]. The course of further legal action is dependent on the nature of the plea, "guilty" or "not guilty," of the accused. See also *McNabb*[1] *v. U.S.*; *Mallory*[1] *v. U.S.*

assault. An illegal threat of immediate bodily harm to another person, a threat made either verbally or physically. See also *battery*[8].

Attorney General. The chief law officer of a national or *state*[3] government[3]. The U.S. Attorney General is a member of the *President's*[6] *Cabinet*[6] and the head of the *Department of Justice*[2]. He furnishes legal counsel to *federal*[3] agencies, directs investigations involving the violation of federal *laws*[8], conducts lawsuits in federal courts on behalf of the U.S., and carries out various other duties. State attorneys general serve in a similar capacity to that of the U.S. Attorney General. In the *majority*[3] of states he is an elective official. In many states the attorney general may issue *advisory opinions*[8] having the general *force*[3] of law. See also *Civil*[9] *Rights Act of 1957*; *Civil*[9] *Rights Act of 1960*.

Austin, John, 1790–1859. The nineteenth-century English jurist whose Province of Jurisprudence determined (1832) and other writings helped form modern analytic ideas of *law*[8]. He believed *positive law*[8] issued from the sanction-bearing command of the sovereign, regardless of the nature of the sovereign.

bail. Money or other security provided a court in exchange for the temporary release of a person awaiting trial. Bail is designed to assure that a person will not be unduly restrained but will, however, appear before a court at the proper time. The *Eighth Amendment*[9] of the U.S. *Constitution*[4] prohibits excessive bail. See also *bond*[8].

battery. An illegal beating or uninvited touching of another person or some object closely associated with another person. See also *assault*[8].

Beccaria, Cesare, 1738–94. The Italian social reformer who is best remembered for his work entitled On Crime and Punishments (1764). Beccaria advocated the *utilitarian*[3] philosophy and used for the first time the phrase "the greatest happiness for the greatest number." He advocated prevention of crime rather than punishment. He also advocated certainty and swiftness of punishment and the abolition of *capital*[8] *punishment*, confiscation, and torture.

Blackstone, William: see Chap. 3.

bond. An amount of money or other surety paid in order to gain the release of another person from official custody or to insure that certain things will or will not be done. See also *bail*[8].

breach of the peace. A violent or disorderly disturbance of public peace. See also *Cantwell*[1] *v. Connecticut*; *Cox*[1] *v. Louisiana*; *Terminiello*[1] *v. Chicago*.

brief. A short written summary of the pertinent legal arguments to be made by counsel during a judicial proceeding.

brief, amicus curiae. A legal *brief*[8] submitted to a court by a person who is not a party to a legal controversy but who wishes, as a "friend of the court," to inform the court on matters of *law*[8].

capital punishment. The imposition of the death penalty on a person for the conviction of specified *crimes*[8]. *Treason*[3], murder, rape, kidnapping, and arson have been the most frequently cited crimes for which social systems have inflicted capital punishment. *Cesare Beccaria*[8] was one of the earliest European social reformers who actively sought the abolition of capital punishment. See also *Furman*[1] *v. Georgia*; *Witherspoon*[1] *v. Illinois*.

certiorari, writ of. A written judicial order from a *Court*[8] *of Appeals* calling for a lower court to send up the records of a particular case for review. Most cases heard by the *U.S. Supreme*[8] Court are heard through the discretionary use of the writ of certiorari. Before a case may be heard by the Court, there must be agreement among at least four justices to issue a writ of certiorari. See also *court*[8] *of record; appellate jurisdiction*[8].

Chief Justice. The presiding judge of a court composed of several justices. The Chief Justice of the U.S. is the presiding judge of the *U.S. Supreme*[8] *Court*. He is appointed by the *President*[6] and *confirmed*[6] by the *Senate*[7]. He is appointed to a life *tenure*[6] and possesses voting *power*[3] equal to other members of the Supreme Court. The Chief Justice presides over regular cases, assigns the writing of opinions, handles routine administrative matters, and presides over the U.S. Senate during *impeachment*[7] trials for U.S. Presidents or *Vice-Presidents*[6]. See also *Charles Evans Hughes*[8]; *John Marshall*[8]; *Roger Brooke Taney*[8].

code. A systematic collection of *laws*[8] or rules of any governmental *jurisdiction*[8]. A code of laws is usually classified according to subject matter and is a collection of laws in effect within the social and political system. See also *black*[9] *code; Code*[8] *of the United States; Hammurabi Code*[8]; *Justinian Code*[8]; *Mosaic Code*[8]; *Napoleonic Code*[8]; *Uniform*[8] *Code of Military Justice*.

Code, Hammurabi. The ancient (approx. 2000 B.C.) Babylonian (Sumerian) codification of legal regulations of economic and social activity. The *code*[8] viewed the ruler as the dispenser of *justice*[8], recognized *property*[10] rights, accepted *feudal*[3] land arrangements, organized a police force, established a postal service, gave women certain rights, recognized religious principles and obligations, regulated trade and travel, regulated family re-

lationships, and established a system of courts and legal justice.

Code, Justinian. The first major codification of the laws of the Roman Empire, an action undertaken under the leadership of Justinian I around 518–534 A.D. The codification was an orderly consolidation of existing *constitutions*[3], edicts, *statutes*[8], judicial decisions, and judicial writings. The basic objective of the *code*[8] was to remove contradictions of law and clarify principles and points of *law*[8] in the most concise fashion.

Code, Mosaic. The Old Testament Jewish *laws*[8] based on God's revelations to Moses and other Hebrew prophets and political leaders. The heart of the Mosaic Code is found in the Ten Commandments, which clarify men's relationship with God and with other men. The Ten Commandments call for a rejection of idolatry and for positive involvement in religious veneration of the God Jehovah. They also call for faithfulness to family and a rejection of murder, adultery, stealing, false witnessing, and covetousness. The lengthy and complex system of laws established sacrificial and symbolic systems of human activity and an essentially priestly court system. The laws regulate marriage, poverty, wages, *usury*[10], *property*[10] ownership, vice, retirement, slavery, worship, kidnapping, family relations, animal usage, food preparation, and other subject areas. The laws, still in effect for orthodox Jews, reflect part of the *Hammurabi Code*[8]. Throughout they reflect the veneration of God and the need for personal morality. The laws greatly influenced Western civilization and various theories of higher law, *natural law*[8], *common law*[8], *natural rights*[3], and *inalienable rights*[3]. They also laid the framework for the religious *theories*[3] of such men as *Saint Augustine*[3], *Thomas Aquinas*[3], *Martin Luther*[3], and *John Calvin*[3]. See also *higher law theory*[3].

Code, Napoleonic. The first comprehensive collection of French *civil law*[8], a collection made by legal advisers commissioned by Napoleon Bonaparte in 1804. The *code*[8] was one of the most ambitious legal undertakings of modern history and served as a model for other civil law *nations*[3].

Code of the United States: see *United*[7] *States Code.*

Commission, Kerner: see *Kerner*[8] *Commission Report.*

Committee on the Judiciary (U.S. Senate). A permanent *standing committee*[7] of the *U.S. Senate*[7] charged with general legislative action concerning the national judiciary. The *committee*[7] is concerned with *federal*[3] judicial *appointments*[6], *jurisdiction*[8], and action. It also investigates and proposes *legislation*[7] related to *constitutional*[3] *amendments*[3], *civil*[9] *rights*, claims against the U.S., *immigration*[3] and *naturalization*[3], *bankruptcy*[10], counterfeiting, and numerous other subjects.

contempt of court. Intentional disobedience of a judicial order or the actual obstruction of the *administration*[6] of *justice*[8] or the fulfillment of the judicial role. A court may cite a person for civil contempt if he refuses to fulfill a *civil law*[8] judgment. A criminal citation may be handed down for the obstruction of court proceedings. A contempt citation may warrant either a fine or imprisonment. See also *contempt*[8] *of Congress*; *immunity*[9] *bath*; *criminal law*[8].

court, admiralty. A judicial body having *jurisdiction*[8] over cases involving maritime or seafaring matters.

court, appellate: see *appellate jurisdiction*[8].

court, circuit: see *Court*[8] *of Appeals.*

court, constitutional. A court authorized and empowered by *constitutional*[3] provisions. The *U.S. federal*[3] court system authorizes constitutional courts in Article III of the *U.S. Constitution*[4]. The constitutional courts provide greater protection for judges in the areas of *tenure*[6] and compensation. The *U.S. Supreme*[8] *Court*, the *Courts*[8] *of Appeals*, and the *District Courts*[8] fit in the Article III category. The *U.S. Congress*[4] has, by *statute*[8], conferred constitutional status on the *Court*[8] *of Claims*, the *Customs Court*[8], and the *Court*[8] *of Customs and Patent Appeals*. See also *legislative court*[8].

Court, Customs (U.S.). A *federal*[3] court created in 1890 and named the Customs Court in 1926. The court is located in New York City and consists of nine judges *appointed*[6] by the *President*[6] and *confirmed*[6] by the *Senate*[7]. The judges serve upon good behavior. The court *adjudicates*[8] conflicts over *tariff*[10] regulations, evaluation of merchandise, and other *customs*[10] *duties* matters. Decisions by the Customs Court may be appealed to the *Court*[8] *of Customs and Patent Appeals*.

Court, District (U.S.). The basic *federal*[3] trial court of *original jurisdiction*[8]. Most federal cases, civil or criminal, originate at the District Court level. There are 88 District Courts having from one to 24 judges. All judges are appointed by the *President*[6], *confirmed*[6] by the *Senate*[7], and serve upon good behavior (judges in *territorial court*[8] districts serve for eight-year periods). See also *civil law*[8]; *United*[8] *States Commissioner*; *United*[8] *States marshall.*

court, legislative. A court created by *statute*[8] rather than by *constitutional*[3] provision. Legislative courts provide less *tenure*[6] and salary protection to judges than do *constitutional courts*[8]. They derive their *power*[3] from the legislative action of the *U.S. Con-*

gress[4]. The *territorial courts*[8] and the *Court*[8] *of Military Appeals* are presently classified as legislative courts.

court-martial. A military court convened for the purpose of hearing cases involving *military*[8] *law*. Court-martial proceedings are usually classified as summary (a single officer hears cases of enlisted men accused of minor violations), special (three officers on the call of a commanding general may hear cases of moderate nature), general (a panel of officers and enlisted men on the call of the U.S. *President*[6] or the Secretary of Defense may hear cases of major violations). See also *Calley*[12] *case*; *Court*[8] *of Military Appeals*; *My Lai*[12] *controversy*; *Uniform*[8] *Code of Military Justice*.

Court of Appeals (U.S.). Any one of the various appellate courts which are part of the systems of courts created in 1891 under the name United States Circuit Courts of Appeals. The system was given its present name, United States Courts of Appeals, in 1948. There are presently 11 numbered courts of appeals in the *states*[3] and the *District of Columbia*[4]. The courts possess *appellate jurisdiction*[8] and hear cases from U.S. *District Courts*[8] and *federal*[3] administrative agencies. A full appeals court has nine judges, although most cases are heard by panels of three judges.

court of chancery. A court having *jurisdiction*[8] over cases in *equity*[8].

Court of Claims (U.S.). A *federal*[3] court created in 1855 in order to expedite the handling of private claims against the U.S. *government*[3]. The Court of Claims has five judges who hear cases concerning damages for injuries, breach of *contract*[10], and other claims against the government. The court was created to relieve the *legislature*[7] of the burden of handling all claims through the regular legislative process.

Court of Customs and Patent Appeals (U.S.). A specialized *federal*[3] court created in 1909 to review cases from the *Customs Court*[8], the Patent Office, and the *United*[2] *States Tariff Commission*. The court is located in *Washington*[4], D.C. and has five judges appointed by the *President*[6] and *confirmed*[6] by the *Senate*[7]. Judges serve on good behavior. Decisions by the court may be heard by the *Supreme*[8] *Court* by *writ of certiorari*[8].

Court of Military Appeals (U.S.). A specialized court created in 1950 to act as a court of appeals for decisions arrived at by *courts-martial*[8]. The Court of Military Appeals is a *legislative court*[8] whose three civilian judges serve terms of 15 years each. Judges are appointed by the *President*[6] with approval by the *Senate*[7]. The court hears appeals on and *adjudicates*[8] conflicts over *military*[8] *law*. The Court of Military Appeals is an independent court attached to the *Department of Defense*[2] for administrative purposes. See also *appellate jurisdiction*[8]; *Uniform*[8] *Code of Military Justice*.

court of record. A court which keeps a permanent record of its proceedings and which may be instructed by *writ of certiorari*[8] or other appropriate action to deliver specific records to a higher court of appeal. A court of record is an independent court possessing *powers*[3] of fine and imprisonment. Lower-level judicial bodies such as *justice*[8] *of the peace* courts and *municipal*[11] courts are generally not classified as courts of record. See also *de*[8] *novo*; *appellate jurisdiction*[8].

court-packing plan (1937). An unsuccessful proposal by *President*[6] *Franklin D. Roosevelt*[6] to compel retirement from *federal*[3] judicial positions those judges attaining the age of 70. In the event that a judge had served at least ten years and had failed to retire at age 70 the President could appoint a new judge to the federal court system. The limit on such *appointments*[6] would be set at 50 at lower levels of the federal court system. The *U.S. Supreme*[8] *Court* could never exceed 15 justices. The plan was proposed as a method to overcome the *conservative*[3] positions of the older justices of the Supreme Court, justices most active in declaring President Roosevelt's *New*[6] *Deal legislation*[7] *unconstitutional*[3]. Popular disfavor of the plan led to its abandonment. However, the Supreme Court suddenly became more *liberal*[3] in the face of such an obvious threat. See also *Carter*[1] *v. Carter Coal Co.*; *Charles Evans Hughes*[8]; *Mulford*[1] *v. Smith*; *National*[1] *Labor Relations Board v. Jones and Laughlin Corp*; *Schechter*[1] *Poultry Corp. v. U.S.*; *Sunshine*[1] *Anthracite Coal Co. v. Adkins*; *U.S.*[1] *v. Butler*; *U.S.*[1] *v. Darby Lumber Co.*; *West*[1] *Coast Hotel Co. v. Parrish.*

court, probate. A court designed specifically to probate (validate) wills and administer estates.

Court, Supreme: see *Supreme*[8] *Court.*

Court, Tax (U.S.). A *quasi-judicial*[8] independent *federal*[3] agency officially known as the Tax Court of the United States. The judicial body was founded in 1924 in order to *adjudicate*[8] controversies involving decisions of the *Internal*[2] *Revenue Service* or other agencies enforcing the Internal Revenue *Code*[8] of the United States. The court contains 16 judges who receive their positions through presidential *appointment*[6] and *Senate*[7] *confirmation*[6]. Judges serve 12-year terms. Decisions of the court may be appealed to the regular federal court system. See also *independent agency*[5]; *appellate jurisdiction*[8].

court, territorial. Any one of the particular courts established in the various dependencies of the U.S. Such *legislative courts*[8] exist in the Virgin Islands, the Panama Canal Zone, Guam, and Puerto Rico. All of those except Puerto Rico hear *federal*[3] cases and cases which could be heard in regular *state*[3] courts. See also *territory*[3].

crime. Any act that breaks a *law*[8] or other official *government*[3] regulation involving the general public. Crimes are ordinarily classified as *misdemeanors*[8] or *felonies*[8] and may be punished by various penalties such as fines, imprisonment, and death. See also *Kerner*[8] *Commission Report*; *malfeasance*[8]; *misfeasance*[8]; *National*[8] *Commission on Violence*; *nonfeasance*[8]; *Walker*[8] *Report*; *treason*[3].

decision. The resolution of a legal controversy by a court of *law*[8] or other appropriate body on the basis of facts presented in relation to *constitutional*[3] or legal principles.

decision, per curium. A judicial announcement of the settlement of a case wtihout a *majority*[3] comment or extensive elaboration on the reasons behind the settlement.

decision, retroactive. A judicial decision applying to a period prior to the decision or to general circumsances closely related to the decision of the court.

de facto. A term used to denote a condition accepted as fact, in contrast to a condition accepted as legal. See also *de*[8] *jure*; *de facto segregation*[9].

defendant. A person who finds legal action brought against himself in a court of *law*[8]. See also *accusatorial*[8] *proceeding*; *immunity*[9] *bath*; *nolo*[8] *contendere*; *plaintiff*[8].

de jure. A term used to denote a condition accepted as legal in contrast to one accepted as existing in fact only. See also *de* [8] *facto*; *de facto segregation* [9].

de novo. The process of "trying anew" a case already heard by a lower court. Since some lower judicial bodies such as *municipal* [11] courts and *justice* [8] *of the peace* courts do not maintain permanent records of proceedings, upon appeal a case must be heard from the beginning, or "de novo." See also *court* [8] *of record*.

dictum (*obiter dictum*). A judicial pronouncement, usually a judge's own legal opinion, which is expressed within a formal decision but which is not a part of the legal judgment of the court.

District of Columbia Court Reform and Criminal Procedure Act of 1970. A *federal* [3] *law* [8] designed as a model for possible *state* [3] anticrime *legislation* [7]. It reorganized court and *bail* [8] procedures, lowered the age at which juveniles can be tried as adults to 16, and called for mandatory five-year sentences for various armed second offenders. Controversial sections of the law permit use of limited *preventative* [8] *detention, no-knock* [8] *searches*, and court-approved *wiretaps* [9] in various matters.

diversity of citizenship question: see Chap. 4.

due process: See Chap. 9.

en banc. The grouping together of all the judges of a particular court (i.e., five judges of the *U.S. Court* [8] *of Claims*) in order to hear a particular case.

equity. The *common law* [8] practice of granting judicial remedy to parties unable to find *justice* [8] through the rigidities of *statutory* [8] provisions or legal actions. Equity originated in English *courts* [8] *of chancery*, which were courts of chivalry or conscience. Equity is often used to prevent a harmful action (*writ of injunction* [8]) or to compel a party to perform some

required function (*writ of mandamus* [8]). There are few separate courts of equity, since most common law courts administer both *law* [8] and equity. See also *writ* [8].

error, writ of. A judicial *writ* [8] which is issued by an appellate court and which demands a lower court to send up the records of a case in order to review the record to determine if an error of *law* [8] was made at the lower level. See also *Court* [8] *of Appeals*; *court* [8] *of record*; *appellate jurisdiction* [8].

ex parte. Judicial action on behalf of one party only without an *accusatorial* [8] *proceeding*. An ex parte action may be sought by an individual (that is, on the request of a court for a *writ of habeas* [8] *corpus*) or it may be undertaken because a possible adverse party fails to appear before the court.

federal question: see Chap. 4.

felony. A major violation of *law* [8] which generally provides for imprisonment or death. A felony contrasts with a minor offense which is known as a *misdemeanor* [8]. See also *crime* [8].

fiction. A legal assumption that a state of facts exists which in reality does not exist (i.e., a person who actually commits a murder and who confesses to the act may be required to plead "not guilty" because the *state* [3] may impose the death penalty for such a *crime* [8]).

gloss. A brief marginal or interlinear annotation to a technical or legal expression which is designed to clarify the meaning of the basic text. On occasion a gloss may be accepted as being as valid as the text itself.

habeas corpus, writ of. A written judicial order demanding legal officials to immediately produce a prisoner and cite the causes for his imprisonment. The *U.S. Constitution*[4] guarantees the right to such a *writ*[8] (Art. I, Sec. 9, Cl. 2) except during times of invasion or domestic violence. See also *Ableman*[1] *v. Booth*; *Endo*[1], *ex parte*; *Korematsu*[1] *v. U.S.*; *McCardle*[1], *ex parte*; *Merryman*[1], *ex parte*; *Milligan*[1], *ex parte*.

hearing, judicial. A trial in an *equity*[8] suit, a preliminary pretrial examination of a person accused of a *crime*[8], or an administrative examination of a party accused of violating the *administrative*[6] *orders* of an administrative agency. See also *administrative adjudication*[6]; *administrative hearing*[6].

Holmes, Oliver Wendell, Jr., 1841–1935. Harvard University professor of *law*[8], editor of The American Law Review, author of The Common Law (1881), *Chief*[8] *Justice* of the Massachusetts Supreme Court, and Associate Justice of the *U.S. Supreme*[8] *Court* from 1902 to 1932. Justice Holmes, frequently referred to as "the Great Dissenter," became known for his *liberal*[3] *dissenting opinions*[8] in favor of individual and human rights. He was considered a *judicial*[8] *activist* on an extremely *conservative*[3] Supreme Court.. In the celebrated case of *Schenck*[1] *v. U.S.*, Justice Holmes, speaking for the *majority*[3], enunciated the *clear*[9] *and present danger doctrine* concerning the freedom of expression. Holmes' basic judicial philosophy was that the Supreme Court should exercise limited *judicial*[4] *review* and permit *federal*[3] and *state*[3] legislative enactments to stand as long as they were within the bounds of good judgment and reasonable *constitutionality*[3]. Some of his more famous dissents, which were later accepted under a more liberal Supreme Court, were in *Lochner*[1] *v. New York*, involving maximum hours of labor; in *Adkins*[1] *v. Children's Hospital*, involving minimum wages; and in *Hammer*[1] *v. Dagenhart*, involving *child*[10] *labor*. See also *Abrams*[1] *v. U.S.*; *maximum*[10] *hour law*; *minimum*[10] *wage law*; *majority opinion*[8]; *reasonable*[9] *man doctrine*.

hot pursuit. The action of a *government*[3] official of one legal *jurisdiction*[8] in crossing into another jurisdiction in order to apprehend a fugitive already being pursued.

Hughes, Charles Evans, 1862–1948. Cornell University professor of *law*[8], New York *state*[3] insurance investigator, reform *governor*[6] of New York, Associate Justice of the *U.S. Supreme*[8] *Court* from 1910 to 1916, presidential candidate in 1916, U.S. Secretary of State, member of the Permanent Court of International Justice, and 11th *Chief*[8] *Justice* of the U.S. Supreme Court from 1930 to 1941. Hughes led the *conservative*[3] Supreme Court in opposition to the *New*[6] *Deal legislation*[7] of *President*[6] Franklin D. Roosevelt[6]. Although he became the focal point of Roosevelt's *court-packing*[8] *plan*, he later moderated his opposition to the New Deal and voted for some social and economic reforms. For example, he voted against the *National*[2] *Recovery Administration* in *Schechter*[1] *Poultry Corp. v. U.S.*, but voted for the *National*[10] *Labor Relations (Wagner) Act* of 1935 in *National*[1] *Labor Relations Board v. Jones and Laughlin Corp.* Hughes, always a strong defender of *civil*[9] *rights* protections, is frequently cited as the greatest Chief Justice since *John Marshall*[8]. See also *International*[12] *Court of Justice.*

indictment. A formal written accusation originating with a prosecuting official and issued by a *grand jury*[8] against a party charged with a legal violation. An indictment is referred to as a "true bill," whereas failure to indict is called a "no bill." An indictment is based on evidence considered sufficient to justify a trial. See also *arraignment*[8]; *Hurtado*[1] *v. California*; *information*[8]; *presentment*[8]; *shocking*[9] *to the conscience doctrine.*

information. A written formal accusation presented under oath to a judicial officer by a prosecuting official charging a party with a legal violation. In most *states*[3] the information may be used in place of a *grand jury*[8] *indictment*[8] to bring a person to trial. See also *Hurtado*[1] *v. California; presentment*[8]; *shocking*[9] *to the conscience doctrine.*

injunction, writ of. A written judicial order issued by a court of *equity*[8] demanding that a specified action cease. On rare occasions an injunction may be "mandatory" and require a certain action. It may be "temporary" or "permanent," depending on the decision of the court. Failure to abide by an injunction may warrant a *contempt*[8] *of court* citation, a fine, or imprisonment.

in re. A judicial designation that legal action is undertaken with regard to a particular party.

judicial activism. The approach to *adjudication*[8] which actively engages judges in problems of *policy*[7] *formulation* and social change. Judicial activism acts aggressively in dealing with *constitutional*[3] interpretations by other branches of *government*[3]. Judicial activists such as *Chief*[8] *Justice Earl Warren*[8] and Associate Justice William O. Douglas admitted a willingness to hear cases involving racial *segregation*[9] and *state*[3] legislative *apportionment*[7], subjects generally left to the states or to other branches of the *federal government*[3]. See also *judicial*[8] *self-restraint.*

Judicial Conference of the United States. An annual conference of the *Chief*[8] *Justice* of the U.S. *Supreme*[8] *Court*, the chief judges of each judicial circuit, selected *District Court*[8] judges from the various circuits, and the chief judge of the *Court*[8] *of Claims.* The Judicial Conference regulates the flow of judicial business within the *federal*[3] court system and makes

recommendations to improve the *administration*[6] of *justice*[8]. See also *Administrative*[2] *Office of the United States Courts.*

judicial review: see Chap. 4.

judicial self-restraint. The approach to *adjudication*[8] which hesitates to engage judges in problems of *policy*[7] *formulation.* Judicial self-restraint permits other branches of *government*[3] to handle problems which, if at all possible, can be dealt with without judicial intervention. Advocates of judicial self-restraint such as Justices Felix Frankfurter and John Marshall Harlan felt some subjects should be avoided because of their "political" nature or their tendency to shift *power*[3] from one area to another. See also *judicial*[8] *activism; political*[4] *question.*

Judiciary Act of 1789: see Chap. 4.

jurisdiction. The right or *authority*[3] of a person, *state*[3], court, *legislature*[7], administrative agency, or other entity to have control over or make decisions with regard to certain matters.

jurisdiction, appellate. The right or obligation of a court to hear and decide cases tried previously in lower courts. Appellate courts do not use *juries*[8] and are designed to analyze *constitutional*[3] questions, correct judicial errors, and give losing parties further opportunities to win their cases. See also *Court*[8] *of Appeals; Judiciary*[4] *Act of 1789; McCardle*[1], *ex parte; Solicitor*[8] *General; writ of appeal*[8]; *writ of certiorari*[8]; *writ of error*[8].

jurisdiction, concurrent. *Authority*[3] of separate courts to hear and decide cases involving the same subject matter.

jurisdiction, denied. The restriction placed on a court which denies it to hear and decide cases involving a particular subject.

jurisdiction, exclusive. The *authority*[3] of a court to exclusively hear and decide cases involving a particular subject.

jurisdiction, original. The right or obligation of a court to hear a case in the first instance. Most courts of original jurisdiction are "lower" courts. The *U.S. Supreme*[8] *Court* has original jurisdiction in cases involving "*ambassadors*[12], other public *ministers*[12], and *consuls*[12]; and those in which a *state*[3] shall be a party" (Art. III, Sec. 2, Cl. 2). See also *Judiciary*[4] *Act of 1789*; *Marbury*[1] *v. Madison.*

jury. A group of persons impaneled by a court to hear evidence in a legal controversy and render a judgment in the case. Juries are used in cases involving both *civil law*[8] and *criminal law*[8]. The *Seventh Amendment*[9] of the *U.S. Constitution*[4] guarantees the right to trial by jury. See also *Duncan*[1] *v. Louisiana*; *grand jury*[8]; *petit jury*[8]; *shocking*[9] *to the conscience doctrine.*

jury, grand. A panel of from 12 to 23 *citizens*[3] who investigate charges made by prosecuting officials against persons charged with violations of *law*[8]. The grand jury deals with serious *crimes*[8] and may determine whether there is enough evidence to justify a trial before a *petit jury*[8]. If the grand jury feels there is enough evidence for trial, it may *indict*[8] the accused party through the issuance of a "true bill." Failure to indict is said to be "no bill." Grand juries may also investigate on their own and issue *presentments*[8] accusing parties of legal violations. In most *states*[3] the grand jury is bypassed in lesser matters and individuals are brought to trial through a device known as an *information*[8]. See also *Fifth Amendment*[9]; *Hurtado*[1] *v. California*; *shocking*[9] *to the conscience doctrine.*

jury, petit. A "small" trial *jury*[8] that is generally composed of 12 persons and which usually requires a stated verdict of "guilty" or "not guilty." The use of the petit jury varies from *state*[3] to state. In many instances the jury must render a unanimous verdict. In most states the petit jury is usually restricted to an examination of facts only. However, in some states the jury may determine *law*[8] and render punishment. Trial by jury is guaranteed by the *U.S. Constitution*[4] (Art. III, Sec. 2, Cl. 3; *Sixth Amendment*[9]; and *Seventh Amendment*[9]) and has been dealt with extensively by the *U.S. Supreme*[8] *Court*. See also *Duncan*[1] *v. Louisiana.*

jus civile. *Civil law*[8] a system of *law*[8] originating from Roman regulations applied specifically to Roman *citizens*[3].

jus gentium. The ancient *law*[8] of the Roman Empire designed for *aliens*[3], a legal system which, it is claimed by some, laid the framework for *international law*[8]. Jus gentium especially emphasized the idea that universal laws exist which apply to all *nations*[3] in interaction with one another. See also *natural law*[8]; *positive law*[8].

justice. The act or quality of doing that which is right or acceptable. The word "justice" is also used as a title for certain judges. As a philosophical, moral, or political abstraction, the word is almost indefinable since concepts of justice differ from one *society*[3] to another. The Greek philosopher Epicurus believed justice changed from time to time but that it basically provided against undue harm or suffering. On the other hand, *Plato*[3] believed that justice meant a balanced and harmonious social structure and interaction in which every person was doing that for which he was best suited. In that sense it was distributive justice. *Thomas Hobbes*'[3] view of justice was, "Whatsoever you do not wish should be done unto you, that do ye not unto another." Jesus had expressed such a thought in positive terms. Sigmund Freud defined justice as "the assurance that a law once made will not be broken in favour of an individual." See also *due*[9] *process of law*; *procedural due*[9] *process*; *substantive due*[9] *process*; *equity*[8].

justice of the peace. A minor judicial official with *jurisdiction*[8] over petty *civil law*[8] and *criminal law*[8] matters. A justice of the peace may be empowered to conduct marriages, fix *bail*[8] for certain offenses, conduct preliminary *hearings*[6] for persons charged with violating criminal laws, investigate traffic deaths, and handle other petty judicial matters. Justices of the peace are most often paid through some form of fee system. See also *court*[8] *of record*.

justiciable question: see Chap. 4.

Kerner Commission Report (1967). The U.S. *government*[3] report officially known as the "Report of the National Advisory Commission on Civil Disorders." The *commission*[6], appointed by *President*[6] *Lyndon B. Johnson*[6] on July 27, 1967, presented within its findings that unemployment, poverty, poor education, and other factors have led to severe social disorders and riots within the U.S. The commission, chaired by *Governor*[6] Otto Kerner of Illinois, particularly indicted white racist superiority and exploitation of blacks as the basic reason for riots within Negro neighborhoods. The commission also made specific recommendations for combating the problems leading to civil disorders. See also *civil*[9] *rights*; *crime*[8].

law (act, statute). A basic rule of conduct prescribed for the social and political *community*[3] by recognized legal *authority*[3] and enforced through *sanctions*[12] available to public officials and public courts. Law may be viewed

as a tradition of predictable order, as a basic document known as a *constitution*[3], as specific *legislation*[7] known as statutes (*acts*[8], *ordinances*[8], etc.), or as administrative regulations (*administrative*[6] orders, rules, etc.). It may be viewed as *criminal law*[8] if it involves the relations between individuals and the *state*[3], or it may be *civil law*[8] if it relates to conflicts between individuals within the state. In the United States *federal government*[3] a *bill*[7] becomes a law by being passed by both houses of the *U.S. Congress*[4] and approved by the *President*[6] under specified conditions. A bill may become a law without presidential signature during any time except during the last ten days of a legislative session (*pocket veto*[7]) or, in the event that the President actually vetoes the bill, by both houses of Congress passing the bill over the *absolute veto*[7] by a two-thirds vote in each house. Laws of the federal government are recorded in the *Statutes*[7] *at Large of the United States* and in the *United*[7] *States Code*. See also *statutory law*[8].

law, administrative. The basic rules of public *policy*[6] surrounding administrative agencies and their practices. Administrative law contains basic *legislation*[7] creating administrative agencies, legislative acts protecting private *citizens*[3] and *corporations*[10] from arbitrary action, *laws*[8] establishing principles of *judicial*[4] *review* of administrative actions, and administrative rules regulating private rights (licensing, *rate-making*[10], etc.). See also *administration*[6].

law, admiralty (maritime). The body of *law*[8] concerned with legal cases involving foreign and *interstate commerce*[10] on navigable waters. The *U.S. Constitution*[4] vests the national *government*[3] with *exclusive jurisdiction*[8] over maritime cases (Art. III, Sec. 2, Cl. 1). See also *Federal*[2] *Maritime Commission*; *Maritime*[2] *Administration*.

law, civil. The legal tradition or body of *law*[8] designed to regulate conflicts over private rights. Civil law originated from Roman regulations of such rights. Such modern regulations differ from *criminal law*[8] in that the *government*[3] simply provides a forum for the settlement of disputes rather than itself charging someone with a *crime*[8] against the *state*[3]. The tradition of Roman civil law contrasts with *common law*[8] in that it is more rigid. Also, it stems more from the rules of legal or administrative *authority*[3] than from judicial decisions and precedent. Such origins led to an early need for arranging *legislation*[7] in *code*[8] form. See also *jus*[8] *civile*.

law, common. The legal tradition and body of *law*[8] derived from English *custom*[3], practices, and judicial decisions. The body of law was termed "common law" because it was applied to the realm in general. Major characteristics of common law have been a belief in *natural laws*[8], the use of right reason, and the acceptance of precedents established in earlier decisions. See also *equity*[8]; *Erie*[1] *Railroad v. Tompkins*; *Mosaic Code*[8]; *stare*[8] *decisis*.

law, constitutional (organic, fundamental). The basic *constitutional*[3] framework of a social or political system, especially a national *state*[3]. Constitutional *law*[8] is most easily interpreted if it is contained within a *written constitution*[3] and it is clearly restricted to the fundamentals of *government*[3]. It is considered superior to *statutes*[8], arbitrary political actions of officials, and private *common law*[8] interpretations of individuals. See also *Ashwander*[1] *v. TVA*; *constitutionalism*[3].

law, criminal. The body of rules designed to regulate the conduct of individuals as members of the *state*[3]. Such rules define *crimes*[8] against the state and public order and prescribe punishment for violators. Criminal

law is generally divided into *misdemeanors*[8] (less serious offenses) and *felonies*[8] (more serious offenses), and contrasts with *civil law*[8] which regulates private rights.

law, customary. A body of regulations established by *custom*[3] and generally recognized as enforceable by the *state*[3].

law, international. The body of legal regulations, *treaties*[12], international judicial decisions, and *custom*[3] generally recognized by the world *community*[3] or particular *nations*[3] as legally binding on sovereign *states*[3] or persons involved in international activities. Because international law does involve sovereign states, it is frequently difficult to enforce without resorting to *force*[3] which easily degenerates into lawlessness. The basic written guideline in international law is the treaty. The concept of *law*[8] in the international community arose among western European nations during the seventeenth century. *Hugo Grotius*[12], Dutch legal *theorist*[3], is generally recognized as the "father of modern international law." See also *jus*[8] *gentium*; and *state (constitutional) sovereignty*[3].

law, martial: see *martial*[8] *law*.

law, military: see *military*[8] *law*.

law, natural. The system of order inherent within the universe and the nature of man, a system which may be partially understood through the use of right reason and moral consciousness. Natural law philosophies may be traced through the Greek Stoics such as *Plato*[3] and *Aristotle*[3], the Church Fathers such as *Augustine*[3] and *Aquinas*[3], the *Enlightenment*[3] thinkers such as *Locke*[3] and *Rousseau*[3], and modern exponents of *civil*[9] disobedience such as *Thoreau*[4] and *Martin Luther King*[9], *Jr.* See also *positive law*[8]; *inalienable rights*[3]; *state*[3] *of nature*; *higher law theory*[3].

law, positive. The concept accepted in some legal and judicial circles that *law*[8] is what is positively commanded by a recognized sovereign. A corollary to the positive law concept is that the sovereign, to maintain his pronouncements as law, must be capable of enforcing his rules and regulations. Judges interpret the law in the light of established standards rather than some amorphous concept of *natural law*[8] or ideal *justice*[8]. See also *John Austin*[8]; *higher law theory*[3]; *legitimacy*[3].

law, Roman civil: see *civil law*[8].

law, statutory. Rules and regulations that take the form of written pronouncements by legally recognized governmental agencies. A *statute*[8] may be an *executive*[6] decree, a legislative enactment, an *administrative*[6] order, a local *ordinance*[8], or other written rule of *government*[3]. In a system of *representative government*[3] the term "statutory law" most often refers to *laws*[8] passed by representative *legislatures*[7]. See also *policy*[7] *formulation*.

litigation: see *adjudication*[8].

magistrate. A minor public official (*justice*[8] *of the peace*, police magistrate, etc.) invested with *authority*[3] to hear cases involving traffic violations, minor criminal offenses, and *civil law*[8] suits involving small sums of money.

malfeasance. The performance of an illegal act, especially on the part of a public official. See also *crime*[8]; *misfeasance*[8]; *nonfeasance*[8].

mandamus, writ of. A written judicial order designed to compel a party to perform a purely ministerial act clearly required by *law*[8]. The writ of mandamus may be issued by any court vested with appropriate *jurisdiction*[8] and may be directed against private *citizens*[3], public officials, *corporations*[10], or lower courts. A court

will not issue such a *writ*[8] if the law clearly leaves room for discretion of action. See also *Kentucky*[1] *v. Dennison*; *Marbury*[1] *v. Madison*; *Mississippi*[1] *v. Johnson*.

Marshall, John, 1755–1835. Virginia *state*[3] *legislator*[7], member of the *U.S. House*[7] *of Representatives*, U.S. Secretary of State, and fourth *Chief*[8] *Justice* of the *U.S. Supreme*[8] *Court*. Marshall, an ardent *Federalist*[4], served as Chief Justice from 1801 to 1835 and elevated the Supreme Court to the position of a major branch of the *federal government*[3] through his exertion of the right of *judicial*[4] *review* over both federal and *state*[3] *laws*[8]. He gave a broad interpretation to the *U.S. Constitution*[4] through the *implied powers*[4], opposed *states'*[4] *rights* doctrines, strictly interpreted *property*[10] rights, and developed strong federal control over commerce. See also *Cohens*[1] *v. Virginia*; *liberal construction*[4]; *Dartmouth*[1] *College v. Woodward*; *Fletcher*[1] *v. Peck*; *Gibbons*[1] *v. Ogden*; *McCulloch*[1] *v. Maryland*; *Marbury*[1] *v. Madison*; *Federalist Party*[5]; *commerce powers*[4].

martial law. Temporary military *government*[3] over a civilian population during a time of civil or military disorder. During such a time, *military*[8] *law* replaces *civil law*[8] and military courts replace civil courts. Martial law is most often used during threats of external invasion, during internal social disorders such as race riots, and during natural disasters. Martial law may be declared by the *U.S. President*[6] or the various *state*[3] *governors*[6] in their appropriate spheres. See also *Duncan*[1] *v. Kahanamoku*; *emergency powers*[4]; *Korematsu*[1] *v. U.S.*; *Milligan*[1], *ex parte*; *police powers*[4]; *Commander-in-Chief powers*[6]; *war*[12] *powers*.

military law. The rules and regulations governing the activities of military agencies and personnel. Military law of the U.S. is formulated by the

U.S. Congress[4] and was unified in the *Uniform*[8] *Code of Military Justice* in 1950. The *code*[8] was thoroughly revised and updated in 1969. See also *Court*[8] *of Military Appeals*; *court-martial*[8]; *martial*[8] *law*; *Reid*[1] *v. Covert*; *Toth*[1] *v. Quarles*; *Trop*[1] *v. Dulles*.

misdemeanor. A minor violation of *law*[8] which generally provides for a fine or a short period of imprisonment in a minor correctional institution. A misdemeanor contrasts with a major offense (a *felony*[8]). See also *crime*[8].

misfeasance. The performance of a lawful act in an illegal manner in such a way as to infringe on the rights of others. See also *crime*[8]; *malfeasance*[8]; *nonfeasance*[8].

Missouri Plan. A distinctive plan designed for selecting judges within *state*[3] judicial systems, a plan inaugurated in Missouri in 1940. The plan combines elective and appointive elements in judicial choice by incorporating the following items: (1) a *nonpartisan*[5] nominating *commission*[6] to recommend a slate of candidates for judicial *appointment*[6] (i.e., three persons); the commission consists of the *Chief*[8] *Justice*, three lawyers named by the state bar association, and three laymen named by the *governor*[6]; (2) appointment by the governor of one of the commission nominees; (3) submission of the judge's name to the people for approval or rejection after a specified time (for example, one year) in order to determine if the judge will be permitted to serve the full term on the bench (12 years); (4) a judge nearing the end of his *tenure*[6] may apply for re-election; a nonpartisan vote from the electorate will determine whether the judge will be retained or removed.

National Commission on Violence. A *federal*[3] investigative *commission*[6] created by *executive*[6] *order* on June 10, 1968 by *President*[6] Lyndon B. *Johnson*[6] to investigate and make rec-

ommendations with respect to the causes and prevention of violence. The broad-based commission, chaired by Dr. Milton Eisenhower, released its final report in December 1969. It revealed that the U.S. is a world leader in social violence. It indicted racism, poverty, easy access to guns, political extremism, *urban*[11] depersonalization, family deterioration, poor education, violence on television, inefficient police *administration*[6], slow judicial procedures, inadequate correctional institutions, and public defiance of law in general. The commission sponsored a private study known as the *Walker*[8] *Report* in 1968, a study of the violence surrounding the *Democratic Party*[5] *convention*[5] in Chicago in August 1968. The commission has also issued numerous staff reports dealing with such topics as the history of violence, black militancy, protest, firearms, assassination, the *mass*[5] *media*, and *justice*[8].

nisi prius. The holding of a trial before a judge and *jury*[8] "in the first instance" rather than on appeal. "Nisi prius" means "unless before" and denotes the concept of clearing cases as they appear before the court. See also *appellate jurisdiction*[8].

no-knock search. A police search of private premises without preliminary action of knocking on the door and announcing a police presence. The *District*[8] *of Columbia Court Reform and Criminal Procedure Act of 1970* provides for such action in the *District of Columbia*[4] without the need for a search *warrant*[8] in the event that the police believe lives would be endangered, evidence destroyed, or suspects could flee. Knowledge of prior possibilities requires court approval for a no-knock entry.

nolo contendere. The admittance by a *defendant*[8] in a *criminal law*[8] case that he does not wish to contest the charges brought against him. Although the defendant does not admit guilt, he accepts the practical results of such a plea since he places himself at the mercy of the court.

nonfeasance. The failure to perform some act required by *law*[8] or other regulation. See also *crime*[8]; *malfeasance*[8]; *misfeasance*[8].

Omnibus Crime Control and Safe Streets Act of 1968. A *federal*[3] law which established the *Law*[2] *Enforcement Assistance Administration* (*LEAA*) and increased federal assistance to *state*[3] and local law enforcement agencies for long-range planning. The *law*[8] authorized *wiretapping*[9] by court order in national security cases, accepted confessions as evidence in court with the right to examine their voluntariness, restricted the importation of firearms, and barred persons convicted as *felons*[8] in riots from holding federal offices for five years.

opinion, advisory. A court opinion rendered in regard to the *constitutionality*[3] or legal effects of a *statute*[8] or proposed *law*[8], even though there exists no judicial controversy between parties contesting the law. *Federal*[3] courts render no advisory opinions, but a few *states*[3] permit their highest courts to render such opinions when called for by another branch of *government*[3]. Only in Colorado do such opinions have the *force*[3] of law. Some states permit their *attorneys*[8] *general* to issue such opinions, which have the force of law unless reversed by court order.

opinion, concurring. A judicial opinion offered by one or more judges who are seated together on a court and who agree with their own court's decision in a case. However, they feel that reasons other than those cited by the *majority*[3] should be listed, reasons that led them to majority agreement on different grounds. See also *Ashwander*[1] v. TVA.

opinion, dissenting. A judicial opinion offered by one or more judges who are seated together on a court and who disagree with the decision rendered by the *majority*[3] of their court. See also *Oliver Wendell Holmes*[8], Jr.; *majority opinion*[8].

opinion, majority. A judicial opinion offered by the judges of a court who voted as a *majority*[3] in deciding a particular case. One justice is generally assigned to write the opinion. In the *U.S. Supreme*[8] *Court*, if voting with the majority, the *Chief*[8] *Justice* assigns himself or another justice to write the opinion. On occasions when the Chief Justice is in the *minority*[3], the senior justice voting with the majority assigns the writing of the majority opinion. A great deal of drafting and compromising takes place during the writing of the opinion. A justice in the majority may differ on reasons for reaching the majority decision and may write a *concurring opinion*[8]. See also *dissenting opinion*[8].

ordinance. A *statute*[8] enacted by a legislative body of a *municipal*[11] *government*[3]. An ordinance may be passed only in accordance with *power*[3] granted to a *municipal corporation*[11] through *state*[3] *constitutional*[3] provisions or state legislative enactments. See also *statutory law*[8].

pardon: see Chap. 6.

parole. Release from prison prior to the expiration of a sentence, on the condition of good behavior.

plaintiff. A person who brings legal action against another party in a court of *law*[8]. See also *accusatorial*[8] *proceeding*; *defendant*[8].

political question: see Chap. 4.

powers, judicial: see Chaps. 6 and 7.

powers, police: see Chap. 4.

presentment. A *grand jury*[8] action, apart from an *indictment*[8], which formally accuses a party of a legal violation. A presentment is issued upon a grand jury's own initiative, whereas an indictment originates with a prosecuting official. See also *information*[8].

preventative (pretrial) detention. The action of holding a person accused of a criminal violation for 60 days upon the determination of a judge that the previous record of the accused warrants temporary denial of *bail*[8]. Such denial ability was granted to *federal*[3] judges in the *District of Columbia*[4] in the *District*[8] of Columbia Court Reform and Criminal Procedure Act of 1970.

prima facie case. Evidence or a collection of evidence deemed sufficient to establish "on first appearence" a fact or a presumption of fact unless otherwise contested.

probation. The conditional suspension of a court sentence upon the guarantee of good behavior by the person convicted of a *crime*[8]. A person on probation remains free, on the condition that he must be regularly supervised by a probation officer.

quasi-judicial. Possessing some of the characteristics of a judicial body or action. Public administrative agencies and their *administrative*[6] orders possess such a characteristic. Such agencies formulate rules and then hold *hearings*[6] and settle conflicts over those rules through decisions recognized as legally binding. See also *independent regulatory commission*[6]; *policy*[7] *formulation*; *quasi-legislative*[7].

reprieve: see Chap. 6.

res judicata (res adjudicata). A "thing decided" by judicial decision which has become a settled principle of *law*[8]. See also *stare*[8] *decisis*.

riot, inciting to. The process of actively and purposely provoking others to violent action. See also *Feiner*[1] *v. New York*; *Terminiello*[1] *v. Chicago*.

rule of law theory: see *theory*[3], *rule of law*.

separability. The concept that if one part of a *statute*[8] is declared *unconstitutional*[3] by judicial action, the other parts are still operable unless all parts are so closely intertwined that none can be separated. Separability may be written into the *law*[8] in the following manner: "TITLE V-SEPARABILITY Sec. 501. If any provision of this Act or the application of any provision thereof to any person or circumstance is judicially determined to be invalid, the remainder of this Act or the application of such provision to other persons or circumstances shall not be affected by such determination."

Solicitor General. The U.S. *Department of Justice*[2] official responsible for representing the U.S. *government*[3] before the *Supreme*[8] *Court*. The Solicitor General must clear all appeals placed on the appellate dockets of all *federal*[3] appeals courts. On the request of the *Attorney*[8] *General*, the Solicitor General may represent the U.S. government before any court, either federal or *state*[3]. See also *appellate jurisdiction*[8].

stare decisis. The *common law*[8] judicial practice of following the precedents established in earlier judicial decisions. See also *res*[8] *judicata*.

statute: see *law*[8].

subpoena. A written legal order of a court or other appropriate body which may require witnesses to appear and produce testimony. Courts, legislative bodies, administrative agencies, and other organized legal agencies are granted the *power*[3] of subpoena in order to assure that *government*[3] will be able to function. A *contempt*[8] of *court* citation and appropriate legal action may face a person who fails to heed a subpoena.

summons. A written legal order issued by a legal or judicial officer to a person who has had a formal legal complaint lodged against him. A summons may also be used to call a prospective *jury*[8] member to service or to warn minor offenders (traffic, etc.) of the responsibility to appear before a *magistrate*[8] at a particular time.

Supreme Court, (U.S.). The highest *federal*[3] court in the U.S. judicial system. Since 1869 the Supreme Court has consisted of a *Chief*[8] *Justice* and eight associate justices. Justices are appointed by the *President*[6], *confirmed*[6] by the *Senate*[7], and hold lifetime *tenure*[6] subject to good behavior. The Supreme Court is the only federal court actually provided for in the *U.S. Constitution*[4] apart from legislative action. The size of the court and its *appellate jurisdiction*[8] are fixed by the *Congress*[4]. Congress first acted on such matters in the *Judiciary*[4] *Act of 1789.* The Court's *original jurisdiction*[8] includes cases affecting *diplomatic*[12] officials and cases in which *states*[3] are parties. The *Eleventh Amendment*[4] removed the *jurisdiction*[8] over cases in which a state is sued by a *citizen*[3] of another state. Certain types of cases involving *federal*[4] *questions* may be appealed from state supreme courts to the U.S. Supreme Court. The Supreme Court exercises a comprehensive *power*[3] of *judicial*[4] *review* over both federal and state governmental operations covered by the U.S. Constitution. The Court hears cases on appeal most often through the discretionary issuance of *writs of certiorari*[8]. Decisions are recorded in the *United*[8] *States Reports.* See also *court-packing*[8] *plan; diversity*[4] *of citizenship question; federal*[4] *question; judicial*[8] *activism; judicial*[8] *self-restraint; justi-*

ciable[4] *question; Marbury*[1] v. *Madison; political*[4] *question.*

Taney, Roger Brooke, 1777–1864. Maryland *state*[3] *legislator*[7], United States *Attorney*[8] *General,* adviser to *President*[6] *Andrew Jackson*[6], Secretary of the Treasury, and fifth *Chief*[8] *Justice* of the U.S. *Supreme*[8] *Court,* 1836 to 1864. Taney opposed a strong *centralized*[3] *government*[3], supported *states'*[4] *rights,* and opposed various economic and *propertied*[10] interests. He was a leading opponent of the *Bank*[10] *of the United States* even though he served as Secretary of the Treasury. He is best remembered as the author of the *majority opinion*[8] in the infamous Supreme Court case of *Dred*[1] *Scott v. Sandford,* a decision which held that Negroes could not be United States *citizens*[3]. In other decisions Taney opposed large *corporate*[10] interests, opposed the use of the *commerce*[4] *clause* to regulate state activities, and opposed extensive growth of judicial *power*[3]. See also *Ableman*[1] v. *Booth; Charles*[1] *River Bridge v. Warren Bridge; Luther*[1] v. *Borden; Merryman*[1], *ex parte.*

tort. A wrongful act involving damages or injury, apart from breach of *contract*[10], for which civil action may be brought against the wrongdoer. See also *civil law*[8].

Uniform Code of Military Justice. A unification of the legal codes regulating the various branches of the U.S. military services. The *code*[8], originally promulgated in 1950, established the *Court*[8] *of Military Appeals,* laid down various regulations for the *administration*[6] of military *justice*[8], and created a system for handling offenses committed by members of the military forces. The code was thoroughly revised in 1969 in order to update the substantive rights guaranteed to military personnel and to modernize procedural practices used in *courts-martial*[8]. The revision was necessitated partially because of various *U.S. Supreme*[8] *Court* rulings involving trial procedures, confessions, *self-incrimination*[9], and other *due*[9] *process of law* guarantees included in the *Constitution*[4]. See also *articles*[12] *of war*; *military*[8] *law*; *procedural due*[9] *process*; *Pueblo*[12] *crisis of 1968*; *substantive due*[9] *process*.

United States attorney. A presidential appointee who serves under the supervision of the *Department of Justice*[2] and who serves in an assigned federal judicial district. A U.S. attorney represents the U.S. in federal cases in which the U.S. *federal government*[3] is a party.

United States commissioner. An official of a federal *District Court*[8] who serves a four-year term and is empowered to issue *warrants*[8], hold preliminary *hearings*[6] for persons accused of *federal*[3] violations, determine whether a person should be held for *grand jury*[8] action, set *bail*[8], administer oaths, and handle various other matters of a judicial nature.

United States marshal. An official of a federal *District Court*[8] who serves a four-year term and who has duties similar to those of a *county*[11] sheriff, except that his activities relate to *federal government*[3] matters. A marshal may arrest violators of federal *law*[8], supervise federal prisoners, serve arrest *warrants*[8] and *jury*[8] notices, maintain order in the court, and fulfill various other needs of the court.

United States Reports. The official record of cases disposed of by the *U.S. Supreme*[8] *Court*. The United States Reports contain the decisions of the Supreme Court, *concurring* or *dissenting opinions*[8], and abbreviated summaries of the legal arguments presented by the various parties. Volumes containing the decisions appear at the end of each session of the Supreme Court.

venue. The *county*[11] or other legal *jurisdiction*[8] in which a *jury*[8] is chosen and in which a trial takes place. A "change of venue" may be granted by the court in question in order to facilitate a fair trial.

Walker Report, (1968). A private report delivered by Mr. Daniel Walker of Chicago, Illinois for the *National*[8] *Commission on Violence*, a body chaired by Dr. Milton Eisenhower. The 1968 report by Mr. Walker, president of the unofficial Chicago *Crime*[8] Commission, examined the violent confrontation of demonstrators and police in the parks and streets of Chicago during the week of the Democratic National Convention in 1968. The report indicted the violent activities of participants on both sides of the confrontation. See also *Democratic Party*[5]; *party convention*[5].

warrant. A judicial *writ*[8] issued to an authorized legal official requiring the official to arrest a designated party, search his premises or his person, or to seize specified *property*[10]. See also *unreasonable search*[9] *and seizure*; *writ*[9] *of assistance*.

Warren, Earl, 1891– . *Attorney*[8] *General* of California, *Republican Party*[5] *Governor*[6] of California, and 14th *Chief*[8] *Justice* of the *U.S. Supreme*[8] *Court*, from 1953 to 1969. Warren is best remembered for his outspoken defense of individual *civil*[9] *rights*. The most famous decision in which he wrote the *majority opinion*[8] was the case of *Brown*[1] *v. Board of Education of Topeka*, a decision which held racially *segregated*[9] public schools *unconstitutional*[3]. A leading *judicial*[8] *activist*, Warren regularly voted in favor of civil liberties protections under *due*[9] *process of law*. He supported protections against *self-incrimination*[9], the right of legal counsel for indigents, protection against *unreasonable search*[9] *and seizure*, and protection of free public expression. He opposed racism, police abuses, intolerance, and legal oppression. He was also a leader in interjecting the Supreme Court into political battles over legislative *reapportionment*[7]. He frequently cited the case of *Reynolds*[1] *v. Sims*, a reapportionment case, as the most significant decision made during his *tenure*[6] on the Court. He felt the case was important because it shifted the political *power*[3] within the *states*[3] to where the people actually lived. After the assassination of *President*[6] John F. Kennedy, the new President, *Lyndon B. Johnson*[6], appointed Warren to chair what came to be known as the *Warren Commission*[6]. The commis-

sion investigated the assassination of President Kennedy and concluded that the assassin, Lee Harvey Oswald, acted alone and that there was no conspiracy involved in the event. See also *Baker*[1] *v. Carr*; *Gideon*[1] *v. Wainwright*; *Miranda*[1] *v. Arizona*; *Wesberry*[1] *v. Sanders*.

writ. A written judicial order prohibiting a designated action (*writ of injunction*[8]) or requiring the cited party to carry out a particular task (*writ of mandamus*[8]). Courts, especially *equity*[8] (chancery) courts, use various types of writs to expedite the judicial process. See also *court*[8] *of chancery*.

Supreme Court cases related to material in this chapter are arranged below by subject. Summaries of the cases are in Chapter One arranged alphabetically by the name of the first party in each case.

CONSTITUTIONAL
   RIGHTS—(Legal)
Gideon v. *Wainwright*
   (1963)

CONSTITUTIONAL
   RIGHTS—(Race)
Brown v. *Board of Education of Topeka* (1954)
Dred Scott v. *Sandford*
   (1857)
Swann v. *Charlotte-Mecklenburg Board of Education* (1971)

ECONOMY—(Contracts)
Dartmouth College v.
   Woodward (1819)
Fletcher v. *Peck* (1810)
Lochner v. *N.Y.* (1905)

ECONOMY—(Intergovernmental Tax Immunity)
McCulloch v. *Md.* (1819)

ECONOMY—(Taxation)
Pollock v. *Farmers' Loan and Trust Co.* (1895)
U.S. v. *Butler* (1936)

EXECUTIVE—
U.S. v. *Curtiss-Wright Export Corp.* (1936)
Youngstown Sheet & Tube v. *Sawyer* (1952)

FEDERALISM—(Diversity of Citizenship)
Chisholm v. *Ga.* (1793)
Cohens v. *Va.* (1821)
Dred Scott v. *Sandford*
   (1857)
Erie Railroad v. *Tompkins*
   (1938)

FEDERALISM—(Implied Powers)
McCulloch v. *Md.* (1819)

FOREIGN POLICY AND
   DEFENSE—
U.S. v. *Curtiss-Wright Export Corp.* (1936)
Youngstown Sheet & Tube v. *Sawyer* (1952)

JUDICIAL REVIEW—
   (General)
Ashwander v. *TVA*
   (1936)
McCardle, Ex parte
   (1869)

Marbury v. *Madison*
   (1808)
Martin v. *Hunter's Lessee*
   (1816)

JUDICIAL REVIEW—
   (Diversity of Citizenship)
Chisholm v. *Ga.* (1793)
Cohens v. *Va.* (1821)
Dred Scott v. *Sandford*
   (1857)
Erie Railroad v. *Tompkins*
   (1938)

JUDICIAL REVIEW—
   (Economy—Contracts)
Fletcher v. *Peck* (1810)

LEGISLATIVE APPOR-
   TIONMENT—
Baker v. *Carr* (1962)
Reynolds v. *Sims* (1964)
Wesberry v. *Sanders*
   (1964)

PUBLIC WELFARE AND
   URBAN PROBLEMS
   —(Welfare)
U.S. v. *Butler* (1936)

Chapter 9

Constitutional Rights

Note to the reader: Cross-referenced terms are in italics. The superscript number refers to the chapter in which the entry may be found. In addition, its placement indicates the word under which the term is alphabetized. (For example, in *electoral*[4] *college*, information on the electoral college may be found in Chapter 4 under "electoral.") Because italics are used in cross-references, they are not used for terms in which they would ordinarily be used: Supreme Court cases and titles of books, journals, plays, and so forth.

> *Supreme Court cases relating to material in this chapter are listed at the end of the chapter (see page 237).*

abolitionist. A *radical*[3] advocate of the extermination of the institution of slavery. Leading abolitionists based their appeal on moral consciousness and Biblical scripture. They were most active in the U.S. between 1830 and 1860. The leading abolitionists were William Lloyd Garrison, Theodore Weld, Harriet Beecher Stowe, and John Brown. See also *Emancipation*[9] *Proclamation*.

academic freedom. The general freedom of academic expression within the academic *community*[3] which is restricted largely by one's own level of professional *expertise*[6] and the institutional rules governing *tenure*[6]. See also *American*[5] *Association of University Professors*; *Barenblatt*[1] *v. U.S.*; *National*[5] *Education Association*.

Alien and Sedition Acts of 1798: see Chap. 4.

Alien Registration (Smith) Act of 1940: see Chap. 4.

Amendment, Eighth (1791). The *amendment*[3] to the *U.S. Constitution*[4] which prohibits excessive *bail*[8], fines, and the use of *cruel and unusual punishment*[9]. See also *Robinson*[1] *v. California*; *Trop*[1] *v. Dulles*.

Amendment, Fifteenth: see Chap. 5.

Amendment, Fifth (1791). The *amendment*[3] to the *U.S. Constitution*[4] which guarantees a *grand jury*[8] in certain cases, prohibits *double*[9] *jeopardy*, prohibits *self-incrimination*[9], guarantees *due*[9] *process of law* in the taking of life, liberty, or *property*[10], and cites the *citizen's*[3] right to just compensation when the *government*[3] exercises its right of *eminent*[9] *domain*. The Fifth Amendment originally applied only to the *federal government*[3]. Protections related to double jeopardy were applied to the *states*[3] in *Benton*[1] *v. Maryland* and self-incrimination in *Malloy*[1] *v. Hogan*. The Fifth Amendment has been "nationalized" through the *due*[4] *process* and *equal*[4] *protection clauses* of the *Fourteenth Amend-*

ment.[4] See also *Albertson[1] v. SACB; Aptheker[1] v. Secretary of State; Barenblatt[1] v. U.S.; Barron[1] v. Baltimore; Bartkus[1] v. Illinois; Bill[9] of Rights nationalization; Brown[1] v. Mississippi; Estes[1] v. Texas; McNabb[1] v. U.S.; Miranda[1] v. Arizona; Palko[1] v. Connecticut; nationalized rights[9]; shocking[9] to the conscience doctrine.*

Amendment, First (1791). The *amendment[3]* to the *U.S. Constitution[4]* which guarantees the freedom of religion, speech, press, assembly, and petition. First Amendment freedoms originally applied only to the *federal government[3]*, a point emphasized by the *Supreme[8] Court* in *Barron[1] v. Baltimore* in 1833. However, since the case of *Gitlow[1] v. New York*, the amendment has been applied judicially to the *states[3]* within the Union through the *due[4] process* and *equal[4] protection clauses* of the *Fourteenth Amendment[4]*. See also *balancing[9] doctrine; Bill[9] of Rights nationalization; child[9] benefit doctrine; clear[9] and present danger doctrine; Everson[1] v. Board of Education; Near[1] v. Minnesota; preferred[9] freedom doctrine; prior[9] restraint doctrine; right of privacy[9]; purchase[9] of services doctrine; released[9] time doctrine; establishment of religion[9] clause; free exercise of religion[9] clause; nationalized rights[9]; subsequent[9] punishment doctrine; wall[9] of separation doctrine.*

Amendment, Fourteenth: see Chap. 4.

Amendment, Fourth (1791). The *amendment[3]* to the *U.S. Constitution[4]* which prohibits *unreasonable search[9] and seizure.* The amendment originally applied only to the *federal government[3]*, but in *Wolf[1] v. Colorado* it was applied to the *states[3]* through the *due[9] process clause* of the *Fourteenth Amendment[4]*. Direct application to the states was further modified in *Mapp[1] v. Ohio.*

Amendment, Ninth (1791). The *amendment[3]* to the *U.S. Constitution[4]*

which states that because certain rights are not mentioned in the Constitution does not mean they do not belong to the people. In *Griswold[1] v. Connecticut* the U.S. *Supreme[8] Court* recognized the *right of privacy[9]* as belonging to the people even though the right is not cited in the Constitution. The amendment states: "The enumeration in the Constitution, of certain rights, shall not be construed to deny or disparage others retained by the people."

amendment, prayer. The popular designation of a *resolution[7]* to amend the *First Amendment[9]* of the *U.S. Constitution[4]* in order to permit prayer and Bible reading on a voluntary basis in public schools and other public institutions. The leading advocates of such an *amendment[3]*, designed to counter several controversial *Supreme[8] Court* decisions, were *Congressman[7]* Frank J. Becker and *Senator[7]* Everett Dirksen. The "Becker Amendment" contained the following language: "Nothing in this Constitution shall be deemed to prohibit the offering, reading from, or listening to prayers or biblical scriptures, if participation therein is on a voluntary basis, in any governmental or public school, institution, or place." After a period of inattention, the movement for support of a similar amendment gained public attention in 1971. See also *Engel[1] v. Vitale; School[1] District of Abington Township v. Schempp.*

Amendment, Second (1791). The *amendment[3]* to the *U.S. Constitution[4]* which guarantees the right of *states[3]* to have militias (*national[12] guard*) and the *citizens[3]* of the states to keep and bear arms.

Amendment, Seventh (1791). The *amendment[3]* to the *U.S. Constitution[4]* which guarantees the right to trial by *jury[8]* in certain cases.

Amendment, Sixth (1791). The *amendment[3]* to the *U.S. Constitution[4]* which guarantees a speedy public trial, the right to confront witnesses, and the right of legal counsel for defense. The amendment originally applied only to the *federal government*[3]. The *Supreme*[8] *Court* held that counsel must be provided for indigents in federal *criminal law*[8] cases in *Johnson*[1] *v. Zerbst* and in *state*[3] criminal cases in *Gideon*[1] *v. Wainwright*. The Court has clarified thousands of legal points related to Sixth Amendment guarantees and has covered many of them with the protection of the *due*[4] *process clauses* of the *Fifth Amendment*[9] and the *Fourteenth Amendment*[4]. See also *Ashcraft*[1] *v. Tennesse*; *Betts*[1] *v. Brady*; *Escobedo*[1] *v. Illinois*; *Estes*[1] *v. Texas*; *Klopfer*[1] *v. North Carolina*; *Miranda*[1] *v. Arizona*; *Moore*[1] *v. Dempsey*; *Pointer*[1] *v. Texas*; *Powell*[1] *v. Alabama*; *Sheppard*[1] *v. Maxwell*.

Amendment, Third (1791). The *amendment*[3] to the *U.S. Constitution*[4] which forbids the quartering of soldiers in private homes during time of peace. See also *Intolerable*[4] *Acts of 1774*; *Quartering*[4] *Act of 1766*; *right of privacy*[9]; *Townshend*[4] *Acts of 1767*.

Amendment, Thirteenth: see Chap. 4.

antimiscegenation law. A legislative enactment which prohibits racially mixed marriages. Miscegenation, the act or practice of persons of different races uniting in marriage, was prohibited by various legal *jurisdictions*[8] in *colonial*[4] America. Numerous *states*[3] maintained such *laws*[8] until they were declared *unconstitutional*[3] by the *U.S. Supreme*[8] *Court* in *Loving*[1] *v. Virginia* in 1967. See also *discrimination*[9]; *segregation*[9]; *white*[5] *citizens' councils*.

anti-Semitism. Dislike of and *prejudice*[9] against persons of Jewish ancestry.

attainder, bill of. A legislative *act*[8] inflicting punishment without the benefit of formal judicial procedures.

Both the *federal*[3] (Art. I, Sec. 9) and *state*[3] (Art. I, Sec. 10) *governments*[3] are prohibited by the *U.S. Constitution*[4] from passing bills of attainder. See also *U.S.*[1] *v. Brown*.

Attorney General's list. A list of *organizations*[6] classified by the U.S. *Attorney*[8] *General* as subversive or largely influenced by subversive elements. The loyalty security list was begun around 1947 and has been regularly revised. It is used primarily to warn persons about organizations they might be considering joining or supporting. See also *Cole*[1] *v. Young*; *loyalty*[9] *oath*.

bad tendency doctrine. A doctrine judicially enunciated by Justice Edward Sanford in the *Supreme*[8] *Court* case of *Gitlow*[1] *v. New York*. Justice Sanford chose such a *theory*[3] for declaring that *states*[3] may not unduly restrict the freedom of speech guarantees of the *First Amendment*[9] and the *Fourteenth Amendment*[4] of the *Constitution*[4]. He did hold, however, that under the *police powers*[4], a state "may punish those who abuse this freedom by utterances inimical to the public welfare, tending to corrupt public morals, incite to *crime*[8], or disturb the public peace. . . ." Justices *Oliver Wendell Holmes*[8], *Jr.* and Louis Brandeis dissented on the grounds that the *clear*[9] *and present danger doctrine* should guide considerations of free expression. They believed such a rule came closer than did the bad tendency rule to dealing with actions rather than *theories*[3] or beliefs. The bad tendency doctrine developed during *World*[12] *War I* on the basis of the *Espionage*[9] *Act of 1917*, *the Sedition*[9] *Act of 1918*, and various state *statutes*[8] regulating actions of *pacifists*[12] and persons advocating *sedition*[12]. The doctrine was used in *Abrams*[1] *v. U.S.*, cited as the bad tendency test in *Pierce*[1] *v. U.S.*, and elaborated on in *Gitlow*[1] *v. New York*. The doctrine is less sympathetic to free speech or criticism of public officials, institutions, and practices than is the clear and present danger doctrine.

balancing doctrine. The judicially oriented doctrine which contends that nearly every case brought before the *U.S. Supreme*[8] *Court* involves a situation wherein freedom must be balanced with security and order. The balancing doctrine was most obvious during the 1950's, a period remembered aş the era of *McCarthyism*[9]. The doctrine holds that freedoms are relative to the need for social order and stability. It is often contrasted to the *preferred*[9] (*absolute*) *freedom doctrine*, which views *First Amendment*[9] freedoms as holding a special place in respect to proposed or actual legislative restrictions. See also *American*[1] *Communications Association v. Douds*; *Barenblatt*[1] *v. U.S.*; *prior*[9] *restraint doctrine*.

Bill of Rights (U.S., 1791): see Chap. 4.

Bill of Rights nationalization. The judicial process through which rights contained within the *U.S. Bill*[4] *of Rights* were formerly viewed as applicable only to the *federal government*[3] but which, since the *Supreme*[8] *Court* case of *Gitlow*[1] *v. New York* in 1925, have been increasingly applied to the *states*[3] through judicial interpretation of the *due*[4] *process clause* of the *Fourteenth Amendment*[4]. See also *Barron*[1] *v. Baltimore*; *Palko*[1] *v. Connecticut*; *selective*[9] *incorporation doctrine*.

black code. A specific piece of *legislation*[7] passed within any southern *state*[3] after the *Civil*[4] *War* and during *Reconstruction*[4] to regulate some aspect of Negro life. The *codes*[8] were part of state *constitutions*[3] and general *statutory law*[8]. They covered vagrancy, labor, contracts, land titles, and almost all areas of legal and *civil*[9] *rights*. *Congress*[4] struck against the

black codes in the *Civil*[9] *Rights Act of 1866* by protecting Negroes' rights to make *contracts*[10], own and dispose of land, and to exercise general rights of *citizenship*[3]. See also *Jim*[9] *Crow law*.

black power. A term used to describe the existence of *power*[3] among black persons. The term became a slogan used by some black Americans seeking to unify the Negro *community*[3] in an attempt to gain political, economic, and social power without deference to the white community and power structure. The movement was stimulated by the cry of "black power" as used around 1966 by Stokely Carmichael and other members of the *Student*[5] *Non-violent Coordinating Committee*. See also *Black*[5] *Panthers*.

blockbusting. A situation wherein a real estate operator picks out a neighborhood where all, or almost all, of the residents are of a single race. He spreads the rumor that persons of another race have either moved into the area or soon will move in and that *property*[10] values will drop. He buys up homes at a depressed price and then resells them to members of the feared racial *minority*[9] *group* at inflated prices and thereby makes a socially manipulated profit.

blue law. Any "puritanical" *law*[8] designed to publicly regulate moral standards, especially Sunday activities of a "questionable" nature. See *Sunday Closing Cases*[1].

censorship. The act of examining a writing, object, or other artifact and determining that the general dissemination or showing of it should be prohibited. Censorship is most frequently exercised by legal authorities on the grounds of morality, military necessity, or the well-being or stability of the *state*[3] or *community*[3]. See also *Burstyn*[1] *v. Wilson*; *Comstock*[9] *law*; *gag*[9] *law*; *Hannegan*[1]

v. Esquire; Hicklin[9] test; John Stuart Mill[3]; John Milton[9]; obscenity[9]; pornography[9]; Pornography[9] Report; prior[9] restraint doctrine; prurient[9] interest; Roth[9] test; subsequent[9] punishment doctrine.

child benefit doctrine. A principle judicially enunciated by Associate Justice Hugo Black in the *majority opinion*[8] of the *U.S. Supreme*[8] *Court* case of *Everson*[1] *v. Board of Education.* The Court upheld a New Jersey state *law*[8] which permitted parents to be reimbursed by the *state*[3] for expenses incurred in providing school bus transportation for children attending parochial schools. Justice Black related that such *legislation*[7] was not in violation of the *establishment of religion*[9] *clause* of the *First Amendment*[9], but was designed to benefit children. Such benefits have subsequently been extended to other areas besides bus transportation. See also *Board*[1] *of Education v. Allen*; *purchase*[9] *of services doctrine*; *wall*[9] *of separation doctrine.*

civil disobedience. The action of an individual or a group which publicly, nonviolently, and with no resistance to arrest breaks a *law*[8] in order to bring about a change in the law or the social structure. See also *Jean Bodin*[3]; *Martin Luther King*[9], *Jr.*; *sit-in*[9]; *Henry David Thoreau*[4].

civil rights. Rights legally belonging to an individual because of his membership within the *state*[3]. Civil rights are generally specified by *constitutional*[3] or *statutory*[8] provisions and are given their basic protection under the concept of *due*[9] *process of law*. See also *Administrative*[2] *Conference of the United States*; *American*[5] *Civil Liberties Union*; *Bill*[4] *of Rights* (*U.S.*); *Bill*[9] *of Rights nationalization*; *Civil*[9] *Rights Acts of 1866, 1875, 1957, 1960, 1964, and 1968*; *Commission on Civil*[2] *Rights*; *Committee*[8] *on the Judiciary* (*U.S. Senate*); *due*[4] *process clause*; *Equal*[2] *Employment Opportunity Commission*; *equal*[4] *protection clause*; *full*[4] *faith and credit clause*; *Kerner*[8] *Commission Report*; *minority*[9] *group*; *National*[5] *Association for the Advancement of Colored People*; *nationalized rights*[9]; *National*[5] *Urban League*; *privileges*[4] *and immunities clause*; *Southern*[5] *Christian Leadership Conference*; *Student*[5] *Nonviolent Coordinating Committee*; *To*[9] *Secure These Rights*; *white primary*[5]; selected case listings on *constitutional*[3] rights at the end of Chap. 9.

Civil Rights Act of 1866. The first *federal*[3] act to define *citizenship*[3] and attempt to guarantee the *civil*[9] *rights* of all persons regardless of race. The *act*[8] guaranteed rights related to *contracts*[10], *property*[10] ownership, civil suits, legal testimony in court, and other basic areas. The *legislation*[7] was designed to destroy the *black*[9] *codes* that had grown up in the southern *states*[3] after the *Civil*[4] *War*. See also *Jones*[1] *v. Alfred H. Mayer Co.*

Civil Rights Act of 1875. A *federal*[3] *law*[8] which made it illegal for any person in any *state*[3] to deny equal public accommodations or services to persons of another race. The major provisions of the civil rights act were declared *unconstitutional*[3] in the Civil Rights Cases of 1883 on the grounds that such *discriminatory*[9] actions are private in nature. See also *black*[9] codes.

Civil Rights Act of 1957. The first *federal*[3] civil rights *law*[8] passed by the *U.S. Congress*[4] since *Reconstruction*[4]. The *legislation*[7] created the *Commission on Civil*[2] *Rights* and guaranteed federal protection for Negroes exercising rights related to voting, education, housing, and other areas. The *act*[8] placed the burden of protection of *civil*[9] *rights* on the U.S. *Department of Justice*[2] rather than the individual Negro. It gave permission for the *Attorney*[8] *General* to institute civil suits in federal *District Courts*[8] to protect the Negro's right to vote. See also *civil law*[8]; *Civil*[9] *Rights Act of 1960*.

Civil Rights Act of 1960. A major piece of *federal*[3] *legislation*[7] which modified the *Civil*[9] *Rights Act of 1957* by strengthening the *Department of Justice*[2] and its *powers*[3] to protect the voting rights of Negroes. The *Attorney*[8] *General* was given the power to halt *state*[3] *discriminatory*[9] practices, require the preservation of voting records, and assign voting referees to protect the *civil*[9] *rights* of all *citizens*[3] of the U.S.

Civil Rights Act of 1964. The most comprehensive single piece of *federal*[3] *civil*[9] *rights legislation*[7] endorsed by the *U.S. Congress*[4] between *Reconstruction*[4] and the civil rights *revolution*[3] of the 1960's. The *law*[8] expanded the *powers*[3] of the *Commission on Civil*[2] *Rights* and extended its life until 1968, created a Community Relations Service within the *Department of Commerce*[2] to help local *communities*[3] deal with racial problems, provided voter *registration*[5] protection for Negroes, forbade *discrimination*[9] in public accommodations engaged in *interstate commerce*[10], forbade discrimination in publicly owned and operated facilities, provided federal financial assistance to public schools seeking to desegregate, created an *Equal*[2] *Employment Opportunity Commission* to investigate charges of discrimination in private hiring practices and *labor*[10] *union* activities, and permitted the withholding of federal funds from federally financed programs within the *states*[3] if discrimination could be proved. Various provisions of the law permit the U.S. *Attorney*[8] *General's* office to bring *desegregation*[9] suits in the name of the U.S., thereby relieving those discriminated against from the burden of bringing legal action themselves.

The "public accommodations" section of the Civil Rights Act of 1964 was upheld by the *U.S. Supreme*[8] *Court* in 1964 in the case of *Heart*[1] *of Atlanta Motel v. U.S.*

Civil Rights Act of 1968. A *federal*[3] law passed partially as a result of the assassination of *Martin Luther King*[9], *Jr.*, a *law*[8] which was primarily directed at prohibiting racial *discrimination*[9] in housing. The act also provided protection to *civil*[9] *rights* workers, regulated riots connected with civil liberties, and guaranteed certain rights for American Indians. See also *open*[9] *occupancy law*.

clear and present danger doctrine. A doctrine judicially developed by Justice *Oliver Wendell Holmes*[8], *Jr.* in the *U.S. Supreme*[8] *Court* case of *Schenck*[1] *v. U.S.*, a case involving the freedom of expression and restrictions placed on expression by the *Espionage*[9] *Act of 1917*. Holmes stated: "The question in every case is whether the words used are used in circumstances and are of such a nature as to create a clear and present danger that they will bring about the substantive evils that Congress has a right to prevent." The clear and present danger doctrine is in contrast to the *bad*[9] *tendency doctrine* which permits officials more leeway in restricting the freedom of expression. See also *Abrams*[1] *v. U.S.*; *Dennis*[1] *v. U.S.*; *Pierce*[1] *v. U.S.*; *sedition*[12]; *Sedition*[9] *Act of 1918*.

Communist Control Act of 1954. A *federal*[3] law which denied any political privileges to the *Communist Party*[5] or any *organization*[6] specifically seeking to overthrow the *federal government*[3] by *force*[3] or violence. The *law*[8] did not make it a criminal offense to belong to the Communist Party, although the party was essentially outlawed through the *legislation*[7]. Various *U.S. Supreme*[8] *Court* decisions of the 1960's opened the door for Communist Party political participation, and the party entered a candidate in the presidential election of 1968, the first such participation since 1940. See also *Alien*[9] *Registration (Smith) Act of 1940*.

Comstock law. The popular designation of any *legislation*[7] which based the determination of *obscenity*[9] on the moral level of a child. Such a view held that isolated passages of written material capable of corrupting a child should be *censored*[9]. The concept was introduced in the English case of Queen v. Hicklin in 1868 and was popularized in the U.S. by the Reverend Anthony Comstock, leader of the New York Society for the Suppression of Vice (founded in 1873). The *Hicklin*[9] *test* and the "Comstock laws" were discredited and a new basis for determining obscenity (the *Roth*[9] *test*) was declared by the *U.S. Supreme*[8] *Court* in 1957 in the case of *Roth*[1] *v. U.S.* See also *pornography*[9].

conscientious objector. A person who refuses to serve in the military forces of a *nation*[3] on the grounds that he has moral or religious convictions against killing. See also *pacificism*[12]; *U.S.*[1] *v. Gillette*; *U.S.*[1] *v. Seeger*.

desegregation. The act or process of abolishing or abandoning the practice of *segregation*[9]. See also *discrimination*[9]; *integration*[9]; case listings on "Racial Rights" at end of Chap. 9.

discrimination. The act of drawing a distinction on the basis of perceived value assumptions. Discrimination in the area of *constitutional*[3] rights generally involves one person or group actively engaging in social and legal practices which work to the detriment of another person or group. See also *antimiscegenation*[9] *law*; *black*[9] *code*; *de facto segregation*[9]; *Equal*[2] *Employment Opportunity Commission*; *fair*[9] *employment practice law*; *grandfather*[5] *clause*; *Jim*[9] *Crow law*; *literacy*[5] *test*; *open*[9] *occupancy law*; *poll*

tax[5]; *segregation*[9]; *separate*[9] *but equal doctrine*; *white primary*[5]; case listings on "Racial Rights" at end of Chap. 9.

double jeopardy. The condition of being placed on trial twice for the same *crime*[8]. Double jeopardy is prohibited to both the national and *state*[3] governments. Trial of a person by both *federal*[3] and state governments for the same offense is not considered double jeopardy if both *governments*[3] have legal *jurisdiction*[8] over the same matter. Trial by both civil and military courts for the same offense might avoid the classification of double jeopardy because of the nature of jurisdiction, especially if it involves a foreign *state*[3]. See also *Bartkus*[1] *v. Illinois*; *Benton*[1] *v. Maryland*; *Fifth Amendment*[9]; *Palko*[1] *v. Connecticut*; *shocking*[9] *to the conscience doctrine*.

due process clauses: see Chap. 4.

due process of law. The guarantee that *government*[3] will not arbitrarily encroach on the basic rights of individuals. Due process originated in *common law*[8] and is the basis of *limited government*[3]. The concept in the U.S. is embodied within the *U.S. Bill*[4] *of Rights* and is applied to the actions of the *federal government*[3] in the *Fifth Amendment*[9] and to the actions of the *states*[3] in the *Fourteenth Amendment*[4]. Due process as a concept has been given basic direction through judicial interpretations of the *U.S. Supreme*[8] *Court*. For example, various rights originally protected from federal violation only, have been "nationalized" through the application of the *due*[4] *process clause* in the Fourteenth Amendment to the due process clause in the Fifth Amendment. Also, on occasion the Supreme Court has viewed the clause as applying to procedures of the *law*[8], a viewpoint referred to as *procedural due*[9] *process*. On other occasions the Court has dealt with the substance of the law, an application known as *substantive due⁹ process.* See also *Barron¹ v. Baltimore; Benton¹ v. Maryland; Bill⁹ of Rights nationalization; Bolling¹ v. Sharpe; Gault¹, in re; Lochner¹ v. New York; Munn¹ v. Illinois; nationalized rights⁹; Palko¹ v. Connecticut.*

due process, procedural. The judicial concept that *government³* officials and courts of *law⁸* should proceed fairly against persons accused of violating the norms of *society³* and the rules of government. Among the positive procedural rights guaranteed in the U.S. *Constitution⁴* are the right to a fair trial, the right to legal counsel, and the right to use of the *writ of habeas⁸ corpus* to avoid arbitrary arrest and confinement. The Constitution places due process restrictions on the use of *bills of attainder⁹, cruel and unusual punishment⁹, double⁹ jeopardy, ex⁹ post facto laws,* and *self-incrimination⁹.* See also *due⁴ process clause; due⁹ process of law; Gault¹, in re; McNabb¹ v. U.S.; Mallory¹ v. U.S.; Miranda¹ v. Arizona; Palko¹ v. Connecticut.*

due process, substantive. The judicial concept that a court of *law⁸* has the responsibility to deal with the substance of *legislation⁷* as well as how legislation is enforced against individuals and *organizations⁶* within the social *community³.* In essence, a court may determine whether a law is "reasonable" and within the scope of governmental *power³.* See also *due⁴ process clause; due⁹ process of law; Dred¹ Scott v. Sandford; Hepburn¹ v. Griswold; Munn¹ v. Illinois; Nebbia¹ v. New York.*

Emancipation Proclamation (1863). A proclamation issued January 1, 1863 by *President⁶ Abraham Lincoln⁶,* stating that all slaves in *territory³* not under *federal³* control should be considered free. See also *abolitionist⁹.*

eminent domain. The *authority³* of *government³* to take private *property¹⁰*

for public use on the condition that just compensation be paid for property. The guarantee of the proper use of eminent domain is covered in the *Fifth Amendment⁹.* Conflicts over what constitutes "just compensation" are usually settled in courts of *law⁸.* See also *Berman¹ v. Parker.*

equal protection clause: see Chap. 4.

Espionage Act of 1917. A *federal³* law passed to restrict open criticism of the U.S. government during *World¹² War I.* The *law⁸* restricted publications, criticism of the military *draft¹²,* and the use of *federal government³* documents and defense information. Various violations of the *act⁸* called for extreme fines, lengthy imprisonment, or the death sentence. The *legislation⁷* was *amended³* by the *Sedition⁹ Act of 1918.* See also *Abrams¹ v. U.S.; bad⁹ tendency doctrine; clear⁹ and present doctrine; Pierce¹ v. U.S.; Schenck¹ v. U.S.*

exclusionary doctrine. The judicial concept or "rule" that any evidence secured through improper means should be barred as evidence in a court of *law⁸.* See also *Mapp¹ v. Ohio; silver⁹ platter doctrine; unreasonable search⁹ and seizure; Weeks¹ v. U.S.; wiretap⁹; Wolf¹ v. Colorado.*

ex post facto law. A retroactive *criminal law⁸* which makes an action illegal after the fact, increases the penalty for an offense already committed, or revises the rules of evidence to the disadvantage of the accused. Ex post facto laws are forbidden to either *state³* or *federal governments³* within the provisions of the U.S. *Constitution⁴* (Art. I, Secs. 9 and 10). See also *Calder¹ v. Bull; retroactive legislation⁷.*

fair employment practice law. Any *law⁸* specifically designed to protect workers and employees from *discriminatory⁹* practices related to race, color, creed, nationality, or other arbitrary criteria. See also *Fair[9] Employment Practices Commission.*

Fair Employment Practices Commission (FEPC). Any commission established by *government[3]* to provide equal employment opportunities for all persons regardless of race, color, creed, nationality, or other arbitrary criteria. During *World[12] War II* the *federal government[3]* used such an agency, which was created through *executive[6] order.* A number of *states[3]* have used such bodies to combat *discriminatory[9]* labor and employment practices. See also *fair[9] employment practice law.*

fairness (equal time) doctrine: see Chap. 5.

Federal Communications Act of 1934. The *federal[3] legislation[7]* which created the *Federal[2] Communications Commission* and granted the agency broad regulatory *powers[3]* over the broadcasting industry. Section 315 of the act is the "equal time" provision which allows equal time under the *fairness[5] doctrine* to major political candidates during an election campaign and rebuttal time outside an election campaign if the airwaves have been used in a *partisan[5]* fashion. Section 605 contains 31 words which allow for *wiretapping[9]* by law enforcement officers. The words are usually interpreted to mean that wiretaps may be made, but that the information gathered may not be used as evidence in a court of *law[8].* The section reads: ". . . no person not being authorized by the sender shall intercept any communication and divulge or publish the existence, contents, substance, purport, effect or meaning of such intercepted communication to any person." See also *Berger[1] v. New York; Katz[1] v. U.S.; Nardone[1] v. U.S.; Olmstead[1] v. U.S.; Red[1] Lion Broadcasting Co. v. FCC.*

First Amendment freedoms: see *First Amendment[9].*

freedom of choice plan. A controversial public educational system used in some southern *states[3]* after 1954 to permit parents to choose between public and private educational institutions for their children's education. A state using such a plan generally authorized state grants up to a set figure ($185, $240, etc. per pupil per school year) in order that children could attend private and nonsectarian schools. Freedom of choice plans helped perpetuate *de facto segregation[9]* and were regularly declared *unconstitutional[3]* by *federal[3]* appeals courts on the grounds that such plans fostered the development of private *segregated[9]* schools and avoided *desegregation[9]* of the public schools as ordered by the *U.S. Supreme[8] Court* in *Brown[1] v. Board of Education* in 1954. In *Green[1] v. County School Board of New Kent County, Virginia,* such plans were questioned unless they actually aided in desegregration. However, such plans were declared unconstitutional by the Supreme Court in the Mississippi case of *Alexander[1] v. Holmes.*

freedom ride. An action whereby an individual or a group embarks on a publicized journey designed to bring about a change in the social structure or *laws[8]* restrictive of personal dignity and freedom. The *Congress[5] of Racial Equality* (CORE) sent the first freedom ride into the South in April 1947. An *integrated[9]* freedom ride movement sponsored by CORE and the *Student[5] Non-violent Coordinating Committee* captured national attention and sympathy for *civil[9] rights* advocates in 1961. See also *Southern[5] Christian Leadership Conference.*

gag law. Any *law[8]* specifically designed to violate any form of the freedom of expression. See also *Bantam[1] Books, Inc. v. Sullivan; censorship[9]; Near[1] v. Minnesota; prior[9] restraint doctrine.*

grandfather clause: see Chap. 5.

guilt by association. Assumption on the part of *government*[3] officials or the general public that a person is guilty of some violation because of his present associations or past memberships in *organizations*[6] or social groups viewed as subversive or socially unacceptable. See also *Adler*[1] *v. Board of Education*; *discrimination*[9]; *McCarthyism*[9]; *Watkins*[1] *v. U.S.*

Hicklin test. The judicial concept related to *obscenity*[9] which was handed down by Lord Cockburn in the English case of Queen v. Hicklin in 1868. The meaning of obscenity was defined as ". . . whether the tendency of the matter charged as obscene is to deprave and corrupt those whose minds are open to such immoral influences and into whose hands a publication of this sort may fall." The concept set obscenity at the moral level of a child. It also held that isolated passages could be considered obscene and dealt with accordingly through *censorship*[9]. The doctrine was accepted in the U.S. largely under the influence of Reverend Anthony Comstock, but was eventually rejected by the *U.S. Supreme*[8] *Court* in 1957 and was replaced with the *Roth*[9] test set forth in *Roth*[1] *v. U.S.* See also *Comstock*[9] *law*; *pornography*[9].

immunity bath. The judicial practice of permitting or requiring a *defendant*[8] or witness in a criminal trial or legislative investigation to testify on matters deemed essential to the proceeding but which could involve *self-incrimination*[9]. A person may be compelled or else face a charge of *contempt*[8] *of court*. However, such compulsion assures a person testifying that he cannot be tried in *federal*[3] or *state*[3] courts on the evidence revealed in testimony. See also *Ullmann*[1] *v. U.S.*

integration. The act or process of taking component parts and making them into one unit. The word "integration" has been used mostly in the political and social context of the U.S. to refer to the removal of legal barriers which previously separated or *segregated*[9] the black and white races. See also *desegregation*[9]; *discrimination*[9]; case listings on "Racial Rights" at the end of Chap. 9.

Internal Security (McCarran) Act of 1950. A *federal*[3] *law*[8] passed over the *absolute veto*[7] of *President*[6] *Harry Truman*[6] in 1950. The *act*[8] prohibited the existence of groups designed to place the U.S. *federal government*[3] under foreign control or a *totalitarian*[3] *dictatorship*[3], required the registration of *Communist*[3] action and Communist *front organizations*[5], and created the *Subversive*[2] *Activities Control Board* to oversee the registration of designated *organizations*[6]. The act sought to regulate Communist involvement in *propaganda*[5] distribution, *labor*[10] *union* activity, foreign travel, public officeholding, and defense employment. However, much of the act has been declared *unconstitutional*[3] and the *power*[3] of the Board has been almost totally destroyed. See also *Albertson*[1] *v. SACB*; *Aptheker*[1] *v. Secretary of State*; *Communist*[1] *Party v. SACB*.

Jencks Act of 1957. A *federal*[3] *law*[8] passed in order to overcome the difficulties stemming from a *U.S. Supreme*[8] *Court* decision involving Clifford E. Jencks, a *labor*[10] *union* official *indicted*[8] for violation of *legislation*[7] regulating *Communist*[3] involvement in labor activities. It was held in *Jencks*[1] *v. U.S.* that *Federal*[2] *Bureau of Investigation* files should be opened to a *defendant*[8] in order that he might build an adequate defense. The legislation permits a trial judge to delete unrelated material from items involving national security before allowing a defendant to examine material relevant to his defense.

Jim Crow law. A *law*[8] designed to *segregate*[9] or systematically *discriminate*[9] against black persons. Jim Crow laws were especially prevalent between 1880 and 1954. They regulated almost every area of the American Negro's life. They were upheld by the *U.S. Supreme[8] Court* in 1896 under the *separate[9] but equal doctrine* and judicially rejected in 1954. See also *black[9] code*; *Brown[1] v. Board of Education*; *Plessy[1] v. Ferguson*; *Reconstruction[4]*.

Kerner Commission Report: see Chap. 8.

King, Martin Luther, Jr., 1929–68. American *civil[9] rights* leader, Baptist minister, and leading modern exponent of the doctrine of *civil[9] disobedience*. King gained national attention in 1956 as the Negro leader of a *boycott[10]* of public bus service in Montgomery, Alabama, a successful boycott designed to *desegregate[9]* public facilities. The Montgomery bus boycott is ordinarily recognized as the first organized civil rights effort in the South. King outlined his civil rights strategy and recounted the story of his activities in such volumes as Stride Toward Freedom (1958), Why We Can't Wait (1964), and Where Do We Go From Here: Chaos or Community? (1967). He served as president of the *Southern[5] Christian Leadership Conference* (SCLC), led major civil rights demonstrations in Birmingham and Selma, Alabama, led a massive civil rights march on *Washington[4]*, D.C. in 1963, and was assassinated during a garbage workers *strike[10]* in Memphis, Tennessee in 1968. See also *sit-in[9]*.

libel. Deliberate defamation of character through any written or visual form which tends to injure the reputation or business of another person or group. Libel may be dealt with under both *civil law[9]* and *criminal law[9]*, depending on the nature of the act of libel. It may be considered group libel if it defames the character of an entire social or *minority[9]* group. See also *Beauharnais[1] v. Illi-*

nois; *legislative[7] immunity*; *Monitor[1] Patriot v. Roy*; *New[1] York Times Co. v. Sullivan*; *question[7] of privilege*; *slander[9]*.

literacy test: see Chap. 5.

loyalty oath. Any oath whereby an individual declares his allegiance to his own *government[3]* and its institutions and disclaims any support of foreign *ideologies[3]* or associations. The usefulness of the loyalty oath has been determined primarily by judicial interpretation. Loyalty oaths have been required of various classifications of public officials and persons working in "sensitive" government positions. However, oaths too vague to clearly specify what constitutes *seditious[12]* acts and utterances have been declared *unconstitutional[3]*. See also *Adler[1] v. Board of Education*; *American[1] Communications Association v. Douds*; *Attorney[9] General's list*; *Cole[1] v. Young*; *Garner[1] v. Board of Public Works*; *Keyishian[1] v. Board of Regents*.

lynch law. A popular term of disputed origin used to describe summary punishment meted out to a person deprived of *due[9] process of law*. Lynch law, frequently carried out by *vigilantes[9]* or members of the *Ku[5] Klux Klan*, was most used against black persons in the U.S. between *Reconstruction[4]* and 1952.

McCarthyism. The indiscriminate use of loose accusations by those seeking to cast doubts on the loyalty of selected public officials and private individuals. The term arose to describe the activities of *Senator[7]* Joseph McCarthy of Wisconsin, a senator who was *censured[7]* by the *Senate[7]* in 1954 for the use of questionable and *slanderous[9]* investigative tactics of "character assassination" and *guilt[9] by association* ostensibly to protect national security from *Communist[3]* subversion. See also *balancing[9] doctrine*.

Mill, John Stuart: see Chap. 3.

Milton, John 1608–74. English poet, social critic, and author of the controversial civil libertarian volume entitled Areopagitica: A Speech of Mr. John Milton for the Liberty of Unlicensed Printing, to the Parliament of England (1644). The work was an unlicensed and unregistered attack on official *censorship*[9]. Milton specifically attacked parliamentary censorship which had replaced the censor of the Court of the Star Chamber, a device that had passed from the scene in 1641. Areopagitica, framed in Greek oratorical form, is a review of the history of censorship, an argument for truth in any form, and an indictment of the ineffectiveness of governmental censorship. Milton would accept censorship of those who definitely threaten the social base ("popery and open superstition"), but he believed that a free *society*[3] can rest only on a free press. Milton's views greatly influenced men such as *John Stuart Mill*[3] and modern defenders of what is known as the *preferred*[9] *(absolute) freedom doctrine.*

minority group. Any group (national, social, political, racial, religious, etc.) that is composed of less than one-half of a total body of persons and which holds a position of relative weakness or inferiority within the larger group. See also *civil*[9] *rights; discrimination*[9]; *Equal*[2] *Employment Opportunity Commission; minority*[3].

Myrdal, Gunnar, 1898– . The Swedish economist, sociologist, and *government*[3] official who wrote The American Dilemma (1944), a classic statement of the racial problems of the American Negro in the U.S. The work, endowed by the Carnegie Corporation, viewed the American dilemma as a "moral lag in the development of the nation." The dilemma became especially apparent after *World*[12] *War I*, a *war*[12] fought in the name of

democracy[3] by a *nation*[3] unwilling to act in a democratic way toward a portion of its own people. The American Dilemma analyzed the nature of democracy, racial attitudes and beliefs, population characteristics, economics, *politics*[3], legal rights, social interaction, and other appropriate variables related to the American Negro.

obscenity. Having the quality of being offensive to accepted *community*[3] standards of decency. See also *Bantam*[1] *Books, Inc. v. Sullivan; Ginsberg*[1] *v. New York; Ginsburg*[1] *v. U.S.; Hicklin*[9] *test; pornography*[9]; *prurient*[9] *interest; Roth*[9] *test; Roth*[1] *v. U.S.; Rowan*[1] *v. U.S. Post Office Department; Stanley*[1] *v. Georgia.*

open occupancy law. Any *law*[8] promulgated to combat racially *discriminatory*[9] practices in housing or public accommodations. Both *federal*[3] and *state*[3] open occupancy laws have been upheld as *constitutional*[3] and not in violation of private rights to own and dispose of *property*[10]. See also *Buchanan*[1] *v. Warley; Civil*[9] *Rights Act of 1866; Civil*[9] *Rights Act of 1968; Heart*[1] *of Atlanta Motel v. U.S.; Jones*[1] *v. Alfred H. Mayer Co.; Reitman*[1] *v. Mulkey; restrictive*[9] *covenant; Shelley*[1] *v. Kraemer.*

peonage. Involuntary servitude based on compulsory service required for the repayment of a debt. Peonage is prohibited by the *Thirteenth Amendment*[4]. See also *Pollock*[1] *v. Williams.*

perjury. The deliberate and willful telling of a lie while under oath in a court of *law*[8] or other appropriate legal body. Responding to a legal affidavit in an untruthful way is also classified as perjury. See also *Harris*[1] *v. N.Y.*

police state. A *state*[3] that maintains *totalitarian*[3] control of *society*[3] through *force*[3] and repressive measures exercised through the pervasive use of police personnel.

pornography. Any written or visual communications specifically designed to excite sexual feelings. See also *Hicklin*[9] *test*; *obscenity*[9]; *Pornography*[9] *Report*; *Roth*[9] *test*.

Pornography Report (1970). A report released in September 1970 by the Federal Commission on Obscenity and Pornography. The report called for the repeal of all *federal*[3], *state*[3], and *municipal*[11] *laws*[8] prohibiting the selling and distribution of materials related to sexual expression. It also called for a massive sex education program, restrictions on materials available to minors, advertising restrictions on sexually explicit materials, and continued research into the the influence of *pornography*[9] on morality. The *commission*[6] which released the report was appointed during the *administration*[6] of *President*[6] *Lyndon B. Johnson*[6] and reported its findings during the adminstration of President Richard Nixon. The commission of 18 members had 5 dissenting members who rejected the highly controversial report on the grounds that the research in the document was "scanty and manipulated." The *minority*[3] upheld traditional views of pornography and its effects on *society*[3] while the *majority*[3] held that pornography cannot be shown to cause *crime*[8], delinquency, sexual deviancy, or emotional disturbance. President Nixon, other adminstration officials, and the single commission member appointed by President Nixon rejected the findings of the majority members before the report was officially released. See also *obscenity*[9].

preferred (absolute) freedom doctrine. The judicial doctrine that the *U.S. Constitution*[4] gives a special place to the *First Amendment*[9] freedoms. The preferred freedom interpretation holds that *legislation*[7] touching on the freedoms of speech, press, and religion must present overwhelming arguments before restrictions may be placed on them. The doctrine was

mentioned by *U.S. Supreme*[8] *Court* Justice Harlan F. Stone in a footnote in *U.S.*[1] *v. Carolene Products Co.*, a case involving *interstate commerce*[10]. After he became *Chief*[8] *Justice*, Stone stated the doctrine in a *dissenting opinion*[8] in Jones v. Opelika (1942), a case involving the fredom to sell religious books without a *municipal*[11] license. When the Court said sales could be restricted, he disagreed and said that the First Amendment freedoms had been placed in a "preferred position." In Murdock v. Pennsylvania (1943), a decision reversing Jones v. Opelika, Justice William O. Douglas emphasized the doctrine by stating: "Freedom of press, freedom of speech, freedom of religion are in a preferred position." See also *balancing*[9] *doctrine*; *John Milton*[9].

prejudice. An emotional state wherein a person or group has unfavorable opinions about another individual group, or thing, without adequate information to determine that the adverse opinions are reasonably or properly held. Numerous prejudices are frequently translated into legally *discriminatory*[9] actions against those persons or groups viewed unfavorably. See also *demagogue*[5]; *segregation*[9].

prior restraint doctrine. The doctrine which stresses that *First Amendment*[9] freedoms may occasionally be legally circumscribed and *censored*[9] on the basis that they might be abused in such a way as to disturb public order. The doctrine of prior restraint has ordinarily been rejected in *U.S. Supreme*[8] *Court* decisions dealing with *First Amendment*[9] freedoms. In the 1971 controversy involving the *Pentagon*[12] *Papers*, the U.S. *federal government*[3] acted through federal courts for the first time to place a prior restraint on publication of materials considered sensitive to the national interest. Such action was declared *unconstitutional*[3] in *New*[1] *York Times v. U. S.* See also *balancing*[9] *doctrine*; *Bantam*[1] *Books, Inc. v. Sullivan*; *Git-*

low[1] *v. New York*; *Near*[1] *v. Minnesota*; *subsequent*[9] *punishment doctrine*; *Times*[1] *Film Corp. v. Chicago*.

privacy, right of. A constitutionally protected and basic human right which is guaranteed by various provisions in the *U.S. Constitution*[4]. Among the protections are prohibitions against the quartering of soldiers, *unreasonable search*[9] *and seizure*, *self-incrimination*[9], and various provisions permitting the freedom of expression and association. In *Griswold*[1] *v. Connecticut* the *Supreme*[8] *Court* specifically cited the right of privacy as a *constitutional*[3] guarantee. The Constitution states in the *Ninth Amendment*[9]: "The enumeration in the Constitution, of certain rights, shall not be construed to deny or disparage others retained by the people."

privileges and immunities clauses: see Chap. 4.

prurient interest. Possessed of lustful or lascivious desires or an extreme obsession with sexual matters. Prurient interest is one of the criteria for determining whether something may be classified as *obscene*[9]. See also *pornography*[9]; *Roth*[9] *test*; *Roth*[1] *v. U.S.*

punishment, cruel and unusual. Any socially unacceptable, arbitrary, or inhumane punishment inflicted on a person accused of or convicted of violating legal regulations formulated by *government*[3] or accepted *authority*[3]. Cruel and unusual punishments are prohibited by the *Eighth Amendment*[9]. See also *Robinson*[1] *v. California*; *Trop*[1] *v. Dulles*.

purchase of services doctrine. The religious-educational concept that governmental revenue funds may be granted to religious schools as long as the funds are used to purchase "secular" services for the religious schools. Such services are usually in the form of textbook loans or educational instruction in the fields of science, modern languages, mathematics, physical education, and other nonreligious subjects. The *U.S. Supreme*[8] *Court* decision of *Lemon*[1] *v. Kurtzman* declared such a plan in the *state*[3] of Pennsylvania *unconstitutional*[3]. See also *child*[9] *benefit doctrine*; *Elementary*[11] *and Secondary Education Act of 1965*; *wall*[9] *of separation doctrine*.

reasonable man doctrine. The judicially enunciated *theory*[3] that legislative enactments in the form of *law*[8] should be upheld by the *U.S. Supreme*[8] *Court* if a "reasonable man" could reach the same conclusions as the *legislature*[7] that passed the law. The doctrine was especially evident in the Supreme Court cases of *Gitlow*[1] *v. New York* and *Lochner*[1] *v. New York*. Justice *Oliver Wendell Holmes*[8], *Jr.*, a leading exponent of the theory, stated in his dissent in the Lochner decision that he would not declare any law *unconstitutional*[3] ". . . unless it can be said that a rational and fair man necessarily would admit that the *statute*[8] proposed would infringe fundamental principles as they have been understood by the traditions of our people and our law." See also *dissenting opinion*[8].

released time doctrine. The doctrine that public school students should be released from regular school classes during the classroom day in order to attend classes of religious instruction. Released time programs using public facilities were declared *unconstitutional*[3] in *McCollum*[1] *v. Board of Education*, whereas those using off-campus facilities were upheld as *constitutional*[3] in *Zorach*[1] *v. Clauson*. See also *wall*[9] *of separation doctrine*.

religion clause, establishment of. The provision within the *First Amendment*[9] of the *U.S. Constitution*[4] which states: "Congress shall make no law respecting an establishment of religion. . . ." The clause prohibits all *laws*[8] respecting such an establishment and acknowledges the *theory*[3] of separation of church and *state*[3]. The principle is not "absolute," but has been given basic development through judicial interpretation. See also *Engel*[1] *v. Vitale*; *Everson*[1] *v. Board of Education*; *Flast*[1] *v. Cohen*; *free exercise of religion*[9] *clause*; *School*[1] *District of Abington Township v. Schempp*; *wall*[9] *of separation doctrine*; *Walz*[1] *v. Tax Commission of the City of New York*.

religion clause, free exercise of. The second portion of the provision of the *First Amendment*[9] within the U.S. *Constitution*[4] which states: "Congress shall make no law respecting an establishment of religion, or prohibiting the free exercise thereof. . . ." The clause prohibits governmental interference with basic and socially acceptable religious practices. The principle is not "absolute," but has been given basic development through judicial interpretation. See also *Cantwell*[1] *v. Connecticut*; *establishment of religion*[9] *clause*; *Flast*[1] *v. Cohen*; *McCollum*[1] *v. Board of Education*; *Minersville*[1] *School District v. Gobitis*; *Pierce*[1] *v. Society of Sisters*; *Reynolds*[1] *v. U.S.*; *Sherbert*[1] *v. Verner*; *Torcasco*[1] *v. Watkins*; *wall*[9] *of separation doctrine*; *Walz*[1] *v. Tax Commission of the City of New York*; *West*[1] *Virginia State Board of Education v. Barnette*; *Zorach*[1] *v. Clauson*.

restrictive covenant. A restrictive clause incorporated within a deed in order to limit the future use of the *property*[10] in question. Restrictive covenants involving race are not illegal, but they may not be enforced in a court of *law*[8] because they violate the *equal*[4] *protection clause* of the *Fourteenth Amendment*[4]. See also *open*[9] *occupancy law*; *Shelley*[1] *v. Kramer*.

rights, absolute. The concept that certain rights should be judicially pro-

tected even if no actual *statutes*[8] grant them such protection. See also *relative rights*[9]; *vested rights*[9].

rights, civil: see *civil*[9] *rights.*

rights, nationalized. Rights contained within the U.S. *Bill*[4] *of Rights* which previously protected individuals only against *federal*[3] encroachment but not against *state*[3] impairment. Through judicial interpretation of the *Fourteenth Amendment*[4] *due*[4] *process clause*, various *civil*[9] *rights* within the Bill of Rights now protect individuals within the states from both *governments*[3]. See also *Barron*[1] *v. Baltimore*; *Bill*[9] *of Rights nationalization*; *equal*[4] *protection clause*; *Fifth Amendment*[9]; *First Amendment*[9]; *Gitlow*[1] *v. New York*; *Palko*[1] *v. Connecticut*; *selective*[9] *incorporation doctrine.*

rights, relative. The concept that rights are relative to social circumstances and other individuals within *society*[3]. The doctrine is in contrast to the idea of *absolute rights*[9].

rights, vested. A doctrine which holds that certain rights such as life and *property*[10] ownership are so fundamental to an individual that *government*[3] has no—or perhaps at most only a minimal—right to control them. Government was originally created to protect such basic rights rather than to regulate them. The doctrine of vested rights grew primarily out of the *natural rights*[3] philosophies of the eighteenth century. See also *absolute rights*[9].

Roth test. The judicial interpretation related to *obscenity*[9] which holds that the determination of what is obscene should be based on the grounds of "whether to the average person, applying contemporary *community*[3] standards, the dominant theme of the material taken as a whole appeals to *prurient*[9] interest." The Roth test as applied by the U.S. *Supreme*[8] *Court* in *Roth*[1] *v. U.S.* marked a turning point in the rejection of the *Hicklin*[9] *test*, a concept which based the determination of obscenity and *pornography*[9] at the level of that which would adversely influence a child. See also *Comstock*[9] *law*.

search and seizure, unreasonable. A search of a person or *property*[10] which is undertaken without proper *warrant*[8] specifying the cause of the search, the area to be searched, or the items to be seized. The concept of unreasonable search and seizure, a *common law*[8] concept largely developed through judicial interpretations of the *U.S. Supreme*[8] *Court*, is prohibited by the *Fourth Amendment*[9]. See also *Berger*[1] *v. New York*; *exclusionary*[9] *doctrine*; *Katz*[1] *v. U.S.*; *Mapp*[1] *v. Ohio*; *Nardone*[1] *v. U.S.*; *Olmstead*[1] *v. U.S.*; *right of privacy*[9]; *Rochin*[1] *v. California*; *Weeks*[1] *v. U.S.*; *Wolf*[1] *v. Colorado*.

Sedition Act of 1918. A *federal*[3] law which *amended*[3] the *Espionage*[9] *Act of 1917*. The *law*[8] prohibited interference with the sale of U.S. *bonds*[10], restricted expression critical of the U.S. *federal government*[3] and its symbols, prohibited obstruction of military recruitment (*draft*[12]), and prohibited anyone from hindering the production of necessary *war*[12] materials. See also *Abrams*[1] *v. U.S.*; *bad*[9] *tendency doctrine*; *clear*[9] *and present danger doctrine*; *Schenck*[1] *v. U.S.*; *sedition*[12]; *World*[12] *War I*.

segregation. A method of *discrimination*[9] among persons or groups which establishes arbitrary social, economic, and political *boundaries*[12] between the persons or groups. Racial and other forms of segregation are usually designed to benefit a group controlling *power*[3] and work to the detriment of some group considered inferior. Segregation of black and white *citizens*[3] of the U.S. was accepted *constitutional*[3] *policy*[6] between 1896 and 1954. See also *antimiscegenation*[9] *law*; *black*[9] *code*; *de facto segregation*[9];

fair[9] *employment practice law*; *integration*[9]; *Jim*[9] *Crow law*; *minority*[9] *group*; *separate*[9] *but equal doctrine*; *white*[5] *citizens' councils*; case listings on "Racial Rights" at the end of Chap. 9.

segregation, de facto. *Segregation*[9] of any categories (race, religion, etc.) "in fact" rather than through legal prescription. De facto segregation is in contrast to *de jure*[8] *segregation*, which is segregation by legal *authority*[3]. See also *freedom*[9] *of choice plan*.

selective incorporation doctrine. The judicially developed doctrine which holds that not all of the individual rights guaranteed in the *U.S. Bill*[4] *of Rights* were automatically "nationalized" by the addition of the *Fourteenth Amendment*[4] to the *U.S. Constitution*[4]. *Nationalized rights*[9] assuring protection against both the *federal government*[3] and the *states*[3] must come under federal protection only as separate cases are decided by the *U.S. Supreme*[8] *Court*. See also *Bill*[9] *of Rights nationalization*; *Palko*[1] *v. Connecticut*.

self-incrimination. The act of implicating oneself in a wrongful or criminal action when testifying before a court of *law*[8] or other legal body. Self-incrimination is forbidden by the *Fifth Amendment*[9] and applies to both *state*[3] and *federal*[3] actions in criminal proceedings unless voluntarily accepted by a *defendant*[8] or witness. See also *criminal law*[8]; *immunity*[9] *bath*; *Malloy*[1] *v. Hogan*; *Marchetti*[1] *v. U.S.*; *right of privacy*[9]; *Twining*[1] *v. New Jersey*; *Ullmann*[1] *v. U.S.*

separate but equal doctrine. The doctrine judicially developed in the *U.S. Supreme*[8] *Court* case of *Plessy*[1] *v. Ferguson* in 1896, a doctrine declaring that *states*[3] could legally require the *segregation*[9] of the races as long as "separate but equal" accommodations were provided. Although the doctrine was originally applied to public passenger train service, the use of segregated facilities reached almost every aspect of life. The doctrine was abandoned in 1954 in the case of *Brown*[1] *v. Board of Education*, on the grounds that segregated facilities are "inherently unequal" and in violation of the *equal*[4] *protection clause* of the *Fourteenth Amendment*[4]. See also *black*[9] *code*; *discrimination*[9]; *Jim*[9] *Crow law*; *Earl Warren*[8].

shocking to the conscience doctrine. The concept that some rights are so basic to human nature and an ordered *society*[3] that to violate them would prove "shocking to the conscience." On various occasions the *U.S. Supreme*[8] *Court* has expressed such an idea, one way or another, in its decision-making. In *Palko*[1] *v. Connecticut* the Court, in deciding a case related to *double*[9] *jeopardy*, held that, "The right to trial by *jury*[8] and the immunity from prosecution except as the result of an *indictment*[8] may have value and importance. Even so, they are not of the very essence of a scheme of ordered liberty. To abolish them is not to violate a principle of *justice*[8] so rooted in the traditions and conscience of our people as to be ranked as fundamental." The situation, according to the Court, did not work "a hardship so acute and shocking that our *polity*[3] will not endure it." Earlier, in *Hurtado*[1] *v. California*, the Court stated that indictment by a *grand jury*[8] was not essential because, ". . . it was the characteristic principle of *common law*[8] to draw its inspiration from every fountain of *justice*[8], we are not to assume that the sources of its supply have been exhausted. On the contrary, we should expect that the new and various experiences of our own situation and system will mould and shape it into new and not less useful form." The new "situation" meant that the *state*[3] could use an *information*[8] to bring a person to trial. The Supreme Court reversed the Palko decision in *Benton*[1] *v. Mary-*

land, holding that protections against double jeopardy "can hardly be doubted" because they are "deeply ingrained in at least the Anglo-American system of jurisprudence." In *Duncan*[1] *v. Louisiana*, the Court held that the *jury*[8] trial is "fundamental to the American scheme of *justice*[8]." See also *Bartkus*[1] *v. Illinois*; *Betts*[1] *v. Brady*; *Fifth Amendment*[9]; *Gideon*[1] *v. Wainwright*; *Malloy*[1] *v. Hogan*; *Twining*[1] *v. New Jersey*.

silver platter doctrine. The practice or "rule" whereby evidence illegally secured by *state*[3] legal officers could be turned over "on a silver platter" to *federal*[3] officials for use in securing federal convictions. Such a practice was declared in violation of the *Fourth Amendment*[9] in Elkins v. U.S. in 1960. See also *exclusionary*[9] *doctrine*.

sit-in. An action whereby an individual or a group is seated in a public place, generally in violation of *law*[8], and refuses to move until certain grievances are considered or objectives reached. *Civil*[9] *rights* sit-ins gained popularity and public notoriety in the 1960's. They developed into one of the most effective civil rights tactics under the leadership of *Martin Luther King*[9], *Jr.* and the *Southern*[5] *Christian Leadership Conference* (SCLC). They were used as a form of *civil*[9] *disobedience* to change social attitudes and public laws related to Negroes.

slander. Deliberate defamation of character through spoken expression which tends to injure the reputation or business of another person or group. See also *libel*[9]; *McCarthyism*[9].

subsequent punishment doctrine. The doctrine that alleged abuses of *First Amendment*[9] freedoms should be dealt with "after the fact." The concept disagrees with *censorship*[9] or the *prior*[9] *restraint doctrine* which might threaten basic freedoms. The doctrine has been a guiding factor in judicial interpretations of the *U.S. Supreme*[8] *Court*. See also *Bantam*[1] *Books, Inc. v. Sullivan; Gitlow*[1] *v. New York; Near*[1] *v. Minnesota; New York Times Co. v. U.S.*

third degree. Severe and tortuous treatment of a prisoner in order to coerce a confession of guilt from the accused. See also *Ashcraft*[1] *v. Tennessee; Brown*[1] *v. Mississippi.*

To Secure These Rights (1947). A 1947 publication released by the President's Commission on Civil Rights, a body appointed by *President*[6] *Harry Truman*[6] to investigate problems of racial *discrimination*[9] and the status of *minority*[9] group rights. The comprehensive and controversial report dealt with arrest, imprisonment, *jury*[8] trial, *contracts*[10], voting rights, expression, and all other major *civil*[9] *rights*. The report laid the modern framework for positive political and legislative acceptance of racial minorities.

vigilante. A member of a vigilance committee informally organized to maintain social order and punish "offenders" not dealt with by recognized legal authorities. A vigilante uses wide discretion in determining what constitutes an "offense" and what method of punishment should be used in dealing with it. See also *Ku*[5] *Klux Klan; lynch*[9] *law.*

Voting Rights Act of 1965: see Chap. 5.

Voting Rights Act of 1970: see Chap. 5.

wall of separation doctrine. The doctrine which holds that functions and institutions of church and *state*[3] should be separated in order to protect both institutions in their appropriate spheres of activities. The doctrine was largely established in the American *colonies*[4] by *Roger Williams*[4] and written into the *First Amendment*[9] of the *U.S. Constitution*[4]

under the leadership of *James Madison*[6] in 1791. The phrase "wall of separation" was first given widespread circulation because of *Thomas Jefferson's*[6] use of it in 1802 in writing to a group of Baptists in Danbury, Connecticut. Judicial interpretations of the wall of separation doctrine have generally held that the "wall" is not absolute. See also *child*[9] *benefit doctrine; establishment of religion*[9] *clause; Everson*[1] *v. Board of Education; free exercise of religion*[9] *clause; Lemon*[1] *v. Kurtzman; purchase*[9] *of services doctrine; released*[9] *time doctrine; Reynolds*[1] *v. U.S.; Walz*[1] *v. Tax Commission of the City of New York.*

wiretap (bug, wiretapping). A concealed listening device capable of intercepting or monitoring conversation or other communications. The use of evidence or other information gained by wiretap has been given basic direction through judicial interpretation. See also *Berger*[1] *v. New York; Federal*[9] *Communications Act of 1934; Katz*[1] *v. U.S.; Nardone*[1] *v. U.S.; Olmstead*[1] *v. U.S.: right of privacy*[9]*; Watergate*[5]*.*

writ of assistance. A general search *warrant*[8] which does not specify the place to be searched or items to be seized by legal authorities. Writs of assistance were used against the American *colonists*[4] by British authorities prior to the *American Revolution*[4]. Such *writs*[8] are prohibited by the *Fourth Amendment*[9]. See also *Townshend*[4] *Acts of 1767.*

Zenger, John Peter, 1697–1746. The *defendant*[8] and principal figure of a 1735 trial in New York that is remembered as the case which established the principle of a free press. Zenger, publisher of the New York Weekly Journal, exposed the corrupt activities of *Governor*[6] William Cosby and was brought to trial for *seditious*[12] *libel*[9]. He was found "not guilty" after the *jury*[8] heard the able defense of Andrew Hamilton of Philadelphia. Hamilton argued that it was no *crime*[8] to publish the truth. In 1791 the principle of a free press was added to the *U.S. Constitution*[4] as part of the *First Amendment*[9]. See also *Bill*[4] *of Rights* (*U.S.*); *censorship*[9]; *gag*[9] *law*; *Near*[1] *v. Minnesota*; *New*[1] *York Times Co. v. U.S.*; *prior*[9] *restraint doctrine*; *subsequent*[9] *punishment doctrine*.

Supreme Court cases related to material in this chapter are arranged below by subject. Summaries of the cases are in Chapter One arranged alphabetically by the name of the first party in each case.

GENERAL—
Barron v. Baltimore (1833)
Civil Rights Cases (1883)
Gitlow v. N.Y. (1925)
Palko v. Conn. (1937)
Slaughterhouse Cases (1873)
U.S. v. Carolene Products Co. (1938)

ASSOCIATION AND ASSEMBLY—
Adderly v. Florida (1967)
Brown v. Louisiana (1966)
Cox v. Louisiana (1965)
Cox v. N.H. (1941)
Griswold v. Conn. (1965)
Hague v. C.I.O. (1939)
Kent v. Dulles (1958)
NAACP v. Alabama (1958)
Scales v. U.S. (1961)
U.S. v. Robel (1967)

CITIZENSHIP—
Afroyim v. Rusk (1967)
Dred Scott v. Sandford (1857)
Fong Yue Ting v. U.S. (1893)
Passanger Cases (1849)
Perez v. Brownell (1958)
Trop v. Dulles (1958)
U.S. v. Wong Kim Ark (1898)

EXPRESSION—(General)
Gitlow v. N.Y. (1925)
Hague v. C.I.O. (1939)
Schenck v. U.S. (1919)

EXPRESSION—(Demonstration)
Adderly v. Florida (1967)
Brown v. Louisiana (1966)
Cox v. Louisiana (1965)
Thornhill v. Alabama (1940)
Tinker v. Des Moines School District (1969)

EXPRESSION—(Films)
Burstyn v. Wilson (1952)
Times Film Corp. v. Chicago (1961)

EXPRESSION—(Libel)
Beauharnais v. Ill. (1952)
Monitor Patriot v. Roy (1971)
N.Y. Times Co. v. Sullivan (1964)

EXPRESSION—(Lobbying)
Red Lion Broadcasting Co. v. FCC (1969)
U.S. v. Harriss (1954)

EXPRESSION—(Obscenity)
Bantam Books, Inc. v. Sullivan (1963)
Chaplinsky v. N.H. (1942)
'Fanny Hill' Case (1966)
Ginsberg v. N.Y. (1968)
Ginzburg v. U.S. (1966)
Hannegan v. Esquire (1946)
Roth v. U.S. (1957)
Rowan v. U.S. Post Office Department (1969)
Stanley v. Georgia (1969)

EXPRESSION—(Press)
Near v. Minnesota (1931)
N.Y. Times Co. v. U.S. (1971)

EXPRESSION—(Religion)
Cantwell v. Conn. (1940)

EXPRESSION—(Right of Privacy)
Griswold v. Conn. (1965)

EXPRESSION—(Riot)
Chaplinsky v. N.H. (1942)
Feiner v. N.Y. (1951)
Terminiello v. Chicago (1949)

EXPRESSION—(Subversive Activities)
Abrams v. U.S. (1919)
Barenblatt v. U.S. (1959)
Communist Party v. SACB (1961)
Dennis v. U.S. (1951)
Lamont v. Postmaster General (1965)
Pierce v. U.S. (1920)
Scales v. U.S. (1961)
Schenck v. U.S. (1919)
Yates v. U.S. (1957)

INVOLUNTARY SERVITUDE AND PEONAGE—
Pollock v. Williams (1944)
Selective Draft Law Cases (1918)

LEGAL RIGHTS—(Bills of Attainder)
U.S. v. Brown (1965)

LEGAL RIGHTS—(Capital Punishment)
Furman v. Georgia (1972)
Witherspoon v. Illinois (1968)

LEGAL RIGHTS—(Confessions)
Ashcraft v. Tenn. (1944)
Brown v. Miss. (1936)
Harris v. N.Y. (1971)
McNabb v. U.S. (1943)
Mallory v. U.S. (1957)
Miranda v. Arizona (1966)

LEGAL RIGHTS—(Counsel)
Argersinger v. Hamlin (1972)
Betts v. Brady (1942)
Escobedo v. Ill. (1964)
Gideon v. Wainright (1963)

Johnson v. *Zerbst* (1938)
Miranda v. *Arizona* (1966)
Powell v. *Alabama* (1932)

LEGAL RIGHTS—(Cruel and Unusual Punishments)
Furman v. *Georgia* (1972)
Robinson v. *Calif.* (1962)
Trop v. *Dulles* (1958)

LEGAL RIGHTS—(Due Process)
Gault, In re (1967)
McNabb v. *U.S.* (1943)
Mallory v. *U.S.* (1957)
Miranda v. *Arizona* (1966)
Palko v. *Conn.* (1937)

LEGAL RIGHTS—(Double Jeopardy)
Bartkus v. *Ill.* (1958)
Benton v. *Maryland* (1969)
Palko v. *Conn.* (1937)

LEGAL RIGHTS— (Eminent Domain)
Berman v. *Parker* (1954)

LEGAL RIGHTS—(Ex Post Facto Laws)
Calder v. *Bull* (1798)

LEGAL RIGHTS—(Grand Jury)
Hurtado v. *Calif.* (1884)

LEGAL RIGHTS—(Habeas Corpus)
Ableman v. *Booth* (1859)
Duncan v. *Kahanamoku* (1946)
Endo, Ex parte (1944)
Korematsu v. *U.S.* (1944)
McCardle, Ex parte (1869)
Merryman, Ex parte (1861)
Milligan, Ex parte (1866)

LEGAL RIGHTS— (Immunity)
Ullman v. *U.S.* (1956)

LEGAL RIGHTS— (Military Law)
Reid v. *Covert* (1957)
Toth v. *Quarles* (1955)

LEGAL RIGHTS—(Search and Seizure)
Berger v. *N.Y.* (1967)
Katz v. *U.S.* (1967)
Mapp v. *Ohio* (1961)
Nardone v. *U.S.* (1939)
Olmstead v. *U.S.* (1928)
Rochin v. *Calif.* (1952)
U.S. v. *U.S .District Court for the Eastern District of Michigan* (1972)
Weeks v. *U.S.* (1914)
Wolf v. *Colorado* (1949)

LEGAL RIGHTS—(Self-incrimination)
Albertson v. *SACB* (1965)
Barenblatt v. *U.S.* (1959)
Brown v. *Miss.* (1936)
Griswold v. *Conn.* (1965)
Harris v. *N.Y.* (1971)
Jencks v. *U.S.* (1957)
Malloy v. *Hogan* (1964)
Marchetti v. *U.S.* (1968)
Miranda v. *Arizona* (1966)
Slochower v. *Board of Education* (1956)
Twining v. *N.J.* (1908)
Watkins v. *U.S.* (1957)

POLITICAL RIGHTS— (General)
Carrington v. *Rash* (1965)
S.C. v. *Katzenbach* (1966)

POLITICAL RIGHTS— (Grandfather Clause)
Guinn v. *U.S.* (1915)

POLITICAL RIGHTS— (Legislative Apportionment)
Avery v. *Midland Co.* (1968)
Baker v. *Carr* (1962)
Colgrove v. *Green* (1946)
Gomillion v. *Lightfoot* (1960)
Gray v. *Sanders* (1963)
Reynolds v. *Sims* (1964)
Wesberry v. *Sanders* (1964)

POLITICAL RIGHTS— (Libel)
Monitor Patriot v. *Roy* (1971)

POLITICAL RIGHTS— (Literacy Test)
Williams v. *Miss.* (1898)

POLITICAL RIGHTS— (Poll Tax)
Harper v. *Va. State Board of Elections* (1966)

POLITICAL RIGHTS— (Primary, General)
Newberry v. *U.S.* (1921)
U.S. v. *Classic* (1941)

POLITICAL RIGHTS— (Primary, White)
Grovey v. *Townsend* (1935)
Nixon v. *Condon* (1932)
Nixon v. *Herndon* (1927)
Smith v. *Allwright* (1944)

PRIVACY—
Griswold v. *Conn.* (1965)

RACIAL RIGHTS— (General)
Civil Rights Cases (1883)

RACIAL RIGHTS— (Association)
NAACP v. *Alabama* (1958)

RACIAL RIGHTS— (Citizenship)
Dred Scott v. *Sandford* (1857)

RACIAL RIGHTS— (Commerce)
Heart of Atlanta Motel v. *U.S.* (1964)
Morgan v. *Virginia* (1946)
Plessy v. *Ferguson* (1896)

RACIAL RIGHTS— (Education)
Alexander v. *Holmes* (1969)
Bolling v. *Sharpe* (1954)
Brown v. *Board of Education of Topeka* (1954)
Cooper v. *Aaron* (1958)
Green v. *County School Board of New Kent County, Virginia* (1968)
Griffin v. *County Board of Prince Edward County* (1964)
McLaurin v. *Oklahoma State Regents* (1950)
Missouri ex rel. Gaines v. *Canada* (1938)
Swann v. *Charlotte-Mecklenburg Board of Education* (1971)
Sweatt v. *Painter* (1950)

RACIAL RIGHTS—
(Housing)
Buchanan v. Warley
(1917)
Jones v. Alfred H. Mayer
Co. (1968)
Reitman v. Mulkey
(1967)
Shelley v. Kraemer
(1948)

RACIAL RIGHTS—
(Marriage)
Loving v. Virginia
(1967)

RACIAL RIGHTS—
(Voting)
Gomillion v. Lightfoot
(1960)
Grovey v. Townsend
(1935)
Guinn v. U.S. (1915)
Nixon v. Condon (1932)
Nixon v. Herndon (1927)
Smith v. Allwright (1944)
S.C. v. Katzenbach
(1966)
Williams v. Miss. (1898)

RELIGION—(General)
Flast v. Cohen (1968)
Walz v. Tax Commission
of the City of New York
(1970)

RELIGION—(Conscien-
tious Objectors)
Gillette v. U.S. (1971)
U.S. v. Seeger (1965)

RELIGION—(Expression)
Cantwell v. Conn. (1940)

RELIGION—(Free
Exercise)
Cantwell v. Conn. (1940)
Pierce v. Society of Sisters
(1925)
Reynolds v. U.S. (1879)
Sherbert v. Verner (1963)
Torcaso v. Watkins
(1961)

RELIGION—(School—
Bible Reading & Lord's
Prayer)
School District of Abing-
ton Township v.
Schempp (1963)

RELIGION—(School—
Child Benefit Theory)
Board of Education v.
Allen (1968)
Everson v. Board of Edu-
cation (1947)

RELIGION—(School—
Flag Salute)
Minersville School District
v. Gobitis (1940)
West Virginia State Board
of Education v. Barnette
(1943)

RELIGION—(School—
Prayer)
Engel v. Vitale (1962)

RELIGION—(School—
Purchase of Services)
Lemon v. Kurtzman
(1971)

RELIGION—(School—
Released Time Doc-
trine)
McCollum v. Board of
Education (1948)
Zorach v. Clauson
(1952)

RELIGION—(School—
Textbooks)
Board of Education v.
Allen (1968)

RELIGION—(School—
Transportation)
Everson v. Board of Edu-
cation (1947)

RELIGION—(Sunday
Closing)
Sunday Closing Cases
(1961)

SUBVERSIVE ACTIVITIES
—(General)
Penn. v. Nelson (1956)

SUBVERSIVE ACTIVITIES
—(Association)
Kent v. Dulles (1958)
Scales v. U.S. (1961)
U.S. v. Robel (1967)

SUBVERSIVE ACTIVITIES
—(Bills of Attainder)
U.S. v. Brown (1965)

SUBVERSIVE ACTIVITIES
—(Expression)
Abrams v. U.S. (1919)
Barenblatt v. U.S. (1959)
Communist Party v.
SACB (1961)
Dennis v. U.S. (1951)
Lamont v. Postmaster
General (1965)
Pierce v. U.S. (1920)
Scales v. U.S. (1961)
Schenck v. U.S. (1919)
Yates v. U.S. (1957)

SUBVERSIVE ACTIVITIES
—(Loyalty Oath)
Adler v. Board of Educa-
tion (1952)
American Communications
Assn. v. Douds (1950)
Cole v. Young (1956)
Garner v. Board of Public
Works (1951)
Keyishian v. Board of
Regents (1967)

SUBVERSIVE ACTIVITIES
—(Registration)
Albertson v. SACB (1965)
Communist Party v. SACB
(1961)

SUBVERSIVE ACTIVITIES
—(Self-incrimination)
Albertson v. SACB
(1965)
Barenblatt v. U.S. (1959)
Jencks v. U.S. (1957)
Slochower v. Board of
Education (1956)
Ullmann v. U.S. (1956)
Watkins v. U.S. (1957)

SUBVERSIVE ACTIVITIES
—(Travel)
Aptheker v. Secretary of
State (1964)
Kent v. Dulles (1958)
Zemel v. Rusk (1965)

TRAVEL—
Aptheker v. Secretary of
State (1964)
Edwards v. Calif. (1941)
Kent v. Dulles (1958)
Zemel v. Rusk (1965)

Chapter 10

The Economy

Note to the reader: Cross-referenced terms are in italics. The superscript number refers to the chapter in which the entry may be found. In addition, its placement indicates the word under which the term is alphabetized. (For example, in *electoral*[4] *college*, information on the electoral college may be found in Chapter 4 under "electoral.") Because italics are used in cross-references, they are not used for terms in which they would ordinarily be used: Supreme Court cases and titles of books, journals, plays, and so forth.

Supreme Court cases relating to material in this chapter are listed at the end of the chapter (see page 269).

---

ability theory. A *theory*[3] of taxation which holds that taxes should be paid primarily by persons and *corporations*[10] most able to pay taxes on the basis of personal worth and income. Advocates of the ability theory generally prefer *progressive taxes*[10] in one form or another.

Agricultural Adjustment Act of 1933. A major *federal*[3] *act*[8] designed to balance agricultural production and consumption within the U.S. The *law*[8], a major piece of *New*[6] *Deal legislation*[7], created the *Agricultural*[2] *Adjustment Administration* (AAA) and provided for production controls on various products. Farmers were offered cash benefits for voluntary reduction of specific products. Payments were financed out of a special tax imposed on processors of farm commodities. The act was declared *unconstitutional*[3] in U.S.[1] *v. Butler* in 1936 on the grounds that its taxing provisions were in violation of the *general*[4] *welfare* clause of the U.S. *Constitution*[4] and the *reserved powers*[4] of the *states*[3]. See also *Agricultural*[10] *Ad-*

justment Act of 1938; *price*[10] *support program*.

Agricultural Adjustment Act of 1938. A federal *law*[8] which replaced the unconstitutional *Agricultural*[10] *Adjustment Act of 1933*. The *act*[8] was designed to regulate agricultural production throughout the U.S. by controlling the interstate shipment of agricultural products and by providing governmental assistance for *conservation*[10] purposes. The *legislation*[7] provided for *parity*[10] arrangements, soil diversion, marketing agreements, crop insurance, and agricultural loans. The funding of the program avoided the earlier *unconstitutional*[3] processing tax and was handled out of the general treasury of the *federal government*[3]. See also *interstate commerce*[10]; *Mulford*[1] *v. Smith*; *price*[10] *support program*.

Amendment, Sixteenth (1913). The *amendment*[3] to the U.S. *Constitution*[4] which empowered the *federal government*[3] to levy and collect a *graduated income tax*[10] without regard to population figures within the separate *states*[3]. The amendment was designed to overcome the decision made by the *Supreme*[8] *Court* in *Pollock*[1] *v. Farmers' Loan and Trust Company*, which declared an income tax *unconstitutional*[3] because it was not a *direct tax*[10] apportioned on the basis of population. See also *Hylton*[1] *v. U.S.*

appropriation. Money or public funds specifically designated, generally by legislative action, for a specific purpose. In the U.S. *constitutional*[3] system all appropriations measures must originate, by *custom*[3], in the *House*[7] *of Representatives*. The *Committee*[7] *on Appropriations* is the major House *committee*[7] regulating such matters.

arbitration, labor. The process in which parties to a labor dispute submit their conflict to examination and judgment by a third party whose judgement is legally binding. See also *collective*[10] *bargaining; Federal*[2] *Mediation and Conciliation Service; mediation*[10]; *National*[2] *Mediation Board; Railway*[10] *Labor Act of 1926.*

Ashurst-Sumners Act of 1935. A *federal*[3] *law*[8] that prohibited the interstate shipment of prison-made goods which were otherwise prohibited by particular *states*[3]. The *U.S. Supreme*[8] *Court* upheld such *legislation*[7] on the basis of what later came to be known as the *divestment*[10] *theory*. See also *interstate commerce*[10]; *Kentucky*[1] *Whip and Collar Co. v. Illinois Central Railroad Co.*

assessed valuation. The value placed on *property*[10] *by government*[3] officials for taxation purposes. Generally, the assessed valuation is a percentage of the actual total value of the property in question. Due to the fluctuating changes in property values, there is constant need for regular revision of assessed valuations. See also *competitive*[10] *underassessment; property tax*[10].

assumption of risk doctrine. The *common law*[8] *theory*[3] which holds that individuals taking employment may not sue the company for damages for personal injury on the job because they knew the risks of production before accepting employment. The assumption of risk doctrine has generally been overcome by *federal*[3] and *state*[3] *workman's*[10] *compensation* and safety *legislation*[7]. See also *fellow*[10] *servant doctrine; Occupational*[11] *Health and Safety Act of 1970.*

audit. An official examination of financial records. An audit of public funds helps maintain fiscal responsibility and integrity. The official auditor of the *U.S. federal government*[3] is the *Comptroller*[10] *General*. See also *General*[2] *Accounting Office.*

balance of payments. The economic arrangement or process in which two or more foreign *nations*[3] attempt to balance imports, exports, and business and private spending abroad in order to maintain favorable credit with one another. Balances are generally maintained on the basis of gold or negotiable instruments acceptable on the world market. See also *devaluation*[10]; *Export-Import*[2] *Bank of the United States; export tax*[10]; *gold*[10] *standard; wage-price*[10] *freeze.*

Bank of the United States. A *federal*[3] bank first chartered in 1791 by the federal *government*[3] under the *implied powers*[4] clause of the *U.S. Constitution*[4]. The charter of the bank expired in 1811. The institution was rechartered in 1816 as a depository for federal funds. The bank's headquarters were located in Philadelphia, and it maintained offices throughout the *country*[3]. The second charter expired in 1836. The Bank, created under the implied powers was the central issue in the *Supreme*[8] *Court* case of *McCulloch*[1] *v. Maryland* in 1819 and a major issue in the election of 1832, an election in which *Andrew*

Jackson[6] opposed the bank's existence. See also *pet bank*[10]; *wildcat bank*[10]; *Roger Brooke Taney*[8].

bank, pet. A *state*[3] bank in which *federal*[3] funds were deposited after the closing of the *Bank*[10] *of the United States* (1833–36). The transfer of funds took place under the leadership of *President*[6] *Andrew Jackson*[6].

bankruptcy. The act of declaring financial insolvency. Bankruptcy is a *concurrent power*[4] regulated by both *federal*[3] and *state*[3] *governments*[3]. In a bankruptcy proceeding a declaration is made by a party, judicial determination is made of the matter, and *administration*[6] of the remaining estate is made in order to divide among the creditors whatever might be left in the estate. A recognized bankruptcy action removes the legal liability for past debts. See also *Securities*[2] *and Exchange Commission*.

bank, soil: see *soil*[10] *bank*.

bank, wildcat. A *state*[3] bank established after the closing of the *Bank*[10] *of the United States* in 1833, which provided easy loans, cheap currency, and widespread opportunities for financial speculation, especially in western land. Numerous wildcat banks collapsed during the *panic*[10] of 1837 because they were unable to redeem their notes on demand.

basing point. A prohibited commercial arrangement in which all producers of a certain commodity agree on a fixed point of distribution and then set their prices according to the price of transportation from that point. Although some distributors have to pay more to transport goods to the particular point, they are able to be part of an arrangement used to manipulate retail prices in a specified area. See also *monopoly*[10]; *restraint of trade*[10].

benefit theory. A *theory*[3] of taxation which holds that taxes should be paid primarily by persons and *corporations*[10] deriving the greatest benefits from certain public expenditures. Persons advocating the use of gasoline taxes ordinarily feel the taxes are being paid by those who use highways built with public revenues earmarked for highway development. See also *earmarking*[10]; *betterment tax*[10].

bimetallism. The economic acceptance of two forms of metal, usually silver and gold, as legal currency in a *nation*[3]. The two metals ordinarily have a legally specified ratio of value between them. The U.S. used bimetallism from 1792 to 1873. The *gold*[10] *standard* was established in the Coinage Act of 1873. Bimetallism was reinstated in the Bland-Allison Act of 1878, but was rejected once again in the Gold Standard Act of 1900. It was reintroduced again in 1934 under the Silver Purchase Act.

blue law: see Chap. 9.

blue sky law. A *law*[8] designed to assure that financial securities offered for public sale are legitimate and negotiable. Numerous *states*[3] have adopted such laws under their *police powers*[4] in order to protect the public against fraudulent securities.

board of equalization. A legal *board*[6] of review which may hear and settle complaints concerning taxation matters within its *jurisdiction*[8]. A board of equalization is generally local or statewide in nature, hears conflicts over *property tax*[10] assessments, and has final *authority*[3] to establish uniform assessment rates. See also *assessed*[10] *valuation*; *competitive*[10] *underassessment*.

bond, financial. A certificate of indebtedness which is issued to a lender of capital expecting repayment of both principal and interest on the loan. Numerous types of bonds are used by private *corporations*[10], public agencies, and other legal entities and institutions to finance various projects of a long-range nature.

boondoggling. A meaningless or useless expenditure of public funds, especially on unnecessary *public*[10] *works* or time-consuming activities simply to keep people employed on the public payroll. The term, of disputed origin, may have come from a Scottish word meaning a "free" marble.

boycott. A deliberate act in which individuals collectively abstain from trading with a person, business, *nation*[3], or other entity in an effort to bring pressure to bear on them. See also *The Association*[4]; *secondary boycott*[10]; *Martin Luther King*[9], *Jr.*

boycott, secondary. A type of *boycott*[10] instituted against one business in order to bring pressure on another business or employer. Secondary boycotts are prohibited by the *Federal*[3] *Labor-Management*[10] *Relations* (*Taft-Hartley*) *Act of 1947*.

Brannan plan. An unsuccessful proposal advocated by U.S. Secretary of Agriculture Charles F. Brannan in 1949 during the *administration*[6] of *President*[6] *Harry Truman*[6]. Under the plan, agricultural price supports would be revised and farmers would sell their basic crops at market prices and receive direct cash assistance from the *federal government*[3] only for crops going below a set figure. The objective of the plan was to abolish the general *price*[10] *support program* based on *parity*[10], lower food prices, and provide adequate compensation for farmers.

budget. A formal estimate of revenues and expenditures considered necessary for financial operation for a specified period of time. Budget development and operation is a complicated process involving departmental estimates, *administrative hearings*[6], *executive*[6] proposals, legislative examination, spending, *auditing*[10], and other elements.

The *Budget*[10] *and Accounting Act of 1921* lists the *President*[6] as the public official responsible for budget preparation for the U.S. *federal government*[3]. See also *debt*[10] *limitation*; *deficit*[10] *financing*; *fiscal*[10] *year*; *Office of Management*[2] *and Budget*.

Budget and Accounting Act of 1921. A federal *law*[8] which established the Bureau of the Budget, the *General*[2] *Accounting Office* (GAO), and a comprehensive federal *budget*[10] under the direction of the *President*[6]. The law requires the presentation of an annual budget by the President to the *Congress*[4]. It also specifies the *fiscal*[10] *year* of the *federal government*[3] as extending from July 1 of one year to June 30 of the next. See also *Office of Management*[2] *and Budget*.

budget, cash. One of the *budgets*[10] used by the *President*[6] to arrange public revenue and spending programs. It reflects the total amount of money going into and out of the U.S. Treasury regardless of the source (trust accounts, loans, repayments, *appropriated*[10] funds, etc.). See also *Department of the Treasury*[2].

budget, dual. A formal budget which is divided in fiscal responsibility between an *executive*[6] and another agency such as the *legislature*[7] or a separate budget *board*[6]. A number of *states*[3] in the U.S. list the *governor*[6] as the chief budget officer, but divide his *power*[3] among other agencies. In some states the governor's *budget*[10] is rarely accepted, since the primary fiscal power resides in another agency of *government*[3].

budget, executive (**administrative**). A formal *budget*[10] arranged by a chief *executive*[6] legally charged with primary responsibility for budgetary matters. The U.S. *President*[6] was charged in the *Budget*[10] *and Accounting Act of 1921* with annually presenting an executive budget. He uses the *Office of Management*[2] *and Budg-*

et to help devise a budget. In the process of budget development different *federal*[3] agencies submit budgetary estimates, *hearings*[6] are conducted, budget examinations are made, and estimates are approved or modified. The budget is formalized and the President delivers his *budget*[6] *message* to the *Congress*[4]. In his message he submits his annual budget. The specific "administrative budget" generally indicates all federal expenditures except trust funds (*Social*[11] *Security*, *Medicare*[11], highways, etc.) and special accounts (old-age retirement payments, etc.). It includes payments such as interest on trust funds that are made entirely within the *government*[3].

budget, hidden. The portion of public funds officially authorized, appropriated, and spent without general public knowledge. In the *U.S. federal government*[3], large sums are spent on defense research, *intelligence*[12], and special operations without public awareness. See also *Pentagon*[12] *Papers*.

budgeting, line item. A narrow, detailed, and specific approach to budgeting which lists specific items to be paid for by a *government*[3] agency. Line item budgeting was used by the U.S. government between 1921 and 1950. See also *Budget*[10] *and Accounting Act of 1921*.

budget, national income accounts. One of the *budgets*[10] used by the *President*[6] to arrange public revenue and spending programs. The budget excludes lending transactions, loans, and repayments. It includes receipts at the time tax liabilities occur and includes *federal*[3] contributions to federal retirement programs. The national income accounts budget is based on the relationship of the *gross*[10] *national product* (GNP) to the total national income.

budget, unified. A federal budget which reflects trust fund revenues and expenditures as well as regular revenues and expenditures. The *budget*[10] also reflects the amount of money the *federal government*[3] lends in excess of what it receives in any given *fiscal*[10] *year*.

budgeting, performance (program). A broad, systematic, and long-range approach to budgeting which considers objectives to be achieved or services to be rendered rather than specific items to be paid by a governmental agency. Performance budgeting was adopted by the U.S. *federal government*[3] in the Budget and Accounting Procedures Act of 1950.

budgeting, PPB. A budgeting system based on systematic planning, programming, and budgeting. The PPB system is a refined and quantative type of *performance budgeting*[10] process which carefully analyzes objectives, costs, possible alternatives, effectiveness, and other important variables. The PPB system was first used by the U.S. *federal government*[3] in the *Department of Defense*[2] under the *administration*[6] of Secretary of Defense Robert McNamara between 1961 and 1967. See also *F–111*[12] *(TFX) controversy*.

capitalism: see Chap. 3.

checkoff. The systematic collection of *labor*[10] *union* dues by an employer who deducts dues from regular individual paychecks. The *Labor-Management*[10] *Relations* (*Taft-Hartley*) *Act of 1947* permits the use of the checkoff if agreed on by *majority*[3] vote of the recognized union members.

child labor. Employment of minor children, generally 16 years of age or younger. Child labor became a social problem and political issue as the U.S. became an industrialized *nation*[3]. *Federal*[3] attempts to regulate child labor were declared *unconstitutional*[3] in the *U.S. Supreme*[8] *Court* cases of *Hammer*[1] *v. Dagenhart* in 1918 and

Bailey[1] *v. Drexel Furniture Co.* in 1922. The *Fair*[10] *Labor Standards Act of 1938* prohibits child labor in the manufacture of goods to be shipped in *interstate commerce*[10]. The *legislation*[7] was upheld in *U.S.*[1] *v. Darby Lumber Company* in 1941.

Clayton Antitrust Act of 1914. A major *federal*[3] law designed to curb *monopoly*[10] and price-fixing practices within the field of private business. The *legislation*[7] supplemented the *Sherman*[10] *Antitrust Act of 1890*. It restricted stock purchases seeking to create monopolies, prohibited *interlocking*[10] *directorates*, made *corporation*[10] officers legally responsible for antitrust violations, prohibited various price-fixing practices, and provided for civil actions designed to block monopolistic practices. The *law*[8] exempted *labor*[10] *unions* and various nonprofit *organizations*[6] which might appear to operate as monopolies. See also *conspiracy*[10] *doctrine*; *restraint of trade*[10]; *U.S.*[1] *v. E. I. Du Pont De Nemours & Co.*

closed shop. A business or industry that employs only *labor*[10] *union* members. See also *open*[10] *shop*; *union*[10] *shop*.

collective bargaining. Working-condition negotiations between an employer and *labor*[10] *union* leaders representing union members. Widespread collective bargaining has been guaranteed *federal*[3] protection since the passage of the *National*[10] *Labor Relations* (*Wagner*) *Act of 1935*. The *National*[2] *Labor Relations Board* (NLRB) regularly supervises collective bargaining practices. See also *Federal*[2] *Mediation and Conciliation Service*; *labor arbitration*[10]; *labor mediation*[10]; *National*[2] *Mediation Board*.

commerce clause: see Chap. 4.

commerce, interstate. Commercial intercourse between two or more *states*[3] or a state and a foreign *nation*[3]. Federal *power*[3] has been developed significantly under the *commerce*[4] *clause* of the *U.S. Constitution*[4], which permits *federal*[3] regulation of interstate commerce. Under the power, the *Congress*[4] has regulated insurance companies, *child*[10] *labor*, race relations, minimum wages, maximum hours, manufacturing, and numerous other subjects. See also: *Commerce*[4] *Compromise*; *Cooley*[10] *doctrine*; *Department of Commerce*[2]; *divestment*[10] *theory*; *Federal*[2] *Maritime Commission*; *Federal*[2] *Mediation and Conciliation Service*; *Federal*[2] *Power Commission*; *intrastate commerce*[10]; *maximum*[10] *hour law*; *minimum*[10] *wage law*; *original*[10] *package doctrine*; *preemption*[4] *doctrine*; case listings on "commerce" at the end of Chap. 10.

commerce, intrastate. Commercial intercourse which takes place wholly within the *boundaries*[12] of a *state*[3] within the *federal*[3] Union. Intrastate commerce is regulated primarily by each state in question. However, intrastate commerce which significantly affects national commerce must be consistent with federal regulations. See also *commerce*[4] *clause*; *Commerce*[4] *Compromise*; *Cooley*[10] *doctrine*; *Department of Commerce*[2]; *divestment*[10] *theory*; *interstate commerce*[10]; *original*[10] *package doctrine*; *preemption*[4] *doctrine*; case listings on "commerce" at the end of Chap. 10.

commission, public service. An authorized *government*[3] body legally charged with general supervision of a *public*[10] *utility* or public service of a particular nature. State *commissions*[6] regulate electrical energy, natural gas service, and other industries. Major functions of such commissions involve *rate-making*[10], safety, routes, and determination of future public needs.

Committee for Economic Development (CED), 1942– . A national, *nonpartisan*[5], and research-oriented association of business leaders in the U.S. The *organization*[6] makes suggestions for national *policy*[6] decisions on the basis of pure economic research. Some of the basic areas of economic interest dealt with by the CED are taxation, unemployment, *tariffs*[10], agricultural *subsidies*[10], and interest rates.

Committee, Joint Economic: see *Joint*[10] *Committee on the Economic Report.*

Committee on Appropriations (U.S. House): see Chap. 7.

Committee on Ways and Means (U.S. House): see Chap. 7.

common carrier. An individual or company that is available for public hire to perform a general public service. A common carrier is generally licensed by the *state*[3], its rates and investment returns are determined by state agencies, and its operating practices are severely circumscribed by state *authority*[3]. See also *public service commission*[10].

Common Market: see *European*[12] *Common Market.*

communism: see Chap. 3.

competitive underassessment. The controversial practice whereby a certified tax assessor underassesses the taxable value of real *property*[10] in order to benefit particular parties. Underassessment generally takes place because of corruption, inexperience, a lack of criteria for assessment, incentive plans to draw industry into an area, and rapid growth in the economic worth of real property in a given area. See also *assessed*[10] *valuation; board*[10] *of equalization; board*[6] *of review; property tax*[10].

Comptroller General. An *executive*[6] official charged with overseeing the disbursement of public funds, book-keeping, *auditing*[10], and other financial details of a governmental *jurisdiction*[8]. The United States Comptroller General .directs the work of the *General*[2] *Accounting Office* and carries on general financial *administration*[6] for the *federal government*[3]. See also *Federal*[5] *Election Campaign Act of 1972.*

conglomerate. A *corporate*[10] arrangement in which investors purchase securities in and gain control of various diversified businesses and industries. See also *merger*[10]; *monopoly*[10].

consent decree (stipulation). The most widely used *federal*[3] enforcement device used to halt antitrust action on the part of particular businesses. A consent decree is an agreement between two parties in a *civil law*[8] suit that one party will halt an illegal action if the other party will drop legal prosecution. The use of consent decrees was legalized in the *Clayton*[10] *Antitrust Act of 1914.* The federal use of consent decrees was upheld in the *Supreme*[8] *Court* case of Swift and Company v. U.S. in 1928. Such devices are used to gain quick compliance with antitrust *legislation*[7] without the burdensome and time-consuming actions required in a court of *law*[8].

conservation. The preservation and planned usage of existing natural resources. See also *Civilian*[2] *Conservation Corps; Department of the Interior*[2]; *Job*[11] *Corps; Mulford*[1] *v. Smith; soil*[10] *bank; Tennessee*[2] *Valley Authority.*

conspiracy doctrine. The doctrine held by some economic and social reformers that some individuals, businesses, and labor groups conspire to violate public rights through illegal business or *labor*[10] *union* activities. *Federal*[3] and *state*[3] legislation has been used to break up such conspiracies. Labor union activities have generally been removed from such a shadow through federal *legislation*[7] such as the *National*[10] *Labor Relations (Wagner) Act of 1935*. Certain business practices such as *monopolies*[10], *trusts*[10], and *holding*[10] *companies* have been prohibited as conspiracies by legislation such as the *Sherman*[10] *Antitrust Act of 1890* and the *Clayton*[10] *Antitrust Act of 1914*.

contract. A formal and legally enforceable agreement between two or more parties to perform or refrain from performing a particular act. The *U.S. Constitution*[4] prohibits *government*[3] from breaking the obligation of contract. See also *contract*[4] *clause*; *contract theory*[3]; case listings on "contract" at the end of Chap. 10.

contract clause: see Chap. 4.

contract, yellow dog. An agreement between a worker and a prospective employer in which the employer states that he will give the worker salaried employment if the worker will agree not to join a *labor*[10] *union*. Yellow dog contracts were first prohibited by the *Norris-LaGuardia*[10] *Act of 1932*.

Cooley doctrine. A doctrine judicially pronounced by Justice Benjamin Curtis in the *U.S. Supreme*[8] *Court* case of *Cooley*[1] *v. Board of Port Wardens of Philadelphia* in 1851. The doctrine held that economic subjects local in nature and not yet regulated by the *Congress*[4] may receive *state*[3] regulation as long as the action does not hinder foreign or *interstate commerce*[10]. As soon as Congress acts on such a subject validity under national *authority*[3], state regulations must conform to *federal*[3] *statutes*[8].

cooling off period. A specified period in which parties in a labor dispute must legally refrain from actions which could lead to a *labor*[10] *union strike*[10]. A cooling off period is most often designated by *federal*[3] or *state*[3] *law*[8]. The *Labor-Management*[10] *Re-* *lations (Taft-Hartley) Act of 1947* authorizes the use of a cooling off period by the *President*[6] in the event that a strike could threaten national security. He may forbid a strike or *lockout*[10] for 60 or 80 days depending on the circumstances of the threatened strike.

cooperative. A voluntary economic arrangement in which persons join together to carry out particular profit-making activities designed to maximize economic returns by servicing a particular and limited membership. A cooperative is usually underwritten through the purchase of shares, eliminates middlemen, distributes profits on the basis of economic return, and is administered by elected directors. See also *American*[5] *Farm Bureau Federation*; *National*[5] *Council of Farmer Cooperatives*.

copyright. An exclusive privilege granted by a recognized governmental *authority*[3] to a person who has created a literary or artistic product. In the U.S. a copyright may be secured by an individual or a business for an initial 28-year period and may be renewed for another 28 years.

corporation. A formal business association created through a charter, composed of stockholders, administered by a *board*[6] of directors or other *executive*[6] officers, and arranged specifically for economic or other purposes. A corporation is considered an artificial person wherein each stockholder has limited liability for the actions of the corporate entity. See also *conglomerate*[10]; *government corporation*[6]; *interlocking*[10] *directorate*; *merger*[10]; *monopoly*[10]; *trust*[10].

customs duties. A tax levied against goods being imported into a *nation*[3]. Customs duties are sometimes used to collect revenue, but in modern times are most frequently used as a *tariff*[10] to protect domestic production. See also *Bureau of Customs*[2]; *Customs Court*[8] (U.S.); *Court*[8] *of Customs and Patent Appeals*; *Department of the Treasury*[2]; *Hampton*[1] *& Co. v. U.S.*; *import tax*[10].

debt limitation. A *constitutional*[3] or *statutory*[8] provision which establishes a limit on government borrowing or indebtedness. The *U.S. federal government*[3] debt limit is established by *law*[8] and is frequently changed as the need arises. In 1971 the U.S. debt limit was over $400 billion. Numerous *states*[3] in the Union establish debt limit by *constitutional*[3] provision. In such a limit the state may be required to operate under a balanced *budget*[10] without *deficit*[10] financing.

deficit financing. The practice of *appropriating*[10] or spending more money than is actually collected in revenues. Some *states*[3] in the Union are *constitutionally*[3] prohibited from using such a fiscal practice. However, the *federal government*[3] frequently uses deficit financing to stimulate a sluggish economy by placing money in the hands of the general public. Deficit financing is a basic cornerstone of *Keynesian economics*[10].

deflation. An economic phenomenon in which general prices of products fall and the purchasing *power*[3] of money increases. The phenomenon generally involves a surplus of products, tight credit, depressed economic conditions, and widespread unemployment. See also *depression*[10]; *inflation*[10].

depletion allowance. A federal *tax*[10] *exemption* permitted "extractive" industries engaged in removing and processing various natural resources such as oil, natural gas, coal, and copper. The industries in question may avoid taxation on a specified percentage of their income due to the expense of the discovery and development of natural reserves. The alleged purpose of such a tax exemption is that industries need to be

encouraged to develop natural resources basic to the national interest. The basic *federal*[3] depletion allowance on oil was reduced from 27.5% to 20% in the Tax Reform Act of 1969. See also *severance tax*[10].

depression. An economic condition wherein businessmen curtail investments and production, unemployment ensues, and market prices fall to a low level. See also *deflation*[10]; *inflation*[10]; *panic*[10]; *recession*[10].

Depression, Great. The catastrophic economic upheaval of the 1930's which began in the U.S. with the crash of the stock market on October 29, 1929. There was extreme curtailment of production, a falling of prices, and widespread unemployment. A major *depression*[10] developed, numerous businesses went *bankrupt*[10], banks closed, farm mortgages were foreclosed, social unrest spread, and personal poverty increased. The major attempts at overcoming the problems created by the Great Depression were contained in the *New*[6] *Deal* programs instituted by *President*[6] *Franklin D. Roosevelt*[6]. The Great Depression was never fully overcome until the economic and industrial recovery which came with *World*[12] *War II*.

determinism, economic: see Chap. 3.

devaluation. A deliberate governmental reduction in the amount of gold or silver maintained as backing for a unit of money. The term may also mean the deliberate reduction of the value of the money in relation to foreign currency. The U.S. officially devalued the dollar by approximately 59 percent with the passage of the Gold Reserve Act in 1939. Devaluation is most often used as a means of gaining an advantage over foreign competitors or in maintaining a favorable *balance*[10] *of payments*. Such a process tends to increase exports and decrease imports. The U.S. dollar was devalued 8 percent in 1971 and 10 percent in 1973. See also *export tax*[10]; *free*[10] *silver*; *gold*[10] *standard*; *import tax*[10]; *wage-price*[10] *freeze*.

dialectical materialism: see Chap. 3.

divestment theory. The process occasionally used by the *federal government*[3] to assist a *state*[3] that wishes to prohibit a particular type of article from entering its *boundaries*[12]. For example, under the *commerce powers*[4] of the *U.S. Constitution*[4], the federal government may "divest" itself of *authority*[3] and permit states to regulate goods entering their boundaries when the interstate movement of such goods would normally be regulated only by the federal government. Divestment has been used in regard to the movement of liquor, prison-made goods, plant life, and various other commercial goods. See also *interstate commerce*[10]; *intrastate commerce*[10]; *Kentucky*[1] *Whip and Collar Co. v. Illinois Central Railroad Co.*; *Leisy*[1] *v. Hardin*; *Webb-Kenyon*[10] *Act of 1913*.

earmarking. The practice of setting aside tax revenues for particular purposes. Earmarking is most evident at the *state*[3] level in the specific areas of highway construction and maintenance, welfare, and education. See also *benefit*[10] *theory*.

Economic Report: see *budget*[6] (*economic*) *message*.

economics, Keynesian: see *John Maynard Keynes*[10].

economics, *laissez faire*: see *laissez*[3] *faire*.

economy, mixed. An economic system which is an informal compromise between strict *laissez*[3] *faire* economics and broad or rigidly controlled or manipulated economics (*communism*[3], *socialism*[3], etc.). In a mixed economic system, the *government*[3] regulates

some areas exclusively, some partially, and others not at all.

eminent domain: see Chap. 9.

Employment Act of 1946. A major federal *law*[8] specifically designed to permit the *federal government*[3] to regulate broad economic matters in the U.S. and thereby avoid major problems of economic dislocation and unemployment. The *legislation*[7] sought to balance manpower, natural resources, economic forces, and other variables in the economic system. It created the *Council*[2] *of Economic Advisers* within the *Executive*[2] *Office* and the *Joint*[10] *Committee on the Economic Report* within the *Congress*[4] in order to coordinate legislative action on economic matters. The *President*[6] delivers an annual *budget*[6] (*economic*) *message* on the status of the economy. He makes recommendations for maintaining full employment of natural resources, persons, and production facilities.

escape clause. A clause in tariff *legislation*[7] which permits the *U.S. President*[6], upon recommendation of the *United*[2] *States Tariff Commission*, to quickly modify *tariff*[10] regulations in order to protect domestic industries from foreign competition. See also *Hampton*[1] *& Co. v. U.S.*

Estes investigation, Billie Sol. A major legal investigation conducted during the early 1960's against Billie Sol Estes of Pecos, Texas. The investigation involved false securities on fertilizer tanks, illegal cotton acreage practices, and the storage of surplus agricultural commodities. The investigation and ensuing scandal uncovered considerable influence peddling, which proved embarrassing to the *Democratic Party*[5] *administration*[6] of *President*[6] *Lyndon B. Johnson*[6]. Estes was convicted of violating various federal *statutes*[8] and was sentenced to a *federal*[3] prison. In the *Supreme*[8] *Court* case of *Estes*[1] *v. Texas*, the

Court declared that Estes' rights to a fair trial had been violated due to the widespread public use of television during the investigation and the trial. Estes was later retried, convicted, and sent to a federal prison. He was released from prison in 1971.

Fair Labor Standards Act of 1938. A *federal*[3] law which prohibited the use of *child*[10] *labor* (under 16 or 18 years of age, depending on the job) and instituted *minimum*[10] *wage laws* and *maximum*[10] *hour laws* for employees engaged in *interstate commerce*[10]. The *law*[8] established 25 cents per hour as the first minimum wage (to increase to 40 cents in three years) and 44 hours per week as the first maximum work week (to drop to 40 hours in three years). The *act*[8] created the Wage and Hour Division in the *Department of Labor*[2] to administer the law. The *legislation*[7] was passed in an effort to balance labor practices in industries across the U.S. and to improve the working conditions of all industrial workers. The Fair Labor Standards Act provision permitting administrative determination of minimum wages was upheld by the *Supreme*[8] *Court* in the case of *Opp*[1] *Cotton Mills v. Administrator of Wage and Hour Division*. The child labor provisions were upheld in *U.S.*[1] *v. Darby Lumber Co.*

fair trade law. Any *law*[8] passed by a *state*[3] which declares that retail prices established by a product manufacturer must be adhered to within the state. Most states have used fair trade laws at one time or another. All state fair trade laws interfering with *interstate commerce*[10] were declared *unconstitutional*[3] by the *Supreme*[8] *Court* in 1951. However, subsequent *federal*[3] *legislation*[7] has reinstated certain fair trade practices.

featherbedding. A "make-work" arrangement between labor and business in which workers are maintained in jobs that are meaningless or that have been outdated due to technological advances. Featherbedding, although difficult to regulate during times of economic uncertainty, is prohibited by the *Labor-Management*[10] *Relations (Taft-Hartley) Act of 1947*. See also *labor*[10] *union*.

Federal Reserve note. U.S. *government*[3] currency note issued by the *Federal*[2] *Reserve System* and backed by gold, government *bonds*[10], or "commercial paper" discounted by the Federal Reserve Board. The Federal Reserve note is the most widely used currency presently in use in the U.S. See also *rediscount*[10] *rate*.

Federal Trade Commission Act of 1914. A major *federal*[3] *law*[8] which created the *Federal*[2] *Trade Commission* (FTC) and charged it with regulating unfair business practices throughout the U.S. The *act*[8] permits investigations of business activities, agency *hearings*[6], rule-making to regulate business operations, and legal action to halt unfair business practices. The FTC is called on to enforce various antitrust laws such as the *Sherman*[10] *Antitrust Act of 1890* and the *Clayton*[10] *Antitrust Act* of 1914. See also *Humphrey's*[1] *Executor (Rathbun) v. U.S.*

fellow servant doctrine. The *common law*[8] doctrine that holds than any individual injured on the job due to the negligence of a fellow employee may not collect damages against the employer himself regardless of how unsafe the overall working conditions. The fellow servant doctrine has generally been abandoned in the U.S. through adoption of *federal*[3] and *state*[3] *workman's*[10] *compensation* and safety *legislation*[7]. See also *assumption*[10] *of risk doctrine*; *Occupational*[11] *Health and Safety Act of 1970*.

feudalism: see Chap. 3.

fiscal year. A 12-month period designated by *government*[3] as a basic arrangement for economic management of public funds. The fiscal year of the U.S. government extends from July 1 of one year to June 30 of the next year. At the present time, some *states*[3] within the Union use the regular calendar year as a fiscal year, as did the U.S. in earlier times. Some states which have legislative *sessions*[7] every other year use a two-year framework for fiscal management. See also *budget*[10].

Food for Peace Program. A *federal*[3] program instituted in 1966 which permits the shipment of surplus agricultural commodities to other *nations*[3] on long-range financing and through outright gifts under the banner of relief. The *U.S. federal government*[3] makes sales through foreign currency exchanges, loans, and other *foreign*[12] *aid* arrangements. See also *Agency*[2] *for International Development*.

Food Stamp Plan: see Chap. 11.

franchise. In the area of business, a franchise is a privilege (license) granted by public *authority*[3] to an individual or an *organization*[6] seeking to operate some public service. See also *public*[10] *utility*.

free enterprise. The belief or practice which holds that private business should be permitted to operate with a minimum of governmental regulation. See also *laissez*[3] *faire*; *Adam Smith*[3]; *Herbert Spencer*[3]; *William Graham Sumner*[10].

free silver. The unlimited and unrestricted coinage of silver currency. The U.S. *government*[3] used silver coins in unlimited quantities between 1834 and 1873. It was restricted in the Demonetization Act of 1873, when the *gold*[10] *standard* was adopted. However, after pressure from agrarian debtor and western interests, silver once again became acceptable currency in 1878 and *bimetallism*[10] was reinstated. The Silver Purchase Act of

1934 nationalized silver and brought foreign and domestic sources under close *federal*[3] regulation in an effort to balance the silver–gold ratio used in the U.S.

futures. A financial arrangement in which a *contract*[10] is signed between a potential producer and a market speculator for future delivery of a particular product at a certain price. Commodity futures, mineral futures, and other types of speculative arrangements are used to help *stabilize*[10] public consumption and market prices.

Galbraith, John Kenneth, 1908– . Former *ambassador*[12] to India, former presidential adviser, author, economist, and Harvard professor. Galbraith was one of the leading advocates of the *Keynesian*[10] "(new) economics" of the post-*depression*[10] and post-*World*[12] *War* II periods. He has consistently supported *liberal*[3] welfare and anti-poverty programs and has been a leader of the *Americans*[5] *for Democratic Action* (ADA). He has written many significant works on economic and welfare problems. Among them are: The Concept of Countervailing Power (1951), American Capitalism (1952), The Great Crash: 1929 (1955), The Affluent Society (1958), and The New Industrial State (1967). Two of his best known works, The Affluent Society and The New Industrial State, question the need for unending production stimulated by artificial advertising and social manipulation. They also describe the social, economic, and political relationships within an industrial *society*[3].

general welfare clause: see Chap. 4.

George, Henry: see Chap. 11.

gold standard. A currency or monetary system backed by gold reserves which may be drawn against the currency at face value upon demand. The

U.S. *federal government*[3] used a bi-metallic (silver and gold) system between 1792 and 1873, at which time the gold standard was adopted. *Bimetallism*[10] was reintroduced in 1878 in the Bland-Allison Act. The Gold Standard Act of 1900 restored the gold standard, but it was rejected in 1934 in the Gold Reserve Act, which permits gold to be held in reserve but does not permit redemption of bills in gold. In the midst of a present international monetary system based on the gold standard, the U.S. is moving away from gold toward a system of trade credits between *nations*[3]. Such a system of international credits could be used to help keep the *balance*[10] *of payments* under control. See also *free*[10] *silver*.

Granger cases: see *Munn*[1] *v. Illinois*.

Granger law. Any *state*[3] law passed in a western state around 1870 in order to protect agrarian interests. The series of *laws*[8], named after the *National*[5] *Grange*, in general regulated railroads, grain storage elevators, and warehouses. Such laws were originally upheld by the *Supreme*[8] *Court* in cases such as *Munn*[1] *v. Illinois*, but were subsequently declared *unconstitutional*[3] in cases such as Wabash, St. Louis and Pacific Railway v. Illinois. See also *Populist Party*[5].

Granger Movement. A U.S. western agrarian reform movement which extended from approximately 1867 until 1900. The movement, led by farmers and debtors, sought and gained *state*[3] and *federal*[3] regulation of railroads, grain storage elevators, warehouses, *monopolies*[10], and other segments of the economy. The movement was given organizational leadership by the *National*[5] *Grange* and political leadership by the *Populist (People's) Party*[5]. The movement was successful in moving some state *legislatures*[7] to pass *Granger*[10] *laws* favorable to

agricultural interests. See also *Munn*[1] *v. Illinois* (1877).

grants-in-aid. Monetary grants made available by one governmental *jurisdiction*[8] to another, usually on the basis of prescribed conditions designed to meet specific program objectives. Grants-in-aid are frequently used in a regulatory way to stimulate *states*[3] or *municipalities*[11] to undertake spending or social programs they could not or would not previously engage in. Grants-in-aid are most often used in programs related to education, highways, health, welfare, and similar matters. See also *Frothingham*[1] *v. Mellon*; *Massachusetts*[1] *v. Mellon*; *Office*[2] *of Intergovernmental Relations*; *revenue*[10] *sharing*; *subsidy*[10].

greenback. A currency note recognized as *legal*[10] *tender* by the U.S. *government*[3]. Greenbacks, backed by government *authority*[3] without precious metal and identified by the green ink used on the back side of the notes, came into existence in 1862 during the *Civil*[4] *War*. They finally received widespread acceptance and backing by precious metal reserves. In 1879 the U.S. government declared greenbacks a permanent part of the U.S. currency system redeemable at face value in gold. See also *Hepburn*[1] *v. Griswold*.

Gresham's Law. A principle enunciated by Sir Thomas Gresham, sixteenth-century English economist and financier. The *theory*[3] holds that money of an inferior nature tends to drive money with a greater intrinsic value out of circulation. Gresham's Law tends to operate in economic systems using full *legal*[10] *tender* and free coinage of money made from different metals. See also *bimetallism*[10]; *free*[10] *silver*; *gold*[10] *standard*.

gross national product (GNP). The total national output of goods and services, public and private, at market prices. In 1970 the U.S. gross national product passed $1 trillion as a gross figure without figuring *inflation*[10].

Hayek, Friedrich August Von, 1899– . Austrian-born English economic *theorist*[3] and university professor. Hayek's influence on the U.S. economic system was felt through such works as Prices and Production (1931), The Pure Theory of Capital (1941), Road to Serfdom (1944), and Individualism and Economic Order (1948). His most famous volume, The Road to Serfdom, warned that rigidly regulated economic systems on either end of the political spectrum (*right*[3] or *left*[3]) tend to become *collectivist*[3] and *totalitarian*[3]. Hayek contended that *democracy*[3] rests essentially on a *capitalistic*[3] and competitive economic structure. He questioned the wisdom of economic reforms that shifted *power*[3] from the individual to the *state*[3], and rejected economic planning, holding that governmental regulation should be directed at protecting the rights of fair competition. He argued for a minimum of *government*[3] control in order to maintain personal and collective freedom. See also *free*[10] *enterprise*.

holding company. A *monopolistic*[10] business structure designed specifically to hold or maintain securities of another or other companies which may be easily dominated. Through such a process, a few *corporate*[10] directors may eliminate competition and manipulate market prices. Holding company practices, although legal, have received *federal*[3] regulation from various anti-monopoly acts such as the *Sherman*[10] *Antitrust Act of 1890* and the *Clayton*[10] *Antitrust Act of 1914*. Holding companies have also been considerably restricted through U.S. *Supreme*[8] *Court* decisions. See also *Public*[10] *Utility Holding Co. Act of 1935*; *restraint of trade*[10]; *Securities*[2] *and Exchange Commission*.

Homestead Act of 1862: see Chap. 11.

inflation. An economic condition in which there is an increase in the money available to the public without a relative increase in the volume of goods or services provided. When such a condition develops, there is usually an increase in prices, with a decrease in purchasing *power*[3]. See also *deflation*[10]; *depression*[10].

injunction, labor. A court order used to prohibit a *labor*[10] *union* or its members from taking disruptive action against an employer. The labor injunction was widely used to hamper union efforts between the passage of the *Sherman*[10] *Antitrust Act of 1890* and the passage of the *Norris-La Guardia*[10] *Act of 1932*, a *federal*[3] *law*[8] which severely restricted the use of injunctions. The *Labor-Management*[10] *Relations* (*Taft-Hartley*) *Act of 1947* permits the *President*[6] to use a *writ of injunction*[8] to require a 60- or 80-day *cooling*[10] *off period* when a *strike*[10] could threaten the national security.

intergovernmental tax immunity: see Chap. 4.

interlocking directorate. A complex *corporate*[10] arrangement in which persons serving on the *board*[6] of directors of one company also serve on the boards of other companies. Such an arrangement is useful for forming a *monopoly*[10] or *trust*[10] and manipulating market prices of particular products. The *Clayton*[10] *Antitrust Act of 1914* prohibits or restricts the operations of most interlocking directorates. See also *merger*[10]; *restraint of trade*[10].

Joint Committee on the Economic Report (**Joint Economic Committee —JEC**). A legislative *committee*[7] created in the *Employment*[10] *Act of 1946* and originally composed of seven members from each house of the U.S. *Congress*[4]. The *joint committee*[7] is charged with studying economic proposals of the *President*[6] and suggesting *legislation*[7] related to the proposals.

Kennedy Round. A three-year international *tariff*[10] negotiating process stimulated by passage of the Kennedy Trade Act of 1962. The eventual *reciprocal tariff*[10] reduction process was agreed on by over 50 *nations*[3]. The negotiations were led by the office of the *General*[12] *Agreement on Tariffs and Trade* (GATT). See also *free*[12] *trade*.

Keynes, John Maynard, 1883–1946. English nobleman, mathematician, *government*[3] official, economic *theorist*[3], Cambridge professor, and author. Keynes, architect of the "Keynesian (new) economics," advocated full employment in an industrial *society*[3] through the use of active governmental interference in *fiscal policy*[10] and *monetary policy*[10]. He advocated *deficit*[10] *financing*, a certain amount of *inflation*[10], government reserves of economic necessities, taxation manipulations, *balance*[10] *of payments* manipulations, artificial stimulation of economic growth, and other controversial devices to maintain a balanced economy. Keynes was especially influential in shaping the ideas of the economic builders of *Franklin D. Roosevelt's*[6] *New*[6] *Deal* and the leaders of John F. Kennedy's *New*[6] *Frontier*. Widespread and strict control of economic institutions, widespread public employment, increased *federal*[3] spending, and deficit financing are all now accepted as basic parts of the economic life of the U.S. Keynes' most significant written works were The Economic Consequences of the Peace (1919), The General Theory of Employment, Interest, and Money (1936), and How to Pay for the War (1940).

Labor-Management Relations (Taft-Hartley) Act of 1947. A major *federal*[3] *act*[8] which enlarged the membership of the *National*[2] *Labor Relations Board* (NLRB), prohibits the *closed*[10] *shop*, permits the *union*[10] *shop* under a *majority*[3] vote of the employees, per-

mits the use of *injunctions*[10] in national emergencies, specifies that a *cooling*[10] *off period* of 60 to 80 days may be used in certain labor disputes, outlaws *jurisdictional strikes*[10], permits the use of breach-of-*contract*[10] suits between employers and *labor*[10] *unions* in certain situations, prohibits *secondary boycotts*[10], prohibits excessive union dues, prohibits direct union contributions to *political party*[5] campaigns, protects the freedom of union and employee expression in labor matters, permits the use of the *check-off*[10] if agreed to by union members, requires non-*Communist*[3] affidavits to be signed by union leaders, and requires the filing of union reports with the *federal government*[3]. Two of the most controversial sections of the act involve the non-Communist oath and the right to work provision. The non-Communist oath section was upheld by the *Supreme*[8] *Court* in 1950 in the case of *American*[1] *Communications Association v. Douds*. Section 14 (b), the *"right*[8] *to work"* law section, permits *states*[3] to prohibit the use of the union shop. The *loyalty*[9] *oath* was repealed in 1959, and various unsuccessful attempts have been made to repeal the right to work provision. See also *Youngstown*[1] *Sheet & Tube Co. v. Sawyer*.

Labor-Management Reporting and Disclosure (Landrum-Griffin) Act of 1959. A major *federal*[3] *law*[8] passed to regulate internal *labor*[10] *union* activities and protect members from unfair practices. The *act*[8], frequently called the Labor Reform Act of 1959, restricts former prison inmates from holding leadership positions within unions, requires regular union reports to *government*[3], prohibits the misuse of union funds, insures the use of the secret ballot and free speech in union procedures, assures rank-and-file access to union records, and permits union members to sue their unions for unfair practices. The law originally barred *Communists*[3] from holding union offices, but this provision was declared *unconstitutional*[3] in the *Supreme*[8] *Court* case of *U.S.*[1] *v. Brown*.

labor theory of value. The economic concept that all economic value originates in the labor which went into the production of the economic value. Leading advocates of such a *theory*[3] were *Adam Smith*[3], David Ricardo, Friedrich Engels, and *Karl Marx*[3]. See also *dialectical*[3] *materialism*; *dictatorship*[3] *of the proletariat*; *proletariat*[3].

labor union. An *organization*[6] composed of workers seeking to better their wages, working conditions, and general benefits through *collective*[10] *bargaining* with employers and through political support of candidates and *political parties*[5] favorable to labor. The largest and most powerful labor union is the *American*[5] *Federation of Labor and Congress of Industrial Organizations* (AFL-CIO). See also *American*[5] *Federation of Teachers*; *Committee*[5] *on Political Education*; *International*[5] *Brotherhood of Teamsters*; *Labor-Management*[10] *Relations* (*Taft-Hartley*) *Act of 1947*; *Labor-Management*[10] *Reporting and Disclosure* (*Landrum-Griffin*) *Act of 1959*; *National*[2] *Labor Relations Board*; *National*[10] *Labor Relations* (*Wagner*) *Act of 1935*; *syndicalism*[3]; *United*[5] *Mine Workers*.

laissez faire: see Chap. 3.

law of capture. The concept that the legal owner of a piece of *property*[10] retains title to the mineral products beneath his land even if some of the products such as oil or gas moved from beneath a neighbor's land. Such legal rights or property may be leased by the legal owner to companies capable of recovering the valuable product.

legal tender. Any form of currency that is legally recognized as acceptable for the payment of all debts, public or private. In 1862 the *U.S. Congress*[4] declared treasury notes known as *greenbacks*[10] (fiat money) to be legal tender even though they were not fully backed by gold or silver. The use of such notes was upheld in the so-called *Legal*[1] *Tender Cases* of 1871. The use of *state*[3] currency notes not recognized as legal tender was restricted by the use of a *federal*[3] *regulatory tax*[10], a tax upheld by the *Supreme*[8] *Court* in 1869. States were *constitutionally*[3] prohibited from recognizing anything as legal tender except gold and silver (Art. I. Sec. 10). See also *free*[10] *silver*; *gold*[10] *standard*; *Hepburn*[1] *v. Griswold*.

Legal Tender Act of 1862. A *federal*[3] act which declared that currency (fiat, *greenback*[10]) notes issued by the U.S. *federal government*[3] during the conduct of the *Civil*[4] *War* could be used to pay debts contracted prior to the outbreak of the *war*[12]. The *act*[8] was declared *unconstitutional*[3] by the *Supreme*[8] *Court* in *Hepburn*[1] *v. Griswold* in 1870, on the grounds that it violated the obligation of *contract*[10] and the *due*[4] *process clause* of the *Fifth Amendment*[9]. In essence, such obligations must be paid in *specie*[10]. The Hepburn ruling was overturned in 1871 in the *Legal*[1] *Tender Cases* and the currency known as *legal*[10] *tender* was declared acceptable on the grounds that the *Congress*[4] may regulate general currency matters and do that which is necessary under the *war*[12] *powers*.

licensing by reciprocity. The process of two or more agencies or governmental units such as *states*[3] agreeing to recognize particular types of licenses in all *jurisdictions*[8] agreeing on the matter. For example, drivers' licenses, public accounting licenses, and other licenses are frequently covered by such interstate agreements. See also *intergovernmental*[11] *agreement*; *interstate*[11] *compact*; *interstate*[11] *relations*; *interstate*[11] *trade barrier*.

lockout. Action taken by an employer which keeps the workers out of the business or industry in question in an effort to come to some agreement between both parties. A lockout is initiated by the employer, whereas, a *strike*[10] is initiated by the employees.

Malthus, Thomas R.: see Chap. 11.

marginal utility theory. The *theory*[3] that the richer a person is, the less need he feels for additional increments of the basic necessities of life and the less he is willing to pay for them. The theory also holds that the richer a person is, the smaller the sacrifice that an additional dollar of taxation makes with regard to his own provision of the basic necessities of life. See also *progressive tax*[10]; *regressive tax*[10].

Marx, Karl: see Chap. 3.

maximum hour law. A *federal*[3] or *state*[3] *law*[8] that requires that private and public businesses must limit the number of daily or weekly hours of employment of workers. The range of hours differs according to place, time, and the circumstances of employment. See also *Bunting*[1] *v. Oregon*; *Fair*[10] *Labor Standards Act of 1938*; *Lochner*[1] *v. New York*; *Muller*[1] *v. Oregon*; *National*[10] *Industrial Recovery Act of 1933*.

McNary-Haugen bill. An unsuccessful, proposed *federal*[3] farm *bill*[7] aimed at artificially raising and stabilizing the prices of farm products. The bill, actively supported by some groups between 1924 and 1928, would have created a federal corporation to purchase surplus farm products and sell them to foreign *nations*[3] or place them in storage. The *government corporation*[6] would have used an "equalization fee" to contrast domestic and international prices in order to pay farmers for commodity losses. See also *price*[10] *support program*.

mediation (conciliation), labor. The process in which parties to a labor dispute submit their dispute to examination and judgment by a third party whose judgment has no legally binding effect. The two major mediation service agencies provided by the *federal government*[3] are the *National*[2] *Mediation Board* and the *Federal*[2] *Mediation and Conciliation Service*.

mercantilism: see Chap. 3.

merger. A business process in which several companies or *organizations*[3] combine into one *corporation*[10] or into an economic arrangement considered mutually beneficial. Mergers are legal as long as they do not obviously operate as a *monopoly*[10] or in such a way as to unfairly manipulate market prices. See also *conglomerate*[10]; *Federal*[2] *Deposit Insurance Corporation*; *interlocking*[10] *directorate*; *trust*[10]; *U.S.*[1] *v. E. C. Knight Co.*

minimum wage law. A *federal*[3] or *state*[3] *law*[8] that requires that private or public businesses must pay workers wages at or above a minimum established by *government*[3]. See also *Adkins*[1] *v. Children's Hospital*; *Fair*[10] *Labor Standards Act of 1938*; *National*[10] *Industrial Recovery Act of 1933*; *West*[1] *Coast Hotel v. Parrish*.

monopoly. An economic or business arrangement in which an economic market is totally controlled by one business. A monopoly makes it possible to eliminate competition and to manipulate market prices. Artificial business monopolies are prohibited by the *federal government*[3] under *legislation*[7] such as the *Sherman*[10] *Antitrust Act of 1890* and the *Clayton*[10] *Antitrust Act of 1914*. Natural business monopolies such as *public*[10] *utility* companies are licensed and regulated by government agencies at various levels of the federal system. See also *Charles*[1] *River Bridge v. Warren Bridge*; *conglomerate*[10]; *in-*

terlocking[10] *directorate*; *Public*[10] *Utility Holding Company* (*Wheeler-Rayburn*) *Act of 1935*; *restraint of trade*[10]; *Securities*[2] *and Exchange Commission*; *trust*[10]; *U.S.*[1] *v. E. C. Knight Co.*; *U.S.*[1] *v. E. I. Du Pont De Nemours & Co.*

Morrill Act of 1862: see Chap. 11.

National Industrial Recovery Act of 1933. A major *federal*[3] *act*[8] of the *New*[6] *Deal* program of *President*[6] *Franklin D. Roosevelt*[6]. The emergency *legislation*[7], passed in the midst of the *Great Depression*[10], established *codes*[8] of fair competition covering wages, prices, *child*[10] *labor*, industrial employment and other items affecting *interstate commerce*[10]. The *Congress*[4] used a legislative *delegation of authority*[6] to permit the President to approve codes submitted to him by various businesses and industries. The *National*[2] *Recovery Administration* (NRA) was created to assist in such practices. The legislation and the NRA were subsequently destroyed by the *Supreme*[8] *Court in Panama*[1] *Refining Co. v. Ryan* and *Schechter*[1] *Poultry Corp. v. U.S.*

nationalization (expropriation) of business: see *nationalized property*[10].

National Labor Relations (Wagner) Act of 1935. A major *federal*[3] *law*[8] which created the *National*[2] *Labor Relations Board* (NLRB), upheld the right of unionization and *collective*[10] *bargaining*, established machinery for collective bargaining procedures, and prohibited unfair employer practices against workers. See also *labor*[10] *union*; *National*[1] *Labor Relations Board v. Jones and Laughlin Corp.*

New Deal: see Chap. 6.

Norris-La Guardia (Anti-Injunction) Act of 1932. A major *federal*[3] *law*[8] which severely limited the use of court *injunctions*[10] to halt peaceful labor *strikes*[10]. The *act*[8] also protected *labor*[10] *union* officials from liability for *radical*[3] unauthorized actions performed by individual union members, forbade the use of *yellow dog contracts*[10], and required trial by *jury*[8] in various *contempt*[8] *of court* cases.

oligopoly. An economic or business arrangement in which an economic market is totally controlled by a few businesses or sellers of a particular product. A condition of oligopoly is not strictly prohibited by *law*[8]. However, such a condition noticeably affects the market price of goods and services offered by companies having little competition. See also *conglomerate*[10]; *interlocking*[10] *directorate*; *merger*[10]; *monopoly*[10]; *trust*[10].

open market operations. An economic practice in which the Federal Reserve Open Market Committee (FROMC) of the United States *Federal*[2] *Reserve System* regulates various financial securities offered for public sale. Open market operations are used to give basic direction to the U.S. economy, especially through the open sale of *government*[3] securities and notes. See also *fiscal policy*[10].

open shop. A business or industry that employs *labor*[10] *union* and nonunion workers. See also *closed*[10] *shop*; *union*[10] *shop*.

original cost theory. A method frequently used by *government*[3] to determine the rate of profit that should be permitted *public*[10] *utility* companies or *common*[10] *carriers* whenever figuring rates that may be charged the public. The *theory*[3] holds that the basic element to be used in figuring rates should be the actual original investment made by stockholders. Lesser factors which are generally considered are expansion investments and depreciation. See also *prudent*[10] *investment theory*; *rate-making*[10]; *re-*

production[10] *cost theory*; *Smyth*[1] *v. Ames.*

original package doctrine. A doctrine judicially pronounced by *Chief*[8] *Justice John Marshall*[8] *in the Supreme*[8] *Court* case of *Brown*[1] *v. Maryland* in 1827. The doctrine held that *interstate commerce*[10] begins as soon as the original package has been delivered to and accepted by a *common*[10] *carrier* for shipment across one or more *state*[3] lines or to a foreign *nation*[3]. Interstate commerce under *federal*[3] regulation continues until the package reaches its destination and is actually opened. Only at that point does the product become a part of *intrastate commerce*[10] under exclusive state regulation. The original package doctrine developed when Maryland sought to impose a rather large license fee on foreign importers doing business within Maryland. Businessmen unwilling to pay the state fee were prohibited from selling imported items within the state. The Supreme Court held that such state action was *unconstitutional*[3]. The doctrine was later modified by the Court through the development of the *divestment*[10] *theory.*

panic. An economic downturn which results in sudden public fear and *radical*[3] and widespread business collapse. A panic is ordinarily characterized by an economic *depression*[10], widespread unemployment, bank closings, *corporate*[10] and private *bankruptcies*[10], agricultural instability, and a decline in foreign trade. See also *wildcat bank*[10]; *Great Depression*[10].

parity. The condition of balanced economic arrangements. The term "parity" is frequently used to contrast the economic significance of two forms of national currency. It is also used to compare agricultural prices of one historical period with prices of an earlier period. The *U.S. federal government*[3] adopted an official agricul-tural *policy*[6] of seeking to maintain parity for American farmers figured on the base period of 1909–1914. The *Department of Agriculture*[2] and the *Congress*[4] determine regularly what parity (the current minimum market price compared to the earlier date) should be for particular crops. See also *price*[10] *support program*; *Wickard*[1] *v. Filburn.*

patent. An official and exclusive *government*[3] grant to a person who has devised a process or invention which could possibly be useful or valuable on the open market. A U.S. patent is currently granted for 17 years on a nonrenewable basis. The term "patent" may also be used to specify a public document or commission granting some exclusive right or position.

peril point. A flexible figure related to *tariff*[10] arrangements, which is used as a guideline to determine when a particular product or the total economic structure of a *nation*[3] is threatened by outside trade. In the U.S., the *United*[2] *States Tariff Commission* makes regular reports to the *President*[6] on the nature of tariff arrangements. The President then makes recommendations to the *Congress*[4]. See also *Hampton*[1] *& Co. v. U.S.*

picket. An organized action of workers designed to stimulate public awareness of grievances of workers against an employer. Picketing generally consists of workers stationing themselves outside a business and advertising by printed signs that employees of the business are on *strike*[10]. Picketing is protected by the *First Amendment*[9] to the *U.S. Constitution*[4] as a form of free speech. See also *Thornhill*[1] *v. Alabama.*

policy, fiscal. The planned governmental management of economic variables within a *society*[3]. Fiscal *policy*[6] of a *government*[3] generally involves decision-making concerning taxes, public spending, money available on the open market, and similar matters. It is designed essentially to maintain a high rate of employment, healthy business activity, and a sound base for the creation of public revenue. The *President's*[6] basic advisory agency in the area of fiscal policy is the *Council*[2] *of Economic Advisers.* See also *monetary policy*[10].

policy, monetary. The planned governmental management of monetary supplies within a political and social system. It consists of balancing the money available within a *society*[3] against the demands made for money by the population. Monetary policy in the U.S. is generally regulated by the *Federal*[2] *Reserve System.* The Federal Reserve Board determines the amount of money available through shifts in the level of the *rediscount*[10] *rate* regulating the cost of borrowing money. The *Congress*[4] sometimes enters the picture of monetary policy through passage of taxation measures which remove money from circulation or make it available. See also *fiscal policy*[10].

pool. A *monopolistic*[10] business arrangement, particularly evident between 1860 and 1880, in which competitive companies in the same business agreed on divided markets and market prices and then pooled the exorbitant profits for division according to established ratios. Pooling in various businesses was prohibited by *federal*[3] *legislation*[7] such as the Interstate Commerce Commission Act of 1883 and the *Sherman*[10] *Antitrust Act of 1890.* See also *Interstate*[2] *Commerce Commission; restraint of trade*[10].

pork barrel: see Chap. 7.

potential output. The maximum output an economy is capable of producing without undue strain on a *society*[3]. In order to maintain a balanced economy, there is generally a public effort to balance output with *total*[10] *demand (spending).*

powers, commerce: see *commerce*[4] *clause.*

powers, taxing: see Chap. 4.

price support program. A complex and controversial federal program to help balance and stabilize farm production and farm prices. The U.S. *federal government*[3] has used various approaches to stabilize agricultural prices since the *New*[6] *Deal,* some of which were declared *unconstitutional*[3], while others were found permissible. The government has used outright purchases of surpluses, crop storage, loan programs, the *soil*[10] *bank, parity*[10], and numerous other systems to help maintain an economic balance in agriculture. See also *Agricultural*[10] *Adjustment Act of 1933; Agricultural*[10] *Adjustment Act of 1938; Brannan*[10] *plan; Farm*[2] *Credit Administration; McNary-Haugen*[10] *bill; Mulford*[1] *v. Smith; stabilizer*[10]; *steadier*[10]; *U.S.*[1] *v. Butler; Wickard*[1] *v. Filburn.*

property. Any tangible or intangible item that belongs legally and exclusively to an individual, group of individuals, *nation*[3], *corporation*[10], or other legal entity. See also *Dartmouth*[1] *College v. Woodward; Dred*[1] *Scott v. Sandford; Olmstead*[1] *v. U.S.*

property, enemy alien. *Property*[10] which is officially taken, temporarily or permanently, from a resident *alien*[3] by a *government*[3] claiming that the owner's homeland is an enemy *nation*[3]. Aliens may find various restrictions on property usage even in times of relative peace. See also *enemy alien*[12]; *nationalized property*[10].

property, nationalized (expropriated). Privately owned *property*[10] that is taken over by *government*[3] for public ownership. *Eminent*[9] *domain* is one form of nationalization of property, which generally requires adequate compensation for the previous owner. The nationalization of *enemy alien property*[10] or general nationalization of major foreign industries operating within a *nation*[3] rarely provide adequate compensation for the property taken. Some nations that have adopted *socialistic*[3] economic practices have nationalized such things as railroads, steel production, health services, and other major segments of the economy. Nations that have adopted *communism*[3] or fallen under its influence generally find all property nationalized. See also *enemy alien*[10]; *Berman*[1] *v. Parker.*

protectionism. The concept and practice of economically protecting local business interests, especially relatively new businesses, from foreign competition through restrictive *tariffs*[10] and trade agreements. See also *Hampton*[1] *& Co. v. U.S.*

prudent investment theory. A method frequently used by *government*[3] to determine the rate of profit that should be permitted *public*[10] *utility* companies or *common*[10] *carriers* whenever figuring rates that may be charged the public. The *theory*[3] holds that rates should be based largely on original cost and subsequent prudent investments in the business. See also *original*[10] *cost theory*; *rate-making*[10]; *reproduction*[10] *cost theory*; *Smyth*[1] *v. Ames.*

public domain: see Chap. 4.

public interest, affected with a. A private business which, by its very nature, has certain attributes of public involvement or which may tend to become a *monopoly*[10]. Such businesses generally receive strict governmental regulation in order to protect the public interest. Examples of such busi-

nesses are *public*[10] *utility* companies, *common*[10] *carriers*, and public warehouses and storage elevators. See also *Munn*[1] *v. Illinois*; *Nebbia*[1] *v. New York.*

public power. Electrical energy produced and distributed by publicly owned facilities. Public power gained public prominence and created political controversy during the *Great Depression*[10] of the 1930's with the building of dams on the Colorado, Columbia, and Tennessee rivers. Although the construction of such electricity-producing facilities was undertaken to provide public employment and *conserve*[10] natural resources, the various production capabilities were viewed as a threat to private *free*[10] *enterprise*. The *Tennessee*[2] *Valley Authority* (TVA) is the largest and most comprehensive public power system in the U.S. Its existence was upheld as *constitutional*[3] in the *Supreme*[8] *Court* case of *Ashwander*[1] *v. Tennessee Valley Authority*. See also *Federal*[2] *Power Commission*; *rural*[10] *electrification*; *Rural*[2] *Electrification Administration*.

public utility. A private business which provides a public service under strict governmental licensing and regulation. Public utilities are under strict legal regulations formulated by both the *federal*[3] and *state*[3] *governments*[3] and are generally administered by *public service commissions*[10] or *independent regulatory commissions*[6]. Examples of public utilities are electrical service, natural gas service, and railroad service. See also *Munn*[1] *v. Illinois*; *proprietary power*[4]; *Public*[10] *Utility Holding Company (Wheeler-Rayburn) Act of 1935*; *rate-making*[10].

Public Utility Holding Company (Wheeler-Rayburn) Act of 1935. A *federal*[3] *law*[8] which brought electrical and gas utility *holding*[10] companies under the securities regulations of the *Securities*[2] *and Exchange Commission*

(SEC) and power regulations of the *Federal*[2] *Power Commission*. The *legislation*[7] restricted holding company structures to the "second degree" (an operating company and two holding companies), permits regulated *rate-making*[10], and carefully supervises the sale of *public*[10] *utility* company securities.

public works. Items built at public expense and through public effort for general public use. Popular items generally built as public works are roads, dams, canals, schools, sewage treatment plants, parks, and public office buildings. See also *boondoggling*[10]; *Corps of Engineers*[2]; *Department of the Interior*[2]; *Federal*[11] *Highway Act of 1956*; *Tennessee*[2] *Valley Authority.*

Railway Labor (Watson-Parker) Act of 1926. A *federal*[3] act which guaranteed the right of labor to organize and bargain collectively within the railway industry. The *act*[8] also designated certain agencies such as the *National*[2] *Mediation Board* to mediate railway labor disputes and outlined certain procedures to be used in settling disputes through *labor mediation*[10] and *labor arbitration*[10]. See also *collective*[10] *bargaining.*

rate-making. The process in which an *independent regulatory commission*[6] or *public service commission*[10] determines the rates a *public*[10] *utility* or *common*[10] *carrier* may charge the public for services. Various criteria are used in determining rates, the most popular being the *original*[10] *cost theory* and the *prudent*[10] *investment theory*. See also *Munn*[1] *v. Illinois*; *Public*[10] *Utility Holding Company (Wheeler-Rayburn) Act of 1935*; *reproduction*[10] *cost theory*; *Smyth*[1] *v. Ames.*

recession. A minor or temporary decline in business activity, a decline that is considered by the public as less severe than a *depression*[10]. See also *panic*[10].

rediscount rate. A lending process which is controlled in the U.S. by the *Federal*[2] *Reserve System* and in which one bank loans funds to another bank on the basis of negotiable instruments or commercial paper previously "discounted." To discount a loan means to subtract the interest on the note in advance. When the rate is raised, the availability of money and credit is restricted on the open market. When it is lowered, money and credit are easier to obtain and there is general stimulation of the total economy. The Federal Reserve Board sometimes adjusts the rate in order to help direct the economy with regard to *inflation*[10] and *deflation*[10]. See also *fiscal policy*[10]; *monetary policy*[10]; *open*[10] *market operations.*

Report on the Subject of Manufacturers (1791). A major and influential volume written by *Alexander Hamilton*[4] in support of governmental promotion and *subsidization*[10] of manufacturing. The work refuted the idea that agriculture is the only productive industry. Hamilton developed systematic arguments in favor of protective *tariffs*[10], exclusion of certain foreign goods, business *tax*[10] *exemptions*, bounties, *patents*[10], and internal improvements such as transportation facilities useful to business. The volume was in direct opposition to what later came to be known as *Jeffersonian democracy*[4].

reproduction cost theory. A method frequently used by *government*[3] to determine the rate of profit that should be permitted *public*[10] *utility* companies or *common*[10] *carriers* whenever figuring rates that may be charged the public. The *theory*[3] holds that rates should be based upon the reproduction cost of current market assets of a company in relation to depreciation of company facilities over a designated period of time. See also *original*[10] *cost theory*; *prudent*[10] *investment theory*; *rate-making*[10]; *Smyth*[1] *v. Ames.*

reserve ratio. The percentage of negotiable assets or cash maintained by a bank as a reserve against the existing deposits. Reserve ratios are set by *federal*[3] and *state*[3] governmental agencies charged with protecting the general public and regulating the banking systems. See also *Federal*[2] *Reserve System.*

revenue (tax) sharing. A condition in which a set percentage of national revenue is automatically returned to the various *states*[3] within the Union to use as they desire without specific conditions attached. Revenue sharing was adopted in 1972 and a $30 billion five-year program was begun in which federal funds will be returned directly to states and local *communities*[3]. The broad program stands in contrast to previous categorical federal *grants-in-aid*[10]. President Richard Nixon supported revenue sharing for *urban*[11] development, *rural*[11] development, transportation, education, job training, and *law*[8] enforcement. Although some *governors*[6] and *mayors*[11] supported revenue sharing, others opposed it because they feared they might receive less money than under previous programs. Some of the key *congressmen*[7] concerned with revenue-raising and *appropriations bills*[7] opposed the program because of the present *deficit*[10] *financing* of the *federal government*[3], because they feared state and local governments might spend the money unwisely, and because they felt their *constituents*[5] would be unable to ascertain who helped them solve specific problems.

revolving fund. A financial fund creted specifically to be used for financial expansion through continual reinvestment use of profits drawn from loans made from the fund.

right to work law. A *statute*[8] which permits employees to work in a business or industry without joining a *labor*[10] union. A right to work law assures the existence of what is known as an *open*[10] *shop*. Section 14(b) of the *Labor-Management*[10] *Relations (Taft-Hartley) Act of 1947* permits individual *states*[3] to have right to work laws. Nineteen states currently have such *legislation*[7].

rural electrification. A formal *federal*[3] program begun in 1935, which is designed to develop and extend the use of electrical power and telephone service in rural areas of the U.S. The *Rural*[2] *Electrification Administration* (REA) administers the program through low-interest loans to rural *cooperatives*[10]. See also *public*[10] *power.*

Sheppard-Towner Act of 1921. A controversial *federal*[3] law which provided *grants-in-aid*[10] to *states*[3] willing to provide practical maternity and infant care. The *act*[8], effective through 1929, was designed to improve medical services within states and reduce the infant and maternal mortality rates within the United States. It was challenged judicially on the grounds that tax funds were being used in violation of the *reserved powers*[4] of the states. The *legislation*[7] and the ensuing *Supreme*[8] *Court* decisions opened the door for widespread *grant-in-aid*[10] programs throughout the U.S. See also *Frothingham*[1] *v. Mellon; Massachusetts*[1] *v. Mellon.*

Sherman Antitrust Act of 1890. A *federal*[3] *law*[8] which forbade all conspiracies "in *restraint of trade*[10]" and all *monopolies*[10] that interferred with *interstate commerce*[10]. The *act*[8] prohibits various types of price-fixing agreements, *contractual*[10] arrangements injurious to commerce. The *legislation*[7] was further expanded with passage of the *Clayton*[10] *Antitrust Act of 1914*. See also *conspiracy*[10] *doctrine; U.S.*[1] *v. E. C. Knight Co.; U.S.*[1] *v. E. I. Du Pont De Nemours & Co.*

Sinclair, Upton, 1878–1969. American *socialist*[3], muckraker, idealist, and prolific author. From 1900 to 1950, Sinclair attacked the excesses of *laissez*[3] *faire capitalism*[3] and defended *liberal*[3] social and economic reforms. He attacked various social abuses in the fields of religion, racial *segregation*[9], education, militarism, the press, private business, and numerous other areas. He gained fame with The Jungle (1906), an expressive novel exposing the unsanitary conditions in the meat-packing industry of Chicago. His exposé led to the passage of the first *federal*[3] pure food *legislation*[7] in the U.S. Sinclair led a movement known as E.P.I.C. (End Poverty in California) and was almost elected *governor*[6] of California on the *Democratic Party*[5] ticket. Among his numerous books were The Metropolis (1908), Jimmie Higgins (1919), The Goose Step (1923), Dragon's Teeth (1942), Wide Is the Gate (1943), and The Cup of Fury (1956). See also *Pure*[11] *Food and Drug Act of 1906*.

Smith, Adam: see Chap. 3.

socialism: see Chap. 3.

soil bank. A *federal*[3] program adopted in 1956 in order to reduce crop surpluses, raise market prices of agricultural products, and *conserve*[10] agricultural land. See also *Commodity*[2] *Credit Corporation*; *price*[10] *support program*.

specie. Coined or metal money. See also *legal*[10] *tender*; *Hepburn*[1] *v. Griswold*.

Spencer, Herbert: see Chap. 3.

stabilizer. A quickly operating economic device or "money stream" used by *government*[3] to help regulate the total economy of a *nation*[3]. Some of the basic stabilizers that move counter to upward or downward economic trends are taxes, *rediscount*[10] *rates*, commodity *futures*[10], *open*[10] *market operations*, and "dumping" of govern-

ment surpluses on the open market. Such actions are used as part of the overall *fiscal policy*[10] and *monetary policy*[10] of the U.S. federal *government*[3]. See also *steadier*[10]; *wage-price*[10] *freeze*.

state debts, assumption of. The economic proposal made by *Alexander Hamilton*[4] while he served as Secretary of the Treasury that the U.S. *government*[3] should pay all of the state debts incurred during the *American Revolution*[4]. The *Congress*[4] assumed such debts in the Assumption Act of 1790.

steadier. A slowly operating economic device or "money stream" used by *government*[3] to help gradually regulate or maintain the total economy of a *nation*[3]. Some of the basic steadiers are large blocks of money such as veterans' benefits, *Social*[11] *Security* payments, agricultural *price*[10] *support programs*, national defense spending, and educational research funding. Spending or withholding of such funds by the *federal government*[3] is part of the overall *fiscal policy*[10] and *monetary policy*[10] employed within the United States. See also *stabilizer*[10].

strike. An act performed by workers which halts business or production, in an effort to achieve certain objectives sought by the workers. The most frequently sought objectives are higher wages, better working conditions, and "fringe benefits" such as sick-leave time and earlier retirement. See also *American*[1] *Communications Association v. Douds*; *Debs*[1], *in re*; *lockout*[10].

strike, jurisdictional. A *strike*[10] undertaken whenever a *labor*[10] *union* feels that its employer has given business to members of another union or in which there is a dispute between two or more unions concerning which group shall represent a group of workers. Jurisdictional strikes were prohibited in the *Labor-Manage-*

ment[10] *Relations (Taft-Hartley) Act of 1947.*

strike, secondary. A *strike*[10] undertaken by a group of workers within one business *organization*[6] in order to bring pressure to bear on another business or employer. For example, a strike against a supplier of parts might be considered effective in influencing labor decisions in another company. Secondary strikes are prohibited by the *Labor-Management*[10] *Relations (Taft-Hartley) Act of 1947.* See also *labor*[10] *union.*

strike, sit-down. An illegal *strike*[10] in which workers stop production and remain inside the plant or business.

strike, sympathy. A *labor*[10] *union* action in which members of a union *strike*[10] in order to benefit a group other than themselves.

strike, wildcat. A *strike*[10] called without approval of *labor*[10] *union* leadership.

subsidy. A financial grant made by *government*[3] to an individual or private business. A subsidy is ordinarily extended in order to stimulate the creation or continued operation of an enterprise viewed as publicly beneficial. See also *grants-in-aid*[10]; *Mulford*[1] *v. Smith*; *parity*[10]; *price*[10] *support program*; *public housing*[11].

Sumner, William Graham, 1840–1910. American clergyman, educator, political scientist, sociologist, economist, and author. Sumner was the leading American advocate of the *theories*[3] of the English economist *Herbert Spencer*[3]. He advocated *laissez*[3] *faire capitalism*[2] and supported *Social*[11] *Darwinism.* He opposed all governmental interference in economic and general social affairs and spoke on behalf of those whose wealth was taken from them through taxes for the support of general welfare needs. He believed poverty indicated some

fault or weakness in those who were poor, that *property*[10] ownership was an *absolute right*[9], and that economic competition, even if fatal, was a basic *law*[8] of nature. Sumner wrote What Social Classes Owe to Each Other (1883), Folkways (1907), and The Science of Society (1927), a posthumous four-volume work which systematically defends his general economic and social theories.

surtax. A tax based on a percentage of a tax figure already in use. The percentage is added to the total tax bill already figured in order to arrive at a new tax figure. For example, a 10 percent surtax on a $1,200 tax bill would be $120; The new tax bill would become $1,320.

tariff. A tax or list of taxes placed by a *government*[3] on exports or imports. The *U.S. Constitution*[4] prohibits the use of *export taxes*[10]. However, the U.S. employs a wide range of taxes on various products imported into the *country*[3] from other *nations*[3]. The *United*[2] *States Tariff Commission*, the *President*[6], the *Congress*[4], and various international agencies help determine tariff levels at any given time. See also *escape*[10] *clause*; *Hampton*[1] *& Co. v. U.S.*; *import tax*[10]; *peril*[10] *point.*

tariff, reciprocal. An international trade agreement in which two or more *countries*[3] agree to raise or lower *tariffs*[10] on particular articles at the same time. Such agreements, sometimes called reciprocal trade agreements, involve the exchange of mutual favors or concessions in the area of international trade. In 1934 the U.S. passed the Reciprocal Trade Agreements Act, which lowered tariffs, permitted the *President*[6] to quickly regulate tariff matters on his own initiative (originally reductions up to 50 percent), and adopted the *most*[12] *favored nation theory* which extends favorable trade relations to all *nations*[3] on the same level. See also *free*[12] *trade*; *General*[12] *Agreement on Tariffs* *and Trade*; *Kennedy*[10] *Round*; *Office*[12] *for Economic Cooperation and Development*; *peril*[10] *point*.

tax, ad valorem. A tax based on the value of a particular item.

tax, betterment (special assessment). A tax levied to pay for particular public improvements which tend to increase the value of adjacent real *property*[10]. For example, homeowners may have to help pay for pavement in front of their homes because such an improvement helps increase the value of the homes themselves. See also *benefit*[10] *theory*.

tax, direct. A tax levied directly on an individual or business and paid directly to the *government*[3] by the person taxed. The most common forms of direct taxes are *graduated income taxes*[10], *inheritance taxes*[10], *gift taxes*[10], *property taxes*[10] *and poll taxes*[5]. Originally the U.S. had to apportion direct taxes on the basis of population among the *states*[3] within the Union, but such an arrangement was changed by the addition of the *Sixteenth Amendment*[10] to the *Constitution*[4] in order to permit individual and *corporate*[10] graduated income taxes. See also *Twenty-fourth Amendment*[5]; *Harper*[1] *v. Virginia State Board of Elections*; *Hylton*[1] *v. U.S.*; *indirect tax*[10]; *Pollock*[1] *v. Farmers' Loan and Trust Co.*; *taxing powers*[4].

tax, estate. A *progressive tax*[10] levied on the *property*[10] of deceased individuals. Estate taxes are used by both the *federal*[3] and *state*[3] governments. The U.S. *government*[3] uses the *tax*[10] *offset* to encourage states to use estate taxes. See also *gift tax*[10].

tax, excess profits. A tax that becomes effective only after a particular value is exceeded on a given item or in a particular taxable area. Excess profits taxes have been used most frequently in the U.S. during wartime in an effort to hold down *war*[12] profiteering.

tax, excise. An *indirect tax*[10] levied on particular products sold within a *country*[3]. Excise taxes are frequently levied on jewelry, alcoholic beverages, tobacco products, and numerous other items. See also *Hylton*[1] *v. U.S.*

tax exemption. Any legal arrangement whereby certain items or matters normally taxed by *government*[3] are are exempted for specific purposes. Some of the most obvious tax exemptions are the oil *depletion*[10] *allowance, municipal*[11] *bonds*[10], religious and benevolent contributions, and minimum child maintenance. See also *Graves*[1] *v. New York ex rel O'Keefe*; *Griffin*[1] *v. County Board of Prince Edward County*; *Helvering*[1] *v. Gerhardt*; *Walz*[1] *v. Tax Commission of the City of New York*.

tax, export. A tax collected on goods being shipped out of a *country*[3]. The *U.S. Constitution*[4] prohibits such a tax.

tax, general sales. An *indirect tax*[10] levied on services or goods available to the general public. General sales taxes ordinarily operate on a graduated scale and are based on the value of particular items. See also *optional municipal sales tax*[10]; *regressive tax*[10].

tax, gift. A *progressive tax*[10] levied on gifts given to individuals, bequeaths generally made in an effort to avoid payment of *inheritance taxes*[10] or *estate taxes*[10].

tax, graduated income. A *direct tax*[10] levied on the income of individuals and businesses. A *federal*[3] income tax was used in the U.S. between 1861 and 1872. However, a graduated income tax *law*[8] passed in 1894 was declared *unconstitutional*[3] by the *U.S. Supreme*[8] *Court* in 1895, on the grounds that it could not be apportioned on the basis of population as called for in Article I, Section 9, Clause 4 of the *Constitution*[4]. The *Sixteenth Amendment*[10] was added to the Constitution in 1913 to permit such a *progressive tax*[10] to be levied directly against individuals and *corporations*[10]. See also *Collector*[1] *v. Day*; *Graves*[1] *v. N.Y. ex rel O'Keefe*; *Helvering*[1] *v. Gerhardt*; *Hylton*[1] *v. U.S.*; *Internal*[2] *Revenue Service*; *Marchetti*[1] *v. U.S.*; *negative income tax*[10]; *Pollock*[1] *v. Farmers' Loan and Trust Co.*

tax, import. A tax collected on goods being shipped into a *country*.[3] See also *Commerce*[4] *Compromise*; *customs*[10] *duties*; *tariff*[10].

tax, indirect. A tax on an article which is collected by one person or agency and passed on to another agency of *government*[3]. Indirect taxes are generally collected by private businesses as *general sales taxes*[10], *tariffs*[10], or other imposts, and are then turned over to the government. The *U.S. federal government*[3] may levy indirect taxes on the basis of geographical uniformity. For example, an indirect tax must be laid at the same rate and on the same basis throughout the U.S. See also *direct tax*[10]; *Hylton*[1] *v. U.S.*; *taxing powers*[4].

tax, inheritance. A *progressive tax*[10] levied on inheritances left to individuals upon the death of friends or relatives. The *U.S. federal government*[3] uses the *tax*[10] *offset* to encourage *states*[3] to use inheritance taxes. See also *gift tax*[10].

tax, negative income. A form of taxation frequently proposed as a possible solution to certain welfare problems. The tax would be a three-way arrangement based on income. A positive *graduated income tax*[10] payable to the *government*[3] would be placed on those persons and families having incomes in excess of their permissible deductions, *tax*[10] *exemptions*, and credits. Those having incomes and legitimate outlays in balance would not have to pay any income taxes. Those having incomes falling below some specified poverty level, generally suggested as $3,200, would be paid by the government.

tax offset. A taxing procedure incorporated by the *federal government*[3] on various occasions to stimulate *states*[3] within the Union to adopt particular programs. For example, in 1926 such a device was used to urge states to adopt *inheritance taxes*[10] with the understanding that those states not having such a tax would find a federal inheritance tax collected within their *boundaries*.[12] In 1935 the device was used as part of the *Social*[11] *Security Act* to urge states to establish *unemployment*[11] *insurance* services. In the case of inheritance taxes, up to 80 percent of the federal tax figure may be offset if the state has an equivalent tax. In the area of unemployment compensation, up to 90 percent of the federal tax may be offset if the state operates unemployment services. The tax offset is useful in helping maintain balanced taxing relationships throughout the U.S. See also *estate tax*[10]; *Steward*[1] *Machine Co. v. Davis.*

tax, optional municipal sales. A sales tax levied at local option which may be added to an existing state *general sales tax*[10]. For example, a state *constitutional*[3] provision may permit a *municipal corporation*[11] to levy a local sales tax of a limited figure (1 cent, 2 cents, etc.) to the existing *state*[3] general sales tax (3 cents, 4 cents, etc.). Both taxes are collected as *indirect taxes*[10] at the time a single purchase is made.

tax, personal property. A tax levied directly on personal *property*[10] owned by a private individual, a group of individuals, or a business. Personal property taxes are generally levied against automobiles, merchandise, stocks, bonds, and other tangible and intangible goods separate from real estate.

tax, poll: see Chap. 5.

tax, progressive. A tax which raises revenue from individuals and businesses most able to pay taxes. A *graduated income tax*[10] is generally considered a progressive tax. See also *marginal*[10] *utility theory*; *regressive tax*[10].

tax, property. A tax levied directly on real *property*[10] owned by a private individual, a group of individuals, or a business. In early U.S. history, property taxes frequently accounted for the bulk of public revenue at the *state*[3] and local levels. One of the major problems in levying and collecting such a tax is that of assessment, due largely to political pressure, administrative difficulties, and the tendency of the value of property to change radically in a short period of time. See also *assessed*[10] *valuation*; *board*[10] *of equalization*; *competitive*[10] *underassessment*.

tax, regressive. A tax which raises revenue from individuals and businesses least able to pay taxes. A *general sales tax*[10] is ordinarily considered a regressive tax. See also *marginal*[10] *utility theory*; *progressive tax*[10].

tax, regulatory. A tax levied for the specific purpose of regulating a particular social, business, economic, or other practice. The *federal*[3] and *state*[3] *governments*[3] have used their *taxing powers*[4] to regulate such things as gambling, the sale of oleomargarine, the issuance of state bank notes, and the production of phosphorus matches. See also *Bailey*[1] *v. Drexel Furniture Co.*; *general*[4] *welfare clause*; *Hampton*[1] *& Co. v. U.S.*; *U.S.*[1] *v. Butler*; *Veazie*[1] *Bank v. Fenno*; *West*[1] *Coast Hotel Co. v. Parrish*.

tax, severance. A tax levied on nonrenewable natural resources (oil, gas, potash, timber, etc.) being used for private profit. Severance taxes are generally used for both *conservation*[10] and revenue-raising purposes. See also *depletion*[10] *allowance*.

tax sharing: see *revenue*[10] *sharing.*

Tax, Single. A tax, sometimes known as the land increment tax, which was popularized by *Henry George*[11], *socialist*[3] author of Progress and Poverty (1879). George advocated placing the ownership of all land in the hands of the *government*[3]. The increased value of the land and its use in a growing *urban*[11] *society*[3] could act as the only revenue source for all public needs.

tax, value-added. A tax, pioneered in France and advocated by some for use in the United States. The tax is based on the value of an article or product at various steps in its production and distribution. The purchaser of the product is taxed primarily on the value at any given step.

tax, withholding. A tax deducted from an employee's paycheck before he receives his salary. Both the *federal*[3] and *state*[3] *governments*[3] may legally withhold certain taxes such as federal and state *graduated income taxes*[10]. See also *Steward*[1] *Machine Co. v. Davis.*

total demand (spending). The sum total of personal spending, residential construction, business investment, and *government*[3] purchases of goods and services within a *society*[3]. In order to maintain a balanced economy, there is generally a public effort to balance total demand with *potential*[10] *output.*

trademark. A registered and governmentally protected name, emblem, or other mark used to identify a particular product. Trademarks are issued in the U.S. by the Patent Office for a 20-year period, renewable for an additional 20 years.

trade, restraint of. An act specifically designed to restrain free competition in an economic market. Various types of restraints are price-fixing, rebating, and *monopolization*[10]. Both *federal*[3] and *state*[3] *governments*[3] place various restrictions on such restraints of trade. See also *basing*[10] *point*; *Clayton*[10] *Antitrust Act of 1914*; *Federal*[2] *Trade Commission*; *free*[10] *enterprise*, *holding*[10] *company*; *interlocking*[10] *directorate*; *pool*[10]; *Sherman*[10] *Antitrust Act of 1890*; *trust*[10].

trust. A business combination of two or more companies in which the control of financial stocks and securities is maintained by a relatively small group of *corporate*[10] executives known as trustees. The trustees ordinarily conduct the businesses in such a way as to *monopolize*[10] a business market or stifle competition. Monopolistic trusts are clearly prohibited by provisions in the *Sherman*[10] *Antitrust Act of 1890* and the *Clayton*[10] *Antitrust Act of 1914*. See also *interlocking*[10] *directorate*; *merger*[10]; *Securities*[2] *and Exchange Commission*.

unemployment insurance: see Chap. 11.

union shop. A business or industry that hires *labor*[10] *union* members and non-union members who agree to join the recognized union within a specified period of time. The *Labor-Management*[10] *Relations* (*Taft-Hartley*) *Act of 1947* guarantees the use of the union shop in all *states*[3] except those specifically passing *right*[10] *to work laws*. See also *closed*[10] *shop*; *open*[10] *shop*.

usury. The practice of lending money at exorbitant, excessive, or illegal rates of interest. Such practices are generally regulated by *state*[3] and *federal*[3] *legislation*[7]. On July 1, 1969 the Federal Consumer Credit Protection Act, the "Truth in Lending Law," went into effect. It requires that lending institutions and installment credit agencies clearly indicate the finance charges made on loans. During 1969 most lending institutions averaged charges of 1.5% of the unpaid monthly balance and an annual percentage rate of 18%.

Veblen, Thorstein, 1857–1929. American historian, biologist, economist, political scientist, and sociologist. Veblen was one of the most caustic social critics of the U.S. during the early part of this century. His most famous critical analysis was contained in The Theory of the Leisure Class (1899), an economic treatise which traced economic affluence from patterns of acquisition of primitive man through modern man's selfish desires for individual ownership. Veblen described man's economic folly as marked by "conspicuous leisure," "conspicuous consumption," and "conspicuous waste." He held that one of man's highest aims is to reveal superiority not only by acquisition per se but by acquisition of goods without physical labor. He contended that competition among those seeking to gain the most through doing the least is destructive of the most meaningful and creative impulses within *society*[3]. He regularly attacked pride, wastefulness, privilege, and materialism. Some of his major *theories*[3] are contained in The Theory of Business Enterprise (1904), The Place of Science in Modern Civilization (1920), and Absentee Ownership and Business Enterprise in Recent Times (1923).

wage-price freeze. A 90-day (August 14, 1971 to November 14, 1971) economic freeze placed on wages, prices, and rents levied by both the public and private sectors throughout the United States. The "freeze" was instituted by *President*[6] Nixon in order to help stabilize the American economy. The action was based on the Economic Stabilization Act of 1971, a *bill*[7] President Nixon originally opposed. It was designed to help check *inflation*[10] and give *federal*[3] officials time to work out details covering broad economic planning. It was also designed to help protect the American dollar abroad because of the *balance*[10] *of payments* deficit. The *Cost*[2] *of Living Council*, headed by Secretary of the Treasury John Connally, was created in order to administer the program. The council immediately reduced federal employment, halted military pay raises, challenged *states*[3] such as Texas which sought to increase teacher salaries in spite of the freeze, and carried out a public relations campaign designed to convince the public to accept the drastic governmental regulation. The 90-day freeze was the beginning of long-range economic control over modern economic problems. See also *fiscal policy*[10]; *monetary policy*[10]; *stabilizer*[10].

Wall Street. The popular designation of the dominant financial *community*[3] in the U.S., a group of individuals and stock brokerage houses located on and near Wall Street in New York City.

Webb-Kenyon Act of 1913. A *federal*[3] *law*[8] which extended earlier federal *legislation*[7] (Wilson Act of 1890) and made it illegal to ship a liquor product in *interstate commerce*[10] if the liquor was used in violation of *state*[3] legislation in the state of destination.

The *act*[8] "divested" the product of its interstate nature even before the product moved from one state to another. The legislation, which emphasized the *divestment*[10] *theory*, was upheld by the *Supreme*[8] *Court* in 1917. See also *Leisy*[1] *v. Hardin*.

workman's compensation. A *government*[3] assistance insurance program basically operated by the separate *states*[3], a program which financially helps employees injured on the job. The extent of payments, the nature of medical assistance, and the nature of job retraining has varied greatly from state to state. In 1970 the *federal government*[3] passed the *Occupational*[11] *Health and Safety Act*, which was designed to protect workers across the *nation*[3]. The *legislation*[7] permits the Secretary of Labor to draft health and safety standards to reduce injuries on the job. Basic workman's compensation is funded primarily through employer payments to a state insurance program, and premiums are ordinarily based on the safety record of the employer. See also *assumption*[10] *of risk doctrine*; *Department of Labor*[2]; *fellow*[10] *servant doctrine*.

Supreme Court cases related to material in this chapter are arranged below by subject. Summaries of the cases are in Chapter One arranged alphabetically by the name of the first party in each case.

CHAPTER 10

COMMERCE—(Interstate)
American Communications
   Assn. v. Douds (1950)
Brown v. Maryland
   (1827)
Carter v. Carter Coal Co.
   (1936)
Cooley v. Board of Port
   Wardens (1851)
Edwards v. Calif. (1941)
Gibbons v. Ogden (1824)
Hammer v. Dagenhart
   (1918)
Kentucky Whip & Collar
   Co. v. Ill. Central Rail-
   road Co. (1937)
Leisy v. Hardin (1890)
Mulford v. Smith (1939)
NLRB v. Jones & Laugh-
   lin Corp. (1937)
Panama Refining Co. v.
   Ryan (1935)
Schechter Poultry Corp.
   v. U.S. (1935)
Sunshine Anthracite Coal
   Co. v. Adkins (1940)
U.S. v. Darby Lumber
   Co. (1941)
Wickard v. Filburn
   (1942)

COMMERCE—(Intrastate)
Brown v. Maryland
   (1827)
Gibbons v. Ogden (1824)

COMMERCE—(Loyalty
   Oath)
American Communica-
   tions Assn. v. Douds
   (1950)

COMMERCE—(Original
   Package Doctrine)
Brown v. Maryland
   (1827)
Leisy v. Hardin (1890)

COMMERCE—(Prison
   Made Goods)
Kentucky Whip & Collar
   Co. v. Ill. Central Rail-
   road Co. (1937)

COMMERCE—(Production
   Regulation)
Carter v. Carter Coal Co.
   (1936)
NLRB v. Jones & Laugh-
   lin Corp. (1937)
Schechter Poultry Corp.
   v. U.S. (1935)
Sunshine Anthracite Coal
   Co. v. Adkins (1940)
U.S. v. Butler (1936)

U.S. v. E. C. Knight Co.
   (1895)
Wickard v. Filburn
   (1942)

COMMERCE—(Race)
Heart of Atlanta Motel v.
   U.S. (1964)
Morgan v. Virginia
   (1946)
Plessy v. Ferguson (1896)

CONTRACT—
Adkins v. Children's
   Hospital (1923)
Charles River Bridge v.
   Warren Bridge (1837)
Dartmouth College v.
   Woodward (1819)
Fletcher v. Peck (1810)
Home Building and Loan
   Assn. v. Blaisdell
   (1934)
Lochner v. N.Y. (1905)
West Coast Hotel Co. v.
   Parrish (1937)

CURRENCY—
Hepburn v. Griswold
   (1870)
Legal Tender Cases
   (1871)
McCulloch v. Md. (1819)
Veazie Bank v. Fenno
   (1869)

EMINENT DOMAIN—
Berman v. Parker (1954)

GRANTS-IN-AID—
Flast v. Cohen (1968)
Frothingham v. Mellon
   (1923)
Massachusetts v. Mellon
   (1923)

LABOR—(Assembly)
Hague v. C.I.O. (1939)

LABOR—(Child)
Bailey v. Drexel Furniture
   Co. (1922)
Hammer v. Dagenhart
   (1918)
U.S. v. Darby Lumber
   Co. (1941)

LABOR—(Collective
   Bargaining)
NLRB v. Jones & Laugh-
   lin Corp. (1937)
U.S. v. E. C. Knight Co.
   (1895)

LABOR—(Maximum
   Hours)
Lochner v. N.Y. (1905)
Muller v. Oregon (1908)
U.S. v. Darby Lumber
   Co. (1941)

LABOR—(Minimum
   Wages)
Adkins v. Children's
   Hospital (1923)
Bunting v. Oregon (1917)
Opp Cotton Mills v. Ad-
   ministrator of Wage &
   Hour Division (1941)
U.S. v. Darby Lumber
   Co. (1941)
West Coast Hotel Co. v.
   Parrish (1937)

LABOR—(Picketing)
Thornhill v. Ala. (1940)

LABOR—(Regulation)
Adkins v. Children's
   Hospital (1923)
Lochner v. N.Y. (1905)

LABOR—(Strike)
American Communications
   Assn. v. Douds (1950)

LABOR—(Unemployment
   Compensation)
Sherbert v. Verner (1963)
Steward Machine Co. v.
   Davis (1937)

LABOR—(Women)
Adkins v. Children's
   Hospital (1923)
Muller v. Oregon (1908)
West Coast Hotel Co. v.
   Parrish (1937)

LEGISLATIVE DELEGA-
   TION OF AUTHOR-
   ITY—
Hampton & Co. v. U.S.
   (1928)
Kentucky Whip & Collar
   Co. v. Ill. Central Rail-
   road Co. (1937)
Panama Refining Co. v.
   Ryan (1935)
Schechter Poultry Corp.
   v. U.S. (1935)

PROPERTY—
Dartmouth College v.
   Woodward (1819)
Dred Scott v. Sandford
   (1857)
Hepburn v. Griswold
   (1870)

Chapter 11

The Urban Society

Note to the reader: Cross-referenced terms are in italics. The superscript number refers to the chapter in which the entry may be found. In addition, its placement indicates the word under which the term is alphabetized. (For example, in *electoral*[4] *college*, information on the electoral college may be found in Chapter 4 under "electoral.") Because italics are used in cross-references, they are not used for terms in which they would ordinarily be used: Supreme Court cases and titles of books, journals, plays, and so forth.

> *Supreme Court cases relating to material in this chapter are listed at the end of the chapter (see page 298).*

adult education program. Any welfare or educational program funded by the *government*[3] in an effort to raise the level of education of adults. The movement for adult education received formal recognition with the creation of the private American Association for Adult Education in 1926. All *states*[3] thereafter made some effort, frequently under *federal*[3] stimulation, to provide remedial education, evening classes, technical training, correspondence courses, and other specialized programs for adults. Adult education and training programs have received the greatest support with passage of the *Economic*[11] *Opportunity Act of 1964.* See also *Volunteers*[11] *in Service to America.*

Aid for Dependent Children (AFDC or ADC). A portion of the categorical assistance program of the *Social*[11] *Security Act of 1935* which gives financial assistance to families with one parent absent or to families or *organizations*[6] caring for dependent children. AFDC is funded through matching funds provided by the *fed-* eral *government*[3] and the *states*[3]. It is one of the most controversial welfare programs because of public charges that such aid stimulates illegitimate births, broken homes, and general welfare dependence. The program increased fivefold between 1940 and 1960 and in recent years has experienced annual increases of even greater percentages. See also *King*[1] *v. Smith.*

Aid to Blind. A portion of the categorical assistance program of the *Social*[11] *Security Act of 1935*, which gives financial assistance to blind persons in financial need. Funding is a joint effort of the *federal government*[3] and the *states*[3]. Qualifications are established by the separate states.

Aid to the Totally and Permanently Disabled. A portion of the categorical assistance program of the *Social*[11] *Security Act of 1935*, which provides financial aid for the physically disabled who are unemployed. The program, begun under a 1950 *amendment*[3] to the Social Security Act, assists persons over 18 years of age. It is jointly funded by the *federal government*[3] and the *states*[3] and is supervised by the separate states.

alderman. A member of a *municipal*[11] council of *government*[3]. An alderman is popularly elected at large or, more commonly, within a particular *district*[7] called a *ward*[5]. In a *bicameral*[7] municipal legislative body an alderman generally serves in a body referred to as a Board of Aldermen. See also *city*[11] council.

Amtrak: see *National*[11] *Railroad Passenger Corporation.*

annexation. The act of an existing unit of *government*[3] expanding its own *boundaries*[12] in order to bring other *territory*[3] under its legal *jurisdiction*[8]. Municipal annexation is ordinarily regulated under state *law*[8] and may in some cases be undertaken through unilateral legal action of the expanding *municipality*[11]. In some *states*[3] annexation may be undertaken only with the consent of the people of the area being annexed.

Appalachia. A term used to describe the poverty-stricken and depressed area of the Appalachian mountain region extending from northern Pennsylvania to northern Alabama. The word became a synonym for "poverty" when the area gained national attention in *Michael Harrington's*[11] book entitled The Other America: Poverty in the United States (1962). The glare of publicity on poverty in the U.S. stimulated passage of the *Economic*[11] *Opportunity Act of 1964*, an act which applied to the entire *nation*[3]. The Appalachian area was specifically designated as "depressed" in the Appalachian Regional Redevelopment Act of 1965. The primary approach used to assist redevelopment came through highway construction.

Area Redevelopment Act of 1961. The first major *act*[8] of the *War*[11] on

Poverty under the Kennedy-Johnson *administrations*[6]. The controversial and short-lived act provided for a four-year attack on the poverty conditions of depressed areas. The *legislation*[7] provided for loans, *grants-in-aid*[10], retraining programs, and other broad redevelopment programs designed to expand business opportunities and jobs in depressed areas. See also *Lyndon B. Johnson*[6]; *urban*[11] *renewal.*

board, county. A relatively small governing *board*[6] charged under state *law*[8] with *administration*[6] of a particular *county*[11] within the *state*[3]. The title of such a structure varies from state to state. The county board may be composed of administrative officials only or of some mixture of administrative and judicial figures. County boards have little or no *executive*[6] leadership, are influenced greatly by the *spoils*[6] *system*, are dominated by nonprofessional personnel, and are charged with general supervision of the county. A few counties in the U.S. have begun to operate under professional administrators through adoption of the *county-manager*[11] *plan*. See also *Avery*[1] *v. Midland County.*

Book of the States. A biennial reference publication of the *Council*[11] *of State Governments* designed to provide comprehensive information on the *governments*[3] of the 50 *states*[3].

borough: see Chap. 7.

Campus Unrest Report (1970). A report issued by the President's Commission on Campus Unrest, an in-depth analysis of various campus disturbances of 1970. The *commission*[6] was appointed by *President*[6] Nixon and was chaired by William W. Scranton, former *governor*[6] of Pennsylvania. Among the most notable campus disturbances analyzed by the "Scranton Report" were conflicts involving the death of four students at Kent State

University in Ohio and the death of two students at Jackson State College in Mississippi. The Kent State disturbance took place in May 1970, soon after President Nixon ordered U.S. military forces into Cambodia. The report on campus unrest criticized the destruction of *property*[10] and disruption of classes by students at Kent State and the use of live ammunition by poorly trained members of the *national*[12] *guard*. In the Jackson State event, the report criticized the Jackson *authorities*[3] and the Mississippi *state*[3] police for overreacting to alleged provocations by Negro college students. See also *Cambodian*[12] *crisis of 1970*.

Central Cities Project. An education program created in 1968 within the Office of Education of the *Department of Health*[2], *Education, and Welfare* and funded by *federal*[3] *grants-in-aid*[10] designed to stimulate large-*city*[11] educational *departments*[6] to develop compensatory education projects in small "subsystems" in neighborhoods where parents could become involved in educational planning and operations. The Central Cities Projects are a conscious effort to decentralize *urban*[11] educational practices and involve *ghetto*[11] parents in educational projects designed to stimulate children toward higher academic achievement. In 1969, in the first *decentralized*[3] project in New York City, the Ocean Hill-Brownsville district of Brooklyn, a major conflict led to the longest teacher's *strike*[10] in the *city's*[11] history. The teachers saw such a program as a threat to the *power*[3] of *labor*[10] union negotiations which they had just gained in the *centralized*[3] administrative offices of New York City. See also *independent school district*[11].

charter, city (municipal). A legal authorization from a *state*[3] to a *municipal corporation*[11] which grants the *powers*[3] of self-government to a local *community*[3]. A charter defines

powers, structures, duties, and other details of a local *government*[3]. States generally grant charters under *special laws*[11], *general laws*[11], *optional laws*[11], or *home*[11] *rule* provisions within their state *constitutions*[3]. The separate types of charters are usually designated by the method used in the original process of *incorporation*[11].

city. A sizable *community*[3] of individuals dwelling within the *boundaries*[12] of an incorporated area possessing *powers*[3] granted to it by the *state*[3]. The term arose originally to describe the total gathering of *citizens*[3] within a given social and political community. See also *municipal corporation*[11].

city classification. The legal process of arranging cities by size in order to determine local governmental structures which may be used to guide local governmental affairs. Many state *legislatures*[7] are given direction by state *constitutional*[3] provisions in seeking to establish reasonable governmental arrangements for cities of various sizes. Once a *city*[11] reaches a particular size it may, under the *general laws*[11] *of the state*[3], choose among several alternative forms of municipal *government*[3] approved by the state. See also *bracket laws*[11].

city council. The basic deliberative and *policy*[7] *formulating* body of a *municipal corporation*[11]. A city council's structure and responsibility are determined largely by the particular form of *city*[11] *government*[3] in use at any given time. In general, a council formulates basic *community*[3] *policy*[6], passes specific municipal *ordinances*[11], and regulates local taxation matters. City councils are most often *unicameral*[7] in structure. They are composed of members (councilmen, aldermen[11], etc.) who are selected in *at-large elections*[5] or within separate *wards*[5]. Many city councils are composed of officials elected through *nonpartisan elections*[5].

city manager. A specialist ordinarily trained in or knowledgeable in administering *municipal corporations*[11]. A city manager is considered the basic figure in the administrative machinery of a *council*[11] *manager* plan of city *government*[3]. A city manager is expected to administer the affairs of the *city*[11] in a *nonpartisan*[5] fashion.

city (municipal, urban) planning. The systematic and comprehensive planning of municipal facilities, public-private relationships, and other physical and social relationships within a *city*[11] or *urban*[11] area. City planning is an ongoing process requiring long-range planning, continual adjustment, and specific proposals. It is directed toward the rational and orderly growth of an urban area. See also *Demonstration*[11] *Cities and Metropolitan Development Act of 1966*; *Model*[11] *Cities Project*; *New Town*[11]; *701 Program*[11]; *regional planning commission*[11].

city-state: see Chap. 3.

commission plan. A structure of *municipal*[11] government, first used in Galveston, Texas in 1901, which places legislative and *executive*[6] *powers*[3] in the same governmental body composed of several commissioners. The *commission*[6] usually consists of five or six members, each administering a separate administrative *department*[6] and each accountable to the commission as a body. Commissioners are ordinarily elected through *at-large elections*[5] on a *nonpartisan*[5] basis. A *mayor*[11] is chosen from among the commissioners to preside over commission meetings and to fulfill ceremonial duties. The form of *government*[3] was most popular and most used in *municipal corporations*[11] in the U.S. between 1901 and 1920.

commission, regional planning. An *urban*[11] governmental agency created for the specific purpose of comprehensive and coordinated regional planning involving several governmental *jurisdictions*[8]. A regional planning commission is generally concerned with land use, transportation, natural resources, environmental problems, and other similar matters. Some regional planning commissions are created by the *state*[3], legally responsible to the state, and composed of individuals selected by state and local processes. See also *city*[11] *planning*; *council*[11] *of governments*.

community: see Chap. 3.

Community Action Agency (CAA), 1964– . A regular federally funded poverty program established in the *Economic*[11] *Opportunity Act of 1964* to enable local *communities*[3] to attack problems of poverty in a comprehensive and coordinated fashion. The programs, part of the *War*[11] *on Poverty*, vary from place to place according to need and resources available. Each community is allowed to establish and administor its own program under a funding arrangement whereby the *federal government*[3] will pay from 80 to 100 percent of the total cost. Funds may be used for research, pilot projects, self-help by the poor, and coordinated services such as job training programs, housing services, legal services (*Legal*[11] *Services Program*), health centers, and educational projects (*Upward*[11] *Bound and Project*[11] *Head Start*). Most programs, scheduled to lose federal funding in 1974, are operated by what are known as Community Action Agencies composed of *government*[3] officials, private associations, and the recipients of assistance.

Comsat. An acronym derived from Communications Satellite Corporation, an *organization*[6] created by the Communications Satellite Act of 1962. The controversial *government corporation*[6] was founded with a 15-member *board*[6] of directors and a combination of private and *government*[3] interests. Comsat was chosen as the exclusive operator of the U.S. portion of an international communications satellite system. The 15-member board contains three presidential appointees, six members elected by private stock holders, and six members representing the *common*[10] *carriers* of the communications industry. Since the creation of the synchronous satellite, Comsat has been involved in a dispute over whether the operations should be commercially competitive or *monopolistic*[10]. There is also disagreement over whether the enterprise should be basically public or private. See also *Early*[11] *Bird*.

Conference of Commissioners on Uniform State Laws, 1892– . An intergovernmental *organization*[6] composed of persons appointed by the various state *governors*[6] in order to seek coordination of legal *statutes*[8] passed by the separate *states*[3]. The three members from each state are known as Commissioners on Uniform State Laws. They work with Commissioners from other states in drafting *legislation*[7] applicable to problems common to more than one state. The Conference works closely with the *American*[5] *Bar Association*. In fact, the annual meetings of both organizations are held at the same time and in the same location. The *executive*[6] agency of the Conference is known as the *Council*[11] *of State Governments*. See also *interstate*[11] *compact*; *interstate*[11] *relations*; *uniform state laws*[11].

consolidation, city-county. A formal *merger*[10] of county *government*[3] with existing *city*[11] governments within the *boundaries*[12] of the *county*[11]. Such a coordinated unit of government must receive approval from the *state*[3] because the county and the *incorporated*[11] cities are all creatures of the state. City-county consolidation may be effectively used where a metropolitan area coincides with the boundaries of the county or in an area where one major city within a county dom-

inates the area. See also *metropolitan*[11] *federation*.

consolidation, school: see *consolidated school district*[11].

corporation, municipal. A legal entity created in response to local initiative and through *incorporation*[11] by the *state*[3] in order to permit the management of local affairs. A municipal corporation acts both as an agency of the state and as a private *corporate*[10] entity. A municipal corporation is generally referred to as a *city*[11], *village*[11], *borough*[11], or an incorporated area. See also *Dillon's*[11] *Rule*.

corporation, quasi-municipal. A local legal entity created by the *state*[3] on its own initiative in order to carry out specific functions of *government*[3]. States may create *counties*[11], *towns*[11], *townships*[11], school districts, and various types of *special districts*[11] to act as quasi-municipal corporations. They may be empowered to handle such things as *law*[8] enforcement, tax collection, water *conservation*[10], education, and public health.

cosmopolis. A *city*[11] inhabited by persons from around the world. A cosmopolitan person is an individual who feels at home in any city or social setting in the world. A cosmopolis is characterized by a mixture of racial stocks, national identities, cultural interests, languages, and social customs.

council-manager plan. A structure of municipal *government*[3], first used in Staunton, Virginia in 1908, which places general *policy*[7] *formulating power*[3] in a small *city*[11] *council* which selects a professional *city*[11] *manager* to develop specific *policies*[6] of *municipal*[11] operation. The council generally ranges in size from five to nine members who are elected in an *at-large election*[5]. The city manager is directly responsible to the council and serves at its pleasure. Within such a system, a *mayor*[11] is elected, generally on a *nonpartisan*[5] basis, and is obligated to fulfill ceremonial functions.

council of governments (COG). A voluntary regional association of local *governments*[3] designed to facilitate regional planning and effective *administration*[6] of *community*[3] services. Numerous *states*[3] have begun to authorize such arrangements in order to better coordinate intergovernmental cooperation. COG's generally do not have the *power*[3] to tax or the power of *eminent*[9] *domain*. They are most useful in regional planning and intergovernmental coordination. They are also useful in structuring an operational base within a state for receipt of *federal*[3] funds directed toward solving particular *urban*[11] regional problems (*crime*[8], pollution, etc.). See also *city*[11] *planning*; *intergovernmental*[11] *agreement*; *regional planning commission*[11].

Council of State Governments. An *organization*[6] of interstate cooperation operated and maintained by the *governments*[3] of the 50 *states*[3] in order to coordinate *interstate*[11] *relations* in all areas of common concern. The Council of State Governments publishes State Government, a monthly magazine, and the *Book*[11] *of the States*, a biennial reference work on state government.

county. A primary subdivision of local *government*[3] within almost all of the *states*[3] within the U.S. There are presently around 3,000 counties throughout the *nation*[3]. They possess *powers*[3] of taxation, *law*[8] enforcement, welfare *administration*[6], electoral procedure, judicial decision-making, road construction and maintenance, and a wide range of other local duties. A county is ordinarily administered by a relatively small *county board*[11] which is primarily administrative in

nature. Most counties do not have a chief *executive*[6] officer. Some receive direction from some form of county manager hired by and responsible to the county board. Other counties are loosely directed by some judicial figure such as a county judge. Numerous counties operate under a *spoils*[6] *system*. Since 1968 county boards have been required to meet the *one-man*[5], *one-vote rule* wherein each member represents approximately the same number of persons. See also *Avery*[1] *v. Midland County*; *county-manager*[11] *plan*.

county-manager plan. A structure of county *government*[3] which places general *policy*[7] *formulating power*[3] in a small *county board*[11] which selects a professional county manager to develop specific *policies*[6] of *county*[11] operation. A few counties in the U.S. use such an arrangement, which is patterned after the *council-manager*[11] *plan* of *municipal*[11] government.

Dahl, Robert A., 1915– . Professor of *political*[3] science at Yale University, political economist, and former president of the *American*[5] *Political Science Association*. Dahl has written a number of significant works, among them: Politics, Economics, and Welfare (1953), A Preface to Democratic Theory (1956), Who Governs? Democracy and Power in an American City (1961), and Modern Political Analysis (1970). His influential volume, Who Governs?, analyzed the *city*[11] of New Haven, Connecticut and the nature of the *community*[3] power structure. He found a *pluralistic*[3] or polycentric structure, in which *power*[3] was dispersed throughout the city and in which power shifted according to the issues being dealt with. His study centered on public education, *urban*[11] renewal, and *municipal*[11] elections. He found that business and economic interests were only one variable in the community decision-making process. He described what has come to be known as a pluralist *theory*[3] of city decision-making. See also *policy*[7] *formulation.*

Demonstration Cities and Metropolitan Development Act of 1966. A federal *law*[8] which created the *Model*[11] *Cities Project* and outlined a coordinated *federal*[3] program for attacking problems of *urban*[11] decay. The *legislation*[7] also created a new federal mortgage insurance program for the creation of *New Towns*[11] and made available federal grants for urban regional planning at the local level. See also *city*[11] *planning.*

Dillon's Rule. A rule articulated by Judge John F. Dillon in Commentaries on the Law of Municipal Corporations (1911). The rule holds that a *municipal corporation*[11] possesses and may exercise only the *powers*[3] expressly granted or fairly implied from those powers expressed or those obviously indispensable to the fulfillment of the purposes of the corporation. All reasonable questions of the exercise of power must be decided in favor of the *state*[3] and in the event of a conflict must be judicially resolved. See also *delegated powers*[4]; *implied powers*[4].

district, common school. A public educational unit that is disappearing from the American scene; it operates primarily under a *county*[11] school *board*[6] and county school superintendent. A common school district is generally *rural*[11], is operated by a very small professional staff, and is inefficient for modern educational purposes. Common school districts arose under primitive educational conditions in the U.S. and were originally loosely organized operations developed by parents in order to receive part of *state*[3] educational money. See also *board of education*[11]; *independent school district*[11].

district, consolidated school. A public educational unit which is formed from separate school systems or districts into one *jurisdictional*[8] unit. School consolidation is ordinarily undertaken in order to provide a more comprehensive and efficient educational program for students within a given geographical area. Such an arrangement may sometimes be operated at a lower cost than it takes to operate several distinct systems. See also *board of education*[11]; *common school district*[11]; *independent school district*[11].

district, economic development (EDD). A geographic area politically organized for economic development purposes through an agency generally in the form of a nonprofit *corporation*[10]. Frequently such districts are given guidance by a national, *state*[3], or *municipal*[11] unit known as a committee for economic development (CED). A formal economic development district is created under the auspices of the Economic Development Administration within the U.S. *Department of Commerce*[2] and must meet certain criteria of need such as high unemployment, low average income, or lack of economic growth. Economic development districts engage in technical assistance, research, loan programs, and *public*[10] *works* projects of various kinds.

district, independent school. A public educational unit in the nature of a *special district*[11], which is directed by an independent *board of education*[11] possessing general administrative and taxing *powers*[3]. The school board is generally popularly elected, establishes basic educational *policies*[6], and chooses a school superintendent to administer the school system. See also *common school district*[11]; *consolidated school district*[11].

district, special. A political unit of local *government*[3] chartered by the *state*[3] to provide a particular service of government within a specified geographical area. The most common special districts deal with education, water distribution and *conservation*[10], sewage disposal, fire and police protection, housing, and similar matters. Special districts generally come into existence because of structural weaknesses of local governments, a desire for political autonomy, lack of initiative in existing units of government, and because they may be organized quickly without prior political and economic problems hanging over them. They are most criticized as adding to the proliferation of government, adding to the tax burden, being undemocratic, and as uneconomical. The creation of a special district is usually approved by the people to be served by the district. It is ordinarily directed by a *board*[6] of directors possessing normal *powers*[3] of taxation and *administration*[6].

Early Bird. The world's first commercial communications satellite, put into orbit by the U.S. on June 2, 1965. The satellite beamed live television pictures across the Atlantic Ocean on the day it was launched. Early Bird was operated by *Comsat*[11] until it was "retired" from active use on January 19, 1969. At that time, more sophisticated equipment was being used for worldwide communications. See also *Sputnik*[11] *I.*

ecology, urban. The interrelationships of *urban*[11] groups, individuals within urban groups, and the urban environment. The urban environment includes geography, culture, economics, *politics*[3], and other physical, psychological, and social factors. See also *Environmental*[2] *Protection Agency.*

Economic Opportunity Act of 1964. The "Anti-poverty Act of 1964," the first *federal*[3] act designed to attack the root causes of poverty in the U.S. The *act*[8], a major part of *President*[6] *Lyndon B. Johnson's*[6] *Great*[6] *Society,* was also the first comprehensive anti-

poverty *legislation*[7] in the U.S. It created the *Office of Economic*[2] *Opportunity* (OEO) and various federal programs such as the *Job*[11] *Corps, Volunteers*[11] *in Service to America* (VISTA), and the *Neighborhood*[11] *Youth Corps* (NYC). The agencies were charged with seeking practical solutions to problems of poverty in America. Major efforts to reach that objective came through *Work*[11] *Study Programs* (*Upward*[11] *Bound*), *Community*[11] *Action Agencies* (CAA), *Legal*[11] *Services Programs, job*[11] *training programs, youth*[11] *education programs* (*Project*[11] *Head Start*), and various loan programs. The basic thrust of the legislation was to conduct a *War*[11] *on Poverty* based on rehabilitation rather than relief. See also *Appalachia*[11]; *Michael Harrington*[11].

education, board of. A *state*[3] or local *board*[6] legally empowered to regulate matters of public education. A board of education is generally composed of persons outside the ranks of professional education, establishes general educational *policy*[6] (teacher certification, building construction, salaries, curriculum, etc.), secures funds for public education, and selects supervisory personnel such as a professional superintendent of education, university *president*[3], or other appropriate official. State boards of education are generally appointed by state *governors*[6] or elected by the state *legislature*[7] or the general electorate. Local boards are generally selected by the local electorate. School boards are nearly always classified as "independent" units, although they frequently become embroiled in state and local *politics*[3]. See also *common school district*[11]; *independent agency*[6]; *independent school district*[11].

Elementary and Secondary Education Act of 1965. The first comprehensive and general *federal*[3] aid to education *act*[8] passed in U.S. history. The *legislation*[7] provides funding for both public and private schools and was passed as part of an overall *War*[11] *on Poverty*. The act, a part of *President*[6] *Lyndon B. Johnson's*[6] *Great*[6] *Society*, provides grants to local school districts serving large numbers of low-income families, for textbooks and library facilities for all income groups, for local resource and educational research centers outside the regular school systems, and for improvement of educational practices at the *state*[3] level. The act covers approximately 95 percent of all school districts in the U.S. Under the act parochial schools receive aid indirectly through the purchase of textbooks in nonreligious subjects and through the use of available resource tools within the *community*[3]. The legislation passed the *Congress*[4] over strong opposition of those fearing a loss of *states'*[4] *rights* and those fearing a breach in the "wall of separation of church and state." See also *child*[9] *benefit doctrine*; *Flast*[1] *v. Cohen*; *Lemon*[1] *v. Kurtzman*; *purchase*[9] *of services doctrine*; *wall*[9] *of separation doctrine*.

Family Assistance Plan (FAP). A welfare proposal advocated by *President*[6] Richard Nixon in 1969 as a replacement for the *Aid*[11] *for Dependent Children* program. The plan, devised primarily by *Daniel Moynihan*[11], suggested a *federally*[3] uniform welfare base for all of the U.S. The base generally suggested was $1,600. The payments would go to primary poverty-level family units regardless of whether the father was employed or even in residence. The level of payments above the base would vary from place to place and according to family size and need.

Federal Aid Road Act of 1916. The first federal *legislation*[7] to provide regular *federal*[3] funds for *state*[3] highway construction. The U.S. Bureau of Public Roads was given considerable *power*[3] to assure that federal transportation funds were used properly within the separate states.

Federal Highway Act of 1944. The major federal *act*[8] which authorized a national system of interstate and defense highways, a system extensively planned and funded in the *Federal*[11] *Highway Act of 1956*. The 1944 *legislation*[7] also authorized *federal*[3] funding for primary and secondary highways within the *states*[3], highways which serve as *urban*[11] extension arteries.

Federal Highway Act of 1956. The major federal legislation which funded the development of a nationwide system of interstate highways. The *legislation*[7], best known as the Interstate Highway Act of 1956, emphasizes the nature of an interdependent *urban*[11] *society*[3] dependent on the movement of people and goods. Interstate highways may be built under a funding ratio whereby the *federal government*[3] pays 90 percent of the construction cost and the *states*[3] pay 10 percent. Upon completion, maintenance is generally funded by the separate states. See also *public*[10] *works*.

Federal-State Joint Action Committee, 1957– . A *committee*[7] organized by the *Governors'*[6] *Conference* in an effort to find ways to slow the shift of governmental *powers*[3] from the *states*[3] to the *federal government*[3]. Most of its recommendations have not been accepted because of continued state and local demands for federal assistance. See also *decentralization*[3]; *intergovernmental*[11] *relations*; *states'*[4] *rights*.

Food Stamp Plan. A *federal*[3] program designed to dispose of agricultural surpluses at the same time certain welfare needs are met. The first food stamp plan in the U.S. began in 1939 as part of the *New*[6] *Deal*. It was dropped after *World*[12] *War II*, but was revised and reinstituted in 1964 as part of the *War*[11] *on Poverty*. Eligible participants in the plan purchase federal food stamps at discount and redeem them at face value for food products at local stores. Families may purchase stamps on the basis of the total family income and the percentage of the family *budget*[10] normally spent for food.

freedom of choice plan: see Chap. 9.

Galbraith, John Kenneth: see Chap. 10.

general assistance. A *state*[3] or local welfare program funded separately from *federal*[3] *public*[11] *assistance* programs. State and local general assistance programs differ considerably across the U.S. Each state may determine its welfare program structure, eligibility criteria, size of payments, administrative practices, and other elements of public welfare within the state.

general welfare clause: see Chap. 4.

George, Henry, 1839–97. Economist, social reformer, author, and leading advocate of the *Single Tax*[10], a proposal advocated by numerous reformist groups around the world. He wrote Our Land and Land Policy (1871), Progress and Poverty (1879), Social Problems (1883), and The Science of Political Economy (1897). George's most famous work was entitled Progress and Poverty: An Inquiry into the Cause of Industrial Depressions, and of Increase of Wealth; the Remedy. The book was one of the major *socialist*[3] indictments of the concentration of wealth in the hands of landed *property*[10] owners. The theme of the work was that as rich men grow richer, the poor grow poorer. Poverty, therefore, is seen as a natural concomitant of progress. George advocated returning the land to the people as part of the *public*[4] *domain*. He said that all of the people should own property, and that its regulation should be based on usage of the property. He felt that the economic

benefits from governmental rental of property could relieve the people of the other standard forms of taxation burdening mankind. This is what he called the Single Tax.

ghetto. A section of a *city*[11] unfavorably restricted to a particular segment of the population. Ghetto, a term originally applied to situations in which European Jews were restricted to wretched sections of cities, has been applied to other *minority*[9] *groups* in the U.S., especially Negroes. A ghetto is usually characterized by homogeneity of race, a condition of poverty, *property*[10] ownership by absentee landlords, and by political, economic, and social repression of the dwellers within the area *boundaries*[12].

government, Metro: see *metropolitan*[11] *federation*.

Governors' Conference: see Chap. 6.

guaranteed annual income. A welfare concept in which *government*[3] should guarantee a basic income level for all families. In 1969 several proposals were advocated which would designate $3,200 for a family of four as the "poverty level" that could be used for such a national welfare program in the U.S. The major criticism of such proposals has been that incentives to work and move off welfare rolls are difficult to build into such a system. A guaranteed annual income pilot project was begun in New Jersey in 1968 with 1,350 working-poor families. A 1970 report revealed that many of those covered under the program were seeking to move their economic status upward on their own initiative.

Harrington, Michael, 1928– . Author, systematic social critic, student of *urban*[11] *society*[3], and *socialist*[3] author of The Other America: Poverty in the United States (1962).

Harrington helped popularize discussion about poverty conditions within the U.S. as he stimulated legislative action which culminated in the *Economic*[11] *Opportunity Act of 1964*. He is frequently cited as one of the few men in American history to move the social conscience in a mass fashion. His name is clearly associated with popular expressions such as the *Other*[11] *America* and the *War*[11] *on Poverty*. A political activist, social worker, and former associate editor of The Catholic Worker, he has also written The Accidental Century (1965) and Toward a Democratic Left (1968).

Head Start: see *Project*[11] *Head Start*.

Hill-Burton Act of 1946. A federal *act*[8] which is officially entitled the Hospital Survey and Construction Act of 1946 and which was designed to finance general hospital construction and modernization across the U.S. The "Hill-Burton Program" is based on matching *grants-in-aid*[10] arrangements between the *federal government*[3] and *state*[3] and local *governments*[3]. On the program's 25th anniversary in 1971 it was revealed that the federal government had contributed over $3.5 billion to match $12 billion from other governmental units involved in hospital projects. *President*[6] Nixon recommended ending the program in 1973.

home rule. The arrangement whereby a *city*[11] or *county*[11] within a *state*[3] may, under state *constitutional*[3] provisions or state *laws*[8], arrange its governmental structures in whatever way it desires as long as the chosen structures do not conflict with national or state *constitutions*[3] or laws. Some states permit cities and counties, particularly cities, to draft their own charters for approval by the local voters. A locally approved *city charter*[11] may be accepted by the state and thereby avoid the use of *general laws*[11] or *special laws*[11] of the state

legislature[7] to structure local *government*[3].

Homestead Act of 1862. A major *federal*[3] act which stimulated settlement of the West through occupancy and improvement of public lands transferrable to private ownership. The *act*[8] specified that persons meeting certain requirements (head of a household, filed application for *citizenship*[3], 21 years of age, veteran, etc.) could receive title of up to 160 acres of public land through payment of a $10 filing fee and residency on the land for five years. A person could also buy the land for $1.25 per acre and waive the residency requirement. The Homestead Act was a culmination of the "free soil" concept advocated by members of the short-lived *Free Soil Party*[5] and opposed by southerners who feared a loss of political *power*[3] through the opening of western land without slavery. See also *Frederick Jackson Turner*[4].

Housing Act of 1937. The first federal *law*[8] which made direct federal *grants-in-aid*[10] to *cities*[11] for *urban*[11] *renewal* and *public housing*[11]. The *act*[8] also established *federal*[3] mortgage insurance programs and designated the *Federal*[2] *Housing Administration* (FHA) and the Public Housing Administration as the principal agencies to administer the programs.

Housing Act of 1949. A federal *act*[8] designed to provide low-cost *public housing*[11] and *urban*[11] *renewal*. The *legislation*[7], amended on numerous occasions, provides the modern basis for *federal*[3] construction of public housing, university housing, and housing for the elderly. It also provides rent *subsidies*[10] and selected *municipal*[11] services. The Housing Act of 1949 built primarily on the groundwork laid in the *Housing*[11] *Act of 1937*.

Housing Act of 1954. A *federal*[3] *law*[8] which primarily extended earlier federal housing programs, broadened the *urban*[11] *renewal* program and re-named it "urban redevelopment," instituted federal *grants-in-aid*[10] for comprehensive *community*[3] planning in what came to be known as *701 Programs*[11], and introduced concepts of urban rehabilitation in place of what had come to be known as "slum clearance." See also *public housing*[11].

Housing and Urban Development Act of 1965. A comprehensive federal *law*[8] which revised earlier *federal*[3] housing *legislation*[7] and created new programs designed to attack *urban*[11] blight and decay. The *act*[8] created the first rent-supplement program for low-income families, extended *Federal*[2] *Housing Administration* (FHA) mortgage insurance programs for low-income families, extended *public housing*[11] programs, made available *grants-in-aid*[10] for *community*[3] facilities development and technical assistance, and made available federal funds for open-space development and "beautification." The legislation placed emphasis primarily on local and regional planning for economic development and alleviation of poverty conditions. See also *city*[11] *planning*.

Housing and Urban Development Act of 1968. A comprehensive federal *law*[8] which authorized the greatest *federal*[3] expenditure for *public housing*[11] in U.S. history, expanded the federal rent supplement program, expanded *Federal*[2] *Housing Administration* (FHA) and other mortgage programs for low- and moderate-income families, and created a federal matching mortgage-assistance program, the so-called *235 Program*[11], wherein the *government*[3] actually pays a portion of a mortgage payment for low-income families. The *act*[8] also revised and broadened *urban*[11] *renewal* programs.

housing, public. Housing built and *subsidized*[10] by *government*[3], generally for famiiles in low-income cate-

gories. The *federal government*[3] began to aid *states*[3] in the development of public housing in the *Housing*[11] *Act of 1937*. A local *community*[3], under state authorization, may create a public housing authority funded by the federal government. Some states and local communities fund their own public housing projects under *local*[11] *public authority* arrangements. Most projects restrict their units to families below certain income levels. In 1971 the *U.S. Supreme*[8] *Court* upheld an *amendment*[3] to the California *constitution*[3] which permits local, popular *referendums*[3] in determining whether to approve federally funded public housing projects. Such a procedure was contested in the courts on the grounds that local referendums may be used to block housing developments and thereby *discriminate*[9] against *minority*[9] *groups* seeking to leave the *ghettoes*[11] of the *cities*[11]. See also *Department of Housing*[11] *and Urban Development*; *Housing*[11] *Act of 1949*; *Housing*[11] *Act of 1954*; *Housing*[11] *Act of 1965*; *Housing*[11] *and Urban Development Act of 1968*; *James*[1] *v. Valtierra*; *urban*[11] *renewal*.

humanitarianism. The belief or practice which emphasizes that man's basic concerns should be directed toward mankind or humanity in general.

Hunter, Floyd, 1921– . Former professor of social work at the University of North Carolina, former executive director of the Atlanta Community Planning Council, and *president*[3] of the Floyd Hunter Company. Hunter's most widely recognized work is entitled Community Power Structure: A Study of Decision Makers (1953). It is a study of Atlanta, Georgia and its levels of *community*[3] *power*[3]. It is also a basic study of the *policy*[7] *formulation* process. Hunter discovered a multi-level power structure within the *city*[11] of Atlanta (which he referred to as a "regional city"). He cited the business community as being most influential in *municipal*[11] decision-making, a portion of the total community which generally acted below the threshold of public attention. The basic power sources were economic, governmental, religious, educational, professional, civic, and cultural. Decision-making tended to flow from top to bottom, with the people at large having little to do with major municipal decisions. City officials were observed as administrators rather than as policy-makers. Hunter popularized what has come to be known as the power structure *theory*[3] of city decision-making. In 1956 he co-authored Community Organization: Action and Inaction and in 1959 wrote Top Leadership.

impacted area. A *community*[3] or region that is severely burdened because of an increase in *government*[3] personnel or government facilities within the area. When the *federal government*[3] feels responsible for placing a burden on local facilities such as schools, sewage plants, etc., it will sometimes assist the community through federal *grants-in-aid*[10].

incorporation, municipal: see *municipal corporation*[11].

insurance, social. A comprehensive welfare plan established by *law*[8], generally compulsory in nature, and based on a program which spreads the cost of benefits among the entire population rather than on individual recipients. The *U.S. federal government*[3] began to use social insurance programs in 1935 with the passage of the *Social*[11] Security Act. The basic federal and *state*[3] approaches to social insurance presently in use throughout the U.S. are *Old*[11] Age, Survivors, and Disability Insurance, unemployment[11] insurance, and workman's[11] compensation. See also Townsend[11] Plan.

intergovernmental (interjurisdictional) agreement. An arrangement,

formal or informal, between two or more governmental units in order to achieve a specific objective or provide reciprocal assistance. A formal agreement is often referred to as an intergovernmental contract. For example, one governmental unit may *contract*[10] with another unit for performance of a specific service such as fire protection or sewage disposal. See also *cooperative federalism*[4]; *licensing*[10] by reciprocity; Office[2] of Intergovernmental Relations.

intergovernmental contract: see *intergovernmental*[11] agreement.

interstate compact. A voluntary agreement between two or more *states*[3] which is designed to meet common problems of the parties concerned. Compacts on major matters must receive the consent of the *U.S. Congress*[4] as specified in Article I, Section 10 of the *Constitution*[4]. They usually relate to such things as *conservation*[10], *boundary*[12] problems, education, port control, flood control, and penal matters. See also *Conference*[11] of Commissioners on Uniform State Laws; cooperative federalism[4]; interstate[11] relations; licensing[10] by reciprocity; Office[2] of Intergovernmental Relations.

Interstate Highway Act of 1956: see *Federal*[11] Highway Act of 1956.

interstate relations. A complex system of interrelationships between the separate *states*[3] and their various governmental agencies. Interstate relations involves Governors'[11] Conferences, interstate[11] compacts, interstate[11] rendition, recognition of the privileges and immunities of the citizens[3] of the various states[3], and acceptance of full faith and credit of the public acts[8] and documents of the separate states. See also Conference[11] of Commissioners on Uniform State Laws; full[4] faith and credit clause; licensing[10] by reciprocity; Office[2] of Intergovernmental Relations; privileges[4] and immunities clause.

interstate rendition (extradition). The legal action of one governmental *jurisdiction*[8] in returning a fugitive from *justice*[8] to the legal jurisdiction from which he fled. Such an action is generally referred to as *extradition*[12] in international relations and as interstate rendition in the U.S. Although the *U.S. Constitution*[4] recognizes interstate rendition, the *Supreme*[8] *Court* has refused to compel any *governor*[6] unwilling to fulfill the obligation to do so. See also *comity*[3]; *Kentucky*[1] *v. Dennison.*

interstate trade barrier. A *state*[3] regulation designed to work to the disadvantage of another state or other states in order to benefit local residents or businesses. See also *Conference*[11] *of Commissioners on Uniform State Laws*; *cooperative federalism*[4]; *interstate*[11] *relations*; *licensing*[10] *by reciprocity.*

Job Corps, 1964– . A *federal*[3] job training program instituted in the *Economic*[11] *Opportunity Act of 1964* as a joint effort between business and *government*[3] to move young people into productive economic positions. The program is administered by the Manpower Administration within the *Department of Labor*[2] and is a voluntary residential training program for disadvantaged educational dropouts between the ages of 16 and 21. Job training centers are located in *urban*[11] areas and in *conservation*[10] centers such as national forests. Once training is completed the Job Corps helps persons find productive employment. The Job Corps was the only federally funded program within the Economic Opportunity Act of 1964 that was created directly by federal initiative rather than local planning.

job training program. Any social and economic program partially or totally funded by the *government*[3] in an effort to train or retrain workers for productive employment. Beginning in 1964, in the *Economic*[11] *Opportunity Act*, the *federal government*[3] has regularly sought to provide job training programs of various types. The *Job*[11] *Corps* provides training for persons between 16 and 21 years of age. The *Neighborhood*[11] *Youth Corps* trains young persons from low-income families. Operation Mainstream was created to improve *rural*[11] areas and small towns through training of low-income persons. New Careers was established to help create new *community*[3] service jobs. Special Impact was established to train adults and the young in poverty *ghetto*[11] areas. Many job training programs were administered through the Bureau of Work Programs within the Manpower Administration of the U.S. *Department of Labor*[2].

Kerr-Mills Act of 1960. *Federal*[3] *legislation*[7] designed to provide federal *grants-in-aid*[10] to *states*[3] seeking to improve hospital services for financially pressed elderly persons. Over half the states participated in the program, but a great deal of confusion resulted early in its *administration*[6] because each state largely determined eligibility of participation and the scope of the total program within the state. The *act*[8] was passed as a legislative compromise to avoid a comprehensive federal health service program, a program eventually instituted in 1965 as *Medicare*[11].

land grant college. A *state*[3] college largely established on the basis of a *federal*[3] land grant provided through the *Morrill*[11] *Act of 1862*. Land grant colleges were originally established to teach agricultural and mechanical arts. Most colleges created under the program came to be known as A. & M. colleges.

laws, bracket. Classification laws sometimes used by *states*[3] to categorize *municipal*[11] responsibilities or benefits on the basis of population size. For example, a state *constitutional*[3] provision or state *law*[8] may provide special privileges for *cities*[11] between 200,000 and 400,000 population, the sponsors knowing that only one or few cities in the state will receive the privileges available. See also *city charter*[11]; *city*[11] *classification.*

laws, general. *Laws*[8] which apply to all geographical regions, persons, or *municipal corporations*[11] of a particular category. A general-law *city*[11] is a municipal corporation chartered under the general laws of the *state*[3], laws which prescribe *powers*[3], duties, and forms of governmental *organization*[6] for cities chartered by the state. Cities and their structures are generally categorized by population size. See also *city charter*[11]; *city*[11] *classification.*

laws, good Samaritan. *Laws*[8] within various *states*[3] of the U.S. which provide immunity from legal liability to persons providing assistance to others in dire need. The state of California enacted the first such law in 1959 in order to protect medical doctors rendering assistance to accident victims. Most states that followed suit passed such *legislation*[7] because of physicians' fears of malpractice suits. Numerous states protect physicians and laymen under such laws as long as individuals render "reasonable first aid."

laws, optional. *Laws*[8] which provide that various types of *city charters*[11] are available to *municipal*[11] areas seeking *municipal incorporation*[11]. A *state*[3] may stipulate that *cities*[11] of certain size may choose between various types of local governmental arrangements. Optional laws are a compromise between incorporation through *special laws*[11] and *home*[11] *rule.*

laws, special. *Laws*[8] which apply to specific regions, persons, or situations such as municipal arrangements within *municipal corporations*[11] chartered

by the *state*[3]. Special laws refer to persons, governmental structures, or cities by name. For example, a *city*[11] may be chartered by a state under a special law and its particular and local affairs structured and regulated to a certain extent through state *legislation*[7]. See also *city charter*[11].

laws, uniform state. *Statutes*[8] written by the *Conference*[11] *of Commissioners on Uniform State Laws* and proposed for adoption by the various *states*[3] within the U.S. The *laws*[8] are useful when adopted without *radical*[3] changes because they help remove confusion and conflict between the states in various subject areas. Only a few Conference proposals have been uniformly adopted across the U.S. Some areas covered in such a manner involve negotiable instruments, stock transfers, bills of lading, business partnerships, and motor vehicle registration. See also *interstate*[11] *relations.*

Legal Services Program 1964– . A *federal*[3] legal aid program created in the *Economic*[11] *Opportunity Act of 1964* as a resource tool for low-income persons needing legal assistance. A basic objective of the program is to inform low-income people of their legal rights and responsibilities. Such programs also advocate changes in the *law*[8] in order to protect the disadvantaged. Legal Service Programs vary according to the needs of the local *community*[3]. Local *Community*[11] *Action Agencies* operate such services under funding through the *Office of Economic*[2] *Opportunity.* Some local Legal Services Programs have become highly controversial when low-income individuals have used such resources to legally challenge slum landlords or others who felt that their taxes were being used against them through federal funding of such services.

local option. An option of self-determination available to a *municipality*[11] or other governmental unit to determine a particular course of action without specific approval from *state*[3] officials. Local option is most visible in local elections used to determine whether the selling and consumption of alcoholic beverages will be permitted in local areas. Local option is also used in many states to permit *county*[11] and municipal *home*[11] *rule* elections for determining the structures of local governmental units.

local public authority (LPA). A federally approved local agency selected to administer a housing or other *urban*[11] program funded partially by the *federal government*[3] under federal *legislation*[7]. An LPA is permitted to make local decisions related to approved programs. A *municipal corporation*[11], an independent redevelopment agency, or other designated *organization*[6] may be selected as a local public authority. LPA's vary from place to place and their responsibilities are generally influenced by a maze of federal, *state*[3], and local structures and regulations.

Malthus, Thomas R., 1766–1834. British historian, economist, Anglican clergyman, and political theorist. Malthus wrote An Essay on the Principle of Population as It Affects the Future Improvement of Society (1798), An Inquiry into the Nature of Progress of Rent (1815), and Principles of Political Economy (1820). He was the first major writer to analyze population increase. His major thesis was that population increases faster than the food supply and that there is a constant need for regular population control. He contended that governmental *policy*[6] should be used so as to avoid the encouragement of population increase and to act as a restraint on population. He believed that *government*[3] should support economic and educational programs which could bring about a higher standard of living for all men.

Through such programs government could avoid some of the social and medical problems found in overpopulated and underfed areas of the world.

Manpower Development and Training Act of 1962. A federal *law*[8] passed in 1962 and subsequently *amended*[3] to assist experienced workers with family obligations to retrain for new employment when displaced by automation or technological changes. The *federal government*[3] assists in the funding of retraining, in transportation or relocation in order to gain retraining, and in family maintenance while retraining. The *act*[8] instituted a broad federal *grant-in-aid*[10] program designed to attack poverty in depressed areas by assisting individual workers. See also *War*[11] *on Poverty*.

mayor. A governmental figure who is generally the principal administrative officer of a *city*[11] or other *municipal*[11] area. The position of mayor, an old *executive*[6] structure, varies from city to city throughout the U.S. In some cities the mayor is a ceremonial figure, while in others he is a major executive official. In some cases he is popularly elected and in others, such as in the *commission*[11] *plan*, he is selected from within the administrative council to serve as a presiding officer and municipal ceremonial figure. See also *city*[11] *council*; *council-manager*[11] *plan*; *mayor-administrator*[11] *plan*; *mayor-council*[11] *plan*.

mayor-administrator plan. A structure of *municipal*[11] government which provides for a *mayor*[11] who may appoint a professional administrator to assist in the *administration*[6] of municipal *policy*[6]. A number of larger American *cities*[11] with strong-mayor systems of *government*[3] use the administrator to assist the mayor in the professional conduct of municipal business. The administrator is appointed by the mayor. His *appointment*[6] may require approval of the *city*[11] *council*, but he is primarily responsible to the mayor. He is given considerable *power*[3] to direct *budgetary*[10] matters, personnel practices, and other essential services. See also *mayor-council*[11] *plan*.

mayor-council plan. A structure of municipal *government*[3] which provides for a popularly elected *mayor*[11] to act as chief *executive*[6] and a *city*[11] *council* which is chosen to act as a legislative body. The plan, the oldest in the U.S., has many variations across the *nation*[3]. However, in general, most mayor-council plans use a *unicameral*[7] council and place some executive *powers*[3] in the mayor's office. The system is called a strong-mayor plan if the mayor dominates the *city*[11] government. It is called a weak-mayor plan if the council dominates the city government and the mayor fulfills a ceremonial role. Among modern American cities using such a plan, the larger cities tend to adopt the strong-mayor plan and the smaller cities tend to adopt the weak-mayor system. See also *mayor-administrator*[11] *plan*.

Medicaid. An abbreviated term meaning "medical care for those needing aid." The Medicaid program was created as part of Title XIX of the *Social*[11] *Security Act amendments*[3] of 1965. It provides *federal*[3] funds for families with dependent children, the generally indigent, and others needing medical assistance regardless of age. Separate *states*[3] determine eligibility levels. Medicaid is a matching program (50-50 in wealthy states and 83-17 in poor states) operated by the separate states. The *Congress*[4] established a 1975 deadline for instituting comprehensive health care for the poor throughout the U.S. See also *Aid*[11] *for Dependent Children*; *American*[5] *Medical Association*; *Medicare*[11]; *socialized medicine*[11].

Medicare. An abbreviated term meaning "medical care insurance." The in-

surance program created in Title XIX of the *Social*[11] *Security Act amendments*[3] of 1965 provides federal *grants-in-aid*[10] to *states*[3] willing to meet *federal*[3] medical standards designed to provide medical care for persons over 65 years of age. Medicare goes beyond the concept established in the *Kerr-Mills*[11] *Act of 1960* and provides services for the elderly regardless of income. Medicare is financed primarily through Social Security payroll *withholding taxes*[10] and covers hospital services, outpatient care, nursing home services, and various other items. Other medical insurance services may be provided through voluntary payments of fees by the recipient of medical aid. The Medicare program is primarily a federal program. It has been severely affected by skyrocketing medical costs and isolated cases of physician abuse related to medical charges. See also *American*[5] *Medical Association*; *Medicaid*[11]; *socialized medicine*[11].

medicine, socialized. The socio-medical process in which the *government*[3] provides basic health and hospital care for the general population through public funds. See also *American*[5] *Medical Association*; *Medicaid*[11]; *Medicare*[11].

megalopolis. A densely populated "great *city*[11]" composed of contiguous overlapping *urban*[11] areas. The three major megalopolises in the U.S. are sometimes cited as Boswash (Boston, Massachusetts to Washington, D.C.), Sansan (San Francisco to San Diego, California), and Chipitts (Chicago, Illinois to Pittsburgh, Pennsylvania). See also *suburbanization*[11]; *urbanization*[11].

metropolis. The dominant *city*[11] in a given region, or a cluster of cities in a given *urban*[11] area.

metropolitan district. A *special district*[11] created by the *state*[3] to assist several local *communities*[3] and local governmental units in coordinating particular programs of common interest to the local units. Metropolitan districts are frequently used to develop and coordinate public transportation systems, parks, cultural centers, sewage disposal, and other public needs.

metropolitan federation. An *urban*[11] arrangement of *government*[3] wherein a central governmental unit is empowered to regulate selected matters of common interest to several local *communities*[3] and wherein local matters are left under local control. Such an arrangement is often called a "metro" government. Dade County (Miami), Florida adopted the first reasonably successful modified *federal*[3] plan in the U.S. through such a *city-county consolidation*[11]. The *county*[11] is a union of 26 *municipalities*[11] and 1 county referred to as Metro. The *city*[11] of Miami is the largest *municipal corporation*[11] in the union. A metropolitan federation was imposed on Toronto, Canada and its 12 *suburbs*[11] in 1954 by the province of Ontario. It preceded Dade County, Florida's Metro, which was adopted by popular *referendum*[3] in 1957.

Model Cities Project. A 1966 program inaugurated in the *Demonstration*[11] *Cities and Metropolitan Development Act.* The Project was a comprehensive attempt to coordinate *federal*[3] programs in housing and *urban*[11] problems, to stimulate urban planning at the local level, and to provide mortgage funding for various housing developments. The program specified approximately 70 *cities*[11] for urban development. However, it received less than adequate funding primarily because of the federal funding of the *Vietnam*[12] *War.* By 1971 over 200 cities were involved in the program in one way or another. See also *city*[11] *planning; urban*[11] *renewal.*

Model City Charter. A model written document for *city*[11] governmental *or-*

ganization[6] which was formulated in 1915 and subsequently revised to meet new *urban*[11] needs. The document was written by the *National*[11] *Municipal League.* It incorporates an appointive chief *executive*[6] in the *council-manager*[11] *plan* of *government*[3], comprehensive and modern *budgetary*[10] practices, a *merit*[6] *system* in personnel selection, *city*[11] *planning*, balanced *zoning*[11] practices, *nonpartisan elections*[5], *Proportional Representation*[5] in *city*[11] *council selection, initiative*[3], *referendum*[3], a *short ballot*[5], and *at-large elections*[5].

Model State Constitution: see Chap. 4.

Morrill Act of 1862. The first major *federal*[3] *act*[8] to give extensive federal aid within the separate *states*[3]. Under the Morrill Act, over 11 million acres of land were given to the states for the establishment of colleges set aside to teach agricultural and mechanical arts. The creation of such colleges (best known as A. & M. colleges) helped the U.S. move into a technological *revolution*[3] in agriculture and into an overall technological development unprecedented in world history. See also *land*[11] *grant college.*

Moynihan, Daniel P., 1927– . Director of the Joint Center for Urban Studies at the Massachusetts Institute of Technology and Harvard University, sociologist, economic historian, welfare specialist, former Assistant Secretary of Labor, and presidential adviser on *urban*[11] and welfare problems. Moynihan co-authored Beyond the Melting Pot: The Ethnic Groups of New York City (1963). He wrote The Negro Family: The Case for National Action (1965), the first racially oriented social and economic study sponsored by the *federal government*[3]. The work, generally known as the Moynihan Report, was published by the *Department of Labor*[2]. The highly controversial report indicted the instability of the Negro family as a basic cause of black poverty. Moynihan contended that as long as the family unit is disoriented, the welfare "cycle of poverty" cannot be broken. On the basis of his significant contributions, he was appointed as a special adviser to *President*[6] Richard Nixon. He helped draft the first comprehensive anti-poverty *legislation*[7] during the *administration*[6] of *Lyndon Johnson*[6], analyzed racial unrest in the United States, became a leading advocate of federal *revenue*[10] *sharing* during the Nixon administration, and helped design the *Family*[11] *Assistance Plan*.

Mumford, Lewis, 1895– . *Urban*[11] sociologist, social critic, *socialist*[3] author, urban philosopher, and editor of journals in *city*[11] *planning* and urban problems. Mumford helped establish the Regional Planning Association of America in 1923. He views the *city*[11] as an organism in need of rational planning and is especially concerned that the city, regardless of how large it gets, continue to maintain a *community*[3] atmosphere. In fact, he sees the city as destructive of human personality and individuality and as a threat to the *democratic*[3] process. He also sees the *rural*[11] and urban segments of the U.S. as highly interdependent in a modern technological setting. His ideas have spanned many years in such publications as The Story of Utopias (1922), Technics and Civilization (1934), The Culture of Cities (1938), The City in History: Its Origins, Its Transformations, and Its Prospects (1961), and The Myth of the Machine: The Pentagon of Power (1970).

municipal incorporation. The creation of a legal body known as a *municipal corporation*[11], "muncipality," *city*[11], *village*[11], or other legal entity created through *state*[3] legislative action. An incorporated area is granted a charter by the state or given the right to devise its own *city charter*[11] through *home*[11] *rule* procedures. Through its charter an incorporated area gains

the *power*[3] to formulate local *policies*[6] and administer governmental needs.

municipality: see *city*[11].

Nader, Ralph, 1934– . Lawyer, author, and self-proclaimed consumer advocate. Nader's exposé of the automobile industry in Unsafe at Any Speed: The Designed-in Dangers of the American Automobile (1965) led directly to passage of the National Traffic and Motor Vehicle Safety Act of 1968. The controversial consumer advocate works with young students and legal researchers in actively *lobbying*[5] the U.S. *Congress*[4] and *state*[3] *legislatures*[7] for consumer protection, workman safety, and other protections for the common man and common *society*[3]. In 1973 he released a major study of the U.S. *Congress*[4].

National Defense Education Act of 1958. A major piece of *federal*[3] *legislation*[7] stimulated by the first successful space flight of the Soviet Union in 1957, an accomplishment remembered as *Sputnik*[12] *I*. The *act*[8], one of the most comprehensive education acts in U.S. history, provides student loans, student fellowships, and *grants-in-aid*[10] to educational institutions willing to support the fields of public education, foreign languages, science, mathematics, psychological counseling and testing, social sciences, engineering, and other specialized areas of importance to an international, technological *society*[3]. The act provides that funds may be made available under specified federal conditions but that states may maintain control over personnel, curriculum, and educational structures. Student loan payments may be "forgiven" if a college graduate in a specified field enters the teaching profession and remains for a certain number of years. After 1968, funding under the act was reduced considerably because of a surplus of trained personnel in the various areas covered in the legislation.

National Municipal League (NML), 1894– . A professional association created in 1894 to seek improvement of *state*[3] and local public *administration*[6] and processes. The NML was the single most important *organization*[6] to stimulate the municipal reform movement between 1900 and 1930. The organization was especially influential in getting widespread adoption of the *council-manager*[11] *plan* of *government*[3]. It stressed during the reform movement that government should be service oriented rather than *partisan*[5] dominated. It supports a *short ballot*[5], *at-large elections*[5], *nonpartisan elections*[5], and the council manager plan of government. The League regularly publishes a *Model*[11] *City Charter*.

National Railroad Passenger Corporation (Amtrak, Railpax), 1971– . A quasi-*government corporation*[6] created in order to improve rail passenger service in the U.S. The *organization*[6] is funded by the *federal government*[3] and private investors. The *President*[6] appoints members of the *board*[6] of directors. The organization began by cutting passenger rail service in half and carrying out a total reorganization of routes across the U.S. It operates trains between major *urban*[11] points across the *country*[3] and directs financial management, public relations, marketing, and related areas.

Neighborhood Youth Corps (NYC), 1964– . A *federal*[3] program created in the *Economic*[11] *Opportunity Act of 1964* as a part-time work experience program for high school dropouts and in-school individuals between the ages of 16 and 21. The program is administered by the *Department of Labor*[2] and is designed to assist local *communities*[3] in training young persons in useful skills and in helping local communities meet specific labor needs.

Occupational Health and Safety Act of 1970. The first comprehensive *federal*[3] *legislation*[7] dealing with the overall working conditions of men and women throughout the U.S. The *act*[8], specifically directed at "healthful working conditions," was passed under the *power*[3] of the *federal government*[3] to regulate *interstate commerce*[10] and anything which might hinder interstate commerce. It was also passed under the power to "provide for the general welfare." The legislation authorizes the Secretary of Labor to establish mandatory occupational safety and health standards for businesses affecting interstate commerce, established an *Occupational*[2] *Safety and Health Review Commission*, provided for research involving safety and medical standards, provided for safety training programs, and provided for penalties of up to $10,000 for each violation or jail sentences of various lengths depending on the violation involved.

Old Age, Survivors, Disability Insurance (OASDI). A major portion of the Social Security program instituted in the *Social*[11] *Security Act of 1935*. OASDI is a federal compulsory *social insurance*[11] program funded through matching payroll *withholding tax*[10] deductions from employers and employees. The program, administered by the *Social*[2] *Security Administration* and handled entirely by the *federal government*[3], pays benefits in the event of old age, death of the head of the family, and in the event of permanent disability. Payments received are based on earnings during the productive years. The OASDI program was created in an effort to avoid the widespread poverty experienced during the unexpected *Great Depression*[10] of the 1930's.

ordinance, zoning: see *zoning*[11].

Ordinances, Northwest: see Chap. 4.

Other America. The popular term used to describe the portion of *society*[3] which is poor, politically ineffectual, and socially invisible to the *majority*[3] of American *citizens*[3]. *Michael Harrington*[11], author and social critic, popularized the term in The Other America: Poverty in the United States (1962) by carefully documenting the problems of the economically depressed portion of American society. See also *Appalachia*[11]; *Economic*[11] *Opportunity Act of 1964*.

powers, proprietary: see Chap. 4.

Program, 235. A controversial *federal*[3] matching mortgage-assistance program created by the *Housing*[11] *and Urban Development Act of 1968* to help low-income families purchase moderate-priced housing. The program, to end in 1973, is based on family income level, a factor reevaluated at regular intervals in order to determine how much of the mortgage should be paid by the *federal government*[3] and how much should be paid by the residents. The program, named for section 235 of the federal *law*[8] providing the assistance, was suspended for a short time in 1970 and 1971 because of alleged abuses in rehabilitation of existing houses. Some critics of the program contend that it creates neighborhood conflicts because the federal government may help several families within a middle-class neighborhood without helping the others who feel they are supporting the neighbor's house payments through *graduated income taxes*[10].

Program, 701. The common designation of the Urban Planning Assistance Program of the *federal government*[3] which was created by section 701 of the *Housing*[11] *Act of 1954* and *amended*[3] in subsequent federal housing *legislation*[7]. Various 701 programs were largely funded by the federal government and created by local governmental *jurisdiction*[8] in order to plan, institute pilot projects, and coordinate various programs aimed at solving *urban*[11] problems. Such pro-

grams dealt with housing, land use, transportation, economic development, environmental problems, and other similar categories. Most 701 programs have been used to *force*[3] urban areas to work on a regionwide basis in solving problems. They have been administered through the *Department of Housing*[2] *and Urban Development* and have created frequent controversy because various *grants-in-aid*[10] have bypassed the *state*[3] and gone directly to local or regional officials. See also *city*[11] *planning*.

Project Head Start, 1964– . A preschool educational program created by the *federal government*[3] in the *Economic*[11] *Opportunity Act of 1964* in order to stimulate culturally disadvantaged children and assist them through basic medical, social, psychological, and nutritional services. The program is given basic direction by the Administrative Office of Child Development within the *Department of Health*[2], *Education, and Welfare*. Most Project Head Start programs receive 80 percent of their funds from the federal government and 20 percent from the *communities*[3] involved. Programs are organized and administered by local communities through the sponsorship of *Community*[11] *Action Agencies*, local *boards of education*[11], voluntary agencies, local governmental agencies, or nonprofit *organizations*[6]. Numerous local Head Start programs originally created under Community Action Agencies were quickly shifted to local school board control because of political conflict over public school *policies*[6].

public assistance. A comprehensive approach to *social insurance*[11] which was incorporated in the *Social*[11] *Security Act of 1935* to assist the elderly, blind, disabled, and dependent children. Public assistance programs are matching *grant-in-aid*[10] programs financed by the *federal government*[3] and the *states*[3]. They may be administered by the state, local agencies under state regulations, or by local agencies regulated by some local governmental unit. Funds are allocated to the states by the federal government on the basis of need. Certain federal standards are imposed upon states receiving federal money for public assistance programs (regular reports, no racial *discrimination*[9], *merit*[6] *system* selection of personnel, and so on), but the basic administrative practices are generally established by the states themselves. See also *Aid*[11] *for Dependent Children*; *Aid*[11] *to Blind*; *Aid*[11] *to the Totally and Permanently Disabled*; *general*[11] *assistance*; *vocational*[11] *rehabilitation*.

Pure Food and Drug Act of 1906. The first major *federal*[3] *legislation*[7] providing consumer protection through restrictions on the preparation and public sale of food and drug products. The series of pure food and drug *acts*[8] regulates the production and movement of such products in *interstate commerce*[10]. The legislation, stiffly opposed by numerous business groups for many years, was stimulated primarily through the publication of *Upton Sinclair's*[11] popular novel, The Jungle (1906), a book which revealed the unsanitary conditions of the meatpacking industry. The legislation has been *amended*[3] on many subsequent occasions. See also *Department of Health*[2], *Education, and Welfare*; *Food*[2] *and Drug Administration*.

regents, board of: see *board of education*[11].

rural. A geographic area containing few persons and dominated by agricultural interests.

Sheppard-Towner Act of 1921: see Chap. 10.

Smith-Hughes Vocational Education Act of 1917. A *federal*[3] *law*[8] which provided federal *grants-in-aid*[10] to

states[3] for public school educational programs in agriculture, home economics, industrial arts, and specialized trades.

Social Darwinism. The concept which holds that the principles of natural selection and the survival of the fittest apply to human history and social arrangements and relationships. The concept was popularized by *Herbert Spencer*[3] in such works as Social Statics (1851) and The Man Versus the State (1884). The term actually derived its name from biological *theories*[3] popularized by Charles Darwin in a book entitled On the Origin of Species by Means of Natural Selection, or the Preservation of Favored Races in the Struggle for Life (1859). See also *Lochner*[1] *v. U.S.*

Social Security Act of 1935. A major piece of federal *legislation*[7] which is regularly *amended*[3] in order to provide a comprehensive program of *social insurance*[11] in the U.S. The legislation, passed in the midst of the *Great Depression*[10], created a system of social insurance for elderly, retired workers and their dependents. The *act*[8] also incorporates programs of categorical *public*[11] *assistance* (blind, disabled, dependent children, needy elderly), *unemployment*[11] *insurance*, *Medicare*[11], *Medicaid*[11], and maternal and child health care. Social Security programs are basically funded through matching payroll *withholding taxes*[10] paid by employers and employees. Some of the programs within the *states*[3] are funded totally by the *federal government*[3] (*Old*[11] *Age, Survivors, and Disability Insurance* (OASDI), and *Medicare*[11], while others are funded jointly by the federal government and the states. See also *King*[1] *v. Smith*; *Social*[2] *Security Administration*; *tax*[10] *offset*.

Standard Metropolitan Statistical Area (SMSA). A geographical area containing a central *city*[11] with a population of at least 50,000 people and a surrounding area of *suburbs*[11], *villages*[11], *towns*[11], and industrial areas. See also *megalopolis*[11]; *metropolis*[11]; *urban*[11]; *urbanization*[11].

substitute father (man-in-the-house) rule. A state *statutory*[8] provision in use in some *states* which permits welfare payments under the *Aid*[11] *for Dependent Children* (AFDC) program to be reduced or dropped if a man other than the father or stepfather is living with the family. In 1968 the *U.S. Supreme*[8] *Court* held in an Alabama case that a state could not deny AFDC payments under such a rule because the state could not regulate the illicit sexual practices of the mother or *force*[3] a person who was not the father to contribute to the support of someone else's children. In 1970 the Supreme Court held in two California cases that a state could not cut child welfare payments under "man-in-the-house" rules unless they could prove he actually contributed toward the support of the children. See also *King*[1] *v. Smith*.

suburb. An area, generally residential in nature, which is on the outskirts of a *city*[11]. Suburbs arose in the U.S. after the close of *World*[12] *War II* with the widespread use of the automobile. The suburbs around major American cities gained population as the cities lost population during the decade 1960 to 1970. Persons living in suburbs are known as "suburbanites." The U.S. census of 1970 revealed that, for the first time in history, persons living in suburbs outnumbered persons living in central cities. See also *suburbanization*[11].

suburbanization. The process, either gradual or rapid, whereby a large number of persons move from a central *city*[11] into outlying residential areas in close proximity to the central city. Suburbanization in the U.S. was most evident between 1960 and 1970. The suburbs have primarily attracted persons or families who are white, middle class, professional "white-collar," *conservative*[3], and socially and geographically mobile.

tax, negative income: see Chap. 10.

Teacher Corps. A *federal*[3] education program created in the Higher Education Act of 1965 as an educational enrichment program for children from low-income areas and as a stimulus for better teacher preparation and recruitment. Teacher Corps teams work in both *urban*[11] and *rural*[11] areas, in *ghettoes*[11], on Indian reservations, in migrant labor camps, correctional institutions, and in other places of educational and cultural deficiency. The Teacher Corps is composed primarily of idealistic liberal arts majors who desire to contribute time and experience to the *War*[11] *on Poverty*.

town. A basic unit of local *government*[3] used in some *states*[3], especially states in the New England area. The New England town is one of the oldest, formal local government structures in the U.S. It includes *urban*[11] and *rural*[11] areas under common supervision of town selectmen chosen during a town meeting. In modern *society*[3], some towns use a professional town manager to assist in governing the area. Some urban areas also use small *representative*[7] town meetings to choose persons to attend the regular town meetings and conduct town business. In many parts of the U.S. the word "town" is used to indicate a group of people living in a *community*[3] smaller than a *city*[11].

Town, New. The term used to describe a formal planned *community*[3] built on a new geographical, social, and architectural base in a selected location. The practical construction of a "New Town" arose in the 1960's with the development of such innovative places as Reston, Virginia and Columbia, Maryland. In those locations, private developers financed by large *corporations*[10] created new *cities*[11] with planned land usage, transportation systems, educational facilities, housing patterns, and other elements. See also *city*[11] *planning*.

Townsend Plan. A controversial *social insurance*[11] plan (Old Age Revolving Pensions, Ltd.) devised and actively promoted by Dr. Francis E. Townsend in 1934. The Townsend Plan advocated a guaranteed monthly income of up to $200 per month for all U.S. *citizens*[3] 60 years of age and over. The cost of such an expenditure would be financed by a 2 percent business transaction tax. The persons receiving the payments were to be legally required to spend the money soon after payment in order to stimulate the total economy. The plan received little public attention, primarily because the *Social*[11] *Security Act of 1935* instituted a comprehensive social insurance program for retired persons.

township. A division of local *government*[3] within a *state*[3], generally a portion of a *county*[11], which is empowered to act on special items of public *policy*[6] and *administration*[6]. The township form of government is found primarily in the northeastern and midwestern states. Townships are frequently 36 square miles in size, *rural*[11] in nature, led by an elected supervisor, regulated by a small township *board*[6], and use an annual town meeting to discuss matters of common interest to people within the area. Township government is falling into disuse in some states as the U.S. becomes more *urban*[11]. In some cases, however, townships are used in urban areas to handle urban problems overlapping several *jurisdictional*[8] areas.

trustees, board of: see *board of education*[11].

unemployment insurance. A nationwide system of *social insurance*[11] stimulated by the U.S. *federal government*[3]

in the *Social*[11] *Security Act of 1935* under the *tax*[10] *offset* provision that the federal government would institute an unemployment insurance program in any *state*[3] not establishing a program of its own. Eligibility, length of payment, size of benefits, and other benefits paid to unemployed workers vary from state to state. Payments are ordinarily not paid to workers who simply quit jobs they dislike. Funds for unemployment insurance *administration*[6] and payments are collected through matching payroll *withholding taxes*[10] paid by employers and employees. The separate states maintain unemployment offices to administer the separate programs and assist recipients in finding new employment. See also *Sherbert*[1] *v. Verner*; *Steward*[1] *Machine Co. v. Davis*.

Upward Bound, 1964– . A *federal*[3] education program instituted in the *Economic*[11] *Opportunity Act of 1964* as a motivation program in order to direct low-income high school students toward college. Upward Bound programs are funded by the *federal government*[3] and operate through accredited institutions of higher learning.

urban. A geographic area containing a large number of persons.

Urban General Plan. A comprehensive, long-range, and formal plan of *urban*[11] growth and development which analyzes the social and economic setting of a *community*[3]. Such a plan, a document in need of constant revision, generally suggests basic urban *policy*[6], indicates options available for implementing policy, points out the significance of physical design within the community, and acts as a public document useful in educating the general public and advising business and *government*[3] leaders on urban policy. See also *city*[11] *planning*.

urbanization. The process, either gradual or rapid, whereby a geographical area becomes heavily populated with people. Urbanization in the U.S. received its greatest impetus from *immigration*[3], a technological *revolution*[3] in agriculture, an industrial revolution in the *cities*[11], mass communications attracting *rural*[11] dwellers to cities, and transportation systems which facilitated the move from rural to *urban*[11] areas. The census of 1920 revealed that slightly over 50 percent of the American population lived in cities. By 1970 the census revealed that over 80 percent of the population lived in urban areas. The modern American *metropolis*[11] (or *megalopolis*[11]) is increasingly taking on the characteristic of a decaying "central city" or urban core populated by black persons, the poor, the elderly, bluccollar laborers, the uneducated, and the underprivileged portion of *society*[3] dependent on welfare. Around that urban core is an unplanned sprawl of middle-class *suburbs*[11] composed largely of white persons.

urban renewal (redevelopment). A comprehensive intergovernmental *urban*[11] rehabilitation program funded by the *federal government*[3] and various private sources within the U.S. Urban redevelopment, as outlined in the *Housing*[11] *Acts of 1937, 1949,* and *1954* (when the term "urban redevelopment" was adopted), provides for slum clearance, open space development, *public housing*[11], neighborhood rehabilitation, and mortgage insurance programs. Land and *property*[10] may be purchased with public funds, occupants may be relocated, and the cleared property may be sold to private developers. In the Housing Act of 1954, not only was the term "urban renewal" dropped in favor of "urban redevelopment," but the idea of "slum clearance" was dropped in favor of "urban rehabilitation." See also *Berman*[1] *v. Parker*; *Department of Housing*[11] *and Urban Development*; *Housing*[11] *and Urban Development Act of 1968.*

village. A small *community*[3], incorporated or unincorporated, which has recognized social and governmental *organization*[6] within a specific geographical setting, but which is smaller than a *city*[11] or a *town*[11]. In many *states*[3] the word "village" has a legal connotation and the community may, under state incorporation, handle basic governmental services such as sewage disposal and street maintenance. See also *municipal corporation*[11].

vocational rehabilitation. A government[3] assistance program used in most *states*[3] to assist persons unable to work at regular employment. Many states extend such assistance and job training to the mentally handicapped, physically incapacitated, prison inmates, and other selected individuals. Vocational rehabilitation programs may involve on-the-job training, remedial education programs, correspondence courses, assistance in locating employment after training, medical services, and other programs of *public*[11] *assistance.* See also *adult*[11] *education program.*

Volunteers in Service to America (VISTA), 1964– . An adult volunteer service program established in the *Economic*[11] *Opportunity Act of 1964.* VISTA volunteers 18 years of age or older may serve in various programs designed as part of the *War*[11] *on Poverty.* Volunteers serve on Indian reservations, in *Job*[11] *Corps* centers, in *Community*[11] *Action Agencies*, in migrant labor camps, in mental institutions, and in various other service projects. VISTA, administered by the *federal*[3] agency known as *ACTION*[2], serves in areas of adult education, remedial education, health, recreation, *community*[3] service, job training, and other categories. See also *adult*[11] *education program.*

War on Poverty. The popular term used to describe the general effort to eradicate the root causes of poverty in the U.S. The term gained public significance during the *administration*[6] of *President*[6] *Lyndon B. Johnson*[6], primarily between 1963 and 1968. The major battle of the War on Poverty came with passage of such *legislation*[7] as the *Manpower*[11] *Development and Training Act of 1962*, the Vocational Education Act of 1963, the *Economic*[11] *Opportunity Act of 1964*, the *Elementary*[11] *and Secondary Education Act of 1965*, the Public Works and Economic Development Act of 1965, and the *Demonstration*[11] *Cities and Metropolitan Development Act of 1966*. A great deal of the legislation was stimulated by *Michael Harrington's*[11] book, The Other America: Poverty in the United States (1962). Some of the major programs of the War on Poverty were the *Job*[11] *Corps*, *Neighborhood*[11] *Youth Corps*, *adult*[11] *education programs*, *Community*[11] *Action Agencies*, *job*[11] *training programs*, *Legal*[11] *Services Programs*, *Work*[11] *Experience Programs*, *Food*[11] *Stamp Plan*, *Teacher*[11] *Corps*, *work*[11] *incentive program*, *Work*[11] *Study Program*, *youth*[11] *education program*, *Project*[11] *Head Start*, *Upward*[11] *Bound*, and *Volunteers*[11] *in Service to America*.

Water Quality Act of 1965. One of the first *federal*[3] water regulatory *acts*[8] in U.S. history. The *legislation*[7] created the Federal Water Pollution Control Administration (FWPCA), developed standards to be maintained on interstate streams and rivers, made available federal *grants-in-aid*[10] for water quality control, and set a deadline for July 1967 for *states*[3] to comply with regulations or face federal action in setting requirements within the separate states.

welfare migration. The movement of persons on public welfare from place to place in order to increase the amount of benefits received from *government*[3]. Welfare migration has most often been stimulated across *state*[3] lines by the fact that some states pay higher benefits than other states for the same welfare problem. In the *Supreme*[8] *Court* case of *Shapiro*[1] *v. Thompson*, it was held that states could not require a one-year residency before granting certain welfare benefits to persons within their legal *jurisdiction*[8]. The decision increased the possibility of more welfare migration and stimulated widespread support for a national welfare program to replace the separate state programs.

welfare state. The *theory*[3] of the *state*[3], which holds that a basic function of the state is to actively promote and care for individual and social needs through governmentally designed and operated programs of economic and social action.

Work Experience Program. A formal program officially created in the *Economic*[11] *Opportunity Act of 1964* and administered by the Welfare Administration within the *Department of Health*[2], *Education, and Welfare*. The Work Experience Program assists needy persons in training, employment counseling, relocation, and other aspects related to employment in a changing and competitive job market.

work incentive program. Any welfare incentive program designed to stimulate persons on welfare to financially contribute toward their own maintenance. For example, a 1967 *amendment*[3] to the *Social*[11] *Security Act of 1935* created a work incentive program that provided child care for welfare mothers wishing to work outside the home, for employment training programs funded by the *federal government*[3], and for special work projects in public or nonprofit agencies. Those under such programs were subject to regular *graduated income taxes*[10] and Social Security taxes. Refusal to work constituted cause for losing certain welfare benefits.

workman's compensation: see Chap. 10.

Work Study Program. A formal program officially created in the *Economic*[11] *Opportunity Act of 1964* and originally administered by the *Office of Economic*[2] *Opportunity*. The program was eventually moved to the Office of Education inside the *Department of Health*[2], *Education, and Welfare*. The Work Study Program provides parttime jobs for needy college students.

youth education program. Any welfare program funded by the *government*[3] in an effort to raise the level of education of young people. In the *Economic*[11] *Opportunity Act of 1964*, the *federal government*[3] formally established several youth education programs such as *Upward*[11] *Bound*, *Project*[11] *Head Start*, and the *Work*[11] *Study Program*. The general objective

of such programs is to place educational advantages at the disposal of persons living in poverty in order that they might become economically productive.

zone of transition. A deteriorating semi-residential and semi-industrial area between or encircling the downtown business district of a *city*[11] and its outlying residential areas and *suburbs*[11].

zoning. The *municipal*[11] practice of legally restricting certain portions of a *city*[11] to particular land uses. *Zoning ordinances*[11] usually regulate general land use and building specifications. The most common zoning categories are residential, commercial, and industrial. They came into existence in order to protect *property*[10] values, health, safety, esthetics, and other publicly acceptable values. Municipal zoning was upheld as *constitutional*[3] in the *Supreme*[8] *Court* case of Euclid v. Ambler Realty Company in 1926, on the grounds that it is a reasonable use of the *police powers*[4] of the *state*[3].

Supreme Court cases related to material in this chapter are arranged below by subject. Summaries of the cases are in Chapter One arranged alphabetically by the name of the first party in each case.

GENERAL—
  Sunday Closing Cases
    (1961)
  U.S. v. Butler (1936)

EDUCATION—(Race)
  Alexander v. Holmes
    (1968)
  Bolling v. Sharpe (1954)
  Brown v. Board of Education of Topeka (1954)
  Cooper v. Aaron (1958)
  Green v. County School
    Board of New Kent
    County, Virginia (1968)
  Griffin v. County Board of
    Prince Edward County
    (1964)
  McLaurin v. Oklahoma
    State Regents (1950)
  Missouri ex rel. Gaines v.
    Canada (1938)

Swann v. Charlotte-
    Mecklenburg Board of
    Education (1971)
  Sweatt v. Painter (1950)

EDUCATION—(Religion)
  Board of Education v.
    Allen (1968)
  Engel v. Vitale (1962)
  Everson v. Board of Education (1947)
  Flast v. Cohen (1968)
  Lemon v. Kurtzman
    (1971)
  McCollum v. Board of
    Education (1948)
  Minersville School District v. Gobitis (1940)
  Pierce v. Society of
    Sisters (1925)
  School District of Abington Township v.
    Schempp (1963)

West Virginia State Board
    of Education v. Barnette
    (1943)
  Zorach v. Clauson (1952)

INTERGOVERNMENTAL
    RELATIONS—(Full
    Faith and Credit)
  Williams v. N.C. (1945)

INTERGOVERNMENTAL
    RELATIONS—
    (Grants-in-aid)
  Flast v. Cohen (1968)
  Frothingham v. Mellon
    (1923)
  Mass. v. Mellon (1923)

INTERGOVERNMENTAL
    RELATIONS—
    (Ingress and Egress)
  Edwards v. Calif. (1941)

INTERGOVERNMENTAL
RELATIONS—(Inter-
state rendition)
Ky. v. *Dennison* (1861)

LABOR—(Child)
Bailey v. *Drexel Furniture
Co.* (1922)
Hammer v. *Dagenhart*
(1918)
U.S. v. *Darby Lumber*
(1941)

LABOR—(Maximum
Hours)
Lochner v. *N.Y.* (1905)
Muller v. *Oregon* (1908)
U.S. v. *Darby Lumber*
(1941)

LABOR—(Minimum
Wages)
Adkins v. *Children's
Hospital* (1923)
Bunting v. *Oregon* (1917)
Opp Cotton Mills v. *Ad-
ministrator of Wage &
Hour Division* (1941)
U.S. v. *Darby Lumber*
(1941)
West Coast Hotel Co. v.
Parrish (1937)

LABOR—(Unemployment
Compensation)
Sherbert v. *Verner* (1963)
Steward Machine Co. v.
Davis (1937)

LABOR—(Women)
Adkins v. *Children's
Hospital* (1923)

Muller v. *Oregon* (1908)
West Coast Hotel Co. v.
Parrish (1937)

PUBLIC HOUSING AND
URBAN RENEWAL—
Berman v. *Parker* (1954)
James v. *Valtierra* (1971)

WELFARE—(Child)
King v. *Smith* (1968)

WELFARE—(Substitute
Father)
King v. *Smith* (1968)

WELFARE—(Welfare
Migration)
Shapiro v. *Thompson*
(1969)

Chapter 12

Foreign Policy and Defense

Note to the reader: Cross-referenced terms are in italics. The superscript number refers to the chapter in which the entry may be found. In addition, its placement indicates the word under which the term is alphabetized. (For example, in *electoral*⁴ *college*, information on the electoral college may be found in Chapter 4 under "electoral.") Because italics are used in cross-references, they are not used for terms in which they would ordinarily be used: Supreme Court cases and titles of books, journals, plays, and so forth.

Supreme Court cases relating to material in this chapter are listed at the end of the chapter (see page 335).

---

abrogation. Action that officially repeals a previous decision or action. For example, a *treaty*¹² may abrogate a previous foreign *policy*⁶ action of a particular *nation*³.

accord. A mutual agreement such as that freely and harmoniously reached by two or more *nations*³.

accredit. To certify or recognize something or someone as officially acceptable. For example, foreign *nations*³ accredit different types of individuals to enter or conduct business within their *boundaries*¹². Nations accredit *ambassadors*¹², *consuls*¹², importers, newsmen, and others acceptable to them.

accretion. A gradual growth or accumulation. National *territory*³ may be increased through accretion whenever soil is gradually deposited along a *boundary*¹² line by a river or an ocean.

adhesion. The act of supporting a particular matter. A *nation*³ that is not an official party to a *treaty*¹² may accept certain principles or provisions of a treaty in force between other nations.

adjutant general. A military officer designated as in control of a particular military staff assignment. A regular army adjutant general ordinarily heads some administrative division within the U.S. military establishment. A *state*³ adjutant general heads the state *national*¹² *guard* and is a political appointee of the state *governor*⁶.

aggression. An unprovoked and violent attack on people, *property*¹⁰, or *territory*³. International aggression has found no common definition generally accepted throughout the world *community*³ because of the difficulty of clearly distinguishing between aggressive and defensive actions. See also *war*¹².

alien: see Chap. 3.

alien, enemy. An *alien*³ who resides in a *country*³ at *war*¹² with his native land.

alliance. A union between two or more *nations*[3] or other political entities which is formed for the mutual benefit of those joining together in a common endeavor. An alliance is generally formed for military or economic benefit in hopes that a combination of national units will tend to discourage outside powers from taking aggressive action. See also *aggression*[12]; *Allied*[12] *powers*; *ANZUS*[12] *Pact*; *Axis*[12] *powers*; *balance*[12] *of power*; *bipolarity*[12]; *Central*[12] *powers*; *Central*[12] *Treaty Organization*; *North*[12] *Atlantic Treaty Organization*; *Rio*[12] *Pact*; *Southeast*[12] *Asia Treaty Organization*; *Warsaw*[12] *Pact*.

Alliance for Progress. A foreign development program organized among Latin American *nations*[3] in 1961 under the sponsorship of the U.S. *government*[3]. President John F. Kennedy led in the formulation of the program designed for social and economic reform in Latin America. The U.S. agreed to invest $20 billion in Latin America over a ten-year period in order to raise the standard of living in the area.

Allied powers. The international *alliance*[12] formed during *World*[12] *War I* between Great Britain, France, the United States, Italy, Japan, and other *nations*[3] engaged in *war*[12] with Germany and other members of the *Central*[12] *powers*. In *World*[12] *War II*, Italy and Japan joined the *Axis*[12] *powers* on the side of Germany. The basic membership of the Allies in World War II consisted of the United States, Great Britain, the Soviet Union, and other nations friendly toward the three major nations. See also *Lend-Lease*[12].

ambassador. The highest-ranking *diplomatic*[12] official *accredited*[12] by a *nation*[3] to represent it before the *government*[3] of another nation. An ambassador extraordinary serves a specific mission, an ambassador plenipotentiary is authorized to negotiate *treaties*[12], and an ambassador-at-large serves at the pleasure of the chief of *state*[3] without serving a particular *country*[3].

angary. The right of a *belligerent*[12] *nation*[3] to appropriate or destroy *neutral*[12] *property*[10] out of alleged necessity, with the understanding that the national or individual owner will be paid for losses incurred.

anti-ballistic missile (ABM). A missile designed to attack and destroy another ballistic missile. A ballistic missile is any projectile directed at a predetermined target by a rocket engine. The ABM gained widespread public attention between 1968 and 1970 when *President*[6] Nixon pushed for funding and development of an expensive, long-range ABM system of defensive protection for the U.S. Proponents claimed the need for protection from the Soviet Union and Communist China; opponents argued that such a system was extremely expensive, unreliable, and would be outdated by the time it became operational. The *Congress*[4] eventually funded a limited ABM system designed as a "thin line" defense against *aggressors*[12]. See also *Cuban*[12] *missile crisis of 1962*; *fail-safe*[12] *system*; *Sputnik*[12] *I*.

ANZUS Pact. A *collective*[12] *security* arrangement between the U.S., New Zealand, and Australia. The *treaty*[12], presently in effect, declares that *aggression*[12] against one of the member *nations*[3] should be considered a threat to the other members and should be dealt with accordingly. The ANZUS (an acronym for Australia, New Zealand, U.S.) Pact was concluded in an effort to provide military stability and strength in the Pacific Ocean. See also *alliance*[12].

appeasement. The act or process of accepting the demands or actions of another person or *nation*[3] in the hope that further trouble may be avoided.

An act of appeasement may involve surrendering a major principle or interest for a minor or temporary respite from difficulty.

arbitration, international. A legal arrangement designed to peacefully dispose of international conflicts through a binding settlement by third-party judges whose decision is accepted as final. The parties in conflict agree on a "compromise" which outlines the nature of the conflict and the rules to be followed in settling the dispute. In 1899 a Permanent Court of Arbitration was established at The Hague. See also *good*[12] *offices*; *The Hague*[12] *Tribunal*.

armistice (truce). A temporary halt of military action on the basis of mutual agreement among *belligerents*[12].

arms race. A condition of keen international competition in which various *nations*[3] seek to maintain weapons superiority over another. *See also atomic*[12] *war*; *Atoms*[12] *for Peace Plan*; *Baruch*[12] *Plan*; *disarmament*[12]; *Nonproliferation*[12] *of Nuclear Weapons Treaty*; *Nuclear*[12] *Test Ban Treaty*; *United*[2] *States Arms Control and Disarmament Agency*.

arrogance of power doctrine. A doctrine of international interaction which stresses the claimed superiority of a particular *nation*[3]. Almost all great powers are guilty of falling victim to such a feeling at one time or another. In a book entitled The Arrogance of Power (1966), *Senator*[7] J. William Fulbright, *chairman*[7] of the *Senate*[7] *Committee*[12] *on Foreign Relations*, claimed that the U.S. had fallen into such a posture and carried it to the extreme during the 1960's. See also *chauvinism*[12]; *ethnocentrism*[3]; *Pax*[12] *Americana*.

articles of war. Legal rules and regulations passed by a *government*[3] in order to maintain and regulate forces.

The *U.S. Constitution*[4] gives the *Congress*[4] the *authority*[3] to formulate such rules related to the army and navy. The basic rules are contained in the *Uniform*[8] *Code of Military Justice*.

asylum. Political protection afforded by a *nation*[3] to persons seeking refuge within its *boundaries*[12].

Atlantic Charter. A joint declaration of foreign *policy*[6] made by *President*[6] *Franklin D. Roosevelt*[6] of the United States and Prime Minister Winston Churchill of the United Kingdom on August 14, 1941. The Atlantic Charter, formulated in secret off the coast of Newfoundland, outlined plans for post-*World*[12] *War II* Europe which incorporated ideas related to peace, freedom, self-determination, *territorial*[3] integrity, equal economic rights, expanded social improvements, and a permanent system of security. The Atlantic Charter became a basic document of free world *public opinion*[5] just prior to U.S. entry into World War II.

Atomic Energy (McMahon) Act of 1946. *Federal*[3] *legislation*[7] which created the *Atomic*[2] *Energy Commission*, created the Joint Committee on Atomic Energy, permitted the exchange of atomic energy information with allies of the U.S., and assured civilian control of atomic energy. See also *atomic*[12] *war*; *Atoms*[12] *for Peace Plan*.

atomic (nuclear) war. Open, violent, and massive military conflict between two or more parties employing atomic or nuclear weapons for destructive purposes. Atomic warfare uses fissionable material readily adaptable to chain reaction releases of tremendous amounts of energy. The only time atomic warfare has actually been used was in 1945 when the U.S. dropped atom bombs on Hiroshima and Nagasaki, Japan and forced a sudden end to *World*[12] *War II*. The highly secret military project which developed the atomic bomb was known as the Manhattan Project. It was made possible by the scientific research of physicist Albert Einstein. See also *arms*[12] *race*; *Atoms*[12] *for Peace Plan*; *Baruch*[12] *Plan*; *conventional war*[12]; *Cuban*[12] *missile crisis of 1962*; *disarmament*[12]; *Hungarian*[12] *crisis of 1956*; *Nonproliferation*[12] *of Nuclear Weapons Treaty*; *Nuclear*[12] *Test-Ban Treaty*.

Atoms for Peace Plan. A 1953 proposal by *President*[6] Dwight D. Eisenhower, which called on the *United*[12] *Nations* and cooperating *nations*[3] to work together in the peaceful development of atomic energy. The proposal was a diversionary plan which sought to shift world emphasis on nuclear energy from *war*[12] to peace. The proposal stimulated the creation of the International Atomic Energy Agency (IAEA) in 1957, but never reached the high objectives sought by President Eisenhower. See also *arms*[12] *race*; *Atomic*[12] *Energy Act of 1946*; *atomic*[12] *war*.

attaché. An individual attached to a *diplomatic*[12] staff serving in a foreign *nation*[3]. An attaché is generally charged with carrying out a specific function. Various types of attachés specialize in such things as engineering, aviation, agriculture, research, labor, and other subjects.

autarchy (autarky): see Chap. 3.

award. A legal settlement or judgment which is made against a *nation*[3] by a recognized international body. An award may take the form of financial remuneration, *territory*[3], or other tangible items. It may be granted to an individual or to his *government*[3].

Axis powers. The international *alliance*[12] formed between Germany, Italy, Japan, and other *nations*[3] during the 1930's and 1940's. The Axis powers, named after the "Rome-Berlin axis," maintained a major warmaking machine which battled the *Allied*[12] *powers* during *World*[12] *War II*. See also *war*[12].

balance of power. A balancing of various international *power*[3] variables considered most important to competing *nations*[3]. The variables generally considered most important are military and economic. On occasion, several nations combine in an *alliance*[12] in order to balance power supposedly existing in another international area. The balance of power concept is ordinarily in a state of continual change. The two major international poles in the modern equation of power are East and West, *Communist*[3] and Free World. The leaders of the two camps are the United States in the West and the Union of Soviet Socialist Republics in the East. See also *bipolarity*[12].

Bamboo Curtain. The real, imaginary, or figurative line that encircles Communist China and behind which restricted *diplomatic*[12], commercial, and social practices take place. The Bamboo Curtain was closed when the *Communists*[3] gained control under *Mao*[3] *Tse-tung* in 1949. It was opened slightly to the Western *nations*[3] in 1971 when a U.S. table tennis team was permitted to enter China for international competition. Soon after that visit, *President*[6] Nixon and other U.S. leaders visited Red China in order to improve relations between China and the U.S. See also *Open*[12] *Door Policy*; *closed society*[3].

Baruch Plan. A plan formulated in 1946 by Bernard Baruch, U.S. *delegate*[5] to the *United*[12] *Nations* and presented to the international *organization*[6] in an effort to develop a workable system of international nuclear *disarmament*[12]. The plan advocated an end to the development of atomic weapons and the destruction of existing nuclear stockpiles. It also advocated that the U.N. regulate ownership, licensing, inspection, enforcement, and general management of nuclear materials. The Plan encountered the basic arguments against nuclear disarmament, arguments which held that no international system could provide adequate inspection and that no agreement could be enforced in a world of sovereign *states*[3]. The plan was never accepted, primarily because of Soviet disapproval. However, it did lay the foundation for later U.N. *treaties*[12] involving the use of nuclear weapons in outer space and treaties which established a partial test ban on nuclear weapons. See also *arms*[12] *race*; *atomic*[12] *war*; *Nonproliferation*[12] *of Nuclear Weapons Treaty*; *Nuclear*[12] *Test-Ban Treaty*; *state* (*constitutional*) *sovereignty*[3].

Bay of Pigs crisis of 1961. An unsuccessful invasion of Cuba by exiled Cubans trained and encouraged by *Central*[2] *Intelligence Agency* personnel of the U.S. *government*[3]. The invasion, aimed at the Cuban government of Fidel Castro, took place at the Bay of Pigs near Cienfuegos, Cuba, on April 15, 1961. It provoked public criticism of *President*[6] John F. Kennedy because of the failure of the U.S. government to clarify the U.S. role in the invasion and the failure of the U.S. to provide air cover for the invaders. See also *Watergate*[5].

belligerency. A condition of violent hostility between two or more *countries*[3]. See also *aggression*[12]; *neutrality*[12]; *war*[12].

benevolent assimilation. The process wherein two or more groups or *countries*[3] peacefully combine or become similar. Benevolent assimilation referred to as *Americanization*[4], is a process in which foreign immigrants peacefully become part of the dominant social and governmental patterns of U.S. *society*[3]. See also *political*[3] *socialization.*

Berlin Airlift. An air operation carried out by the *Allied*[12] *powers* between June 1948 and May 1949, in an effort to supply basic human necessities to the people of Berlin, West Germany after general ground access to the whole *city*[11] was closed off in a *blockade*[12] by the Soviet Union. The U.S.S.R. controlled East Germany and all *territory*[3] through which ground transportation had to pass before reaching Berlin. The Berlin Airlift proved to be a basic factor in the creation of the West German Republic and the *North*[12] *Atlantic Treaty Organization.*

Big Stick Policy. The foreign *policy*[6] doctrine advocated by *President*[6] *Theodore Roosevelt*[6]; especially with regard to Latin American *nations*[3]. President Roosevelt's theme of "speak softly and carry a big stick" emphasized the fact that the U.S. intended to exert strong pressure in guiding military and economic affairs throughout the world. See also *Good*[12] *Neighbor Policy*; *dollar diplomacy*[12]; *Platt*[12] *Amendment*; *Roosevelt*[12] *corollary.*

bipartisan (**bipartisanship**): see Chap. 5.

bipolarity. The condition of international affairs in which the *nations*[3] of the world or a major portion of the world tend to group together around two rival *power*[3] centers. The condition of bipolarity was especially evident after *World*[12] *War II*, when nations viewed their interests in terms of the interests of the United States or the Soviet Union. See also *alliance*[12]; *balance*[12] *of power*; *Cold*[12] *War*; *polarization*[3].

blockade. The obstructive or *forceful*[3] closing of a *boundary*[12]. Blockades are sometimes useful to prevent supplies from reaching military troops, to prevent *neutral*[12] *countries*[3] from trading with a *belligerent*[12] *nation*[3], and to prevent basic necessities from reaching civilian populations whose ultimate plight could help those carrying out the blockade to achieve desired objectives. See also *Berlin*[12] *Airlift*; *blockade*[12] *runner*; *Cuban*[12] *missile crisis of 1962*; *quarantine*[12].

blockade, Berlin: see *Berlin*[12] *Airlift*.

blockade runner. Any person or vessel that actively engages in crossing a *blockaded*[12] *boundary*[12] line.

boundary. A line, marked or imaginary, which specifies geographical, legal, or social limits. International boundaries may be determined through informal acceptance, negotiation, *war*[12], or some other acknowledged and accepted practices. Boundaries reflect the desire for a particular population to delineate its sphere of social and political control. See also *gerrymander*[7]; *territory*[3].

boycott: see Chap. 10.

Bricker Amendment. An unsuccessful, proposed *amendment*[3] to the *U.S. Constitution*[4] which would have limited the treaty-making *authority*[3] of the *President*[6]. The amendment, sponsored in the early 1950's by *Senator*[7] John Bricker, would have required that presidential *executive*[12] *agreements* receive congressional approval before becoming effective as *international law*[8]. The amendment would have required that *treaties*[12] be consistent with provisions in the U.S. Constitution. If it had been accepted, the Bricker Amendment would have reversed the rule adopted in the *Supreme*[8] *Court* case of *Missouri*[1] *v. Holland*, which permits international treaties to override the *police powers*[4] of the *states*[3].

brinkmanship. The practice of permitting or actively encouraging human or international situations to move to the verge of *war*[12] without actually engaging in violence or military action. U.S. Secretary of State John Foster Dulles brought the concept to public attention during the Eisenhower *administration*[6] when he declared in 1956 that the U.S. had deliberately engaged in such a *diplomatic*[12] practice in the *Cold*[12] *War* with *Communism*[3]. See also *Formosan*[12] *crisis of 1958*; *massive retaliation strategy*[12].

Calley case. The controversial and lengthy *court-martial*[8] of Lieutenant William L. Calley, Jr., during 1970–71. Calley, one of the principal figures in the *My*[12] *Lai controversy* during the *Vietnam*[12] *War* was charged with murdering over 100 South Vietnamese civilians on March 16, 1968. The Calley court-martial, the longest military trial in U.S. history, ended on March 29, 1971 with a guilty verdict for the murder of 22 persons. Calley was sentenced to life in prison. General and overwhelming *public opinion*[5] supporting Calley led *President*[6] Nixon to declare that he would, under the *Commander-in-Chief powers*[6], eventually determine Calley's fate after all appeals were exhausted. The Calley case raised the issue of new *war*[12] *crimes trials* similar to those held at the end of *World*[12] *War II*. It also raised questions about military obedience to commanding officers giving orders on the field of battle. During 1971 Calley's sentence was reduced to twenty years in prison by a military appeals officer, a decision upheld by the Army Court of Military Review in 1973.

Calvo clause: see *Calvo*[12] *doctrine*.

Calvo doctrine. An international doctrine elaborated on by Argentine Prime Minister Carlos Calvo during the 1880's and 90's. The doctrine, occasionally built into public *contracts*[10] as a national and domestic protective clause, holds that monetary claims by private *citizens*[3] of one *nation*[3] against the *government*[3] or citizens of another nation should not be collected by external *diplomatic*[12] pressure or *force*[3] of arms.

Cambodian crisis of 1970. A U.S. and South Vietnamese military operation frequently cited as the Cambodian invasion, or Cambodian incursion, of 1970, an operation ordered by *President*[6] Richard M. Nixon in an effort to destroy *Viet*[12] *Cong* (see *National*[12] *Liberation Front*) and North Vietnamese military supplies in the *neutralist*[12] *territory*[3] of Cambodia. The operation was ordered in early May 1970, soon after the *leftist*[3], corrupt Cambodian *government*[3] of Prince Norodom Sihanouk fell from *power*[3]. President Nixon announced that it was necessary to enter Cambodia in order to clear out privileged enemy sanctuaries and supply lines operating along the Ho Chi Minh Trail. The movement was justified on the grounds that U.S. troops could not turn the *Vietnam*[12] *War* over to the South Vietnamese as long as such supply sanctuaries existed. Divided and vocal *public opinion*[5] surfaced in the U.S., congressional opposition to the Vienam War increased, internal conflicts developed inside the Nixon *administration*[6], and student demonstrations on university campuses erupted into violence and death, particularly at Kent State University. The U.S. government gave massive political and military support to a new pro-Western Cambodian government led by General Lon Nol. The Nixon administration also began to announce that the U.S. government would do "whatever necessary" to protect the lives of American fighting men abroad. The Cambodian incursion and the use of U.S. troops lasted only a few months. However, after U.S. forces withdrew, the U.S. government continued to give military aid to the Cambodian government, and large contingents of South Vietnamese troops

remained in Cambodia. The crisis stimulated extensive debate in the *Congress*[4] concerning the *power*[3] of the President to make *war*[12] without a congressional *declaration of war*[12]. See also *Campus Unrest Report*[11]; *Cooper-Church*[12] *Amendment*; *Nixon*[12] *doctrine*.

Central powers. The international *alliance*[12] formed during *World*[12] *War I* between Germany, Austro-Hungary, Turkey, Bulgaria, and other *nations*[3] engaged in military conflict with the *Allied*[12] *powers* led by the United States, Great Britain, and France.

Central Treaty Organization (CENTO). A diplomatic *alliance*[12] in the Middle East which includes Great Britain, Iran, Pakistan, and Turkey. The mutual security alliance was formalized in 1959 and presently receives extensive financial and *diplomatic*[12] support from the U.S. although the U.S. is not a formal member. The *organization*[6] is designed to counter *Communist*[3] influence in the Middle East. See also *collective*[12] *security*; *Eisenhower*[12] *doctrine*.

Chamizal Treaty. A *diplomatic*[12] agreement between the U.S. and Mexico which was formalized in a *treaty*[12] in 1963 in order to adjust a *boundary*[12] dispute between the two *nations*[3]. The dispute involved 600 acres of land in the El Chamizal area between El Paso, Texas, and Juarez, Mexico. Portions of the land had been shifted by a change in the Rio Grande River in 1864. An arbitration *commission*[6] declared in 1911 that the land should be returned to Mexico, but the U.S. did not accept the *arbitration*[12] decision. In the final exchange in 1963 approximately 435 acres were returned to Mexico and the remaining acres were returned to the U.S.

charge d'affaires. A *diplomatic*[12] official temporarily empowered to conduct the affairs of an *embassy*[12] or *legation*[12] in the absence of an *ambassador*[12] or *minister*[12].

chauvinism. An extreme, exaggerated, boastful, and unquestioning patriotic expression which reveals total support for a *nation*[3]. See also *arrogance*[12] *of power doctrine*; *ethnocentrism*[3]; *nationalism*[3]; *Pax*[12] *Americana*.

civil defense (CD). A system of domestic civilian and military protection designed to provide a maximum of military security for civilian populations. Civil defense presently involves coordinated and voluntary public action, public warning systems, shelters, and educational programs designed to assist civilians during military attacks and natural disasters. See also *mobilization*[12]; *Office of Emergency*[2] *Preparedness*.

Civil War. (U.S.): see Chap. 4.

Clausewitz, Karl Von, 1780–1831. Prussian general, military historian, and military philosopher. Clausewitz, son of a Prussian officer, became director of the German War School in 1818. He helped reorganize the Prussian army, assisted Russian military forces against France, and helped develop basic modern military concepts adopted throughout the world. His volume, entitled On War (1833), is commonly recognized as the first modern analysis of total warfare. It is considered the classic on land warfare. Clausewitz's major concepts stemmed from Napoleon's use of total war as national *policy*[6]. His most famous statement is, "War is not merely a political act, but also a political instrument . . . a continuation of policy by other means." Some of Clausewitz's major military concepts were: completely annihilate the enemy's armies first, avoid sentimentality and human feelings, actively defend your own resources and men, heed the psychological factors of military

combat, and use *war*[12] for accomplishing political purposes. He believed that war was simply one portion of foreign policy and a natural part of the activities of the *state*[3]. See also *psychological warfare*[12].

coexistence, peaceful. A doctrine popularized in the Soviet Union and called to world attention by Soviet Premier Nikita Khruschev between 1958 and 1964. The *theory*[3] holds that *Communism*[3] will eventually triumph over all other political and economic systems. However, for the sake of expediency, both Communism and *capitalism*[3] may peacefully and indefinitely exist alongside one another. The theory is essentially a *liberal*[3] reinterpretation of the doctrines of *Karl Marx*[3] and *Lenin*[3]. It was formulated with an understanding of the possible consequences of a total *atomic*[12] *war* between Free World and Communist *nations*[3]. See also *coexistence*.[3]

Cold War. Military, *diplomatic*[12], political, and economic challenges that create severe international tension between two or more *nations*[3], tension which falls short of open and violent hostility. A period known as the Cold War began at the end of *World*[12] *War II* and was a *bipolarization*[12] of *Communist*[3] and Free World nations. The leading powers of the Cold War were the U.S. and the Soviet Union. The Cold War was characterized by a nuclear *arms*[12] *race*, economic competition, *propaganda*[5] barrages, pervasive *intelligence*[12] operations, and military face-offs such as that experienced during the *Cuban*[12] *missile crisis of 1962*. A gradual thaw in the Cold War began to develop during the 1960's when the *administration*[6] of *President*[6] *Lyndon B. Johnson*[6] publicly rejected continuation of Cold War *politics*[3]. The Cold War appeared to end almost completely with *President*[6] Nixon's trips to China and the Soviet Union in 1972. See also *ideological warfare*[12].

collective security. A comprehensive and worldwide *diplomatic*[12] and military system designed to maintain international order through collective action against any *nation*[3] threatening world peace through *aggression*[12]. The *League*[12] *of Nations* and the *United*[12] *Nations* were both founded on the idea of collective security. Collective action of the United Nations may take the form of public expression of displeasure, economic *sanctions*[12], military action, or other agreed upon devices. Various regional *alliances*[12] have been formed in Europe, Asia, Latin America, and the Middle East as collective security arrangements. See also *ANZUS*[12] *Pact*; *Central*[12] *Treaty Organization*; *North*[12] *Atlantic Treaty Organization*; *Rio*[12] *Pact*; *Southeast*[12] *Asia Treaty Organization*; *Warsaw*[12] *Pact*.

comity: see Chap. 3.

Committee on Foreign Relations (U.S. Senate). One of the most influential *standing committees*[7] in the U.S. *Senate*[7], a *committee*[7] responsible for congressional actions related to approval of *treaties*[12] negotiated by the *President*[6] and approval of presidential *appointments*[6] in the area of foreign affairs. The committee also deals with matters related to military *policy*[6], international *organizations*[6], international economic relations, and similar matters.

Connally Amendment. A *treaty*[12] *reservation* by the United States to the 1946 *treaty*[12] covering the *jurisdiction*[8] of the *International*[12] *Court of Justice*. The reservation, named for *Senator*[7] Tom Connally, *chairman*[7] of the *Senate*[7] *Committee*[12] *on Foreign Relations*, forbade compulsory handling by the Court of any matters that were "essentially within the domestic jurisdiction of the United States of America as determined by the United States of America."

conscientious objector: see Chap. 9.

consul. A foreign service official appointed to handle various commercial, minor *diplomatic*[12], and service functions on behalf of a *nation*[3].

containment. A U.S. foreign *policy*[6] position enunciated by *President*[6] *Harry S Truman*[6] in 1947, a *pragmatic*[3] and activist policy specifically designed to "contain" *Communism*[3] within existing *boundaries*[12]. President Truman hoped that if Communism could be contained, it would die from internal inconsistencies and weaknesses. The policy of containment has been implemented through regional security agreements, foreign economic aid, trade agreements, and various other devices. See also *collective*[12] *security*; *domino*[12] *theory*; *Truman*[12] *doctrine*.

contraband. *Property*[10] of a commercial nature which is prohibited to a *belligerent*[12]. Contraband shipped by a *neutral*[12] to a belligerent is generally considered "contraband of war" and may be seized by another belligerent.

Cooper-Church Amendment. A proposed but unsuccessful *amendment*[3] to the Foreign Military Sales bill of 1970, which was offered by *Senators*[7] Frank Church and John Sherman Cooper. The amendment was attached to a *bill*[7] permitting weapons sales to friendly, underdeveloped countries. Cosponsored by 30 senators, it sought to prohibit the use of any funds to retain U.S. forces or advisers in Cambodia after July 1, 1970 unless specifically authorized by the *Congress*[4]. Originally the amendment passed the *Senate*[7] by a 58-37 *roll call vote*[7], but failed in the *House*[7] *of Representatives*, 237 to 153. The proposed amendment was considered a major challenge to the *Commander-in-Chief powers*[6] and *diplomatic*[6] *powers* of the *President*[6]. See also *Cambodian*[12] *crisis of 1970*; *rider*[7]

counterinsurgency. *Intelligence*[12] and military action used to combat internal subversion, *guerrilla war*,[12] and *insurgency*[12] against a recognized *government*[3].

country mission. A particular foreign *policy*[6] post overseas or in a foreign *nation*[3]. A *country*[3] mission is generally headquartered in a foreign *embassy*[12], directed by an *ambassador*[12], and staffed by various *diplomatic*[12] specialists. Each country mission operates under the U.S. *Department of State*[2] and receives instructions from an appropriate section ("desk") or *bureau*[6] in *Washington*[4], D.C. The country mission staff is generally provided by the *Foreign*[2] *Service* within the State Department.

coup d'etat: see Chap. 3.

credibility gap: see Chap. 6.

Cuban missile crisis of 1962. The international confrontation in 1962 between the United States and the Soviet Union over the Soviet placement of intermediate-range missiles in Cuba. *President*[6] John F. Kennedy placed a *quarantine*[12] on Cuba and demanded that Soviet Premier Khrushchev remove the missiles or else face a strong reaction from the U.S. The missiles were promptly dismantled and returned to the Soviet Union. The crisis highlighted the true nature of a nuclear face-off and introduced a new type of *blockade*[12] in which a third party was restricted in movement apart from a period of declared *war*[12]. See also *atomic*[12] *war*; *anti-ballistic*[12] *missile*; *credibility*[6] *gap*; *declaration of war*[12]; *massive retaliation strategy*[12].

détente. A term used to describe a relaxation of international tensions between two or more *nations*[3].

deterrence. Action by one *nation*[3] to discourage or deter other nations from undertaking *aggressive*[12] or harmful action. Deterrence usually involves

military weapons development, *propaganda*[5], *diplomatic*[12] maneuvers, and other military and diplomatic tactics.

diplomacy. The art and science of conducting basic political, social, and economic relationships between two or more *nations*[3]. Each nation generally maintains some form of foreign service *organization*[6] in order to carry out basic diplomatic needs such as communications, negotiations, and trade relations. See also *Department of State*[2]; *diplomatic*[6] *powers*; *diplomatic*[12] *recognition*; *Foreign*[2] *Service*; *Rogers*[12] *Act of 1924*.

diplomacy, dollar. The concept that foreign *policy*[6] decisions should be designed primarily to bring economic benefit to the *nation*[3] or particular private interests within the nation. The term was originally used to describe the United States foreign policy stance of *President*[6] *Theodore Roosevelt*[6]. Dollar diplomacy implied U.S. military intervention whenever necessary to protect U.S. economic interests in foreign nations. See also *Big*[12] *Stick Policy*; *free*[10] *enterprise*; *Good*[12] *Neighbor Policy*; *Roosevelt*[12] *corollary*.

diplomatic immunity. Exemption of a *diplomatic*[12] representative of one *country*[3] from certain internal regulations of the country in which the *representative*[7] resides. Diplomatic immunity is generally agreed on by the respective chiefs of *state*[3] of the two *nations*[3] in question, without formal *treaty*[12] negotiations. Examples of diplomatic immunity are sanctity of residence, freedom from civil and legal prosecution, and freedom of travel. See also *extraterritorality*[12].

diplomatic recognition. The act or process wherein one *government*[3] accepts the existence or legality of another government. Recognition is generally accorded by a chief of state when he sends an official *ambassador*[12] or other *diplomatic*[12] official to the *state*[3] being recognized. Recognition is termed *de*[8] *facto* when it is a provisional action which recognizes tenuous governmental control over particular *territory*[3] or people. It is termed *de*[8] *jure* when all qualifications are removed and the government is recognized as exercising full legal *authority*[3] over the general population. The *President*[6] possesses the *power*[3] of recognition as part of his *diplomatic*[6] powers. See also *de facto government*[3]; *de jure government*[3]; *U.S.*[2] *v. Belmont.*

disarmament. The act or process of reducing or destroying military weapons and weapons systems. Modern concepts of disarmament ordinarily point to self-destruction of a *nation's*[3] own weapons. Disarmament actions may be taken unilaterally or through multilateral *treaty*[12] agreements. A basic problem is mutual distrust among those considering disarmament. There is always the possibility that one or more parties to a disarmament agreement will not disarm. There is also the problem of realistic inspection behind international *boundary*[12] lines. Another problem involves enforcement if one party to an agreement is found in violation of the agreement. *Hague*[12] *Tribunal* conferences and *United*[12] *Nations* discussions regularly bring up the possibility of disarmament, especially nuclear disarmament. However, only limited success has been made in certain areas related to nuclear and *chemical and biological warfare*[12]. See also *atomic*[12] *war*; *Nonproliferation*[12] *of Nuclear Weapons Treaty*; *Nuclear*[12] *Test Ban Treaty*; *Strategic*[12] *Arms Limitation Talks*; *United*[2] *States Arms Control and Disarmament Agency.*

Dominican crisis of 1965. A *revolutionary*[3] uprising in 1965 which led to unilateral U.S. intervention in the Dominican Republic. U.S. military forces upheld the existing *government*[3] while claiming to protect American lives and *property*[10]. The action

was obviously directed at keeping *Communist*[3] leaders from gaining control of the government of the Dominican Republic. The action emphasized the *Johnson*[12] *corollary* of the *Monroe*[12] *Doctrine* and was severely criticized by numerous American and Latin American officials as weakening indigenous movements of social and political reform in certain Latin American *nations*[3] and as weakening collective action by the *Organization*[12] *of American states.* See also *collective*[12] *security.*

domino theory. The *theory*[3] that if one *country*[3] falls to *Communist*[3] control, adjacent countries in the same area will eventually fall in successive order. With regard to Asia, *President*[6] John F. Kennedy elaborated on the theory in 1956 by stating, "Vietnam represents the cornerstone of the free world in Southeast Asia, the keystone to the arch, the finger in the dike. Burma, Thailand, India, Japan, the Philippines, and obviously Laos and Cambodia would be threatened if the red tide of communism overflowed into Vietnam." See also *containment*[12]; *Vietnam*[12] *War.*

draft **(conscription).** Compulsory military service, generally for a specified length of time. The drafting of military personnel is exercised under the *implied powers*[4] of the *U.S. Congress*[4]. See also *pacifism*[12]; *Selective*[2] *Service System*; *war*[12] *powers.*

Drago doctrine. A statement in 1902 by Luis M. Drago, Foreign Minister of Argentina, that one *nation*[13] should not intervene in another nation's affairs or use *force*[3] in order to recover debts owed to its *citizens*[3] residing in that foreign *state*[3].

Eisenhower doctrine. A foreign *policy*[6] doctrine enunciated by *President*[6] Dwight D. Eisenhower in 1957, in which the President declared that all *nations*[3] have the *inalienable right*[3] to determine their own political and economic systems. He specifically offered economic and military assistance to Middle Eastern nations seeking to avoid internal *Communist*[3] subversion or external Communist control. A *joint resolution*[7] of the *Congress*[4] authorized the President to initially spend $200 million for economic and military aid upon request by Middle Eastern nations. See also *Central*[12] *Treaty Organization*; *foreign*[12] *aid*.

embargo. A *government*[3] order which prohibits commercial trade with individuals or businesses of other *states*[3]. Numerous types of embargoes (total, limited, etc.) may be used to achieve various objectives (*diplomatic*[12] *recognition*, economic advantage, military *reprisal*[12], etc.). See also *sanction*[12].

embassy. An official *diplomatic*[12] mission headed by an *ambassador*[12] and appointed by one *nation*[3] or *government*[3] to conduct business with another nation or government. The term "embassy" also denotes the official residence of an ambassador or other high-ranking diplomatic representative serving in a foreign nation. The embassy is generally located in the national capital and is the working headquarters for the *country*[12] *mission*.

European Common Market (European Economic Community). An economic agreement entered into in 1958 by Belgium, France, Italy, the Netherlands, West Germany, and other western European *nations*[3] in an effort to balance economic and trade relations throughout Europe. The European Common Market is concerned with equitable *tariff*[12] regulations, employee movement, capital investments, and other vital economic variables. The greatest controversy concerning the arrangement involved French refusal to permit Great Britain to join the market in 1961. Great Britain finally entered the economic community in 1972.

executive agreement. An official international agreement between the chief *executive*[6] officers of two national *states*[3] or *governments*[3]. Executive agreements are executed under the fundamental and *inherent powers*[4] of the chief of state or under the *power*[3] of the commander-in-chief of the armed services. They are binding in *international law*[8] and do not require *U.S. Senate*[7] approval. They are most frequently used to expedite minor international business and they avoid complicated and time-consuming struggles generally associated with formal treaty *ratification*[3]. Examples of executive agreements include trade agreements, commitments to provide military advisers to a friendly government, and actions designed to implement prior *treaty*[12] agreements. See also *Commander-in-Chief powers*[6]; *war*[12] *powers*.

expansionism. The active process of expanding political and *governmental*[3] influence over additional *territory*[3] and populations. Expansionism may proceed through military conquest, *annexation*[11], economic domination, or other similar processes. See also *Manifest*[4] *Destiny*; *Mexican*[12] *War*.

extradition (rendition). The legal action of one *governmental*[3] jurisdiction in returning a fugitive from *justice*[8] to the legal *jurisdiction*[8] from which he fled. Such an action is generally referred to as extradition in international relations and as *interstate*[11] *rendition* within the United States. Extradition is largely dependent on international *treaties*[12] between the *nations*[3] involved. Treaties generally specify offenses for which persons may be extradited. Political offenses are usually not covered by such legal agreements.

extraterritoriality. The foreign *policy*[6] arrangement whereby one national *state*[3] is granted permission to exercise *jurisdiction*[8] on its *citizens*[3] or designated subjects within another *territory*[3] or national state. *Diplomatic*[12] *immunity* and merchant vessel status under a national flag on the high seas are examples of extraterritoriality.

F-111 (TFX) controversy. A complex and extended controversy involving the F-111 jet fighter plane designed and built by General Dynamics *Corporation*[10] during the 1960's. General Dynamics received the *contract*[10] in a heated dispute with Boeing Corporation, which actually made a lower bid on development and construction. The F-111 was developed in Fort Worth, Texas. It became the center of controversy for Secretary of Defense Robert McNamara and his *PPB budgeting*[10] system. The finished F-111, a swing-wing plane designed with commonality features for both Air Force and Navy use, eventually cost much more than originally estimated, experienced numerous early flight failures and crashes, and received a cold reception from the Navy, which wanted a lighter airplane for carrier use. See also *Department of Defense*[2].

fifth column. A secret political *faction*[3] within a *nation*[3] which gives moral or material support to an external enemy. The term was coined in 1936 by General Emilio Mola of the rebel faction led by Francisco Franco during the Spanish *civil war*[12] of the 1930's. General Mola said that he had four columns of troops with which to attack Madrid, but that a fifth column of sympathizers was already in the *city*[11] working against the Spanish *republic*[3]. See also *rebellion*[3].

foreign agent: see Chap. 5.

foreign aid. Any material or economic assistance granted by one *government*[3] or other international or private *organization*[6] to another government or national population. Foreign aid is ordinarily granted under the banner of fighting poverty, disease, hunger,

and illiteracy. In reality, U.S. foreign aid is frequently given to dispose of surplus agricultural commodities and to maintain friendship with *nations*[3] being courted by *Communist*[3] powers. Foreign aid may take any number of forms, ranging from military assistance to surplus food distribution. Aid may consist of outright gifts, private investments, technical or military advice, *tariff*[12] concessions, loans, and a wide range of other devices. See also *Agency*[2] *for International Development*; *autarchy*[3]; *Department of State*[2]; *Food*[10] *for Peace Program*; *Lend-Lease*[12]; *Marshall*[12] *Plan*; *Office*[12] *for Economic Cooperation and Development*; *Point*[12] *Four Program*; *Truman*[12] *doctrine*.

Formosan crisis of 1958. An international crisis sparked by regular military bombardment by Communist China of two small islands, Quemoy and Matsu, just off the mainland of China and claimed by Formosa's Nationalist Chinese *government*[3]. U.S. Secretary of State John Foster Dulles employed the doctrine of *brinkmanship*[12] and threatened massive retaliation against Communist China for the *aggressive*[12] action. Overwhelming expressions of United States *public opinion*[5] forced Dulles to shift his position to one of lesser consequences. The crisis passed when Communist China ended its firing on the two small islands, areas which eventually became Formosan observation outposts along the Chinese border. The crisis highlighted the *power*[3] of public opinion in international affairs and the weakness of the doctrines of brinkmanship and massive retaliation. See also *massive retaliation strategy*[12].

Fourteen Points. The popular designation of *President*[6] *Woodrow Wilson's*[6] 1918 proposals for ending *World*[12] *War I* and establishing a permanent peace. The major provisions of the plan were for open *covenants*[3] openly arrived at, freedom of the seas, removal of international economic barriers, international regulation of *colonies*[4], settlement of *boundary*[12] disputes, self-determination for *nations*[3], and the creation of an international organization (*League*[12] *of Nations*) designed to assure peace. Part of Wilson's idealistic proposals were written into the *Treaty of Versailles*[12] which formally ended World War I.

free trade. A condition of international trade which is generally unfettered by rigid *tariff*[10] or trade regulations designed to protect particular industries. See also *General*[12] *Agreement on Tariffs and Trade*; *Kennedy*[10] *Round*; *most*[12] *favored nation theory*; *Office*[12] *for Economic Cooperation and Development*.

functionalism, international. The *theory*[3] of international relations which holds that common world problems and economic programs tend to *integrate*[9] international *communities*[3] apart from separate *nationalistic*[3] political forces. The ultimate design visualized by the functional theory is a *world government*[3] based on mutual interests and cooperation. See also *internationalism*[12].

General Agreement on Tariffs and Trade (GATT). An international agreement among numerous nations designed to reduce *tariffs*[10] and *discriminatory*[9] trade practices. GATT was formed in Geneva in 1947 and operates largely through *executive*[12] *agreements*. The *organization*[6] meets regularly to adjust trade differences of the member *nations*[3]. See also *free*[12] *trade*; *Kennedy*[10] *Round*; *reciprocal tariff*[10].

Geneva Conventions (Agreements, Accords) of 1949. A major modernization and revision of international rules of warfare formulated in Geneva, Switzerland in 1949. The Geneva Conventions, which began in 1864, deal with *chemical and biological warfare*[12], prisoner treatment, the sick and wounded, civilian populations, *refu-*

gees[12], and other areas related to human sensibilities evident in a world of *war*[12].

Geneva Conventions (Agreements, Accords) of 1954. A multilateral agreement between various world powers concerning military and social conflict in Indochina and Korea. The Geneva Conference held during the French military defeat at Dienbienphu in Indochina partitioned the area into North and South Vietnam by dividing the two at the 17th parallel. The parallel was established as a "provisional" *boundary*[12]. General elections were scheduled for July 1954 in order to reunify the two areas. The elections were never held and the entire region eventually erupted into what came to be known as the *Vietnam*[12] (*Indochina*) *War*.

genocide. The deliberate and systematic destruction of a particular race, culture, or national group. See also *Nazism*[3]; *war*[12] *crimes trials*.

G.I. Bill of Rights. A series of *federal*[3] *laws*[8] begun in 1944 which guarantee educational funds, loans, *veterans'*[6] *preference* in the *civil*[6] *service*, unemployment compensation, and other benefits for veterans of U.S. military forces. See also *Veterans*[2] *Administration*.

Good Neighbor Policy. The popular designation of the U.S. foreign policies advocated by *President*[6] *Franklin D. Roosevelt*[6], policies particularly directed toward regaining the friendship and support of Latin American *nations*[3]. The Good Neighbor Policy was an attempt to overcome foreign *policy*[6] fears generated in Latin America by the *Platt*[12] *Amendment, dollar diplomacy*[12], the *Big*[12] *Stick Policy* of *Theodore Roosevelt*[6], and other earlier, questionable foreign policy practices of the U.S. *government*[3].

good offices. A practice involving two parties in dispute and a third, *neutral*[12] party offering to assist the disputants in rebuilding lines of communication and understanding. The third party may informally suggest possibilities of settlement of the dispute with the understanding that the disputants do not have to accept the offer. See also *international arbitration*[12].

government, world: see Chap. 3.

Grotius, Hugo, 1583–1645. Dutch jurist, theologian, poet, historian, government official, and international legal scholar. Grotius is generally recognized as the father of modern *international law*[8], which he became interested in when he served as a member of the Dutch *diplomatic*[12] mission to France in 1598, when he wrote about Portuguese and English conflicts in 1604, and when he helped *arbitrate*[12] English and Dutch trade conflicts in 1611. He also actively worked toward religious reunification of Christian churches in various *nations*[3], especially in churches split over issues of church and state and predestination. Grotius is best remembered for a volume entitled On the Law of War and Peace (1625). Written in an age of international lawlessness and political intrigue, the work is sometimes cited as the first systematic and comprehensive analysis of international law. It deals more with principles of *law*[8] than with specific international controversies. Grotius bases his system of law on *natural law*[8]. His basic assumption lies in the idea of sovereignty of separate *states*[3] claiming certain territorial *boundaries*[12] and international privileges. He wrote that every *community*[3] must at some point recognize certain rights of existence and social interaction. The international community is no different. In his work on war, Grotius analyzed international conduct, rules of *war*[12], and the nature of *justice*[8]. See also *state (constitution) sovereignty*[3].

Hague Tribunal, The. The international tribunal located in the Nether-

lands capital (The Hague) on the North Sea. Since 1899 the tribunal has acted as a place for the settlement of international disputes. Hague conferences have formulated agreements or discussed problems related to rules of *war*[12], international debts, settlement of conflicts, *disarmament*[12], and similar matters. The Permanent Court of Arbitration was established at The Hague to assist in diminishing international conflict. Hague peace conferences in 1899 and 1907 presented the first international opportunities for general agreement on various problems affecting world stability. The *United*[12] Nations agency known as the *International*[12] Court of Justice (World Court) presently sits at The Hague. See also *international arbitration*[12]; *international law*[8].

hot pursuit: see Chap. 8.

Hungarian crisis of 1956. A *revolutionary*[3] crisis provoked in Hungary when anti-Stalinist demonstrations turned into public renunciations of the Soviet Union and the *Warsaw*[12] *Pact*. The public demonstrations turned into riots and were quickly put down by the Soviet Army. Hundreds of persons died, many fled the *country*[3], and a puppet *government*[3] was installed by Soviet *authority*[3]. In spite of public outrage around the world, the Free World *nations*[3] were unable to respond effectively to the Soviet action. The Hungarian crisis emphasized the *totalitarian*[3] tactics of the Soviet Union and the desire for freedom among eastern European nations. It also emphasized the possibilities of total nuclear destruction and the weakness of *brinkmanship*[12] and the doctrine of massive retaliation enunciated by U.S. Secretary of State John Foster Dulles. See also *atomic*[12] *war*; *massive retaliation strategy*[12]; *Joseph Stalin*[3].

insurgency. A *rebellion*[3] or revolt against a recognized *government*[3] which is smaller and less organized than a full-scale *revolution*[3]. See also *counterinsurgency*[12].

intelligence. Information acquired, secretly or openly, for the specific purpose of knowing in detail about a rival or potential enemy. *Governments*[3] generally conduct intelligence (spy) operations in order to assess the nature of *power*[3] at any given time. Military intelligence generally involves acquisition of information related to troop strength, supplies, movement, production, weapons locations, and similar data. Intelligence-gathering in the U.S. is most noticeably carried out by the *Central*[2] *Intelligence Agency*, the United States Army, the National Security Agency, the *Federal*[2] *Bureau of Investigation*, and the *Department of State*[2]. See also *committees*[4] *of correspondence*; *Watergate*[5].

International Court of Justice (World Court). The primary judicial structure of the *United*[12] *Nations*. The ICJ, located at The Hague, replaced the Permanent Court of International Justice (World Court) when the U.N. was formed in 1945. The Court may interpret international *treaties*[12], *customs*[3], *laws*[8], and other items and principles recognized in the world *community*[3]. The Court is not particularly effective because only national *states*[3] willing to accept the *jurisdiction*[8] of the Court may be dealt with. The Court is composed of 15 justices chosen by the *General*[12] *Assembly* and *Security*[12] *Council* of the U.N. Judges serve for nine-year terms, and no more than one justice at a time may be seated from any one *nation*[3]. See also *The Hague*[12] *Tribunal*; *Charles Evans Hughes*[8].

internationalism. The concept that *nations*[3] should and can interact in a world *community*[3] in a peaceful way. See also *international functionalism*[12]; *world government*[3].

Iron Curtain. The real, imaginary, or figurative line that encircles *territory*[3]

dominated and controlled by the Union of Soviet Socialist Republics and behind which restricted *diplomatic*[12], communications, social, and political practices take place. British Prime Minister Winston Churchill coined the term in 1946 after Soviet dictatorial action taken by *Joseph Stalin*[3]. The curtain opened somewhat in 1972 with the visit of *President*[6] Nixon to the Soviet Union. See *closed society*[3]; *encirclement theory*[3].

irrendentism: see Chap. 3.

isolationism. The concept or practice of remaining relatively separated from the international interactions of other *nations*[3]. The first official foreign *policy*[6] stance of the U.S. enunciated by *President*[6] *George Washington*[6] was one of isolationism. See also *alliance*[12]; *Washington's*[12] *Farewell Address*.

Johnson corollary. The corollary of the *Monroe*[12] *Doctrine* enunciated by *President*[6] *Lyndon B. Johnson*[6] in 1965, a foreign *policy*[6] stance which held that the use of *force*[3] in international relations in the Western Hemisphere may be necessary to keep out *Communist*[3] governments. President Johnson sent troops into the Dominican Republic in 1965 to assure that the Dominican *government*[3] would not fall under Communist control. See also *Dominican*[12] *crisis of 1965*.

Kellogg-Briand Pact. An international *treaty*[12] officially entitled the General Treaty for the Renunciation of War. It was first signed in Paris, France on August 27, 1928 and has come to be known as the Kellogg-Briand Pact or the Pact of Paris. Actually a series of treaties formulated by U.S. Secretary of State Frank B. Kellogg and French Foreign Minister Aristide Briand, the pact declared that the signatory *nations*[3] renounced *war*[12] as an "instrument of national policy." It also declared that international conflicts should be settled through peaceful methods. Numerous nations, the U.S. included, adopted *treaty*[12] *reservations* on the Kellogg-Briand Pact, which stated that the reserving nation could use military *force*[3] in an offensive way. Since there was little agreement on what constituted offensive or defensive military actions, the treaty did little to halt *aggressive*[12] actions, which eventually led to *World*[12] *War II*. See also *Stimson*[12] *doctrine*.

Kennedy Round: see Chap. 10.

Korean War. A period of military action from 1950 to 1953 that involved the question of dividing North and South Korea at the 38th parallel. The North Korean Army of the People's Democratic Republic of Korea crossed the 38th parallel and initiated military action on June 25, 1950. The U.S. and other forces under *United*[12] *Nations authority*[3] responded by sending troops to assist South Korea. *President*[6] *Truman*[6] named General Douglas MacArthur to head the United Nations forces. The U.S. and South Korean forces carried the weight of the *war*[12] against North Korea. Communist China gave major military personnel assistance and the Soviet Union gave financial and weapons assistance to North Korea. The war ended in a stalemate in July 1953. The conflict emphasized a major problem of *bipolarity*[12] between East and West, the presidential *power*[3] to make major military troop commitments without a *declaration of war*[12], and presidential control over a military commander (MacArthur) at odds with the military authority of the civilian leader (Truman) of American troops. See also *Commander-in-Chief powers*[6]; *MacArthur*[12] *controversy*; *executive war*[12]; *Youngstown*[1] *Sheet and Tube Co. v. Sawyer*.

law, admiralty: see Chap. 8.

law, international: see Chap. 8.

law; martial: see martial[8] law.

law; military: see military[8] law.

League of Nations. An international *organization*[6] created at the end of *World*[12] *War I* in an effort to maintain world peace. It was the first international organization specifically designed as a world forum for maintaining peace. The organization was originally proposed in the *Fourteen*[12] *Points* of *Woodrow Wilson*[6] and became a part of the *Treaty of Versailles*[12] in 1919. The League functioned from 1920 to 1946, when the *United*[12] *Nations* superseded it. A major weakness of the League was that the U.S. never became a formal member due to U.S. rejection of the Treaty of Versailles. The organization acted as a communications clearinghouse in dealing with various political, economic, social, and *diplomatic*[12] problems brought before it by member *nations*[3]. It was totally unsuccessful in halting *aggressive*[12] actions, which eventually led to *World*[12] *War II*. See also *collective*[12] *security*; *mandate territory*[12].

legation. A secondary *diplomatic*[12] assignment, ranking beneath an *embassy*[12]. The term "legation" is also used to designate the residence of the diplomatic official assigned as a legation or legate.

Lend-Lease. A U.S. foreign assistance program begun in 1941 in which the United States *government*[3] supplied essential *war*[12] products (food, oil, services, etc.) to *Allied*[12] *powers* on terms other than cash payments. Lend-Lease, instituted by the Lend-lease Act of 1941, was based on mutual and reciprocal action among the various Allied powers in conflict with the *Axis*[12] *powers* and on the idea that the stability of certain *nations*[3] greatly affected the national interest of the U.S. See also *foreign*[12] *aid*; *World*[12] *War II*.

letter of marque. A governmental commission or document issued to a private individual to carry out acts of *war*[12] on behalf of the *government*[3]. The most common type of letter of marque throughout history has been the commission which calls on private ship owners to engage in acts of war or *reprisal*[12].

MacArthur controversy. The political conflict between *President*[6] *Harry S Truman*[6] and General Douglas MacArthur in 1951–52. The controversy culminated in the dismissal of MacArthur as commander of U.S. forces in the Far East. President Truman removed his commanding general for failure to follow *executive*[6] *orders* in the conduct of the *Korean*[12] *War*, for public criticism of *executive*[6] action, and for his open declaration supporting an invasion of China in spite of the limited nature of the *war*[12]. The controversy led to a complete *U.S. Senate*[7] investigation of the removal of MacArthur. See also *Commander-in-Chief powers*[6]; *limited war*[12].

Manifest Destiny: see Chap. 4.

Marshall Plan (European Recovery Program). An economic assistance plan formulated by U.S. Secretary of State George C. Marshall for the economic recovery of western Europe after *World*[12] *War II*. The plan, put into effect in 1948, was a comprehensive and coordinated recovery program known as the European Recovery Program. The program involved the expenditure of between $12 and $15 billion. The program was designed primarily to assist European *nations*[3] in economic recovery in order that they would not turn to *Communist*[3] philosophy or economic structures. It also proved a useful tool for disposing of American agricultural surpluses. The entire effort was coordinated by the Organization for European Economic Cooperation. See also *foreign*[12] *aid*.

Mexican War. A declared *war*[12] fought between the U.S. and Mexico

between April 1846 and September 1847. The highly controversial war was officially closed with the signing of the *Treaty*[12] of Guadalupe Hidalgo on February 2, 1848. A basic cause of the Mexican War was the doctrine of *Manifest*[4] *Destiny* and the desire to extend slavery and the cotton economy. Texas, a former Mexican possession, entered the Union in 1845 and emphasized the problem of disputed *territory*[3] between the Rio Grande River and the Nueces River. Mexico broke *diplomatic*[12] relations, and military conflict erupted inside the disputed area when American troops moved into it. The Mexican forces were overwhelmed and agreed to cede over 500,000 square miles of territory to the victorious United States. The Mexican *government*[3] also relinquished all claims to Texas above the Rio Grande and agreed to end all claims against the U.S. or its nationals. In exchange it was agreed that Mexico would receive $15 million for relinquishing the territory and ending the claims. The peace settlement extended the U.S. to the Pacific Ocean. It also renewed the controversy over balancing slave and free-state growth within the Union. See also *Compromise*[4] *of 1850*; *expansionism*[12].

military-industrial complex. An interrelated, highly complex, and controversial arrangement of economic and military *policy*[7] *formulation* and public spending which involves *corporate*[10] business, public educational institutions, private research *organizations*[6], and military services. The military-industrial complex has become especially apparent in an age of increasing technology, expanding governmental operations, and international tensions due to the nuclear *arms*[12] *race*. Upon retirement from the presidency in 1961, General Eisenhower publicly warned the U.S. of the increasing and pervasive strength of the military-industrial complex. He warned against the "acquisition of unwarranted influence, whether sought or unsought, by the military-industrial complex."

minister. A *diplomatic*[12] official of secondary ranking. The term is also used to describe a *government*[3] official who serves as head of a particular *department*[6].

mobilization. The act of preparing for *war*[12], generally through widespread and comprehensive planning of total manpower and material resources. See also *civil*[12] *defense*; *Office of Emergency*[2] *Preparedness*.

Monroe Doctrine. A foreign *policy*[6] statement made by *President*[6] James Monroe in 1823, which declared that the U.S. would not permit further European *colonization*[4] or political influence in North or South America. In return, the U.S. declared that it would make no attempts to establish colonies in Europe. The doctrine was specifically designed to urge Russians to stay away from the northern coast of North America and to warn European *nations*[3] to stay out of Latin American *wars*[12] for independence. The U.S. indicated a willingness to become militarily involved if Latin American nations were not left to determine their own institutions. See also *Johnson*[12] *corollary*; *Roosevelt*[12] *corollary*.

most favored nation theory. The idea of reciprocal guarantees to *citizens*[3] of two or more *nations*[3] on the basis that commercial, political, or social privileges will be granted on the same level as that given to all other nations. For example, the Jay *Treaty*[12] of 1794 was based on such a *theory*[3] in covering trade regulations with Great Britain which involved U.S. trade in the British East Indies. The same principle was used in the Burlingame Treaty of 1868 with China. The U.S. and China agreed to reciprocally guarantee to citizens of each other's *country*[3] certain rights of travel, residence,

religion, commerce, and *politics*[3]. In *tariff*[10] negotiations the most favored nation theory generally acts to avoid trade *discrimination*[9]. All parties to an agreement receive equal treatment accorded to the most favored nation. See also *free*[12] *trade*; *Open*[12] *Door Policy*; *quid*[12] *pro quo*; *reciprocal tariff*[10].

My Lai controversy. An emotional controversy related to the *Vietnam*[12] *War* in which several American soldiers were accused of murdering ("massacring") over 100 Vietnamese civilians at a small village named My Lai. The controversy over the alleged massacre of 1968 broke in 1970 when a former Army veteran, Ronald Ridenhauer, corresponded with various *government*[3] officials and related his own experiences in Vietnam. Another Vietnam veteran, an army photographer, sold private pictures of the incident at My Lai to Life magazine and brought the issue to public attention. Originally the U.S. Army charged 14 officers and enlisted men with murder or with suppressing information of the My Lai action. The controversy eventually centered on Lieutenant Calley and Captain Ernest Medina, both of whom faced *courts-martial*[8] during 1970 and 1971. Calley was eventually found guilty of murder and Medina was found innocent. The My Lai controversy focused public attention on the nature of military orders, the personal psychological difficulties of the Vietnam War and the depersonalization of modern warfare. See also *Calley*[12] *case*; *psychological warfare*[12].

national guard (state militia). A volunteer state *organization*[6] largely funded and trained by the U.S. *federal government*[3] and available for general *state*[3] and national emergencies. Each state's national guard is commanded by the *governor*[6], generally through a state *adjutant*[12] *general*. In the event of national emergency, the *President*[6] may act under the Army Organization Act of 1920 and activate (nationalize) the national guard as part of national military forces. Under national *authority*[3], the national guard is subject to general congressional regulation and presidential leadership. See also *Second Amendment*[9]; *national*[12] *guard nationalization.*

national guard nationalization: see Chap. 6.

National Liberation Front (NLF). The political arm of a guerrilla force formed in South Vietnam in 1960, a force also known as the Viet Cong (an abbreviation for Vietnamese Communist). The NLF, billed as a "popular uprising," was especially powerful in the southern portion of South Vietnam. It terrorized and intimidated villagers, extorted money for political and military operations, *drafted*[12] military recruits, and carried out a general *propaganda*[5] program supporting the objectives of North Vietnam. See also *guerrilla war*[12]; *pacification*[12]; *Vietnamization*[12]; *wars*[12] *of national liberation.*

neutrality. The legal condition of a *state*[3] which has publicly declared itself unwilling to support any parties engaged in *belligerent*[12] actions against one another. Neutrality is ostensibly supposed to protect commercial relations, *territory*[3], and political integrity of the declared neutral. See also *Cambodian*[12] *crisis of 1970.*

Nixon (Guam) doctrine. An ambiguous and controversial foreign *policy*[6] stance enunciated by *President*[6] Nixon on the island of Guam in July 1969. The doctrine holds essentially that Asian *nations*[3] must depend less on the U.S. for fending off international *Communist*[3] expansion. President Nixon announced that the U.S. military forces in Asia should be reduced, especially ground combat troops, and that the U.S. should continue to help

friendly Asian nations prepare to defend themselves. The extent of help is the major point in dispute. The doctrine has hinted that a nuclear "shield" would be placed around friendly nations if Communist aggressors threatened to use nuclear *force*[3] to achieve victory. The doctrine also seems to leave open the possibility of long-range use of air and sea *power*[3] in Asia and the possibility of the use of ground combat forces if U.S. "interests" are threatened. Major critics of the policy hold that the doctrine really means that the U.S. should give arms to Asians in order that Asians can fight Asians in *conventional wars*[12]. See also *atomic*[12] *war*; *Vietnam*[12] *War.*

Nonproliferation of Nuclear Weapons Treaty. An international *treaty*[12] designed to prevent the spread of nuclear weapons to nonnuclear countries. The treaty, originally circulated by the *United*[12] *Nations*, was signed by the U.S., the U.S.S.R., Great Britain, and other major *nations*[3]. The two major world powers not signing the treaty were France and Communist China. The treaty is generally considered the best hope for limiting the nuclear *arms*[12] *race* and the possible spread of nuclear might into the hands of irresponsible parties. See also *atomic*[12] *war*; *Baruch*[12] *Plan*; *disarmament*[12].

North Atlantic Treaty Organization (NATO). A regional *organization*[6] created by *treaty*[12] in 1949 to protect the security of American and Allied interests in the north Atlantic area. The *collective*[12] *security* arrangement was originally composed of the U.S. and 11 other *nations*[3] and had its headquarters in France. In 1966, under the direct influence of President Charles de Gaulle of France, the headquarters were moved from France to Belgium. See also *alliance*[12]; *Warsaw*[12] *Pact.*

Nuclear (Partial, Limited, Moscow) Test-Ban Treaty. An international agreement in 1963 among over 100 major world powers which halted all nuclear weapons testing in the atmosphere, outer space, and under water. The *treaty*[12] permitted underground nuclear testing. The three major powers to sign the treaty were the U.S., the U.S.S.R. and the U.K. The only two major powers that did not sign the treaty were France and Communist China. The treaty makes provisions for inspection of nuclear testing covered in the treaty in all cases except underground tests. The treaty was the first international treaty specifically aimed at limiting the nuclear *arms*[12] *race*. Any signatory *nation*[3] may withdraw from the treaty agreement on three months' notice if it feels its national interests are threatened. See also *atomic*[12] *war*; *Baruch*[12] *Plan*; *disarmament*[12].

Office for Economic Cooperation and Development (**OECD**). An international economic arrangement created in 1961 in order to improve and facilitate economic trade among various world *powers*[3], especially non-*Communist*[3] powers. The OECD regularly seeks to adjust *tariff*[10] differences, acts as a clearinghouse on international economic information, helps handle *balance*[10] *of payment* problems, and assists in guiding *foreign*[12] *aid* programs and international economic development. See also *free*[12] *trade*; *reciprocal tariff*[10].

Open Door Policy. A basic U.S. foreign *policy*[6] enunciated in China in 1853 by U.S. Commodore Matthew C. Perry and in 1899 by U.S. Secretary of State John Hay. The policy, directed by the *most*[12] *favored nation theory*, demanded equal treatment for U.S. interests and a weakening of the various "spheres of influence" controlled by particular *nations*[3] operating in China. The policy also demanded *territorial*[3] and political integrity for China. The U.S. sought to be a part of the Oriental commercial trade and

gain some of the privileges enjoyed by various European powers such as Great Britain and France. The policy died at the end of *World*[12] *War II* when China turned to *Communism*[3] and closed itself off behind the *Bamboo*[12] *Curtain*.

Organization of American States (**OAS**). A Western Hemisphere regional *organization*[6] created in 1948 as a successor to previous organizations designed to facilitate economic development, protective security, and social stability throughout Latin America. The Inter-American Conference, which meets in *Washington*[4], D.C. every five years, acts as the principal administrative agency of the OAS. The Pan American Union, also located in Washington, acts as a general secretariat to carry out basic programs of the organization. The Organization of American States has continually been concerned with the threat of *Communist*[3] subversion throughout Latin America. Cuba was expelled from the OAS in 1962 when it fell to a Communist *government*[3] led by Fidel Castro. Another major concern of the OAS has been general economic development of the various member *states*[3] and coordination of economic relations throughout Latin America.

Outer Space Treaty. An international agreement among numerous world powers to coordinate and regulate exploratory activities in outer space. The *treaty*[12], formulated within the *United*[12] *Nations*, was signed by 84 nations in 1967. The treaty prohibits military use of outer space and any claims of national sovereignty over any portion of outer space. It provides for international exchange of information about space, joint efforts in recovery of space vehicles and personnel, and general cooperation in conquering the unknown reaches of outer space. See also *Sputnik*[12] *I*; *state (constitutional) sovereignty*[3].

pacification. The act or process of stabilizing and making peaceful a violent or disorderly condition. The term "pacification" gained prominence as a major concept of military strategy in the *Vietnam*[12] *War*, especially with regard to guerrilla activities in politically unstable rural hamlets. See also *guerrilla war*[12]; *National*[12] *Liberation Front*; *Vietnamization*[12].

pacifism. The philosophical, religious, or practical rejection of all *war*[12] and violence as a means of settling conflicts or achieving particular objectives. See also *conscientious*[9] *objector*; *U.S.*[1] *v. Gillette*; *U.S.*[1] *v. Seeger*.

passport. An official *government*[3] document which grants a *citizen*[3] of a national *state*[3] the right to travel to other states or specified areas. An official passport is generally recognized as basic for personal and national identification and for legal and *diplomatic*[12] protection while traveling abroad. See also *Aptheker*[1] *v. Secretary of State*; *Kent*[1] *v. Dulles*; *Zemel*[1] *v. Rusk*.

Pax Americana. The doctrine that world stability and peace are largely dependent on U.S. *power*[3] and influence. The period of Pax Americana is not clearly defined. Some defenders of the doctrine hold that the period began with the *Spanish-American*[12] *War* in 1898 and extends up to the present. See also *arrogance*[12] *of power doctrine*; *chauvinism*[12]; *ethnocentrism*[3].

Pentagon. A five-sided public building in Arlington, Virginia, which contains the offices of the U.S. *Department of Defense*[2] and is the operational center for all U.S. military operations throughout the world. The Pentagon has become the major symbol of the entire U.S. defense establishment. It represents the largest single *bureaucratic*[6] *organization*[6], public or private, presently in operation anywhere in the world. See also *Pentagon*[12] *Papers*.

Pentagon Papers. A 47-volume *Pentagon*[12] study of U.S. involvement in Vietnam between the close of *World*[12] *War II* and 1968. The top-secret study of the *Vietnam*[12] *War* is entitled "History of U.S. Decision-Making Process on Vietnam Policy." It was revealed to the American public throughout June of 1971 after Daniel Ellsberg, a former Pentagon research specialist, released major portions of the document to the New York Times and various other newspapers. Once selected portions of the Pentagon Papers appeared in print, the *U.S. Department of Justice*[2] gained a *writ of injunction*[8] from a federal *District Court*[8] on the grounds that publication of the materials could do "irreparable injury to the national defense." The Washington Post, the Boston Globe, the Los Angeles Times, and other major papers began to publish series based on the documents, and they too faced *federal*[3] action. The *U.S. Supreme*[8] *Court* extended its 1971 term and quickly acted on the matter, the first federal prior restraint on published material in U.S. history. It upheld the doctrine that under the *First Amendment*[9], no prior restraint may be placed on the publication of such materials. The encounter became a classic battle between the right of *government*[3] to maintain secrecy and the right of the public to know what *government*[3] is doing. The basic substance of the Pentagon Papers revealed U.S. acceptance of the *domino*[12] *theory* during the *administration*[6] of *Harry S Truman*[6], rejection of Vietnam reunification during the Eisenhower *administration*[6], advisory troop commitments during the Kennedy administration, and large-scale military involvement during the *Johnson*[6] administration. The published documents raised significant questions about the credibility of various government officials and advisers, since what the public was told at the time did not correspond with what the documents indicated the government officials were actually contemplating, especially through what is commonly known as "contingency planning." See also *credibility*[6] *gap*; *hidden budget*[10]; *prior*[9] *(previous) restraint doctrine*; *New*[1] *York Times v. U.S.*; *Watergate*[5].

persona non grata. A *diplomatic*[12] official declared unacceptable by the *government*[3] of the *nation*[3] to which he is assigned. An acceptable diplomatic official is referred to as persona grata.

Platt Amendment. An *amendment*[3], or *rider*[7], on an army *appropriations bill*[7] in 1901, which declared that the U.S. *government*[3] possessed the right to intervene in domestic Cuban affairs in order to protect Cuban "independence" and "life, *property*[10], and individual liberty." The amendment, named after *Senator*[7] Orville Platt, became a part of the Cuban *constitution*[3] of 1901. Cuba reluctantly agreed to avoid *treaties*[12] with foreign powers which would threaten independence. Cuba also agreed to avoid extreme indebtedness and to permit the U.S. government to operate naval bases on the island of Cuba. The Platt Amendment was repealed in 1934. See also *Big*[12] *Stick Policy*; *Spanish-American*[12] *War*.

Point Four Program. A U.S. *foreign*[12] *aid* program proposed by *President*[6] *Harry S Truman*[6] in 1949 and put into effect in 1950 in an effort to raise the social, economic, and technical standards of underdeveloped *countries*[3] friendly with the U.S. The Point Four Program, fourth in a listing of priorities established by President Truman, achieved popular success both at home and abroad. The major weakness of the program was that some of the underdeveloped countries receiving technical assistance were not ready for such *expertise*[6]. See also *Third*[12] *World*.

positivism, international. The international legal *theory*[3] which holds that sovereign *states*[3] may be bound only to that to which they give their consent. See also *state (constitutional) sovereignty*[3]; *treaty*[12] *reservation*.

powers, advice and consent: see Chap. 7.

powers, Commander-in-Chief: see Chap. 6.

powers, diplomatic (foreign policy): see Chap. 6.

powers, emergency: see Chap. 4.

powers, inherent: see Chap. 4.

protectorate: see Chap. 3.

protocol. A formal *diplomatic*[12] document which indicates preliminary agreement between two or more international parties, agreement which occasionally serves as the basis for *treaty*[12] negotiations. The word "protocol" is also used to indicate ceremonial formalities and courtesies basic to *government*[3].

Pueblo crisis of 1968. An unexpected and embarrassing crisis provoked when the People's Republic of Korea (North Korea) fired on and captured a U.S. *intelligence*[12] ship, the U.S.S. Pueblo, in international waters in January 1968. One crewman was killed and 82 were taken captive and held for 11 months. North Korean officials agreed to release the crew in exchange for an admission of guilt by the U.S. *government*[3]. Once the crew was free, the U.S. government denounced its admission of guilt. The *Communist*[3] *bloc*[7] countries made capital of its latest *propaganda*[5] victory. The crisis accentuated the widespread intelligence-gathering operations of the U.S. government, the ability of a small *nation*[3] to publicly embarrass the U.S., the limited possibilities of effective retaliation on any nation, the cruel brutality of North Korean psychological interrogation methods, and the need to revise the *Uniform*[8] *Code of Military Justice* to permit certain kinds of confessions under special circumstances. See also *massive retaliation strategy*[12]; *psychological warfare*[12].

Punta del Esta Conference (1961). A Latin American conference held at Punta del Esta, Uruguay in 1961 under the sponsorship of the *Organization*[12] *of American States.* The Conference projected long-range economic and social reforms for Latin America. The U.S. pledged $20 billion toward the economic development of the region, principally in an effort to promote *capitalism*[3] and avoid *Communist*[3] influence in Latin America.

quarantine. The international process of one *state*[3] stopping another state from delivering goods detrimental to its national interests, even though those goods are destined for a third state. During the Cuban missile crisis of 1962, the U.S. used a new type of *blockade*[12] under the title of "quarantine." The U.S. restricted the movement of Soviet ships to a third party, Cuba, without an actual condition of *war*[12]. See also *Cuban*[12] *missile crisis of 1962.*

quid pro quo. The personal, national, or international concept that interactions should be balanced in such a way as to provide equal benefits to all parties concerned. In international relations a quid pro quo is a reciprocal arrangement where one thing is exchanged for another. See also *most*[12] *favored nation theory.*

rapprochement. The rebuilding of lines of communication and cordial feelings after a period of ill will or military conflict.

rebellion: see chap. 3.

rebus sic stantibus. A *theory*[3] of *international law*[8] which holds that a *treaty*[12] is valid only as long as conditions remain essentially as they were when the treaty was signed. The controversial theory is sometimes used as a basis for repudiation of a treaty and may be viewed by other *nations*[3] as a violation of international law and order.

refugee. A person who is expelled from or flees from political, religious, social, military, or other persecution or conflict. Large numbers of civilian refugees created international social and economic problems after *World*[12] *War I*, *World*[12] *War II*, and during the *Cold*[12] *War* of international conflict between *Communism*[3] and the Free World. See also *Geneva*[12] *Conventions of 1949.*

reparations. Payments or indemnities made for damages or wrongs done to another party. After the conclusion of a military conflict the victorious powers ordinarily demand reparations as payment for military damages, especially if the losing *nations*[3] initiated the conflict. See also *Treaty of Versailles*[12].

reprisal. A forceful act of retaliation against another party for a claimed injury. An act of reprisal is generally carefully scaled to coincide with the alleged injury. The reprisal falls short of outright *war*[12] and is ordinarily of the same magnitude as the injury or slightly greater than the injury. Violence, *boycotts*[10], *blockades*[12], economic *sanctions*[12], and various other devices may be used as acts of vengeance, as well as to deter further injury.

Reserve Officers Training Corps (ROTC), 1916– . A military-educational training program operating on selected secondary public school and university campuses throughout the U.S. ROTC students participate in general educational programs and specialized programs of military training. They receive *government*[3] allowances and benefits and are required to attend summer training camps. Upon graduation from college and completion of the basic ROTC program, the students are commissioned as second lieutenants (army and air force) or ensigns (navy), depending on their branch of service. Most graduates are commissioned in the U.S. Army Reserve. Distinguished military graduates are afforded regular military commissions.

reserves. Military troops trained, armed, and supported as ready replacements for regular military forces. The U.S. Army maintains organized reserve units which are generally composed of personnel who previously served in the regular military services or persons serving extended periods of reserve training. The *state*[3] *national*[12] *guard* units are also availabe for national service whenever the *President*[6] wishes to "nationalize" them and call them to active duty under his command. See also *national*[6] *guard nationalization*.

revolution: see Chap. 3.

Rio Pact. A regional security agreement formalized in the Inter-American Treaty of Reciprocal Assistance. The *treaty*[12] was signed at Rio de Janeiro, Brazil on September 2, 1947. The pact is composed of numerous Latin American and North American *nations*[3] committed to collective action against *Communist*[3] *aggression*[12] in the Western Hemisphere. The pact is a formal *alliance*[12] calling for group action in the event that a particular signatory nation is threatened or attacked by external powers. See also *collective*[12] *security*.

Rogers Act of 1924. The *federal*[3] legislation which created the *Foreign*[2] *Service*, consolidated *diplomatic*[12] and *consular*[12] missions, established a *merit*[6] *system* for choosing personnel,

established Foreign Service classifications, and guaranteed retirement and other benefits for career diplomatic officials. The *legislation*[7] was modified in the Foreign Service Act of 1946 through classification of Career Ministers and the creation of a Foreign Service Reserve. See also *diplomatic*[6] *power*.

Roosevelt corollary. The popular designation of the Latin American foreign *policy*[3] formulated by *President*[6] *Theodore Roosevelt*[6] in 1904, a policy holding that the *Monroe*[12] *Doctrine* should work in reverse and the U.S. should protect European *nations*[3] against abuses from Latin American nations. The *theory*[3] held essentially that in a condition of *anarchy*[3] in international relations, the dominant civilized *state*[3] must act as an international police force. The practical result of the doctrine was that the U.S. intervened in the internal affairs of Latin American nations in order to protect U.S. and European interests. See also *Big*[12] *Stick Policy*; *dollar diplomacy*[12].

sanctions. An action taken by one party or collective group to coerce another party into abiding by particular *customs*[3] or legal regulations. In *international law*[8] some sanctions frequently employed are *boycotts*[10], *embargoes*[12], economic coercion, withdrawal of *diplomatic*[12] *recognition*, and internal intervention.

sedition. Language or action which engenders disrespect or incites *rebellion*[3] against the *state*[3] or the recognized *government*[3] of the state. See also *Abrams*[1] *v. U.S.*; *Alien*[4] *and Sedition Acts of 1798*; *clear*[9] *and present danger doctrine*; *Federal*[2] *Bureau of Investigation*; *Pennsylvania*[1] *v. Nelson*; *Schenck*[1] *v. U.S.*; *Sedition*[9] *Act of 1918*.

Selective Service System: see Chap. 2.

self-executing treaty. Any *treaty*[12] that becomes effective upon negotiation by the chief of *state*[3] and, in the case of the United States, upon acceptance by two-thirds of the *Senate*[7]. Such a treaty does not require any additional legislative action to implement the international agreement.

Southeast Asia Treaty Organization (SEATO). A regional security arrangement established in 1954 as an *alliance*[12] between Pacific Ocean *nations*[3] seeking to avoid *Communist*[3] domination and control. In the event that one of the member *states*[3] is attacked, the other member states will respond collectively as they think befits their defense needs. SEATO headquarters is located in Bangkok, Thailand. The major member states are the U.S., France, Great Britain, Australia, New Zealand, the Philippines, and Pakistan. South Vietnam, Cambodia, and Laos are not members of SEATO, but collective protection of them was later guaranteed by the member states. See also *collective*[12] *security*; *Vietnam*[12] *War*.

Spanish-American War. A declared *war*[12] between the U.S. and Spain from April 1898 to August 1898. The conflict was officially ended by the Treaty of Paris, a *treaty*[12] accepted by the *Senate*[7] on February 6, 1899. The war, conducted during the *administration*[6] of *President*[6] William McKinley, was fought ostensibly because of *humanitarian*[11] interests in the oppressed people of Cuba, oppression made public in the "yellow journalism" of *William Randolph Hearst*[5] and Joseph Pulitzer. A basic objective of the war was to protect U.S. economic interests in Cuba during a time of *revolutionary*[3] instability under Spanish rule. While seeking to protect those interests, the U.S.S. Maine was sunk in Havana harbor on February 15, 1899. The war was a major element in the growth of U.S. involvement in world affairs. *Expansionist*[12] sentiment in the U.S. favored U.S. influence throughout Latin America. As a result of the war the U.S. acquired Puerto Rico and Guam, paid $20 million for the Philippine Islands, and gained control over Cuba. See also *Platt*[12] *Amendment*.

Sputnik I. The first space satellite to be successfully fired into outer space, a vehicle developed and controlled by the Soviet Union in 1957. The satellite amplified the nature of the *Cold*[12] *War* between the East and West, acted as a major *propaganda*[5] device for world *Communism*[3], emphasized the achievements of science and technology, and launched a race for outer space between the U.S. and the Soviet Union. See also *anti-ballistic*[12] *missile*; *Comsat*[11]; *National*[11] *Defense Education Act of 1958*.

state, buffer. A small or weak *state*[3] located between two rival powers which acts as a deterrent to outright conflict between the two major states.

state, garrison. A *state*[3] which is continually preparing for *war*[12] or engaged in military conflict.

state, satellite: see Chap. 3.

status quo: see Chap. 3.

status quo ante bellum. A condition which is essentially the same as before military action took place. See also *War*[12] *of 1812*.

Stimson doctrine. A foreign *policy*[6] stance publicly announced by U.S. Secretary of State Henry L. Stimson in 1931. The doctrine, occasionally credited to *President*[6] Herbert H. Hoover, held that any *treaty*[12] or agreement *forced*[3] from another *nation*[3] in violation of existing treaties of non-*aggression*[12] need not be recognized by the U.S. The specific event provoking the Stimson Doctrine was the Japanese invasion of Manchuria in 1931 in violation of the *Kellogg-Briand*[12] *Pact of 1928*.

Strategic Arms Limitation Talks (SALT). A series of *disarmament*[12] negotiations which began in April 1970 in Helsinki, Finland. The talks, led by the U.S. and the Soviet Union, were begun as the first step toward practical reduction of nuclear arms development. Some of the major nuclear concerns involved intercontinental ballistic missiles (IBM), *anti-ballistic*[12] *missiles* (ABM), and multiple individually targetable reentry vehicles (MIRV). Underlying the talks held in Helsinki in 1970 and in Vienna in 1971 were the possibility of accidental nuclear warfare and the tremendous expense required to develop questionable nuclear weapons systems. See also *arms*[12] *race*; *Nuclear*[12] *Test-Ban Treaty*; *Outer*[12] *Space Treaty*.

strategy, flexible response. The military strategy advocated by *President*[6] John F. Kennedy, which emphasized the balancing of military threats to Free World *nations*[3] with conventional weapons, *counterinsurgency*[12] forces, and other tactics short of outright nuclear war. The strategic concept holds that each military threat should be met with counterforce specifically designed to cope with that particular level of threat. See also *atomic*[12] *war*; *conventional war*[12]; *insurgency*[12]; *massive retaliation strategy*[12].

strategy, massive retaliation. The military strategy advocated by U.S. Secretary of State John Foster Dulles during the *administration*[6] of *President*[6] Dwight D. Eisenhower. The strategic concept held that ground combat with Communist forces would be meaningless in places such as Asia. Therefore *Communism*[3] should be dealt with through threats of massive retaliation by a major world power allied with any *nation*[3] threatened by Communist control. It was generally accepted that the U.S. arsenal of nuclear weapons would be part of the massive retaliation against a Communist enemy. See also *Cuban*[12] *missile crisis of 1962*; *flexible response strategy*[12]; *Formosan*[12] *crisis of 1958*; *Hungarian*[12] *crisis of 1956*; *Pueblo*[12] *crisis of 1968*.

Suez crisis of 1956. An international crisis provoked when Gamal Abdel Nasser of Egypt nationalized the Suez Canal in 1956 after the U.S. decided against helping Egypt construct a high dam on the Nile River. The British and French, primary stockholders in the Suez Canal and dependent on it for trade routes, attacked Egypt against the advice of U.S. Secretary of State Dulles. Outraged world *public opinion*[5] was focused at the *United*[12] *Nations*, threats of *war*[12] with the Soviet Union were sounded, the French, British, and Israeli troops were withdrawn, and a United Nations peacekeeping force was installed along the Suez Canal. See also *nationalized property*[10].

system, fail-safe. A complex technological weapons control system designed to automatically compensate for technological or human error within a particular weapon. The fail-safe system became absolutely essential with the advent of the *Cold*[12] *War* and the development of sophisticated and totally destructive nuclear weapons. A fail-safe system which fails within a guided missile is sometimes referred to as a "broken arrow." See also *anti-ballistic*[12] *missile*; *atomic*[12] *war*.

tactics, overland (horizontal). The traditional approach to ground warfare, which involves the movement of troops over physical terrain, generally through face-to-face confrontation with the enemy. Such tactics were developed throughout history by such military figures as Philip of Macedonia, Alexander the Great, Julius Caesar, Napoleon, Frederick the Great, and *Karl Von Clausewitz*[12].

tactics, vertical envelopment. The airlifting of men, supplies, and military hardware into enemy *territory*[3]. Vertical envelopment tactics came into use with the development of the airplane and the training of parachutists. It became more sophisticated with the development of the helicopter. The *Vietnam*[12] *War* was the testing ground for full-scale employment of such a military tactic.

territory, mandate. A term used after *World*[12] *War I* to designate a *country*[3] whose internal governmental affairs were supervised by a member *state*[3] of the *League*[12] *of Nations* after peace had been established. Former possessions of Germany and Turkey were administered under such an arrangement.

territory, trust. A term used after *World*[12] *War II* to designate a *country*[3] whose internal governmental affairs were supervised by a member *state*[3] of the *United*[12] *Nations* after peace had been established. Former possessions of Japan and Italy were administered under such an arrangement. See also *United*[12] *Nations Trusteeship Council.*

Third World. A popular term used to describe the underdeveloped *countries*[3] of the world and the countries not rigidly aligned with one of the two major sides in the *Cold*[12] *War*. Some of the nations viewed as the keystone of the Third World are India and numerous African republics. Many of the countries are not strongly committed to either *Communist*[3] or *democratic*[3] value systems.

Tonkin Gulf Resolution. A *resolution*[7] passed by both houses of the U.S. *Congress*[4] in August 1964, which gave the *President*[6] broad *authority*[3] to take "all necessary steps, including the use of armed forces" to "prevent further aggression" in Southeast Asia. The resolution received broad congressional support and was based on what appeared to be a clear case of *aggression*[12] by North Vietnam on U.S. vessels in international waters of the Tonkin Gulf of the South China Sea. Officials of the U.S. destroyers (and *intelligence*[12]-gathering vessels) U.S.S. Maddox and U.S.S. Turner Joy claimed that between August 2 and August 4, several torpedo boats attacked them without provocation in international waters. Visual confirmation of destroyed enemy torpedo boats was never made, although the U.S. vessels revealed minor damages. President *Lyndon Johnson*[6] used the Tonkin Gulf Resolution as the basis for ordering massive bombing of North Vietnam in 1965 and the sending of hundreds of thousands of American ground combat troops into South Vietnam. The resolution became, according to the *Department of State*[2], the "functional equivalent" of a *declaration of war*[12] against North Vietnam. The resolution came into question during congressional investigations held by the *Senate*[7] *Committee*[12] *on Foreign Relations* in 1967. Questions were raised as to the seriousness of the incident described in official navy reports, the reliability of information collected, and the truthfulness of military and naval personnel. The Tonkin Gulf Resolution was repealed by President Richard M. Nixon on January 12, 1971, when he signed a military credit sales *bill*[7] which permitted easy credit on U.S. weapons sold to friendly foreign powers. President Nixon held that the resolution was already meaningless since he was acting under his *Commander-in-Chief powers*[6] to protect U.S. military forces already in South Vietnam. The resolution is officially called the Southeast Asia Resolution. See also *Nixon*[12] *doctrine*; *Vietnam*[12] *War*.

treaty. A legal *contract*[10] or agreement between two or more *nations*[3]. Treaties most often involve mutual *alliance*[12], cessation of *war*[12], economic trade, *disarmament*[12], arms control, and similar matters. The U.S. *President*[6] may negotiate a treaty, but it does not become an official document until it has been *ratified*[3] by two-thirds of the *Senate*[7]. Once a treaty is ratified it becomes, according to Article VI of the *Constitution*[4], a part of the "supreme law of the land." See also *national*[4] supremacy clause; *rebus*[12] sic stantibus; self-executing[12] *treaty*; *treaty*[12] reservation.

treaty reservation. A formal *amendment*[3] or addition to a *treaty*[12] which is added by one party in order to modify a particular portion of the treaty to that party's own advantage. An international *state*[3] adding a reservation may wish to deny application of the treaty to certain matters. Before a reservation is accepted as *international law*[8], all other parties to the treaty must accept the reservation of the individual state. See also *Connally*[12] Amendment; international positivism[12].

Truman doctrine. The 1947 foreign *policy*[6] statement of *President*[6] Harry S Truman[6] which pledged U.S. economic and military assistance to Greece and Turkey specifically and other *nations*[3] indirectly in their efforts to avoid a Communist takeover. The Truman doctrine presented the first occasion for the U.S. to actually commit itself to the policy of *containment*[12] in combating *Communism*[3]. See also *foreign*[12] aid.

two-China theory. The belief that both the People's Republic of China (Communist China) and the Nationalist Republic of China (Taiwan) should be generally recognized by the world *community*[3] as legal *governments*[3] in full control of their respective *territories*[3] and populations. At one time, such a *theory*[3] implied the possibility of seating both governments in the United Nations, although both countries rejected the idea. The issue became especially important during 1971 as world powers began to lean toward accepting Communist China as a member of the U.N. In spite of U.S. opposition, Nationalist China was expelled from the U.N. on October 25, 1971 by a *United*[12] Nations General Assembly vote of 76 to 35. Communist China thereby gained the China seat in the *United*[12] Nations Security Council, and Taiwan became the first *country*[3] to be expelled from the U.N.

U-2 crisis of 1960. An international crisis created by the crash of a U.S. U-2 *intelligence*[12] plane "brought down" in the Soviet Union on May 1, 1960. The highly secret aircraft, piloted by Francis Gary Powers, contained microfilm of high-flight reconnaissance missions over the Soviet Union. The pilot was eventually sentenced to ten years in a Soviet prison, but was released in 1962 in exchange for a convicted Soviet spy. The crash of the plane made the world aware of the U.S. intelligence operations, clearly indicted the U.S. for breaking *international law*[8], provided the Soviet Union with a major piece of *propaganda*[5], and wrecked a series of scheduled meetings in Paris between *President*[6] Eisenhower and Premier Khrushchev of the Soviet Union.

Ugly Americanism. The social, political, and *diplomatic*[12] concept that generally unacceptable actions commited by Americans who travel abroad or serve abroad reflect on the general character of the U.S. The term gained widespread popularity and usage after publication of a popular novel entitled The Ugly American, by William J. Lederer and Eugene Burdick in 1958. Ugly Americanism may be engendered for any number of reasons, real or imagined. Among the most cited reasons are *paternalism*[3], immorality, *chauvinism*[12], economic dominance, and general political influence.

Uniform Code of Military Justice: see Chap. 8.

United Nations (U.N.). The major international *organization*[6] which was established in 1945 as a forum for maintaining world peace. The organization maintains permanent headquarters in New York City and is composed of six major organs: the *United*[12] *Nations General Assembly*, the *United*[12] *Nations Security Council*, the *United*[12] *Nations Secretariat*, the *United*[12] *Nations Trusteeship Council*, the Economic and Social Council, and the *International*[12] *Court of Justice*. The United Nations also sponsors and supports numerous specialized agencies and projects. All U.N. services are designed to provide international stability and to improve the human condition around the world. General operations of the U.N. are directed from New York City. However, the International Court of Justice sits at The Hague and various specialized agencies such as UNESCO have operating secretariats at locations outside New York City. The U.N. has acted as the primary international forum for discussion of world issues. It acted as a basic organizational structure in guiding the military forces which helped South Korea avoid military conquest by North Korean forces between 1950 and 1953. It has also led in achieving international *treaty*[12] commitments designed to avoid international nuclear warfare. The U.N. has little *authority*[3] to intervene in internal matters of sovereign *states*[3]. However, through international treaties and through social and cultural programs it is evident that the U.N. has some influence on the international scene. See also *collective*[12] *security*; *The Hague*[12] *Tribunal*; *Korean*[12] *War*; *state (constitutional) sovereignty*[3].

United Nations Educational, Scientific, and Cultural Organization (UNESCO). A specialized *United*[12] *Nations* agency responsible for promotion and coordination of various educational, scientific, and cultural programs undertaken by the international *community*[3]. UNESCO pro-

grams are coordinated through a Secretariat in Paris. They generally involve research, teaching, cultural exchanges, data exchanges, *mass*[5] *media* productions, and other assorted and stimulating programs.

United Nations General Assembly. The *United*[12] *Nations* body composed of all the member *states*[3] of the U.N. The *organization*[6] allows each *delegation*[5] ten members and one vote. The General Assembly reviews any international matters presented by its own membership. Most decisions are agreed on by a simple *majority*[3] vote of members present and voting. The General Assembly may issue *resolutions*[7] and recommend action, but it may not make regulations binding on any member or nonmember national state. In the light of this fact, it has been more effective as a world forum for discussion of international matters.

United Nations Secretariat. The general administrative and *bureaucratic*[6] machinery of the *United*[12] *Nations*. The Secretariat serves as the staff agency in the United Nations headquarters in New York City and various field offices throughout the world. The principal officer of the Secretariat is the Secretary-General, an official nominated by the *United*[12] *Nations Security Council* and chosen by *popular vote*[5] in the *United*[12] *Nations General Assembly*. The Secretariat plans and coordinates numerous service functions such as translation services, personnel services, transportation services, and postal services.

United Nations Security Council. One of the principal agencies within the *United*[12] *Nations*, an agency composed of the five major and permanent powers responsible for the creation of the United Nations (United States, Great Britain, France, Soviet Union, and China) and ten temporary nations selected for two-year terms of office. The Security Council is responsible for seeking peaceful solutions to international conflicts. Decisions related to peacekeeping are made by unanimous vote of the body. The Soviet Union has been especially noted for using its *veto*[7] in various matters brought before the Security Council. However, the agency still acts as a primary public forum for discussing issues of world peace. The *presidency*[3] of the Security Council rotates on a regular monthly basis in order to avoid procedural domination by any one power.

United Nations Trusteeship Council. A primary *United*[12] *Nations* agency charged with general administrative regulation of trust territories under U.N. jurisdiction. The Trusteeship Council began acting immediately upon creation to assist the trust territories to achieve independence. By 1971 the agency had helped 9 out of 11 *territories*[3] to reach independence. See also *trust territory*[12].

Versailles, Treaty of. The peace *treaty*[12] that officially ended *World*[12] *War I*. The treaty, signed on June 28, 1919 and formed partially under the leadership of *President*[6] *Woodrow Wilson*[6], was rejected by the *U.S. Senate*[7]. The provisions of the treaty stripped Germany of various *colonies*[4], forced her to admit error in starting the *war*[12], required *reparations*[12] of $56 billion, and stripped her of the *power*[3] to make war. The treaty also created the *League*[12] *of Nations*. The U.S. rejected the treaty, refused to join the League of Nations, and declared an end to World War I by a *joint resolution*[7] of *Congress*[4] and separate treaties with Germany, Austria, and Hungary. The U.S. and China were the only two major powers involved in World War I that did not sign the Treaty. See also *Fourteen*[12] *Points*.

veterans' preference: see Chap. 6.

Viet Cong: see *National*[12] *Liberation Front*.

Vietnamization. The U.S. military and *foreign*[12] *aid* program designed to turn the primary fighting duties in the *Vietnam*[12] *War* over to military troops and provincial leaders of the Republic of South Vietnam. The term "Vietnamization" gained widespread popularity during the presidential election of 1968 due to public desires to remove U.S. troops from the Vietnam War.

Vietnam (Indochina) War. A prolonged, complex, and controversial military conflict in Indochina. The conflict primarily involved the United States, South Vietnam, and North Vietnam. The political and military involvement of the U.S. began in the area primarily in 1954 when the *Geneva*[12] *Conventions of 1954* divided North and South Vietnam at the 17th parallel. That involvement deepened in 1956 when the French occupation forces were defeated by the Viet Minh (*Communist*[3]) forces at Dienbienphu. Elections designed to reunify North and South Vietnam were never held as scheduled in 1956. Most observers predicted that Ho Chi Minh, the Communist candidate who led the Viet Minh to victory over the French, would win the elections. In the light of political instability in the area and the fear of Communist control, the U.S. eventually entered the *guerrilla war*[12] through *executive*[12] *agreements* and under a *protocol*[12] to the *Southeast*[12] *Asia Treaty Organization* agreements. The U.S. began to supply military "advisers" in 1961 in order to assist South Vietnam against Communist controlled forces coordinated by the *National*[12] *Liberation Front*, or Viet Cong. The U.S. began to bomb North Vietnam in 1965 soon after the *Congress*[4] passed the *Tonkin*[12] *Gulf Resolution* of 1964. The U.S. *federal government*[3] had sent over 500,000 troops to the war zone and sustained almost 40,000 casualties by 1968. The *limited war*[12] divided the *nation*[3] and forced *President*[6] *Lyndon B. Johnson*[6] to retire from office in 1968. The *war*[12] spread to Cambodia in 1970 and Laos in 1971, the American public began to call for an end to the conflict, and President Nixon began a gradual withdrawal of American forces. The U.S. committed itself to the Vietnam War primarily on the basis that the war was a test of U.S. "integrity" and a challenge to the U.S. as the "backbone of free-world security." It was also seen as a testing ground for *wars*[12] *of national liberation.* U.S. government advisers argued that if Vietnam fell to the Communists, all Asian Free World nations would fall under the *domino*[12] *theory.* They also argued that the South Vietnamese should be permitted to "shape their political and economic institutions according to patterns of their own choosing." The psychological trauma and confusion of the conflict was amplified in the *My*[12] *Lai controversy* which culminated in the *Calley*[12] *case.* When the ground war ended in early 1973 the U.S. had sustained almost 46,000 deaths.

war. Open and violent military conflict between two or more parties. War may exist under a formal declaration of hostilities or under practical conditions of violence without reference to legality. War between *belligerents*[12] generally *abrogates*[12] existing *treaty*[12] agreements, severs *diplomatic*[12] relations, urges belligerents to abide by various international rules of military and *humanitarian*[11] conduct, and demands total *mobilization*[12] of all national resources. War may be carried out for almost any political, social, economic, *ideological*[3], or religious reason. It may take almost any form of destructive and violent activity known to man. War, as general anti-social conduct, is practiced on a mass scale apart from basic biological need only among human beings and army ants. See also *aggression*[12]; *Karl Von Clausewitz*[12]; *Coup*[12] *d'état*; *declaration of war*[12]; *rebellion*[3]; *revolution*[3].

war, civil. A military conflict between various segments of a *state*[3] or an existing *government*[3] for control of the government. See also *Civil*[4] *War (U.S.).*

war, conventional. A military conflict that employs "conventional" weapons not dependent on atomic or nuclear energy. Some standard conventional weapons are rifles, heavy armor (tanks, cannons, etc.), non-nuclear explosives (grenades, bombs, etc.), napalm, tear gas, and bayonets. See also *atomic*[12] *war*; *flexible response strategy*[12]; *limited war*[12].

war crimes trials. A series of trials conducted at the conclusion of *World*[12] *War II* in Nuremberg, Germany, and Tokyo, Japan. The Nuremberg trials, conducted by the victorious *Allied*[12] *powers*, found 22 former high German military officers guilty on the grounds that they had perpetrated various war crimes and *crimes*[8] against humanity. The Tokyo trials found 25 major individuals guilty. In both settings, many lesser individuals were also tried and found guilty and imprisoned or executed. The war crimes trials presented the first occasion for military victors to try individuals for violating world stability and peace. *Aggression*[12], *genocide*[12], atrocities against civilian populations, and mistreatment of prisoners of war were items generally classified as war crimes. War crimes were listed as those against nationals of a *state*[3] or those against the international *community*[3]. See also *Calley*[12] *case.*

war, declaration of. A formal declaration of hostilities made by one *state*[3] or *nation*[3] against another state or nation. In the United States, only the *Congress*[4] may issue a formal declaration of *war*[12] by a *joint resolution*[7] of Congress signed by the *President*[6]. Out of the 11 serious and extended wars the U.S. has been engaged in, only five were officially declared by Congress: the *War*[12] *of 1812*, the *Mexi-*

[12] *War*, the *Spanish-American*[12] , *World*[12] *War I*, and *World*[12] *War II*. See also *war*[12] *powers*; *executive war*[12].

war, executive. A condition of *war*[12] instituted by or entered into through the *powers*[3] of a chief *executive*[6] without legislative approval. The *U.S. President*[6] may take action that involves the *nation*[3] in hostilities even though the *U.S. Constitution*[4] states that the *Congress*[4] is the branch of *government*[3] responsible for declaring war. In 1970 the *Senate*[7] debated the *Cooper-Church*[12] *Amendment*, an *amendment*[3] to a foreign military sales bill which would have restricted the President's power to conduct *war*[12] without congressional approval. See also *executive*[12] *agreement*; *declaration of war*[12]; *Vietnam*[12] *War*.

warfare, chemical and biological (CBW). The deliberate military usage of harmful and destructive chemical and bacteriological elements. Various chemical and biological elements are useful in destroying persons, animals, and plants for military purposes. A Geneva Convention *protocol*[12] formulated in 1925 outlaws chemical and biological warfare. The U.S. signed the protocol in 1970 and began destroying stockpiles of chemical and biological weapons. See also *Geneva*[12] *Conventions of 1949*.

warfare, ideological. Military, political, or social conflict which reveals the presence of strong *ideological*[3] commitments and values. The religious *wars*[12] of the Middle Ages were some of the most vivid and violent ideological conflicts in world history. The *Cold*[12] *War* which began at the end of *World*[12] *War II* emphasized the ideological conflict between *Communism*[3] and *capitalism*[3], personified by the U.S. and the Soviet Union. The major weapons of ideological warfare are *propaganda*[5], *diplomatic*[12] ploys, threats, intrigue, indoctrination, and careful regulation of public expression.

warfare, psychological. Any psychologically violent action undertaken in an effort to gain political or military advantage during a time of military or social conflict. Psychological warfare may take the form of subtle *propaganda*[5], a sudden and unexpected change in military tactics, *third*[9] *degree* mental torture, or any number of devices which affect the psychological equilibrium of military troops and political leaders. See also *Cold*[12] *War*; *hot war*[12]; *My*[12] *Lai controversy*; *Pueblo*[12] *crisis of 1968*.

war, guerrilla. Irregular, violent, and voluntary military action undertaken by small groups of individuals not directed by recognized or legal military authorities. Guerrilla activity is ordinarily directed at existing *government*[3] officials and structures. It is often carried out in *rural*[11] areas, supplied by outside sources, based on rapid strikes, and employs various *propaganda*[5] devices. Guerrilla warfare depends on extreme terror tactics such as kidnappings and unexpected bombings designed to disrupt regular governmental operations and to maintain support of the general population out of fear. See also *National*[12] *Liberation Front*; *Vietnam*[12] *War*.

war, hot. *War*[12] which is characterized more by open and violent conflict between belligerents than by systematic and planned tension based on psychological, propagandistic, or *ideological*[3] factors. See also *ideological warfare*[12]; *psychological warfare*[12].

war, limited. A military conflict that is deliberately waged at a particular level of violence which falls short of the total destruction or surrender of a *belligerent*[12]. In a limited war all belligerents carefully determine objectives, the scope of military activity, the type of weapons to be used, and the status of particular portions of the population. The *theory*[3] of limited war arose at the end of *World*[12] *War II* and with the possibility of nuclear destruction of the entire world. A limited war is basically dependent on conventional weapons which do not use atomic or nuclear energy. Some strategists argue that there could be a limited use of field-sized nuclear weapons. However, others argue that there is no such thing as a "limited" nuclear weapon. See also *atomic*[12] *war; conventional war*[12]; *Korean*[12] *War; MacArthur*[12] *controversy; Vietnam*[12] *War.*

War of 1812. A declared *war*[12] between the United States and Great Britain which was fought between June 18, 1812 and January 8, 1815, when General *Andrew Jackson*[6] defeated the British at New Orleans, Louisiana. The Treaty of Ghent, which was signed on December 24, 1814, officially ended the war before the last major battle was fought. The war, fought during the *administration*[6] of *President*[6] *James Madison*[6], was conducted by the U.S. on the grounds that Great Britain had "impressed" U.S. seamen into British service, had violated *territorial*[3] rights, had *blockaded*[12] U.S. ports, and had refused to revoke the commercially restrictive Orders in Council which directed U.S.-bound *neutral*[12] goods through British ports. Although the British destroyed the U.S. Capitol building, engaged various Indian tribes in support against the U.S., and fought effectively on the open seas, the U.S. ground and naval forces defeated the British in such places as Lake Erie, the Northwestern Territory, Canada, and New Orleans. In the Treaty of Ghent it was decided that hostilities would end and that the U.S. and Canadian boundaries would remain the same (*status*[12] *quo ante bellum*). The issues of impressment, fishing rights, and other commercial subjects were ignored in the settlement. Plans were made for a *boundary*[12] *commission*[6] to deal with the northeastern boundary dispute between the U.S.

and Canada. The treaty dealt with almost no substantive issues, but simply restored the peace. See also *Hartford*[4] *Convention.*

war powers. The recognized and legal *authority*[3] to provide for national defense or conduct *war*[12] against another national *state*[3] or population. In the United States *constitutional*[3] *system* the *Congress*[4] is granted the *power*[3] to declare war, to raise funds for the support of military forces, and to make rules for the various military services. A primary restriction on congressional warmaking power is that funds for the army may be appropriated for two-year periods of time. The *President*[6] is *constitutionally*[3] listed as the Commander-in-Chief of the armed forces. As leader of the armed forces and of foreign *policy*[6], the President may act through *executive*[12] *agreements* and *executive*[6] *orders*, which may lead the U.S. into direct military conflict with other *nations*[3] without a formal *declaration of war*[12]. Under the war powers, the U.S. *government*[3] may suspend certain *civil*[9] *rights* protections (*writ of habeas*[8] *corpus*, speedy trial, etc.), carry out *public*[10] *works* projects (*Tennessee*[2] *Valley Authority*, war roads, etc.), regulate international trade and travel (quota restrictions, *embargoes*[12], etc.), *draft*[12] persons into military service, and do many other things considered essential for national defense. See also *Ashwander*[1] *v. TVA; Commander-in-Chief powers*[6]; *emergency powers*[4]; *exclusive powers*[4]; *Korematsu*[1] *v. U.S.; martial*[8] *law; military*[8] *law.*

Warsaw Pact. A regional security agreement formalized in the Eastern European Mutual Assistance Treaty signed by eight *Communist*[3] nations of eastern Europe in 1955. The pact is a formal *alliance*[12] which calls for group action in the event that a particular signatory *nation*[3] is threatened or attacked by external powers. It serves as a Communist military and economic alliance designed to counter the influence and *power*[3] of the *North*[12] *Atlantic Treaty Organization,* an *alliance*[12] between several western European nations. See also *collective*[12] *security.*

wars of national liberation. Military and political conflicts deliberately provoked by subversive and *insurgent*[12] forces and designed to maximize *Communist*[3] influence and control in selected areas of the world, especially the underdeveloped areas of the world which have historically been dominated by colonialism. Such "popular uprisings" are doctrinally justified by Communist powers as being essential for the destruction of *capitalism*[3] and the fulfillment of a worldwide classless Communist *society*[3]. The *war*[12] in Algeria, which led to independence from France, and the *Vietnam*[12] *War* are regularly cited as wars of national liberation. See also *guerrilla war*[12]; *National*[12] *Liberation Front*; *Third*[12] *World*.

Washington's Farewell Address. A public statement by *President*[6] *George Washington*[6] which was made upon his retirement from office in 1796. President Washington declined to accept a third term in office and thereby established the no-third-term tradition. His basic farewell advice to the American people involved foreign *policy*[6]. He warned against domestic *factionalism*[3] and against entangling *alliances*[12], "intrigues," and *wars*[12] with foreign powers which might prove detrimental to the national interest. He set the basic framework for *isolationism*[12] during his *administration*[6]. He said that the U.S. should hold its involvement with foreign powers to the commercial level.

World War I. A major international upheaval which raged between August 1914 and November 1918. The *war*[12] pitted the *Central*[12] *powers* led by Germany against the *Allied*[12] *powers* led by the United States, France, and Great Britain. The war was sparked by various complex political, social, and economic issues which were intertwined throughout continental Europe. Feelings of *nationalism*[3], expressions of militarism, entangling *alliances*[12], and petty jealousies were all evident before and during the struggle. The U.S. led by *President*[6] *Woodrow Wilson*[6], hoped to remain *neutral*[12] but entered the conflict on the side of Great Britain and France in 1917 after it ran into commercial difficulties with German submarine warfare. After experiencing extensive losses of military personnel and equipment, the Allied forces eventually defeated the Central powers. An *armistice*[12] was signed on November 11, 1918, and all fighting stopped. The *Treaty of Versailles*[12] was signed on June 28, 1919; all the major powers except the U.S. and China agreed to its terms. See also *Abrams*[1] *v. U.S.*; *bad*[9] *tendency doctrine*; *clear*[9] *and present danger doctrine*; *Espionage*[9] *Act of 1917*; *Pierce*[1] *v. U.S.*; *Schenck*[1] *v. U.S.*; *Sedition*[9] *Act of 1918*.

World War II. The second major international military and social upheaval of the twentieth century, a conflagration which raged between 1939 and 1945. The seeds of the *war*[12] lay in the unwise and harsh conditions imposed on Germany after *World*[12] *War I*, the worldwide *depression*[10] of the 1930's, economic warfare between European *nations*[3], the breakdown of the *League*[12] *of Nations*, the rearming and industrialization of Germany, and renewed *nationalism*[3] and the development of *fascism*[3] in Germany, Italy, and Japan. After numerous *aggressive*[12] invasions of peaceful Oriental and European nations (Manchuria by Japan in 1931, Poland by Germany in 1939, etc.), visible and *genocidal*[12] actions on the part of Germany, the development of German submarine warfare, the German air war on England, and the Japanese attack on Pearl Harbor, the United States entered the war on December 8, 1941. The United States, led by *President*[6] *Franklin D.*

Roosevelt[6], was already giving financial assistance to the *Allied*[12] *powers* engaged in conflict against the *Axis*[12] *powers.* The war raged throughout the Atlantic Ocean, the Pacific Ocean, in Africa, in Asia, in western Europe, and in most land areas except the Western Hemisphere. The U.S. underwent total *mobilization*[12] and economic regulation in order to conduct the war. The war ended in Europe on May 8, 1945 as a result of the Allied invasion led by General Dwight D. Eisenhower. It ended in Asia on September 2, 1945 as a result of the atomic attacks on Hiroshima and Nagasaki, Japan. *War*[12] *crimes trials* were held in both Germany and Japan and peace *treaties*[12] were signed with Japan on September 8, 1951, and with Germany on May 26, 1952. See also *atomic*[12] *war*; *Lend-Lease*[12].

xenophobia: see Chap. 3.

Supreme Court cases related to material in this chapter are arranged below by subject. Summaries of the cases are in Chapter One arranged alphabetically by the name of the first party in each case.

GENERAL—
  Ashwander v. TVA (1936)
  Debs, In re (1895)

CONSCIENTIOUS
  OBJECTORS—
  Gillette v. U.S. (1971)
  U.S. v. Seeger (1965)

DIPLOMATIC
  RECOGNITION—
  U.S. v. Belmont (1936)

DRAFT—
  Selective Draft Law Cases
  (1918)

EXECUTIVE AGREE-
  MENTS—
  U.S. v. Belmont (1936)

HABEAS CORPUS—
  Duncan v. Kahanamoku
  (1946)
  Endo, Ex parte (1944)
  Korematsu v. U.S. (1944)
  Merryman, Ex parte
  (1861)
  Milligan, Ex parte (1866)

MARTIAL LAW—
  Duncan v. Kahanamoku
  (1946)
  Korematsu v. U.S. (1944)
  Milligan, Ex parte (1866)

MILITARY LAW—
  Reid v. Covert (1957)
  Toth v. Quarles (1955)
  Trop v. Dulles (1958)

PRESIDENTIAL
  POWERS—(Inherent)
  U.S. v. Curtiss-Wright
  Export Corp. (1936)

Youngstown Sheet & Tube
  v. Sawyer (1952)

PRESIDENTIAL
  POWERS—(War)
  Ashwander v. TVA
  (1936)
  Korematsu v. U.S. (1944)
  N.Y. Times Co. v. U.S.
  (1971)
  Prize Cases (1863)

SUBVERSIVE ACTIVITIES
  —(General)
  Penn. v. Nelson (1956)
  U.S. v. U.S. District Court
  for the Western District
  of Michigan (1972)

SUBVERSIVE ACTIVITIES
  —(Association)
  Kent v. Dulles (1958)
  Scales v. U.S. (1961)
  U.S. v. Robel (1967)

SUBVERSIVE ACTIVITIES
  —(Bills of Attainder)
  U.S. v. Brown (1965)

SUBVERSIVE ACTIVITIES
  —(Expression)
  Abrams v. U.S. (1919)
  Barenblatt v. U.S. (1959)
  Communist Party v.
  SACB (1961)
  Dennis v. U.S. (1951)
  Lamont v. Postmaster
  General (1965)
  Pierce v. U.S. (1920)
  Scales v. U.S. (1961)
  Schenck v. U.S. (1919)
  Yates v. U.S. (1957)

SUBVERSIVE ACTIVITIES
  —(Loyalty Oath)
  Adler v. Board of Educa-
  tion (1952)
  American Communications
  Assn. v. Douds (1950)
  Cole v. Young (1956)
  Garner v. Board of Public
  Works (1951)
  Keyishian v. Board of
  Regents (1967)

SUBVERSIVE ACTIVITIES
  —(Registration)
  Albertson v. SACB (1965)
  Communist Party v.
  SACB (1961)

SUBVERSIVE ACTIVITIES
  —(Self-incrimination)
  Albertson v. SACB (1965)
  Barenblatt v. U.S. (1959)
  Jencks v. U.S. (1957)
  Slochower v. Board of
  Education (1956)
  Ullman v. U.S. (1956)
  Watkins v. U.S. (1957)

SUBVERSIVE ACTIVITIES
  —(Travel)
  Aptheker v. Secretary of
  State (1964)
  Kent v. Dulles (1958)
  Zemel v. Rusk (1965)

TARIFFS—
  Hampton & Co. v. U.S.
  (1928)

TREATIES—
  Missouri v. Holland
  (1920)

THE CONSTITUTION
OF THE UNITED STATES

Adopted September 17, 1787

Effective March 4, 1789

We the people of the United States, in order to form a more perfect union, establish justice, insure domestic tranquillity, provide for the common defense, promote the general welfare, and secure the blessings of liberty to ourselves and our posterity, do ordain and establish this Constitution for the United States of America.

ARTICLE I

SECTION 1. All legislative powers herein granted shall be vested in a Congress of the United States, which shall consist of a Senate and House of Representatives.

SECTION 2. 1. The House of Representatives shall be composed of members chosen every second year by the people of the several States, and the electors in each State shall have the qualifications requisite for electors of the most numerous branch of the State legislature.

2. No person shall be a representative who shall not have attained to the age of twenty-five years, and been seven years a citizen of the United States, and who shall not, when elected, be an inhabitant of that State in which he shall be chosen.

3. Representatives and direct taxes[1] shall be apportioned among the several States which may be included within this Union, according to their respective numbers, which shall be determined by adding to the whole number of free persons, including those bound to service for a term of years, and excluding Indians not taxed, *three fifths of all other persons*.[2] The actual enumeration shall be made within three years after the first meeting of the Congress of the United States, and within every subsequent term of ten years, in such manner as they shall by law direct. The number of representatives shall not exceed one for every thirty thousand, but each State shall have at least one representative; and until such enumeration shall be made, the State of New Hampshire shall be entitled to choose three, Massachusetts eight, Rhode Island and Providence Plantations one, Connecticut five, New York six, New Jersey four, Pennsylvania eight, Delaware one, Maryland six, Virginia ten, North Caroline five, South Carolina five, and Georgia three.

4. When vacancies happen in the representation from any State, the executive authority thereof shall issue writs of election to fill such vacancies.

[1] See the 16th Amendment.
[2] See the 14th Amendment.

5. The House of Representatives shall choose their speaker and other officers; and shall have the sole power of impeachment.

SECTION 3.   1. The Senate of the United States shall be composed of two senators from each State, *chosen by the legislature thereof,*[3] for six years; and each senator shall have one vote.

2. Immediately after they shall be assembled in consequence of the first election, they shall be divided as equally as may be into three classes. The seats of the senators of the first class shall be vacated at the expiration of the second year, of the second class at the expiration of the fourth year, and of the third class at the expiration of the sixth year, so that one third may be chosen every second year; and if vacancies happen by resignation, or otherwise, during the recess of the legislature of the State, the executive thereof may make temporary appointments until the next meeting of the legislature, which shall then fill such vacancies.[3]

3. No person shall be a senator who shall not have attained to the age of thirty years, and been nine years a citizen of the United States, and who shall not, when elected, be an inhabitant of that State for which he shall be chosen.

4. The Vice President of the United States shall be President of the Senate, but shall have no vote, unless they be equally divided.

5. The Senate shall choose their other officers, and also a president *pro tempore,* in the absence of the Vice President, or when he shall exercise the office of the President of the United States.

6. The Senate shall have the sole power to try all impeachments. When sitting for that purpose, they shall be on oath or affirmation. When the President of the United States is tried, the chief justice shall preside: and no person shall be convicted without the concurrence of two thirds of the members present.

7. Judgment in cases of impeachment shall not extend further than to removal from office, and disqualifications to hold and enjoy any office of honor, trust or profit under the United States: but the party convicted shall nevertheless be liable and subject to indictment, trial, judgment and punishment, according to law.

SECTION 4.   1. The times, places, and manner of holding elections for senators and representatives, shall be prescribed in each State by the legislature thereof; but the Congress may at any time by law make or alter such regulations, except as to the places of choosing senators.

2. The Congress shall assemble at least once in every year, and such meeting shall be on the first Monday in December, unless they shall by law appoint a different day.

SECTION 5.   1. Each House shall be the judge of the elections, returns and qualifications of its own members, and a majority of each shall constitute a quorum to do business; but a small number may adjourn from day to day, and may be authorized to compel the attendance of absent members, in such manner, and under such penalties as each House may provide.

2. Each House may determine the rules of its proceedings, punish its members for disorderly behavior, and, with the concurrence of two thirds, expel a member.

3. Each House shall keep a journal of its proceedings, and from time to time publish the same, excepting such parts as may in their judgment require secrecy; and the yeas and nays of the members of either House on any question shall, at the desire of one fifth of those present, be entered on the journal.

4. Neither House, during the session of Congress, shall, without the consent of the other, adjourn for more than three days, nor to any other place than that in which the two Houses shall be sitting.

[3] See the 17th Amendment.

SECTION 6.   1. The senators and representatives shall receive a compensation for their services, to be ascertained by law, and paid out of the Treasury of the United States. They shall in all cases, except treason, felony, and breach of the peace, be privileged from arrest during their attendance at the session of their respective Houses, and in going to and returning from the same; and for any speech or debate in either House, they shall not be questioned in any other place.

2. No senator or representative shall, during the time for which he was elected, be appointed to any civil office under the authority of the United States, which shall have been created, or the emoluments whereof shall have been increased during such time; and no person holding any office under the United States shall be a member of either House during his continuance in office.

SECTION 7.   1. All bills for raising revenue shall originate in the House of Representatives; but the Senate may propose or concur with amendments as on other bills.

2. Every bill which shall have passed the House of Representatives and the Senate, shall, before it becomes a law, be presented to the President of the United States; if he approves he shall sign it, but if not he shall return it, with his objections to that House in which it shall have originated, who shall enter the objections at large on their journal, and proceed to reconsider it. If after such reconsideration two thirds of that House shall agree to pass the bill, it shall be sent, together with the objections, to the other House, by which it shall likewise be reconsidered, and if approved by two thirds of that House, it shall become a law. But in all such cases the votes of both Houses shall be determined by yeas and nays, and the names of the persons voting for and against the bill shall be entered on the journal of each House respectively. If any bill shall not be returned by the President within ten days (Sundays excepted) after it shall have been presented to him, the same shall be a law, in like manner as if he had signed it, unless the Congress by their adjournment prevent its return, in which case it shall not be a law.

3. Every order, resolution, or vote to which the concurrence of the Senate and the House of Representatives may be necessary (except on a question of adjournment) shall be presented to the President of the United States; and before the same shall take effect, shall be approved by him, or being disapproved by him, shall be repassed by two thirds of the Senate and House of Representatives, according to the rules and limitations prescribed in the case of a bill.

SECTION 8.   The Congress shall have the power

1. To lay and collect taxes, duties, imposts, and excises, to pay the debts and provide for the common defense and general welfare of the United States; but all duties, imposts, and excises shall be uniform throughout the United States;

2. To borrow money on the credit of the United States;

3. To regulate commerce with foreign nations, and among the several States, and with the Indian tribes;

4. To establish a uniform rule of naturalization, and uniform laws on the subject of bankruptcies throughout the United States;

5. To coin money, regulate the value thereof, and of foreign coin, and fix the standard of weights and measures;

6. To provide for the punishment of counterfeiting the securities and current coin of the United States;

7. To establish post offices and post roads;

8. To promote the process of science and useful arts, by securing for limited times to authors and inventors the exclusive right to their respective writings and discoveries;

9. To constitute tribunals inferior to the Supreme Court;

10. To define and punish piracies and felonies committed on the high seas, and offenses against the law of nations;

11. To declare war, grant letters of marque and reprisal, and make rules concerning captures on land and water;

12. To raise and support armies, but no appropriation of money to that use shall be for a longer term than two years;

13. To provide and maintain a navy;

14. To make rules for the government and regulation of the land and naval forces;

15. To provide for calling forth the militia to execute the laws of the Union, suppress insurrections and repel invasions;

16. To provide for organizing, arming, and disciplining the militia, and for governing such part of them as may be employed in the service of the United States, reserving to the States respectively, the appointment of the officers, and the authority of training the militia according to the discipline prescribed by Congress.

17. To exercise exclusive legislation in all cases whatsoever, over such district (not exceeding ten miles square) as may, by cession of particular States, and the acceptance of Congress, become the seat of the government of the United States, and to exercise like authority over all places purchased by the consent of the legislature of the State in which the same shall be, for the erection of forts, magazines, arsenals, dockyards, and other needful buildings; and

18. To make all laws which shall be necessary and proper for carrying into execution the foregoing powers, and all other powers vested by this Constitution in the government of the United States, or in any department or officer thereof.

SECTION 9.   1. The migration or importation of such persons as any of the States now existing shall think proper to admit, shall not be prohibited by the Congress prior to the year one thousand eight hundred and eight, but a tax or duty may be imposed on such importation, not exceeding ten dollars for each person.

2. The privilege of the writ of *habeas corpus* shall not be suspended, unless when in cases of rebellion or invasion the public safety may require it.

3. No bill of attainder or *ex post facto* law shall be passed.

4. No capitation, or other direct, tax shall be laid, unless in proportion to the census or enumeration hereinbefore directed to be taken.[4]

5. No tax or duty shall be laid on articles exported from any State.

6. No preference shall be given by any regulation of commerce or revenue to the ports of one State over those of another: nor shall vessels bound to, or from, one State be obliged to enter, clear, or pay duties in another.

7. No money shall be drawn from the treasury, but in consequence of appropriations made by law; and a regular statement and account of the receipts and expenditures of all public money shall be published from time to time.

8. No title of nobility shall be granted by the United States: and no person holding any office of profit or trust under them, shall, without the consent of the Congress, accept of any present, emolument, office, or title, of any kind whatever, from any king, prince, or foreign State.

SECTION 10.   1. No State shall enter into any treaty, alliance, or confederation; grant letters of marque and reprisal; coin money; emit bills of credit; make anything but gold and silver coin a tender in payment of debts; pass any bill of attainder, *ex post facto* law, or law impairing the obligation of contracts, or grant any title of nobility.

2. No State shall, without the consent of the Congress, lay any imposts or

---

[4] See the 16th Amendment.

duties on imports or exports, except what may be absolutely necessary for executing its inspection laws: and the net produce of all duties and imposts laid by any State on imports or exports, shall be for the use of the treasury of the United States; and all such laws shall be subject to the revision and control of the Congress.

3. No State shall, without the consent of the Congress, lay any duty of tonnage, keep troops, or ships of war in time of peace, enter into any agreement or compact with another State, or with a foreign power, or engage in war, unless actually invaded, or in such imminent danger as will not admit of delay.

ARTICLE II

Section 1. 1. The executive power shall be vested in a President of the United States of America. He shall hold his office during the term of four years, and, together with the Vice President, chosen for the same term, be elected as follows:

2. Each State shall appoint, in such manner as the legislature thereof may direct, a number of electors, equal to the whole number of senators and representatives to which the State may be entitled in the Congress: but no senator or representative, or person holding an office of trust or profit under the United States, shall be appointed an elector.

The electors shall meet in their respective States, and vote by ballot for two persons, of whom one at least shall not be an inhabitant of the same State with themselves. And they shall make a list of all the persons voted for, and of the number of votes for each; which list they shall sign and certify, and transmit sealed to the seat of the government of the United States, directed to the president of the Senate. The president of the Senate shall, in the presence of the Senate and House of Representatives, open all the certificates, and the votes shall then be counted. The person having the greatest number of votes shall be the President, if such number be a majority of the whole number of electors appointed; and if there be more than one who have such majority, and have an equal number of votes, then the House of Representatives shall immediately choose by ballot one of them for President; and if no person have a majority, then from the five highest on the list the said House shall in like manner choose the President. But in choosing the President, the votes shall be taken by States, the representation from each State having one vote; a quorum for this purpose shall consist of a member or members from two thirds of the States, and a majority of all the States shall be necessary to a choice. In every case, after the choice of the President, the person having the greatest number of votes of the electors shall be the Vice President. But if there should remain two or more who have equal votes, the Senate shall choose from them by ballot the Vice President.[5]

3. The Congress may determine the time of choosing the electors, and the day on which they shall give their votes; which day shall be the same throughout the United States.

4. No person except a natural born citizen, or a citizen of the United States, at the time of the adoption of this Constitution, shall be eligible to the office of President; neither shall any person be eligible to that office who shall not have attained to the age of thirty-five years, and been fourteen years a resident within the United States.

5. In case of the removal of the President from office, or of his death, resignation, or inability to discharge the powers and duties of the said office, the same shall devolve on the Vice President, and the Congress may by law provide for the case

[5] Superseded by the 12th Amendment.

of removal, death, resignation, or inability, both of the President and Vice President, declaring what officer shall then act as President, and such officer shall act accordingly, until the disability be removed, or a President shall be elected.

6. The President shall, at stated times, receive for his services a compensation, which shall neither be increased nor diminished during the period for which he shall have been elected, and he shall not receive within that period any other emolument from the United States, or any of them.

7. Before he enter on the execution of his office, he shall take the following oath or affirmation:—"I do solemnly swear (or affirm) that I will faithfully execute the office of President of the United States, and will to the best of my ability, preserve, protect and defend the Constitution of the United States."

SECTION 2.   1. The President shall be commander in chief of the army and navy of the United States, and of the militia of the several States, when called into the actual service of the United States; he may require the opinion, in writing, of the principal officer in each of the executive departments, upon any subject relating to the duties of their respective offices, and he shall have power to grant reprieves and pardons for offenses against the United States, except in cases of impeachment.

2. He shall have power, by and with the advice and consent of the Senate, to make treaties, provided two thirds of the senators present concur; and he shall nominate, and by and with the advice and consent of the Senate, shall appoint ambassadors, other public ministers and consuls, judges of the Supreme Court, and all other officers of the United States, whose appointments are not herein otherwise provided for, and which shall be established by law: but the Congress may by law vest the appointment of such inferior officers, as they think proper, in the President alone, in the courts of law, or in the heads of departments.

3. The President shall have power to fill up all vacancies that may happen during the recess of the Senate, by granting commissions which shall expire at the end of their next session.

SECTION 3.   He shall from time to time give to the Congress information of the state of the Union, and recommend to their consideration such measures as he shall judge necessary and expedient; he may, on extraordinary occasions, convene both Houses, or either of them, and in case of disagreement between them with respect to the time of adjournment, he may adjourn them to such time as he shall think proper; he shall receive ambassadors and other public ministers; he shall take care that the laws be faithfully executed, and shall commission all the officers of the United States.

SECTION 4.   The President, Vice President, and all civil officers of the United States, shall be removed from office on impeachment for, and conviction of, treason, bribery, or other high crimes and misdemeanors.

ARTICLE III

SECTION 1.   The judicial power of the United States shall be vested in one Supreme Court, and in such inferior courts as the Congress may from time to time ordain and establish. The judges, both of the Supreme and inferior courts, shall hold their offices during good behavior, and shall, at stated times, receive for their services, a compensation, which shall not be diminished during their continuance in office.

SECTION 2.   1. The judicial power shall extend to all cases, in law and equity, arising under this Constitution, the laws of the United States, and treaties made, or which shall be made, under their authority;—to all cases affecting ambassadors, other public ministers and consuls;—to all cases of admiralty and maritime jurisdiction;—to controversies to which the United States shall be a party;—to controversies between two or more States; between a State and citizens of another State[6] —between citizens of different States;—between citizens of the same State claiming lands under grants of different States, and between a State, or the citizens thereof, and foreign States citizens or subjects.

2. In all cases affecting ambassadors, other public ministers and consuls, and those in which a State shall be party, the Supreme Court shall have original jurisdiction. In all the other cases before mentioned, the Supreme Court shall have appellate jurisdiction, both as to law and to fact, with such exceptions, and under such regulations as the Congress shall make.

3. The trial of all crimes, except in cases of impeachment, shall be by jury; and such trial shall be held in the State where the said crimes shall have been committed; but when not committed within any State, the trial shall be at such place or places as the Congress may by law have directed.

SECTION 3. 1. Treason against the United States shall consist only in levying war against them, or in adhering to their enemies, giving them aid and comfort. No person shall be convicted of treason unless on the testimony of two witnesses to the same overt act, or on confession in open court.

2. The Congress shall have power to declare the punishment of treason, but no attainder of treason shall work corruption of blood, or forfeiture except during the life of the person attainted.

ARTICLE IV

SECTION 1. Full faith and credit shall be given in each State to the public acts, records, and judicial proceedings of every other State. And the Congress may by general laws prescribe the manner in which such acts, records and proceedings shall be proved, and the effect thereof.

SECTION 2. 1. The citizens of each State shall be entitled to all privileges and immunities of citizens in the several States.[7]

2. A person charged in any State with treason, felony, or other crime, who shall flee from justice, and be found in another State, shall on demand of the executive authority of the State from which he fled, be delivered up to be removed to the State having jurisdiction of the crime.

3. No person held to service or labor in one State under the laws thereof, escaping into another, shall in consequence of any law or regulation therein, be discharged from such service or labor, but shall be delivered up on claim of the party to whom such service or labor may be due.[8]

SECTION 3. 1. New States may be admitted by the Congress into this Union; but no new State shall be formed or erected within the jurisdiction of any other State, nor any State be formed by the junction of two or more States, or parts of States, without the consent of the legislatures of the States concerned as well as of the Congress.

2. The Congress shall have power to dispose of and make all needful rules and regulations respecting the territory or other property belonging to the United States;

[6] See the 11th Amendment.
[7] See the 14th Amendment, Sec. 1.
[8] See the 13th Amendment.

and nothing in this Constitution shall be so construed as to prejudice any claims of the United States, or of any particular State.

SECTION 4. The United States shall guarantee to every State in this Union a republican form of government, and shall protect each of them against invasion; and on application of the legislature, or of the executive (when the legislature cannot be convened) against domestic violence.

ARTICLE V

The Congress, whenever two thirds of both Houses shall deem it necessary, shall propose amendments to this Constitution, or, on the application of the legislature of two thirds of the several States, shall call a convention for proposing amendments, which in either case, shall be valid to all intents and purposes, as part of this Constitution when ratified by the legislatures of three fourths of the several States, or by conventions in three fourths thereof, as the one or the other mode of ratification may be proposed by the Congress; Provided that no amendment which may be made prior to the year one thousand eight hundred and eight shall in any manner affect the first and fourth clauses in the ninth section of the first article; and that no State, without its consent, shall be deprived of its equal suffrage in the Senate.

ARTICLE VI

1. All debts contracted and engagements entered into, before the adoption of this Constitution, shall be as valid against the United States under this Constitution, as under the Confederation.[9]

2. This Constitution, and the laws of the United States which shall be made in pursuance thereof; and all treaties made, or which shall be made, under the authority of the United States, shall be the supreme law of the land; and the Judges in every State shall be bound thereby, anything in the Constitution or laws of any State to the contrary notwithstanding.

3. The senators and representatives before mentioned, and the members of the several State legislatures, and all executive and judicial officers, both of the United States and of the several States, shall be bound by oath or affirmation to support this Constitution; but no religious test shall ever be required as a qualification to any office or public trust under the United States.

ARTICLE VII

The ratification of the conventions of nine States shall be sufficient for the establihsment of this Constitution between the States so ratifying the same.

Done in Convention by the unanimous consent of the States present the seventeenth day of September in the year of our Lord one thousand seven hundred and eighty-seven, and of the independence of the United States of America the twelfth. In witness whereof we have hereunto subscribed our names.

[Names omitted]

---

[9] See the 14th Amendment, Sec. 4.

Articles in addition to, and amendment of, the Constitution of the United States of America, proposed by Congress, and ratified by the legislatures of the several States pursuant to the fifth article of the original Constitution.

AMENDMENTS

First Ten Amendments passed by Congress Sept. 25, 1789.
Ratified by three-fourths of the States December 15, 1791.

ARTICLE I

Congress shall make no law respecting an establishment of religion, or prohibiting the free exercise thereof; or abridging the freedom of speech, or of the press; or the right of the people peaceably to assemble, and to petition the government for a redress of grievances.

ARTICLE II

A well regulated militia, being necessary to the security of a free State, the right of the people to keep and bear arms, shall not be infringed.

ARTICLE III

No soldier shall, in time of peace be quartered in any house, without the consent of the owner, nor in time of war, but in a manner to be prescribed by law.

ARTICLE IV

The right of the people to be secure in their persons, houses, papers, and effects, against unreasonable searches and seizures, shall not be violated, and no warrants shall issue, but upon probable cause, supported by oath or affirmation, and particularly describing the place to be searched, and the persons or things to be seized.

ARTICLE V

No person shall be held to answer for a capital, or otherwise infamous crime, unless on a presentment or indictment of a grand jury, except in cases arising in the land or naval forces, or in the militia, when in actual service in time of war or public danger; nor shall any person be subject for the same offense to be twice put in jeopardy of life or limb; nor shall be compelled in any criminal case to be a witnesses against himself, nor be deprived of life, liberty, or property, without due process of law; nor shall private property be taken for public use without just compensation.

ARTICLE VI

In all criminal prosecutions, the accused shall enjoy the right to a speedy and public trial, by an impartial jury of the State and district wherein the crime shall have been committed, which district shall have been previously ascertained by law, and to be informed of the nature and cause of the accusation; to be confronted with the witnesses against him; to have compulsory process for obtaining witnesses in his favor, and to have the assistance of counsel for his defense.

ARTICLE VII

In suits at common law, where the value in controversy shall exceed twenty dollars, the right of trial by jury shall be preserved, and no fact tried by a jury shall be otherwise reëxamined in any court of the United States, than according to the rules of the common law.

ARTICLE VIII

Excessive bail shall not be required, nor excessive fines imposed, nor cruel and unusual punishments inflicted.

ARTICLE IX

The enumeration in the Constitution of certain rights shall not be construed to deny or disparage others retained by the people.

ARTICLE X

The powers not delegated to the United States by the Constitution, nor prohibited by it to the States, are reserved to the States respectively, or to the people.

ARTICLE XI

Passed by Congress March 5, 1794. Ratified January 8, 1798.

The judicial power of the United States shall not be construed to extend to any suit in law or equity, commenced or prosecuted against one of the United States by citizens of another State, or by citizens or subjects of any foreign State.

ARTICLE XII

Passed by Congress December 12, 1803. Ratified September 25, 1804.

The electors shall meet in their respective States, and vote by ballot for President and Vice President, one of whom, at least, shall not be an inhabitant of the same State with themselves; they shall name in their ballots the person voted for as President, and in distinct ballots, the person voted for as Vice President, and they shall make distinct lists of all persons voted for as President and of all persons voted for as Vice President, and of the number of votes for each, which lists they shall sign and certify, and transmit sealed to the seat of the government of the United States, directed to the President of the Senate;—The President of the Senate shall, in the presence of the Senate and House of Representatives, open all the certificates and the votes shall then be counted;—The person having the greatest number of votes for President, shall be the President, if such number be a majority of the whole number of electors appointed; and if no person have such majority, then from the persons having the highest numbers not exceeding three on the list of those voted for as President, the House of Representatives shall choose immediately, by ballot, the President. But in choosing the President, the votes shall be taken by States, the representation from each State having one vote; a quorum for this purpose shall consist of a member or members from two thirds of the States, and a majority of all the States shall be necessary to a choice. And if the House of Representatives shall not choose a President whenever the right of choice shall devolve upon them, before the fourth day of March next following, then the Vice President shall act as President, as in the case of the death or other constitutional disability of the President. The person having the greatest number of votes as Vice President shall be the Vice President, if such number be a majority of the whole number of electors appointed, and if no person have a majority, then from the two highest numbers on the list, the Senate shall choose the Vice President; a quorum for the purpose shall consist of two thirds of the whole number of Senators, and a majority of the whole number shall be necessary to a choice. But no person constitutionally ineligible to the office of President shall be eligible to that of Vice President of the United States.

ARTICLE XIII

Passed by Congress February 1, 1865. Ratified December 18, 1865.

SECTION 1.   Neither slavery nor involuntary servitude, except as punishment for crime whereof the party shall have been duly convicted, shall exist within the United States, or any place subject to their jurisdiction.

SECTION 2.   Congress shall have power to enforce this article by appropriate legislation.

ARTICLE XIV

Passed by Congress June 16, 1866. Ratified July 23, 1868.

SECTION 1.   All persons born or naturalized in the United States, and subject to the jurisdiction thereof, are citizens of the United States and of the State wherein they reside. No State shall make or enforce any law which shall abridge the privileges or immunities of citizens of the United States; nor shall any State deprive any person of life, liberty, or property, without due process of law; nor deny to any person within its jurisdiction the equal protection of the laws.

SECTION 2.   Representatives shall be apportioned among the several States according to their respective numbers, counting the whole number of persons in each State, excluding Indians not taxed. But when the right to vote at any election for the choice of electors for President and Vice President of the United States, representatives in Congress, the executive and judicial officers of a State, or the members of the legislature thereof, is denied to any of the male inhabitants of such State, being twenty-one years of age, and citizens of the United States, or in any way abridged, except for participation in rebellion, or other crime, the basis of representation therein shall be reduced in the proportion which the number of such male citizens shall bear to the whole number of male citizens twenty-one years of age in such State.

SECTION 3. No person shall be a senator or representative in Congress, or elector of President and Vice President, or hold any office, civil or military, under the United States, or under any State, who having previously taken an oath, as a member of Congress, or as an officer of the United States, or as a member of any State legislature, or as an executive or judicial officer of any State, to support the Constitution of the United States, shall have engaged in insurrection or rebellion against the same, or given aid or comfort to the enemies thereof. But Congress may by a vote of two thirds of each House, remove such disability.

SECTION 4. The validity of the public debt of the United States, authorized by law, including debts incurred for payment of pensions and bounties for services in suppressing insurrection or rebellion, shall not be questioned. But neither the United States nor any State shall assume or pay any debt or obligation incurred in aid of insurrection or rebellion against the United States, or any claim for the loss or emancipation of any slave; but all such debts, obligations, and claims shall be held illegal and void.

SECTION 5. The Congress shall have power to enforce, by appropriate legislation, the provisions of this article.

ARTICLE XV

Passed by Congress February 27, 1869. Ratified March 30, 1870.

SECTION 1. The right of citizens of the United States to vote shall not be denied or abridged by the United States or by any State on account of race, color, or previous condition of servitude.

SECTION 2. The Congress shall have power to enforce this article by appropriate legislation.

ARTICLE XVI

Passed by Congress July 12, 1909. Ratified February 25, 1913.

The Congress shall have power to lay and collect taxes on incomes, from whatever source derived, without apportionment among the several States, and without regard to any census or enumeration.

ARTICLE XVII

Passed by Congress May 16, 1912. Ratified May 31, 1913.

The Senate of the United States shall be composed of two senators from each state, elected by the people thereof, for six years; and each senator shall have one vote. The electors in each State shall have the qualifications requisite for electors of the most numerous branch of the State legislature.

When vacancies happen in the representation of any State in the Senate, the executive authority of such State shall issue writs of election to fill such vacancies: *Provided,* That the legislature of any State may empower the executive thereof to make temporary appointments until the people fill the vacancies by election as the legislature may direct.

This amendment shall not be so construed as to affect the election or term of any senator chosen before it becomes valid as part of the Constitution.

ARTICLE XVIII

Passed by Congress December 17, 1917. Ratified January 29, 1919.

After one year from the ratification of this article, the manufacture, sale, or transportation of intoxicating liquors within, the importation thereof into, or the exportation thereof from the United States and all territory subject to the jurisdicion thereof for beverage purposes is hereby prohibited.

The Congress and the several States shall have concurrent power to enforce this article by appropriate legislation.

This article shall be inoperative unless it shall have been ratified as an amendment to the Constitution by the legislatures of the several States, as provided in the Constitution, within seven years from the date of the submission hereof to the states by Congress.

ARTICLE XIX

Passed by Congress June 5, 1919. Ratified August 26, 1920.

The right of citizens of the United States to vote shall not be denied or abridged by the United States or by any State on account of sex.

The Congress shall have power by appropriate legislation to enforce the provisions of this article.

ARTICLE XX

Passed by Congress March 3, 1932. Ratified January 23, 1933.

SECTION 1. The terms of the President and Vice President shall end at noon on the 20th day of January, and the terms of Senators and Representatives at noon on the 3d day of January, of the years in which such terms would have ended if this article had not been ratified; and the terms of their successors shall then begin.

SECTION 2. The Congress shall assemble at least once in every year, and such meeting shall begin at noon on the 3d day of January, unless they shall by law appoint a different day.

SECTION 3. If, at the time fixed for the beginning of the term of the President, the President-elect shall have died, the Vice President-elect shall become President. If a President shall not have been chosen before the time fixed for the beginning of his term, or if the President-elect shall have failed to qualify, then the Vice President-elect shall act as President until a President shall have qualified; and the Congress may by law provide for the case wherein neither a President-elect nor a Vice President-elect shall have qualified, declaring who shall then act as President, or the manner in which one who is to act shall be selected, and such person shall act accordingly until a President or Vice President shall have qualified.

SECTION 4. The Congress may by law provide for the case of the death of any of the persons from whom the House of Representatives may choose a President whenever the right of choice shall have devolved upon them, and for the case of the death of any of the persons from whom the Senate may choose a Vice President whenever the right of choice shall have devolved upon them.

SECTION 5. Sections 1 and 2 shall take effect on the 15th day of October following the ratification of this article.

SECTION 6. This article shall be inoperative unless it shall have been ratified as an amendment to the Constitution by the legislatures of three-fourths of the several States within seven years from the date of its submission.

ARTICLE XXI

Passed by Congress February 20, 1933. Ratified December 5, 1933.

SECTION 1. The Eighteenth Article of amendment to the Constitution of the United States is hereby repealed.

SECTION 2. The transportation or importation into any State, Territory, or possession of the United States for delivery or use therein of intoxicating liquors in violation of the laws thereof, is hereby prohibited.

SECTION 3. This article shall be inoperative unless it shall have been ratified as an amendment to the Constitution by conventions in the several States, as provided in the Constitution, within seven years from the date of the submission thereof to the States by the Congress.

ARTICLE XXII

Passed by Congress March 24, 1947. Ratified February 26, 1951.

SECTION 1. No person shall be elected to the office of the President more than twice, and no person who has held the office of President, or acted as President, for more than two years of a term to which some other person was elected President shall be elected to the office of the President more than once. But this article shall not apply to any person holding the office of President when this article was proposed by the Congress, and shall not prevent any person who may be holding the office of President, or acting as President, during the term within which this article becomes operative from holding the office of President or acting as President during the remainder of such term.

SECTION 2. This article shall be inoperative unless it shall have been ratified as an amendment to the Constitution by the legislatures of three-fourths of the several States within seven years from the date of its submission to the States by the Congress.

ARTICLE XXIII

Passed by Congress June 16, 1960. Ratified March 29, 1961.

SECTION 1.   The district constituting the seat of Government of the United States shall appoint in such manner as the Congress may direct:

A number of electors of President and Vice President equal to the whole number of Senators and Representatives in Congress to which the District would be entitled if it were a State, but in no event more than the least populous State; they shall be in addition to those appointed by the States, but they shall be considered, for the purposes of election of President and Vice President, to be electors appointed by a State; and they shall meet in the District and perform such duties as provided by the twelfth article of amendment.

SECTION 2.   The Congress shall have the power to enforce this article by appropriate legislation.

ARTICLE XXIV

Passed by Congress August 27, 1962. Ratified January 23, 1964.

SECTION 1.   The right of citizens of the United States to vote in any primary or other election for President or Vice President, for electors for President or Vice President, or for Senator or Representative in Congress, shall not be denied or abridged by the United States or any State by failure to pay any poll tax or other tax.

SECTION 2.   The Congress shall have the power to enforce this article by appropriate legislation.

ARTICLE XXV

Passed by Congress July 6, 1965. Ratified February 10, 1967.

SECTION 1.   In case of the removal of the President from office or of his death or resignation, the Vice President shall become President.

SECTION 2.   Whenever there is a vacancy in the office of the Vice President, the President shall nominate a Vice President who shall take office upon confirmation by a majority vote of both Houses of Congress.

SECTION 3.   Whenever the President transmits to the President pro tempore of the Senate and the Speaker of the House of Representatives his written declaration that he is unable to discharge the powers and duties of his office, and until he transmits to them a written declaration to the contrary, such powers and duties shall be discharged by the Vice President as Acting President.

SECTION 4.   Whenever the Vice President and a majority of either the principal officers of the executive departments or of such other body as Congress may by law provide, transmit to the President pro tempore of the Senate and the Speaker of the House of Representatives their written declaration that the President is unable to discharge the powers and duties of his office, the Vice President shall immediately assume the powers and duties of the office as Acting President.

351

Thereafter, when the President transmits to the President pro tempore of the Senate and the Speaker of the House of Representatives his written declaration that no inability exists, he shall resume the powers and duties of his office unless the Vice President and a majority of either the principal officers of the executive department or of such other body as Congress may by law provide, transmit within four days to the President pro tempore of the Senate and the Speaker of the House of Representatives their written declaration that the President is unable to discharge the powers and duties of his office. Thereupon Congress shall decide the issue, assembling within forty-eight hours for that purpose if not in session. If the Congress, within twenty-one days after receipt of the latter written declaration, or, if Congress is not in session, within twenty-one days after Congress is required to assemble, determines by two-thirds vote of both Houses that the President is unable to discharge the powers and duties of his office, the Vice President shall continue to discharge the same as Acting President; otherwise, the President shall resume the powers and duties of his office.

ARTICLE XXVI

Passed by Congress March 23, 1971. Ratified June 30, 1971.

SECTION 1. The right of citizens of the United States, who are eighteen years of age or older, to vote shall not be denied or abridged by the United States or by any State on account of age.

SECTION 2. The Congress shall have power to enforce this article by appropriate legislation.

Index

The superscript number refers to the chapter in which the entry may be found. In addition, its placement indicates the word under which the term is alphabetized.